THE ENCYCLOPAEDIA OF ISLAM
THREE

THE ENCYCLOPAEDIA OF ISLAM

THREE

Edited by

Kate Fleet, Gudrun Krämer, Denis Matringe,
John Nawas, and Everett Rowson

With

Roger ALLEN, Edith AMBROS, Thomas BAUER, Johann BÜSSOW,
Ruth DAVIS, Ahmed EL SHAMSY, Maribel FIERRO, Najam HAIDER,
Konrad HIRSCHLER, Nico KAPTEIN, Alexander KNYSH,
Corinne LEFÈVRE, Scott LEVI, Roman LOIMEIER, Daniela MENEGHINI,
Negin NABAVI, M'hamed OUALDI, D. Fairchild RUGGLES,
Ignacio SÁNCHEZ, and Ayman SHIHADEH

TUTA SUB AEGIDE PALLAS 1683

BRILL

LEIDEN • BOSTON
2020

Library of Congress Cataloging-in-Publication Data

A C.I.P. record for this book is available from the Library of Congress.

EI3 is published under the patronage of the international union of academies.

ISSN: 1873-9830
ISBN: 978-90-04-41346-7

This book is printed on acid-free paper and produced in a sustainable manner.

LIST OF ABBREVIATIONS

A. Periodicals

AI = *Annales Islamologiques*
AIUON = *Annali dell' Istituto Universitario Orientale di Napoli*
AKM = *Abhandlungen für die Kunde des Morgenlandes*
AMEL = *Arabic and Middle Eastern Literatures*
AO = *Acta Orientalia*
AO Hung. = *Acta Orientalia (Academiae Scientiarum Hungaricae)*
ArO = *Archiv Orientální*
AS = *Asiatische Studien*
ASJ = *Arab Studies Journal*
ASP = *Arabic Sciences and Philosophy*
ASQ = *Arab Studies Quarterly*
BASOR = *Bulletin of the American Schools of Oriental Research*
BEA = *Bulletin des Études Arabes*
BEFEO = *Bulletin de l'Ecole Française d'Extrême-Orient*
BEO = *Bulletin d'Études Orientales de l'Institut Français de Damas*
BIE = *Bulletin de l'Institut d'Égypte*
BIFAO = *Bulletin de l'Institut Français d'Archéologie Orientale du Caire*
BKI = *Bijdragen tot de Taal-, Land- en Volkenkunde*
BMGS = *Byzantine and Modern Greek Studies*
BO = *Bibliotheca Orientalis*
BrisMES = *British Journal of Middle Eastern Studies*
BSOAS = *Bulletin of the School of Oriental and African Studies*
BZ = *Byzantinische Zeitschrift*
CAJ = *Central Asiatic Journal*
DOP = *Dumbarton Oaks Papers*
EW = *East and West*
IBLA = *Revue de l'Institut des Belles Lettres Arabes, Tunis*
IC = *Islamic Culture*
IHQ = *Indian Historical Quarterly*
IJAHS = *International Journal of African Historical Studies*
IJMES = *International Journal of Middle East Studies*

ILS = *Islamic Law and Society*
IOS = *Israel Oriental Studies*
IQ = *The Islamic Quarterly*
JA = *Journal Asiatique*
JAIS = *Journal of Arabic and Islamic Studies*
JAL = *Journal of Arabic Literature*
JAOS = *Journal of the American Oriental Society*
JARCE = *Journal of the American Research Center in Egypt*
JAS = *Journal of Asian Studies*
JESHO = *Journal of the Economic and Social History of the Orient*
JIS = *Journal of Islamic Studies*
JMBRAS = *Journal of the Malaysian Branch of the Royal Asiatic Society*
JNES = *Journal of Near Eastern Studies*
JOS = *Journal of Ottoman Studies*
JQR = *Jewish Quarterly Review*
JRAS = *Journal of the Royal Asiatic Society*
JSAI = *Jerusalem Studies in Arabic and Islam*
JSEAH = *Journal of Southeast Asian History*
JSS = *Journal of Semitic Studies*
MEA = *Middle Eastern Affairs*
MEJ = *Middle East Journal*
MEL = *Middle Eastern Literatures*
MES = *Middle East Studies*
MFOB = *Mélanges de la Faculté Orientale de l'Université St. Joseph de Beyrouth*
MIDEO = *Mélanges de l'Institut Dominicain d'Études Orientales du Caire*
MME = *Manuscripts of the Middle East*
MMIA = *Majallat al-Majmaʿ al-ʿIlmi al-ʿArabi, Damascus*
MO = *Le Monde Oriental*
MOG = *Mitteilungen zur Osmanischen Geschichte*
MSR = *Mamluk Studies Review*
MW = *The Muslim World*
OC = *Oriens Christianus*
OLZ = *Orientalistische Literaturzeitung*
OM = *Oriente Moderno*
QSA = *Quaderni di Studi Arabi*
REI = *Revue des Études Islamiques*
REJ = *Revue des Études Juives*
REMMM = *Revue des Mondes Musulmans et de la Méditerranée*
RHR = *Revue de l'Histoire des Religions*
RIMA = *Revue de l'Institut des Manuscrits Arabes*
RMM = *Revue du Monde Musulman*
RO = *Rocznik Orientalistyczny*
ROC = *Revue de l'Orient Chrétien*
RSO = *Rivista degli Studi Orientali*
SI = *Studia Islamica (France)*
SIk = *Studia Islamika (Indonesia)*
SIr = *Studia Iranica*

TBG = *Tijdschrift voor Indische Taal-, Land- en Volkenkunde* (of the Bataviaasch Genootschap van Kunsten en Wetenschappen)
VKI = *Verhandelingen van het Koninklijk Instituut voor Taal-, Land en Volkenkunde*
WI = *Die Welt des Islams*
WO = *Welt des Orients*
WZKM = *Wiener Zeitschrift für die Kunde des Morgenlandes*
ZAL = *Zeitschrift für Arabische Linguistik*
ZDMG = *Zeitschrift der Deutschen Morgenländischen Gesellschaft*
ZGAIW = *Zeitschrift für Geschichte der Arabisch-Islamischen Wissenschaften*
ZS = *Zeitschrift für Semitistik*

B. Other
ANRW = *Aufstieg und Niedergang der Römischen Welt*
BGA = *Bibliotheca Geographorum Arabicorum*
BNF = Bibliothèque nationale de France
CERMOC = Centre d'Études et de Recherches sur le Moyen-Orient Contemporain
CHAL = *Cambridge History of Arabic Literature*
CHE = *Cambridge History of Egypt*
CHIn = *Cambridge History of India*
CHIr = *Cambridge History of Iran*
Dozy = R. Dozy, *Supplément aux dictionnaires arabes*, Leiden 1881 (repr. Leiden and Paris 1927)
EAL = *Encyclopedia of Arabic Literature*
EI1 = *Encyclopaedia of Islam*, 1st ed., Leiden 1913–38
EI2 = *Encyclopaedia of Islam*, 2nd ed., Leiden 1954–2004
EI3 = *Encyclopaedia of Islam Three*, Leiden 2007–
EIr = *Encyclopaedia Iranica*
EJ1= *Encyclopaedia Judaica*, 1st ed., Jerusalem [New York 1971–92]
EQ = *Encyclopaedia of the Qurʾān*
ERE = *Encyclopaedia of Religion and Ethics*
GAL = C. Brockelmann, *Geschichte der Arabischen Litteratur*, 2nd ed., Leiden 1943–49
GALS = C. Brockelmann, *Geschichte der Arabischen Litteratur, Supplementbände I–III*, Leiden 1937–42
GAP = *Grundriss der Arabischen Philologie*, Wiesbaden 1982–
GAS = F. Sezgin, *Geschichte des Arabischen Schrifttums*, Leiden 1967–
GMS = *Gibb Memorial Series*
GOW = F. Babinger, *Die Geschichtsschreiber der Osmanen und ihre Werke*, Leipzig 1927
HO = *Handbuch der Orientalistik*
İA = *İslâm Ansiklopedisi*
IFAO = Institut Français d'Archeologie Orientale
JE = *Jewish Encyclopaedia*
Lane = E. W. Lane, *Arabic-English Lexicon*
RCEA = *Répertoire Chronologique d'Épigraphie Arabe*
TAVO = *Tübinger Atlas des Vorderen Orients*
TDVİA = *Türkiye Diyanet Vakfi İslâm Ansiklopedisi*
UEAI = Union Européenne des Arabisants et Islamisants
van Ess, *TG* = J. van Ess, *Theologie und Gesellschaft*
WKAS = *Wörterbuch der Klassischen Arabischen Sprache*, Wiesbaden 1957–

A

al-Ashqar, ʿUmar Sulaymān

ʿUmar b. **Sulaymān al-Ashqar** (1940–2012) was a Palestinian Salafī scholar whose writings concentrate on a wide variety of issues and contributed to the political development of the Jordanian Muslim Brotherhood. Born in Burqa, near Nablus, on 26 November 1940, according to his own account al-Ashqar grew up in a pious middle-class home (al-Ashqar, *Ṣafaḥāt*, 13–24). In 1953, his family moved to Saudi Arabia, where ʿUmar focussed on Islamic subjects at university, studied with prominent Salafī scholars such as ʿAbd al-ʿAzīz b. Bāz (d. 1999) and Muḥammad Nāṣir al-Dīn al-Albānī (d. 1999), married a cousin from his home village, and obtained an administrative job at the Islamic University of Medina (al-Ashqar, *Ṣafaḥāt*, 25–48).

In Medina, al-Ashqar became involved in calling people to Islam *(daʿwa)* and in attempts to practise commanding right and forbidding wrong *(al-amr bi-l-maʿrūf wa-l-nahy ʿan al-munkar)* by verbally reprimanding people for their sinful behaviour. As al-Ashqar himself relates the story, this effort once turned violent, when—against his will—other activists came armed with sticks, presumably to enforce their views upon others. Al-Ashqar was arrested and imprisoned for over four months and was afterwards banned from the country (al-Ashqar, *Ṣafaḥāṭ*, 70–3, 81–5). After a brief period in the West Bank, al-Ashqar moved to Kuwait in 1965, as many Palestinians did in that period (Lesch). There, he became a teacher at a government school, engaged in *daʿwa* activities again, and left for Cairo to study at al-Azhar University for several years, where he obtained a master's degree in Islamic legal theory *(uṣūl al-fiqh)* in 1974 and a Ph.D. in comparative *fiqh* in 1980. The same year, he returned to Kuwait to teach at the law faculty and started teaching at the *sharīʿa* faculty in 1982 (al-Ashqar, *Ṣafaḥāt*, 89–98, 120–1).

The Iraqi invasion of Kuwait in 1990 forced the Palestinian community—most of whose members held Jordanian citizenship, having left from the Jordanian-controlled West Bank in the 1950s and 1960s—to leave the country. As a result, some 300,000 of them ended up in Jordan in the early 1990s (Le Troquer and Hommery al-Oudat). Al-Ashqar was among these Palestinians, and he immediately obtained a teaching position at the *sharīʿa* faculty of the University of Jordan, Amman, in 1990. In 2002, he was fired for what he describes as unknown reasons and, apart from a two-year job at the *sharīʿa* faculty of the University of al-Zarqāʾ, also in Jordan (2003–5), he remained unemployed, dedicating the rest of his life to his studies (al-Ashqar, *Ṣafaḥāt*, 101–7, 113–21). Al-Ashqar died in Amman on 10 August 2012.

Al-Ashqar's body of work is extensive and very broad, encompassing many books on topics that range from fasting to witchcraft, from rituals to marriage, and from *ḥadīth* to the Islamic economy. These books, al-Ashqar claims, were quite influential, and some of them were translated into numerous languages (al-Ashqar, *Ṣafaḥāt*, 132–65). Although his work has not been much researched in Western academia, some of his publications are mentioned in studies on Islamic bio-ethical subjects, such as abortion (Rispler-Chaim). He also published a series of books on various aspects of the Salafī creed (*ʿaqīda*), including several studies on Muslim views on Paradise and Hell that have received some academic attention (Lange).

More typical of his Salafī leanings are his works on the supposedly true path represented by the *ahl al-sunna wa-l-jamāʿa* (Sunnīs). According to him, this group has remained faithful to the method of the first generations of Muslims *(manhaj al-salaf)* and therefore, al-Ashqar claims, differs from deviant trends like the Khārijīs, on the one hand, and the Murjiʾa, on the other, representing the golden mean between them (al-Ashqar, *Ahl al-sunna*, 23–79). The same attitude can be seen in his work on *fiqh*, in which he distinguishes between the different jurisprudential methods of the people of considered opinion *(ahl al-raʾy)*, the Ẓāhirīs, and the people of (the Prophetic) tradition *(ahl al-ḥadīth)*. Al-Ashqar criticises the first two and clearly sides with the third, which he portrays as the ideal middle way between ignoring the texts and emphasising them too much (al-Ashqar, *Madkhal*, 11–37). In the theological sphere, his Salafī credentials are seen in his insistence that God's names and attributes *(al-asmāʾ wa-l-ṣifāt)* must be affirmed as they appear in the text, yet without resorting to anthropomorphism *(tashbīh)* or other means of explaining them (al-Ashqar, *Asmāʾ*). He was particularly against the use of metaphorical interpretation *(taʾwīl)* as a means to explain God's names and attributes (al-Ashqar, *Taʾwīl*).

While clearly Salafī in outlook, al-Ashqar was never a major scholar in the Jordanian Salafī community. This may have had to do with the highly polarised relations within this trend (Wagemakers, *Salafism*), to which al-Ashqar was a complete outsider and in which he perhaps did not want to get involved. In any case, while not closely involved with the Jordanian Muslim Brotherhood either, he did serve as an adviser to that organisation. He was a major influence on its decision to participate in parliament and government, which was a controversial topic for it in the early 1990s. Unlike others, al-Ashqar argued that such political involvement was permissible (al-Ashqar, *Ḥukm*), thereby paving the way for a greater inclusion of the Muslim Brotherhood in Jordan (Schwedler; Wagemakers, *Muslim Brotherhood*).

Bibliography

Works

Ahl al-sunna wa-l-jamāʿa. Aṣḥāb al-manhaj al-aṣīl wa-l-ṣirāṭ al-mustaqīm, Amman 1993; *al-Asmāʾ*

wa-l-ṣifāt fī muʿtaqad ahl al-sunna wa-l-jamāʿa, Amman 1994²; *Ḥukm al-mushāraka fī l-wizāra wa-l-majālis al-niyābiyya*, Amman 2009²; *al-Madkhal ilā dirāsat al-madāris wa-l-madhāhib al-fiqhiyya*, Amman 1998²; *Ṣafaḥāt min ḥayātī*, Amman 2010; *al-Taʾwīl. Khuṭūratuhu wa-āthāruhu*, Amman 1992.

Studies

Christian Lange, Contemporary Salafi literature on Paradise and Hell. The case of ʿUmar Sulaymān al-Ashqar, in Elisabeth Kendall and Ahmad Khan (eds.), *Reclaiming Islamic tradition. Modern interpretations of the classical heritage* (Edinburgh 2016), 247–62; Ann M. Lesch, Palestinians in Kuwait, *Journal of Palestine Studies* 20 (1991), 42–54; Vardit Rispler-Chaim, Between Islamic law and science. Contemporary muftis and Muslim ethicists on embryo and stem cell research, *Comparative Islamic Studies* 2 (2006), 27–50; Jillian Schwedler, *Faith in moderation. Islamist parties in Jordan and Yemen* (Cambridge 2006), 155–64; Yann Le Troquer and Rozenn Hommery al-Oudat, From Kuwait to Jordan. The Palestinians' third exodus, *Journal of Palestine Studies* 28 (1999), 37–51; Joas Wagemakers, *The Muslim Brotherhood in Jordan*, Cambridge 2020; Joas Wagemakers, *Salafism in Jordan. Political Islam in a quietist community* (Cambridge 2016), 95–175.

Joas Wagemakers

ʿAttāb b. Asīd

ʿAttāb b. Asīd b. Abī l-ʿĪṣ b. Umayya (d. 13/634) was the first Muslim governor *(amīr)* of Mecca. Initially an opponent of the prophet Muḥammad, he accepted Islam at the conquest of Mecca (8/630). Before the Battle of Ḥunayn (8/630), Muḥammad appointed ʿAttāb (only 18–21 years old at the time) as governor, a position whose duties included leading prayers, coordinating the annual pilgrimage *(ḥajj)*, and regulating financial transactions—one of the few *ḥadīth* attributed to him concerns assessing *zakāt* (religious tax) on raisins as it is assessed on date palms. When some Meccans, opposing ʿAttāb and the Muslims, continued to perform their customary pilgrimage, Muḥammad dispatched Abū Bakr (the Prophet's father-in-law, close companion, and eventual first caliph, d. 13/634) to bolster ʿAttāb and to inform the Meccans that their pilgrimage was no longer permissible. Shortly thereafter, Muḥammad sent ʿAlī b. Abī Ṭālib (the Prophet's cousin and son-in-law and eventual fourth caliph, d. 40/661) with a new Qurʾānic revelation, from Sūrat Barāʾa, alternatively known as Sūrat al-Tawba ("The Repentance," Q 9), confirming Abū Bakr's message.

In spite of ʿAttāb's Umayyad lineage, later Shīʿī sources praise him, noting his support of ʿAlī and the family of the Prophet. Al-Majlisī (d. 1110/1699) recorded Muḥammad's purported speech at ʿAttāb's appointment as governor, in which Muḥammad praised ʿAttāb's devotion to him, ʿAlī, and their family, while discounting ʿAttāb's young age: "The oldest is not the best; rather, the best is the greatest [in terms of capability]" *(fa-laysa al-akbar huwa al-afḍal bal al-afḍal huwa al-akbar)*. This was a clear rebuttal of those who rejected ʿAlī, in part because of his young age, as Muḥammad's successor (al-Majlisī, 21:123). ʿAttāb's close connection to both Muḥammad and ʿAlī was demonstrated when ʿAlī became engaged to Juwayriya bt. Abī Jahl. Neither Muḥammad nor Fāṭima, Muḥammad's daughter and the wife of ʿAlī, approved of this potential marriage. ʿAttāb, at the behest of Muḥammad, agreed to marry Juwayriya, who was ʿAttāb's cousin through his paternal aunt, in ʿAlī's stead.

On Muḥammad's death, ʿAttāb went into hiding because of renewed Meccan opposition. He resurfaced only through the support of Suhayl b. ʿAmr b. ʿAbd Shams (d. 18/639), an influential Meccan orator who embraced Islam after the Battle of Ḥunayn. ʿAttāb's ostensible weakness contrasts with the image portrayed in a forceful speech he allegedly delivered at his appointment as governor, in which he threatened to punish the Quraysh if they failed to obey God, as mediated through his leadership, if only by neglecting prayer (al-Majlisī, 21:124). Abū Bakr kept ʿAttāb as governor of Mecca and even added al-Ṭāʾif to his jurisdiction for a short time, as had Muḥammad previously. ʿAttāb is described as pious and frugal. One tradition claims that he received from Muḥammad an allowance of one dirham per day for his service as governor (Ibn Hishām, 4:139). Another tradition states that he received two woven garments, which he then gave as a gift to his servant (Ibn Saʿd, 635).

According to most sources, ʿAttāb died on the same day as Abū Bakr. Al-Ṭabarī, however, includes a tradition which claims that ʿAttāb remained governor of Mecca until 22/643, into the reign of ʿUmar b. al-Khaṭṭāb (r. 13/634–23/644), the second caliph (al-Ṭabarī, *Taʾrīkh*, 5:2671–2). This claim is rejected by other sources (al-Balādhurī, *Ansāb*, ed. ʿAbbās, 4/1:456).

Bibliography

Sources

al-Azraqī, *Akhbār Mecca*, ed. Ferdinand Wüstenfeld (Beirut 1964), 1:127–8; al-Balādhurī, *Ansāb al-ashrāf*, ed. Muḥammad Ḥamīdallāh (Cairo 1959), 1:303, 364–8, 529; al-Balādhurī, *Ansāb al-ashrāf*, ed. Iḥsān ʿAbbās (Wiesbaden 1979), 4/1:456; al-Bukhārī, *Kitāb al-taʾrīkh al-kabīr* (Hyderabad 1941), 4/1:54; al-Bukhārī, *Ṣaḥīḥ*, ed. Muṣṭafā Dīb al-Bughā (Beirut 1993[5]), 3:1364, 5:2004; Ibn ʿAbd al-Barr, *al-Istīʿāb fī maʿrifat al-Aṣḥāb*, ed. ʿAlī Muḥammad al-Bajjāwī (Cairo 196-), 3:1023–4; Ibn al-Athīr, *Usd al-ghāba fī maʿrifat al-Ṣaḥāba* (Beirut 2012), 812–3; Ibn Ḥajar, *al-Iṣāba fī tamyīz al-Ṣaḥāba*, ed. ʿĀdil Aḥmad ʿAbd al-Mawjūd and ʿAlī Muḥammad Muʿawwaḍ (Beirut 1995), 4:356–7; Ibn Ḥajar, *Tahdhīb al-tahdhīb*, ed. Ibrāhīm al-Zaybaq and ʿĀdil Murshid (Beirut 2001), 3:47–8; Ibn Hishām, *al-Sīra al-nabawiyya*, ed. ʿUmar ʿAbd al-Salām Tadmurī (Beirut 1990[3]), 4:56, 139, 317; Ibn Qutayba, *al-Maʿārif*, ed. Tharwat ʿUkāsha (Cairo 1969[2]), 283; Ibn Saʿd, *Ṭabaqāt al-kubrā*, ed. ʿAlī Muḥammad ʿUmar (Cairo 2001), 6:34–5, 8:8; Khalīfa b. Khayyāṭ, *Ṭabaqāt*, ed. Akram Ḍiyāʾ al-ʿUmarī (Baghdad 1967), 2:277; al-Majlisī, *Biḥār al-anwār* (Beirut 1983), 22:122–4; al-Mizzī, *Tahdhīb al-kamāl* (Beirut 1992), 19:282–6; al-Ṭabarī, *Taʾrīkh al-rusul wa-l-mulūk*, ed. M. J. de Goeje (Leiden 1897–1901, repr. 1964), 3:1369, 1659, 1670, 1685, 4: 2128, 2135, 5:2671–2, trans. Ismail K. Poonawala, *The history of al-Ṭabarī. The last years of the Prophet*, vol. 9 (New York 1990), 21; al-Wāqidī, *Kitāb al-maghāzī*, ed. Marsden Jones (Oxford 1966), 1:6, 3:889, 959.

Lyall Armstrong

al-ʿAẓīmī

Abū ʿAbdallāh Muḥammad b. ʿAlī b. Muḥammad al-Tanūkhī **al-ʿAẓīmī** (483–556/1090–1161) was a historian, poet, and school teacher from Aleppo. He was a poet and eulogist for Turkmen rulers, such as the Saljūqs of Damascus and the Artuqids of Aleppo, composing in support of their *jihād* against the Crusaders. Around the year 535/1140 al-ʿAẓīmī joined the entourage of ʿImād al-Dīn Zengi (r. 521–41/1127–46) the ruler of Aleppo (Ḥalab), in northern Syria and northern Iraq. Zengi was the patron of al-Aẓīmī until his death in 541/1146.

Al-ʿAẓīmī wrote three works of history but only one survives, namely, *Taʾrīkh al-ʿAẓīmī*, which is a very brief history of Aleppo and northern Syria along with accounts of other Muslim populated regions. The book is subdivided in yearly accounts and is abstract and rather wearisome, with some sentences being difficult to understand. *Taʾrīkh al-ʿAẓīmī* starts with stories of several Abrahamic prophets and presents the genealogy of the prophet Muḥammad. A lengthy list of the titles and names of Muslim rulers from the Umayyad and ʿAbbāsid dynasties up to the year 538/1144 is also presented. The significance of *Taʾrīkh al-ʿAẓīmī* stems from the fact that many of the events it chronicles are not mentioned elsewhere, especially for the last five decades covered by the book. It is one of the rare historical materials of Syrian historiography dating from between the mid-fifth/eleventh and sixth/twelfth centuries to survive, bridging the gap to other later sources. In 1984, Ibrāhīm Zaʿrūr edited it in full and titled it *Taʾrīkh Ḥalab* ("The history of Aleppo"). This edition has disappointingly few annotations on rulers and geographic places.

Another work on the history of Aleppo authored by al-ʿAẓīmī was *Taʾrīkh Ḥalab*, a work which was is no longer extant. Chroniclers such as Ibn al-ʿAdīm (d. 660/1261) and Ibn Khallikān (d. 681/1282) extensively relied on several parts of this voluminous book.

The second lost work, titled *al-Muʾassal ʿalā l-aṣl al-mawṣūl* ("The well-founded on the solid ground work"), was a biographical dictionary of rulers and scholars, and Ibn al-ʿAdīm would have read the original manuscript in al-ʿAẓīmī's own handwriting. In addition, Ibn al-ʿAdīm relied on this work in his extensive work on Aleppo, *Bughyat al-ṭalab*. Claude Cahen edited and translated the part of *al-Muʾassal* which starts from the year 455/1063.

Al-Aẓīmī was an eye witness chronicler to the Saljūqs, Artuqids, and Zengi. His lost works influenced other leading chroniclers like Ibn al-ʿAdīm, Ibn Khallikān, and Ibn al-Furāt (d. 807/1405). Through them portions of these work have survived and continue to serve as an important source of North Syrian historiography of the sixth/twelfth century.

Bibliography

al-Aẓīmī, *Taʾrīkh Ḥalab*, ed. Ibrāhīm Zaʿrūr, Damascus 1984; Claude Cahen, La chronique abregee d'al-Azimi, *JA* 230 (1938), 353–448; Carole Hillenbrand, The establishment of the Artuqid power in Diyar Bakr in the twelfth century, *SI* 54 (1981), 129–53; Taef El-Azhari, *Zengi and the Muslim response to the crusades. The politics of jihad*, Routledge 2016.

Taef El-Azhari

B

Baalbek

Baalbek (Ar., Baʿlabakk, known in Greek and Roman times as Heliopolis, the city of the sun; Duval 128) is a city and archaeological site in the northern Bekaa (Biqāʿ) valley of Lebanon, a part of the Syrian-African rift. Since the ʿAbbāsid period, initially in narratives of the Islamic conquests *(futūḥāt)* (Donner), the place has been named in Arabic chronicles, biographical dictionaries, and geographical texts. Its archaeological remains attracted the attention of travellers whose writings spread Baalbek's fame, as early as the middle Islamic period (334–656/945–1258). Baalbek has experienced several destructive earthquakes, notably in 598/1202 and 1172/1759, but its Roman past is still visible. According to the 2013 Lebanese census, it had 81,000 inhabitants and was the tenth largest city in Lebanon.

The Arab armies of the emerging Islamic state conquered Baalbek in 16/637 (Kaegi). The pre-Islamic monumental remains of Baalbek were known to Arab and European readers already in the period of the Crusades. Rabbi Benjamin of Tudela (d. 568/1173) (trans. Adler, 48) and al-Sharīf al-Idrīsī (d. c.560/1164–5) (ed. Bombaci et al., 369–70) recorded local traditions that the site was built by King Solomon, traditions that had circulated in earlier Syriac writings (*heikhelā de-Shelīmūn de-Baʿalbek medīnatā*; Minov, 62). Since the twelfth/eighteenth century these ruins have been admired also by European visitors (Pococke, 106–13; Wood; Volney, 2:232–47). These marvels are echoed in contemporary travel literature, as in the visit of Kaiser Wilhelm II to Baalbek in 1898, on his way to Jerusalem (Sader et al., 27–33), and in Marcel Proust's Balbec (Benhaïm).

During the Mamlūk period (658–923/1260–1516), the city was under the shadow of Damascus, as attested by chronicles, biographies, geographies, and other documents (*maḥḍar*s, reports) (Frenkel). It housed Sunnī institutions of learning and sacred places—the best known being the mausoleum of the Ṣūfī *shaykh* al-Yūnīnī (d. 617/1219)—and was a modest Shīʿī centre of learning. The shrine of Khawla bt. al-Ḥusayn (d. 61/680) attracted many Shīʿī pilgrims, who, however, kept a low public profile in those days. The political situation and administrative practices did not change with the Ottoman conquest of Syria (922/1516), as evidenced by various contemporary sources (Abdel Nour, 346–9).

With the reorganisation of the Ottoman administration in Bilād al-Shām (Syria) in about 956/1549—during the reign of Sulṭān Süleyman (Süleymān) I (r. 926–74/1520–66)—its southern part, named Eyalet-i Arab (Iyālat al-ʿArab), was divided into eight provinces. Its central *sancak* (Ar., *sanjak*, administrative district) was Damascus, within which Baalbek was administered as a county *(nahiye/ naḥiya)*. The district's population was predominantly Shīʿī, but Baalbek itself was inhabited also by Sunnīs and members of several Christian denominations. During those first centuries of Ottoman rule, commercial networks connected Baalbek and its Bekaa hinterland to Tripoli and Hama. At the same time, Baalbek had a close relationship with Damascus.

The dominant regional force in the northern Bekaa valley during those centuries was the Twelver Shīʿī Ḥarfūsh clan (in the plural, al-Ḥarāfisha), which had played a political role since the last decades of the Mamlūk sultanate. In 940/1534 ʿAlī b. Mūsā l-Ḥarfūsh (d. 998/1589) was named governor of Baalbek. He was succeeded, upon his death, by his son Mūsā b. ʿAlī al-Ḥarfūsh (d. 1016/1608) (al-Duwayhī, 160, 184, 189; Winter, 45–53). The clan's power forced the Ottoman authorities occasionally to appoint members of the family as semi-autonomous local governors, in return for which they supplied the Sublime Porte and its Syrian representative with services, including collection of taxes, and provided labour and military manpower. The situation changed with the Tanzimat, the modernising reforms of 1839 to 1876, when the Ḥarāfisha lost their power in Baalbek, and the area came under direct Ottoman rule.

In the eleventh/seventeenth century, when ʿAbd al-Ghanī al-Nābulusī (d. 1143/ 1731) visited Baalbek, its population was about five thousand, of various denominations (Ibn Maḥāsin, 38–9; al-Nābulusī, 97–100). It had two baths *(ḥammāms)*, and, during the twelfth/eighteenth century, a third was opened, perhaps indicating economic improvement or increasing investment by the rulers in the public welfare. Travelogues by local travellers, notably Badr al-Dīn Muḥammad al-Amīrī al-Ghazzī al-Dimashqī (d. 984/1577; 41–2), and al-Nābulusī, reveal the strong political and cultural link between Sunnī Shāmī religious scholars and Baalbek, which could, in this respect, be regarded as a satellite of Damascus, the *sanjaq*'s capital.

With the rapid and profound changes that swept Ottoman Bilād al-Shām in the thirteenth/nineteenth century, Baalbek was transformed. New governmental and foreign schools (American, English, and Jesuit) for boys and girls were established to serve the local communities. The political implications of this development can be seen in the Baalbek native Rustum Ḥaydar's (1889–1940) joining the Young Arab Society (al-Fatāt) in Istanbul in 1909 (Provence, 70). The local demographic stagnation in the second half of the thirteenth/nineteenth century can probably be explained by the migration of Christians to the newly emerging town of Zahlé (Ar., Zaḥla), in the southern Bekaa.

Following the emergence of independent Lebanon (1946), Baalbek was associated with opposing trends. In the 1950s it came to play an important part in the national classicisation of tradition. Baalbek was chosen as the venue of the folkloric Lebanese Nights, which came to be associated with the famous singer Fayrūz (b. 1934), the Rahbānī brothers (Assi, d. 1986, and Manṣūr, d. 2009), and a brand of Lebanese Christian nationalism that seeks to demonstrate that the Maronites have an ethno-nationalist pre-Islamic and pre-Arabisation identity (Phares).

Baalbek and the Bekaa were synonymous with the marginalised Shīʿī community. The speech delivered by Imām Mūsā l-Ṣadr (d. 1978) in Baalbek in March 1974 symbolises the revolutionary turn in the city's place in the modern history of Lebanon and its Shīʿī community. In about 1982, ʿAbbas Mūsāwī (d. 1992) returned to Lebanon from Najaf, in Iraq, and established in Baalbek a Shīʿī religious seminary (*ḥawza*), which became closely associated with the rising Ḥizballāh (Party of God, often spelt Hizbullah), but power struggles within the local Shīʿī community in the 1990s prevented the party from controlling the city. In 2003 Baalbek was separated from the Bekaa governorate and the administrative division of Baalbek-Hermel was created. In 1984 UNESCO recognised Baalbek as a world cultural heritage site.

Bibliography

Sources

Badr al-Dīn Muḥammad al-Amīrī al-Ghazzī al-Dimashqī, *al-Maṭāliʿ al-Badriyya fī l-manāzil al-Rūmiyya*, ed. Mahdī ʿĪd al-Rawwaḍiyya, Abu Dhabi 2004; Benjamin of Tudela (Benyamīn al-Tuṭīlī), *Riḥla*, ed. and trans. Marcus Nathan Adler, *The itinerary of Benjamin of Tudela*, London 1907, repr. New York 1964; Rubens Duval (ed.), *Lexicon syriacum auctore Hassano bar Bahlule voces syriacas græcasque cum glossis syriacis et arabicis complectens*, Paris 1888–1901; Isṭifanūs al-Duwayhī, *Taʾrīkh al-ṭāʾifa al-Mārūniyya*, Beirut 1890; al-Idrīsī, *Nuzhat al-mushtāq fī ikhtirāq al-āfāq (Opus geographicum, sive Liber ad eorum delectationem qui terras peragrare studeant)*, ed. Alessio Bombaci et al., Naples 1970–; Yaḥyā b. Abī l-Ṣafā Ibn Maḥāsin, *al-Manāzil al-Maḥāsiniyya fī l-riḥla al-Ṭarābulusiyya*, ed. Muḥammad ʿAdnān al-Bakhīt, Beirut 1401/1981; ʿAbd al-Ghanī al-Nābulusī, *al-Tuḥfa al-Nābulusiyya fī l-riḥla al-Ṭarābulusiyya*, ed. Heribert Busse, Beirut 1971; Richard Pococke, *A description of the East and some other countries*, 2 vols. in 3, London 1743–5; Constantin-François Volney, *Travels through Syria and Egypt, in the years 1783, 1784, and 1785*, London 1787, 1788[2]; Robert Wood, *The ruins of Balbec, otherwise Heliopolis in Cœlosyria*, London 1757.

Studies

Antoine Abdel Nour, *Introduction à l'histoire urbaine de la Syrie ottomane (XVIe–XVIIIe siècle)*, Beirut 1982; N. N. Ambraseys and Muawia Barazangi, The 1759 earthquake in the Bekaa Valley. Implications for earthquake hazard assessment in the eastern Mediterranean region, *Journal of Geophysical Research* 94/B4 (1989), 4007–13; André Benhaïm, From Baalbek to Baghdad and beyond. Marcel Proust's foreign memories of France, *Journal of European Studies* 35 (2005), 87–101; Franziska Bloch, Verena Daiber, and Peter Knötzele, *Studien zur spätantiken und islamischen Keramik. Ḫirbat al-Minya, Baalbek, Resafa*, Rahden, Westphalia 2004; Fred McGraw Donner, *The early Islamic conquests*, Princeton 1981; Anne Marie Eddé, Bilād al-Shām, from the Fāṭimid conquest to the fall of the Ayyūbids (359–658/970–1260), in Maribel Fierro (ed.), *The new Cambridge history of Islam*, vol. 2, *The western Islamic world, eleventh to eighteenth centuries*, Cambridge 2010; Yehoshua Frenkel, Mapping the Mamluk sultanate, in Stephan Conermann (ed.), *History and society during the Mamlūk period (1250–1517)* (Bonn 2014), 37–60; Walter Emil Kaegi, *Byzantium and the early Islamic conquests*, Cambridge 1992, repr. 2000; Sergey Minov, The story of Solomon's palace at Heliopolis, *Le Muséon* 123/1–2 (2010), 61–89; Roy P. Mottahedeh, The eastern travels of Solomon. Reimagining Persepolis and the Iranian past, in Michael Cook, Najam Haider, Intisar Rabb, and Asma Sayeed (eds.), *Law and tradition in classical Islamic thought. Studies in honor of Professor Hossein Modarressi* (New York 2013), 247–67; Augustus R. Norton, *Hezbollah. A short history*, Princeton 2007, 2014[2];

Walid Phares, *Lebanese Christian nationalism. The rise and fall of an ethnic resistance*, Boulder 1995; Michael Provence, *The last Ottoman generation and the making of the modern Middle East*, Cambridge 2017; Qāsim al-Shammāʿī al-Rifāʿī, *Baʿlabakk fī l-taʾrīkh. Dirāsa shāmila li-taʾrīkhihā wa-masājidihā wa-madārisihā wa-ʿulamāʾihā*, Beirut 1404/1984; Hélène Sader, Thomas Scheffler, and Angelika Neuwirth (eds.), *Baalbek. Image and monument 1898–1998*, Stuttgart 1998; Ziad Sawaya, *Histoire de Bérytos et d'Heliopolis d'après leurs monnaies (Ier siècle av. J.-C.–IIIe siècle apr. J.-C.)*, Beirut 2009; J. Sourdel-Thomine, Baʿlabakk, *EI2*; Alexander Toepel, Late paganism as witnessed by the Syriac *Cave of treasures*, *Greek, Roman, and Byzantine Studies* 59 (2019), 507–28; Stefan Winter, *The Shiites of Lebanon under Ottoman rule, 1516–1788*, Cambridge 2010.

YEHOSHUA FRENKEL

Banjārās

The majority of **Banjārās** are Hindu nomads. Henry Elliot (1869) was perhaps the first to report on Muslim Banjārās in the region stretching from Hardwar in the state of Uttaranchal through the districts of Muradabad, Rampur, and Bareilly, to Gorakhpur in Uttar Pradesh. The Muslim Banjārās, then known as Turkiyā and Mukerī Banjārās, comprised about two-thirds of the Banjārā population in the then United Provinces. They were reported to be quite orthodox in their social and religious conduct and less wandering grain traders than the Hindu Banjārās. Present-day Muslim Banjārās are known as Turks, Banjārās, and Makrānīs, and they reside in predominantly sedentary mercantile rural communities. Since the beginning of twentieth century, they have undergone many socio-economic and educational changes.

Banjārās have a variety of origins, ways of life, and identities. Various etymologies have been proposed for the word Banjārā (Varady, 4), but, according to Irfan Habib, the Urdu name Banjārā—derived from Sanskrit *vaṇij* (merchant, also the etymon of "Baniyās," the name for the Indian mercantile caste)—was apparently first used in the tenth/sixteenth century for large communities inhabiting the plains of India, whose members combined pastoralism and trade (Habib, 374). Known in Urdu as *kārvānīs* (caravan people) and *nāyaks* (caravan headmen) in early mediaeval history, they were first described in an account of the price-control measures of the Delhi sultan ʿAlāʾ al-Dīn Khaljī (r. 695–715/1296–1316) (Habib, 374). Being inland traders and long-distance transporters, Banjārās appear to have had a virtual monopoly on the grain trade and supplies to the military, until the construction of metalled roads and the introduction of railways in the mid-nineteenth century.

Banjārā communities, mostly in the Deccan plateau in central and western India, were described in reports of colonial administrators (e.g., Russell) as polytheist "nomads" or "gypsies," as residing in mobile *t'āṇḍ'ās* (caravan encampments) under the absolute authority of a *nāyak*, and as practising many peculiar customs, such as the consumption of alcohol and hashish decoctions by men and women, the collection of water only from holes dug on river banks or from wells, the celebration of marriages only in the rainy season when sedentary in a village, and the marriage of an elder brother's widow to a younger brother of her deceased husband (Deogaonkar and Deogaonkar, 49–50). They were also said to be descended from Chāraṅs (wandering actors or singers) and B͟hāt's (bards and panegyrists) of Rajasthan. Henry Elliot (1869) was perhaps the first scholar who not only identified Muslim Banjārās in the region comprising present-day Uttar Pradesh and Uttaranchal but also described them in detail. According to him, Banjārās of this region fell into five major divisions—the Baids, the Lavāṅās, the Bahrūps, the Turkiyās, and the Mukerīs, the latter two divisions consisting of Muslims. These Banjārās, unlike those of the Deccan, "were not always wandering merchants but denizens of the large tract of country under the Northern hills from Gorakhpur to Hardwar" (Elliot, 51). They resided in villages, much intermixed with local sedentary people; many deserted their homes in order to join the "Banjārā fraternity" (Elliot, 51). The Indian census of 1891 enumerated 66,828 Banjārās, divided into nine subgroups—Chauhan, Bahrup, Gaur, Jadon, Panwar, Rather, Tanwar, Others, and Muslims—in thirty-six districts of the United Provinces, of whom 26,953 were Muslims (Crook, 166–7). These figures do not include the Muslim Banjārā population of Rampur district, then a princely state, where they were reported to number approximately ten thousand in 1901 *(Gazetteer of Rampur).*

Turkiyā Banjārās asserted that they came from Multan (in Panjāb), having "left their newly chosen country of the Deccan under a leader called Rustam Khan, and first of all took their abode at Badlitanda, near Moradabad, from where they have gradually spread to Bilaspur, Riccha, and the neighbouring tracts" (Elliot, 54). Mukerī Banjārās claimed a Meccan origin. "Leaving Mecca, they came and resided at Jhajjar, where their illustrious name became corrupted from Meccai into Mukerī" (Elliot, 54), a popular etymology with no linguistic basis. They were reported in eastern and southern districts of Uttar Pradesh and in the neighbouring areas of Bihar and from what is now Madhya Pradesh. The Turkiyā and Mukerī Banjārās were divided into various tribes having both Indian and foreign names—such as Tomar, Badan, Chakirahā, Chawhān, Gahlot, Dilvarī, Aghvān, Bechrarī, Durkī, Shaykh, Alwī (ʿAlawī), and Khiljī—suggesting diverse origins. Although Muslim Banjārās apparently had many similarities with Hindu Banjārās, whether from northern or southern India—as suggested by the names of their tribes and by their way of life involving *t'āṇd'ās* and *nāyaks*—they were reported to be less wandering and more orthodox in rites, rituals, and social conduct (Elliot; Crook). They were large-scale transporters, dealers in food grains, and cattle traders. In the Rohilkhand region, in the northern districts of Uttar Pradesh, where the rice trade flourished, Banjārās brought paddy from villages on their ponies and seasoned and prepared it for trade in local markets and in the markets of distant towns and cities such as Delhi. They controlled almost all the grain trade of Rohilkhand and employed a shrewd practice known as *badnī*, under which cash advances were made by the Banjārās at a fixed rate while the crop was still standing; this rate was maintained, irrespective of the actual crop production *(Gazetteer of Rampur).*

Decennial census and district reports of independent India provide no information about Muslim Banjārās, and the latter have not been studied by scholars or civil-society organisations, limiting our knowledge of their present distribution and socio-economic condition to some northern districts of Uttar Pradesh. Known by various names, such as Turks, Banjārās, and Makrānīs, in these districts, they form distinctive rural and urban

Muslim communities or *barādarīs* (patrilineal endogamous groups), having no global unity or identity. They are Ḥanafī Sunnīs. Some of the men wear beard and cap, and most of the women wear the burqa or veil. They celebrate, in addition to both ʿĪd festivals and the birthday of the Prophet, *shab-i barāt* (commemorating the entry of the Prophet into Mecca); many visit Ṣūfī shrines. Many offer *namāz* (prescribed prayers) five times a day, fast for one month each year, and make the *ḥajj*. They still control the grain trade of their villages and towns, although most are wage labourers, small peasants, self-employed mechanics, vendors, small traders, and shop keepers. Some have succeeded in trade and commerce and become stockbrokers, transporters, contractors, and owners of rice mills, brick kilns, cold-storage facilities, and other small-scale businesses. A growing consciousness of the importance of modern education is apparent in the increasing numbers of students, male and female, in modern educational institutions, although few have achieved white-collar positions or government employment. They participate in local and state elections, but they are not politically empowered, for, like other Muslims in present-day India, they encounter prejudice, discrimination, insecurity, and exclusion in their daily lives and business (Waheed, Muslim Banjaras; Waheed, *Social structure*).

Bibliography

William Crook, *The tribes and castes of the North Western India*, vol. 1, Calcutta 1896, repr. Delhi 1974–5; Shashishekar Gopal Deogaonkar and Shailaja Shashishekar Deogaonkar, *The Banjara*, New Delhi 1992; Henry Elliot, *Memoirs on the history, folk-lore, and distribution of the races of the North Western Provinces of India, being an amplified edition of the original supplemental glossary of Indian terms*, ed. John Beames, 2 vols., London 1869, cited here in repr. in one volume, Osnabrück 1976; *Gazetteer of the Rampur state*, Allahabad 1911; Irfan Habib, Merchant communities in precolonial India, in James D. Tracy (ed.), *The rise of merchant empires. Long-distance trade in the early modern world, 1350–1750* (New York 1990), 371–99; Robert Vane Russel, *The tribes and castes of the Central Provinces of India*, vol. 2, London 1969; Robert Gabriel Varady, North Indian Banjaras. Their evolution as transporters, *South Asia. Journal of South Asian Studies* 2 (1979), 1–17; Abdul Waheed, Muslim Banjaras. Peddlers of Uttar Pradesh. A socio-historial study, *Man in India* 89/4 (2009), 619–35; Abdul Waheed, *Social structure and economy of an urban Muslim community. A case study of Muslim Banjaras of Baheri, district Bareilly*, Ph.D. diss., Aligarh Muslim University 2000.

Abdul Waheed

al-Bazzī

Abū l-Ḥasan Aḥmad b. Muḥammad b. ʿAbdallāh b. al-Qāsim b. Nāfiʿ b. Abī Bazza **al-Bazzī** (b. 170/786–7, d. 250/864–5), a client of the Banū Makhzūm, was the chief Qurʾān reciter and *muʾadhdhin* (caller to prayer) of al-Masjid al-Ḥarām (the Holy Mosque) of Mecca for over 40 years. His forefather, Abū Bazza, was of Persian descent reportedly converted to Islam at the hands of al-Sāʾib b. Abī al-Sāʾib Ṣayfī al-Makhzūmī (d. after 8/638), a Companion of the Prophet and one of his trade partners.

Al-Bazzī studied Qurʾānic recitation with ʿIkrima b. Sulaymān (d. 181–90/798–806) and Abū l-Ikhrīṭ Wahb b. Wāḍiḥ (d. 190/806) both of whom were considered to be the chief Qurʾān reciters of Mecca during their time. Alongside Qunbul (d. 291/904), al-Bazzī is considered to be the second canonical *rāwī* (transmitter) of Ibn Kathīr (d. 120/738), the eponymous Meccan reader. Neither Qunbul nor al-Bazzī were directly connected to Ibn Kathīr; they were separated from him by two generations of transmitters.

Al-Bazzī stands out from the rest of the eponymous readers and their *rāwī*s due to his unique practice of performing *takbīr* (the saying of the formula *Allāhu Akbar*; God is Great) at the end of each *sūra* between *sūra* 93 ("Forenoon") and *sūra* 114 ("The people"). In addition to transmitting a *ḥadīth* to this effect, he promulgated the practice in Mecca and integrated it into the principles of the reading of Ibn Kathīr. The *ḥadīth* was deemed weak by Muslim scholars, even though the renowned *ḥadīth* scholar al-Ḥākim al-Nīsābūrī (d. 405/1014) considered it to be sound according to the criteria of the highly regarded *ḥadīth* collectors Muslim (d. 261/875) and al-Bukhārī (d. 256/870). Indeed, al-Bazzī was deemed to be weak and faulty as a *ḥadīth* transmitter (*munkar al-ḥadīth*). Nevertheless, his practice of performing *takbīr* at the end of each *sūra* between *sūra* 93 and *sūra* 114 has continued until today in the Meccan tradition of recitation, and it is taught, in accordance with *al-Shāṭibiyya*—the didactic poem on the seven canonical readings of the Qurʾān written by the Andalusian Qirāʾāt scholar Abū Muḥammad al-Shāṭibī (d. 590/1194)—as an integral part of al-Bazzī's rendition of Ibn Kathīr's eponymous reading.

Bibliography

Sources

Ibn al-Athīr, *al-Lubāb fī tahdhīb al-Ansāb* (Beirut 1972), 1:149; al-Dhahabī, *Maʿrifat al-qurrāʾ al-kibār ʿalā l-ṭabaqāt wa-l-aʿṣār*, ed. Ṭayyār Āltīqūlāg (Istanbul 1995), 1:365–70; al-Ḥākim al-Nīsābūrī, *al-Mustadrak ʿalā l-Ṣaḥīḥayn* (Cairo 1997), 3:373; Ibn Abī Ḥātim al-Rāzī, *al-Jarḥ wa-l-taʿdīl* (Beirut 1953), 2:71; Ibn al-Jazarī, *Ghāyat al-nihāya fī ṭabaqāt al-qurrāʾ*, ed. Gotthelf Bergsträsser (Cairo 1932–5, repr. Beirut 2006), 1:109–10; Ibn Mujāhid, *Kitāb al-sabʿa fī l-qirāʾāt*, ed. Shawqī Ḍayf (Cairo 1980), 65–6; Ibn al-Sallār, *Ṭabaqāt al-qurrāʾ al-sabʿ*, ed. Aḥmad ʿInāya (Beirut 2005), 39–40; al-ʿUqaylī, *al-Ḍuʿafāʾ al-kabīr*, ed. ʿAbd al-Muʿṭī Qalʿajī (Beirut 1984), 1:127.

Studies

T. I. Ḍamra, *al-Ṭarīq al-munīr ilā qirāʾat Ibn Kathīr bi-riwāyatay al-Bazzī wa-Qunbul* (Amman 2006), 33–6; Shady Hekmat Nasser, *The transmission of the variant readings of the Qurʾān. The problem of* tawātur *and the emergence of* shawādhdh (Leiden 2013), 138–46; ʿAbd al-Fattāḥ ʿA. al-Qāḍī, *al-Wāfī fī sharḥ al-Shāṭibiyya* (Jeddah 1999[5]), 383–6; J. C. Vadet, Ibn Kathīr, *EI2*.

Shady H. Nasser

C

Conakry

Conakry, once a small village on a peninsula (three by five kilometres) where the French settled in 1885, is the capital of Guinea, with a population of 1.5 to 2 millions, stretching from east to west more than thirty kilometres. The Baga, considered autochthonous, and the Susu arrived in several waves, beginning as early as the twelfth/eighteenth century. They were later joined by Fulani. Over the years, migrants coming from further away moved to Conakry in search of work.

One of the earliest photographs of Conakry shows a group of villagers standing around a Nimba (Baga) fertility mask, some wearing Muslim gowns and caps, revealing much about the religious diversity of the place. The growth of the colonial city attracted clerks, traders, and skilled labourers coming especially from Senegal and Sierra Leone; forced labour was also employed. The arrival of new migrants introduced new religious practices or reinforced existing ones. Krio from Freetown had built their temple by the late 1890s, and Senegalese had their mosque affiliated with the Tijāniyya Ṣūfī order (the Tijāniyya was founded in Tlemcen in Algeria in 1195/1781 by the *shaykh* and religious scholar Aḥmad b. Muḥammad al-Tijānī, d. 1815, and gained influence in large portions of North and West Africa and, later and to a lesser extent, in Egypt, Sudan, and Ethiopia). Meanwhile the Catholic congregations of the Holy Ghost Fathers and the Sisters of St Joseph of Cluny acquired large tracts of land, and Protestant missionaries arrived.

During the first two decades of the twentieth century, the population grew from a few hundred to about ten thousand. The colonisers were eager to plan the city in accord with contemporary urban planning theory and racist discourse. After a period in which they welcomed all newcomers, they imposed a segregated division, first into two zones (1901), then into three (1905). The criterion was not overtly "race" but purchasing power. Some well-to-do Africans bought plots of land in the administrative and residential quarter. The intent was, however, clearly to separate Africans from Europeans and concentrate investment and infrastructure in the "first zone," around Government House, next to which, appropriately, the cathedral was built in the 1930s. The grid pattern was adopted without taking into account existing African neighbourhoods: Almamya, Sandervalia, Boulbinet, Timenetaye, Tombo, and Coronthie. Because of this urban policy, Conakry became known as "the pearl of Africa" and was considered a colonial model, with its prevalent dualism. A colonial municipality presided over the whole city from 1904 to 1956, while chieftainships were recognised in the African quarters.

Conakry remained a modest city in the interwar period, with about fifty thousand inhabitants. It was not until the 1940s that it expanded onto the mainland and suburbs grew. In 1948, a master plan was drawn up, including the transfer of the railway station and all administrative services from the old first zone to the new suburbs. Because of the political turmoil and the cost, however, the plan was not implemented. During Sékou Touré's regime (1958–84), minimal state intervention took place, despite the fact that the geographical site, an elongated piece of land, was a handicap to expansion and new road infrastructure was greatly needed. A few symbolic buildings were constructed, such as the People's Palace built by the Chinese in 1965. In 1983, the Fayçal Mosque, with its international Arab architecture and four minarets, was financed by Saudi Arabia and Morocco, in a city where Islam is the predominant religion. Islamic reformist movements influenced by Saudi Arabia, sometimes known as Wahhabism, are gaining in importance.

Under presidents Lansana Conté (in office 1984–2008) and Alphé Condé (in office since 2010) economic liberalism has prevailed. Transverse roads, linking the two shores of the peninsula, have been built. Private properties have mushroomed. The population exploded from 115,000 in 1960 to between 500,000 and 700,000 in 1983 and more than a million in 1996. Conakry was previously administered by a governor, but administrative reform in 1991 established five municipalities with elected councils and mayors, tightly controlled by the central government: Kaloum (the old city centre on the peninsula), Dixinn, Matam, Ratoma, and Matoto.

Population density, the lack of infrastructure, unemployment, the growing heterogeneity of the population, and the use of ethnicity discourse as a means of control have led to frequent clashes.

Bibliography

Odile Goerg, Conakry, in Simon Bekker and Göran Therborn (eds.), *Capital cities in Africa. Power and powerlessness* (Cape Town and Dakar 2011), 8–29 (www.codesria.org/IMG/pdf/Capital_Cities_in_Africa_-_Chapter_2__Conakry.pdf); Odile Goerg, *Pouvoir colonial, municipalités et espaces urbains. Conakry et Freetown, des années 1880 à 1914*, vol. 1, *Genèse des municipalités*, vol. 2, *Urbanisme et hygiénisme*, Paris 1997; Thomas O'Toole, *Historical dictionary of Guinea*, Metuchen and London 1978, with Janice E. Baker, 2005[4]; Alain Richard, Emile Tompapa, and Mamadou Aliou Bah, *Conakry, porte de la Guinée*, Conakry and Vanves 1998.

Odile Goerg

E

Epics, Persian

Persian epics are the product of a long-lasting oral and then written transmission of myths, stories, and beliefs. Its pre-eminent literary product is the *Shāh-nāma* ("Book of kings"), a long epic poem written down by Abū l-Qāsim Firdawsī (d. c.410/1020) of Ṭūs.

1. Indo-Iranian roots

Iranian peoples maintained an unbroken transmission of their heroic epics, reaching back to a common Indo-Iranian and even a more distant Indo-European past (Skjærvø, Importance; Watkins, 14–6, 57–8; Dumézil, 1:9–27, 2:137–45). The themes of epic narratives rooted in mythology, together with the specifics of their poetic language and composition, bear witness to their oral origins. The formation of Persian epic texts should be perceived as a dynamic process that developed through oral transmission, for several millennia, and then, from the Sāsānid period on (226–651 C.E.), developed in two parallel, mutually interfering channels, oral and written.

Epic mythology served as raw material for the construction of sacral Zoroastrian history and official Iranian dynastic histories, hence a tendency towards its ossification (religious and official royal tradition tend to become canonical and are thus not easily changed). On the other hand, because their epics had a symbolic and emotional value for the Iranians, they should be viewed as a live and productive source of literary, cultural, and ideological patterns and a token of common identity.

The earliest, brief references to the epic heroes and their exploits are found in the *Avesta*, the Zoroastrian holy book. What is known by the Persians as their own mytho-epic heritage was thus inherited in its East Iranian version, diffused in the Iranian Plateau through Zoroastrianism, which originated somewhere in southern Central Asia or present-day Afganistan (Skjærvø, *Avesta*, 171–2; Grenet; Hintze, 36). The Avestan texts relevant to mytho-epic heroes and events are, most importantly, the *Yasht*s (hymns to Indo-Iranian gods) with their catalogues of sacrifiers (Yt V, IX, XV, XVII, XIX) and of ancestral souls (Yt XIII), the *Vīdēvdāt*

II and *Hōm-yasht* (*Yasna* IX) (*Zend-Avesta*, trans. Darmesteter). The deeds of mythical heroes in the *Avesta* are mentioned only allusively, which suggests a common knowledge of their oral narrative background by their singers and audience. Middle Persian (Pahlavi) religious books, in particular the *Bundahishn* (chaps. 29–32) and *Dēnkard* (bks. 8, 9)—recorded only after the Arab conquest of Iran (third-fourth/ninth-tenth centuries) but based on the lost parts of the *Avesta*—convey more developed versions of those myths (for textual sources, see Christensen, *Premier homme*, 1:11–30; 2:3–31; Christensen, *Kayanides*, 10–69). Several minor Pahlavi texts telling the stories of mythical or historical mythologised figures were known to the authors of early Islamic literature, but only a few survived, such as *Kārnāmag-i Artakhsher-i Pabāgān*, ("The exploits of Artakhsher, son of Pabāg") and *Ayādgār-i Zarīrān* ("Memorial of Zarīr"), the only surviving example of a Middle Persian heroic poem (apparently of Parthian origin), reconstructed as metrical by Benveniste (Benveniste; Akbarzāda, *Shāh-nāma*, 129–62). Several lost Middle Persian texts are listed by Islamic sources, for instance, *al-Fihrist* by the Baghdadi bibliophile Ibn al-Nadīm (377/987), an encyclopedic Arabic-language catalogue of the knowledge and literature of mediaeval Islam in the fourth/tenth century.

Some motifs and heroes of Iranian epic mythology have been identified with their Indian counterparts, although we still have no comprehensive study of common Indo-Iranian epic mythology. Such characters as Vedic Yama/Avestan Yima (New Persian Jamshīd), Ved. Trita/Avest. Thrita, Thraētaona (N. Pers. Farīdūn), and Ved. Kavi Uśanas/Avest. Kavi Usan (N. Pers. Kay Kāvūs) are common to both traditions (Darmesteter, Points de contact; Christensen, *Premier homme*, 2:3–62; Wikander; Dumézil, 2:132–238; Watkins, 314–20). More parallels between Iranian and Indian epics are discussed by, for example, Molé (Deux notes, 141–7), Skjærvø (Eastern Iranian), Kiyyā, and Krasnowolska (*Mythes, croyances*, 171–89).

Under Sāsānid rule, the Avestan heroes were included in the official written history of the dynasty. The catalogues of mythical ancestors were transformed into a genealogical tree of fictitious dynasties of the Pishdadids and Kayanids, to which Ardashīr I (r. 226–41 C.E.), the founder of the ruling house, became connected through intermediary links. The final recension of the Sāsānid history, *Khᵛadāy-nāmag* ("Book of kings"), which combined the narrative on mythical heroes with dynastic chronicles, was completed towards the end of the Sāsānid reign (Hämeen-Antilla, 1–9). Extant are neither its original Middle Persian version nor its Arabic translations, the most important of which is the *Kitāb siyar al-mulūk al-Furs* by Ibn al-Muqaffaʿ (d. 139/757), a Persian translator, author, and thinker who wrote in Arabic. The content of the *Khᵛadāy-nāmag* may be partly inferred from the Arabic and New Persian works of Islamic authors, amongst them Dīnavarī (d. between 281/894 and 290/903), grammarian, lexicographer, astronomer, mathematician, and Islamic traditionist of Persian origin who lived in Iraq; al-Ṭabarī (d. 310/923), pre-eminent Iranian scholar and author of a celebrated commentary on the Qurʾān and an important classical Arabic historical text *(Taʾrīkh al-rusul wa-l-mulūk)*; Balʿamī (d. between 382/992 and 387/997), Persian historian, writer, and vizier of the Sāmānids

(r. 204–395/819–1005); al-Thaʿālibī (d. 961/1038), author from Nīshāpūr best known for a huge Arabic anthology of prose and poetry; and Gardīzī (d. c.453/1061), Persian geographer and historian from Gardīz, in modern Afghanistan (Nöldeke, 142–6; Yarshater, 359–66; Shahbazi, Hämeen-Antilla, 59–130, 147–52). Local histories such as the *Tārīkh-i Bukhārā* by al-Narshakhī' (d. 348/959), Ibn al-Balkhī's *Fārsnāma* (early sixth/twelfth century), and the anonymous *Tārīkh-i Sīstān* (fifth-seventh/eleventh-thirteenth century) contribute to the knowledge of the lost Middle Persian mytho-historical accounts.

2. New Persian

In the third-fourth/ninth-tenth centuries, when the revival of Persian literature began under local Iranian dynasties, repeated efforts were made to record in the New Persian language the epic heritage that was believed to be the true history of Iran. Little remains of these attempts. Early sources mention a now lost prose *Shāh-nāma* ("Book of kings") by Abū l-Muʿayyad Balkhī, an early Persian poet and writer of the Sāmānid period whose works have almost entirely disappeared (Lazard, Abu 'l-Muʾayyad Balxi); another prose version was the so-called *Shāh-nāma-yi Abū Manṣūrī*, compiled on the order of Abū Manṣūr b. ʿAbd al-Razzāq, governor of Khurāsān, towards the middle of the fourth/tenth century, of which only an introduction survives (Qazvīnī, 2:5–90; Monchi-zadeh, 1–39). From Masʿūdī Marvazī's versified *Shāh-nāma* (turn of the third-fourth/ninth-tenth centuries) three couplets remain (Lazard, *Premiers poètes*, 1:73; 2:47), and some one thousand couplets by Abū Manṣūr Daqīqī (d. c.366/976) were incorporated by Firdawsī into his work (Nöldeke, 147–8; Lazard, 1:32–6).

3. Firdawsī's *Shāh-nāma* and the oral tradition

Persian epos acquired its refined literary form in the *Shāh-nāma* by Abū l-Qāsim Firdawsī, completed in about 400/1010. Firdawsī's *Shāh-nāma* is a *mathnavī*, a type of poem of unlimited length, consisting of pair-rhymed verses. It contains more than sixty thousand *bayt*s (couplets) in eleven-syllable *mutaqārib* verse, probably a continuation of a Pahlavi epic metre, adapted to the quantitative prosodic system of Arab origin (Mār, 190–7; Kuryłowicz, 97–101).

The *Shāh-nāma* comprises two unequal parts, a mytho-heroic one (two-thirds of the text) and an historical one, the two parts differentiated in content and structure. The first part corresponds roughly to the scope of Avestan mythology: it tells the stories of the first man and the world's first ruler, Gayūmarth (Avest. Gayō Maretan), the rise and fall of King Jamshīd, and the tyranny of Ḍaḥḥāk (the anthropomorphised three-headed dragon Azhī Dahāka of the *Avesta*) and his defeat by Farīdūn; Farīdūn's division of the world amongst his three sons and the murder of Īraj by his envious brothers Salm and Tūr, resulting in a blood feud between the Iranian and Turanian branches of the family; a series of Kayanid kings (in the *Avesta* tribal leaders titled *kavi*), most importantly Kay Kāvūs, his son Sīyāvush (Avest. Kavi Syāvarshan) murdered by the Turanian king Afrāsyāb (Avest. Franrasyān) and Sīyāvush's son Kay Khusraw (Avest. Kavi Haosravah), the avenger; the reign of Gushtāsp (Avest. Kavi Vishtāspa, Zarathushtra's patron and follower), his son Isfandīyār (Avest. Spentōdhāta), and his grandson Bahman. The wars between

Iranians and Turanians, the two hostile but closely related clans (the latter early identified as Turks), dominate the mytho-epic part of the poem. The central figure of these wars is the superhero Rustam, the Iranian kings' best ally and rescuer from troubles. With his death the heroic age comes to an end. Rustam is unknown to the *Avesta*, but he and his father Zāl and grandfather Sām inherited some features of the Avestan dragon-slayer Sāma Keresāspa (N. Pers. Garshāsp). Local variants of the saga of the Sāma house were popularised in Iran by the Saka (Scythian) conquerors of Drangiana, the future Sakastān/Sīstān, towards the end of the second century B.C.E. (Nöldeke, 138–40; Coyajee, 139–40, 158–61; Yarshater, 373–7). Other protagonists of epic tales, such as Gūdarz, Gīv, Bīzhan, and Milād, have been incorporated into the mainstream Persian epics from the once rich but forgotten Parthian heroic tradition (Coyajee, 138–58; Yarshater, 453–61).

The "historical" part of the poem concentrates on the Sāsānid dynasty. The Achaemenids, founders of the Persian empire (559–330 B.C.E.) have been reduced to two mythologised kings, Dārāb (Darius I, r. 522–486 B.C.E.) and Dārā (Darius III, r. 336–30); the Parthian Ashkanids (247 B.C.E.-226 C.E.) are merely listed, except for the last, Ardavān IV (r. 213–24 C.E.), who plays a role in the story of Ardashīr. On the contrary, a long chapter is devoted to Alexander the Great (Iskandar, r. 331–23 B.C.E.), whose fabulous adventures follow the Middle Eastern versions of ps.-Callistenes romance (Bertel's, 283–9, Hanaway, 609–10). The stories about Sāsānid rulers, derived from their dynastic records, although partly mythologised, are a valuable source of information on the history and culture of the period. Realistic descriptions of the life of the common people become numerous and the poet's references to his worsening personal situation more frequent. The poem ends with a dramatic account of the Arab invasion, the death of the last Sāsānid king, Yazdigard III (30/651), and the fall of Persian Empire.

There is no doubt that Firdawsī had at his disposal a New Persian prose version of the *Khʷadāy-nāmag* (apparently the *Shāh-nāma-yi Abū Manṣūrī*) and probably some other written texts, so that the majority of his stories can be referred to literary sources, directly or indirectly known. The authors of classical works on the Persian epos believed the poetical form of the *Shāh-nāma* to be Firdawsī's own contribution, preceded by the less successful attempts of earlier poets (Nöldeke, 164–5; Mīnuvī, 80; Safā, 192–203). The development of research on orality—begun by Milman Parry (d. 1935), the American scholar of epic poetry and founder of the discipline of oral tradition, and Albert B. Lord (d. 1991), the Harvard professor of Slavic and comparative literature who carried on Parry's research on epic literature—prompted the study of the oral roots of Persian poetry. The results of their work applied to the *Shāh-nāma* material led to the conclusion that Firdawsī's poetic art is derived from a long-lived oral tradition and that he himself must have been familiar with the techniques of oral performance (Boyce; Davidson; Skjærvø, Importance; Krasnowolska, Elementy; Yamamoto). If we accept Albert Lord's definition of a formula as "a group of words ... regularly employed under the same metrical conditions to express a given essential idea" (Lord, 4; see Watkins, 16–8), Firdawsī's language is densely formulaic; it uses poetical figures such as hyperbole, metaphor, and simile, as well as frequently repeated epithets and repeatable rhymes. Themes that recur in the *Shāh-nāma* include, amongst others, conventional descriptions of an advancing army and individual combat; brief metaphorical descriptions of approaching day and night (indicators of the passage of time); images of handsome men and beautiful women, ideal landscapes, and magic strongholds; catalogues of gifts, war booty, and treasures; messages, coronation speeches, last wills, and mourning laments; and moral admonitions and reflections on the relentlessness of fate (an influence of the fatalistic current in Zoroastrian thought; cf. Ringgren; Josephson); and dreams. Such stylistic devices, worked out in the process of oral transmission, enable a singer to build the action quickly during a performance (Lord, 38–98; Bowra, 254–98; Watkins, 12–9). Similar themes and poetic figures typical of oral epic composition are found already in the Middle Persian *Ayādgār ī Zarērān* ("Memorial of Zarīr"), the only surviving specimen of epic poetry in Pahlavi, preserved in a unique manuscript dated 1322 C.E. (e.g., Pagliaro).

Apart from its formal division into chapters, a regular, informal segmentation of the pre- Sāsānid part of *Shāh-nāma* into a series of parallel-shaped textual units testifies to its cyclisation during oral transmission. The recurrent narrative pattern originates from the calendar myth that has as its hero a nature deity, dying and being reborn (cf. Grintzer, 178–9). In Iranian epics the myth evolved into the three-generation story of a sinful king, his innocently murdered young son compared to a sacrificial animal, and the dead hero's son who takes revenge on his father's killer. Regular components of this scenario are the miraculous childhood of a hero in exile; a trip of initiation (by overcoming its obstacles a young hero proves his power and charisma); marriage to one or more brides, preceded by wedding trials (tests that enable the hero to marry); an expedition to rescue a person who has disappeared; and the killing of an enemy with demonic attributes (Krasnowolska, Elementy, 140–6; Krasnowolska, Heroes, 176–87). Larger narrative units (*dāstāns*), which belong to the main plot or accompany it as side stories, are framed with conventional opening and closing passages, a place for the poet's comments, reflections, and direct addresses to his public.

In the "historical" part of the poem the formulaic, heroic idiom is retained, but the rules of its inner division change. Some elements of the mytho-epic scenario survive—for instance, in the stories of Dārāb and Ardashīr—but regular narrative patterns atrophy. In their place is a series of short anecdotes (Alexander's and Bahrām Gūr's adventures) and clusters of wisdom sentences (testament of Ardashīr; the wise sayings of Būzurjmihr).

The great popularity of Firdawsī's poem resulted in the proliferation of its manuscripts, of varying length and content. The oldest known are dated some two hundred years after the poet's life (the Florence manuscript is dated 614/1217; the second oldest, London 675/1276). A first attempt at reconstruction of Firdawsī's original text was made on the order of the Tīmūrid sultan Bāysunqur (d. 836/1433) of Herat, himself also a calligrapher, in 832/1429. A pre-modern critical edition by Turner Macan (1829), based on several Indian manuscripts, was followed by those by the French Jules Mohl (d. 1876) and his continuator Charles Barbier de Meynard

(d. 1908), with parallel French translation in prose (1838–78), and the unfinished edition (1877–84) of the German Johann August Vullers (d. 1880), completed as the Barukhīm Tehran edition (1313–5sh/1934–6). The Moscow *Shāh-nāma* of E. Ė. Bertel's (d. 1957) in nine volumes (1960–71) was the first modern critical edition, based on a group of the oldest manuscripts then known. Jalal Khaleghi-Motlagh's (b. 1937) edition (New York 1987–2008) which takes into account the most recently discovered (1977), and the oldest known (614/1217) Florence manuscript is the most comprehensive to date.

4. After Firdawsī

Several post-Firdawsī heroic *mathnavī* poems emerged between the fifth/eleventh and the sixth/twelfth centuries. Most of those epics, traditionally referred to as "secondary," contain material that is not included in Firdawsī's work but that is, in some instances, old and valuable. The *Garshāsp-nāma* (458/1066), by Firdawsī's compatriot Asadī Ṭūsī (d. 465/1073), treats of the war exploits and exotic travels of Garshāsp, the Avestan Keresāspa (Molé, L'épopée iranienne, 380–3), almost absent from the epic mainstream. Several poems, mainly anonymous, such as *Farāmarz-nāma*, *Borzū-nāma*, *Shahrīyār-nāma*, *Bānū Gushāsp-nāma*, and *Bahman-nāma*, tell the stories of Rustam's descendants, partly repeating the *Shāh-nāma* narrative patterns. The action of the *Kush-nāma*, like that of the *Garshāsp-nāma*, takes place in the mythical times of Jamshīd and Ḍaḥḥāk but seems to have preserved some memories of the Central Asian Kushan empire (first-second century C.E.) (Ethé, 233–5; Molé, Épopée, 384–90; Safā, 283–343; de Blois, 475–6). Akbarzāda notes a connection between the frequent references to India in Persian "secondary" epics and the Zoroastrian migration to the Subcontinent in the first centuries of Islam, which leads him to ascribe the authorship of these works to Parsee authors. The adventures of Iskandar have been dealt with by several poets, most importantly Niẓāmī Ganjavī (d. 602/1209) in his two-part *Iskandar-nāma*, then reworked by Amīr Khusraw Dihlavī (d. 725/1325) in his *Āyina-yi Iskandarī*, ʿAbd al-Rahmān Jāmī (from Herat, d. 898/1492) in his *Khirad-nāma-yi Iskandarī* ("The book of wisdom of Alexander"), and Abū Ṭāhir Ṭarsūsī (fl. fifth/eleventh or possibly sixth/twelfth century) in his *Dārāb-nāma* (Bertel's, 286–367).

As de Blois observes (475), "the distinction between the heroic and the romantic epic is not clear-cut," but romantic epic may be singled out as a genre long established in Persian literature. The origin of *Vīs-u Rāmīn* (446/1054) by Fahkr al-Dīn Gurgānī (d. 446/1054, Isfahan), the story of a love triangle, comparable to *Tristan and Isolde*, has been recognised by Minorsky (22–31) as Parthian and seems, like other early romantic narratives, such as ʿUnṣurī's (d. c.430/1039) partly preserved *Vāmiq-u ʿAdhrā* and ʿAyyuqī's (fl. fifth/eleventh century) *Varqa u Gulshāh*, to be influenced by late antique Greek romance (Davis). The most famous examples of romantic epos are three poems from Niẓāmī's *Khamsa* ("Quintet"). Two of them, *Haft paykar* ("Seven beauties") and *Khusraw va Shīrīn* ("Khusraw and Shīrīn") have their prototypes in the Sāsānid part of the *Shāh-nāma*; the third is an ancient Arab love story, *Laylī va Majnūn*.

Heroic Firdawsī-style verse was used from the ninth/fifteenth century on in poems about the conquests of the Prophet, the Shīʿī Imāms, and other religious figures (Ṣafā, 377–90) and in the works in praise of contemporary rulers, from the Khārazm-shāh Muḥammad ʿAlāʾ al-Dīn (r. 596–617/1200–20) to the Qājārs (r. 1779–1925) (Ṣafā, 354–76). Firdawsī's influence was also considerable in Persianate India, where numerous manuscripts of the *Shāh-nāma* were copied with illustrations and where epic poems were written in its style and metre, such as the *Taʿrīf-i Ḥusayn Shāh* ("Eulogy for Ḥusayn Shāh") by Aftābī (fl. under the Niẓām Shāhī kings of Ahmadnagar in the Deccan Burhān Shāh, r.915–961/1509–54, and Ḥusayn Shāh, r. 961–72/1554–65), dedicated to the victory of Ḥusayn Shāh over the great South Indian Hindu kingdom of Vijayanara.

Firdawsī's work established a canon for literary form and content of Persian epics. Nevertheless, analogously to the manuscript transmission of the *Shāh-nāma*, its oral diffusion continued. It has been sung by traditional singers in its versified form *(Shāh-nāma-khᵛānī)*, and fragments have been sung as accompaniment to athletic exercises in *zūr-khāna*s (Iranian traditional gymnasia). The *Shāh-nāma* stories are performed also in rhythmic prose interlaced with verse *(naqqālī)*, in some cases with pictures painted on large canvas scrolls or on the walls of tea houses (for modern performers and their texts and techniques, see Maḥjūb, 1079–1113).

Bibliography

Sources

Murtaḍā Mīr Aftābī, *Taʿrīf-i bādshāh-i Dakan*, ed. and trans. G. T. Kulkarni and M. S. Mate, *Tarif-i-Husain Shah, Badshah Dakhan*, Pune 1987; *Avesta. Die heiligen Bücher der Parsen*, ed. Karl F. Geldner, 3 vols., Stuttgart 1885–95; Abū ʿAlī Balʿamī, *Tārīkh-i Balʿamī* (a free translation of the *Tārīkh-i Ṭabarī*), ed. Muḥammad Taqī Bahār, Tehran 1380sh/2001; Abū l-Qāsim Firdawsī, *Shāh-nāma*, ed. E. Ė. Bertel's, 9 vols., Moscow 1960–71; Abū l-Qāsim Firdawsī, *Shāh-nāma*, ed. Jalāl Khāliqī Muṭlaq, 8 vols., New York 1366–86sh/1987–2008; Abū Saʿīd Gardīzī, *Zayn al-akhbār*, ed. ʿAbd al-Ḥayy Ḥabībī, Tehran 1347sh/1968–9; Fahkr al-Dīn Gurgānī, *Vīs-u Rāmīn*, ed. Māgalī Tudūā (Magali Tʿodua) and Aliksāndar Guvakhārīā (Alekʿsandre Gvaxaria), ed. K. S. Aīnī, Tehran 1349sh/1970–1; Ibn al-Balkhī, *The Fársnáma of Ibnu'l-Balkhí*, ed. Guy Le Strange and Reynold A. Nicholson, Cambridge 1921; Abū Bakr Muḥammad al-Narshakhī, *Tārīkh-i Bukhārā*, ed. Mudarris Raḍavī, Tehran 1351/1972; *Pahlavi texts*, trans. Edward William West, 5 vols., Oxford 1880–97; al-Ṭabarī, *Taʾrīkh al-rusul wa-l-mulūk*, ed. M. J. de Goeje et al., *Annales quos scripsit Abu Djafar Mohammed ibn Djarir at-Tabari*, vol. 1, Leiden 1879–81, vol. 2, 1881–2; *Tārīkh-i Sīstān*, ed. Muḥammad Taqī (Malik al-Shuʿarāʾ) Bahār, Tehran 1314/1935; Abū Ṭāhir al-Ṭarsūsī, *Dārāb-nāma-yi Ṭarsūsī*, ed. Dhabīḥallāh Safā, 2 vols., Tehran 1977; al-Thaʿālibī, *Histoire des rois des Perses*, ed. and trans. Hermann Zotenberg, Paris 1900; Ḥakīm Asadī Ṭusī, *Garshāsb-nāma*, ed. Ḥabīb Yaghmāʾī, Tehran 1317sh/1938; *The Zend-Avesta*, trans. James Darmesteter and Lawrence Heyworth Mills, 3 vols., Oxford 1882–7(?).

Studies

Dāryūsh Akbarzāda, *Shāh-nāma va zabān-i Pahlavī*, Tehran 1379sh/2000–1; Dāryūsh Akbarzāda, Yāddāshtī bar jāygāh-i Hind dar barkhī mutūn-i hamāsī, *Pazhūhish-nāma-yi Adab-i Hamāsī* 13/2 (1396sh/2017), 53–64; Émile Benveniste, Le mémorial de Zarēr. Poème pehlevi, *JA* 220 (1932), 245–93; E. Ė. Bertel's, *Navoi i dzhami*, Moscow 1965; François de Blois, Epics, *EIr*; Mary Boyce, The Parthian *gōsān* and Iranian minstrel tradition, *JRAS* 1–2 (1957), 10–45; Arthur Christensen, *Les Kayanides*, Copenhagen 1931; Arthur Christensen, *Les types du premier homme et du premier roi dans l'histoire légendaire des Iraniens*, 2 vols., Stockholm 1917 and Leiden 1934; Jehangir Cooverji Coyajee, Studies in the *Shāhnāmeh*, *J. K. R. Cama Oriental Institute* 33 (1939), 1–325; James Darmesteter, Points de contact entre le *Mahābhārata* et le *Shāhnāmeh*, *JA* 3 (1887), 38–75; Olga M. Davidson, *Poet and hero in the Persian Book of kings*, Ithaca and London 1994; Richard Davis, Greece, ix, Greek and Persian romances, *EIr*; Georges Dumézil,

Mythe et épopée, 3 vols., Paris 1968–73; Hermann Ethé, Neupersische Literatur, in Wilhelm Geiger and Ernst Kuhn (eds.), *Grundriss der iranischen Philologie*, 2 vols. (Strassburg 1895–1904), 2:212–370; Frantz Grenet, Zarathustra's time and homeland. Geographical perspectives, in Michael Stansberg and Yuhan Sohrab-Dinshaw Vevaina (eds.), *The Wiley Blackwell companion to Zoroastrianism* (Chichester 2015), 21–30; P. A. Grintser, Epos drevnego mira, in P. A. Grintser (ed.), *Tipologiia i vzaimosvazi literatur drevnego mira* (Moscow 1971), 134–205; Jaakko Hämeen-Anttila, *Khwadāynāmag. The Middle Persian Book of kings*, Leiden 2018; William L. Hanaway, Eskandar-nāma, *EIr*; Djalal Khaleghi-Motlagh, Ferdowsi, Abu'l-Qasem, i, Life, *EIr*; Khujasta Kiyyā, Rakhsh-i Rustam asb-i qurbānī?, in ʿAlī Muḥammad Ḥaqqshinās et al. (eds.), *Yād-i Bahār. Yād-nāma-yi Duktur Mihrdād Bahār*, (Tehran 1376sh/1997–8), 373–82; Almut Hintze, Zarathustra's time and homeland: Linguistic perspectives, in Michael Stansberg and Yuhan Sohrab-Dinshaw Vevaina (eds.), *The Wiley Blackwell companion to Zoroastrianism* (Chichester 2015), 31–8; Judith Josephson, Fate, wisdom and the king in book three of the *Denkard* and the *Shāhnāme* by Ferdowsi, in Forogh Hashabeiky (ed.), *International Shāhnāme Conference. The second millenium* (Uppsala 2015), 99–116; Anna Krasnowolska, Elementy stylu epiki ustnej w Šāh-nāme Ferdousiego, in Andrzej Czapkiewicz (ed.), *Poetyka orientalna i jej recepcja w Europie* (Krakow 1989), 137–54; Anna Krasnowolska, The heroes of Iranian epic tale, *Folia Orientalia* 24 (1987), 173–89; Anna Krasnowolska, *Mythes, croyances populaires et symbolique animale dans la littérature persane*, Paris 2012; Jerzy Kuryłowicz, *Metrik und Sprachgeschichte*, Wroclaw 1975; Gilbert Lazard, *Les premiers poètes persans*, 2 vols., Tehran and Paris 1964; Gilbert Lazard, Abu 'l-Muʾayyad Balxi, in Jiži Bečka (ed.), *Yádnáme-ye Jan Rypka* (Prague 1967), 95–101; Albert Bates Lord, *The singer of tales*, Cambridge MA 1960; Muḥammad Jaʿfar Maḥjūb, *Adabiyāt-i ʿāmiyāna-yi Īrān*, Tehran 1382sh/2003; Y. N. Mār, Vazn-i shiʿr-i Shāh-nāma, in I. Sidīqī (ed.), *Hazāra-yi Firdawsī* (Tehran 1322sh/1943), 188–98; H. Massé, Ḥamāsa, ii, Littérature persane, *EI2*; V. Minorsky, Vīs u Rāmīn. A Parthian romance (conclusion), *BSOAS* 12/1 (1947), 20–35; Mujtabā Mīnuvī, *Firdawsī va shiʿr-i ū*, Tehran 1354sh/1975; Marijan Molé, Deux notes sur le Rāmāyaṇa, in *Hommages à Georges Dumézil* (Brussels 1960), 140–50; Marijan Molé, L'épopée iranienne après Firdōsī, *La Nouvelle Clio* 5 (1953), 377–93; Davoud Monchi-zadeh, *Topographisch-historische Studien zum iranischen Nationalepos*, Wiesbaden 1975; Theodor Nöldeke, Das iranische Nationalepos, *Grundriss der iranischen Philologie*, ed. Wilhelm Geiger and Ernst Kuhn (Strassburg 1895–1904), 2:130–211; Antonio Pagliaro, *Il testo pahlavico Ayātkār-i Zarērān*, Rome 1925; Mīrzā Muḥammad Qazvīnī, *Bīst maqāla*, ed. ʿAbbās Iqbāl and Ibrāhīm Pūrdāʾūd, 2 vols., Tehran 1332 sh/1953; Helmer Ringgren, *Fatalism in Persian epics*, Uppsala 1952; Dhabīḥallāh Ṣafā, *Hamāsa-sarāyī dar Īrān*, Tehran 1321/1942, 1352/1973[3]; A. Shapur Shahbazi, On the Xwadāy-nāmag, in *Iranica varia. Papers in honor of Professor Ehsan Yarshater* (Leiden 1990), 208–29; Prods Oktor Skjærvø, The Avesta as source for the early history of the Iranians, in George Erdosy (ed.), *The Indo-Aryans of ancient South Asia* (Berlin and New York 1995), 155–76; Prods Oktor Skjærvø, Eastern Iranian epic traditions, ii, Rostam and Bhīṣma, *AO Hung.* 51/1–2 (1998), 159–70; Prods Oktor Skjærvø, The importance of orality for the study of Old Iranian literature and myth, *Nāma-yi Irān-i Bāstān* 5/1–2 (2005–6), 9–31; Calvert Watkins, *How to kill a dragon. Aspects of Indo-European poetics*, New York and Oxford 1995; Stig Wikander, Sur le fonds commun indo-iranien des épopées de la Perse et de l'Inde, La Nouvelle Clio 1–2 (1949), 310–29; Kumiko Yamamoto, *The oral background of Persian epics. Storytelling and poetry*, Leiden 2003; Ehsan Yarshater, Iranian national history, *CHIr* 3/1 (Cambridge 1983), 359–477.

Anna Krasnowolska

F

al-Faḍl b. Dukayn

Abū Nuʿaym al-Mulāʾī **al-Faḍl b. Dukayn** was a Kufan traditionist. He was reportedly born in 129/746–7 or late in 130/mid-748 and died late in 218/833–4 or perhaps at the end of Shaʿbān or in Ramaḍān 219/September-October 834. He was a client to the family of Ṭalḥa b. ʿUbaydallāh (d. 36/656). He was cross-eyed or had some other visual defect, for which he was nicknamed al-Aḥwal. His name of affiliation *(nisba)* al-Mulāʾī refers to his partnership with another Kufan traditionist, ʿAbd al-Salām b. Ḥarb (d. 187/803), in a shop selling wraps of some sort (wraps of some sort (*mulāʾ*)). Yaḥyā b. Maʿīn (d. 233/848) is said to have come to the shop to test him by reading to him thirty *ḥadīth* reports that he said al-Faḍl had previously related, interpolated with three spurious additions. Al-Faḍl recognised the interpolated reports but, when he realised that Yaḥyā was testing him, angrily withdrew to his house behind the shop (al-Khaṭīb, 14:315–6).

One son of his is known, named ʿAbd al-Raḥmān, who took charge of his funeral (Ibn Saʿd, 6:279–80), and one daughter, named Ṣulayḥa or Ṭulayḥa, who related reports of his affirming that the Qurʾān was the increate word of God (al-Mizzī, 23:215).

Al-Faḍl b. Dukayn was a leading transmitter from Sufyān al-Thawrī (d. 161/778?). He appears 175 times in the *Ṣaḥīḥ* of al-Bukhārī (d. 256/870), more than twice as often as any other immediate Kufan source, and 161 times in the *Musnad* of Aḥmad b. Ḥanbal (d. 241/855), where he is in sixth place amongst immediate Kufan sources. Al-Bukhārī also quotes him often in *al-Taʾrīkh al-kabīr* regarding the death dates of earlier traditionists. He was praised for relating *ḥadīth* verbatim, although he was also sometimes blamed for *tadlīs* (disguising weak *ḥadīth)* and for taking payment to relate *ḥadīth*, a practice he justified by pointing to his thirteen dependents.

Ibn al-Nadīm (d. 385/995) lists al-Faḍl amongst the traditionist-jurisprudents *(fuqahāʾ aṣḥāb al-ḥadīth)* and attributes to him two books that do not survive: *Kitāb al-manāsik* ("Book of pilgrimage rituals"), presumably a collection of *ḥadīth* concerning the pilgrimage rituals, and *Kitāb al-masāʾil fī l-fiqh* ("Book of questions on jurisprudence"), presumably a collection of legal opinions. Another collection of *ḥadīth* is extant and has been published under the title *Kitāb al-ṣalāt* ("Book of prayer"). It comprises rules concerning ritual prayer going back to the Prophet (about one-fifth), his Companions (about two-fifths), and his Followers (about two-fifths). About eight-tenths of al-Faḍl's immediate sources are Kufan, one-tenth Basran, and the remainder from Medina, Mecca, and elsewhere.

Al-Faḍl b. Dukayn was sometimes suspected of Shīʿism but denied ever having insulted Muʿāwiya. Near the end of this life, he was interrogated as part of the inquisition *(miḥna)* in Kufa. He refused to endorse the doctrine of the createdness of the Qurʾān. His historical significance is mainly as an example, like Abū Bakr b. Abī Shayba (d. 235/849), of Kufan traditionalism. As such, he was partial to earlier Kufan traditionist figures such as Ibrāhīm al-Nakhaʿī (d. 96/714?) and Sufyān al-Thawrī, whom he often quoted in comparison with Abū Ḥanīfa (d. 150/767) or his teacher Ḥammād b. Abī Sulaymān (d. 120/738?). Al-Faḍl's approach to determining the law was to amass *ḥadīth*—that is, past sayings with chains of transmission *(asānīd)*—as opposed to elaborating by analogy a complete, self-consistent law.

Bibliography

al-Faḍl b. Dukayn, *Kitāb al-ṣalāt*, ed. Ṣalāḥ b. ʿĀyiḍ al-Shallāḥī, Medina 1417/1996; Ibn al-Nadīm, *Kitāb al-fihrist*, ed. Ayman Fuʾād al-Sayyid, 4 vols. (London 1435/2014²), 2:90; Ibn Saʿd, *Kitāb al-ṭabaqāt al-kabīr*, ed. E. Sachau et al. (Leiden 1912–40), 6:279–80; al-Khaṭīb al-Baghdādī, *Taʾrīkh Madīnat al-Salām*, ed. Bashshār ʿAwwād Maʿrūf (Beirut 1422/2001), 14:307–20; *GAS*, 1:101; al-Mizzī, *Tahdhīb al-Kamāl*, ed. Bashshār ʿAwwād Maʿrūf, 35 vols. (Beirut 1402–13/1982–92), 23:197–220.

Christopher Melchert

H

Ḥāshid

Ḥāshid is the name of a set of tribes in northern Yemen. In genealogies from the Islamic period, Ḥāshid and Bakīl appear as brothers descended from Hamdān b. Zayd, and Hamdān had been the name of the leading Ḥāshid family before Islam. The fourth/tenth-century account of the geographer and genealogist al-Ḥasan al-Hamdānī (d. 334/945) suggests complex layering of identity. Khārif, for example, now a major Ḥāshid tribe, is depicted as widely scattered rather than a discrete entity, yet Khārif sent a delegation to the prophet Muḥammad. Until at least the early seventh/thirteenth century most of Khārif's present-day territory was identified with a tribe named al-Ṣayad, which itself later figures as one of the three sections of Khārif.

The four major Ḥāshid tribes in the post-mediaeval period are Khārif, al-ʿUṣaymāt, ʿIdhar, and Banī Ṣuraym, which between them occupy most of the area between ʿAmrān and Ḥūth. Al-ʿUṣaymāt's territory contains much of the area of al-Baṭana, west of Ḥūth, where run-off from the mountains allows intensive sorghum cultivation. At all periods, however, the Ḥāshid tribes depended largely on rain-fed farming and were thus vulnerable to drought. All four of the tribes mentioned were repeatedly in alliance or dispute with non-tribal rulers, often over control of richer land elsewhere in Yemen. In recent times Sanḥān (originally seen as part of Madhḥij), Hamdān Ṣanʿāʾ, and Bilād al-Rūs have also been considered Ḥāshidī.

The Ḥāshid tribes are less extensive than those of Bakīl but have often been more coherent politically. The al-Aḥmar family, from al-ʿUṣaymāt, have been recognised as paramount *shaykhs* (sing., *shaykh al-mashāyikh*) since the early twelfth/eighteenth century. The grave of ʿAlī b. Qāsim al-Aḥmar (d. 1140/1727), probably the second of the al-Aḥmar line, is at al-Khamrī, near Ḥūth. The family was prominent throughout the nineteenth century. The recognition of Yaḥyā b. Muḥammad Ḥamīd al-Dīn as Zaydī *imām* in 1904 is said to have owed much to the support he received from Nāṣir b. Mabkhūt al-Aḥmar.

In 1960 Imām Aḥmad, who had succeeded his father, Yaḥyā, as *imām* in 1948, executed Ḥusayn al-Aḥmar and his son Ḥamīd. During the Yemeni civil war (1962–70) most of Ḥāshid supported the Republic. ʿAbdallāh b. Ḥusayn al-Aḥmar, the paramount *shaykh* during this period, emerged as a major figure in Republican politics. After the war he was chair of North Yemen's Consultative Council for several years and, after the unification of the two Yemens, was speaker of the national parliament from 1993 until his death in 2007. He was one of the founders of the reformist al-Iṣlāḥ party. Some parts of Ḥāshid benefitted from involvement with government in the last decades of the twentieth century. Other parts remained extremely poor.

After ʿAlī ʿAbdallāh Ṣāliḥ, an army officer from Sanḥān, became President of North Yemen in 1978, many authors described the country as being ruled by Ḥāshid. The prominence of Sanḥān owed more to the history of Yemen's regular army than to tribal considerations, and the ruling group's relations with most of Ḥāshid were in fact distant. Sometimes confusion arose because certain members of the ruling group had the surname al-Aḥmar. They were not, however, related to the paramount *shaykhs* of Ḥāshid.

Bibliography

ʿAbdallāh b. Ḥusayn al-Aḥmar, *Mudhakkirāt, qaḍāyā wa-mawāqif*, Ṣanʿāʾ 2007; Paul Dresch, *Tribes, government, and history in Yemen*, Oxford 1989; al-Ḥasan al-Hamdānī, *al-Iklīl min akhbār al-Yaman, al-kitāb al-ʿāshir*, ed. Muḥibb al-Dīn al-Khaṭīb, Cairo 1368/1948; al-Ḥasan al-Hamdānī, *Ṣifat Jazīrat al-ʿArab*, ed. D. H. Müller, Amsterdam 1968; Ibrāhīm b. Aḥmad al-Maqḥafī, *Muʿjam al-buldān wa-l-qabāʾil al-Yamaniyya*, 2 vols., Ṣanʿāʾ 2002; Robert Wilson, Al-Hamdānī's description of Ḥāshid and Bakīl, in *Proceedings of the Seminar for Arabian Studies* 11 (1981), 95–104.

Paul Dresch

I

Ibn Abī l-Ḍiyāf

Aḥmad **Ibn Abī l-Ḍiyāf** (1802–74) was, from 1827 to 1867, the personal secretary to the Ḥusaynid governors who had ruled the Ottoman province of Tunis since 1117/1705. He wrote an important chronicle in Arabic about the history of Tunisia and played a major role in 1861 in the promulgation of the first national constitution in a Muslim country.

His family was part of the Awlād ʿŪn tribe in the Silyāna, southwest of Tunis. Ḍiyāf's father moved to Tunis and became, by the end of the twelfth/eighteenth century, the private secretary of prominent local dignitaries and statesmen such as the *wazīr* and *mamlūk* Yūsuf Ṣāḥib al-Ṭābiʿ (d. 1230/1815). Aḥmad's father was ousted from office when his patron, the former *wazīr*, was killed in 1815.

Disregarding the advice of his father, who feared that his son would similarly fall into political disfavour, Ḍiyāf decided to become a scribe and adviser to the beys and was charged with crucial tasks, including political missions to the imperial capital, Istanbul, in 1830 and 1842. He also followed the bey Aḥmad (r. 1837–55) during his journey in France in 1846, the first such trip made by a North African and Muslim sovereign.

Ḍiyāf was, above all, deeply involved in the implementation of the Ottoman reforms in Tunis. He was one of the main authors of two major legal texts implemented under European pressure: the 1857 *ʿahd al-amān*, which established legal equality and full security for all inhabitants of Tunisia—whether Muslims, Jews, or Christians—and the 1861 constitution, the first such document in the Muslim world. While drawing up these major legal transformations, Ibn Abī l-Ḍiyāf wanted to involve the *ʿulamāʾ* whom he had known since his training at the Great Mosque of the Zaytūna, but the Islamic scholars kept their distance from the implementation of laws that did not originate with God and the *sharīʿa*.

Ḍiyāf was shunted aside, especially from 1867 to 1873, as he was less and less comfortable endorsing the policy of Muḥammad al-Ṣādiq Bāshā Bey (r. 1859–82), whom he criticised for becoming an absolute monarch. Having written some poetry and a great number of administrative letters, he spent the last years of his life completing his *ta'rīkh* (chronicle) titled *Itḥāf ahl al-zamān bi-akhbār mulūk Tūnis wa-ʿahd al-amān* ("Presenting to contemporaries the history of the rulers of Tunis and the fundamental pact"), a major source for the history of modern Tunisia.

The *Itḥāf* narrates the history of Tunisia from the mediaeval period to 1872. It becomes more interesting when its author reaches the end of the twelfth/eighteenth century and narrates events that he and his father experienced. Ḍiyāf does not rely solely on his own memory but also quotes administrative documents and relies on other eyewitness accounts. As a former servant of the Ḥusaynid dynasty, he praises his masters who were able to establish themselves in Tunis, but he also warns his readers against the danger of absolute power, which, according to him, ruined every dynasty that had ruled this part of the Maghrib.

Bibliography

Works by Ibn Abī l-Ḍiyāf

Dīwān Aḥmad b. Abī l-Ḍiyāf min Majmaʿ al-dawāwīn al-Tūnisiyya, ed. Muḥammad b. ʿUthmān al-Sanūsī and Aḥmad al-Ṭawīlī, Tunis 2002; *Itḥāf ahl al-zamān bi-akhbār mulūk Tūnis wa-ʿahd al-amān*, 8 vols., Tunis 1963–6, excerpts selected and trans. L. Carl Brown, *Consult them in the matter. A nineteenth century Islamic argument for constitutional government. The muqaddima (introduction) to Ithaf ahl al-zaman*, Fayetteville AR 2005; *Rasāʾil Aḥmad ibn Abī l-Ḍiyāf al-sirriyya ilā Maḥmūd ibn ʿAyyād, 1850–1853*, ed. Yūnus Waṣīfī, Tunis 2005; *Risālat al-Mannāʿī ilā l-Mushīr al-Awwal Aḥmad Bāy fī l-shakwā min Aḥmad Ibn Abī l-Ḍiyāf wa-sāʾir aʿdāʾih*, ed. Aḥmad al-Ṭawīlī, Tunis 1977.

Studies

Ahmed Abdesselem, *Les historiens tunisiens des XVIIe, XVIIIe, et XIXe siècles*, Tunis 1973; André Demeerseman, *Aspects de la société tunisienne d'après Ibn Abî l-Dhiyâf*, Tunis 1996; Ahmed Jdey, *Ahmed ibn Abi Dhiaf. Son œuvre & sa pensée. Essai d'histoire culturelle*, Zaghouan 1996; Muḥammad Maḥfūz, *Ibn Abī Ḍiyāf. Ḥayātuhu, naẓarāt fī ta'rīkhihi*, Tunis 1983; Béchir Tlili, Note sur la notion d'état dans la pensée de Ah'mad Ibn Abi ad'-D'iyâf, *RMMM* 8 (1970), 141–70.

M'hamed Oualdi

Ibn Abī Shayba

Abū Bakr ʿAbdallāh b. Muḥammad **Ibn Abī Shayba** al-ʿAbsī (d. 235/849) was a prominent Sunnī *ḥadīth* scholar who lived most of his life in Kufa. His grandfather was a *qāḍī* (judge) in Wāsiṭ (Iraq), his father was a *qāḍī* in Fārs province (Iran), and his brother ʿUthmān (d. 239/853–4) was a respected *ḥadīth* scholar.

Ibn Abī Shayba was born in Kufa in 156/773, where he collected reports from numerous Iraqi teachers, especially Wakīʿ b. al-Jarrāḥ (d. 197/813), whose *Muṣannaf* (a collection of reports arranged topically) may have been incorporated into Ibn Abī Shayba's own writings. Ibn Abī Shayba appears to have avoided the *miḥna* (inquisition) concerning the createdness of the Qurʾān that the ʿAbbāsid caliph al-Maʾmūn (r. 189–218/813–33) initiated, and he was among the handful of *ḥadīth* scholars whom the caliph al-Mutawakkil (r. 232–247/847–61) brought to Baghdad to narrate anti-Muʿtazilī *ḥadīth*s in 234/848–9, the year in which he ended the inquisition. Ibn Abī Shayba had numerous students, and more than one thousand of his *ḥadīth*s are found in the canonical collections of Muslim (d. 261/875) and Ibn Māja (d. 273/887). Later *ḥadīth* critics viewed him favourably and considered him one of the most erudite scholars of his generation, along with Aḥmad b. Ḥanbal (d. 241/855), ʿAlī ibn al-Madīnī (d. 234/849), and Yaḥyā b.

Maʿīn (d. 233/848). Ibn Abī Shayba died in Muḥarram 235/ July–August 849.

Three books are ascribed to Ibn Abī Shayba: *al-Muṣannaf*, *al-Musnad*, and a Qurʾān commentary that is no longer extant. Sections of Ibn Abī Shayba's *Muṣannaf* have been transmitted as independent books, such as his *Kitāb al-īmān* ("Book on faith"), which was edited by the Salafī scholar Nāṣir al-Dīn al-Albānī (d. 1999).

Ibn Abī Shayba's *Muṣannaf* is the largest extant collection of *ḥadīth* from the early period of Islam. It survives only in the recension of Baqī b. Makhlad (d. 276/889), who carried it back to his native city of Córdoba, Spain, where it was transmitted for about three hundred years, before it was brought to the Levant by the Egyptian merchant ʿAbd al-Raḥmān b. Makkī (d. 599/1202–3). The 2006 Riyadh edition of the *Muṣannaf* contains 38,939 reports, with full *isnād*s (chains of transmission), in thirty-nine books. The vast majority of these reports are statements attributed to Companions (*ṣaḥāba*) and Successors (*tābiʿūn*), and the editors of Ibn Abī Shayba's *Muṣannaf* estimate that only one in six of its reports is a Prophetic *ḥadīth*. Some of the most important religious authorities Ibn Abī Shayba cites are the Successors al-Ḥasan al-Baṣrī (d. 110/728), Ibrāhīm al-Nakhaʿī (d. 95/114), and ʿĀmir al-Shaʿbī (d. between 103/721 and 110/728), as well as the Companions ʿUmar b. al-Khaṭṭāb (d. 23/644) and ʿAlī b. Abī Ṭālib (d. 40/661). Remarkably, Ibn Abī Shayba does not cite in his *Muṣannaf* the opinions of any post-Successor scholars, such as Sufyān al-Thawrī (d. 161/778) or Mālik b. Anas (d. 179/795). He cites 125 opinions of Abū Ḥanīfa (d. 150/767) only in order to demonstrate that they contradict the Prophet's *sunna*; that section is titled "Refutation of Abū Ḥanīfa."

Ibn Abī Shayba's *Muṣannaf* is distinguished from the *Muṣannaf* of ʿAbd al-Razzāq al-Ṣanʿānī (d. 211/827) in terms of both scale and breadth of topics covered. In addition to books on the standard legal topics and the Prophet's expeditions (*maghāzī*), which are common to both *Muṣannaf*s, Ibn Abī Shayba includes substantial books on morals and manners (*adab*), supplications (*duʿāʾ*), renunciation (*zuhd*), special qualities of select early Muslims (*faḍāʾil*), and apocalyptic prophesies (*fitan*), along with shorter books on faith, necrology of *ḥadīth* narrators (*taʾrīkh*), the aforementioned refutation of a selection of Abū Ḥanīfa's legal opinions, and precedents (*awāʾil*).

The *Muṣannaf* is an excellent example of what Joseph Schacht called "Traditionist jurisprudence." Ibn Abī Shayba was an independent scholar who displayed no loyalty to any of the emerging legal schools of his day. His primary method was to collect as many Prophetic, Companion, and Successor opinions as possible for each legal topic, each with a complete *isnād*, in order to show the range of rulings that the earliest Muslims proposed. His approach identifies topics upon which the earliest Muslim authorities were in consensus, and the far larger array of legal topics over which there was disagreement. Ibn Abī Shayba rarely provides explicit legal opinions of his own, nor does he indicate his preference in cases of disagreement. His primary contribution to Islamic law is the preservation and clear presentation of thousands of legal opinions ascribed to the Prophet, Companions, and Successors. These provide historical insight into the nature of Muslim jurisprudence prior to the crystallisation of the classical Sunnī schools of law.

Ibn Abī Shayba also compiled a substantial *Musnad* (a collection of *ḥadīth* arranged according to who narrated each report), only two fragments of which survive and have been published. One fragment contains the *ḥadīth*s Ibn Abī Shayba narrated through 32 Companions, while the other one contains *ḥadīth*s narrated through 256 Companions, each of whom contributed just one or two *ḥadīth*s. Altogether, the published edition of Ibn Abī Shayba's *Musnad* contains 998 *ḥadīth*s, 258 of which are narrated by the famous Companion who settled in Kufa, ʿAbdallāh b. Masʿūd (d. 32/652–3).

Bibliography

Works

Kitāb al-īmān, ed. Nāṣir al-Dīn al-Albānī, Damascus 1983; *al-Muṣannaf*, ed. Ḥamad al-Jumʿa and Muḥammad Laḥīdān, 16 vols., Riyadh 2006; *al-Muṣannaf* (with cross-references for each *ḥadīth*), ed. Abū Muḥammad Usāma b. Ibrāhīm, 15 vols., Cairo 2008, available at https://archive.org/details/waq110421; *Musnad Ibn Abī Shayba*, ed. Aḥmad al-Mazīdī and ʿĀdil al-Ghazāwī, 2 vols., Riyadh (n.d.).

Sources

al-Khaṭīb al-Baghdādī, *Taʾrīkh Madīnat al-Salām*, ed. Bashshār Maʿrūf (Beirut 2001), 11:259–67; al-Dhahabī, *Siyar aʿlām al-nubalāʾ*, ed. Shuʿayb Arnāʾūṭ (Beirut 2001), 11:122–7; al-Dhahabī, *Tadhkirat al-ḥuffāẓ* (Beirut 1998), 2:16–7; Ibn Ḥajar al-ʿAsqalānī, *Tahdhīb al-tahdhīb* (Beirut 2004), 3:636–7.

Studies

Scott C. Lucas, Where are the legal ḥadīth? A study of the Muṣannaf of Ibn Abī Shayba, *ILS* (2008), 283–314; Scott C. Lucas, Principles of traditionist jurisprudence reconsidered, *MW* (2010), 145–56; Joseph Schacht, *The origins of Muhammadan jurisprudence*, Oxford 1953; *GAS* 1:108–9.

Scott C. Lucas

Ibn Faḍlallāh al-ʿUmarī

Shihāb al-Dīn Abū l-ʿAbbās Aḥmad b. Yaḥyā **Ibn Faḍlallāh** b. Mujallī b. Daʿjān al-Qurashī al-ʿAdawī **al-ʿUmarī** (d. 9 Dhū l-Ḥijja 749/28 February 1349) was the most renowned member of an illustrious family of chancery officials who served the Mamlūk sultanate for over a century. By the time of Ibn Faḍlallāh's birth in Damascus on 3 Shawwāl 700/11 June 1301, the family had already seen its sons attain high office, including his father, Muḥyī l-Dīn Yaḥyā b. Faḍlallāh (d. 738/1337), who spent over twenty years as the secretary of state (*kātib al-sirr*) of the chanceries of Damascus and Cairo. Shihāb al-Dīn worked in the Damascus chancery as a young man under the tutelage of the great littérateur Shihāb al-Dīn Maḥmūd al-Ḥalabī (d. 725/1325), and he received a comprehensive education in the scribal arts, law, prosody, rhetoric, *ḥadīth*, and other subjects.

In 729/1329, Ibn Faḍlallāh accompanied his father to Cairo, where the latter was appointed head of the chancery, a post he held until his death. During these years, Ibn Faḍlallāh assisted his father in the service of the Mamlūk sultan al-Nāṣir Muḥammad (third and final reign, 709–41/1310–41), reading the sultan his correspondence and authoring official letters and decrees. In 736/1336, at the request of the powerful viceroy of Syria Sayf al-Dīn Tankiz (d. 740/1340), Nāṣir al-Dīn appointed one Ibn al-Quṭb as head of the chancery in Damascus, a position that Ibn Faḍlallāh coveted. Unable to disguise his disdain, he protested Nāṣir al-Dīn's demand that he write the letter of investiture, claiming that Ibn al-Quṭb was a converted Copt. The sultan was furious and ordered Muḥyī al-Dīn to replace his impetuous son with a more obedient one, ʿAlāʾ al-Dīn ʿAlī (d. 769/1368). Shihāb al-Dīn was put under house arrest and later imprisoned in the citadel (Shaʿbān 739-Rabīʿ I 740/February 1339-September 1339) for again inciting the displeasure of the sultan.

Unlike ʿAlāʾ al-Dīn, who eventually succeeded his father as *kātib al-sirr* in Cairo and remained in this position for over thirty years, Shihāb al-Dīn was not adept at finding steady work in the Mamlūk administration. His fortunes apparently changed after emerging from prison, when he was appointed *kātib al-sirr* in Damascus. He entered the chancery on ʿĀshūrāʾ 741 (6 July 1340) and shortly thereafter hired the great poet Ibn Nubāta (d. 768/1366), who had long-standing ties to the Ibn Faḍlallāh family. Within another year, though, Shihāb al-Dīn was stripped from his post and replaced by another brother, Badr al-Dīn Muḥammad (d. 746/1345). He was given a position at the Falakiyya *madrasa* in Damascus, but that was also short-lived, as he was summoned to Cairo to answer for the great number of complaints about him. After his brother ʿAlāʾ al-Dīn intervened on his behalf, he was able to return to Damascus, where he spent the rest of his life without employment, composing his literary works. When the Black Death arrived in Syria, Ibn Faḍlallāh left Damascus for Mecca with his family but changed course and went to Jerusalem instead, where his wife succumbed to the plague. He died soon thereafter and was buried in his family's mausoleum in Damascus.

Ibn Faḍlallāh was famous among his contemporaries for his brilliance as a prose stylist and his prodigious memory. Al-Ṣafadī (d. 764/1363) reckoned him among the greatest chancery writers since al-Qāḍī l-Fāḍil (d. 596/1200), mentioning him in the same company as Muḥyī l-Dīn Ibn ʿAbd al-Ẓāhir (d. 692/1293) and Shihāb al-Dīn Maḥmūd al-Ḥalabī. His professional difficulties notwithstanding, Ibn Faḍlallāh authored one of the most important chancery manuals of the Mamlūk period, *al-Taʿrīf bi-l-muṣṭalaḥ al-sharīf* ("The explanation of noble protocols"), which provided appropriate formulae for writing letters to dignitaries, as well as guidelines for penning oaths, official decrees, letters of investiture, truces, agreements, annulments, and other documents. The book was popular among bureaucrats and prompted an updated version in Ibn Nāẓir al-Jaysh's (d. 786/1384) *Tathqīf al-Taʿrīf* ("The cultivation of *The explanation*") and a totalising compendium of scribal practice in al-Qalqashandī's (d. 821/1418) *Ṣubḥ al-aʿshā fī ṣināʿat al-inshāʾ* ("Dawn of the night-blind, on the art of epistolography").

Ibn Faḍlallāh is best known for his monumental *Masālik al-abṣār fī mamālik al-amṣār* ("The routes of insight into the civilised realms"), an encyclopaedic 27-volume compendium. The title and preface suggest that it fits within the venerable genre of geographical writing known as *masālik wa-mamālik* (routes and realms); however, the work incorporates so many elements from other genres and knowledge practices that it appears to represent a different genre altogether. The *Masālik* is divided into two uneven sections of four and twenty-three volumes. The first section addresses geographical topics; the second is devoted mainly to history. A considerable proportion of the work consists of biographies of famous individuals of the Islamic world, arranged by professional category (for example, Qurʾān reciters, jurists, lexicographers, grammarians, philosophers, singers, chancery scribes, and poets) and organised along the conceit of judging the merits of the Islamic East and West *(al-inṣāf bayna l-mashriq wa-l-maghrib)*. Ibn Faḍlallāh was not agnostic on this question; much of the *Masālik* seems to have been a response to the famous compendium by Ibn Saʿīd al-Maghribī (d. 685/1286), *al-Mughrib fī ḥulā l-Maghrib* ("The extraordinary [book] on the delights of the Maghrib"), which exalted the history and literature of the Islamic West.

In light of Ibn Faḍlallāh's rebellious personality, it is unsurprising that in the *Masālik* he is often dismissive of the opinions of his predecessors in the discipline of geography. As he writes in the preface,

> Having consulted all of the books written about the states and contents of the terrestrial climes, I did not find any that scrutinised their conditions or depicted their forms, for most of these books only contain old reports and [stories] about the conditions of long-gone kings, extinct civilisations, and customs that have vanished along with their peoples. There is not much benefit or purpose in merely recounting them, for the best statement is the truest one, and people resemble their contemporaries more than they do their own ancestors.

Partly because of this concern with contemporary knowledge, the work has been exploited by scholars of the Mamlūk period for its historical data.

In addition to the *Taʿrīf* and the *Masālik*, Ibn Faḍlallāh authored various other lesser-known texts, including a four-volume history of the family of ʿUmar b. al-Khaṭṭāb—the second of the Rightly Guided caliphs (r. 13–23/634–44), from whom the Banū Faḍlallāh claimed descent—a collection of poems praising the prophet Muḥammad, and several anthologies.

Bibliography

Works

Masālik al-abṣār fī mamālik al-amṣār, ed. ʿAbdallāh b. Yaḥyā l-Sarīḥī et al., Abu Dhabi 2001–; *Masālik al-abṣār fī mamālik al-amṣār*, ed. Kāmil Salmān al-Jubūrī et al., Beirut 2010; *Masālik al-abṣār fī mamālik al-amṣār*, vol. 1, *L'Afrique moins l'Egypte*, trans. Gaudefroy-Demombynes, Paris 1927; *al-Taʿrīf bi-l-muṣṭalaḥ al-sharīf*, ed. Samīr al-Durūbī, al-Karak 1992; *Kitāb al-durar al-farāʾid min ghurar al-qalāʾid*, Amman 2015; *Dhahabiyyat al-ʿaṣr*, ed. Ibrāhīm Ṣāliḥ, Beirut 2011.

Sources

Ibn Ḥajar al-ʿAsqalānī, *al-Durar al-kāmina*, Hyderabad 1972², 1:393–5; al-Kutubī, *Fawāt al-wafayāt*, ed. Iḥsān ʿAbbās, Beirut 1973, 1:157–61; al-Ṣafadī, *al-Wāfī bi-l-wafayāt*, ed. Aḥmad al-Arnāʾūṭ and Turkī Muṣṭafā, Beirut 2000, 8:163–75.

Studies

Régis Blachère, Quelques réflexions sur les formes de l'encyclopédisme en Égypte et en Syrie du VIIIᵉ/XIVᵉ siècle à la fin du IXᵉ/XVᵉ siècle, *BEO* 23 (1970), 7–19; Richard Hartmann, Politische Geographie des Mamlūkenreichs. Kapitel 5 und 6 des Staatshandbuchs Ibn Faḍlallāh al-ʿOmarī, *ZDMG* 70/1–2 (1916), 1–40, and 3–4 (1916), 477–511; Dorothea Krawulsky, al-Badw fī Miṣr wa-l-Shām fī l-qarnayn al-sābiʿ wa-l-thāmin al-hijriyayn ʿind al-ʿUmarī fī *Masālik al-abṣār*, *al-Ijtihād* 4/17 (1992), 35–72; Dorothea Krawulsky, *Masālik al-abṣār fī mamālik al-amṣār* li-Ibn Faḍlallāh al-ʿUmarī (700–749 H./1301–1349 M.). Muḥāwala fī sīra taʾrīkhiyya li-makhṭūṭātih, *Dirāsāt: al-Silsila A, al-ʿUlūm al-insāniyya* 17 (1990), 169–85; Klaus Lech, *Das mongolische Weltreich. Al-ʿUmarī's Darstellung der mongolischen Reiche in seinem Werk* Masālik al-abṣār fī mamālik al-amṣār, Wiesbaden 1968; Rüdiger Lohlker, Al-ʿUmarīs Bericht über Indien. Eine Studie zur arabisch-islamischen Geographie des 14. Jahrhunderts, *ZDMG* 156/2 (2006), 339–67; Etienne Quatremère, Notices de l'ouvrage entitulé *Masâlek-el-absâr*, *Notices et extraits des manuscrits de la Bibliothèque du roi* 13 (1838), 151–384; D. S. Rice, A miniature in an autograph of Shihāb al-Dīn Ibn Faḍlallāh al-ʿUmarī, *BSOAS* 13/4 (1951), 856–67.

Elias Muhanna

Ibn al-Furāt

Abū l-Ḥasan ʿAlī b. Muḥammad **Ibn al-Furāt** (241–312/855–924) was an ʿAbbāsid scribe (*kātib*) and *wazīr* from a famous Shīʿī secretarial family, the Banū l-Furāt. He served the caliph al-Muqtadir (r. 295–320/908–32) as *wazīr* on three separate occasions. Contemporaries praised him for his financial expertise and generosity, but he was also criticised, especially for his harsh conduct against colleagues during his third and last wazīrate (311–2/923–4), the so-called "year of destruction."

1. Background

Members of the Banū l-Furāt figure in the sources since the days of the caliph al-Muʿtamid (r. 256–79/870–92). Some identify Muḥammad b. Mūsā b. al-Furāt (fl. third/ninth century), the father of Abū l-Ḥasan ʿAlī, as the first scribe within the family; others mention his elder brother Abū l-ʿAbbās Aḥmad (d. 291/904) as the first to enter state service. The Banū l-Furāt was a family of merchants and financiers, probably originating from upper Nahrawān, on the eastern shore of the Tigris (al-Hamadhānī, 246; Ibn al-Najjār, 19:66; al-Ṣābiʾ, 8).

Some of the family's members seem to have been prominent figures within the Shīʿī community of Muḥammad b. Nuṣayr al-Namīrī (d. 270/883), a Basran who claimed to be either a prophet or the *bāb* (literally "gate," a leading disciple of the Imām). He is alleged to have believed in the divine nature of the Imām. Muḥammad b. Nuṣayr was affiliated with the tenth and eleventh of the Twelver Shīʿī Imāms, ʿAlī al-Hādī (d. 254/868) and al-Ḥasan al-ʿAskarī (d. 260/874), and later may have founded the Nuṣayriyya movement which remains, however, contested by scholars (Massignon, Les origins; Massignon, Recherches).

2. Early career

The two brothers Abū l-ʿAbbās Aḥmad and Abū l-Ḥasan ʿAlī b. al-Furāt were recruited by the *wazīr* Ismāʿīl b. Bulbul (d. c.278/892), who served the caliph al-Muʿtamid (r. 256–79/870–92). Ismāʿīl b. Bulbul had Shīʿī sympathies and hired the two brothers for their financial expertise. The elder brother, Aḥmad, became head of the *dīwān al-dār* (the coordinating bureau for the land tax administration of the entire caliphate) under the caliph al-Muʿtaḍid (r. 279–89/892–902) and continued as financial director of the *dīwān al-sawād* (bureau of the land tax of Iraq) under the caliph al-Muktafī (r. 289–95/902–8; van Berkel, Bureaucracy, 89–90; Bowen, 324; Sourdel, *Vizirat*, 334–5, 590–1, 737; Sourdel, Gouvernement, 49–50). His younger brother ʿAlī assisted him (al-Ṣābiʾ, 131; al-Tanūkhī, 8:24).

After Aḥmad's death in 291/904, ʿAlī became the director of the *dīwān al-sawād* himself, serving under the *wazīr* al-ʿAbbās b. al-Ḥasan (d. 296/908). As one of the most important *kuttāb* (scribes) of the ʿAbbāsid administration, he played an important role in the selection of the next caliph after the death of al-Muktafī. He supported the young prince Jaʿfar (the later caliph al-Muqtadir) against the more-experienced ʿAbdallāh b al-Muʿtazz. According to the chronicler Miskawayh (d. 421/1030), Ibn al-Furāt explained his motivation with the words: "Why should you appoint a man who will govern, who knows our resources, who will administer affairs himself, and will regard himself as independent? Why do you not entrust this matter to someone who will leave you to manage it?" (Miskawayh, 1:3)

The main competitors of the Banū l-Furāt in the Baghdadi administration of the late third/ninth and early fourth/tenth centuries were the Banū l-Jarrāḥ, a secretarial family of Christian descent from Dayr Qunnā, a town some ninety kilometres south of Baghdad. The head of the Banū l-Jarrāḥ in the days of Abū l-Ḥasan ʿAlī b. al-Furāt was ʿAlī b. ʿĪsā (d. 334/946), the so-called "good *wazīr*". ʿAlī b. ʿĪsā had been trained by the brothers Aḥmad and ʿAlī b. al-Furāt, but, over the course of al-Muqtadir's reign, the families became each other's main competitors for positions and influence (See also van Berkel, ʿAlī b. ʿĪsā; Bowen). During the early years of the caliph al-Muqtadir's reign, the wazīrate often alternated between them. The Banū l-Jarrāḥ had supported Ibn al-Muʿtazz, and consequently, after the failed coup of Ibn al-Muʿtazz in 296/908, it was Ibn al-Furāt and not one of the members of the Banū l-Jarrāḥ who was rewarded with the wazīrate.

3. Three wazīrates

Ibn al-Furāt's first wazīrate (296–9/908–12) was relatively successful. The prosperous province of Fārs was brought back under the control of Baghdad and the *wazīr* was able to reach agreements with local rebels such as al-Ḥusayn b. Ḥamdān (d. 306/918) from Mosul and Ibn Abī l-Sāj (d. 315/928) from Azerbaijan and Armenia. Ibn al-Furāt largely maintained very good relations with members of the caliphal family and the court attendants. He showered them with gifts and allowances (see, for example, Miskawayh, 1:13). He was particularly close to the queen mother, Shaghab (d. 321/933), a highly influential woman at the court of her young son. At her request, Ibn al-Furāt called al-Muqtadir "his son," took him on his lap, and spoke for him during meetings (al-Ṣābiʾ, 117). Ibn al-Furāt's first wazīrate ended as the result of an immediate shortage of cash in the treasury—a recurrent theme of al-Muqtadir's reign—which prevented the *wazīr* from organising for the *ḥajj* (ʿArīb, 32–40; Miskawayh, 1:7–20; al-Ṣābiʾ, 25–9; al-Ṭabarī, 3:2287).

As a result of these monetary problems and the wazīr's subsequent request for a loan from the private purse of the caliph, his administration fell. Ibn al-Furāt was arrested and his house placed under surveillance. After his release from a five-year confinement, Ibn al-Furāt was appointed to the wazīrate for a second time, in 304/917. This term in office was less successful than his first. The army lost an important battle against Ibn Abī l-Sāj, the leader of Armenia and Azerbaijan, and Ibn al-Furāt's administration was plagued by constant shortages. At the same time, Ibn al-Furāt raised the allowances of the caliphal family and amassed enormous riches for himself and his family (Miskawayh, 1:64). His former protégé, Ibn Muqla (d. 328/940), betrayed his patron by revealing details of his hidden assets to his political enemy, the chamberlain (*ḥājib*) Naṣr (d. 316/928). In 306/918, he was accused of treason and taken into custody once again (ʿArīb, 59–70; Ibn al-Athīr, 8:98–111; Ibn al-Jawzī, 13:166; Miskawayh, 1:41–59; al-Ṣābiʾ, 30–3).

In 311/923, Ibn al-Furāt returned to the political arena—after years of confinement in the palace—when he was reinstated as *wazīr* for a third term in office. All sources agree that this third wazīrate was disastrous. At the beginning of his term, Ibn al-Furāt convinced the caliph al-Muqtadir to confiscate huge sums from his predecessors Ḥāmid b. al-ʿAbbās (d. 311/923) and ʿAlī b. ʿĪsā and their dependents to solve the financial problems of the caliphate. The *wazīr* and his son Muḥassin (d. 312/924) then harshly interrogated, tortured, and eventually even killed some of the former officials to extract money from them. The brutality of these interrogations led chroniclers to call 312/924 "the year of destruction" (ʿArīb, 97). At the same time, the Qarāmiṭa, an Ismāʿīlī group operating in the Syrian desert and northeastern Arabia, sacked the city of Basra and attacked the *ḥajj* caravan. Because of his Shīʿī background, the *wazīr*'s political enemies accused him of secretly collaborating with this sect. In 312/924, Ibn al-Furāt and his son al-Muḥassin were arrested, interrogated and, finally, executed. Their heads were shown to the caliph before being thrown into the river. Ibn al-Furāt's age on the day of his execution was seventy-one years. (ʿArīb, 97–107; Ibn al-Athīr, 8:139–55; Ibn al-Jawzī, 13:219–20, 238–44; Miskawayh, 1:91–139; al-Ṣābiʾ, 34–62).

Bibliography

Sources

Muḥammad b. ʿAbd al-Malik Ibn al-Athīr al-Hamadhānī, *Takmilat taʾrīkh al-Ṭabarī*, ed. Muḥammad Abū l-Faḍl Ibrāhīm, Cairo 1977[2]; Ibn al-Athīr, *al-Kāmil fī l-taʾrīkh*, ed. Carolus J. Tornberg, 14 vols., Leiden 1851–76, reprint Beirut 1979–82; Ibn al-Jawzī, *al-Muntaẓam fī taʾrīkh al-mulūk wa-l-umam*, ed. Muḥammad ʿAbd al-Qādir ʿAṭāʾ and Muṣṭafā ʿAbd al-Qādir ʿAṭāʾ, 19 vols., Beirut 1992–3; Ibn al-Najjār al-Baghdādī, *Dhayl taʾrīkh Baghdād*, ed. Muṣṭafā ʿAbd al-Qādir ʿAṭāʾ, Beirut 1997; Miskawayh, *Tajārib al-umam. The eclipse of the Abbasid caliphate*, ed. H. F. Amedroz, trans. D. S. Margoliouth, 6 vols., Oxford 1920–1; ʿArīb b. Saʿd al-Qurṭubī, *Ṣilat taʾrīkh al-Ṭabarī*, ed. Muḥammad Abū l-Faḍl Ibrāhīm, Cairo 1977[2]; Hilāl al-Ṣābiʾ, *Tuḥfat al-umarāʾ fī taʾrīkh al-wuzarāʾ. The historical remains of Hilâl al-Ṣâbī. First part of his Kitab al-wuzara (Gotha MS., 1756) and fragment of his history 389–393 A.H. (B. M. MS, add. 19360)*, ed. H. F. Amedroz, Beirut 1904; Abū Bakr al-Ṣūlī, *Mā lam yunshar min awrāq al-Ṣūlī. Akhbār al-sanawāt 295–315 h.*, ed. Hilāl Nājī, Beirut 2000; al-Ṭabarī, *Taʾrīkh al-rusul wa-l-mulūk*, ed. M. J. de Goeje et al., 15 vols., Leiden 1879–1901; al-Tanūkhī, *Nishwār al-muḥāḍara*, ed. ʿAbbūd al-Shālijī, 8 vols., Beirut 1971–3.

Studies

Maaike van Berkel, The bureaucracy, in Maaike van Berkel, Nadia Maria El Cheikh, Hugh Kennedy, and Letizia Osti (eds.), *Crisis and continuity at the Abbasid court. Formal and informal politics in the caliphate of al-Muqtadir (295–320/908–32)* (Leiden 2013), 87–109; Maaike van Berkel, ʿAlī b. ʿĪsā b. Dāʾūd b. al-Jarrāḥ, *EI3*; Maaike van Berkel, Nadia Maria El Cheikh, Hugh Kennedy, and Letizia Osti (eds.), *Crisis and continuity at the Abbasid court. Formal and informal politics in the caliphate of al-Muqtadir (295–320/908–932)*, Leiden 2013; Irit Irene Blay-Abramski, *From Damascus to Baghdad. The ʿAbbāsid administrative system as a product of the Umayyad heritage (41/661–320/932)*, Ph.D. dissertation, Princeton University 1982; Harold Bowen, *The life and times of ʿAlī b. ʿĪsā, the "Good Vizier,"* Cambridge 1928; ʿAbd al-Azīz al-Dūrī, *Taʾrīkh al-ʿIrāq al-iqtiṣādī fī l-qarn al-rābiʿ al-hijrī*, Beirut 1999; Nadia Maria El Cheikh, The Court of al-muqtadir. its space and its occupant, in John Nawas (ed.), *ʿAbbāsid studies II. Occasional papers of the School of ʿAbbāsid Studies, Leuven 28 June–1 July, 2004* (Leuven 2010), 319–36; Paul L. Heck, *The construction of knowledge in Islamic civilization. Qudāma b. Jaʿfar and his Kitāb al-kharāj wa-ṣināʿat al-kitāba*, Leiden 2002; Frede Løkkegaard, *Islamic taxation in the classical period. With special reference to circumstances in Iraq*, Copenhagen 1950; David Bruce Jay Marmer, *The political culture of the ʿAbbāsid court, 279–324 (A.H.)*, Ph.D. diss., Princeton University 1994; Louis Massignon, Les origines shīʿites de la famille vizirale des Banū l-Furāt, in William Marçais (ed.), *Melanges Gaudefroy-Demombynes* (Cairo 1935–40), 25–9; Louis Massignon, Recherches sur les shīʿites extrémistes à Baghdad à la fin du troisième siècle de l'Hégire', *ZDMG* 92 (New Series 17) (1938), 378–382; Louis Massignon, La politique islamo-chrétienne des scribes nestoriens de Deïr Qunnä a la court de Baghdad au ixe siècle de notre ère, *Vivre et Penser*, 2nd series (1942), 7–14; Letizia Osti, The wisdom of youth. Legitimising the caliph al-Muqtadir, *Al-Masāq* 19 (2007), 17–27; Letizia Osti, ʿAbbāsid intrigues. Competing for influence at the caliph's court, *al-Masāq* 20/1 (2008), 5–15; Dominique Sourdel, *Le vizirat ʿabbāside de 749 à 936 (132 à 324 de l'hégire)*, 2 vols., Damascus 1959–60; Dominique Sourdel, Gouvernement et administration dans l'Orient islamique jusqu'au milieu du xie siècle, in Domique Sourdel and J. Bosch Vilá (eds.), *Regierung under Verwaltung des vorderen Orients in Islamischer Zeit* (Leiden 1988), 1–70.

Maaike van Berkel

Ibn al-Qaysarānī, Abū l-Faḍl

Abū l-Faḍl Muḥammad b. Abī l-Ḥusayn Ṭāhir b. ʿAlī b. Aḥmad al-Maqdisī al-Shaybānī (448–507/1056–1113), known by his contemporaries as **Ibn al-Qaysarānī** or Ibn Ṭāhir, was a renowned transmitter of Prophetic traditions and the author of many works, including Ṣūfī treatises. Born in Jerusalem in Shawwāl 448/December 1056 to a family from Caesarea, in Palestine (whence his *nisba*s al-Maqdisī and Ibn al-Qaysarānī), he first heard *ḥadīth* recited in his native town at the age of twelve. After his first pilgrimage to Mecca and his visit to Baghdad on his way back in 467/1074–75, he travelled the central and eastern Islamic world, from Egypt to Khurāsān, collecting *ḥadīth* from numerous *shaykh*s. He acquired fame as a transmitter, and his biographers list almost seventy of his *ḥadīth* masters, seven of whom he heard in Syria and Palestine, four in Egypt, five in Arabia, eleven in Iraq and Jazīra, and about forty in Iran. He himself transmitted to numerous disciples, including important *shaykh*s, such as Abū Ṭāhir al-Silafī (d. 576/1180) and the Ibn Nāṣir (d. 550/1155) of Baghdad.

Ibn al-Qaysarānī settled in Hamadhān but continued to travel in search of *ḥadīth*. He left many anecdotes about the daily life of a travelling *muḥaddith*, stressing the difficulties and pains endured by the passionate seeker of traditions, stating that he twice urinated blood during his journeys, always travelled on foot, and accepted no financial assistance. Like many of his contemporaries, he copied books, especially *ḥadīth* collections, for his living and was known as a fast and elegant copyist. His biographers emphasise his ability to walk seventeen to twenty farsangs in twenty-four hours. Such detailed anecdotes are found in his *Kitāb al-manthūr* ("Book written in prose"), and some are quoted by al-Dhahabī (d. 749/1348) in his *Taʾrīkh al-Islām* ("History of Islam") and *Siyar aʿlām al-nubalāʾ* ("Lives of the most famous noble men"). Ibn al-Qaysarānī died in Baghdad on his return from his yearly pilgrimage to Mecca in Rabīʿ I 507/August 1113, aged fifty-nine, in the Ṣūfī lodge *(ribāṭ)* of al-Bisṭāmī, on the west side of the city, and was buried in the adjacent cemetery.

Ibn al-Qaysarānī was a prolific writer, author of dozens of treatises (the *Hadiyat al-ʿārifīn* ("Present to the learned ones") lists sixty-seven titles), dedicated in large part to the science of *ḥadīth* and Qurʾānic studies. He also wrote historical, biographical, and geographical works, such as a *Taʾrīkh ahl al-Shām wa-maʿrifat al-āʾimma min-hum wa-l-aʿlām* ("History of the people of Shām [Syria], and knowledge of their *imām*s and famous men"), a *Lubāb* ("Quintessence"), a *Muʿjam al-bilād* ("Dictionary of the countries"), and *al-Muʾtalif wa-l-mukhtalif* ("The similar and the distinct"), an alphabetical dictionary of homonymous *nisba*s; only the latter seems to have come down to modern times. About twenty of his works have been edited; they consist mainly of *ḥadīth* treatises, both thematic and methodological, including *tarājim* (biographical records), *rijāl* (knowledge of *ḥadīth* transmitters), *ansāb* (geographical adjectives), and *alqāb* (nicknames and honorific titles) collections. The *Shurūṭ al-āʾimma al-sitta* ("Criteria of the six authorities") is a short essay investigating the criteria adopted by the authors of the six canonical *ḥadīth* collections (al-Bukhārī, Muslim, Abū Dāwud, al-Tirmidhī, al-Nasāʾī, and Ibn Māja) for selecting traditions, and the *Masʾalāt al-ʿulū wa-l-nuzūl fī l-ḥadīth* focuses on "high" or "low" chains of transmission *(isnād)*, the "high" *isnād*s (with a low number of intermediaries between the primary authority and the last transmitter) being preferred over the "low" ones, which have a larger number of sequential transmitters. The *Tadhkirat al-mawḍūʿāt* ("Mention of forged traditions") records alphabetically traditions transmitted by weak or controversial transmitters.

Although the fact is, not surprisingly, concealed or criticised by many of his mediaeval biographers, Ibn al-Qaysarānī was learned in mystical knowledge *(taṣawwuf)*. Al-Dhahabī mentions him as a disciple of Saʿd al-Zanjānī (d. 471/1078) in Mecca; another of his mystic masters was Hayyāj b. ʿUbayd al-Ḥiṭṭīnī. Ibn al-Qaysarānī wrote two treatises on mystical practices and composed mystical poetry. His short *Kitāb al-samāʿ* is a defence of *samāʿ* (musical audition) based on Prophetic traditions. It, along with other specialised Ṣūfī literature (Ṣūfī manuals and biographies), is similar to other treatises on this topic from the fourth-fifth/tenth-eleventh centuries, and it received a polemic response from the Ḥanbalī scholar Ibn Qudāma (d. 620/1223). Ibn al-Qaysarānī's main work on mystical practices is the *Ṣafwat al-taṣawwuf* ("The finest of mystical knowledge," c. 480/1087), a practical and ethical manual for Ṣūfīs built entirely upon quotations of *ḥadīth* and Qurʾānic verses. The book examines and defends all kinds of Ṣūfī practice, ranging from personal devotion *(ʿibādāt)* to the way mystics dressed, ate, or travelled, and it exalts the ethical values they professed. Like the *Kitāb al-samāʿ*, it advocates debated practices such as *samāʿ* and *raqṣ* (dancing). This treatise, which does not elaborate spiritual or mystical themes, belongs to the genre of Ṣūfī *adab* manuals and reflects the formation of Ṣūfī institutions and practices during the fifth/eleventh century.

Ibn al-Qaysarānī belonged to the Dāwūdī (or Ẓāhirī) *madhhab*, a Sunnī juridical and theological school named for its founder, Dāʾūd b. Khalaf (d. 270/883), and known for its literalist ideas. He acquired fame as a *ḥadīth* transmitter and was praised for his wide knowledge, excellent memory, and reliability. He was, however, strongly criticised by some traditionalists: Ibn ʿAsākir (d. 571/1176) found Ibn al-Qaysarānī "highly deceptive," and the Ḥanbalī Ibn al-Jawzī (d. 597/1201) attacked his liberal views on music and Ṣūfism and held his opinions licentious and the *Ṣafwat al-taṣawwuf* "laughable." Ibn al-Qaysarānī was accused also of a poor command of Arabic grammar and of committing linguistic barbarisms. Amongst his biographers, he was defended by Ibn al-Samʿānī (d. 562/1166) and al-Dhahabī as a reliable transmitter of Prophetic traditions.

Ibn al-Qaysarānī left at least one son, Abū Zurʿa Ṭāhir b. Muḥammad b. Ṭāhir (d. 566/1170), a minor *ḥadīth* transmitter who had, amongst his disciples, the

Ḥanbalī *wazīr* of Baghdad Ibn Hubayra (d. 560/1165) and who made a living as a trader. Ibn al-Dimyāṭī reports that Abū Zurʿa had so little interest in knowledge that he gave all the books written by his father to a scholar in Hamadhān, so that they could be of some use to the public.

Bibliography

Works of Ibn al-Qaysarānī

1) *Ḥadīth* and authorities

Aṭrāf al-gharāʾib wa-l-afrād min ḥadīth Rasūl Allāh lil-Imām al-Dāraquṭnī, ed. Maḥmūd Muḥammad Maḥmūd Ḥasan Naṣṣār, 5 vols., Beirut 1998; *Dhakhīrat al-ḥuffāẓ min al-Kāmil li-Ibn al-ʿAddī*, ed. ʿAbd al-Raḥmān al-Farīwāʾī, 5 vols., Riyadh 1416/1996; *Īḍāḥ al-ishkāl*, ed. Bāsim Fayṣal Jawābira, Kuwait 1988; *al-Jamʿ bayn kitābay Abī Naṣr al-Kalābādhī wa-Abī Bakr al-Iṣbahānī fī rijāl al-Bukhārī wa-Muslim*, 2 vols. in one, Hyderabad 1323/1905; *Masʾalat al-ʿulū wa-l-nuzūl fī l-isnād*, ed. Ṣalāḥ al-Dīn Maqbūl Aḥmad, Kuwait 1401/1981; *Shurūṭ al-āʾimma al-sitta*, ed. ʿAbd al-Fattāḥ Abū Ghadda, in *Thalāth rasāʾil fī ʿilm muṣṭalaḥ al-ḥadīth* (Beirut 1417/1997), 83–106; *Tadhkirat al-ḥuffāẓ. Aṭrāf aḥādīth kitāb al-Majrūḥīn li-Ibn Ḥibbān*, ed. Ḥamdī ʿAbd al-Majīd Salafī, Riyadh 1415/1994; *Tadhkirat al-mawḍūʿāt*, ed. Ziyād al-Naqshabandī al-Atharī, Beirut 2013.

2) Other religious topics

Masʾalat al-tasmiya = Tawḍīḥ al-masʾala wa-taḥqīq al-ḥaqq fī l-jarḥ bi-l-basmala, ed. ʿAbdallāh b. ʿAlī Murshid, Cairo 1992; *al-Ḥujja ʿalā tārik al-maḥajja*, ed. ʿAbd al-ʿAzīz b. Muḥammad al-Sadḥān, 2 vols., Riyadh 1429/2008 (*ʿaqīda*, Muslim creed).

3) *Ansāb* and *alqāb*

Kitāb al-ansāb al-muttafiqa fī l-khaṭṭ al-mutamāthila fī l-nuqaṭ wa-l-ḍabṭ = al-Muʾtalif wa-l-mukhtalif = Homonyma inter nomina relativa, ed. P. de Jong, Leiden 1865; *Maʿrifat al-alqāb*, ed. ʿAdnān Ḥammūd Abū Zayd, Cairo 1421/2001.

4) Anthologies and poetry

Shiʿr Ibn al-Qaysarānī, ed. ʿĀdil Jābir Ṣāliḥ Muḥammad, al-Zarqāʾ, Jordan 1991; *al-Manthūr min al-ḥikāyāt wa-l-suʾālāt*, ed. Jamāl ʿAzzūn, Riyadh 1430/2009; *Muntakhab al-manthūr*, ed. ʿAbd al-Raḥmān b. Ḥasan b. Qāʾid, Riyadh 2009.

5) Mystical (Ṣūfī) practices

Kitāb al-samāʿ, ed. Abū l-Wafāʾ Muṣṭafā al-Marāghī, Cairo 1414/1994; *Ṣafwat al-taṣawwuf*, ed. Ghāda al-Muqaddam ʿAdra, Beirut 1416/1995.

Primary sources on Ibn al-Qaysarānī

Ibn ʿAsākir, *Taʾrīkh Dimashq*, ed. ʿUmar Gharāma al-ʿAmrawī (Beirut 1415–1421/1995–2000), 53:280–3; Ibn al-Jawzī, *al-Muntaẓam*, ed. Muḥammad ʿAbd al-Qādir ʿAṭā and Muṣṭafā ʿAbd al-Qādir ʿAṭā (Beirut 1412/1992), 16:136–8; Ibn Nuqṭa, *al-Taqyīd* (Beirut 1435/2014), 1:199–200; Sibṭ Ibn al-Jawzī, *Mirʾāt al-zamān*, ed. Ibrāhīm al-Zaybaq (Damascus 1434/2013), 20:71–3; Ibn Khallikān, *Wafayāt al-aʿyān*, ed. Iḥsān ʿAbbās (Beirut 1968), 4:287–8; Ibn ʿAbd al-Hādī, *Ṭabaqāt ʿulamāʾ al-ḥadīth*, ed. Akram al-Bushrī and Ibrāhīm al-Zaybaq (Beirut 1417/1996–7), 4:13–7; al-Dhahabī, *Tadhkirat al-ḥuffāẓ* (Hyderabad 1377/1957^3), 4:1242–5; al-Dhahabī, *Taʾrīkh al-Islām*, ed. ʿUmar ʿAbd al-Salām Tadmurī (Beirut 1410–1421/1990–2000), 35:168–81 (with full bibliography); al-Dhahabī, *Siyar aʿlām al-nubalāʾ*, ed. Shuʿayb al-Arnāʾūṭ (Beirut 1405/1985), 19:361–71; Ibn al-Dimyāṭī, *al-Mustafād*, ed. Bashshār ʿAwwād Maʿrūf (Beirut 1406/1986), 112–5; Ibn Kathīr, *al-Bidāya*, ed. ʿAbdallāh b. ʿAbd al-Muḥsin al-Turkī (Cairo 1419/1998), 16:222–3; al-Ṣafadī, *al-Wāfī bi-l-wafayāt*, vol. 3, ed. Sven Dedering (Beirut and Wiesbaden 1394/1974^2), 166–8; Ibn Ḥajar al-ʿAsqalānī, *Lisān al-mīzān*, ed. Salmān ʿAbd al-Fattāḥ Abū Ghadda (Beirut 1423/2002), 7:211–6.

Studies about Ibn al-Qaysarānī

Daphna Ephrat, *Spiritual wayfarers, leaders in piety. Sufis and the dissemination of Islam in medieval Palestine* (Cambridge MA 2008), 86–8; Ahmet T. Karamustafa, *Sufism. The formative period* (Edinburgh 2007), 86, 163; Joseph Schacht, Ibn al-Ḳaysarānī, *EI2; GAL*, 1:436.

Vanessa Van Renterghem

Ibn al-Shajarī

Ḍiyāʾ al-Dīn Abū l-Saʿādāt Hibatallāh b. ʿAlī (450–542/1058–1148), known as **Ibn al-Shajarī**, was a famous grammarian and an authority on poetry from Baghdad.

He was a descendant of the cousin of the Prophet and the last of the Rightly Guided Caliphs, ʿAlī b. Abī Ṭālib (r. 35–40/656–61), and thus he was known as al-Sharīf al-Ḥasanī al-ʿAlawī (for his genealogy see al-Suyūṭī, *Tuḥfat al-adīb*, 2:541). He was born in Baghdad and spent his entire life in al-Karkh, a quarter in western Baghdad. After studying philology, poetry, and other subjects in the classical canon under ʿAlī b. al-Faḍḍāl al-Mujāshiʿī (d. 479/1086) and al-Khaṭīb al-Tibrīzī (d. 502/1109; for the list of his teachers, see Ibn al-Shajarī's *al-Amālī*, ed. al-Ṭanāḥī, 1:20–1), he became an accomplished and widely known authority on grammar and classical poetry. Over the course of seventy years of teaching, he had many disciples, including al-Samʿānī (d. 562/1167), the author of the biographical dictionary *al-Ansāb*, and the grammarians Ibn al-Khashshāb (d. 567/1172) and Abū l-Barakāt Ibn al-Anbārī (d. 577/1181; see the list in *al-Amālī*, ed. al-Ṭanāḥī, 1:23–5, with an additional eleven scholars). His academic merits guaranteed him a prominent position in society, and his reputation was further enhanced when he followed his father in assuming the function of syndic (*naqīb*) of the ʿAlids in al-Karkh. He lived to an advanced age.

Four of his books have survived:

1. *Amālī Ibn al-Shajarī*, dictated in eighty-four sessions (*majālis*), are his main work. This compilation lacks an introduction, a feature shared with the works listed in numbers 2–4 below; one might conclude from this omission that these additional works were dictations too. The *Amālī* were printed in two volumes in Hyderabad in 1349/1930; for the missing parts of this edition, see *Mā lam yunshar min al-Amālī l-Shajariyya*, ed. Ḥātim Ṣāliḥ al-Ḍāmin, *al-Mawrid* 3 (1974), 1:183–206, 2:171–98, repr. Beirut 1405/1984; *Nuṣūṣ muḥaqqaqa fī l-lugha wa-l-naḥw*, Baghdad 1991, 391–542; a very good and complete edition is that of Maḥmūd Muḥammad al-Ṭanāḥī in 3 vols., Cairo 1413/1992.

2. *Al-Ḥamāsa al-Shajariyya* consists of poetry fragments from pre-Islamic times up until the ʿAbbāsid era (from 132/750). It is divided into fifteen sections (sing. *bāb*) and twenty subsections (sing. *faṣl*) and follows in structure Abū Tammām's (d. 231/845) *Ḥamāsa*. The work is edited in two volumes by ʿAbd al-Muʿīn al-Mallūḥī and Asmāʾ al-Ḥimṣī, Damascus 1970.

3. *Mā ttafaqa lafẓuhu wa-khtalafa maʿnāhu*, a dictionary of 1,670 alphabetically arranged homonyms, with explanations of their meaning; ed. ʿAṭiyya Rizq, Beirut 1413/1992.

4. *Mukhtārāt shuʿarāʾ al-ʿArab* is an anthology in three parts. The first part contains twelve and the second part twenty-five poems by famous poets of previous generations, with philological notes by the author; the third part includes twelve *qaṣīda*s by al-Ḥuṭayʾa (fl. first half of the first/seventh century), ed. ʿAlī Muḥammad al-Bijāwī, Cairo 1975.

Bibliography

Sources

Ibn al-Anbārī, *Nuzhat al-alibbāʾ fī ṭabaqāt al-udabāʾ*, ed. Ibrāhīm al-Sāmarrāʾī (Baghdad 1970²), 299–302; ʿImād al-Dīn al-Iṣfahānī, *Kharīdat al-qaṣr. Qism shuʿarāʾ al-ʿIrāq*, ed. Muḥammad Bahja al-Atharī (Baghdad 1396/1976), 3/1:52–4; Ibn al-Jawzī, *al-Muntaẓam fī tawārīkh al-mulūk wa-l-umam*, ed. Suhayl Zakkār (Beirut 1415/1995), 10:5278–9;

Yāqūt, *Muʿjam al-udabāʾ*, ed. Iḥsān ʿAbbās (Beirut 1993), 6:2775–6; al-Qifṭī, *Inbāh al-ruwāt*, ed. Muḥammad Abū l-Faḍl Ibrāhīm (Cairo 1369–93/ 1950–73), 3:356–7; Ibn Khallikān, *Wafayāt al-aʿyān*, ed. Iḥsān ʿAbbās (Beirut 1968), 6:45–50; al-Yamānī, *Ishārat al-taʿyīn*, ed. ʿAbd al-Majīd Diyāb (Riyadh 1406/1986), 370; al-Dhahabī, *Siyar aʿlām al-nubalāʾ*, ed. Shuʿayb al-Arnāʾuṭ et al. (Beirut 1406/1986[3]), 20:194–6; al-Dhahabī, *Taʾrīkh al-Islām*, ed. ʿUmar ʿAbd al-Salām Tadmurī (Beirut 1415/1995), 37:128–30; al-ʿUmarī, *Masālik al-abṣār*, facsimile edition (Frankfurt 1408/1988), 7:93–5; al-Ṣafadī, *al-Wāfī bi-l-wafayāt*, ed. Otfried Weintritt (Beirut 1418/ 1997), 27:294–9; al-Suyūṭī, *Bughyat al-wuʿāt*, ed. Muḥammad Abū l-Faḍl Ibrāhīm (Cairo 1384/1964), 2:324; al-Suyūṭī, *Tuḥfat al-adīb fī nuḥāt Mughnī l-labīb*, ed. Ḥasan al-Malkh and Suhā Naʿja (Irbid 1426/2005), 2:541–6.

Studies

ʿAbd al-ʿAzīz ʿArafa, *Fann al-taʿbīr fī Mukhtārāt shuʿarāʾ al-ʿArab l-Ibn al-Shajarī Hibatallāh ʿAlī Abī l-Saʿādāt al-ʿAlawī*, Cairo 1975–6; ʿAbd al-Munʿim Aḥmad al-Tikrītī, *Ibn al-Shajarī wa-manhajuhu fī l-naḥw*, Baghdad 1974; Ramzi Baalbaki, *The Arabic lexicographical tradition. From the 2nd/8th to the 12th/18th century* (Leiden and Boston 2014), 200–2; *GAL* 1:280; *GALS* 1:492–3; *GAS* 2:74, 78, 85.

Reinhard Weipert

Ibn Sharīf al-Rundī

Abū l-Ṭayyib Ṣāliḥ b. Yazīd **Ibn Sharīf al-Rundī** (601–84/1204–85) was an Andalusī prose writer, poet, jurist, and arithmetician, renowned especially for his elegy for the loss, during his lifetime, of the most important cities of al-Andalus (Valencia, Játiva, Jaén, Murcia, Córdoba, and Seville). Since the nineteenth century and the first translations of this poem, he has been better known as Abū l-Baqāʾ al-Rundī, as he was referred to by the historian and anthologist al-Maqqarī (d. 1041/1632) in introducing his poem (*Nafḥ al-ṭīb*, 4:486). Arabic sources—including al-Maqqarī in other passages of *Nafḥ al-ṭīb* and in his *Azhār al-riyāḍ* (1:47–50), where he again quotes the elegy—are, however, unanimous in omitting the name Abū l-Baqāʾ (father of survival).

The most nearly complete biography of Ibn Sharīf is that by the Andalusī *wazīr* and historian Ibn al-Khaṭīb (d. 776/1375), who quotes the Andalusī traditionist and historian Ibn al-Zubayr (d. 708/1308) and the biographer Ibn ʿAbd al-Malik al-Marrākushī (d. 703/1303) and presents some thirty poems or fragments and a piece of rhymed prose from Ibn Sharīf's *Rawḍat al-uns* ("Garden of sociability").

Ibn Sharīf was born in Muḥarram 601/September 1024 to a family from the Berber tribe of Nafza that was apparently well established in Ronda, hence his two Arabic gentilics, al-Nafzī and al-Rundī. It is assumed that he was born and lived in Ronda, a city he yearned for when he was absent from it. He studied with his father and others jurists and men of letters, and Ibn al-Zubayr reports that Ibn Sharīf attended his classes in Málaga. He travelled to other cities in al-Andalus and North Africa—Granada, Fez, Marrakech, and Ceuta—praising their rulers or asking their help against the Christian kings of the Iberian Peninsula.

As a transmitter of Prophetic traditions, Ibn Sharīf wrote a book, now lost, on Muḥammad's sayings about Jibrīl (Gabriel). He also was an expert on the Islamic law of inheritance and composed some useful handbooks on this subject in prose and verse, but he was known primarily as a poet, a writer of prose, and a theoretician of poetry. As a poet he frequented the Naṣrid court of Granada, and some of his poems were composed at the request of its rulers. He excelled in love poetry and panegyrics but was also inclined towards mysticism *(taṣawwuf)*; his unaffected poetic style was esteemed.

Arabic sources assert that Ibn Sharīf wrote a treatise on prosody *(ʿarūḍ)*, but no such work is extant. His *al-Wāfī fī naẓm al-qawāfī* ("All about rhymes") is a kind of Arabic poetics in which he quotes many of his own poems. Although it has been frequently described, only its first section, on poetry, poets, and poetic genres, has been published. He also wrote an encyclopaedic work of *adab* (belles lettres) in twenty chapters, *Rawḍat al-uns wa-nuzhat al-nafs* ("Garden of sociability and recreation of the soul"). It is as yet unpublished, and its surviving manuscript seems to be incomplete (Zamāma refers to only nine chapters). Ibn Sharīf dedicated the work to Muḥammad I Ibn al-Aḥmar (r. 629–71/1232–73), the first Naṣrid ruler of Granada, and included in it some of his own *maqāmāt* or epistles.

Ibn Sharīf owes his lasting fame to his elegy, composed in 665/1266 (Ibn Abī Zaʿr, 127–9), for the hundred lost cities and fortresses of al-Andalus that were surrendered by Ibn al-Aḥmar to Alfonso X, king of Castille (r. 1252–84). Ibn al-Khaṭīb never mentions this poem, probably because it was an embarrassing reminder of the weakness of his patrons. More than two centuries later, less gifted poets added some verses to Ibn Sharīf's poem in order to mention the loss of other cities, such as Baza (Basṭa) (894/1489) and Granada (897/1492).

Bibliography

Works by Ibn Sharīf

Inqādh ʿAṭāʾallāh Muḥsin, *al-Wāfī fī naẓm al-qawāfī* li-Abī l-Baqāʾ Ṣāliḥ b. al-Sharīf al-Rundī (601H-684H), *Majallat Jāmiʿat al-Anbār lil-Lughāt wa-l-Ādāb* 1 (2009), 21–160 (www.iasj.net/iasj?func=fulltext&aId=63727) (contains only the first section); *Dīwān Abī l-Ṭayyib Ṣāliḥ b. Sharīf al-Rundī... fī aʿmālihi l-adabiyya, al-shiʿr wa-l-nathr*, ed. Ḥayāt Qāra, Alexandria, Egypt 2010.

Sources

Ibn al-Zubayr, *Kitāb ṣilat al-ṣila*, ed. ʿAbd al-Salām al-Harrās and al-Shaykh Saʿīd Aʿrāb (Mohammedia, Morocco 1413/1993), 3:84–5 (biography no. 119); Ibn ʿAbd al-Malik al-Marrākushī, *al-Dhayl wa-l-takmila li-kitābay al-Mawṣūl wa-l-Ṣila*, vol. 4, ed. Iḥsān ʿAbbās (Beirut 1973), 136–9 (biography no. 263), and vol. 8, ed. Muḥammad b. Sharīfa (Rabat 1984), 528–9 (biography no. 38); Ibn Abī Zarʿ, *al-Dhakhīra al-saniyya*, ed. Mohammed Ben Cheneb, *Ad-Daḫīrat as-saniyya (Le trésor magnifique). Chronique anonyme des Mérinides* (Algiers 1921), 127–9; Ibn al-Khaṭīb, *al-Iḥāṭa fī akhbār Gharnāṭa*, ed. Muḥammad ʿAbdallāh ʿInān (Cairo 1975), 3:360–76; al-Maqqarī, *Azhār al-riyāḍ fī akhbār ʿIyāḍ*, ed. Muṣṭafā l-Saqqā, Ibrāhīm al-Abyārī, and ʿAbd al-Ḥafīẓ Shalabī (Cairo 1939), 1:47–50; al-Maqqarī, *Nafḥ al-ṭīb*, ed. Iḥsān ʿAbbās (Beirut 1388/1968), 2:694, 3:347, 4:147, 486–9, 5:602.

Studies

Ahmed Benhamouda, al-Wāfī fī naẓm al-ḳawāfī d'Abū l-Baḳāʾ b. Šarīf al-Rundī, in *Mélanges offerts à Gaudefroy-Demombynes par ses amis et anciens élèves* (Cairo 1935–45), 189–95; Muḥammad Riḍwān al-Dāya, *Abū l-Baqāʾ al-Rundī, shāʿir rithāʾ al-Andalus*, Beirut 1976, 1986[2] (including an anthology of poetry and prose by Ibn Sharīf, 117–67); Raymond K. Farrin, Seville, where *miḥrābs* weep and pulpits lament. Al-Rundī's elegy in the classic poetic tradition, in Michelle M. Hamilton and David A. Wacks (eds.), *The study of al-Andalus. The scholarship and legacy of James T. Monroe* (Boston and Washington DC 2018), 97–121; Fernando de la Granja, La venta de la esclava en el mercado en la obra de Abū l-Baqāʾ de Ronda, *Revista del Instituto de Estudios Islámicos en Madrid* 13 (1965–6), 119–36 (repr. in Fernando de la Granja, *Maqāmas y risālas andaluzas*, Madrid 1976, 139–60, and Fernando de la Granja, *Estudios de historia de Al-Andalus*, Madrid 1999, 41–63); Zubair Mohammad Ehsanul Hoque, Elegy for lost kingdoms and ruined cities in Hispano-Arabic poetry, *Journal of the Asiatic Society of Bangladesh* (Humanities) 52 (2007), 235–66; ʿAbdallāh Kannūn,

Abū l-Baqāʾ al-Rundī wa-kitābuhu *l-Wāfī fī naẓm al-qawāfī*, *Revista del Instituto de Estudios Islámicos en Madrid* 6 (1958), 206–20; Jaʿfar Mājid, Abū l-Baqāʾ al-Rundī, nāqidan wa-shāʿiran, in *Actas del II Coloquio Hispano-Tunecino de Estudios Históricos (Madrid/Barcelona, mayo 1972)* (Madrid 1973), 261–86; Jaʿfar Mājid, *Kitāb al-Wāfī fī naẓm al-qawāfī* li-Abī l-Baqāʾ al-Rundī, *Ḥawliyyāt al-Jāmiʿa al-Tūnisiyya* 6 (1969), 171–201 (includes an edition of the chapter on descriptive poetry, 179–201); al-Ṭāhir Aḥmad Makkī, Abū l-Baqāʾ al-Rundī wa-nūniyyatuhu fī rithāʾ al-Andalus, in Ṭāhir Aḥmad Makkī, *Dirāsāt andalusiyya fī l-adab wa-l-taʾrīkh wa-l-falsafa* (Cairo 1980), 307–60; J. M. Puerta Vílchez, Al-Rundī, Abū l-Baqāʾ, in *Enciclopedia de la cultura andalusí*, 1/7, *Biblioteca de al-Andalus*, vol. 7 (Almería 2012), 194–208 (no. 1663); Ḥayāt Qāra, Nubdha min shiʿr Abī l-Ṭayyib al-Rundī wa-naẓmihi laysat fī dīwānihi l-maṭbūʿ, *Majallat Maʿhad al-Makhṭūṭāt al-ʿArabiyya* 60 (2016), 62–87; ʿAbd al-Qādir Zamāma, *Kitāb Rawḍat al-uns wa-nuzhat al-nafs* li-Abī l-Baqāʾ Ṣāliḥ b. Sharīf al-Rundī (601–684 H./1204–85 M.), *Majallat Maʿhad al-Makhṭūṭāt* 18 (1392/1972), 331–7 (www.ahlalhdeeth.com/vb/showthread.php?t=272015); ʿAbdallāh Muḥammad al-Zayyāt, *Rithāʾ al-mudun fī al-shiʿr al-andalusī* (Benghazi 1990), 363–81, 746–50.

Teresa Garulo

Ibn al-Zibaʿrā, ʿAbdallāh

ʿAbdallāh b. al-Zibaʿrā (d. c.15/636) was an anti- then a pro-Islamic poet. He was a contemporary of the prophet Muḥammad and became one of the harshest critics of the new religion. His full name was ʿAbdallāh b. al-Zibaʿrā b. Qays b. ʿAdī b. Saʿd b. Sahm. He was a descendant of the Quraysh tribe, the tribe of Muḥammad, albeit from a different branch, the Sahm, which was one of the noblest and most powerful groups of Quraysh.

Ibn al-Zibaʿrā's enmity against Islam was expressed in his poetry as well as in his actions. He argued with Muḥammad, trying to demonstrate that in the Qurʾān there are some verses that are neither logical nor true (Ibn Hishām, 1:359–61). During Muḥammad's prayers, Ibn al-Zibaʿrā smeared the face of the Prophet with animal blood and faeces (Ibn Abī Ḥātim, 12:370). According to one interpretation of Q 17:47, he described Muḥammad as a man "deprived of reason" (*masḥūr*) (al-Māwardī, 4:134). In the Qurʾān there are some veiled references to the poet that rail against him. He is referred to as a *ẓālim*, "one who treats [himself and the others] wrongly," or simply as a "disbeliever" (Q 17:47); and he was also considered to be one of the poets who "went astray, leading their followers along the wrong path" (Q 26:224; al-Zamakhsharī, 3:344).

During the conquest of Mecca by the Muslims in the year 8/630, Ibn al-Zibaʿrā fled to Najrān, a city in southwestern Arabia. After hearing verses satirising him by Ḥassān b. Thābit (d. 54/674), the Prophet's poet, and feeling betrayed by other friends from his tribe who had decided to join the Muslims (poem no. 18, in the Jubbūrī collection), he made his way to Muḥammad and converted to Islam.

The *dīwān* (collection of poems) of Ibn al-Zibaʿrā was compiled by Yaḥyā l-Jubbūrī; it includes twenty-seven short poems, ranging in length from one to seventeen verses. The themes in his *dīwān* are divided into four main groups: the first includes poems related to a pre-Islamic quarrel between the poet and the Quṣayy branch of Quraysh. He composed invective verses against them, then—since he was likely to be punished—he composed some poems expressing his apologies (poem nos. 2, 8, 11). The second theme is praise for some members and branches of the Quraysh tribe (nos. 13, 14, 16, 21, 25,

28). The third theme incorporates poems that describe the battles of the anti-Muslim Qurashīs against Muḥammad (nos. 1, 3, 12, 15, 17). Here the poet often eulogises his tribe's victory against the Muslims in the battle of Uḥud, which took place in the year 3 or 4/624–5 (other battles are also mentioned). In one poem he laments the death of some Qurashī leaders in the battle of Badr, which they lost to Muḥammad one year before the battle of Uḥud (no. 20). The fourth main theme is the apology the poet made to Muḥammad after his conversion to Islam (nos. 10, 19, 26). The *nasīb* (the love theme usually found at the beginning of the classical Arabic poem) is marginal in his poetry. It appears in three poems only (nos. 1, 3, 12) and varies from one to four verses long, followed by the battle eulogy theme (nos. 1, 3, 12).

Bibliography
ʿAbdallāh b. al-Zibaʿrā, *Shiʿr ʿAbdallāh b. al-Zibaʿrā*, ed. Yaḥyā l-Jubbūrī, Beirut 1981[2] (an older version appears in Yaḥyā l-Jubbūrī, ʿAbdallāh b. al-Zibaʿrā. Ḥayātuh wa-shiʿruh, *Majallat Maʿhad al-Makhṭūṭāt al-ʿArabiyya* 24/1 (1978), 43–98); J. W. Fück, *Ibn al-Zibaʿrā*, *EI2*; Ibn Abī Ḥātim, *Tafsīr al-Qurʾān al-ʿaẓīm*, ed. Asʿad Muḥammad al-Ṭayyib, 14 vols., Riyad 1419[/1999]; Ibn al-Athīr, *Usd al-ghāba fī maʿrifat al-ṣaḥāba*, ed. ʿAlī Muḥammad Muʿawwaḍ and ʿĀdil Aḥmad ʿAbd al-Mawjūd (Beirut 1994), 3:293; Ibn Hishām, *al-Sīra l-nabawiyya*, ed. Muṣṭafā l-Saqqā, Ibrāhīm al-Ibyārī, and ʿAbd al-Ḥafīẓ al-Shalabī (Cairo 1955), 1:57–8, 312, 359–61, 593–4; 2:15–6, 136–7, 141–2, 166–7, 256–8, 278–9, 325, 418–20, 502; Ibn Qudāma al-Maqdisī, *Kitāb al-tawwābīn* (n.p. 2003), 75–6; al-Māwardī, *al-Nukat wa-l-ʿuyūn*, ed. Ibn ʿAbd al-Maqṣūd b. ʿAbd al-Raḥīm (Beirut n.d.), 4:134; Paolo Minganti, Il Poeta meccano ʿAbd Allāh ibn az-Zibaʿrà as-Sahmī. Notizie biografiche e raccolta dei frammenti, *RSO* 38/4 (1963), 323–59; al-Ṭabarī, *Jāmiʿ al-bayān fī taʾwīl al-Qurʾān*, ed. Aḥmad Muḥammad Shākir (Beirut 2000), 18:539; al-Zamakhsharī, *al-Kashshāf ʿan ḥaqāʾiq ghawāmiḍ al-tanzīl*, 4 vols., Beirut 1407/1986–7; *EAL* 1:385; *GAS* 2:275–6.

Ali Ahmad Hussein

Ijāra (protection)

Ijāra is an Arabic verbal noun (from the root *j-w-r*), that denotes the formal extension of temporary **protection** *(jiwār)* to the life and property of a specified person (the *mustajīr*) who is in physical proximity to the protector (the *mujīr*). The concept of *ijāra* also works in conjunction with such lexically related terms as *istijāra* (requesting protection) and *jār* (a protected person, neighbour, or, less often, protector). These terms were prominent in the pre-Islamic and early Islamic periods, whereafter conceptual analogues such as *amān* (a temporary pledge of security, usually made to individuals) and *dhimma* (an indefinite pact of security, usually contracted with a group, in exchange for tribute and submission) came to be employed more frequently to convey concepts related to the granting of protection. *Ijāra* has, however, experienced a quiet revival in modern treatments of refugees and asylum in Islam.

1. In pre-Islamic Arabia

Ijāra is cognate with words signifying parallel concepts in several ancient Semitic languages, including Hebrew, Ugaritic, and Akkadian. In the tribal societies of pre-Islamic Arabia, when a free man or woman granted formal protection to an outsider—often a traveller or an outcast from another tribe—the tribe of the *mujīr* was honour-bound to protect the *mustajīr* as they would members of their own tribe. Such *ijāra* was announced publicly. A sacred area *(ḥaram)* or tomb could confer de facto protection of much the same kind. Certain tribes have maintained similar customs of protection to the present day, for which they sometimes use *ijāra* terminology (Dresch, 59–61, 118; Layish).

2. In the Qurʾān and *ḥadīth*

Of the thirteen occurrences of the root *j-w-r* in the Qurʾān, eight pertain to the concept of *ijāra* (excluding two occurrences of *jār* that do not specify protection, and three conceptually distinct forms of the root). God alone is able to protect believers, by *ijāra*, from "a painful chastisement" (Q 46:31; cf. 8:48, 67:28, 72:22). Indeed, although He makes *ijāra*, no one can protect another person against Him by *ijāra* (23:88). Believers are instructed to make *ijāra* for pagans who request it, so that (or until) they hear God's word (9:6). The exegetes regarded the protection granted by *ijāra* according to 9:6 as synonymous with *amān*. Indeed, the verse became the basic proof-text for the classical Islamic practice of granting *amān* to foreigners, even though it features the language of *ijāra* more prominently than that of *amān* (Shoukri, 66–85).

Ijāra is also encountered in the Prophetic *ḥadīth*. As in the Qurʾān, God "grants protection" from various dangers: "The Messenger of God said, 'God has protected you *(ajārakum)* from three sorts of harm: your Prophet will not imprecate against you so that you all perish; the people of falsehood will not overcome the people of truth; and you will not all agree upon error" (Abū Dāwūd, 6:307, no. 4253, *Kitāb al-fitan*). *Ijāra* also appears regularly in the *sīra* accounts of the Prophet's life. In the Meccan period, when the first believers flee to Ethiopia from the persecution of the Meccan pagans, the protection extended to them by the Christian Negus is described as *ijāra: wa-qad aḥsana l-najāshī jiwārahum* (and the Negus protected them well). A short time later, the Prophet's companion Abū Bakr (d. 13/634) also flees Mecca but soon obtains *jiwār* from a pagan called Ibn al-Dughunna and so is able to return. When Ibn al-Dughunna, at the Meccans' behest, asks Abū Bakr to cease his public Muslim worship, the latter renounces Ibn al-Dughunna's *jiwār* in favour of "the *jiwār* of God" (Ibn Hishām, 1:330, 333, 372–3).

Ijāra appears frequently also in reports concerning events that postdate the *hijra*. The clauses that comprise the agreement now commonly known as the Constitution of Medina declare that "the *dhimma* of God is one; the least of [the parties to it] may make *ijāra* on behalf of them [all]" *(wa-inna dhimmata llāhi wāḥidatun yujīru ʿalayhim adnāhum)*. The latter clause also appears in a well-known *ḥadīth*. The "Constitution" also stipulates that "no pagan may make *ijāra* for the property or lives of the Quraysh" *(wa-innahu lā yujīru mushrik^{un} māl^{an} li-Quraysh^{in} wa-lā nafs^{an})*, that the *jār* is owed the same protection as that enjoyed by the parties to the agreement, and that *ijāra* is not to be made for any woman without the permission of her people or for members of Quraysh or their allies under any circumstances. The text concludes by stating that God is the protector *(jār)* of those who keep the agreement (Serjeant, 17, 23, 35, 37, 39).

3. In the Islamic state

The concept of *ijāra* was thus fundamental to the state established by the Prophet. Similarly, according to relatively early sources, the pact that Muḥammad concluded with the Christians of Najrān, in Yemen, promised them "the *jiwār* of God and the *dhimma* of Muḥammad the prophet" in perpetuity. That this arrangement was understood as one of *ijāra* is made explicit in a text by which Abū Bakr, now caliph, reportedly confirmed the pact with the Najrānīs. He writes that Muḥammad had "granted them *(ajārahum)* the *jiwār* of God," but a third text, in which ʿUmar b. al-Khaṭṭāb (d. 23/644) confirms and amends the pact after having forcibly transferred the Najrānīs to Iraq, uses *amān* instead of *jiwār* (al-Shaybānī, 7:550–7; Milka Levy-Rubin, 32–4). After the conquest of Mecca, Umm Hāniʾ bt. Abī Ṭālib (d. after 40/661), the Prophet's cousin and elder sister of his son-in-law and close companion ʿAlī (d. 40/661), extends protection by *ijāra* to her two non-Muslim brothers-in-law. The Prophet upholds her *ijāra* despite ʿAlī's desire to kill them (Ibn ʿAbd al-Barr, 234).

Where the concept and practice of *ijāra* had formerly functioned in a tribal society, the advent of Islam thus initially reinscribed it in a society where membership was conditioned more upon shared belief and practice than upon shared kinship and which now enjoyed the *jiwār* of God. However, the terminology of *ijāra*, which had coexisted with overlapping notions—for example, *walī* (friend, protector), *ḥalīf* (ally) (see further Schick)—was gradually eclipsed by that of *amān* and *dhimma* (Schmucker, 10, 13–5, 34, 194). The reasons for this shift require additional study. Levy-Rubin, who connects *amān* to non-tribal notions of formal protection that prevailed outside pre-Islamic Arabia, has proposed that the "implications [of *jiwār*] were too far-reaching and were too suggestive of insider status where non-Muslims were concerned" (Levy-Rubin, 34; cf. Wansbrough, 133–5). Until the modern period, therefore, *ijāra* had a low profile in Islamic discourses, save in discussions of the important early texts in which it occurs. The terms *jār* and *jiwār*, by contrast, were widely discussed by jurists in relation to the general concept of "neighbour," particularly as it pertains to the rights and duties of individual neighbours in their relations with one another (Ibn Fāyiʿ).

The positive association of *ijāra* with the Prophet's era, combined with the reluctance of Islamic tradition to elaborate the term's precise significance for later generations, has left it available for modern reclamation, particularly by Muslims concerned with forced migration. The numerous military conflicts of the twentieth and twenty-first centuries have lent urgency to Islamic ethical thought regarding refugees and asylum. In this context, Muslim and non-Muslim writers have invoked the early *ijāra* tradition to trace an authentically Arabian and Islamic pedigree for the liberal extension of protection, combined with non-refoulement, to refugees.

Bibliography

Sources

Abū Dāwūd, *Sunan*, ed. Shuʿayb al-Arnāʾūṭ and Muḥammad Kāmil Qara Balilī, Beirut 2009; Ibn ʿAbd al-Barr, *al-Durar fī ikhtiṣār al-maghāzī wa-l-siyar*, ed. Shawqī Ḍayf, Cairo 1386/1966; Ibn Hishām, *al-Sīra al-nabawiyya*, ed. Muṣṭafā al-Saqqā, Ibrāhīm al-Ibyārī, and ʿAbd al-Ḥafīẓ Shalabī, 2 vols., Cairo 1936, 1375/1955[2]; al-Shaybānī, *al-Aṣl*, ed. Muḥammad Buynūkālin, Beirut 1433/2012.

Studies

Ghassan Maârouf Arnaout, *Asylum in the Arab-Islamic tradition*, Geneva 1987; Paul Dresch, *Tribes, government, and history in Yemen*, Oxford 1989; Melissa Finn, Asylum, in Gerhard Böwering et al. (eds.), *The Princeton encyclopedia of Islamic political thought* (Princeton 2012), 47–8; ʿAbd al-Raḥmān b. Aḥmad b. Muḥammad Ibn Fāyiʿ, *Aḥkām al-jiwār fī l-fiqh al-Islāmī*, Jidda 1995; Aharon Layish, *Dār ʿadl*. Symbiosis of custom and *sharīʿa* in a tribal society in process of sedentarization, *JSAI* 19 (1995), 198–213; Jean Lecerf, Djiwār, *EI2;* Milka Levy-Rubin, *Non-Muslims in the early Islamic empire*, Cambridge 2011;

J. Schacht, Amān, *EI2;* Robert Schick, Protection, *EQ;* Werner Schmucker, *Untersuchungen zu einigen wichtigen bodenrechtlichen Konsequenzen der islamischen Eroberungsbewegung*, Bonn 1972; R. B. Serjeant, The Sunna Jāmiʿah, pacts with the Yathrib Jews, and the *taḥrīm* of Yathrib, *BSOAS* 41/1 (1978), 1–42; Arafat Madi Shoukri, *Refugee status in Islam*, London 2011; J. E. Wansbrough, *Lingua Franca in the Mediterranean*, Richmond, Surrey 1996; W. Montgomery Watt, Idjāra, *EI2*.

Luke Yarbrough

Imām (technical term)

The etymological meaning of ***imām*** (pl. *aʾimma*) is someone who leads a group, such as the chief of a caravan, or something that guides, such as a roadway (as in Q 15:79) or a book or register (Q 17:71). It is used occasionally to denote bad examples to be eschewed (Q 9:12). In Islam, the word has retained these meanings. Besides the Qurʾānic examples already given, it is commonly used as an epithet for the founders of law schools, leading theologians, and other religious authorities, as well as for other important figures and intellectuals. Ibn Sīnā (Avicenna, d. 428/1037), for instance, is nicknamed Imām al-Ḥukamāʾ (leader of the wise men). The term has also acquired several specific, technical meanings.

1) In Islamic ritual practice the *imām* is the leader, normally a man and rarely a woman (Apostolidou; Sadeghi), of the congregational *ṣalāt* prayers, most importantly the obligatory Friday prayers. A prerequisite of all *ṣalāt* prayers performed by at least two men is that they be led by an *imām*, whose utterances and gestures the congregation imitates. Thus, the *imām* usually says aloud those parts of the prayer that the congregants must imitate inaudibly (al-Jazīrī, 1:228, 237). The *imām* stands in front of the assembly, which is aligned in rows, all facing Mecca (but see al-Muqaddasī, 202, who mentions a case of the assembly praying in front of the *imām*). The exception to this rule is when there is only one supplicant besides the *imām*, in which case the former stands to the *imām*'s right. Jurists have established the conditions of the imāmate, which are largely agreed upon: the *imām* must be of good intellectual and religious repute and sufficiently knowledgeable of the Qurʾān and its recitation, and his imāmate must not be contested by the congregation. While the *imām* often acts as the *khaṭīb* (preacher) in Friday prayers as well, it is considered improper for him to combine the imāmate with certain other offices of the mosque, such as that of muezzin. He is, nonetheless, responsible for initiating the prayers at the proper times (al-Ghazālī; al-Jazīrī, 1:367–402).

2) The *imām* is the ruler or leader of the community *(umma)*, especially in the formative period of Islam, in whom political, military, and religious authority were united. The doctrine of the imāmate in this sense developed radically differently in the three major sects of Islam. In (proto-) Sunnī Islam the imāmate coincided with the caliphate. Geographical and demographical expansion soon necessitated the appointment of delegates to lead the *ṣalāt* prayers, gradually isolating the office of the *imām* of a mosque from worldly leadership *(mulk)*, for which the title "caliph" came to prevail. In Shīʿism, the *imāms* are the venerated ʿAlī b. Abī Ṭālib (d. 40/661) and several of his descendants. According to Shīʿī doctrine, they are infallible, endowed with a unique esoteric knowledge, and they continue the Prophet's divinely inspired leadership in religious and worldly affairs. Finally, in Khārijism

(both the first/seventh century sectarian groups retroactively labeled *khawārij* and medieval and modern Ibāḍism), the community leader holds his position by popular consent.

3) In the study of the various codices and readings *(qirāʾāt)* of the Qurʾān, *al-imām* denotes the Medina Standard Codex, one of the mother copies or possibly the archetype of the Codex of ʿUthmān (e.g., Ibn Qutayba, 36, al-Naḥḥās, 431; for a discussion, see Nöldeke et al. , and Cook).

Bibliography

Sources

al-Ghazālī, *Iḥyāʾ ʿulūm al-dīn* (Beirut 1426/2005), 204–10; Ibn Qutayba, *Taʾwīl mushkil al-Qurʾān*, ed. al-Sayyid Aḥmad Saqr, Cairo 1954–5; ʿAbd al-Raḥmān al-Jazīrī, *Kitāb al-fiqh ʿalā l-madhāhib al-arbaʿa*, 5 vols., Beirut 2003; al-Muqaddasī, *Aḥsan al-taqāsīm fī maʿrifat al-aqālīm*, ed. M. J. de Goeje, Leiden 1906; Abū Jaʿfar al-Naḥḥās, *Iʿrāb al-Qurʾān*, ed. Khālid al-ʿAlī, Beirut 2008.

Studies

Anna Apostolidou, China's "nu ahong." The female imams of Ningxia, *Centre for Mediterranean, Middle East & Islamic Studies, Middle East Bulletin* 21 (2010), 14–5; Michael Cook, The stemma of the regional codices of the Koran, *Graeco-Arabica* 9–10 (2004), 89–104; Theodor Nöldeke, Friedrich Schwally, Gotthelf Bergsträsser, and Otto Pretzl, *Geschichte des Qorāns* (Leipzig 1909–38²), 3:6–19; Behnam Sadeghi, *The logic of law making in Islam. Women and prayer in the legal tradition* (Cambridge 2013), chap. 4.

Stijn Aerts

ʿInāyat Allāh Khān

ʿInāyat Allāh Khān Kashmīrī (d. 1139/1726) was born into an intellectual family. His mother, Ḥāfiẓa Maryam, instructed several pre-eminent Mughal nobles in Islamic subjects. Amongst them was Awrangzīb's favourite daughter, the princess Zīb al-Nisāʾ Makhfā (d. 1113/1702), who is said to have memorised the Qurʾān by the age of seven, thus becoming a *ḥāfiẓa* (fem. of Ar. *ḥāfiẓ*, a term used of Muslims who memorise the entire Qurʾān). That pleased the emperor and eased the introduction of ʿInāyat Allāh Khān into the empire's higher administrative apparatus through his mother and Zīb al-Nisāʾ. This was the starting point of ʿInāyat Allāh Khān's successful career at the Mughal court under five Mughal emperors: Awrangzīb ʿĀlamgīr (r. 1068–1118/1658–1707), Shāh ʿĀlam Bahādur (r. 1118–24/1707–12), Jahāndār Shāh (1124–5/1712–3), Farrūkh Siyar (r. 1124–31/1712–9), and Muḥammad Shāh (r. 1131–61/1719–48). From 1114/1702 onwards, ʿInāyat Allāh Khān was Awrangzīb's official *munshī* (secretary) and participated in many important governmental meetings and served as the ruler's official representative in several ceremonies, such as the *dīvān-i khāṣṣ* (private audience chamber) in the Red Fort, where the Mughal emperor received high courtiers and official guests. Several contemporary witnesses emphasise his close friendship with Awrangzīb (Navāz Khān, 2:828–30) and the emperor's trust in him (Navāz Khān, 1:310–21).

After Awrangzīb's death, in 1118/1707, ʿInāyat Allāh Khān skilfully navigated amongst factions at court struggling for power, and he was able to consolidate his position in the post-Awrangzīb period. From his early youth on, he maintained a strong connection to Kashmir, which led to his promotion to its governor during the short reign of Jahāndār Shāh (which overlapped for some weeks with that of Farrūkh Siyar) and made him popular as

ʿInāyat Allāh Khān, called Kashmīrī. He later reached the highest Mughal ranks and acted as deputy vizier.

ʿInāyat Allāh Khān was not only a highly respected and successful courtier and politician but was also intimately familiar with literary and historical works. He collected and edited various materials, notably Awrangzīb's orders, notes, and letters. The results of his efforts include, for example, the *Aḥkām-i ʿĀlamgīrī* ("Orders of ʿĀlamgīr"), distinct from the eponymous text written by Ḥamīd al-Dīn Khān and translated by Jadunath Sarkar, and the *Kalimāt-i ṭayyibāt* ("Nice sayings") and *Kalimāt-i Awrangzīb* ("Sayings of Awrangzeb"). ʿInāyat Allāh Khān's appreciation for and interest in literature and historiography led him also to patronise Mustaʿidd Khān's *Maʾāthir-i ʿĀlamgīrī* ("Heroic deeds of ʿĀlamgīr," completed 1122/1710), an important chronicle of Awrangzīb's reign.

Bibliography

Sources

Ḥamīd al-Dīn Khān, *Aḥkām-i ʿĀlamgīrī* (Pers. text with Eng. trans., notes and a life of Awrangzīb), ed. J. N. Sarkar, Calcutta 1912; ʿInāyat Allāh Khān, *Aḥkām-i ʿĀlamgīrī*, Rampur State Library and Patna O.P.L. MSS; ʿInāyat Allāh Khān Kashmīrī, *Kalimāt-i ṭayyibāt*, ed. S. Azizuddin Husain, Delhi 1982; Mustaʾidd Khān, *Maʾāthir-i ʿĀlamgīrī*, ed. Āghā Aḥmad ʿAlī, *The Maāsir-i-ʿālamgiri of Muhammad Sāqī Mustaʾidd Khān*, 2 vols., Calcutta 1870–3; Shāh Navāz Khān, *Maʾāthir al-umarāʾ*, ed. Mīrzā Ashraf ʿĀlī, vol. 2 (Calcutta 1890), 828–32.

Studies

Muhammad Athar Ali, *The Mughal nobility under Aurangzeb*, Aligarh 1966, rev. ed. Delhi 1997; Stephan Conerman, *Historiographie als Sinnstiftung. Indo-persische Geschichtsschreibung während der Mogulzeit (932–1118/1516–1707)*, Wiesbaden 2002; S. M. Azizuddin Husain, Inayatullah Khān Kashmīrī. A biographical study, *Studies in Islam. Quarterly Journal of the Indian Institute of Islamic Studies* 18 (1981), 9–19; S. M. Azizuddin Husain, *Structure of politics under Aurangzeb 1658–1707*, Delhi 2002; S. M. Azizuddin Husain, *Kalimat-i-Aurangzeb*. A source of Aurangzeb's reign, *Proceedings of the Indian History Congress* 40 (1979), 314–8; Annie Krieger-Krydnicki, *Captive princess. Zebunissa, daughter of Emperor Aurangzeb*, trans. from the French by Enjum Hamid, Karachi 2005; Tilmann Kulke, *A Mughal munshī at work. Conflicts and emotions in Mustaʿidd Ḫān's Maʾāṯir-i ʿĀlamgīrī. A narratological investigation*, Ph.D. diss., European University Institute, Florence 2016; Sayyid Athar Abbas Rizvi, *Shāh Walī-Allāh and his times. A study of eighteenth century Islām, politics and society in India*, Canberra 1980; Jadunath Sarkar, *History of Aurangzeb, mainly based on Persian sources*, 5 vols., Calcutta 1912–30.

Tilmann Kulke

ʿĪsā b. ʿUmar

Abū ʿUmar **ʿĪsā b. ʿUmar** al-Thaqafī (d. 149/766) was a reader of the Qurʾān and a grammarian of the Basran school. (His *kunya* is given as Abū Sulaymān in Ibn al-Anbārī, 28). The son of a client (*mawlā*) of Khālid b. al-Walīd al-Makhzūmī (d. 21/642), more often designated as simply "*mawlā Khālid*," he settled at Basra among the Banū Thaqīf, a relationship he claimed with his *nisba*. He studied the Qurʾān and philology under ʿAbdallāh b. Abī Isḥāq al-Ḥaḍramī (d. 117/735), Yaḥyā b. Yaʿmar (d. 129/746), and Abū ʿAmr Ibn al-ʿAlāʾ (d. 154/771 or 157/774), and profited from many meetings with the poet Dhū l-Rumma (d. c.117/735), an older contemporary, who explained many rare and uncommon words to him. Among his disciples were some of the most prominent Arabic grammarians: al-Khalīl b. Aḥmad (d. 175/791), Sībawayh (d. 177/793), Abū ʿUbayda (d. 210/825), al-Aṣmaʿī (d. 213 or 216/828 or 831), and Quṭrub (d. 206/821). The fact that he was the fifth most frequently quoted scholar in Sībawayh's

Kitāb ranks him among the very important pre-Khalīlian grammarians, although we have no clear idea of his views on issues in grammar. Some sources say that he wrote more than seventy books, but their titles and their contents are not provided. Two of them, namely (1) *al-Jāmiʿ* and (2) *al-Mukmil/al-Mukammil* or *al-Ikmāl*, are known by their titles and seem to have really existed. The title *al-Jāmiʿ* may indicate that it is a *summa* of ʿĪsā's grammatical knowledge and the title of the second work may indicate that it was written as a supplement to the first. Unfortunately both fell soon into oblivion and left no traces in the works of later grammarians. Occasional notes in the biographical literature point out that ʿĪsā b. ʿUmar gave preference to the method of *qiyās* (analogy) for solving grammatical questions *(masāʾil)*, following herewith his teacher ʿAbdallāh b. Abī Isḥāq (see Fück), and to the use of the accusative instead of the nominative in certain constructions, which is all the biographers had to say about ʿĪsā as grammarian. They took more interest in ʿĪsā's way of speaking, which was characterised by the constant use of *iʿrāb* (desinential inflections) and obsolete and extremely rare words *(taqʿīr)* for ordinary objects and activities of daily life, habits that provided amusing anecdotes for the biographers (see Weipert, 32–4, 73–8).

Bibliography

Sources

Abū l-Ṭayyib al-Lughawī, *Marātib al-naḥwiyyīn*, ed. Muḥammad Abū l-Faḍl Ibrāhīm (Cairo 1394/1974²), 43; al-Sīrāfī, *Akhbār al-naḥwiyyīn al-Baṣriyyīn*, ed. Fritz Krenkow (Beirut and Paris 1936), 31–3; al-Zubaydī, *Ṭabaqāt al-naḥwiyyīn*, ed. Muḥammad Abū l-Faḍl Ibrāhīm (Cairo 1392/1973), 40–5; Ibn al-Nadīm, *al-Fihrist*, ed. Ayman Fuʾād Sayyid (London 1430/2009), 1/1:109–11; al-Yaghmūrī, *Nūr al-qabas*, ed. Rudolf Sellheim (Wiesbaden 1964), 46–7; ʿAlī b. Ḥasan, *al-Mukhtār min al-Muqtabas*, facsimile edition (Frankfurt 1990), 49–73; al-Tanūkhī, *Taʾrīkh al-ʿulamāʾ al-naḥwiyyīn*, ed. ʿAbd al-Fattāḥ Muḥammad al-Ḥulw (Riyadh 1401/1981), 135–8; Ibn al-Anbārī, *Nuzhat al-alibbāʾ*, ed. Ibrāhīm al-Sāmarrāʾī (Baghdad 1970²), 28–30; Yāqūt, *Muʿjam al-udabāʾ*, ed. Iḥsān ʿAbbās (Beirut 1993), 5:2141–3; al-Qifṭī, *Inbāh al-ruwāt*, ed. Muḥammad Abū l-Faḍl Ibrāhīm (Cairo 1369–93/1950–1973), 2:374–7; Ibn Khallikān, *Wafayāt al-aʿyān*, ed. Iḥsān ʿAbbās (Beirut 1968), 3:486–8; al-Yamānī, *Ishārat al-taʿyīn*, ed. ʿAbd al-Majīd Diyāb (Riyadh 1406/1986), 249–50; al-Dhahabī, *Siyar aʿlām al-nubalāʾ*, ed. Shuʿayb al-Arnaʾūṭ et al. (Beirut 1406/1986⁴), 7:200; al-Dhahabī, *Taʾrīkh al-Islām*, ed. ʿAbd al-Salām Tadmurī (Beirut 1411/1991), 9:561–3; al-Ṣafadī, *al-Wāfī bi-l-wafayāt*, ed. Monika Gronke (Beirut 1431/2010), 23:484–8; Ibn al-Jazarī, *Ghāyat al-nihāya*, ed. Gotthelf Bergsträsser (Cairo 1351/1932), 1:612; al-Suyūṭī, *Bughyat al-wuʿāt*, ed. Muḥammad Abū l-Faḍl Ibrāhīm (Cairo 1384/1964), 2:237–8; al-Suyūṭī, *Tuḥfat al-adīb fī nuḥāt Mughnī l-labīb*, ed. Ḥasan al-Malkh and Suhā Naʿja (Irbid 1426/2005), 2:586–9.

Studies

GAL 1:99; *GALS* 1:158; *GAS* 9:37–9; Ṣāliḥ Muḥammad ʿAlī Abū Shārib, *Qirāʾat ʿĪsā b. ʿUmar al-Thaqafī*, Amman 1435/2014; Ramzi Baalbaki, *The early Islamic grammatical tradition*, Aldershot 2007; Johann Fück, ʿĪsā b. ʿUmar, *EI2*; Ṣabāḥ ʿAbbās al-Sālim, *ʿĪsā b. ʿUmar al-Thaqafī. Naḥwuhu min khilāl qirāʾatihi*, Baghdad and Beirut 1395/1975; Rafael Talmon, *Eighth-century Iraqi grammar. A critical exploration of pre-Ḫalīlian Arabic linguistics*, Winona Lake IN 2003; Cornelis H. M. Versteegh, *Arabic grammar and Qurʾānic exegesis in early Islam*, Leiden 1993; Reinhard Weipert, *Altarabischer Sprachwitz. Abū ʿAlqama und die Kunst, sich kompliziert auszudrücken* (Munich 2009), 32–4, 73–8.

Reinhard Weipert

Ismāʿīl b. Yasār

Abū Fāʾid **Ismāʿīl b. Yasār** al-Nisāʾī (d. 130/748) was a minor poet from Medina who composed panegyrical odes and elegies, most notably on the Zubayrids.

His father, an Iranian from Azerbaijan, went to al-Ḥijāz and settled in Medina, where he prepared wedding dinners; hence his *nisba* al-Nisāʾī ("concerned with women"), which was subsequently applied to Ismāʿīl as well. Ismāʿīl, who became a *mawlā* (client) of the Banū Taym b. Murra, a branch of the Banū Quraysh, was a poet, as were his son Ibrāhīm and his brothers Ibrāhīm, Muḥammad, Mūsā Shahawāt, and Sulaymān. A few of their verses are found scattered in the literature, but it seems that the belletrist Abū l-Faraj al-Iṣfahānī (d. 356/967) was the only one to devote entire chapters to Ismāʿīl and Mūsā Shahawāt, providing extensive information about them in *al-Aghānī* (4:408–27 and 3:351–65 respectively). Even so, the rather limited number of verses and fragments of poems does not permit a well-grounded judgement on the quality of their poetical skills.

What can be said is that both poets earned their living by composing panegyrical odes and elegies on prominent personalities. Ismāʿīl, for instance, gave preference to the members of the Zubayrid family, whose eager partisan he had been: He praised Abū Bakr b. Ḥamza, a grandson of ʿAbdallāh b. al-Zubayr (2–73/624–92) and mourned him in two *qaṣīdas*, and he composed further elegies on Muḥammad and Yaḥyā, sons of the famed traditionist ʿUrwa b. al-Zubayr (23–93/643–711). After the death of ʿAbdallāh b. al-Zubayr, Ismāʿīl went to Damascus and tried to gain the favour of the Umayyad caliphs ʿAbd al-Malik b. Marwān (r. 65–86/685–705) and, much later, al-Walīd b. Yazīd (r. 125–6/743–4), as well as al-Walīd's brother al-Ghamr, with his panegyrical poems. The poems were gladly accepted, but once, when Ismāʿīl was bold enough to praise himself and his Iranian roots in front of Hishām b. ʿAbd al-Malik (r. 105–25/724–43), the caliph became furious and ordered him thrown into a pond: he nearly drowned and, as additional punishment, was banished to the Ḥijāz.

Ismāʿīl b. Yasār lived a very long life and died shortly before the reign of the Umayyad dynasty ended in 132/750.

His surviving verses, about seventy, were collected by Yūsuf Ḥusayn Bakkār, Beirut 1404/1984, nearly exclusively from *al-Aghānī*; see also the short supplement to this edition by ʿIrfān ʿAbd al-Qādir al-Ashqar, *MMIA* 61 (1986), 3:628–33.

Bibliography

Sources

al-Jumaḥī, *Ṭabaqāt fuḥūl al-shuʿarāʾ*, ed. Maḥmūd Muḥammad Shākir (Cairo 1974), 1:408–9, 2:675–6; al-Zubayr b. Bakkār, *Jamharat nasab Quraysh wa-akhbārihā*, ed. Maḥmūd Muḥammad Shākir (Riyadh 1419/1999[2]), passim; al-Balādhurī, *Ansāb al-ashrāf*, ed. Iḥsān ʿAbbās (Beirut 1417/1996), 5:230–1; Abū l-Faraj al-Iṣfahānī, *al-Aghānī* (Cairo 1345–94/1927–74), 4:408–27; Ibn Manẓūr, *Mukhtaṣar Taʾrīkh Dimashq l-Ibn ʿAsākir*, ed. Riyāḍ ʿAbd al-Ḥamīd Murād and Rawḥiyya al-Naḥḥās (Damascus 1404/1984), 4:376–8 (the biography is missing in Ibn ʿAsākir's main work); al-Ṣafadī, *al-Wāfī bi-l-wafayāt*, ed. Josef van Ess (Wiesbaden 1394/1974), 9:241–4; al-Baghdādī, *Sharḥ shawāhid Shāfiyat Ibn al-Ḥājib*, Muḥammad Nūr al-Ḥasan, Muḥammad al-Zafzāf, and Muḥammad Muḥyī l-Dīn ʿAbd al-Ḥamīd (Beirut 1395/1975[2]), 318–20.

Studies

Charles Pellat, Ismāʿīl b. Yasār, *EI2*; Maḥmūd al-Miqdād, Ismāʿīl b. Yasār mawlā Banī Taym b. Murra, *al-Turāth al-ʿArabī* (Damascus 1986), 24:190–210; *GAL* 1:62; *GALS* 1:95; GAS 2:429–30.

Reinhard Weipert

J

al-Jaghmīnī

Sharaf al-Dīn Abū ʿAlī Maḥmūd b. Muḥammad b. ʿUmar **al-Jaghmīnī** (al-Chaghmīnī) al-Khwārazmī (d. c.618/1221–2) composed multiple scientific works (in astronomy, arithmetic, astrology, and medicine) in Arabic in the late sixth/twelfth and early seventh/thirteenth centuries under the auspices of the Khwārazmshāhs in Central Asia. Two of his compositions in particular became popular textbooks: an introduction to Ptolemaic theoretical astronomy, *al-Mulakhkhaṣ fī ʿilm al-hayʾa al-basīṭa;* and a medical treatise, *al-Qānūnča* ("The 'little *Qānūn*'"), an abridgement of Ibn Sīnā's (Avicenna, d. 428/1037) famous compendium *al-Qānūn fī l-ṭibb* ("The canon of medicine"). The impact and longevity of their influence are evidenced by the plethora of extant copies, and by their many commentaries and translations, which continued to be studied extensively for over seven centuries and disseminated widely throughout the Islamic world and South Asia.

1. Dating al-Jaghmīnī to the late sixth/twelfth and early seventh/thirteenth centuries

Numerous modern sources erroneously date al-Jaghmīnī to the first half of the eighth/fourteenth century. Some list two Jaghmīnīs, distinguishing between an early seventh/thirteenth-century astronomer/mathematician (d. c.618/1221–2), who authored the *Mulakhkhaṣ (GAL,* 1:473; *GALS,* 1:865), and an eighth/fourteenth-century physician (d. 745/1344–5), who wrote the *Qānūnča (GAL,* 1:457; *GALS,* 1:826).

The error that one Jaghmīnī (who authored both the *Mulakhkhaṣ* and the *Qānūnča*) died in 745/1344–5 originates with Heinrich Suter (Zur Frage, 539–40), who relied on a specious marginal note in a *Qānūnča* copy (Gotha, Forschungsbibliothek, MS Or. A 1930, fol. 1b) reported in a catalogue (Pertsch, 3/3:468). Suter was emboldened because *Mulakhkhaṣ* commentaries first appeared around that time and because the sources suggesting 618/1221–2 for al-Jaghmīnī's floruit (e.g.,

Gottwaldt, 245, no. 169) provided no evidence to support this date. Contributing further to the misdating of al-Jaghmīnī was not recognising how commonplace it was for copyists to modify a scientific treatise over time in such a way that it incorporated material from later sources, thus making it appear that it depended on these later sources (F. J. Ragep, On dating Jaghmīnī).

Suter's interpretation was perpetuated (e.g., Suter [Vernet], al-Djaghmīnī; *GAS*, 5:115, no. 56) despite mounting contradictory evidence, such as the discovery of an early copy of the *Mulakhkhaṣ*, dated 644/1246–7 (Istanbul, Süleymaniye Library, Laleli MS 2141, fol. 81a), by Max Krause (Krause, 510). This led some scholars to raise the possibility of two Jaghmīnīs (e.g., Richter-Bernburg, 373). Thus, several sources list al-Jaghmīnī under two categories, astronomy and medicine, with different dates. However, the two-Jaghmīnī hypothesis is refuted by several colophons of extant *Qānūnča* manuscripts bearing seventh/thirteenth-century copy dates, the earliest of which was copied in Konya in 601/1205 (Istanbul, Süleymaniye Library, Ayasofya MS 3735, fol. 25a). In sum, the content and extant copy dates of several of al-Jaghmīnī's works, in conjunction with the floruits of his dedicatees, support the notion that he flourished in the late sixth/twelfth and early seventh/thirteenth centuries, during the reigns of the Khwārazmshāhs ʿAlāʾ al-Dīn Tekish (r. 567–96/1172–1200) and ʿAlāʾ al-Dīn Muḥammad (r. 596–617/1200–20).

Al-Jaghmīnī's works contain two dedicatees. Both his *Mulakhkhaṣ* and a short treatise on planetary sizes and distances are dedicated to Imām Badr al-Dīn al-Qalānisī, who hailed from a prominent Damascene family of Shāfiʿī scholars, and who composed a pharmaceutical treatise, *Aqrābādhīn al-Qalānisī* (c.590/1194; Ibn Abī Uṣaybiʿa, 2:31; Fellmann, 1–3). Some versions of the *Mulakhkhaṣ* include a dedicatory poem al-Jaghmīnī composed to him. Al-Jaghmīnī dedicated two works to Shihāb al-Dīn Abū Saʿd Ibn ʿImrān al-Khwārazmī al-Khīwaqī (d. c.616–7/1220), a renowned Shāfiʿī scholar and trusted adviser *(wakīl)* to ʿAlāʾ al-Dīn Muḥammad (al-Nasawī, *Sīrat al-sulṭān*, 109–15 [=al-Nasawī, *Histoire du sultan*, 82–9]). The thirteen-year span of their composition dates—from 602/1205, for an astrological treatise, to 615/1218, for a mathematical work—indicates a longstanding relationship between al-Jaghmīnī and Shihāb al-Dīn and falls within the long reign of ʿAlāʾ al-Dīn Muḥammad.

Where al-Jaghmīnī lived throughout his life is not at all clear, though most likely he lived in the environs of Merv. Given the last composition date we have for him (615/1218), he may have witnessed the ushering in of the reign of the last Khwārazmshāh, Jalāl al-Dīn (r. 617–28/1220–31). It is plausible that al-Jaghmīnī ultimately died during one of the many battles of the Mongol onslaught that devastated the regions of Khurāsān and Khwārazm during that time, which destroyed major centres of learning, including the cities of Merv and Gurgānj. Hence, we have a viable explanation to support the 618/1221–2 date for al-Jaghmīnī's death, a date that appears (without explanation) in numerous Islamic sources.

A full discussion of al-Jaghmīnī's dates can be found in S. Ragep, *Jaghmīnī's* Mulakhkhaṣ, 5–26.

2. Works by al-Jaghmīnī

All of al-Jaghmīnī's known works were originally composed in Arabic and all are extant (S. Ragep, 281–3).

2.1 *Astronomy*

1. *al-Mulakhkhaṣ fī ʿilm al-hayʾa al-basīṭa*

An introductory work on the discipline of *hayʾa*, this work was composed in 602–3/1205–6 at the behest of Imām Badr al-Dīn al-Qalānisī, who proposed that al-Jaghmīnī write a concise and succinct work on the subject. The structure and content offer a physical configuration *(hayʾa)* of the universe as a coherent whole glorifying God's entire creation, both His celestial realm (*hayʾat al-samāʾ*; part 1, in five chapters) and the sublunary terrestrial region (*hayʾat al-arḍ*; part 2, in three chapters). The *Mulakhkhaṣ* lacks a discussion of planetary sizes and distances of the celestial bodies, often found in *hayʾa* works; this may have led al-Jaghmīnī to compose treatise no. 2. Al-Jaghmīnī mentions only two authorities, Ptolemy's (d. c.168 C.E.) *Almagest* and al-Battānī's (d. 317/929) *Zīj* or astronomical handbook, but the *Mulakhkhaṣ* is also highly reliant on ʿAbd al-Jabbār al-Kharaqī's *al-Tabṣira fī ʿilm al-hayʾa* (composed c.526–7/1132–3). The *Mulakhkhaṣ*, categorised as a "famous abridgement" *(mukhtaṣar)* on the discipline of *hayʾa* (Ṭāshkubrīzāda, 349), served as the starting point for over 60 commentaries, supercommentaries, glosses, and translations (into Persian, Turkish, and Hebrew) that were composed and studied for over seven centuries (S. Ragep, 284–91). Ṭāshkubrīzāda (Taşköprüzade, d. 968/1561) highlights four: one by Faḍlallāh al-ʿUbaydī (d. 751/1350), a student of Quṭb al-Dīn al-Shīrāzī (d. 710/1311 who cites the *Mulakhkhaṣ* in his *Nihāyat al-idrāk*; F. J. Ragep, Shīrāzī's *Nihāyat*, 51, 55); a second by Kamāl al-Dīn al-Turkmānī (composed in 755/1354); a third by al-Sayyid al-Sharīf al-Jurjānī (d. 816/1413); and a fourth by Qāḍīzāde al-Rūmī (d. after 844/1440; composed in 814/1412 and dedicated to the Tīmūrid ruler Ulugh Beg, d. 853/1449). The influence of Qāḍīzāde's commentary (İhsanoğlu et al., 1:8–21, no. 3) deserves special mention, in that it inspired at least 24 supercommentaries or glosses and was studied well into the thirteenth/nineteenth century. Qāḍīzāde's *Sharḥ al-Mulakhkhaṣ* became a favoured intermediate-level textbook in Ottoman *madrasas*, often studied with the gloss by ʿAbd al-ʿAlī al-Bīrjandī (d. 935/1528) (İhsanoğlu et al., 1:101–4, no. 1; İzgi, 1:381–2, d.1). For a critical edition and English translation of *al-Mulakhkhaṣ*, see S. Ragep, *Jaghmīnī's* Mulakhkhaṣ.

2. *Risāla fī aqdār ajrām al-kawākib wa-abʿādihā*

A treatise on planetary distances and sizes, dedicated to Badr al-Dīn al-Qalānisī, and composed after the *Mulakhkhaṣ* (S. Ragep, 16, 36 n. 141).

3. *Taḥrīr al-qawāʿid li-taḥlīl astār al-farāʾid*

A treatise on rules for clarifying miscellaneous items in astronomy.

2.2 *Astrology*

4. *al-Kitāb fī quwā l-kawākib wa-ḍaʿfihā*

A short astrological treatise on the strengths and weaknesses of the planets, dedicated to Shihāb al-Dīn. Al-Jaghmīnī composed this work one year prior to the *Mulakhkhaṣ*. Al-Jaghmīnī discusses the positions of the apogees for each of the planets in both works, but here his listings begin with Dhū l-Qarnayn 1516 (the era of Alexander the Great), whereas the date he gives in the *Mulakhkhaṣ* is Dhū l-Qarnayn 1517 (=602–3/1205–6) (S. Ragep, 21, 37 n. 148).

2.3 *Mathematics*

5. *Talkhīṣ Kitāb Ūqlīdis*

An epitome of Euclid's *Elements*, composed at the request of Shihāb al-Dīn Abū Saʿd Ibn ʿImrān al-Khwārazmī al-Khīwaqī, and completed on 22 Ṣafar 615 / 19–20 May 1218. For a facsimile of this work, see *Talkhīṣ Kitāb Ūqlīdis*, 15–246 (S. Ragep, 21, 24).

6. *al-Mūjaz fī l-ḥisāb*

A summary on arithmetic.

7. *Risālat ṣuwar al-ḥisāb al-tisʿ* (=*Risāla laṭīfa fī ḥisāb*?=*Risāla fī l-ḥisāb*?)

A treatise on nine types of arithmetic. Also referred to as *Risāla mukhtaṣara fī l-ḥisāb* (King, *Survey*, 150 [G17, 6.3.11]; Rosenfeld and Ihsanoğlu, 198, M1).

8. *Sharḥ ṭuruq al-ḥisāb fī masāʾil al-waṣāyā*

A commentary on using arithmetic in questions related to inheritance.

9. *Manẓūma fī l-jabr wa-l-muqābala*

A treatise in rhyme on algebra. A poem in 25 verses on problems about algebraic equations.

2.4 *Medicine*

10. *al-Qānūnča* ("The 'little *Qānūn*'")

This ten-part medical treatise states that it contains the "choicest parts" from "books of the Ancients"; however, al-Jaghmīnī relies principally on Book One (On general principles of medicine) of Ibn Sīnā's *al-Qānūn fī l-ṭibb*. An extant copy of the *Qānūnča*, dated 601/1205 (Istanbul, Süleymaniye Library, Ayasofya MS 3735), indicates that al-Jaghmīnī composed it prior to the *Mulakhkhaṣ*. According to the commentary of Ḥusayn b. Muḥammad b. ʿAlī al-Astarābādhī, written in 831/1427, the *Qānūnča* was "currently used in all countries, and, indeed, students were as familiar with it as with the midday sun" (Iskandar, 56–7). The base text and ensuing commentaries and translations (into Persian, Turkish, English, and Urdu) continued to be studied and copied well into the thirteenth/nineteenth century throughout Anatolia, as well as in Central and South Asia. The *Qānūnča* was also transliterated into Hebrew characters (Langermann, 148). A Persian *Qānūnča* commentary by Muḥammad Akbar Arzānī (d. 1134/1722) is titled *Mufarriḥ al-qulūb* (Keshavarz, 57–8) (for the *Qānūnča* *see* Iskandar, 56–64, 166–70; S. Ragep).

2.5 *Other*

11. A poem *(qaṣīda)*

12. A small fragment of a mathematical work attributed to al-Jaghmīnī (Leiden, Leiden University Library, MS Or. 204[2], fol. 30a; Witkam, 88).

3. Misattributions

1. *al-Kitāb al-qiwāmī fī l-ḥisāb*

This is an arithmetical treatise on extracting roots and operations with decimal fractions. The author may be Abū Naṣr Samawʾal b. Yaḥyā l-Maghribī, who completed a treatise with a similar title in 568/1172–3 (Ibn Abī Uṣaybiʿa, 2:31).

2. *al-Risāla al-mawsūma bi-Ṭibb al-Nabī*

This is a treatise on the medicine of the Prophet. The author has been identified as Jaʿfar b. Muḥammad al-Mustaghfirī (d. 432/1040). The misattribution (e.g., Elgood) may have occurred because this work and al-Jaghmīnī's *Qānūnča* were copied together in some codices.

Bibliography

Works

Talkhīṣ Kitāb Ūqlīdis, ed. Ṣādiq Ḥusaynī al-Ishkavarī, Qum 1384/2006; Sally P. Ragep, *Jaghmīnī's* Mulakhkhaṣ. *An Islamic introduction to Ptolemaic astronomy*, New York 2016.

Sources

Irene Fellmann, *Das Aqrābādīn al-Qalānisī. Quellenkritische und begriffsanalytische Untersuchungen zur arabisch-pharmazeutischen Literatur*, Beirut 1986; Josephus M. E. Gottwaldt, *Opisanie arabskich rukopisej prinadležavšich bibliotekě Imperatorskago Kazangskago Universiteta* (Kazan 1855), 245, no. 169; Ibn Abī Uṣaybiʿa, *ʿUyūn al-anbāʾ fī ṭabaqāt al-aṭibbāʾ*, ed. August Müller (Cairo 1882), 2:31; Ekmeleddin İhsanoğlu et al. (eds.), *Osmanlı astronomi literatürü tarihi* (=History of astronomy literature during the Ottoman period), 2 vols., Istanbul 1997; A. Z. Iskandar, *A catalogue of Arabic manuscripts on medicine and science in the Wellcome Historical Medical Library*, London 1967; Cevat İzgi, *Osmanlı Medreselerinde İlim*, 2 vols., Istanbul 1997; Fateme Keshavarz, *A descriptive and analytical catalogue of Persian manuscripts in the library of the Wellcome Institute for the History of Medicine* (London 1986), 57–8; David A. King, *A catalogue of the scientific manuscripts in the Egyptian National Library*, vol. 2, *Descriptive catalogue arranged chronologically according to subjects. Indexes of authors and titles*, Cairo 1986; David A. King, *A survey of the scientific manuscripts in the Egyptian National Library*, Winona Lake IN 1986; Max Krause, Stambuler Handschriften islamischer Mathematiker, *Quellen und Studien zur Geschichte der Mathematik, Astronomie und Physik* B/3 (1936), 437–532, repr. as Fuat Sezgin (ed.), *Islamic mathematics and astronomy* (Frankfurt am Main 1998), 83:237–332; Y. Tzvi Langermann, Arabic writings in Hebrew manuscripts. A preliminary relisting, *ASP* 6/1 (1996), 137–60; Muḥammad b. Aḥmad al-Nasawī, *Histoire du sultan Djelal ed-Din Mankobirti, prince du Kharezm*, trans. Octave Houdas, Paris 1895; Muḥammad b. Aḥmad al-Nasawī, *Sīrat al-sulṭān Jalāl al-Dīn Mankubirtī li-Muḥammad b. Aḥmad al-Nasawī*, ed. Ḥāfiẓ Aḥmad Ḥamdī, Cairo 1953; Wilhelm Pertsch, *Die orientalischen Handschriften der Herzoglichen Bibliothek zu Gotha* (Gotha 1881), 3/3:468–9 (no. 1928), 469–71 (no. 1930); Boris A. Rosenfeld and Ekmeleddin İhsanoğlu, *Mathematicians, astronomers and other scholars of Islamic civilization and their works (7th–19th century)*, Istanbul 2003; Aḥmad b. Muṣṭafā Ṭāshkubrīzāda, *Miftāḥ al-saʿāda wa-miṣbāḥ al-siyāda* (Beirut 1985), 3:348–9; Jan Just Witkam (comp.), *Inventory of the oriental manuscripts of the library of the University of Leiden*, vol. 1, *Manuscripts Or. 1-Or. 1000. Acquisitions in the period between 1609 and 1665*, Leiden 2007.

STUDIES

Cyril Elgood, Tibb-ul-Nabbi or Medicine of the Prophet, *Osiris* 14 (1962), 33–192 (misattribution); F. Jamil Ragep, On dating Jaghmīnī and his *Mulakhkhaṣ*, in Mustafa Kaçar and Zeynep Durukal (eds.), *Essays in honour of Ekmeleddin İhsanoğlu* (Istanbul 2006), 461–6; F. Jamil Ragep, Shīrāzī's *Nihāyat al-idrāk*. Introduction and conclusion, *Tarikh-e Elm* 11 (2013), 41–57; Sally P. Ragep, *Jaghmīnī's* Mulakhkhaṣ (see under WORKS); Lutz Richter-Bernburg, Jaġmini, Maḥmud, *EIr* 14/4:373; Heinrich Suter, Zur Frage über die Lebenszeit des Verfassers des Mulaḫḫaṣ fî'l-hei'a, Maḥmûd b. Muḥ. b. ʿOmar al-Ǵaġmînî, *ZDMG* 53 (1899), 539–40, repr. as Fuat Sezgin (ed.), *Islamic mathematics and astronomy*, vol. 77, *Miscellaneous texts and studies on Islamic mathematics and astronomy* (Frankfurt am Main 1998), 2:305–6; Heinrich Suter, al-Djaghmīnī, *EI1*; Heinrich Suter (rev. J. Vernet), al-Djaghmīnī, *EI2*; *GAL* 1:457, 473; *GALS* 1:826, 865; *GAS* 5:115, no. 56.

SALLY P. RAGEP

Japheth

Japheth is not mentioned in the Qurʾān. The Qurʾān mentions the story of Noah in several passages but offers little regarding his family. There is reference to a wicked wife (Q 66:10) and an impious son (Q 11:40–6), the latter usually identified in later traditions as Canaan or Yām. Japheth is named amongst the three sons of Noah (Shem, Japheth, and Ham) only in a few later reports and traditions relating mainly to the genealogies of peoples after the Flood.

Few details about Japheth appear in Islamic literature. Japheth was one of seven or eight saved in the Ark (al-Ṭarafī, § 79, 81). He was the youngest of Noah's sons and lived nine hundred years. Noah had him when he was five hundred years old (Ibn Qutayba, 24). Japheth, Ham, and Shem helped Noah build the Ark (al-Thaʿlabī, 56). Some literary sources, historiographical works, and *qiṣaṣ al-anbiyāʾ* (tales of the prophets) collections give the names of Japheth's wife and progeny, adding only a few details, such as the number of the languages they spoke. Japheth's wife was named Arbasīsa, who bore him seven sons and one daughter (al-Ṭabarī, 1:211). It was Japheth who, while Ham laughed and was consequently cursed for doing so, covered the private parts of Noah when the wind lifted his robe while he was sleeping (al-Rabghūzī, 1:48). An isolated attestation in al-Thaʿlabī's *Qiṣaṣ al-anbiyāʾ* (151) maintains that Japheth had planted the pine (*ṣanawbar*) tree called Shāt Dirakht (Pers. *dirakht*, "tree") that was worshipped by the mysterious People of the Rass named in Q 25:38.

The main interest in Japheth in the Islamic sources lies in his descendants and, implicitly, the peoples originating from them. Japheth had seven sons, like his brothers, and they scattered in every direction, from east to west (al-Dīnawarī, 2; Ṣibṭ Ibn al-Jawzī, 249). According to other sources, in the division of humankind originating from Noah's offspring, Japheth is said to have been the father of the Turks, Romans, and Byzantines (Rūm), Gog and Magog, the Chinese, and the people of Khurāsān as far as Ḥulwān, in western Iran (Muqātil, 4:453). According to a report attested in the *ḥadīth*s (sayings of Muḥammad), Japheth is the father of the Rūm (Aḥmad b. Ḥanbal, Beirut 2001, 33:292f., nos. 20099–100). Various versions of these traditions emphasise other details. Japheth was sent to Turkestan, making all Turks descendants of Japheth (al-Rabghūzī, 1:49). Further, while the descendants of Shem are reddish-white and those of Ham are black, the descendants of Japheth are reddish-brown (al-Ṭabarī, 1:199). Islamic literature also includes details drawn literally from the Bible, such as Noah's invocation that God make numerous (the descendants of) Japheth and allow him to dwell in the places of Shem (al-Masʿūdī, 45, from Gen., 9, 27).

Bibliography

Sources

al-Dīnawarī, *Akhbār al-ṭiwāl*, ed. ʿAbd al-Munʿim ʿĀmir (Cairo 1960), 2; al-Masʿūdī, *Murūj al-dhahab wa-maʿādin al-jawhar*, ed. Charles Pellat (Beirut 1965), 1:45; Ibn Qutayba, *al-Maʿārif* (Cairo 1992), 23–6; Muqātil b. Sulaymān, *Tafsīr*, ed. ʿAbdallāh Maḥmūd Shiḥāta (Cairo 1979–89), 4:453; al-Rabghūzī, *The stories of the prophets.* Qiṣaṣ al-anbiyāʾ. *An eastern Turkish version*, ed. H. E. Boeschoten and John O'Kane, *The stories of the prophets* (Leiden 2015[2]), 1:48–9, 2:57; Sibṭ Ibn al-Jawzī, *Mirʾāt al-zamān fī taʾrīkh al-aʿyān*, ed. Iḥsān ʿAbbās (Beirut 1985), 1:245–9; al-Ṭabarī, *Taʾrīkh al-rusul wa-l-mulūk*, ed. M. J. de Goeje et al. (Leiden 1879–1901), 1:195–200, 211, trans. Franz Rosenthal, *The history of al-Ṭabarī*, vol. 1, *General introduction and from the Creation to the Flood* (Albany 1989), 365–8; al-Ṭarafī, *Qiṣaṣ al-anbiyāʾ*, ed. Roberto Tottoli, *The stories of the prophets by Ibn Muṭarrif al-Ṭarafī* (Berlin 2003), 31 (Ar.), 37 (Eng.); al-Thaʿlabī, *Qiṣaṣ al-anbiyāʾ* (Cairo 1954), 56, 151, trans. William M. Brinner, *ʿArāʾis al-majālis fī Qiṣaṣ al-anbiyāʾ or Lives of the prophets as recounted by Abū Isḥāq Aḥmad ibn Muḥammad ibn Ibrāhīm al-Thaʿlabī* (Leiden 2002), 95, 251.

Study

Max Grünbaum, *Neue Beiträge zur semitischen Sagenkunde* (Leiden 1893), 86–7.

Roberto Tottoli

K

Kabul art and architecture

Kabul, capital and principal city of modern Afghanistan, has a history of **art and architecture** spanning over two millennia but only few material remains survived. Kabul blossomed at times as a provincial garrison town and major trade post, at other times as the centre of the various pre-Islamic and Islamic empires that dominated the Hindu Kush region, the proverbial "crossroads of Asia" and "gateway to India," amalgamating cultural influences from Hellenic, Persian, Arabo-Islamic, Central Asian, and Indian civilisations.

Numerous remains and archaeological finds both within, and in the vicinity of, Kabul's historic settlement area clearly attest a period of prosperity in the first centuries C.E. under Buddhist Kushano-Sāsānian rule (for site distribution, see Ball and Gardin). The relatively peaceful and prosperous times under the Kushans and later under Sāsānian suzerainty came to an end in the early second half of the fifth century C.E., when warlike Hephtalite tribes from the Central Asian steppes started to push southward across the Hindu Kush barrier and subsequently into the Indus Valley. The fall of the Hephtalites was eventually brought about in the mid-sixth century C.E. by a coalition of Western Turks and Sāsānians known to the Arab chroniclers as the Kābul Shāhīs.

The first lengthy Muslim occupation occurred in the third/ninth century followed in the fourth/tenth century by the semi-autonomous non-Muslim Hindū Shāhīs. In 366/977, Kabul fell to Sebüktigin (d. 387/997), founder of the Ghaznavid dynasty (r. 366–582/977–1186). At the time, the town reportedly possessed a strong citadel, the Bālā Ḥiṣār, built on an eastern spur of the Shīr Darvāza mountain; it was connected with defensive walls that ran along the ridges of the Shīr Darvāza and the Kūh-i Āsamā'iyya on the opposite, northern bank of the Kabul river, circumscribing a settlement area of approximately four to five square kilometres. While the citadel had already been firmly in the hands of Muslims, the town at the foot of the citadel and the populous suburbs within the wider walled-in area were still inhabited by a Hindu-Buddhist population (al-Iṣṭakhrī, 120).

When the Ghaznavids took full control over the city, Hindu–Buddhist culture was eradicated with temples either destroyed or built over with mosques and Muslim shrines. While Kabul had outrivalled Kāpisa as the region's paramount city in the centuries leading up to the final Islamisation, for the next five centuries it was eclipsed again by other centres of gravity, such as Ghaznī and later Herāt in particular. The waning of Kabul was ensured by the successive rule of the Ghaznavids, the Ghūrids, the Khwārazmshāhs, and after their defeat by Chingis Khan's Mongol armies in 617/1220, the Chaghatai Khāns (r. 623–771/1226–1370) and the Tīmūrids (r. 771–912/1370–1506). Tellingly enough, no pre-Tīmūrid monuments from the Islamic period have survived at Kabul, certainly also in part because of the devastating Mongol incursions of the eighth/thirteenth century and the region's slow recovery thereafter. According to Ibn Baṭṭūṭa, who passed by in 733/1333 on his way to India, Kabul, formerly a vast town, had been reduced to the size of a mere village (Ibn Baṭṭūṭa, 180).

The oldest surviving Islamic monument is a mausoleum on the Shuhudā-yi Ṣāliḥīn cemetery grounds, and stylistically dates from the late ninth/fifteenth century. This square, single-domed baked brick building is known as the Ziyārat-i Seh Oghor, which presumably is a corruption of Seh Ulugh (Einzmann, 198–9) as it holds descendants of Ulugh Beg b. Abī Saʿīd ("Kābulī"), who from 865/1461 to 907/1501 was the Tīmūrid governor of Kabul and Ghaznī. As at other Tīmūrid centres, Kabul's urban area was expanded in the late tenth/fifteenth century by a broad belt of suburban residential garden estates (sing. *bāgh*) following the design pattern of the quadripartite *chahār bāgh*. They concentrated along an open water canal built at the skirts of the Tākht-i Shāh and Shīr Darvāza mountains (Bābur, 200). It can safely be assumed that several of the gardens Kabul became famed for later in the Mughal period had earlier phases. An excavated vaulted brick tomb in the Bāgh-i Bābur, tentatively dated to the late-Tīmūrid period, suggests that also the funeral garden, a prominent feature of Mughal architecture, had an early predecessor at Kabul (Franke-Vogt et al., 545).

In 910/1504, Ẓahīr al-Dīn Bābur (d. 937/1530), a Tīmūrid-Chaghatayid prince from the Ferghana Valley in present-day Uzbekistan and progenitor of the Mughal dynasty (r. in India 932–1273/1526–1857), captured Kabul and established his new kingdom there. The city gained unprecedented importance as the royal seat and residence of the harem, the base for campaigns into the Indian subcontinent (until the dynasty was established in northern India), and later, until the decline of Mughal power in the early twelfth/eighteenth century, as a provincial capital, a thriving commercial entrepôt well incorporated within the web of imperial highroads, as well as an administrative, cultural, and military outpost at the north-western border with the Ṣafavid Empire (906–1134/1501–1722). Perhaps most importantly, however, the possession of Kabul had great symbolic value for the Mughal rulers as the cradle of their dynasty and only territory of the former Tīmūrid Empire permanently under their control.

However, only few traces of the Mughal era remain today. The most significant of these is the Bāgh-i Bābur on the western slope of the Shīr Darvāza mountain, an eleven-hectare hillside garden of fifteen terraces in which Bābur and four of his

Illustration 1. The rebuilt grave enclosure of Bābur's (d. 937/1530) tomb inside a rebuilt brick wall, near Kabul. © Agha Khan Trust for Culture / Ratish Nanda (architect, photographer).

relatives were buried (Parpagliolo; Franke-Vogt et al.). The garden measures approximately 400 metres in length and was founded on a strict symmetry with emphasis on the central axis. From the twelfth terrace downwards, a water canal was laid out within a raised walkway or central avenue, with water chutes and basins connecting the terraces and with larger water reservoirs at the ninth and tenth terrace as well as near the entrance at the bottom of the slope, built in the course of a general embellishment of the site (ʿAbd al-Ḥamīd Lāhūrī in Bābur, appendix V, ixxx) by the order of Shāh Jahān (r. 1037–68/1628–58). It also included the construction of a caravanserai; three water basins; a small marble mosque (built between 1056/1646 and 1058/1648) located on the thirteenth terrace; an enclosed tomb for Bābur's granddaughter Ruqayya Sulṭān Begum (the first wife and chief consort of the third Mughal emperor Akbar and foster-mother of Shāh Jahān) on the uppermost fifteenth terrace; and a marble-screen *(jālī)* funerary enclosure around Bābur's tomb on the penultimate terrace (Zajadacz-Hastenrath) [Illustrations 1 and 2].

The splendour of Mughal Kabul becomes tangible only in the chronicles of the period and memoirs of the emperors themselves. During Bābur's reign, the focus lay on the foundation or reconstruction of walled-in pleasure gardens for the royal encampments. In Humāyūn's reign (937–46/1530–40 and 962–3/1555–6)

Illustration 2. Carved *jālī* screens flank the opening on the marble enclosure around Bābur's (d. 937/1530) grave. © Agha Khan Trust for Culture / Christian Richters (photographer).

the Shāh-i Du Shāhmshīrhā mosque was built near the river. In Jahāngīr's reign (1014–37/1605–27), the citadel was refurbished. But the most intensive remodelling of Kabul was done under the auspices of Shāh Jahān's governor ʿAlī Mardān (in office 1050–60/1641–50). Besides the reshaping of Bābur's tomb-garden, the citadel was substantially rebuilt. The old citadel on the hilltop (referred to as the Bālā Ḥiṣār-i Bālā or Upper Citadel) was largely abandoned as a royal residence and instead the separately walled precinct below, the Bālā Ḥiṣār-i Pāyīn (destroyed in 1880), was transformed into a formidable palace city. In the light of early thirteenth/nineteenth century sources, it appears as a proper township with the palace complex in the core, divided into various courts and quadrangles and accommodating the residences of the ruling family built against the northern perimeter wall, a double-sided hall of audience *(dīvān-i ʿām)* facing both a large ceremonial courtyard and a court garden, a mosque, stables, and barracks, a street bazaar, and two residential neighbourhoods of nearly one thousand houses reserved for courtiers, servants, soldiers, and minority groups such as Arabs and Armenian Christians (Masson II, 255). Another important building project of the 1050s/1640s was the construction of the famous Chahār Chatta Bāzār (destroyed in 1842), a straight arcaded market street of four roofed passages *(chatta)*.

As the Mughal Empire waned in the early twelfth/eighteenth century, Kabul witnessed less tranquil times. In

1151/1738, it became a domain of Nādir Shāh Afshār (d. 1160/1747). At least one of the Mughal gardens was appropriated for the foundation of a new quarter, which rose west of the existing town for his Qizilbāsh troops. Nādir Shāh's empire was inherited by his Afghān general Aḥmad Shāh Durrānī (d. 1186/1772), whose coronation in 1160/1747 is commonly regarded as the birth of the Afghān state. The capital was moved several times but returned to Kabul in 1187/1773 after Aḥmad Shāh's son Tīmūr Shāh had ascended the throne. The Durrānī Empire disintegrated soon after Tīmūr Shāh's death in 1207/1793 and, following decades of civil war and unrest, the Ṣadūzāī branch of the Durrānīs was replaced in 1826 by the Muḥammadzāī Durrānī *amīr*s and later kings (r. 1826–1973) of Afghanistan. In the course of the nineteenth century, which saw two British occupations of Kabul, in 1839–42 and 1879–80, the country became wedged between the encroaching British and Russian empires and was eventually forged in 1880 as a semi-independent (until full independence in 1919) buffer state between the respective colonial spheres of influence.

During the long period of instability following Tīmūr Shāh's death, Kabul emerged as the dominant political and cultural centre of the Hindu Kush and was substantially rebuilt. The most important monument from the Durrānī period is the mausoleum of Tīmūr Shāh near the riverbank (begun presumably after Tīmūr Shāh's demise, possibly even as late as 1817, shortly before the dynasty's end). Albeit never completed, it is an imposing structure in the tradition of the Tīmūrid–Mughal imperial funeral architecture and was modelled after its immediate predecessor, the Aḥmad Shāh mausoleum at Qandahār (date of construction unknown, but likely between 1182/1768 and 1186/1772), with an inner and outer dome resting on a two-storey octagonal base. At the time of Dūst Muḥammad's reign (1826–39 and 1845–63) and the first British campaign, most monuments from former times had already fallen into neglect and decay. Still, private construction continued at a good pace and the oldest surviving neighbourhood mosques and townhouses, mostly two-storey dwellings with wings flanking an inner courtyard, date from this period, clearly borrowing their delicately carved wooden shutter window façades and intricate floral plasterwork in the interior from the late Mughal repertoire of architectural decoration and ornamentation.

Towards the close of the nineteenth century, the ruling elite's increasing contact with European architecture inspired them to reconstruct the capital. In the 1870s, Amīr Shīr ʿAlī (r. 1863–6 and 1868–79) embraced the idea of founding an extensive new residential city in the plain to the north of Kabul, but the second British invasion ended this project abruptly and only the outer defensive walls of "Shīrpūr" materialised. After the Bālā Ḥiṣār complex had been demolished by the British, one of the first measures taken by Amīr ʿAbd al-Raḥmān (r. 1880–1901) was the foundation of a square, fortified palace city, the Arg, just north of the river. This spurred a further expansion of the city northwards as fashionable quarters with palaces and houses of the royal family, officials, and other well-to-do people developed around the Arg. ʿAbd al-Raḥmān was a prolific builder, employing the skills of Central Asian artisans and Indian draftsmen. He commissioned about thirty major construction projects—including palaces, administrative, and religious buildings—all in a hybrid style incorporating elements of Central Asian, Mughal, and European architecture. The first building that was fully European in style, modelled after the Dorchester House in London, was Prince Naṣrallāh's residence, the Zayn al-ʿImāra ("Beautiful Building;" built in 1896–7). Under Amīr Ḥabīballāh (r. 1901–18), the westernisation of Kabul's architecture and interiors continued, mainly along British-colonial lines, and for the first time European planners (such as Finlayson and Miller) were employed.

The reign of Amīr Amānallāh (r. 1919–29) is commonly seen to mark the end of Islamic traditions of architecture and urbanism in Kabul. The reformer king attempted to radically modernise Afghanistan on Western designs, and although he was eventually ousted by conservative tribal and religious forces, he managed to initiate dramatic political and social change. European and Turkish architects and engineers (such as Godard, Brix, Harten, De Gado, and Tewfiq Bey) helped him with the ambitious project of a fully Western-looking new capital city, Dār al-Amān, in the Chahārdih Valley, 10 km west of the existing town, and the summer resort Paghmān. Mosques were built in late-Ottoman style (such as the reconstruction of the Masjid-i Du Shamshīrhā) or plainly modelled after European secular architecture (such as the Paghmān Mosque). Of Dār al-Amān, only a few buildings such as the parliament, the king's palace (Tāj Beg), and the municipality were realised. Instead, Kabul continued to develop under the guidance of foreign planners around its historic core, which gradually fell into disrepair and eventually was almost completely laid to ruins during the fighting between Mujahideen factions in the early 1990s.

Bibliography

Sources

Ẓahīr-al-Dīn Bābur, *The Bābur-Nāma (Memoirs of Bābur)*, ed. and trans. Annette Susannah Beveridge, London 1922 (reprinted Delhi 1998); Inayat Khan, *The Shah Jahan Nama of 'Inayat Khan*, ed. Wayne Edison Begley and Ziyaud-Din A. Desai, Delhi, Oxford, and New York 1990; al-Iṣṭakhrī, *Das Buch der Länder*, trans. Andreas David Mordtmann, Hamburg 1845 (reprinted Frankfurt 1995); Ibn Baṭṭūṭa, *Travels in Asia and Africa 1325–1354*, trans. and ed. H. A. R. Gibb, London 1929 (reprinted Karachi 1986); Nūr-al-Dīn Muḥammad Jahāngīr, *The Tūzuk-i-Jahāngīrī, or memoirs of Jahāngīr*, trans. Alexander Rogers, ed. Henry Beveridge, 2 vols., London 1909–19 (reprinted New Delhi 2006); Charles Masson, *Narrative of various journeys in Balochistan, Afghanistan, and the Panjab*, 4 vols., London 1842; John Alfred Gray, *At the court of the Amir*, London 1895; ʿAbd al-Raḥmān, *The Life of Abdur Rahman*, ed. Sultān Muḥammad Khān, 2 vols., London 1900 (reprinted Karachi 1981); Oskar von Niedermayer and Ernst Diez, *Afganistan*, Leipzig 1924; John Burke, *Afghan war album, 1878–79*, India Office Select Materials, British Library, London, photograph 430/3; Bengal Sappers and Miners, *Photographs of Kabul and its environs, 1879–80*, India Office Select Materials, British Library, London, photograph 197/1–66.

Studies

Warwick Ball and Jean-Claude Gardin, *Archaeological gazetteer of Afghanistan*, 2 vols., Paris 1982; Nancy Hatch Dupree, Early twentieth century Afghan adaptations of European architecture, *Art and Archaeology Research Papers* 11 (1977), 15–21; Nancy Hatch Dupree, A building boom in the Hindukush. Afghanistan 1921–1928, *Lotus International* 26/1 (1980), 115–21; Harald Einzmann, *Religiöses Volksbrauchtum in Afghanistan. Islamische Heiligenverehrung und Wallfahrtswesen im Raum Kabul*, Wiesbaden 1977; Ute Franke-Vogt et al., Bagh-e Babur, Kabul. Excavating a Mughal garden, *South Asian Archaeology* (Bonn 2005),

541–55; Gérard Fussman, *Monuments Bouddhiques de la région de Caboul*, 2 vols., Paris 2008; Joseph Hackin and Jean Carl, *Recherches archéologiques au col de Khair Khaneh près de Kābul*, Paris 1936; Jonathan Lee, Kabul, V. Monuments of Kabul city, *EIr*; Maria Teresa Shephard Parpagliolo, *Kābul. The Bāgh-i Bābur*, Rome 1972; Marcus Schadl, Die Grabbauten der Durrani in Kandahar und Kabul, in Herta Hafenrichter, Anja Heidenreich, and Daniel Redlinger (eds.), *Beiträge zur islamischen Kunst und Archäologie* (Wiesbaden 2008), 1/71–82; Marcus Schadl, Tradition and transformation of the Kabuli courtyard house, in Nasser Rabbat (ed.), *The courtyard house from cultural reference to universal relevance* (London 2010), 47–64; Marcus Schadl, From pre-industrial to industrial Kabul. The bazaars and the manufactories, in Mohammad Gharipour (ed.), *The bazaar in the Islamic city. Design, culture, and history* (Cairo and New York 2012), 185–202; Marcus Schadl, The illusion of nature. The image of the garden in Mughal architectural decoration and its reception in the late Mughal period, in Lorenz Korn and Anja Heidenreich (eds.), *Beiträge zur islamischen Kunst und Archäologie* (Wiesbaden 2012), 3/304–20; May Schinasi, *Kaboul 1773–1948. Naissance et croissance d'une capitale royale*, Naples 2008; William Woodburn, *The Bala Hissar of Kabul. Revealing a fortress-palace in Afghanistan*, Chatham 2009; William Woodburn and Ian Templeton, From the Bala Hissar to the Arg. How royal fortress palaces shaped Kabul, 1830–1930, *The Court Historian* 17 (2012), 171–88; Salome Zajadacz-Hastenrath, A note on Babur's lost funerary enclosure at Kabul, *Muqarnas* 14 (1997), 136–42.

Marcus Schadl

Kaftārū, Aḥmad

Aḥmad Kaftārū (1912–2004) was the grand *muftī* of Syria (1963–2004) and the leader of the Naqshbandiyya-Mujaddidiyya-Khālidiyya-Kaftāriyya Ṣūfī order (*ṭarīqa*) in Syria. He was a devoted supporter of the regime of Ḥāfiẓ al-Asad (r. 1970–2000) and Bashshār al-Asad (r. beginning 2000).

Aḥmad Kaftārū was born around 1912 in Damascus, the son of Amīn Kaftārū (1877–1938) and Nājiyya Sinjābī. His father was a Kurd, whose family had moved from Karma, near al-Ḥasaka, in northeastern Syria, to Damascus in 1878 (al-Ḥāfiẓ and Abāẓa, 290, 515). After primary school and Islamic studies with prominent Damascene scholars, such as ʿAlī al-Takrītī (d. 1942), Abū l-Khayr al-Mīdānī (d. 1961), and Amīn al-Warrānī al-Zamalkānī (d. 1927), Aḥmad Kaftārū gradually began preaching and teaching Islam in Damascus. His father initiated him into the Naqshbandiyya-Mujaddidiyya-Khālidiyya *ṭarīqa* of Shaykh ʿĪsā al-Kurdī (d. 1912) and his successor, Amīn al-Warrānī al-Zamalkānī, which was the dominant Ṣūfī order in Syria. It was not until al-Zamalkānī's death, in 1927, that Amīn Kaftārū took over as the leader of what then became the Naqshbandiyya-Mujaddidiyya-Khālidiyya-Kaftāriyya order. He remained in that position until his death, in 1938, when Aḥmad assumed leadership of this branch of the order (al-Bānī, 41, 62, 100; al-Ḥabash, 46–9).

During the same period, Aḥmad Kaftārū began his career as a state-employed religious scholar. In 1948 he worked as a mosque teacher in Qunaytra and from 1950 onwards in the capital, Damascus. Two years later, he was nominated *muftī* of the Shāfiʿī *madhhab* of Damascus and a member of the Supreme *iftāʾ* Council (Majlis al-Iftāʾ al-Aʿlā) (Böttcher, *Syria's Sunni Islam*, 20–1; Kuftaro (Kaftārū), *Way of truth*, vii; al-Ḥabash, 83), the highest decision-making body in the *iftāʾ*-administration before it was incorporated into the newly created Ministry of Islamic Foundations (Wizārat al-Awqāf) in 1961. In 1955, Kaftārū publicly supported a candidate of the Baʿth Party against the candidate of the Muslim Brotherhood. He also had a weekly programme on Islam that was broadcast on the Syrian state-run radio station from 1959 to 1964 (Böttcher, *Syrische Religionspolitik*, 152; Pierret, 47).

In 1963 the Baʿth Party seized power, and on 30 March 1963 the grand *muftī* of Syria, Muḥammad Abū l-Yusr ʿĀbidīn (d. 1981), was dismissed from his position, an action that referenced military order (*amr ʿaskarī*) no. 1 of 8 March 1963. ʿAbd al-Razzāq al-Ḥumṣī was appointed as interim until 28 October 1963. In the meantime, the new rulers passed a legislative decree on 19 August 1964 to limit the tenure of the grand *muftī* to three years. On 26 October 1964, Kaftārū was elected grand *muftī* of Syria by a committee of thirty-six members, including the the Minister of Justice and the new Minister of Awqāf, Dr. ʿAbd al-Raḥmān al-Kawākibī. He won by one vote, defeating Shaykh Ḥasan Ḥabannaka al-Mīdānī (d. 1978), who was a well-known Muslim scholar. Shaykh Kaftārū held this position until his death, in 2004 (Böttcher, *Syrische Religionspolitik*, 54–9).

Kaftārū's influence as the leader of the Naqshbandiyya-Mujaddidiyya-Khālidiyya-Kaftāriyya in Syria grew after Ḥāfiẓ al-Asad seized power in 1970. Over the years his interpretation of Ṣūfī Islam developed into an important pillar of the regime's official Sunnī Islam (Böttcher, *Syrische Religionspolitik*, 154–65; Habibis, 212). The friendship that developed between the two men provided Kaftārū with the necessary backing to expand his *ṭarīqa* and his Islamic centre, the Majmaʿ Abī l-Nūr al-Islāmī, which comprised the Institute for Islamic Mission and Guidance (Maʿhad al-Daʿwa wa-l-Irshād), founded in 1975. The centre included primary and secondary schools for girls and boys, as well as branches in four foreign universities based in Libya, Lebanon, Sudan, and Pakistan. His centre also included a library, a charitable organisation, an Arabic language institute, and space for lessons, daily and weekly training in *dhikr* and other rituals of Ṣūfī Islam, and a mosque.

Kaftārū focused on his weekly teaching and audio output and published very little. (See bibliography.)

Despite the Naqshbandiyya's inherent anti-Shīʿī stance, Kaftārū complemented the regime's pro-Iranian policies by developing close cooperation with the Iranian Cultural Centre in Damascus, as well as with Iranian and Lebanese Shīʿī clerics. Kaftārū also strongly promoted the involvement and education of women in his movement. Prominent Syrian Ṣūfī female leaders, such as his daughter, Wafāʾ Kaftārū, and Munīra al-Qubaysī, were among his disciples (Khatib, 170–1).

Kaftārū neglected his role as head of the *iftāʾ*-administration, leaving the position of his *fatwā*-secretary *(amīn al-fatwā)* vacant for a decade. While the Ministry of Islamic Foundations was gradually taken over by the Syrian regime, Kaftārū focused on public relations and visits of foreign diplomats, dignitaries, journalists, and politicians. During his tours abroad he promoted his centre and Ṣūfī network (Pierret, 76).

Kaftārū was married twice and had ten children by his first wife, Ḥawwa Millī (al-Ḥabash, 48). After his death, on 3 September 2004, in Damascus, his centre was renamed Ahmad Kaftaru Academy (Mujammaʿ al-Shaykh Aḥmad Kaftārū). His son Salāḥ al-Dīn (b. 1957) took over the administrative leadership, while the spiritual succession of the Kaftāriyya Ṣūfī network was distributed among his prominent disciples (Pierret 75–6).

Bibliography

Selected works of Aḥmad Kaftārū
Min hudā l-Qurʾān al-karīm, Damascus 1990; with Muḥammad Rajab Dīb and Rajab Dīb, *Dhikr Allāh taʿālā kamā fī l-Kitāb wa-l-Sunna*, Beirut 1993; *Zād al-duʿāt min al-ʿilm wa-l-āyāt*, Damascus 1995; with ʿImād ʿAbd al-Laṭīf Naddāf, *al-Shaykh Aḥmad Kaftārū yataḥaddathu*, Damascus 1997; Ahmad Kuftaro, *The way of truth*, Damascus 1997, 2004³; with Muḥammad Sharīf Ṣawwāf and Mundhir Aḥmad Daqr, *al-Ḥayāt al-zawjiyya min manẓār al-sharīʿa al-Islāmiyya*, Damascus 2001; *Ḥiwārāt fī l-fikr al-Islāmī maʿa al-Shaykh Aḥmad Kaftārū*, Damascus 2009.

Studies
Muḥammad Bashīr al-Bānī, *al-Murshid al-mujaddid*, Damascus 1979; Annabelle Böttcher, *Syrische Religionspolitik unter Asad*, Freiburg im Breisgau 1997; Annabelle Böttcher, Islamic teaching among Sunni women in Syria, in Donna Lee Bowen and Evelyn Early (eds.), *Everyday life in the Muslim Middle East* (Bloomington 2001²), 290–9; Annabelle Böttcher, *Syria's Sunni Islam under Hafiz al-Asad*, Kindle-Amazon 2015; Muḥammad al-Ḥabash, *al-Shaykh Aḥmad Kaftārū wa-manhajuhu fī l-tajdīd wa-l-iṣlāḥ*, Damascus 1996²; Daphne Habibis, *A comparative study of the workings of a branch of the Naqshbandi Sufi order in Lebanon and the UK*, Ph.D. diss., London School of Economics, University of London 1984; Muṭīʿ al-Ḥāfiẓ and Nizār Abāẓa, *Taʾrīkh ʿulamāʾ Dimashq fī l-qarn al-rābiʿ ʿashar al-hijrī*, vol. 1, Damascus 1986; Line Khatib, *Islamic revivalism in Syria*. The rise and fall of Baʿthist secularism, London 2011; Thomas Pierret, *Religion and state in Syria. The Sunni ulama from coup to revolution*, Cambridge 2013.

Annabelle Böttcher

al-Kāmiliyya

Al-Kāmiliyya was a Shīʿī sect that emerged in the aftermath of the First Civil War (35–40/656–61). During the first centuries of Islam, the claims to leadership (*imāma*) raised by the Shīʿa—supporters of the descendants of ʿAlī b. Abī Ṭālib (r. 35–40/656–61), the Prophet's cousin and son-in-law, and Fāṭima (d. 11/632), the Prophet's daughter, and of their political and religious right to rule—gave rise to a wide range of opinions and religious sects. Starting in the fourth/tenth century, heresiographers record the ephemeral existence of a sect called al-Kāmiliyya, allegedly founded by Abū Kāmil Muʿādh al-Nabhānī (fl. in Kufa, first decade of the second/eighth century).

Abū Kāmil was a supporter of Zayd b. ʿAlī (d. 122/740), the founder of the Zaydī branch of Shīʿism, according to whose tenets a legitimate Imām had a religious duty to declare publicly his claim to the imāmate and to fight for his rights. Abū Kāmil adopted the Zaydī view of the imāmate, which held that it was restricted to the descendants of Fāṭima, but stressed the politico-religious value of taking up arms as the mark of a just ruler. He applied this criterion retrospectively even to ʿAlī and his son al-Ḥasan (d. 50/670), providing an example of a recurrent feature of the political and religious confrontations of the first centuries of Islamic history: the accusation of unbelief (*takfīr*). In his opinion, opposing ʿAlī's right to lead after the death of the prophet Muḥammad caused the Muslim community to fall into unbelief. According to the account of the heresiographer Saʿd b. ʿAbdallāh al-Qummī (d. 301/913–4), Abū Kāmil held that ʿAlī himself became an unbeliever because of his initial refusal to rise up in order to summon people to pledge allegiance to him and returned to the fold of Islam only after fighting his adversaries.

The political tenets of the Kāmiliyya seem to be a radical interpretation of the

Zaydī doctrine known as *imāmat al-afḍal* (the leadership of the most excellent), according to which the Imām should demonstrate his excellence and display the mark of divine grace by rising up to claim his rightful place as ruler. Later heresiographical sources depict Abū Kāmil and his followers as one of the extreme Shīʿī currents that envisaged the transmission of the imāmate as the transmigration of the soul (*tanāsukh*), conceiving of it as a divine light passing from one Imām to the next. This led the heresiographers to classify the Kāmiliyya as one of the extremist sects (*ghulāt*). The poet Bashshār b. Burd (d. 166/783) appears to have been a follower of the sect.

Bibliography

al-Ashʿarī, *Maqālāt al-islāmiyyīn*, ed. Hellmut Ritter (Wiesbaden 1963[2]), 176; al-Qummī, *al-Maqālāt wa-l-firaq*, ed. Muḥammad Jawād Mashkūr (Tehran 1963), 14; al-Shahrastānī, *al-Milal wa-l-niḥal*, ed. William Cureton (London 1842–6), 1:133, trans. Daniel Gimaret and Guy Monnot, *Livre des religions et des sectes* (Paris 1986), 1:511–2; Joseph Van Ess, Die Kāmiliyya: zur Genese einer häresiographischen Tradition, *WI* 28 (1988), 141–53; Joseph Van Ess, *TG*, 1:269–72.

Leonardo Capezzone

Karadjordje

Karadjordje (b. unknown, probably 1182/1768–d. 1232/1817) was the leader of the first Serbian uprising (1218–29/1804–13), which took place in a prolonged period of upheaval that ultimately lead to the establishment of the autonomous Serbian state on previously Ottoman-controlled territories. He was the founder of the Karadjordjević dynasty, whose members ruled Serbia and the Kingdom of Yugoslavia at various points throughout the thirteenth-fourteenth/nineteenth-twentieth century until 1945. He bore the title *vožd* ("chief").

Djordje Petrović, popularly known as Karadjordje ("Black Djordje"), was born in a village in the Šumadija district of what is now central Serbia to a poor family descended from Montenegrin migrants. During the Ottoman-Habsburg war of 1202–5/1788–91, Karadjordje served with other Serbs in the Habsburg Freikorps militia. After the amnesty, he returned home to work in agriculture as a livestock merchant, but the turbulent events of that era saw him take up arms again soon after.

Sultan Selim III (Sulṭān Selīm III, r. 1203–22/1789–1807) saw the end of the war with the Habsburgs as an opportunity to restore central authority to the area of Belgrade that had come under janissary rule. There were similar situations elsewhere in Ottoman territories. At the time, the Ottoman Empire was extremely decentralised and most provincial territories were under the effective authority of notables (*ayans*). The Serbian revolt should be considered in the context of these rivalries and revolutionary upheaval rather than, as traditional nationalist historiographies suggest, an expression of exclusively nationalist aspirations. The Serbian revolt began as a movement for ending janissary rule and, initially, Serbian forces acted in alliance with the sultan's forces. It was only later that they defied Ottoman authority altogether. The international context was also important, particularly the Napoleonic Wars and the Russo-Ottoman War of 1221–7/1806–12.

The new Ottoman governor of the area found a common cause with the local Serbs in his bid to drive the janissaries out of Belgrade. Acting on behalf of the sultan, Serbian forces participated in military campaigns against the janissaries and their ally, Osman Pazvantoğlu (r. 1209–10–1221/1795–1807), the *ayan* of Vidin, in present-day north-west Bulgaria. Karadjordje was one of the commanders of Serbian forces. However, under the pressure of crises elsewhere (such as Napoleon's invasion of Egypt in 1213/1798), the Ottoman government was forced to reinstall the janissaries' authority. They rebelled and killed the Ottoman governor.

In 1216/1802, the Serbs took part in another campaign to end janissary misrule, partly in response to a call for action by the sultan. Similar rebellions took place elsewhere under various leaders in the Serbian lands. In 1219/1804, the whole area of the paşalık of Belgrade apart from Belgrade itself was under the control of Serbian forces who recognised Karadjordje as their supreme leader. At this stage, they were still acting as loyalists. Relations with the Ottoman authorities soured when the Serbs presented a number of demands, which included recognising Karadjordje as a supreme leader, banning Ottomans from settling outside Belgrade without permission, and staffing fortresses with equal numbers of Serbian and Ottoman troops. In exchange, Serbs would pay a yearly tribute to the sultan. Crucially, they demanded that the treaty should be guaranteed by foreign powers. This was difficult for the Ottoman government to accept, as it would bring the Serbian question into international focus. While the Ottoman authorities pondered alternatives, the janissaries revolted again. In 1220/1805, Karadjordje abandoned Belgrade and launched another rebellion, this time against the sultan. The sultan declared him a rebel and launched a military campaign in retaliation. The first Ottoman attempts to suppress the rebellion failed and the Serbs retained control of the area, apart from Belgrade itself. Karadjordje even collaborated with Osman Pazvantoğlu briefly, but the two sides ultimately remained bitter rivals.

For some time, Constantin Ypsilantis (d. 1231/1816), Prince of Wallachia and Moldova, had encouraged the Serbs to fight for full independence. Russia, at war with the Ottomans between 1221–7/1806–12, expressed similar encouragement and dispatched military officers to help train Serbian forces. But this aid was intermittent and fluctuated according to Russia's own strategic considerations. For example, Russia withdrew direct support for the Serbs after the signing of the Treaty of Tilsit in 1222/1807, then resumed support a couple of years later when hostilities with the Ottomans recommenced. Karadjorje was ready to ally with Russia in these endeavors. Once the Serbs had gained control of enough territory, they established the basis of state institutions, such as a governing council and an assembly. However, Karadjordje maintained extensive personal control, which provoked considerable antagonism amongst other rebel leaders.

Meanwhile, upheaval broke out in the Ottoman capital when Selim III was overthrown and replaced by Mustafa IV (Muṣṭafā, r. 1221–3/1807–8). A year later, pro-reformist notables led another palace coup, bringing Mahmud II (Maḥmūd, r. 1222–54/1808–39) to power.

In 1227/1812 and under the threat of a French invasion, Russia sought to end the war with the Ottomans. According to the Treaty of Bucharest, the Ottomans were to re-occupy the fortifications that existed in Serbia before 1218/1804. Serbs were granted control over the administration of their own affairs and tax collection. As the Ottomans retreated, they suppressed rebellious activities among the Serbs. In Receb (Rajab) 1228/July 1813, Karadjorje fled to Austria with other Serbian leaders. Thus, the first Serbian uprising ended in defeat. A few months later, the Ottomans declared a general amnesty. One of the rebel commanders, Miloš Obrenović (d. 1277/1860), returned to Serbia and became the leader of the second Serbian uprising (1230–3/1815–17). Obrenović negotiated an agreement with the Ottoman government that granted limited autonomy to the lands of the former *paşalık* of Belgrade and recognised him as the *knez* ("supreme prince").

In 1232/1817, Karadjordje secretly crossed into Serbia in a bid to seek support for a Greek anti-Ottoman uprising. Fearing a challenge to his authority and a threat to the precarious agreement, Miloš Obrenović ordered Karadjordje's death and sent his head to the Ottoman governor of Belgrade. The incident instigated a bitter rivalry between the Karadjordjević and Obrenović families that had lasting political ramifications.

Bibliography

Frederick Anscombe, The Balkan revolutionary age, *The Journal of Modern History*, 84/3 (2012), 572–606; Charles and Barbara Jelavich, *The establishment of the Balkan national states, 1804–1920*, Seattle 1977; Stanford Shaw, *Between old and new. The Ottoman Empire under Selim III, 1789–1807*, Cambridge MA 1971; Wayne Vucinich (ed.), *The first Serbian uprising, 1804–1813*, Boulder 1982; Milenko Vukičević, *Karadjordje*, vol. 1, *1752–1804* Belgrade 1988; Milenko Vukičević, *Karadjordje*, vol. 2, *1804–1807*, Belgrade 1988.

Milena Methodieva

al-Karrāmiyya

Al-Karrāmiyya were an ascetic missionary movement centred on north-eastern Iran and neighbouring regions from the third/ninth to the sixth/twelfth centuries.

1. The founder

Abū ʿAbdallāh Muḥammad b. Karrām (d. 20 Ṣafar 255/7 February 869) was born to a family from Sijistān (Sīstān), in what is now south-eastern Iran, around 184/800—according to one Karrāmī tradition—in Mecca while his parents were on pilgrimage there (Zysow, Karrāmiya). He was said by his followers to have been of Arab stock, but this was sometimes called into question by his opponents, who loved to make fun of his Persian accent when he spoke Arabic (van Ess, *Ungenützte Texte*, 50, n. 208). His father may have worked as a vinedresser *(karrām)*, but we cannot be sure of this, especially as an alternative reading of his name was Kirām. Apparently, he studied law with ʿUthmān b. ʿAffān al-Sijistānī (d. 255/896), a leading authority of the Ḥanafī law school in Sijistān, with whom he then fell out (van Ess, *Ungenützte Texte*, 21; Zysow, Karrāmiya).

Ibn Karrām had what we might call a public career only relatively late in life. Sometime after 225/840 he was important enough to be called in front of the governor of Sijistān and accused of heterodox views, whose precise nature we cannot specify. Although sources hostile to the movement admit that he already commanded a large following at that point, they try to show that his problematic views had nothing to do with Ḥanafism. This effort to distance Ḥanafism from Ibn Karrām is unsurprising, given that many

Ḥanafis were, later, important enemies of Ibn Karrām's movement.

Ibn Karrām is said to have claimed divine inspiration. Exiled from his country of origin, he moved to Khurāsān (approximately, the north-east of modern Iran and the neighbouring regions to the north and east), where he studied law and the interpretation of the Qurʾān at different places until finally settling in Nīshāpūr, at the time the most important town of the province, which became the centre for his sect during the following centuries (Zysow, Karrāmiya).

In Nīshāpūr he studied with the traditionist Aḥmad b. Ḥarb (d. 234/849), a leading figure among local ascetics. On his return from a pilgrimage to Mecca, Ibn Karrām is said to have used the opportunity of the death of the governor of Sijistān who had exiled him to liquidate his assets there. Back in Nīshāpūr, he started a very successful missionary movement. The movement was active amongst the rural population in Khurāsān, not least in the mountainous regions of what is now Afghanistan. As was typical for many ascetic figures of the time, he is said to have spent some time also at the Muslim-Byzantine frontier in the north of Syria (Zysow, Karrāmiya).

During his stay in Nīshāpūr, Ibn Karrām seems to have once again run into trouble with the authorities, for reasons that are unclear. The Ṭāhirid rulers of Khurāsān (r. 205–59/821–73) had him imprisoned for at least one prolonged period. After his release, a final exile took him and a great number of followers to Palestine. In Jerusalem he taught Prophetic tradition. Once again, however, he fell foul of the local governor, who had him expelled to Ẓughar (Zoara), south-east of the Dead Sea. He died there but was brought back by his disciples to Jerusalem for burial. His followers continued to visit his grave for some centuries (Zysow, Karrāmiya).

2. A religious movement

The movement that Ibn Karrām founded spread as far as Cairo and Jerusalem already in his lifetime. Apparently, though, most adherents in the West were eastern Iranian migrants to these places, and the Karrāmiyya ultimately remained a phenomenon of the East, where they played an important role in the political struggles in cities like Herat, in present-day Afghanistan, and Nīshāpūr. With the spread of the movement, a splintering into subsects was to be expected. Mediaeval sources cite quite a number of them, but it is very difficult to establish the exact content of their respective teachings; at any rate, they seem not to have had very conflictual relations with one another (Zysow, Karrāmiya).

Seemingly, one of the reasons for the Karrāmiyya movement's success was the very active preaching of its preachers, who did not shy away from instilling fear into their audience; Ibn Karrām himself was the author of *ʿAdhāb al-qabr* ("The torment of the grave": according to majority Muslim belief, sinners undergo an episode of torment in the grave before resurrection), which unfortunately is not extant. The Karrāmiyya used lively anecdotes, of which we still have a sample in ʿUmar b. Abī l-Ḥusayn al-Naysābūrī al-Samarqandī's (fl. ninth/fifteenth century) *Rawnaq al-qulūb* ("Splendour of the hearts"), also known as *Rawnaq al-majālis* ("Splendour of the gatherings") (van Ess, *Ungenützte Texte*, 30–41). Ideological enemies criticised them for their propensity to use weak Prophetic traditions as long as those traditions helped to achieve homiletic success. It is not for nothing that Ibn Karrām was said by scholars of *ḥadīth* to have been under the spell of Maʾmūn b. Aḥmad al-Sulamī (fl. mid-third/ninth century), a notorious forger of traditions (van Ess, *Ungenützte Texte*, 31, 48–50).

As regards the question of how to define belief, the Karrāmiyya's positions generally matched those of mainstream early Khurāsānian and Transoxanian Islam, specifically the adherents of the Ḥanafī school of law and, in particular, the theological school of the Murjiʾa (those who leave the judgment on sinners, and particularly on the conflicting parties during the civil wars of early Islam, to God and his reckoning on the Day of Resurrection). For the Karrāmiyya, belief was mere confession with the tongue, to the exclusion of understanding, inner conviction, and works. This was not to say, though, that mere formal belief might lead to paradise (Zysow, Karrāmiyya, 254). At the same time, they were not particularly strict in matters of ritual purity, thereby easing the way for converts (van Ess, *Ungenützte Texte*, 18).

While the rank and file thus did not have to perform great deeds to be accepted as believers, the leading members of the movement were known for their feats of glaring asceticism. This asceticism went so far as to prohibit all efforts to gain a livelihood *(taḥrīm al-makāsib)*, be it by way of work or even begging, as they thought it to be contrary to true trust in God *(tawakkul)*. In practice, it seems, some Karrāmīs at least admitted that gaining one's livelihood by working or begging was allowed by God's leave *(rukhṣa)*. Nonetheless, their brazen *tawakkul* led to strong reactions by political authorities and religious rivals (Bonner; Madelung, 43; Zysow, Karrāmiya). *Taḥrīm al-makāsib* was not a conviction held by the Karrāmiyya alone; it was ascribed as well to the ascetic movement of the so-called *ṣūfiyyat al-muʿtazila* (the Ṣūfīs among the Muʿtazilites, the latter being one of the theological schools of early Islam; van Ess, *Der Eine*, 1339). The religious prestige their preaching and asceticism had earned the Karrāmīs allowed them to fund houses of common life (Persian *khānqāhs*), probably with donations from supporters. The Karrāmiyya is the first movement that is associated with this institution, which in later centuries was central to Ṣūfism all over the Islamic world (Chabbi, Remarques; Chabbi, Réflexions; Madelung, 45).

It seems that, in the beginning at least, the Karrāmiyya had certain eschatological overtones that may explain the choice of Jerusalem as place of exile by the movement's founder (Zysow, Karrāmiya). This may have played a role in explaining the negative stance many pre-modern Muslim authors took regarding the movement. Even more problematic for its critics seems to have been the fact that the Karrāmiyya held great appeal for the lower classes, in city and countryside alike, as well as for certain members of the military elite of the Ghaznavid dynasty, who ruled in what is now eastern Iran, Afghanistan, and parts of the Indian subcontinent from 367/977–8 to 583/1187. The leaders of the movement used this appeal in the factional conflicts that plagued places like Nīshāpūr and Herat. These conflicts were often framed along religious lines. The prominent Karrāmī Abū Bakr Muḥammad b. Isḥāq b. Maḥmashādh (d. 421/1030) and his family played a leading role in this infighting, while the otherwise conflicting Ḥanafī and Shāfiʿī notables and their supporters at times worked in unison against the Karrāmiyya (Berger, 25–34; Bulliet; Bosworth).

Ibn Maḥmashādh was known particularly for his missionary work among the

Zoroastrians of the region. Although this work may have played a role in the support the movement received from the Ghaznavid dynasty, the Karrāmīs' decidedly anti-Shīʿī stance may have been even more important (Zysow, Karrāmiya). In the long run, though, the Karrāmiyya lost out, on the one hand, to those Ḥanafīs who supported either the Muʿtazila or the theological school of al-Māturīdī (d. c.333/944) and, on the other hand, to the Shāfiʿīs associated with the theology of al-Ashʿarī (d. 324/935–6). It is unclear why the movement, which at times had been dominant in many places, disappeared completely. What can be said is that after the Ghaznavids and their Ghūrid successors (r. sixth/twelfth-early seventh/thirteenth centuries), Karrāmī leaders failed to win the support of rulers. Anti-Shīʿī positions were not much appreciated by the Mongol rulers of seventh/thirteenth-century Iran. The disappearance of the movement must therefore have been a consequence of both a lack of royal patronage and also the disdain it was held in by many scholars for its populist attitudes. At the same time, institutions and practices that were typical of Karrāmī Islam, and which had made them popular with the masses, survived or reappeared in other movements, not least in post-fourth/tenth-century Ṣūfism.

3. The Karrāmiyya and Islamic mysticism

Ṣūfism spread from Iraq to the east during the fourth/tenth century in close association with the Shāfiʿī school of law. In Khurāsān and Transoxania, this Iraqi school of Islamic mysticism encountered local forms of asceticism and mysticism that then became integrated into the Ṣūfī tradition and appeared in later mystical literature simply as the eastern branches of a single, pan-Islamic form of spirituality. The authors who reconstructed the history of Ṣūfism in this way, most notably the Shāfiʿī Abū ʿAbd al-Raḥmān al-Sulamī (d. 412/1021) and his disciples, saw themselves in the tradition of the Khurāsānian Malāmatiyya (the people of blame, who out of modesty avoided being seen in a positive light by others) in asceticism and of the Ashʿarīs in theology. As such, they strongly opposed both the ostentatiousness of Karrāmī asceticism and what they held to be their theological anthropomorphism. Even more, the bourgeois supporters of the Malāmatiyya disliked the Karrāmīs as rabble-rousers and enemies of theirs in the aforementioned civil conflicts. The Karrāmiyya movement was therefore largely excluded from the mainstream view of the history of Khurāsānian and Transoxanian mysticism (Chabbi, Remarques; for a more nuanced view, Melchert; Zysow, Karrāmiya). The Karrāmiyya nonetheless had certain features that continued to play a role in many strands of Islamic mysticism, not least their ostentatiousness and their active proselytising among non-Muslims. Another central idea that continued to find support in some Ṣūfī circles was the movement's view that the friends *(awliyāʾ)* of God (meaning the ascetics and mystics) ranked higher even than the prophets, whose rank was saved by seeing them as friends as well (Chabbi, Remarques, 45; on later developments of this motif, Addas, 50). The institution of the *khānqāh*, which was formative for later Ṣūfism, has already been mentioned.

4. Theological views

Because of their growing isolation in factional conflicts, the Karrāmiyya were excluded from the mainstream not only of the history of mysticism but also of the Ḥanafī school of law. As mentioned above, the founder received his education in a Ḥanafī environment. It seems, nonetheless, that members of the Karrāmiyya movement held a number of views that did not become part of mainstream Ḥanafism, and that the divorce between the two groups became increasingly pronounced (Zysow, Karrāmiya). Still, the Karrāmiyya held the typically Ḥanafī opinion that belief could neither grow nor diminish. Some of their theological positions were close to those of the Muʿtazilīs', who were very strong among eastern Ḥanafīs at the time. Like them, they believed that humans can discern the good and evil character of actions by their own reasoning. Yet they rejected the typically Muʿtazilī proposition that God is obliged always to do what is best for humans (Zysow, Karrāmiyya). Other issues where they were famously at variance with the Muʿtazilīs were their strong reliance on—and, according to their enemies, loose handling of—Prophetic tradition and their willingness to define and describe God in a concrete way, which for others smacked of anthropomorphism, but was later lauded by Ibn Taymiyya (d. 728/1328), the paradigmatic figure of tradition-minded Islam (Madelung). The Karrāmīs' anthropomorphism is to be understood in the context of the strong position of the Jahmiyya (a theological school that tended to have a very abstract view of God) in the eastern Islamic world. The ideas of the Karrāmiyya in this respect were not the product of naïve acceptance of a literal understanding of the Qurʾān and *ḥadīth*; rather, their ideas about the corporeality of God show that they were steeped in Stoic philosophical ideas, which were influential in early Islam in general. According to these concepts, all real things must have corporeal features. Another question is that of the changeability of the divine attributes. For the Karrāmiyya, God's seeming mutability, as manifested in his changing creation of things, is not what it seems. All these are manifestations of God's power that as such does not come to an end and therefore they do not involve a change in God's eternal attributes (e.g., his capacity to create as against a single act of creation. Zysow, Karrāmiyya).

Being at the same time strongly rationalist and very *ḥadīth*-minded (Zysow, Karrāmiyya) was not a common combination in the later Ḥanafī school. This contributed to the marginalisation of the movement in the religious field and in the memory of later Muslim authors. As most original works of Karrāmī authors are lost, we know this tradition largely through the lenses of outsiders to the movement who tried to refute their views (van Ess, *Der Eine;* van Ess, *Ungenützte Texte).* This explains why the important contribution of the Karrāmiyya to the history of Muslim religious institutions and Islamic thinking was long forgotten and has only been unearthed by modern scholarship during the last decades.

Bibliography

Sources

ʿAbd al-Qāhir al-Baghdādī, *Kitāb al-milal wa-l-niḥal*, ed. A. Nader, Beirut 1970; Ibn Fūrak, *Sharḥ al-ʿĀlim wa-l-mutaʿallim*, ed. Aḥmad ʿAbd al-Raḥīm al-Sāyiḥ and Tawfīq ʿAlī Wahba, Cairo 1430/2009; Abū l-Muẓaffar Shāhfūr al-Isfarāyīnī, *al-Tabṣīr fī l-dīn*, ed. Majīd al-Khalīfa, Beirut 2008; al-Ḥusayn b. Ibrāhīm al-Jūraqānī, *al-Abāṭil wa-l-manākir*, ed. ʿAbd al-Raḥmān al-Farīwāʾī, Riyadh 1422/2002; al-Juwaynī, *al-Shāmil fī uṣūl al-dīn*, ed. ʿAlī al-Nashshār, Alexandria 1969; Abū l-Muʿīn al-Nasafī, *Tabṣirat al-adilla*, ed.

Claude Salamé, 2 vols., Damascus 1990–3; Abū l-Qāsim Salmān al-Naysābūrī, *al-Ghunya fī l-kalām*, ed. Muṣṭafā Ḥusayn ʿAbd al-Hādī, 2 vols., Cairo 2010; al-Muqaddasī, *Kitāb aḥsan al-taqāsīm fī maʿrifat al-aqālīm*, ed. M.J. de Goeje, Leiden 1906[2]; Abū l-Ḥasan ʿAlī b. al-Ḥusayn al-Sughdī, *al-Nutaf fī l-fatāwā*, ed. Ṣalāḥ al-Dīn al-Nāhī, 2 vols., Beirut 1984[2]; ʿUmar b. Abī l-Ḥusayn al-Naysābūrī al-Samarqandī, *Rawnaq al-qulūb*, Paris, BNF, MSS Ar. 6674 and 4929.

Studies

Claude Addas, *Ibn Arabî et le voyage sans retour*, Paris 1996; Lutz Berger, *Geschieden von allem außer Gott*, Hildesheim 1998; C. E. Bosworth, The rise of the Karāmiyyah in Khurasan, *MW* 50/1 (1960), 5–14; Michael Bonner, The *Kitāb al-kasb* attributed to al-Shaybānī. Poverty, surplus, and the circulation of wealth, *JAOS* 121/3 (2001), 410–27; Richard W. Bulliet, *The patricians of Nishapur*, Cambridge MA 1972; Jacqueline Chabbi, Remarques sur le développement historique des mouvements ascétiques et mystiques en Khurasan. IIIe/IXe siècle–IVe/Xe siècle, *SI* 46 (1977), 5–72; Jacqueline Chabbi, Réflexions sur le soufisme Iranien primitif, *JA* 266 (1978), 37–55; Josef van Ess, *Ungenützte Texte zur Karrāmīya*, Heidelberg 1980; Josef van Ess, *Der Eine und das Andere. Beobachtungen an islamischen häresiographischen Texten*, Berlin 2011; Wilferd Madelung, *Religious trends in early Islamic Iran*, Albany NY 1988; Christopher Melchert, Sufis and competing movements in Nishapur, *Iran* 39 (2001), 237–47; Aron Zysow, Two unrecognized Karrāmī texts, *JAOS* 108/4 (1988), 577–87; Aron Zysow, Karrāmiyya, in Sabine Schmidtke (ed.), *Oxford handbook of Islamic theology* (Oxford 2016), 252–62; Aron Zysow, Karrāmiya, *EIr*.

Lutz Berger

Kelantan

Kelantan is a major centre of Malay life and culture on the Malay Peninsula. Once an autonomous sultanate that maintained a distinct identity over several centuries, it is now, after several changes of legal status, one of the states of the Federation of Malaysia. Like most Malay sultanates, its lands were and still are a physical and social catchment area surrounding a river that once provided the principal means of communication in the areas over which, with varying degrees of plausibility and effect, the sultan claimed political control. The capital, whose position rested on the control of internal riverine and external water-borne trade, has long been Kota Baru, near the deltaic mouth of the Kelantan River. The entire Kelantan delta and the larger adjacent alluvial plain has long had a dense Malay population, whose subsistence was based upon rice cultivation, fishing and related food production, and a variety of handicrafts (including batik-cloth printing and silver- and copper-ware) and local artistic performances (including shadow play and several forms of folk opera and recitation arts).

1. Early history, facing eastward

Lying on the eastern side of the mountainous and densely-jungled Malay peninsula, Kelantan, before the development of modern communication and transport, faced the outside world eastward from Kota Baru onto the Gulf of Siam. Its main trading connections were with the Malay sultanates of Patani and Singgora (Songkhla, in Thai) to the north and Terengganu and Pahang to the south and, beyond that, to the Siamese and the Muslim Cham Cambodian areas north and east on the gulf coast and to Johor and Singapore to the south. Because of the difficulties of travel and communications across the peninsula, Kelantan was part of and well integrated into the culturally diverse Gulf of Siam region, rather than with what were, or became, the heartlands of the Malay world on the west coast of the peninsula and, beyond, in Sumatra and Java. Its eastward orientation helped shape the sultanate's cultural distinctiveness and political identity amongst the peninsular Malay states from premodern times into the colonial and postcolonial eras.

2. Increasing Siamese influence

The claimed political autonomy of Kelantan—together with the smaller sultanates of the Malay cultural zone in southern Thailand centred on Patani—was eroded as it came under increasing Siamese influence from the eleventh/seventeenth century and direct political pressure following the imposition of Siamese control upon Patani, in the nineteenth century. An older tributary relationship, symbolised by the periodic presentation to Bangkok of the *bunga mas* (lit., golden flowers; certain symbolic gold and silver valuables in branch-like form), was ever more insistently redefined by the Siamese as one of direct subservience and fealty. Siamese pressure placed a lasting stamp on Kelantanese society and identity. Feeling increasingly beleaguered, many Kelantanese came to see themselves defiantly as Malays, not merely distinct from but culturally opposed to the Siamese and, together with the Malays of the Patani, Songkhla, Narathiwat, and Yala regions of what has been called Siam's "remote southeast," under assault from expanding Thai-Buddhist domination. They understood themselves increasingly as Malays whose identity was grounded in what might now be termed a premodern, local form of political Islam.

This sense of Kelantanese cultural and political identity was cultivated by two generations of refugee Islamic scholars from the Patani region who fled to Kota Baru in the mid- and late nineteenth century, set up their *madrasas*, and spread their influence in the large and growing traditional *pondok* schools (analogous to the Javanese *pesantren*) throughout the Kelantan coastal plain. It was further strengthened by the policies of political centralisation of Kelantan under Sultan Muhammad II (r. 1844–86) and the imposition of what was considered normative Islam, allied with the growing influence of "correct" Sunnī Islamic scholarship as mediated through some notable families from the Kelantanese community in Mecca.

3. British colonial rule and the growth of a rigorous Islamism

These developments continued when, after a period of political instability and further Siamese interventions following the death of Sultan Muhammad II, Kelantan came under British colonial rule after 1909 as one of the indirectly ruled Unfederated Malay States. The new arrangements buttressed the social and political position of the leading Kelantanese royal and noble families, gave modern expression to the state's distinctive Malay identity, and helped generate new elite forms of Malay political self-assertion. These developments soon found expression in the creation in 1915 of a new bureaucratic institution for the centralisation of Islamic administration, education, and taxation, the Majlis Agama Islam dan Adat Istiadat Melayu (Council for Islamic Religion and Malay Custom), the first of its kind in Malaya and a model adopted later in other Malay states.

The colonial years saw the further development of orthodox Sunnī scholarly and educational activity under some notable local *ʿulamāʾ* (religious scholars) along with an increasing assertion of pan-Islamic connections, as well as the development of a lively modern, largely anti-elite, Malay literary intelligentsia and related publishing institutions. After independence in 1957, these two tendencies—that inclined towards "*sharīʿa*-minded" rigour and the anti-elitist Malay vernacular radicalism—would converge within and drive populist support for the Pan-Malayan Islamic Party (Parti Islam SeMalaya, PAS), which had emerged in 1951. Under colonial rule, Kelantanese life continued to be largely inwardly focused, detached from the material development then transforming the west-coast states of the Malay peninsula. Attracting little outside imperial investment and experiencing little of the economic dynamism and the associated non-Malay immigration of those other states—where the activities of non-Malay, especially Chinese and Indian, immigrants had a huge transformative effect—Kelantan remained an overwhelmingly peasant-based agrarian state notable for the retention and "traditionalising" of its Malay culture and character. More than ninety-five percent of the population was Malay, largely of Kelantanese and Patani origins. The local dialect of the Malay language was and is largely incomprehensible to Malays from the other Malayan states; it is more closely related to the Malay dialects of Patani and southern Thailand.

4. Independence and the ascendancy of the PAS

Occupied by Japan and Thailand from 1941 to 1945, Kelantan returned to British control after World War II and, as one of its eleven constituent states (nine of them sultanates), became independent from colonial rule as part of the Federation of Malaya in 1957. Its demographic and sociocultural characteristics contributed to a distinctive Islamic sensibility and a style of Malay-Islamic politics often at odds with, if not antagonistic to, the overall politics of Malaysia and its governing party. In Malaya's first post-independence elections, in 1959, the PAS won a landslide victory in Kelantan, the first time anywhere in the world an Islamic party came to power via democratic elections. When in 1963 the Federation of Malaya was expanded to include, as the Federation of Malaysia, the Borneo states of Sarawak and Sabah, Kelantan, under PAS leadership, unsuccessfully opposed the federation's enlargement as a diminution of its constitutional prerogatives and a dilution of the nation's Malay-Islamic character.

Except for an interlude from 1978 to 1990—following a period of unhappy cooperation and coalition with its main political adversary, the United Malays National Organisation (UMNO)—PAS has exercised power in Kelantan from 1959 to the present. Insisting that Malaysia has, since independence, been constitutionally an "Islamic state in the making," it has used its position to drive UMNO and Malaysian politics generally ever more forcefully towards the implementation of *sharīʿa* law, including the canonical *ḥudūd* punishments.

5. The increasing domination of Islam in the life of Kelantan

Over two centuries, Islam, in its local form, has become an increasingly prominent and defining feature of public and everyday life in Kelantan. This has been due partly to the growing enforcement by PAS of what it sees as proper Islamic morality, in the form of dress codes and gender segregation in public places, combined with the suppression of what it denounces as the un-Islamic aspects of Kelantanese Malay culture, such as the ironically gender-flexible folk opera with its musical appeal to carnal desires *(nafsu*, from Ar. *nafs)*. The growing influence of Islam is also attributable to the promotion of Sunnī orthodoxy through education, including *pondok*s and traditional *madrasa*s, modern primary and secondary "*madrasa*-type" Arabic-Islamic schools, and tertiary institutions, such as Akademi Pengajian Islam Nilam Puri (the Nilam Puri Academy of Islamic Studies), once an independent PAS-government initiative but now a branch of the University of Malaya. PAS has further enhanced the central role of Islam in Kelantan civic culture through the vernacular sermons, homilies, and lectures (widely available as tapes and texts) of its leader "Tok Guru" (lit., honoured teacher) Haji Nik Abdul Aziz bin Haji Nik Mat, who served as chief minister of Kelantan from 1990 until his death in 2015.

Remote two centuries ago from the mainstream of peninsular Malay life, Kelantan has now, thanks largely to its commitment under PAS guidance to the politics of conspicuous piety, become central to Malaysian Islamic life. It still strives to set its terms to the nation's Muslim and non-Muslim citizens alike. This stands in stark contrast to conditions in a society that, when the first great modern Malay writer Munshi Abdullah visited Kota Baru in 1839, shocked him with its scandalous standard of immodesty and public immorality and its disregard for the basic precepts of the faith.

Bibliography

Munshi Abdullah bin Abdul Kadir, *The voyage of Abdullah. Being an account of his experiences on a voyage from Singapore to Kelantan*, trans. A. E. Coope, Singapore 1949, Kuala Lumpur 1967; Walter Armstrong Graham, *Kelantan. A state of the Malay Peninsula. A handbook of information*, Glasgow 1908; Abdullah Alwi Haji Hassan, *The administration of Islamic law in Kelantan*, Kuala Lumpur 1996; "Ibrahim Syukri" (pseud.), *History of the Malay kingdom of Patani (Sejarah Kerajaan Melayu Patani)*, trans. Conner Bailey and John N. Miksic, Athens OH 1985, Chiang Mai 2005; Clive S. Kessler, *Islam and politics in a Malay state. Kelantan 1838–1969*, Ithaca NY 1978; Clive S. Kessler, Remembering "Tok Guru," *New Mandala* (Australian National University), 16 February 2015, www.newmandala.org/remembering-tok-guru/; Farish A. Noor, The localization of Islamic discourse in the *Tafsir* of Tuan Guru Nik Aziz Nik Mat, *Mursyid'ul Am* of PAS, in Virginia Hooker and Norani Othman (eds.), *Malaysia. Islam, society, and politics* (Singapore 2003), 195–235; Farish A. Noor, *The Malaysian Islamic Party 1951–2013. Islamism in a mottled nation*, Amsterdam 2014; William R. Roff (ed.), *Kelantan. Religion, society and politics in a Malay state*, Kuala Lumpur 1974 (esp. the chapter by Roff, The origins and early years of the Majlis Ugama, 101–52); Shahril Talib, *History of Kelantan, 1890–1940*, Kuala Lumpur 1995.

Clive S. Kessler

L

Lakhm

The **Lakhm** were a Qaḥṭānī Arab tribe of southern Syria closely connected to the Judhām and ʿĀmila. According to the traditional genealogy, the eponym Lakhm was of Qaḥṭānī origin and the brother of Judhām and ʿĀmila, although some argued that the tribe was actually from the Nizār (Caskel, 2:53–6; Ibn Durayd, 225–7). In historical times, these three "sister tribes" were political allies and occupied the same region in southern Syria. The Lakhm were considered the most ancient and illustrious of the three, with links to biblical figures such as Abraham and Joseph. In early Islamic times, the Lakhm became less important and were absorbed by the Judhām, who played a leading role under the Umayyads. Whereas the *nisba* "Judhamī" remained frequent, "Lakhmī" gradually disappeared and was reduced to little more than an archaic-sounding honorific title that evoked the tribe's glorious past.

The connection of the tribe of Lakhm in Syria with the Lakhmids, the celebrated kings of al-Ḥīra in the Middle Euphrates, remains a matter of dispute. Mesopotamia was probably the Lakhm's original dwelling area in the third century C.E. until they migrated to Syria in the early fourth century C.E. In fact, there is no evidence of the Lakhm in the area dominated by the kings in al-Ḥīra in the late fourth century C.E. The dynasty probably kept the name of Lakhm because of the tribe's prestige, and some scholars assume that only the first kings were Lakhmīs (Retsö, 473–80). Arabic tradition, however, continued to associate the tribe of Lakhm with the kings of al-Ḥīra. Later groups who claimed descent from the prestigious kings of al-Ḥīra, such as the Banū ʿAbbād of Seville (Ramírez, 195–203) and the present-day Druze in Lebanon (Hitti, 31), did so by asserting their affiliation with the tribe of Lakhm.

Bibliography

Source

Ibn Durayd, *al-Ishtiqāq*, ed. ʿAbd al-Salām Muḥammad Hārūn, Cairo 1378[/1958].

Studies

Philip Hitti, *The origins of the Druze people*, New York 1928, repr. 1966; Werner Caskel, *Ǧamharat an-nasab. Das genealogische Werk des Hišām ibn Muḥammad al-Kalbī*, Leiden 1966;

José Ramírez del Río, *La orientalización de al-Andalus*, Seville 2002; Jan Retsö, *The Arabs in antiquity* (London 2003), index; Isabel Toral-Niehoff, *Al-Ḥīra. Eine arabische Kulturmetropole im spätantiken Kontext* (Leiden 2014), index.

Isabel Toral-Niehoff

Lexicography, Arabic

The tradition of premodern **Arabic lexicography** extended for about a millennium and embraced a wide variety of genres and numerous methods of arrangement. The *Kitāb al-ʿayn* of al-Khalīl b. Aḥmad (d. 175/791), which represents both the first extant thematic monograph and the first lexicon to include all Arabic roots, dates from the second half of the second/eighth century. Though not strictly premodern in terms of chronology, al-Zabīdī's (d. 1205/1790) voluminous *Tāj al-ʿarūs* is regarded as the most comprehensive work that crowns this long period of Arabic lexicographical writing.

1. Emergence

Interest in lexicography was part of a more general interest in linguistic matters and, in particular, grammar. The lexicographical and grammatical traditions share a common background and both are closely connected to the study of the Qurʾānic text. It is therefore no coincidence that the first and most influential work of grammar, *al-Kitāb*, was authored by Sībawayh (d. 180/796), whose principal teacher was al-Khalīl. Furthermore, just as the grammarians *(naḥwiyyūn)* were deeply interested, among other things, in explaining syntactical issues pertaining to Qurʾānic usage, the lexicographers *(lughawiyyūn)* tried to explain Qurʾānic words that were either not familiar to many Arabs or had a specific meaning in a Qurʾānic context, and to identify words of non-Arabic origin that occur in the Qurʾān. In both disciplines, *shawāhid* (instances of attested usage) from poetry and the speech of the Arabs were cited in the study of the syntax and word meanings of the Qurʾān. Poetry was also an important stimulus for Arabic lexicography, due to many words found within poems that became increasingly unfamiliar to people who were becoming more settled and urbanised.

The lexicographers identified the speech of the Bedouin *(aʿrāb)* as the "purest" and most eloquent form of Arabic and thus competed in recording data from them, mainly in their desert abodes. This process of data collection was known as *jamʿ al-lugha* and took place over the course of most of the second/eighth century and the first half of the third/ninth century. The collected data provided much of the raw material for authors of thematic monographs, as well as authors of lexica that aspired to include all attested roots. Accordingly, the lexicographers preserved much of the linguistic and cultural heritage of the Arabs that might have otherwise been lost. Yet they largely focussed on usage of *gharīb* (strange; pl. *gharāʾib*) or even *nādir* (rare; pl. *nawādir*) types. This explains the numerous works on *gharāʾib*, such as the *Kitāb al-gharībayn* of Abū ʿUbayd Aḥmad b. Muḥammad al-Harawī (d. 401/1011), which covers *gharīb* material in the Qurʾān and *ḥadīth*, and the *nawādir*, such as Abū Zayd al-Anṣārī's (d. 215/830) *al-Nawādir* and Abū Misḥal al-Aʿrābī's (d. 231/845) book by the same title.

According to biographical sources as of the third/ninth century, early lexicographical and grammatical activity was prompted by the spread of *laḥn* (solecism).

This may partially explain why lexicographers and grammarians alike were eager to identify criteria for "correct" usage. With the spread of Arabic as a spoken language throughout much of the Islamic world and following the Arabisation of the *dawāwīn* (official registers) during the reign of the caliph ʿAbd al-Malik b. Marwān (r. 65–86/685–705), grammarians responded to the growing need to study Arabic by exploring its phonological, morphological, and syntactical characteristics. For their part, lexicographers focussed mainly on two aspects of semantic study. The first was the classification into themes of the vast number of lexical items that the process of data collection yielded (for example, plants, animals, the human body, rain, wind, clouds, swords, wells, saddles, etc.) and the exploration of several semantic phenomena (for example, *gharīb* and *nādir*, homonyms, synonyms, Arabised words, and so forth). The second aspect was the formal *(lafẓī)* arrangement of the material according to a certain principle that helps the user locate the desired lexical item or root.

These two aspects of semantic study very quickly gave rise to two types of lexica that continued throughout the lexical tradition, since each serves a different purpose than the other. Perhaps the most lucid distinction between these two types was given by Ibn Sīda (d. 458/1066) in the introduction to his *al-Mukhaṣṣaṣ* (1:10–12). The two terms he uses are *mubawwab* and *mujannas*, which correspond to onomasiological and semasiological, respectively. In the former, meaning leads to sign, as found with thematically arranged monographs and thesauri, whereas in the latter, sign leads to meaning, as with lexica that are arranged based on formal criteria. Ibn Sīda himself authored a multi-volume lexicon of each type. He explains that having authored his *mujannas* lexicon, *al-Muḥkam*, which guides the user to the exact place in which a word occurs, he wanted to match it with *al-Mukhaṣṣaṣ*, a *mubawwab* lexicon that better befits the needs of the orator *(khaṭīb)* and poet *(shāʿir)*, since it allows them to choose the *mot juste* from among a number of listed adjectives and synonyms.

The distinction between *mubawwab* and *mujannas* lexica is a useful tool in studying the lexicographical tradition. Yet the boundaries between the two types are often blurred. For example, in many *mubawwab* monographs the material is arranged alphabetically, as in some works on proverbs or Arabised words. In contrast, Ibn Durayd's (d. 321/933) *mujannas* lexicon, *Jamharat al-lugha*, contains towards its end a miscellany of short chapters that are not alphabetically arranged and that deal with thematic issues, including morphological patterns, dialectal features, rare usage, and several semantic fields, such as food, bows and arrows, blades, and footwear. Generally speaking, unlike *mubawwab* lexica, *mujannas* lexica tend to be exhaustive of all Arabic roots and, in certain extensive works, aspire to include all their attested derivatives. Yet, despite this characterisation, a book such as the *Kitāb al-jīm* of Abū ʿAmr al-Shaybānī (d. 206/821), for example, is best classified as a *mujannas* lexicon because it is generally recognised as the first to use an alphabetical arrangement (albeit on first-letter basis only) even though its author focuses on *gharīb* material and does not aim at exhausting all the roots of the language.

It is also noteworthy that throughout the tradition of premodern Arabic lexicography, bilingual and multilingual dictionaries were quite rare, given that lexicographers were seldom interested in a comparative approach to linguistic study. There are, however, a few Arabic–Persian and Arabic–Mongolian glossaries, as well as other word lists (Naṣṣār, *al-Muʿjam al-ʿArabī*, 1:91–6; Carter, 108). Also noteworthy is al-Zamakhsharī's (d. 538/1144) *Muqaddimat al-adab*, an Arabic–Persian lexicon arranged according to nominal and verbal patterns.

2. *Mubawwab* (onomasiological) lexica

Mubawwab lexica include specialised works that deal with a specific theme, as well as multi-themed thesauri. The earliest extant monographs were authored by lexicographers of the latter part of the second/eighth century and the early part of the third/ninth, that is, by contemporaries of al-Khalīl and Abū ʿAmr al-Shaybānī, authors of the two earliest *mujannas* lexica, *al-ʿAyn* and *al-Jīm* respectively. Also contemporaneous with both types of lexicon were the earliest multi-themed works, such as the *al-Gharīb al-muṣannaf* ("Classified strange usage") of Abū ʿUbayd al-Qāsim b. Sallām al-Harawī (d. 224/838). It would, therefore, be anachronistic to suggest that single-topic monographs belong to a stage that precedes that of multi-themed works and that *mujannas* lexica appeared only in a third stage of development (cf. Amīn, 2:263ff.; Marçais, 149–51; Abū Sharīfa et al., 116–8; Ghurāb, 48–50). Furthermore, throughout much of the tradition, authors of *mujannas* lexica incorporated into their works material derived from *mubawwab* lexica, and vice versa. For example, three of Ibn Fāris's (d. 395/1004) five main sources in his *mujannas* lexicon, *Maqāyīs al-lugha*, are *mubawwab* works, namely, the *Gharīb al-ḥadīth* and *al-Gharīb al-muṣannaf* of Abū ʿUbayd al-Qāsim b. Sallām and the *Iṣlāḥ al-manṭiq* of Ibn al-Sikkīt (d. 244/858; see *Maqāyīs al-lugha*, 1:4–5). On the other hand, both *mujannas* lexica, *al-ʿAyn* and *Jamharat al-lugha*, are among the main sources from which Ibn Sīda derived the material of *al-Mukhaṣṣaṣ*.

Among the earliest *mubawwab* lexica to appear were books on proverbs *(amthāl)*, with the earliest two extant works whose attribution is not in doubt being *Amthāl al-ʿArab* by al-Mufaḍḍal al-Ḍabbī (d. 168?/784?) and *al-Amthāl* by Muʾarrij al-Sadūsī (d. between 193/808 and 198/813). Soon after the appearance of these two seminal works Abū ʿUbayd al-Qāsim b. Sallām authored his own *al-Amthāl*, which includes 1,386 proverbs grouped into major themes that are further divided into 270 chapters, a level of ordering that was unprecedented. Alphabetical arrangement of proverb collections was first introduced by Ḥamza al-Iṣfahānī (d. after 351/962) in his *al-Durra al-fākhira*, but the *Majmaʿ al-amthāl* of al-Maydānī (d. 518/1124) is probably the most famous in the genre and includes 4,765 proverbs arranged on first-letter basis only.

Other than their historical and cultural significance, proverbs were the subject of lexicographical interest due to their linguistic idiosyncrasies and the strong bond between them and *gharīb* material (cf. Abū Hilāl al-ʿAskarī, 1:5). The genre of *gharīb* includes works on *gharīb* material in the Qurʾān and *ḥadīth* in addition to the more general *gharīb* that occurs in the speech of the Arabs and in poetry. It is noteworthy that most works on Qurʾānic *gharīb* do not only explain words that may well not be readily understood by some speakers of Arabic, but also more commonly used words, such as *khizy* (disgrace), *ukul* (fruit), and *nabaʾ* (news) (Ibn Qutayba, *Tafsīr gharīb al-Qurʾān*, 61, 97, 154). The reason for including such words seems to be the desire to identify their exact meanings within a Qurʾānic context. This phenomenon is far less frequent in works on *gharīb* in the *ḥadīth*. Outside the sphere of Qurʾān and *ḥadīth*, the *Laysa fī kalām al-ʿArab* (lit., "There is not in the speech of the Arabs [except]...") of Ibn Khālawayh (d. 370/980) is unique in that it consists of 188 short chapters in each of which are cited words that are the only examples of a rare morphological pattern or phenomenon.

Apart from proverbs and *gharīb* material, a number of other genres (as outlined below) dominated the *mubawwab* lexicographical tradition for several centuries.

2.1. *Specific semantic fields*

Data collection in the second half of the second/eighth century generated a vast amount of vocabulary related to a variety of topics. Specialised monographs were thus authored on themes that included *nabāt* (plants in general), *zarʿ* (planting), *shajar* (trees), *kalaʾ* (herbage), *ʿushb* (grass), *nakhl* (palm trees), *tamr* (dates), *karm* (vineyards), *ḥayawān* (animals in general), *usd* (lions), *dhiʾāb* (wolves), *khayl* (horses), *ibil* (camels), *shāʾ* (sheep), *wuḥūsh* (wild animals), *ḥasharāt* (insects), *hawāmm* (creeping things, reptiles), *naḥl* (bees), *ʿasal* (honey), *khalq al-insān* (human body), *maṭar* (rain), *rīḥ* (wind), *saḥāb* (clouds), *al-layl wa-l-nahār* (day and night), *silāḥ* (weapons), *ābār* (wells), *khamr* (wine), and even *dawāhī* (calamities) and *maysir* (gambling). Much of the material in these monographs was incorporated into multi-themed works (see 2.6 below), as well as *mujannas* lexica.

2.2. *Arabised words* (al-muʿarrab)

Early lexicographers held conflicting views as to whether the Qurʾān contains loan words or not and thus developed criteria to distinguish these from words of Arabic origin (al-Suyūṭī, 1:268ff.). However, due to their limited knowledge of foreign languages, lexicographers did not always correctly ascribe loan words to their true origins. The most famous work in the genre, al-Jawālīqī's (d. 540/1145) *al-Muʿarrab min al-kalām al-aʿjamī*, appeared relatively late in comparison with seminal works in other genres. It contains 743 words that are alphabetically arranged by first letter only, and are mostly repeated in later works.

2.3. *Solecism* (laḥn al-ʿāmma)

Given their puristic approach and their conviction that the norms of correctness and eloquence *(faṣāḥa)* should be derived from Qurʾānic usage, pre-Islamic poetry, and the speech of the Bedouin, lexicographers readily considered speech departing from these norms as deficient. Contrary to the literal meaning of *laḥn al-ʿāmma* (errors committed by the generality of people), the material cited in this genre often includes errors ascribed to the *khāṣṣa* (elite), including writers, poets, Qurʾānic readers *(qurrāʾ)*, jurists, physicians, and so forth. Among the earliest works are al-Kisāʾī's (d. 189/805) *Mā talḥan fīhi l-ʿāmma* and Thaʿlab's (d. 291/904) *al-Faṣīḥ*. Most works are arranged based on the type of error in question, for example, semantic changes and changes in vowels, consonants, and morphological patterns. Of particular note in this genre is the *Tathqīf al-lisān* of Ibn Makkī (d. 501/1107) due to its discussing, among other topics, the difference in *laḥn* between the east and west of the Arab world.

2.4. *Semantics*

The lexicographers focussed on three major semantic phenomena: *al-aḍdād* (words with two contradictory meanings), *al-mushtarak* (homonyms), and *al-mutarādif* (synonyms).

The earliest extant monographs on *al-aḍdād* go back to the early third/ninth century. Quṭrub (d. 206/821), al-Aṣmaʿī (d. 216/831), and Ibn al-Sikkīt, among other early scholars, authored monographs on the subject, but these used neither thematic nor alphabetical arrangements. The largest collection of *aḍdād*, which contains a total of 357 items, is found in Abū Bakr Ibn al-Anbārī's (d. 328/940) *al-Aḍdād*, but the first to arrange the words alphabetically based on the first letter of their roots was Abū l-Ṭayyib al-Lughawī (d. 351/962) in his *al-Aḍdād fī kalām al-ʿArab.*

The term *al-mushtarak* is used for homonymous polysemic words that, unlike *al-aḍdād*, do not indicate contradictory meanings. The title of one of the earliest monographs in this genre, Abū l-ʿAmaythal's (d. 240/854) *Mā ttafaqa lafẓuhu wa-khtalafa maʿnāhu* ("What agrees in form and differs in meaning"), succinctly describes this semantic phenomenon. Ibn al-Shajarī's (d. 542/1148) book with the same title is the largest of its kind and includes 1,670 words of this type, arranged alphabetically according to the first letter of the word, rather than its root.

Monographs on *al-mutarādif* normally list several synonymous words, unlike *mujannas* lexica, which usually cite only one synonym for any given word or often explain a word without giving any synonym. Al-Aṣmaʿī's *Mā khtalafat alfāẓuhu wa-ttafaqat maʿānīhi* ("What differs in form and agrees in meaning") is the first extant work in the genre. Ibn al-Sikkīt soon followed this work with *al-Alfāẓ*, best known through al-Tibrīzī's (d. 502/1109) commentary on it, *Kanz al-ḥuffāẓ fī Kitāb tahdhīb al-alfāẓ*. It is thematically arranged in 148 chapters, each of which contains words and expressions that pertain to a specific semantic field (such as wealth, poverty, fertility, infertility, stinginess, colour, old women, death, water, etc.). Abū l-Ḥasan al-Hamadhānī's (d. c.320/932) *al-Alfāẓ al-kitābiyya* is similarly divided into 365 short chapters that embrace a wide variety of semantic fields.

2.5. *Letters, particles, and morphological patterns*

Several monographs deal with specific letters of the alphabet *(ḥurūf al-hijāʾ)*. Among these letters is the *hamza (ʾ)*, also referred to as *alif*, due to its dialectal and orthographic peculiarities. Examples include Abū Zayd al-Anṣārī's *al-Hamz* and Ibn Khālawayh's *al-Alifāt.* Similarly, the *lām (l)* is discussed in several works, such as al-Zajjājī's (d. 337/949) *al-Lāmāt*, mostly for its syntactical characteristics. A host of monographs are also devoted to *ḍād (ḍ)* and *ẓāʾ (ẓ)* given that they were widely confused at the levels of both pronunciation and orthography. Ibn al-Sīd al-Baṭalyawsī (d. 521/1127), in his *al-Farq bayna l-ḥurūf al-khamsa*, covered the letters *dhāl (dh)*, *ṣād (ṣ)*, and *sīn (s)* in addition to *ḍād* and *ẓāʾ.* Other monographs deal specifically with *idghām* (assimilation), *ibdāl* (consonantal substitution), and *qalb* (metathesis).

Although *ḥurūf al-maʿānī* (literally, letters with meaning, that is, particles) are an essential part of Arabic grammatical theory, to them are devoted numerous monographs of the *mubawwab* type. Based on their arrangement or lack thereof, these can be divided into three groups: (i) those that lack any arrangement, such as al-Zajjājī's *Ḥurūf al-maʿānī* and ʿAlī b. Muḥammad al-Harawī's (d. c.415/1025) *al-Uzhiyya fī ʿilm al-ḥurūf;* (ii) those in which particles are arranged alphabetically irrespective of their form, such as al-Mālaqī's (d. 702/1302) *Raṣf al-mabānī fī sharḥ ḥurūf al-maʿānī;* and (iii) those in which particles are grouped based on their number of letters and then each group is arranged alphabetically, for example, al-Rummānī's (d. 384/994) *Maʿānī l-ḥurūf.*

At the level of morphology, the topics to which monographs were devoted include *al-ishtiqāq* (derivation of proper nouns or attributes of God), *al-mudhakkar wa-l-muʾannath* (masculine and feminine), *al-maqṣūr wa-l-mamdūd* (abbreviated and prolonged words that end with *-ā* or *-āʾ* respectively), and *al-muthallathāt* (triplets). The latter subgenre cites groups of three words that share the same root and pattern but differ in the vowel of one of their consonants. One example from the earliest work, Quṭrub's *al-Muthallathāt* (48–9) is *jadd* (grandfather), *jidd* (earnestness), and *judd* (old well). There are also extensive works that list and explain nominal and verbal patterns. Isḥāq b. Ibrāhīm al-Fārābī's (d. 350/961) *Dīwān al-adab* is unprecedented in combining both types of patterns in one lexicon. The two most comprehensive lexica that exclusively include verbal patterns share the same title, *al-Afʿāl*, and are authored by the Andalusian scholars al-Saraqusṭī (d. after 400/1010) and Ibn al-Qaṭṭāʿ (d. 515/1121).

2.6. *Multi-themed lexica or thesauri*

Many of the above genres are included in multi-themed lexica or thesauri, which drew much of their material from single topic monographs as well as from *mujannas* lexica. Several early authors are reported to have used the term *muṣannaf* (classified) in the titles of their works to indicate that they embrace many topics. The one book that has survived from the early period is Abū ʿUbayd al-Qāsim b. Sallām's *al-Gharīb al-muṣannaf*, which consists of twenty-six sections that are further divided into about nine hundred mostly short chapters. Its material includes vocabulary related to specific themes (such as women, food, wine, weapons, animals, plants, etc.) as well as purely philological topics, such as phonological matters, morphological patterns, and Arabised words. Ibn Qutayba's (d. 276/889) *Adab al-kātib* also includes a mixture of vocabulary and philological topics. Another famous work is al-Thaʿālibī's (d. 429/1038) *Fiqh al-lugha*, which is made up of thirty chapters that embrace about six hundred topics. But the most comprehensive multi-themed lexicon in the tradition is Ibn Sīda's *al-Mukhaṣṣaṣ*, and the impressive list of sources listed in its introduction (1:11–3) demonstrates its extremely wide scope. Ibn Sīda proudly highlights the unique arrangement of his book, which he believes to be unmatched by any previous work on lexicography (Introduction, 1:10, 12, 14). After *al-Mukhaṣṣaṣ*, multi-themed works became quite rare, most probably because there was precious little to be added to its extensive material.

3. *Mujannas* (semasiological) lexica

Mujannas lexica, arranged on the basis of formal criteria, are typically unspecialised and usually exhaustive of all Arabic roots. Accordingly, perhaps with the exception of the comprehensive thesauri, authoring a *mujannas* lexicon is a much more laborious task than compiling a *mubawwab* one. This might explain the paucity of lexica of the former type compared to the latter. (The present survey excludes lexica that are not philological in nature, such as works on *buldān* [cities, regions, etc.], *tarājim* [biographies], philosophical and medical terms, names of drugs, etc.)

There are three types of arrangement of roots in the *mujannas* lexica: the phonetic-permutative, the alphabetical, and the rhyme systems. These types do not correspond to separate historical stages, and although the rhyme system eventually became dominant, the last major lexica of the phonetic-permutative and the alphabetical types were authored as late as the fifth/eleventh and sixth/twelfth centuries respectively, as the following survey demonstrates.

3.1. *The phonetic-permutative system*

The earliest lexicon using the phonetic-permutative form of arrangement was the *Kitāb al-ʿayn* of al-Khalīl b. Aḥmad. A number of scholars as early as the third/ninth century expressed their doubts as to the true identity of *al-ʿAyn*'s author. Schoeler convincingly argues that although al-Khalīl is the intellectual creator of the work and large parts of it are based on his teachings, it was probably his disciple al-Layth b. al-Muẓaffar (d. 190/805) who compiled the vast majority of the lexicon's entries (Schoeler, 142–63). The book's introduction, written by an unknown disciple of al-Khalīl, presents the latter's phonetic and morphological views that form the foundations of the lexicon (Baalbaki, *Lexicographical tradition*, 282ff.). His aim was to devise a system that would exhaust *all* Arabic roots to be included in a lexicon. For this purpose, he identified three basic principles, namely, (i) that the letters of the alphabet form a closed set, (ii) that the number of radicals in Arabic words ranges from two to five, and (iii) that the possible permutations of roots are readily identifiable. The number of these permutations—referred to as *taqālīb* in later works—is two in biliterals (e.g., *KD, DK*) and six in triliterals (e.g., *ʿNT, ʿTN, NʿT, NTʿ, TʿN, TNʿ*). Those that are in use are called *mustaʿmal* (e.g., *ʿNT, NʿT*), whereas those that are not used are called *muhmal* (e.g., *ʿTN, TNʿ*). In quadriliterals and quinqueliterals, the theoretical number of permutations is 24 and 120 respectively, but very few of these are actually used.

By applying *dhawāq* (sampling of letters), al-Khalīl arranged the letters of the alphabet according to their points of articulation, starting at the source of the airstream and working outward, in the following order: *ʿ, ḥ, h, kh, gh, q, k, j, sh, ḍ, ṣ, s, z, ṭ, d, t, ẓ, dh, th, r, l, n, f, b, m, w, alif, y, hamza*. Al-Khalīl most probably steered away from the two customary arrangements that would have been known to him (that is, the *ʾ, b, j, d, h, w, z*, etc. and the *ʾ, b, t, th, j, ḥ, kh*, etc. arrangements) because they lack any linguistic justification. The suggestion that al-Khalīl was influenced by Indian parallels is flawed, given the substantial differences between the Arabic and Indian phonetic traditions (Law, 215–27). In fact, al-Khalīl's intuitive and experimental approach to discovering the phonetic traits of the letters and his exploration of Arabic morphological peculiarities are not at all suggestive of borrowing from a readily available system that merely had to be Arabised.

Apart from a number of minor modifications, al-Khalīl's phonetic arrangement of roots, his chapters that are based on the number of radicals in words, and his method of listing together the various permutations of the roots were faithfully followed by authors of lexica of the phonetic-permutative type. These include the first *mujannas* lexicon in Arab Spain, *al-Bāriʿ fī l-lugha* by al-Qālī (d. 356/967), *Tahdhīb al-lugha* by al-Azharī (d. 370/981), *al-Muḥīṭ fī l-lugha* by al-Ṣāḥib b. ʿAbbād (d. 385/995), and *al-Muḥkam* by Ibn Sīda. Yet these works considerably expand *al-ʿAyn*'s material, often including derivatives ignored by al-Khalīl and citing more *shawāhid* (attested material), particularly from poetry. Al-Azharī in particular was keen on adhering to what he considered to be correct usage, and the title of his lexicon ("Correction of language") reflects his critical approach to earlier authors. Ibn Sīda, on the other hand, is probably the first author of any *mujannas* lexicon to set clear norms to be followed in the organisation of data in the lemmata. These include what the author should regularly mention or ignore within the lemmata as well as several economies that would contribute to the formulation of definitions in a concise and systematic manner.

3.2. *The alphabetical system*

Lexicographers who arranged their lexica alphabetically often cited the widespread familiarity of this approach (Kurāʿ al-Naml, 1:31; Ibn Durayd, 1:40). Outside the sphere of philology, this system was frequently used, for instance in *ḥadīth* scholarship, as exemplified by al-Bukhārī's (d. 256/870) biographical work, *al-Taʾrīkh al-kabīr*. In this system, the letters are arranged (in the tradition dominant in the eastern part of the Arab world) as follows: *ʾ, b, t, th, j, ḥ, kh, d, dh, r, z, s, sh, ṣ, ḍ, ṭ, ẓ, ʿ, gh, f, q, k, l, m, n, h, w, y* (or *w, h, y*). The first *mujannas* lexicon to adopt this system, although on first-letter basis only, was the *Kitāb al-jīm* of al-Shaybānī. Given that this work begins with *alif*, rather than *jīm*, the choice of title for this work is puzzling. Unlike most *mujannas* lexica, *al-Jīm*, as noted earlier, is not intended to be exhaustive of all Arabic lexical items. This notwithstanding, it is essential to list it with *mujannas* lexica in order to demonstrate the emergence of the alphabetical systems at a very early stage of lexicographical writing. Furthermore, it does not seem to be a finished book, since it consists of provisional notes that were possibly meant to be the subject of further revision. Although al-Shaybānī died a few decades after al-Khalīl, it is not improbable, given al-Shaybānī's long life (he lived 119 years according to some sources), that he authored his lexicon at the same time that *al-ʿAyn* was written, if not even slightly earlier.

Ibn Durayd arranged the roots in most parts of his *Jamharat al-lugha* by taking the initial, medial, and final radicals into consideration. Yet he followed al-Khalīl's method of listing together all the permutations of the roots and of dividing his chapters—though not without certain modifications—in accordance with the number of radicals of the roots. A few decades later, Ibn Fāris in his *Maqāyīs al-lugha* adopted the alphabetical system and, like Ibn Durayd, took all the radicals of the roots into consideration in their arrangement and observed the number of radicals in the division of the chapters, but abandoned the permutations. In both *al-Maqāyīs* and the more concise *Mujmal al-lugha*, Ibn Fāris follows a unique system of alphabetical arrangement, not known in other lexica. In biliterals, for example, he begins the letter *r* not with *rʾ, rb*, and so forth, but with *rz, rs, rsh*, and so forth (since *r* is immediately followed by *z* in the alphabet, then *s, sh*, and so on). The root that is made up of *r* and the last letter of the alphabet (in this case, *rh*) is then followed by *rʾ, rb, rt... rdh*. The same principle of cyclical arrangement is applied in triliterals, not only between the first and second letters but also between the second and third.

Al-Zamakhsharī's (d. 538/1144) *Asās al-balāgha* is the first *mujannas* lexicon in which full alphabetical order is applied without any consideration for the permutations or root length. As far as content is concerned, *al-Asās* is unique in that its main objective is to distinguish between the tropical *(majāzī)* and the literal or veridical *(ḥaqīqī)* meanings of words. This is primarily achieved by the author's focus on contextual usage, rather than lexical items in isolation.

3.3. *The rhyme system*

This system is also alphabetical, but roots are arranged starting with the last, followed by the first, then the intermediate radicals, that is, 3rd, 1st, 2nd in triliterals and 4th, 1st, 2nd, 3rd in quadriliterals. Al-Jawharī (d. c.400/1010) perfected this system in his *al-Ṣiḥāḥ* by adopting a sole criterion of arrangement, that is, the order of radicals irrespective of any morphological consideration. However, the arrangement of roots by their final letters preceded him by more than one and a half centuries. Like his maternal uncle al-Fārābī (d. 350/961) in *Dīwān al-adab*, al-Jawharī took all the radicals of the root into consideration in his arrangement, but he abandoned al-Fārābī's division of chapters based on nominal and verbal patterns.

Prior to al-Fārābī, al-Bandanījī (d. 284/897) had authored *al-Taqfiya fī l-lugha* ("Rhyming in language"), which is believed to be the first *mujannas* lexicon to follow the rhyme system, even though it does not go beyond the final radical in the arrangement. The title of the book strongly suggests a link with poetry. In fact, al-Bandanījī's unidentified disciple who wrote its introduction clearly indicates that it is based on *qawāfī* (sg. *qāfiya*), which he defines as a line of poetry. The book's chapters are further divided into sections that are devoted to rhyming patterns, referred to in the introduction as *afāʿīl* and grouped in the text under the term *qāfiya*. Each section embraces a number of words (that is, not roots) that are not necessarily of the same morphological pattern, but which can serve as final words in the same poem, such as *raʾb, tabb, sibb, aqabb, shiqb, shurb (al-Taqfiya*, 127ff.; cf. Baalbaki, The influence, 20–30).

In the development of the rhyme system in lexica even al-Bandanījī is preceded, as has been recently demonstrated (Baalbaki, A precursor, 5–14; Baalbaki, *Lexicographical tradition*, 363–72), by Ibn al-Sikkīt, who arranged lexical items according to their final radicals in a lengthy chapter of *Iṣlāḥ al-manṭiq* (37–84). This chapter seems to have been used by al-Bandanījī as a template for *al-Taqfiya.* Furthermore, the remarkable statement of Abū Ḥanīfa Aḥmad al-Dīnawarī (d. before 290/902–3) that he preferred arranging lexical items based on their first, rather than last, letters (*al-Nabāt*, 397) strongly indicates that by the third/ninth century the rhyme system was more commonly employed than has been hitherto acknowledged.

The approach taken by al-Jawharī in his *al-Ṣiḥāḥ*, as stated in its short introduction, was to only include material that he deemed to be correct. However, most later authors of *mujannas* lexica aimed at achieving comprehensiveness and thus restored much of the material that al-Jawharī had omitted. By way of contrast, *al-Ṣiḥāḥ* contains 5,618 roots, whereas Ibn Manẓūr's (d. 711/1311) *Lisān al-ʿArab* and al-Zabīdī's *Tāj al-ʿarūs* contain 9,273 and 11,978 roots respectively (Mūsā, 149).

Among the lexica that follow al-Jawharī's rhyme system, al-Ṣaghānī's (d. 650/1252) *al-ʿUbāb al-zākhir* ("The flowing torrent") is quite impressive, not only in its comprehensiveness and reliance on a very large number of sources, but also in the internal arrangement of its lemmata. Most importantly, al-Ṣaghānī separates the ground form of the verb from the augmented forms, and lists each verbal pattern with its nominal derivatives. Another major lexicon of his is *al-Takmila wa-l-dhayl wa-l-ṣila* ("The supplement, sequel, and link"), which broadly expands the material of *al-Ṣiḥāḥ*.

The better known *Lisān al-ʿArab*, as Ibn Manẓūr explains in its introduction, brings together five sources, namely, al-Azharī's *al-Tahdhīb*, Ibn Sīda's *al-Muḥkam*, al-Jawharī's *al-Ṣiḥāḥ*, Ibn Barrī's (d. 582/1187) *al-Tanbīh wa-l-īḍāḥ* (known as *al-Ḥawāshī)*, and Ibn al-Athīr's (d. 606/1210) *al-Nihāya fī gharīb al-ḥadīth wa-l-athar*. Although Ibn Manẓūr adds little to the material available in these sources, he normally tries to group together semantically related lexical items within each lemma. In this respect, he relies mainly on Ibn Sīda's arrangement of the material in *al-Muḥkam* (Baalbaki, *Lexicographical tradition*, 390–91)

No less famous than *Lisān al-ʿArab* is al-Fīrūzābādī's (d. 817/1415) *al-Qāmūs al-muḥīṭ*, the name of which stemmed from the Greek *ōkeanós* (ocean). *Qāmūs* subsequently became synonymous with *muʿjam* (lexicon) in general. To achieve his aim of comprehensiveness, al-Fīrūzābādī supplements *al-Ṣiḥāḥ*'s content mainly with material derived from *al-Muḥkam* and *al-ʿUbāb*. The lemmata are systematised and well organised, and several economies—including abbreviations—are employed to keep the lexicon to a manageable length.

The last major lexicon of the *mujannas* type in the premodern tradition, *Tāj al-ʿarūs*, is the most comprehensive of all and, like *Lisān al-ʿArab*, is truly encyclopaedic in scope. But unlike Ibn Manẓūr, who restricts his sources to five, al-Zabīdī uses more than a hundred sources, which he lists in his introduction. The lexicon is based on al-Fīrūzābādī's *al-Qāmūs*, but al-Zabīdī expands it considerably and amends some of the author's errors of explanation, vocalisation, and *taṣḥīf* (erroneous dotting of letters).

Each of the systems of arrangement in *mujannas* lexica exhausted the roots of the language, at least theoretically. On the other hand, the inclusion in the lemmata of all derivatives was a much more arduous task. Various authors had different approaches to this methodological problem, in accordance with their views on issues of correctness and authenticity. Another serious methodological problem was the internal arrangement of the lemmata. The lexica vary considerably in this respect, but even the most organised ones (such as *al-ʿUbāb* and *al-Qāmūs*) do not systematically apply their norms for the arrangement of lexical items within the lemmata. In most lexica the reader often has to read through much of the material to find the sought after word, primarily because of the absence of a rigorous system of arranging the verbal and nominal derivatives, place names, proper nouns, and so forth. Furthermore, towards the end of the fourth/tenth century, as we learn from Ibn Jinnī (d. 392/1002; *al-Khaṣāʾiṣ*, 2:5), it was difficult to find a Bedouin individual who could be a reliable source of linguistic information, and thus the lexicographical corpus was effectively closed. Accordingly, authors of later lexica had to rely on material provided by their predecessors and only sporadically recorded neologisms and the semantic development of lexical items. This notwithstanding, the premodern Arabic lexicographical tradition, throughout its long history of development, represents a major achievement on the part of its philologists and provides contemporary

Arabic speakers and linguists alike with a rich linguistic heritage. Firmly rooted since its inception in the Arabic–Islamic culture and closely related to grammatical study, lexicography—like grammar—was to numerous authors much more than a craft—it was a passion and a powerful expression of cultural belonging.

Bibliography

Sources

Abū l-ʿAmaythal al-Aʿrābī, *Mā ttafaqa lafẓuhu wa-khtalafa maʿnāhu*, ed. Maḥmūd Shākir Saʿīd, Jedda 1991; Abū Misḥal al-Aʿrābī, *al-Nawādir*, ed. ʿIzzat Ḥasan, 2 vols., Damascus 1961; Abū l-Ṭayyib al-Lughawī, *al-Aḍdād fī kalām al-ʿArab*, ed. ʿIzzat Ḥasan, 2 vols., Damascus 1963; Abū ʿUbayd al-Qāsim b. Sallām al-Harawī, *al-Amthāl*, ed. ʿAbd al-Majīd Qaṭāmish, Damascus 1980; Abū ʿUbayd al-Qāsim b. Sallām al-Harawī, *Gharīb al-ḥadīth*, ed. Muḥammad ʿAbd al-Muʿīd Khān, 4 vols., Hyderabad 1964–7; Abū ʿUbayd al-Qāsim b. Sallām al-Harawī, *al-Gharīb al-muṣannaf*, ed. Muḥammad al-Mukhtār al-ʿUbaydī, 3 vols., Carthage 1989–96; Abū Zayd al-Anṣārī, *al-Hamz*, ed. Louis Cheikho, *al-Mashriq* 13 (1910), 696–703, 750–7, 843–9, 907–15; Abū Zayd al-Anṣārī, *al-Nawādir fī l-lugha*, ed. Muḥammad ʿAbd al-Qādir Aḥmad, Beirut 1981; Abū Hilāl al-ʿAskarī, *Jamharat al-amthāl*, ed. Muḥammad Abū l-Faḍl Ibrāhīm and ʿAbd al-Majīd Qaṭāmish, 2 vols., Beirut 1988[2]; al-Aṣmaʿī, *al-Aḍdād*, in August Haffner (ed.), *Thalāthat kutub fī l-aḍdād* (Beirut 1913), 5–70; al-Aṣmaʿī, *Mā khtalafat alfāẓuhu wa-ttafaqat maʿānīhi*, ed. Mājid Ḥasan al-Dhahabī, Damascus 1986; al-Azharī, *Tahdhīb al-lugha*, ed. ʿAbd al-Salām Hārūn et al., 15 vols., Cairo 1964–7; Abū Bishr al-Bandanījī, *al-Taqfiya fī l-lugha*, ed. Khalīl Ibrāhīm al-ʿAṭiyya, Baghdad 1976; Ibn al-Sīd al-Baṭalyawsī, *al-Farq bayna l-ḥurūf al-khamsa*, ed. ʿAlī Zuwayn, Baghdad 1985; al-Bukhārī, *al-Taʾrīkh al-kabīr*, 4 vols., Hyderabad 1360–84/1941–65; al-Mufaḍḍal al-Ḍabbī, *Amthāl al-ʿArab*, ed. Iḥsān ʿAbbās, Beirut 1981; Abū Ḥanīfa al-Dīnawarī, *al-Nabāt*, ed. Bernhard Lewin, Wiesbaden 1974; Isḥāq b. Ibrāhīm al-Fārābī, *Dīwān al-adab*, ed. Aḥmad Mukhtār ʿUmar, 5 vols., Cairo 1974–9; al-Fīrūzābādī, *al-Qāmūs al-muḥīṭ*, 4 vols., Cairo 1952; al-Jawālīqī, *al-Muʿarrab min al-kalām al-aʿjamī ʿalā ḥurūf al-muʿjam*, ed. Aḥmad Muḥammad Shākir, Cairo 1361/1942; al-Jawharī, *al-Ṣiḥāḥ*, ed. Aḥmad ʿAbd al-Ghafūr ʿAṭṭār, 6 vols., Beirut 1979[2]; Abū l-Ḥasan al-Hamadhānī, *al-Alfāẓ al-kitābiyya*, ed. Louis Cheikho, Beirut 1913[9]; ʿAlī b. Muḥammad al-Harawī, *al-Uzhiyya fī ʿilm al-ḥurūf*, ed. ʿAbd al-Muʿīn al-Mallūḥī, Damascus 1982[2]; Abū ʿUbayd Aḥmad b. Muḥammad al-Harawī, *Kitāb al-gharībayn fī l-Qurʾān wa-l-ḥadīth*, ed. Aḥmad Farīdī al-Mazyadī, 6 vols., Mecca 1999; Abū Bakr Ibn al-Anbārī, *al-Aḍdād*, ed. Muḥammad Abū l-Faḍl Ibrāhīm, Kuwait 1960; Ibn al-Athīr, *al-Nihāya fī gharīb al-ḥadīth wa-l-athar*, ed. Ṭāhir Aḥmad al-Zāwī and Maḥmūd Muḥammad al-Ṭanāḥī, 5 vols., Beirut 1979[2]; Ibn Barrī, *al-Tanbīh wa-l-īḍāḥ ʿammā waqaʿa fī l-Ṣiḥāḥ*, ed. Muṣṭafā Ḥijāzī and ʿAbd al-ʿAlīm al-Ṭaḥāwī, 2 vols., Cairo 1980–1; Ibn Durayd, *Jamhrat al-lugha*, ed. Ramzī Munīr Baʿalbakī, 3 vols., Beirut 1987–8; Ibn Fāris, *Muʿjam maqāyīs al-lugha*, ed. ʿAbd al-Salām Muḥammad Hārūn, 6 vols., Cairo 1946–52; Ibn Fāris, *Mujmal al-lugha*, ed. Zuhayr ʿAbd al-Muḥsin Sulṭān, 4 vols., Beirut 1984; Ibn Jinnī, *al-Khaṣāʾiṣ*, ed. Muḥammad ʿAlī al-Najjār, 3 vols., Cairo 1952–6; Ibn Khālawayh, *al-Alifāt*, ed. ʿAlī Ḥusayn al-Bawwāb, Riyad 1982; Ibn Khālawayh, *Laysa fī kalām al-ʿArab*, ed. Aḥmad ʿAbd al-Ghafūr ʿAṭṭār, Beirut 1979[2]; Ibn Makkī al-Ṣiqillī, *Tathqīf al-lisān wa-talqīḥ al-janān*, ed. ʿAbd al-ʿAzīz Maṭar, Cairo 1981; Ibn Manẓūr, *Lisān al-ʿArab*, 15 vols., Beirut 1968; Ibn al-Qaṭṭāʿ, *al-Afʿāl*, 4 vols., Hyderabad 1360–4/1941–5; Ibn Qutayba, *Adab al-kātib*, ed. Muḥammad Muḥyī l-Dīn ʿAbd al-Ḥamīd, Cairo 1963[4]; Ibn Qutayba, *Tafsīr gharīb al-Qurʾān*, ed. al-Sayyid Aḥmad Ṣaqr, Cairo 1958; Ibn al-Shajarī, *Mā ttafaqa lafẓuhu wa-khtalafa maʿnāhu*, ed. ʿAṭiyya Rizq, Stuttgart 1992; Ibn Sīda, *al-Muḥkam wa-l-muḥīṭ al-aʿẓam*, ed. ʿAbd al-Ḥamīd Hindāwī, 11 vols., Beirut 2000;Ibn Sīda, *al-Mukhaṣṣaṣ*, 17 vols., Būlāq 1316–21/1898–1903; Ibn al-Sikkīt, *al-Aḍdād*, in August Haffner (ed.), *Thalāthat kutub fī l-aḍdād* (Beirut 1913), 163–220; Ibn al-Sikkīt, *Iṣlāḥ al-manṭiq*, ed. Aḥmad Muḥammad Shākir and ʿAbd al-Salām Muḥammad Hārūn, Cairo 1956[2]; Ḥamza al-Iṣfahānī, *al-Durra al-fākhira fī l-amthāl al-sāʾira*, ed. ʿAbd al-Majīd Qaṭāmish, 2 vols., Cairo 1972–6; al-Khalīl b. Aḥmad,

Kitāb al-ʿayn, ed. Mahdī al-Makhzūmī and Ibrāhīm al-Sāmarrāʾī, 8 vols., Baghdad 1980–5; al-Kisāʾī, *Mā talḥan fīhi l-ʿāmma*, ed. Ramaḍān ʿAbd al-Tawwāb, Cairo 1982; Kurāʿ al-Naml, *al-Mujarrad fī gharīb kalām al-ʿArab wa-lughātihā*, ed. Muḥammad b. Aḥmad al-ʿUmarī, Cairo 1409–14/1988–93; Aḥmad b. ʿAbd al-Nūr al-Mālaqī, *Raṣf al-mabānī fī sharḥ ḥurūf al-maʿānī*, ed. Aḥmad Muḥammad al-Kharrāṭ, Damascus 1975; al-Maydānī, *Majmaʿ al-amthāl*, ed. Muḥammad Muḥyī l-Dīn ʿAbd al-Ḥamīd, 2 vols., Cairo 1955; al-Qālī, *al-Bāriʿ fī l-lugha*, ed. Hāshim al-Ṭaʿʿān, Baghdad 1975; Quṭrub, *al-Aḍdād*, ed. Hans Kofler, *Islamica* 5 (1931–2), 241–84, 385–461, 493–544; Quṭrub, *al-Muthallathāt*, ed. Riḍā l-Suwaysī, Libya and Tunisia 1978; al-Rummānī, *Maʿānī l-ḥurūf*, ed. ʿAbd al-Fattāḥ Ismāʿīl Shalabī, Cairo n.d.; Muʾarrij al-Sadūsī, *al-Amthāl*, ed. Ramaḍān ʿAbd al-Tawwāb, Beirut 1983; al-Ṣaghānī, *al-Takmila wa-l-dhayl wa-l-ṣila li-Kitāb tāj al-lugha wa-ṣiḥāḥ al-ʿArabiyya*, ed. ʿAbd al-ʿAlīm al-Ṭaḥāwī et al., 6 vols., Cairo 1970–9; al-Ṣaghānī, *al-ʿUbāb al-zākhir wa-l-lubāb al-fākhir*, ed. Muḥammad Ḥasan Āl Yāsīn, 5 vols., Baghdad 1977–87; ed. Fīr Muḥammad Ḥasan, Baghdad 1978; al-Ṣāḥib b. ʿAbbād, *al-Muḥīṭ fī l-lugha*, ed. Muḥammad Ḥasan Āl Yāsīn, 11 vols., Beirut 1994; Saʿīd b. Muḥammad al-Saraqusṭī, *al-Afʿāl*, ed. Ḥusayn Muḥammad Muḥammad Sharaf, 4 vols., Cairo 1975–9; Abū ʿAmr al-Shaybānī, *Kitāb al-jīm*, ed. Ibrāhīm al-Abyārī et al., 4 vols., Cairo 1974–83; Sībawayh, *al-Kitāb*, ed. ʿAbd al-Salām Muḥammad Hārūn, 5 vols., Cairo 1977; al-Suyūṭī, *al-Muzhir fī ʿulūm al-lugha wa-anwāʿihā*, ed. Muḥammad Aḥmad Jād al-Mawlā, ʿAlī Muḥammad al-Bijāwī, and Muḥammad Abū l-Faḍl Ibrāhīm, 2 vols., Cairo n.d.; al-Thaʿālibī, *Fiqh al-lugha*, ed. Louis Cheikho, Beirut 1903; Thaʿlab, *Faṣīḥ Thaʿlab*, ed. Muḥammad ʿAbd al-Munʿim al-Khafājī, Cairo 1949; al-Tibrīzī, *Kanz al-ḥuffāẓ fī Kitāb Tahdhīb al-Alfāẓ*, ed. Louis Cheikho, Beirut 1895; Muḥammad Murtaḍā l-Zabīdī, *Tāj al-ʿarūs min jawāhir al-Qāmūs*, 10 vols., Cairo 1306/1888; al-Zajjājī, *Ḥurūf al-maʿānī*, ed. ʿAlī Tawfīq al-Ḥamad, Beirut 1984; al-Zajjājī, *al-Lāmāt*, ed. Māzin al-Mubārak, Damascus 1969; al-Zamakhsharī, *Asās al-balāgha*, Beirut 1965; al-Zamakhsharī, *Muqaddimat al-adab*, ed. Ioannes Godofredus Wetzstein, Leipzig 1850.

Studies

ʿAbd al-Qādir Abū Sharīfa, Ḥusayn Lāfī, and Dāwūd Ghaṭāsha, *ʿIlm al-dalāla wa-l-muʿjam al-ʿArabī*, Amman 1989; Muḥammad Ḥusayn Āl Yāsīn, *al-Dirāsāt al-lughawiyya ʿind al-ʿArab ilā nihāyat al-qarn al-thālith*, Beirut 1980; Aḥmad Amīn, *Ḍuḥā l-Islām*, 3 vols., Cairo 1938[2]; Aḥmad ʿAbd al-Ghafūr ʿAṭṭār, *al-Ṣiḥāḥ wa-madāris al-muʿjamāt al-ʿArabiyya*, Mecca 1990[4]; Ramzi Baalbaki, The influence of poetry on the rhyme system in lexicography, Evidence from Bandanīǧī's (d. 284/897) *Kitāb al-taqfiya*, *Journal of Arabic Linguistics Tradition* 10 (2012), 20–30; Ramzi Baalbaki, A precursor to the rhyme system in Arabic lexicography. Ibn al-Sikkīt's chapter on *faʿl* and *faʿal* in *Iṣlāḥ al-manṭiq*, *al-Abḥāth* 60–1 (2012–3), 5–14; Ramzi Baalbaki, *The Arabic lexicographical tradition from the 2nd/8th to the 12th/18th century*, Leiden 2014; Thomas Bauer, *Das Planzenbuch des Abū Ḥanīfa ad-Dīnawarī. Inhalt, Aufbau, Quellen*, Wiesbaden 1988; Michael G. Carter, Arabic lexicography, *Religion, learning and science in the ʿAbbasid period, CHAL*, 106–17; ʿAbdallāh Darwīsh, *al-Maʿājim al-ʿArabiyya maʿa ʿināʾ khāṣṣ bi-muʿjam al-ʿAyn lil-Khalīl b. Aḥmad*, Cairo 1956; Werner Diem, *Das* Kitāb al-Ǧīm *des Abū ʿAmr aš-Šaybānī. Ein Beitrag zur arabischen Lexicographie*, Munich 1968; Henri Fleisch,La lexicographie arabe au IVe siècle de l'hégire, *MFOB* 50 (1984), 173–88; Helmut Gätje, Arabische Lexikographie. Ein historischer Überblick, *Historiographia Linguistica* 12 (1985), 105–47; ʿIzzat Ḥusayn Ghurāb, *al-Maʿājim al-ʿArabiyya. Riḥla fī l-judhūr wa-l-taṭawwur wa-l-huwiyya*, Damietta 2005; Ḥilmī Khalīl, *Muqaddima li-dirāsat al-turāth al-muʿjamī al-ʿArabī*, Beirut 1997; John A. Haywood, *Arabic lexicography. Its history and its place in the general history of lexicography*, Leiden 1965; Vivien Law, Indian influence on early Arab phonetics—or coincidence? *Studies in the History of Arabic Grammar II. Proceedings of the 2nd Symposium on the History of Arabic Grammar, Nijmegen, 27 April–1 May 1987*, ed. Michael G. Carter and Kees Versteegh (Amsterdam 1990), 215–27; William Marçais, *Articles et conférences*, Paris 1961; ʿAlī Ḥilmī Mūsā, Dirāsa tiqniyya muqārana li-maʿājim al-Ṣiḥāḥ wa-Lisān al-ʿArab wa-Tāj al-ʿarūs, *Majallat al-Muʿjamiyya* 5/6 (1989–90), 147–58; Ḥusayn Naṣṣār, *al-Muʿjam al-ʿArabī. Nashʾatuhu wa-taṭawwuruhu*, 2 vols., Cairo 1968[2]; Ḥusayn Naṣṣār, *Maʿājim ʿalā l-mawḍūʿāt*, Kuwait 1985; Riyāḍ Zakī Qāsim, *al-Muʿjam al-ʿArabī. Buḥūth fī l-mādda wa-l-manhaj wa-l-taṭbīq*, Beirut 1987; Solomon I. Sara, The classical Arabic lexicographical tradition, in Jonathan Owens (ed.), *The Oxford handbook of Arabic linguistics* (Oxford 2013), 520–38; Gregor Schoeler, Who is the author of the Kitāb al-ʿayn? in James E. Montgomery (ed.), *The oral and the written in early Islam* (London and New York 2006), 142–63; Tilman Seidensticker, Die einheimische arabische Lexikographie. Ein Überblick, in Norbert Nebes (ed.), *Neue Beiträge zur Semitistik* (Wiesbaden 2002), 147–66; *GAS*, 8, *Lexicographie bis ca. 430 H.*; Reinhard Weipert, *Classical Arabic philology & poetry. A bibliographical handbook of important editions from 1960 to 2000*, Leiden 2002; Stefan Wild, *Das* Kitāb al-ʿAin *und die arabische Lexikographie*, Wiesbaden 1965.

Ramzi Baalbaki

Libraries of Arabic and Persian texts in late imperial China

Libraries of Arabic and Persian texts in late imperial China owed their existence to the mobility of people across Asia. Changes in China's engagement with Arabic and Persian texts were shaped by the socio-political environment and attitudes in China towards foreign knowledge in general and knowledge from the Islamicate world in particular.

The earliest application of the Chinese term Hui (translated here as "Arabo-Persian") appears to have been to the Uyghur population, but the meaning changed in the early centuries of the second millennium to encompass the cultural, linguistic, religious, and geographical features of the Islamicate world. When used to refer to written texts, the term denoted both Arabic and Persian (and from the twelfth/eighteenth century onwards also Eastern Turki) texts in China.

China's engagement with Arabic and Persian texts has a long history. As an early example, Ibn al-Nadīm's *Kitāb al-fihrist* (376/987) mentions a Chinese student of Muḥammad b. Zakariyā al-Rāzī (d. 313/925 or 323/935) who wished to copy Galen's sixteen-volume work, presumably in its Arabic translation, in order to take it back to China after completing his studies.

The Mongol conquest of China, during the thirteenth century, and the sweeping movements of people, texts, and artefacts across the vast Mongol empire were significant in China's importation of Arabic and Persian texts. The Mongol Yuan dynasty (r. China 1279–1368) established imperial bureaus to apply Arabo-Persian knowledge in fields such as astronomy and medicine. These imperial bureaus housed libraries of relevant Arabic and Persian texts. A list of Arabic books (and perhaps also their Persian translations) that were housed in the northern branch of the imperial astronomical observatory in Xanadu dates to the tenth year of the Zhiyuan reign (672/1273). It gives the transliterated titles—represented phonetically by Chinese characters—and their Chinese translations of twenty-two works, including Arabic translations of Euclid's (d. 286 B.C.E.) *Elements*, Ptolemy's (d. c.168 C.E.) *Almagest*, and ʿAbd al-Raḥmān al-Ṣūfī's (d. 376/986) *Ṣuwar al-kawākib* (Tasaka, 1546–7; Ma Jian, 194; Yang and Yu, 179–81).

In 769/1368, the troops of Zhu Yuanzhang, a rebel leader who fought the Yuan and eventually united China under the Ming dynasty (r. 1368–1644), took over the Yuan capital Dadu (present-day Beijing). The imperial libraries of the Yuan were then transferred to the newly established Ming capital, Nanjing. Amongst these books were reportedly hundreds of Arabic and Persian works (Weil, Fourteenth-century transformation). While the fate of most Arabic and Persian texts held in the Ming imperial repositories is unclear, several texts on astronomy, calendar-making, and pharmaceuticals were translated into Chinese between the late fourteenth and early fifteenth centuries. Many of these translations included the term Huihui (Arabo-Persian, synonymous with "Hui") in their titles, in order to indicate their foreign sources. From the mid-fifteenth century onwards, the use of Arabic and Persian texts by imperial bureaus decreased dramatically.

Arabic and Persian texts were not only held by imperial libraries but circulated amongst Chinese Muslims and were found in private libraries throughout China. A movement—often attributed to Hu Dengzhou (d. c.1005/1597), a Muslim savant from Shaanxi province in northwestern China—that advocated a systematic study of Arabic and Persian texts, mainly on Arabic grammar, logic, Islamic theology, and jurisprudence, emerged during the mid-sixteenth century amongst Chinese Muslims in northwestern China. By the early seventeenth century it had spread through Ming China. The movement promoted the search for Arabic and Persian texts in Chinese private libraries, the importation of texts from Islamic scholarly centres in other parts of Asia, and the copying and study of these texts (Ben-Dor Benite; Weil, Islamicated China). Translations into Chinese of Arabic and Persian works, prepared outside the court by local savants, began in the mid-seventeenth century, making them accessible to readers who did not command the source languages. Liu Zhi (d. c.1142/1730), a prominent Chinese Muslim scholar who translated several Persian texts into Chinese and published commentaries on others, described his visits to private libraries in China and the Arabic and Persian texts he discovered in them. Together with an extensive list of Arabic and Persian sources he used for his publications, Liu Zhi's descriptions bring to light the richness of Arabo-Persian repositories during the seventeenth and eighteenth centuries.

Analyses of the Arabic and Persian texts that circulated in China during the seventeenth and eighteenth centuries suggest that the total corpus included almost equal numbers of works in Arabic and Persian, with a concentration on Arabic and Persian grammar—such as Chang Zhimei's *Hawā-i minhāj* (also known as *Minhāj al-ṭalab*), a work on Persian grammar and morphology, originally composed in China—and Arabic translation of texts on logic—such as the Isagog, al-Shamsiyya, or unidentified works titled *Man-tui-ge* (滿退格, *Manṭiq*)—as well as Islamic theology, Ḥanafī jurisprudence, and the natural sciences (Morimoto; Takashi et al.; Weil, Islamicated China). By the mid-nineteenth century, intensified contacts with the Arabic-speaking world resulted in a gradual increase in the number of Arabic texts circulating in China, which came to outnumber Persian texts (Peterson).

Bibliography

For more information on Arabic and Persian texts circulating in China during the Ming and Qing periods, see Morimoto, Takashi et al., and Weil, Islamicated China. On Chinese translations of Arabic and Persian texts, see Leslie and Murata. On surveys of Arabic and Persian texts in mosques and libraries in present-day China, see Afshār, 479–93, 568–74; al-ʿAlawī; Bakhtyar; Blodget, xxi–xxii; d'Ollone; Dānishpazhūh; and Sharīʿat.

Studies

Īraj Afshār, Jung-i Chīnī yā safīna-i "Pūsī" (Īlānī), *Āyande* 8/8 (1361sh/1982), 479–93, and 8/9 (1361sh/1982), 568–74; Hādī al-ʿAlawī, al-Makhṭūṭāt al-ʿArabiyya fī jāmiʿ Bikīn, *Majallat Majmaʿ al-Lugha al-ʿArabiyya bi-Dimashq* 53/2 (1978), 474–81; Mozafar Bakhtyar, China, in Geoffrey Roper (ed.), *World survey of Islamic manuscripts* (London 1994), 1:63–116; Zvi Ben-Dor Benite, *The dao of Muhammad. A cultural history of Chinese Muslims in late imperial China*, Cambridge MA 2005; Henry Blodget, Arabs in Peking. From a letter of Rev. Henry Blodget to Prof. H. A. Newton of New Haven, dated Peking, Feb 19, 1863, *JAOS* 8 (1866), xxi–xxii; Lucien Bouvat, La littérature musulmane en Chine, pt. 1, *RMM* 3 (1908), 510–21; Philibert Dabry de Thiersant, *Le mahométisme en Chine et dans le Turkestan orientale*, Paris 1878; Muḥammad Taqī Dānishpazhūh, Nigāhī-yi guẓarā bih payvandfarhangī-i Īrān va Chīn, *Nuskhahā-yi Khaṭṭī* 11–12 (1362/1983), 1006–26; Morimoto Kazuo, Kaimin ga mochita arabia bun, perusha bun tenkyo. 17–18 seiki kōtaiki kannanshō no hibun no kentō kara ("The Arabic and Persian sources used by the Hui people. An examination of a stele from Henan province dated to the transitional period between the 17th and 18th centuries"), *Slavic Eurasia Papers* 5 (2012), 149–61; Tasaka Kōdō, *Chūgoku ni okeru kaikyō no denrai to sono kōtsū* ("The transmission of Islam to China and its routes"), Tokyo 1964; Takashi Kuroiwa, Nakanishi Tatsuya, and Morimoto Kazuo, 17–18 seki kōtaiki no chūgoku furuyokiha isurāmu. Kaifonshusenchin no arabia go hibun no kentō kara ("A study of China's Old Sect of Islam in the transitional period of the 17th and 18th centuries from the Kaifeng and Zhuxianzhen inscriptions"), *Memoirs of the Institute for Oriental Culture* 162 (2012), 223–88; Donald D. Leslie, *Islamic literature in Chinese*, Canberra 1981; Ma Jian, Yuan mishujian zhi *Huihui shuji* shiji ("Interpreting *The list of Islamic books* in Yuan's annal of the imperial archive"), *Guangming Ribao* (1955), 193–8; Henri d'Ollone et al., *Recherches sur les musulmans chinois*, Paris 1911; Kristian Petersen, Shifts in Sino-Islamic discourse. Modelling religious authority through language and travel, *Modern Asian Studies* 48 (2014), 340–69; Murata Sachiko, *Chinese gleams of Sufi light. Wang Tai-Yü's "Great learning of the pure and real" and Liu Chih's "Displaying the concealment of the real realm,"* Albany 2000; Muḥammad Javād Sharīʿat, The library of the Tung-hsi mosque at Peking, *Asian Affairs* 11 (1980), 68–70; Dror Weil, The fourteenth-century transformation in China's reception of Arabo-Persian astronomy, in Patrick Manning and Abigail Owen (eds.), *Knowledge in translation. Global patterns of scientific exchange, 1000–1800 CE* (Pittsburg 2018), 262–74; Dror Weil, Islamicated China. China's participation in the Islamicate book culture during the seventeenth and eighteenth centuries, in Sabine Schmidtke (ed.), *Histories of books in the Islamicate world*, in *Intellectual History of the Islamicate World* 4 (2016), 36–60; Yang Huaizhong and Yu Zhen'gui, *Yisilan yu zhongguo wen hua* ("Islam and Chinese culture"), Yinchuan 1995.

Dror Weil

Literacy, in Arabic and Persian, in late imperial China

Literacy in **Arabic and Persian** became more common **in late imperial China**, specifically during the Ming and Qing periods (roughly, from the fourteenth to the twentieth century). Three reasons for this development can be identified. First, the Chinese court used Arabic and Persian for diplomacy and desired access to scientific knowledge originating from the Islamicate world. Second, religious communities, most notably Muslims and Jews, persisted in their use of Arabic and Persian (and their related scripts and variants). Third, from the mid-sixteenth century onwards, local Chinese savants, many of whom were either practising Muslims or of Muslim descent, were interested in a deeper understanding of Arabic and Persian philosophical and religious texts.

Those Chinese people who either professed the Islamic religion or who had Muslim ancestry were often referred to as *"huihui,"* a term also used for the entire Muslim population of western and central

China. Both Arabic and Persian (and, by the late-eighteenth century, also Eastern Turki) were collectively referred to in Chinese sources during much of China's late imperial period as *"huiwen,"* that is, the written language of the *huihui*.

Literacy in Arabic was principally used for accessing the Qurʾān, Islamic law, and Arabic philology whereas literacy in Persian granted access to Islamic theology and natural philosophy. Increased contact with the Middle East during the second half of the nineteenth century resulted in a greater number of Arabic and Persian texts being circulated in China.

In the Ming and Qing courts, speakers of Persian (and, to a lesser degree, Arabic) served a number of functions. They were instrumental in the translation of Persian (and possibly also Arabic) texts on astronomy, astrology, and medicine for the benefit of the relevant Chinese governmental bureaus. A notable translation project of Persian texts was launched by the first Ming emperor in the 1380s. Among the texts translated was *al-Madkhal fī ṣināʿat aḥkām al-nujūm* ("Introduction to astrology") by Kūshyār b. Labbān (fl. c.400/1010) (Yano; Weil, The fourteenth-century transformation). Training in Persian was carried out in the Bureau of Translators *(huihui guan)*, mainly for the purpose of diplomatic correspondence with the rulers of the Persianate world. A number of Chinese-Persian lexicons, prepared for the training of translators at the Arabo-Persian division of the Bureau of Translators have survived (Honda; Liu). These lexicons organise the Persian vocabulary in thematic categories and present it in Arabic script with an accompanying Chinese transliteration. Bilingual compilations from the Arabo-Persian division shed light on the methodologies of translation between Persian and Chinese by these official translators.

Mosque schools thoughout China provided basic training in recitation of the Qurʾān and the daily prayers for which they used a number of manuals in Persian and Arabic. Graduates of these schools received the titles *ahong* (from the Persian *ākhund*) and *manla* (from the Persian *mullā*) to denote their level of literacy in religious texts. Similarly, basic training in Judeo-Persian (in addition to Hebrew) seems to have taken place in the Kaifeng synagogue, as indicated by available Judeo-Persian texts (Leslie, *The survival*).

By the mid-sixteenth century, Hu Dengzhou (1522–97), a Chinese Muslim from Shaanxi province, founded an education network that aimed to improve traditional mosque education by promoting a more comprehensive study of Arabic and Persian and texts written in these languages (Ben-Dor Benite; Weil, Islamicated China). Hu and his disciples drafted curricula for the study of language and literature, making use of the Arabic and Persian texts that circulated in China at the time. The curricula varied from master to master, and differed in the selection of texts. Generally, the language training included the study of Arabic and Persian grammar (divided into morphology (*ṣarf*) and syntax (*naḥw*)), logic *(manṭiq)*, and rhetoric *(balāgha)*. A long list of Arabic and Persian textbooks were used in these schools, including the *Miṣbāḥ* ("The lamp on grammar") of Muṭarrizī (d. 610/1213), the *Ḍawʾ al-miṣbāḥ* ("The lamp of light") of Isfarāyīnī (d. 610/1213), the *ʿAwāmil* ("Governing entities") of Jurjānī (d. 474/1081), the *al-Fawāʾid al-ḍiyāʾiyya bi-sharḥ al-kāfiyya* ("The enlightening benefits in the commenting on *al-Kāfiyya*") of ʿAbd al-Raḥmān Jāmī (d. 898/1492), the

Miftāḥ al-ʿulūm ("Key to the sciences") of al-Sakkākī (d. 626/1229), and the *Taṣrīf al-Zanjānī* ("al-Zanjānī's treatise on the inflection of Arabic verbs") of ʿIzz al-Dīn al-Zanjānī (fl. 655/1257) (Weil, Appendix 2). A number of Arabic and Persian dictionaries and lexicons were used as well, including the *al-Ṣaḥḥāḥ* of al-Jawharī (d. 393/1002) and the *Kitāb muqaddimat al-adab* of al-Zamakhsharī (d. 538/1143). Chang Zhimei, a teacher in a Shandong branch of the network, who was known also by his Arabic name Muḥammad b. al-Ḥakīm al-Zināmī al-Shandūnī al-Ṣīnī (fl. early seventeenth century), compiled a Persian grammar and dictionary with the title *Minhāj al-ṭalab* (Kauz). Interestingly, in his introduction to the work, Chang goes against a tendency to privilege Arabic learning over Persian in the other schools of the network. Later members of this network produced direct and paraphrased translations of selected works, mainly from Persian into Chinese (Murata; Petersen).

In addition to the use of Arabic and Persian, some Chinese Muslims developed original writing systems that used the Arabic script to write a mixture of Chinese and Arabo-Persian vernacular discourse. This system became to be known as *Xiaoer jing*. Evidence for the use of this system in Muslim communities in northern and north-western China dates back to the late eighteenth century.

Bibliography

For more information on Arabic and Persian texts circulating in China during the Ming and Qing periods, see Leslie and Wassel, Arabic and Persian sources; Morimoto, Kaimin ga mochita arabia bun; Takashi et al., 17–18 seki kōtaiki no chūgoku furuyokiha isurāmu; Weil, Islamicated China; Weil, *The vicissitudes*. On Chinese translations of Arabic and Persian texts, see Leslie, *Islamic literature* and Murata, *Chinese gleams*. On surveys of Arabic and Persian texts in contemporary mosques and libraries in China, see Afshār, Jung-i Chīnī, 479–93, 568–74; al-ʿAlawī, al-Makhṭūṭāt; Bakhtyar, China; Blodget, Arabs in Peking, xxi–xxii; D'Ollone, *Recherches*; Dānishpazhūh, Nigāhī; and Sharīʿat, Nusakh. On Persian dictionaries in China, see Kauz, Chang Zhimei; Tin, *Farhang-i Fārsī*; ʿĀbidīnī, *Minhāj al-ṭalab*. On the history of *Xiaoer jing*, see Bausani, Un caso estremo; Feng, "Xiaoerjin" chutan.

Studies

Īraj Afshār, Jung-i Chīnī yā safīna-i 'Pūsī' (Īlānī), *Āyande* 8/8 (1361sh/1982), 479–93 and 8/9 (1361sh/1982), 568–74; Abū Ṭālib Mīr ʿĀbidīnī (ed.), *Minhāj al-ṭalab*, Tehran 1388sh/2009; Hādī al-ʿAlawī, al-Makhṭūṭāt al-ʿArabiyya fī jāmiʿ Bikīn, *Majallat Majmaʿ al-Lugha al-ʿArabiyya bi-Dimashq* 53/2 (1978), 474–81; Mozafar Bakhtyar, China, in G. Roper (ed.), *World survey of Islamic manuscripts* (London 1994), 1:63–116; Zvi Ben-Dor Benite, *The dao of Muhammad*, Cambridge MA 2005; Henri Blodget, Arabs in Peking. From a Letter of Rev. Henry Blodget to Prof. H. A. Newton of New Haven, dated Peking, Feb 19, 1863, communicated with remarks and explanations by the president, *JAOS* 8 (1866), xxi–xxii; Lucien Bouvat, La littérature musulmane en Chine (i), *Revue du Monde Musulman* 3 (March 1908), 510–21; Alessandro Bausani, Un caso estremo di diffusione della scrittura Araba. II, "Sino-Arabo", *OM* 48 (1968), 857–76; Henri D'Ollone et al., *Recherches sur les musulmans chinois*, Paris 1911; Claude-Philibert Dabry de Thiersant, *Le Mahométisme en Chine et dans le Turkestan oriental*, Paris 1878; Muḥammad Taqī Dānishpazhūh, Nigāhī-yi gudharā bih payvand farhangī-yi Īrān va-Chīn, *Nuskhahā-yi khaṭṭī* 11–12 (1362sh/1983), 1006–26; Feng Zenglie, "Xiaoerjin" chutan—jieshao yizhong alabo zimu de hanyu pinyin wenzi, *Alabo Shijie* 1 (1982), 37–47; Honda Minobu, "Kaikaikan yakugo" ni tsuite, *Hokkaidō daigaku bungakubu kiyō* 11 (Feb 1963), 150–224; Ralph Kauz, Chang Zhimei und der Islam in Shandong im 17. Jahrhundert. Akkulturation oder Abgrenzung? Zur Geschichte einer persischen Grammatik, *Saeculum* 60/1 (2010), 91–113; Donald D. Leslie, *Islamic literature in Chinese*, Canberra 1981; Donald D. Leslie, *The survival of the Chinese Jews. The Jewish community of Kaifeng*, Leiden 1972; Donald D. Leslie and Mohamed Wassel, Arabic and Persian sources used by Liu Chih, *CAJ* 26/1–2 (1982), 78–104; Liu Yingsheng, *"Huihuiguan zazi" yu "huihuiguan yiyu" yanjiu*, Beijing 2008; Morimoto Kazuo, Kaimin ga mochita arabia bun, perusha bun tenkyo—17–18 seiki kōtaiki kannanshō no hibun no kentō kara, *Chūgoku yūrashya genkyū wo hiraku—Hokkaidō chūō yūrashya genkyūkai dai 100kai kinen* (2012), 149–6; Sachiko Murata, *Chinese gleams of Sufi light. Wang Tai-Yü's great learning of the Pure and Real and Liu Chih's displaying the concealment of the Real Realm*, Albany 2000; Kristian Petersen, Shifts in Sino-Islamic discourse. Modelling religious authority through language and travel, *Modern Asian Studies* 48 (2014), 340–69; Takashi Kuroiwa, Nakanishi Tatsuya, and Morimoto Kazuo, 17–18 seki kōtaiki no chūgoku furuyokiha isurāmu. Kaifon—shusenchin no arabia go hibun no kentō kara, *Memoirs of the Institute for Oriental Culture* 162 (2012), 223–88; Tasaka Kōdō, *Chūgoku ni okeru kaikyō no denrai to sono kōtsū*, Tokyo 1964; Tin Huī Jū [Teng Huizhu] (ed.), *Farhang-i Fārsī. Bar asās-i nushkhahā-yi khaṭṭī mawjūd dar Chīn*, Tehran 1374sh/1995; Muḥammad Javād Sharīʿat, Nusakh khaṭṭī dar Chīn, *Rāhnāmah-i kitāb* 20/8 (1356sh/1977), 584–9; Muḥammad Javād Sharīʿat, The library of the Tung-hsi Mosque at Peking, *Asian Affairs* 11 (1980), 68–70; Dror Weil, Islamicated China. China's participation in the Islamicate book culture during the seventeenth and eighteenth centuries, in Sabine Schmidtke (ed.), *Histories of books in the Islamicate world. Intellectual history of the Islamicate world*, vol. 4 (Leiden 2016), 36–60; Dror Weil, The fourteenth-century transformation in China's reception of Arabo-Persian astronomy, in Patrick Manning and Abigail Owen (ed.), *Knowledge in translation. Global patterns of scientific exchange, 1000–1800 CE* (Pittsburg 2018), 262–74; Dror Weil, *The vicissitudes of late imperial China's accommodation of Arabo-Persian knowledge of the natural world*, 16th–18th centuries, Ph.D. diss., Princeton University 2016; Yang Huaizhong and Yu Zhen'gui, *Yisilan yu zhongguo wenhua*, Yinchuan 1995; Michio Yano, *Kūshyār Ibn Labbān's introduction to astrology*, Tokyo 1997.

Dror Weil

Literary criticism, Urdu

The beginning of **literary criticism** (in the modern sense) in **Urdu** *(tanqīd)* is usually attributed to two authors of the late nineteenth century, Mawlānā Muḥammad Ḥusayn Āzād (d. 1910) and Alṭāf Ḥusayn Ḥālī (d. 1914). Literary criticism did, however, exist in Urdu before the colonial encounter.

1. The prehistory of modern Urdu criticism

The earliest sources of critical ideas/criteria are brief asides in verses and prefaces to collections of poetry. Thus, Fārūqī regards Amīr Khusraw (d. 725/1325)—although he wrote predominantly in Persian—as a founder of theoretical writing on poetics, who fused Arabic, Persian, and Sanskrit elements and exerted a lasting influence on later poets in both Persian and Urdu (Faruqi, 826–7). He considers the distinction between theme *(maḍmūn)* and meaning *(maʿnī)* drawn by the Dakhinī poet Nuṣratī Bījāpūrī (d. 1085/1674) as a major achievement of literary theory in Urdu (Fārūqī, 828) and sees a steady expansion of literary theory from Valī (d. 1119?/1707?) to Shaykh Nāsikh (d. 1838) (Dakhinī is an archaic variety of Urdu that flourished as a literary language in the Deccan sultanates from the ninth/fifteenth century to the eleventh/seventeenth).

Pronouncements in criticism and ideas on Urdu poetics are abundant in the *tadhkiras* (annotated anthologies of poetry) written in Persian and later also in Urdu throughout the eighteenth and nineteenth centuries. Although these utterances had not been collected in any systematic compendium, they served as important source material for later writers. Initially, most of these *tadhkiras* were written in Persian and arranged alphabetically by the first letter of the poets' names. Important *tadhkiras* written by Urdu poets are Mīr Taqī Mīr's (d. 1810) *Nikāt al-shuʿarā* ("Subtle points of the poets," 1165/1752), Khᵛāja Khān b. Turktāz Khān "Ḥamīd" Awrangābādī's *Gulshan-i guftār* ("The rose garden of language," 1165/1752), Fatḥ ʿAlī al-Ḥusaynī Gardīzī's *Tadhkira-yi rīkhta gūyāṃ* ("Biographies of *rīkhta* (the former Persian designation of Urdu, lit., mixed, Urdu *rekhta*) authors," 1165/1752), Qāʾim Chāndpūrī's (d. 1208/1793–4) *Makhzan-i nikāt* ("The storehouse of subtleties," 1167/1754), and Shafīq Lachmī Narāyan Awrangābādī's (d. 1808) *Chamanistān-i shuʿarā* ("Poets' garden," 1175/1761–2). *Makhzan-i nikāt* was claimed by its author to be the first *tadhkira* on Urdu poets, and, judging by its preface, he had indeed begun to write it in 1157/1744. It was the first to attempt a periodisation of poets (Fatiḥpūrī, 129). Some of the critical concepts that evolved in the pre-modern period were *īhām* (double entendre, punning), already a term widely used in classical Persian criticism, *ravānī* (fluidity, melodious flow), *maḍmūn āfirīnī* (creation of themes), and *maʿnī āfirīnī* (creation of meaning).

Criticism and theoretical pronouncements were found also in the prefaces or introductions of poets, such as that of Shāh "Ḥātim" (d. 1197/1783) to his *Dīvān-zāda* (selections from his *dīvān*, 1168/1755), which, however, dealt predominantly with the correct use of language.

Institutions that served as vehicles for literary criticism were the often highly competitive *mushāʿiras* (ritualised poetry readings) and the relationship between a poetic mentor *(ustād)* and his pupil *(shāgird)*, a special feature of Urdu literary culture. Mirzā Asadallāh Khān Ghālib's (d. 1869) letters provide interesting insights into how the *ustād* taught his *shāgird* the rules and criteria of poetics and how he suggested improvements *(iṣlāḥ)*.

2. The colonial challenge

A paradigmatic shift occurred in the last decades of the nineteenth century, under the influence of the political and social circumstances created by colonial rule. These developments are closely linked to the Aligarh Movement—an educational-reform movement launched by the modernist socio-religious reformer Sayyid Aḥmad Khān (d. 1898), who, by 1872, called for a new type of "natural poetry"—and a new type of *mushāʿira* initiated by Colonel William Rice Morland Holroyd (d. 1913) at a meeting of the Anjuman-i Panjāb (Panjāb Society) in Lahore in 1874, after Muḥammad Ḥusayn Āzād (d. 1910) had delivered his famous lecture on the reform of Urdu poetry. Sayyid Aḥmad Khān congratulated him and encouraged him in a letter to get even closer to "nature" (the English word used in the Urdu letter), to discard anything fanciful and unreal, which was an attack particularly on the ghazal, and to reproduce ideas from English poetry in Urdu.

In his seminal *Āb-i ḥayāt* ("The water of life," 1880), Āzād attempted to present a chronological history of Urdu literature on modern lines, but, in the discussion of the poetry mentioned in this selective canon, he still followed traditional criteria.

The Urdu poet and writer Alṭāf Ḥusayn Ḥālī (d. 1914) was another follower of Sayyid Aḥmad Khān. His *Muqaddama-yi shiʿr-u shāʿirī* ("Introduction to verse and poetry," 1893) was intended as a kind of guide book to poetry in the new context, but his study of Ghālib and his poetry, *Yādgār-i Ghālib* ("A memoir of Ghālib," 1897), was virtually free of references to Western authors and concepts, and his *Muqaddama* contained numerous passages on "Eastern" poetics that were largely ignored by later critics.

3. Progressives and modernists

Further change came with the Progressive Writers' Association (PWA, Anjuman Taraqqī Pasand Muṣannifīn), which developed into the most influential literary movement from the late 1930s to the late 1940s. Under changed historical and geopolitical circumstances, young writers, some of whom had studied in England and were influenced by communist ideas as well as by psychoanalysis and modernist English writing, continued the utilitarian approach to literature initiated by the Aligarh Movement but with a new agenda. The *ghazal* again came under fierce attack as a decadent form born of feudalism, while the critics of this school advocated realism with a clear element of social criticism. Towards 1949 they developed extreme and rigid prescriptions for progressive literature that alienated and excluded several great writers of the time, such as Saʿādat Ḥasan Mant'o (d. 1955), N. M. Rāshid (d. 1975) and "Mīrājī" (Thanāʾallāh Ďār, d. 1949).

There has been a lengthy debate about the relationship between the PWA and the Ḥalqa-yi Arbāb-i Dhawq (lit., circle of persons of taste), which has often been construed as one of opposition and even enmity. In its beginnings in 1939, the Ḥalqa was simply a forum for the discussion of literary works, mainly short stories but also poetry. Its sessions were attended by writers of diverse persuasions, and there were close friendships between authors from the two camps. Thus, Muḥammad Ḥasan ʿAskarī (d. 1978), one of the strongest critics of progressivism in later years, in the early 1940s strongly defended many young poets against criticism by traditionalists and edited a collection of poems that included many prominent progressives. ʿAskarī, who knew French, discussed Rimbaud's and Baudelaire's poetry in great detail in his Urdu essays and advocated a self-confident appropriation of influences from other literatures in all languages of the world. The main distinction, however, was the stress on the aesthetic, formal aspects of literature in ʿAskarī's writing and in the Ḥalqa, an aspect that was often deliberately downplayed in critical pronouncements by progressives.

An innovation introduced by Mīrājī in the Ḥalqa in its first session and one which continues to this day is *majlisī tanqīd* (criticism in a gathering, collective criticism). The author presented his poem, short story, or extract from a longer text, and this was commented upon immediately by the audience, thus establishing the direct interaction between author and recipient that was also typical of the classical *mushāʿira*. This practice has its own pitfalls and limitations, and the audience's reaction was limited initially to superficial impressions and praise. Inspired by trends in Western criticism, however, it put the main stress on the text rather than the author. Of seminal importance in this regard are the critical writings of Mīrājī who, probably inspired by the English educator, literary critic, and rhetorician Ivor Armstrong Richards (d. 1979), initiated the close analytical reading of contemporary Urdu poetry, including psychological criticism, and established these principles in the meetings of the Ḥalqa. Often, however, he also included the social context of literary production and the author's personality/biography in his interpretations. As a key to a better understanding of his own and some contemporaries' unfamiliar poetic practice, he formulated a new poetics for modern Urdu poetry, as well as highlighting innovative elements in classical poetry. In his applied criticism he failed to hint at the creation of multiple meanings in poetry and to distinguish between the poet and the lyrical self/persona of the poem.

The controversy between the aestheticism and subjectivity/individualism of the Ḥalqa and the ideological and formal regimentation propagated by the progressives broke out in Pakistan in full force after Partition in 1947 and led to the dwindling influence of the PWA in India, particularly after its conference of 1949. Leaving behind the dogmatic tendencies of this period, the progressive movement produced some eminent literary critics, amongst them the poets ʿAlī Sardār Jaʿfrī (d. 2000), Iḥtishām Ḥusayn (d. 1972), and the critic, novelist, and playwright Muḥammad Ḥasan (d. 2010) in India, and Muḥammad ʿAlī Ṣiddīqī (d. 2013) in Pakistan.

4. Urdu criticism since 1947

After 1947 the discussion of cultural identity in Pakistan acquired central importance. While ʿAskarī stressed the Islamic nature of Urdu literature in Pakistan, followed by critics such as Salīm Aḥmad (d. 1983), Vazīr Āghā (d. 2010) dealt in depth with the Indic element in Urdu poetry. Influenced also by New Criticism, he based his interpretations of Urdu poetry on close reading but allowed for contextualisation.

Modern trends in poetry and the short story since the late 1950s inspired heated debates on modernism *(jadīdiyat)* in Urdu literature, which was defined by most critics as based exclusively on the author's individual experience and thus as opposed to progressivism. These debates were occasionally influenced by major Western schools of thought—such as Marxism, psychoanalysis, existentialism, structuralism, logical positivism, post-structuralism, New Criticism, reader-response criticism, deconstruction, and feminist criticism—but Urdu criticism often transformed such theories according to the historical and cultural context and developed its own concepts and trajectories of literary schools and traditions, for instance in a critical appraisal of the *dāstān* (prose romance) and *ghazal* tradition and reconstruction of their poetics. Thus Gyān Chand Jayn (d. 2007), Vaqār ʿAẓīm (d. 1976), and others published several studies on the history of the Urdu *dāstān* in the 1960s. In 1999 Shams al-Raḥmān Fārūqī (b. 1935), in his discussion of the *dāstān*—based on his reading of the entire forty-six volumes of the *Dāstān-i Amīr Ḥamza*, a legendary narrative of the exploits of an uncle of the prophet Muḥammad, of which the Mughal emperor Akbar (r. 963–1014/1556–1605) commissioned an enormous illustrated manuscript in Persian in about 969/1562—presented a theoretical basis for its analysis on modern lines (narratology, reader-response critique, Bakhtin's heteroglossia, and dialogicity) but, nevertheless, on its own cultural terms. Equally important are his reconstruction of classical Urdu poetics in the light of modern theory in his study of the classical Urdu poet Mīr Taqī Mīr and of Gopī Chand Nārang's (b. 1931, Indian) new reading of Ghālib.

Postcolonial approaches were reinforced after the military strikes of the

United States following 9/11 and the destabilisation resulting from these military adventures. These events not only turned into subjects of creative literature but also sharpened the sense of the postcolonial predicament and triggered a reassessment of the colonial intervention in Urdu literature and literary criticism. At the same time, critics have begun to analyse the effect of the pervasive influence of modern electronic media on Urdu writers. Another new trend is feminist criticism, mostly written by well known Pakistani women poets and writers, such as Fahmīda Riaḍ (d. 2018), Kishvar Nāhīd (b. 1940), Zāhida Ḥinā (b. 1946), Adhrā ʿAbbās (b. 1950), and Fāṭima Ḥasan (b. 1953), some of it later by Riaḍ also self-styled as feminist deconstruction.

In Urdu, a terminological distinction is drawn between criticism *(tanqīd)* and research *(taḥqīq)*, which comprises the search for texts, critical editions of works of the past, and literary historiography. While many authors combine the two, Jamīl Jālibī (b. 1929, Pakistan) is particularly noteworthy in historiography. Amongst the younger generation, Nāṣir Abbās Nayyar (b. 1965, Pakistan) has published books and articles on the history of Urdu criticism, its theoretical foundations, the application of modern theories in Urdu, and critical studies of Urdu authors.

Bibliography

Sources

Muḥammad Ḥasan ʿAskarī, *Majmūʿa*, Lahore 1994; Muḥammad Ḥusayn Āzād, *Āb-i ḥayāt*, Lahore 1907, facs. Lucknow 1993[3], trans. and ed. Frances Pritchett with Shamsur Rahman Faruqi, *Āb-e ḥayāt. Shaping the canon of Urdu poetry*, New Delhi 2001; Shams al-Raḥmān Fārūqī, *Shiʿr-i shūr angīz*, 4 vols., New Delhi 1990–4; Shams al-Raḥmān Fārūqī, *Saḥirī, shāhī, ṣāḥib qirānī. Dāstān-i Amīr Ḥamza kā muṭāliʿa*, vol. 1, *Naẓrī mabāḥith*, New Delhi 1999; Alṭāf Ḥusayn Ḥālī, *Muqaddama-yi shiʿr-u shāʿirī*, ed. Rashīd Ḥasan Khān, Delhi 1969; Gopī Chand Nārang, *Ghālib. Maʿnī āfirīnī, jadaliyātī vaḍaʿ, shūnyatā awr shiʿriyāt*, New Delhi 2013; Mīrājī (Thanāʾallāh Ḍār), *Is naẓm meṃ*, Karachi 2002.

Studies

Purnima Dhavan and Heidi Pauwels, Controversies surrounding the reception of Valī "Dakhanī" (1665?-1707?) in early *tażkirahs* of Urdu poets, *JRAS* 25/4 (2015), 625–46; Mehr Afshan Farooqi, *Urdu literary culture. Vernacular modernity in the writing of Muhammad Hasan Askari*, New York 2012; Shamsur Rahman Faruqi, A long history of Urdu literary culture, pt. 1, Naming and placing a literary culture, in Sheldon Pollock (ed.), *Literary cultures in history. Reconstructions from South Asia* (Berkeley 2003), 805–63; Farmān Fatihpūrī, *Urdū shuʿarā ke tadhkire awr tadhkira nigārī*, Karachi 1998; Marcia K. Hermansen and Bruce B. Lawrence, Indo-Persian *tazkiras* as memorative communications, in David Gilmartin and Bruce B. Lawrence (eds.), *Beyond Turk and Hindu. Rethinking religious identities in Islamicate South Asia* (Gainesville 2000), 149–75; Nāṣir ʿAbbās Nayyar, *Jadīd awr mābaʿd jadīd tanqīd*, Karachi 2004; Frances W. Pritchett, A long history of Urdu literary culture, pt. 2, Histories, performances, and masters, in Sheldon Pollock (ed.), *Literary cultures in history. Reconstructions from South Asia* (Berkeley 2003), 864–92; Frances W. Pritchett, *Nets of awareness. Urdu poetry and its critics*, Berkeley 1994.

Christina Oesterheld

Louis IX

Louis IX (25 April 1214–25 August 1270; r. 1226–70), known as Saint Louis, is the popular French king who led two failed crusades against the Muslim world. Louis's main achievement was imposing his authority on his vassals in feudal France; his two crusades, however, ended disastrously. He led the Seventh Crusade to Egypt in 647/1249, where he was captured and then released after a ransom was paid. In 668/1270, Louis attacked Tunis, where he died from disease. The Roman Catholic Church canonised him in 1297.

The Seventh Crusade had a deep impact on both sides of the Mediterranean. Its financial and military burden fell on the French kingdom and caused widespread uprisings. Nevertheless, the crusade led the king to consolidate his rule in southern France, establish diplomatic contacts with the Mongols, and commence reform of the royal justice system and fiscal administration of his kingdom. On the other hand, the Seventh Crusade witnessed, and arguably enabled, major political change in Egypt, as it coincided with the death of the last effective Ayyūbid sultan of Egypt, al-Malik al-Ṣāliḥ II Najm al-Dīn Ayyūb (r. in Egypt 637–47/1240–49) and the rise of the Mamlūks.

Muslim and Christian mediaeval sources concur on the overall unfolding of the events of the Seventh Crusade (Eddé, passim; Jackson, chapters 5 and 6). After a grave illness, Louis took the crusading vow in 1244. He completed meticulous preparations and set sail for Cyprus in August 1248. His ten-month stay in Cyprus was ill-advised, especially as al-Ṣāliḥ Ayyūb, the sultan of Egypt, was being constantly informed of the crusaders' movements. On 20 Ṣafar 647/4 June 1249, Louis's fleet reached Dimyāṭ (Damietta); by 6 June/22 Ṣafar the town was taken in a stunning victory made possible by the panicking defenders. Yet this success was not seized upon, as Louis delayed his next movement while the Nile began its rise. Meanwhile, al-Ṣāliḥ Ayyūb died on 14 Shaʿbān 647/22 November 1249. His death was kept secret by his wife Shajar al-Durr until the return of his son Tūrānshāh (d. 648/1250) from Ḥiṣn Kayfā in Mesopotamia. On 20 November, King Louis led his army upstream towards Cairo. Incessantly harassed by the Egyptian army and fleet, and hindered by a difficult terrain riddled with canals, the crusaders finally reached al-Manṣūra a month later. On 4 Dhū l-Qaʿda 647/8 February 1250, the king's brother, Robert of Artois, launched an attack on al-Manṣūra without Louis's knowledge. The Ayyūbid army's elite Baḥrī-Mamlūk corps distinguished itself in battle and the attack was repelled decisively; Artois was killed, along with many French notables. When the newly installed sultan Tūrānshāh arrived in al-Manṣūra, the road to Cairo was now firmly blocked by his army and the Nile controlled by his fleet. Famine and disease struck the crusader camp and Louis decided to retreat to Dimyāṭ, but it was too little too late. On 2 Muḥarram 648/6 April 1250, the French king was captured and his army routed at the battle of Fāriskūr.

Tūrānshāh's negotiations with his royal prisoner were interrupted when he was assassinated by his father's Mamlūk corps on 28 Muḥarram 648/2 May 1250. The negotiations quickly resumed, as the Mamlūks were eager for the ransom money. The king was freed on 2 Ṣafar 648/6 May 1250 and sailed for Acre, and Dimyāṭ was returned to Muslim hands. He spent the next four years in the Latin East fortifying Acre, Caesarea, Jaffa, and Sidon. Back in France, the situation had deteriorated because of the financial burden of the crusade, the English threat, and popular disturbances. The death of the king's mother, Blanche of Castile, in 1252, hastened his return in 1254.

The Eighth Crusade was tragically short. In 1267, Louis took his crusading vows again. He landed in Tunis on 27 Dhū l-Qaʿda 668/18 July 1270. An epidemic of dysentery struck the crusader camp and killed Louis's son, John Tristan (1250–70). The king was next; he died on 6 Muḥarram 669/25 August 1270, probably from dysentery.

Mamlūk sources were well informed about King Louis. He was referred to as al-Fransīs and less frequently al-Ifransīs, that is, "the Frenchman" (al-Dhahabī, 47:50 and 53). The Syrian historian Ibn Wāṣil (d. 697/1298) described him as "Raydāfrans, the leader of the French people among the Franks"; he also said of him:

> This Raydāfrans is one of the greatest kings of the Franks and the most powerful among them; Ifrans is a Frankish nation (*umma*); Raydāfrans means the king of Ifrans, since *rayd* means king in their language; he was an ardent follower of Christianity. (Ibn Wāṣil, 9)

Moreover, Louis was described as *ʿaẓīm al-naṣrāniyya*, i.e., the leader of Christianity (al-Dhahabī, 47:52). The French royal regalia were used to celebrate the Egyptian victory. Tūrānshāh sent King Louis's cloak to be paraded in Damascus, where it was described as a scarlet mantle with fur and a golden buckle, "*Saqrlāṭ aḥmar bi-farū sinjāb*" (al-Dhahabī, (years 641–50), 47:54) and "*wa-fīhā buklat dhahab*" (Ibn al-Dawādārī, 7:381) [Illustration 1]. Around the time of the Eighth Crusade, the Cairene chancery secretary, Ibn ʿAbd al-Ẓāhir (d. 692/1292) mentioned, "*al-Fransīs, Lūwīs bin Lūwīs*" (Ibn ʿAbd al-Ẓāhir, 370). His brother Charles of Anjou (r. 1266–85, d. 1285,) was referred to by Baybars al-Manṣūrī (d. 725/1325) both as "King Sharl, brother of al-Fransīs" and "Jārlā, brother of Raydāfrans" (al-Manṣūrī, 89 and 117). Additionally, Louis was described in terms of European mediaeval metrics of power by Ibn al-Dawādārī (d. after 736/1335–6), who said of him, "Al-Fransīs is the greatest among the kings of the inner Franks (*al-dākhila*), with the greatest number of castles and troops" (Ibn al-Dawādārī, 7:365).

Arabic authors attempted to explain the French king's motives for the Eighth Crusade. Ibn al-Dawādārī believed Louis held a grudge against Egypt: "Following his release, he returned home, but in his heart there existed an inextinguishable fire because of what had happened to him. He had intended to return to Egypt for revenge." Explaining the choice of Tunis, Ibn al-Dawādārī related:

> [Louis's] counselors warned him, "You have tried Egypt once before, you know more than anyone else what happened there! It is wiser that you head for Tunis.... Once you conquer Ifrīqiya, you will be able to attack Egypt by land and sea." He followed their advice and attacked Tunis with a [large army] along with a group of Frankish kings. But God struck his camp with disease, so the accursed one [King Louis] perished, along with a number of other kings and most of his [army]. (Ibn al-Dawādārī, 8:101–2)

Al-Dhahabī (d. 748/1348) considered trading rights with Tunis to be Louis's main drive: "The Franks landed in Tunis to support the Genoese, whose money has been seized [by the ruler of Tunis]." Referring to John Tristan, he mentions that Louis's son had died and that "it was said that al-Fransīs perished and they [the Franks] no longer had a king to rule them. The Franks asked for a truce and it was agreed on the condition that they [those in power in Tunis] returned to the Genoese their money" (al-Dhahabī, 49:60).

Arabic sources provide an inconsistent portrayal of Louis. They depict him as

Illustration 1. Louis IX depicted in the *Moralized Bible*, written and illuminated in Paris, France, between 1227 and 1234. The Morgan Library & Museum, New York, MS M.240.

religiously overzealous, obstinate, and arrogant, and as an unfit military leader. Such an image may have been aggravated by Sicilian Hohenstaufen propaganda against Louis, which was disseminated via prominent Muslims connected to the courts of Frederick II (1194–1250) and his son Manfred (r. 1258–66; El-Merheb, passim). Nonetheless, there was a less adversarial image of Louis in the Arabic sources. The king's bravery in battle and his refusal to abandon his people were qualities that the Muslims admired (Eddé, 105–7). Even his devotion to his Christian faith was on occasion noted favourably. What persisted the most in Arabic writings was, however, the famous poem of the Egyptian poet and public servant Ibn Maṭrūḥ (d. 649/1251), scorning the French king and his crusade (Ibn Wāṣil, 71–2).

Bibliography

Sources

Baybars al-Manṣūrī, *Zubdat al-fikra fī taʾrīkh al-Hijra*, ed. D. S. Richards, Beirut 1998; al-Dhahabī, *Taʾrīkh al-Islām wa-wafayāt al-mashāhīr wa-l-aʿlām*, ed. ʿUmar ʿAbd al-Salām Tadmurī, vol. 47 (years 641–50) and vol. 49 (years 661–670), Beirut 1987; Ibn ʿAbd al-Ẓāhir, *al-Rawḍ al-zāhir fī sirāt al-malik al-Ẓāhir*, ed. ʿAbd al-ʿAzīz al-Khuwayṭir, Riyad 1976; Ibn al-Dawādārī, *Kanz al-durar wa-jāmiʿ al-ghurar*, 9 vols., Cairo 1972; Ibn Wāṣil, *Die Chronik des ibn Wasil. Ǧamāl ad-Dīn Muḥammad ibn Wāṣil, Mufarriǧ al-Kurūb fī Aḫbār Banī Ayyūb. Kritische Edition des letzten Teils (646/1248–659/1261) mit Kommentar. Untergang der Ayyubiden und Beginn der Mamlukenherrschaft*, ed. Mohamed Rahim, Wiesbaden 2010; Jean de Joinville, *Vie de Saint Louis*, ed. Jacques Monfrin, Paris 1995.

Studies

Anne-Marie Eddé, Saint Louis et la Septième Croisade vus par les auteurs Arabes, in Françoise Micheau (ed.), *Les relations des pays de l'Islam avec le monde latin. Du milieu du Xe siècle au milieu du XIIIe siècle*, (Paris 2000), 72–111; Mohamad El-Merheb, Louis IX in medieval Arabic sources. The saint, the king, and the Sicilian connection, *Al-Masāq* 28/3 (2016), 282–301; Peter Jackson (ed.), *The Seventh Crusade, 1244–1254. Sources and documents*, Farnham 2009; Jacques Le Goff and Gareth Evan Gollrad, *Saint Louis*, Notre Dame IN 2009; Jean Richard, *Saint Louis. Crusader king of France*, trans. Jean Birrell, Cambridge 1992.

Mohamed El-Merheb

Lucknow art and architecture

The city of **Lucknow**, which became, in 1189/1775, the second capital of the Twelver (Ithnāʿasharī) Shīʿī nawabs of Awadh (Oudh), featured a magnificent built environment and a robust tradition of painting. A distinctive Awadhi style of painting was initially established at Faizabad (Fayḍābād, in present-day Uttar Pradesh), Awadh's first capital. Painting in Lucknow was heavily indebted to artists working in Faizabad, but, by the nineteenth century, reflected European styles. Lucknow's architecture followed a similar path, but new building types, some of them monumental, constructed for its Shīʿī patrons gave the city a unique visual appeal.

Lucknow was a significant place before the rule of the nawabs of Awadh. There are remains of pre-Mughal structures; a tomb for the Mughal emperor Akbar's (r. 963–1014/1556–1605) governor of Lucknow, Shaykh Ibrāhīm Chishtī; and, on a high hill, a three-domed mosque said to have been built by Awrangzīb (r. 1068–1118/1658–1707) [Illustration 1]. It now appears as a sober structure representing Sunnī Islam overlooking the more flamboyant Shīʿī *imāmbāras*—centres for Twelver Shīʿī religious rituals—and mosques provided by various nawabs in

Illustration 1. Awrangzīb's (r. 1068–1118/1658–1707) mosque, early twelfth/late seventeenth century, Lucknow. Photograph courtesy of Catherine Asher.

the city below. A Mughal fort known as the Machchi Bhavan (destroyed in 1857), consisting of a group of buildings within walled courtyards, was begun under the Mughals. The British constructed a trading station (factory) known as the Farangi Mahal (foreigner's hall), which was later given by Awrangzīb to a Muslim religious scholar and is today an Islamic college.

1. Architecture in Faizabad

The first nawabs of Awadh looked not to earlier buildings of Lucknow for inspiration but to Delhi, as they considered themselves the cultural successors of the Mughals (r. 932–1275/1526–1858). Few buildings in Faizabad, their first capital, remain from this time, although English artists have left impressions of Nawab Shujāʿ al-Dawla's palace, Lal Bagh, built during his reign (1168–89/1754–75). Like a typical Mughal palace, Lal Bagh comprised multiple courtyards with gardens and pavilions enclosed by high walls. The gate leading to the palace is elaborately decorated with stucco, for stone quarries were distant and stucco was less expensive. The architecture of both Faizabad and Lucknow comprised a brick core covered with stucco that could be sculpted with floral forms, the exaggerated arches and royal emblems giving the architecture of Awadh an exuberant air. The square-plan tombs in Faizabad built for Shujāʿ al-Dawla and his wife, while adhering in form to Mughal traditions, are decorated with the elaborate stucco work that became a hallmark of Awadhi architecture.

2. Painting in Faizabad and Lucknow and European influence

While little remains of Faizabad's built environment, much evidence of painting survives. Artists trained in Mughal Delhi came to Faizabad in search of new patrons. Some stand out, notably Mīr Kalān Khān (fl. 1147–84/1734–70), Mihr Chand (fl. 1179–89/1765–75), and Nidha Mal (fl. 1148–63/1735–50). The early painting of Awadh, especially portraits of nawabs and/or other elite seated on terraces, is so similar to styles employed at Delhi that it difficult to tell the origins of such works. Over time, styles peculiar to Awadh emerged. One important factor was the presence of several Europeans in Faizabad and later in Lucknow, who were keenly interested in painting and, perhaps more than the nawabs, promoted local artists. Jean-Baptiste Gentil (d. 1799) and Antoine-Louis Polier (d. 1795), amongst others, collected older and contemporary Indian paintings and encouraged artists such as Mīr Kalān Khān and Mihr Chand by establishing studios. Polier's collection was compiled in at least twelve albums comprising Awadhi paintings as well as those from Deccani and Mughal courts. Artists such as Mīr Kalān Khān, who worked in both Faizabad and Lucknow, studied these works. His own output often combined very different styles placed together artfully on a single page. His work has been likened to *kichari*, an Indian dish consisting of a mixture of ingredients. His *Lovers in a landscape*, executed in about 1173–83/1760–70 in Lucknow, and now held by the David Collection, in Copenhagen, is a mixture of Ṣafavid, European, and multiple schools of Indian painting, including Rājpūt and Bījāpūrī on a single page [Illustration 2]. The development of painting first in Faizabad and later in Lucknow was further enriched by European artists who came to make their fortunes, in particular the English artist Tilly Kettle (active in India 1769–76), whose many oil paintings of Nawab Shujāʿ al-Dawla were copied by Awadhi artists in water colour.

3. Awadh becomes artistically less dependent on Mughal Delhi

Artists, patrons, and workshops can move from venue to venue, so it is not always clear whether a painting was produced in Faizabad or in Lucknow. In the case of architecture, however, the location is known. Shujāʿ al-Dawla died in 1189/1775 and was succeeded by his son, Āṣaf al-Dawla (r. 1189–1211/1775–97), who, eager to flee his domineering mother, established himself in Lucknow. Under Āṣaf al-Dawla, Awadhi culture, while originally based on Mughal prototypes, became increasingly distinct from that of Mughal Delhi. Urdu poetry flourished, extolling love and the female body. Awadhi cuisine became famous for its kababs, biryanis (rice dishes), curries, flat breads, and snacks such as samosas (stuffed savoury pastries). Luxury arts, such as enamelled metalwork, elaborate jewellery with precious gems, and jade-handled weapons (some ceremonial), were produced throughout the *nawābī* period. Modelled on Mughal styles these arts took on an added exuberance. The precise dates of most luxury artefacts are unknown, but a sword presented to the British soldier and colonialist Lord Clive (d. 1774) is dated 1201/1786–7. Textiles and dress were often lavishly embroidered or embellished with gold. Summer wear consisted of a finely woven cotton, almost translucent, that was exquisitely embroidered in a manner known as *chikankārī*.

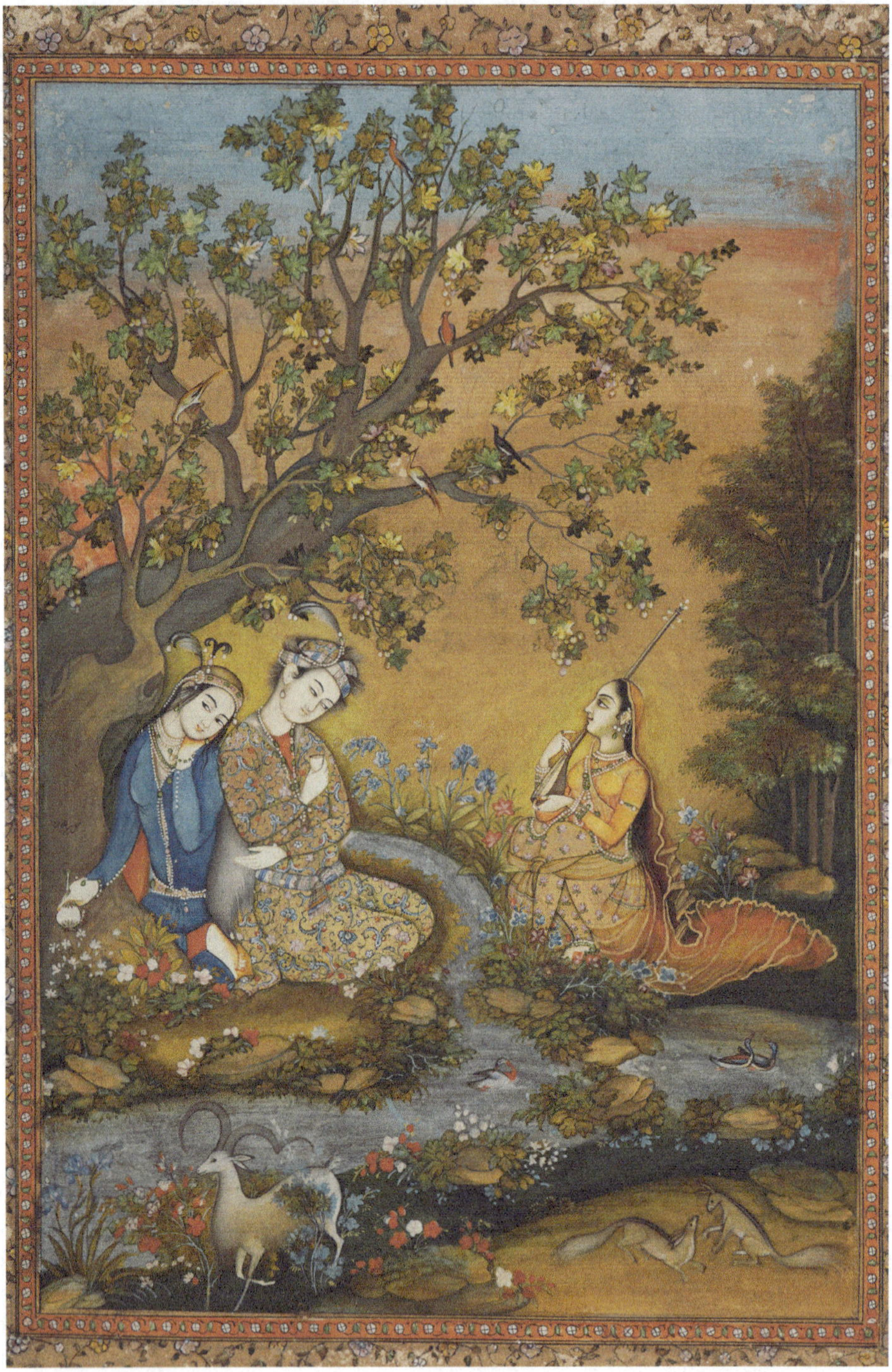

Illustration 2. Mīr Kalān Khān (fl. 1147–84/1734–70), *Lovers in a landscape*, Lucknow c.1173–83/1760–70. Miniature, 22.2 x 15.2 cm, pasted on an album leaf. Image courtesy of The David Collection, Copenhagen, inv. no. 50/1981, photographer Pernille Klemp.

Illustration 3. Āṣaf al-Dawla's (r. 1189–1211/1775–97) Bara Imāmbāra (large *imāmbāra*), commissioned in 1198/1784, Lucknow. Photograph courtesy of Catherine Asher.

4. *Imāmbāras*

Architecture under Āṣaf al-Dawla surpassed earlier works in scale, decoration, and design. In about 1198/1784, Āṣaf al-Dawla ordered the construction of a massive *imāmbāra* complex, the largest ever built up to that time, for the ritual mourning of Imām al-Ḥusayn's martyrdom at Karbalāʾ in 61/680 [Illustration 3]. *Imāmbāra*s (also known as *Ḥusayniyya*s) were venues for reciting poetry mourning al-Ḥusayn *(marsiya*, Ar., *marthiya)* but were also used for the storage of *taʿziya*s (here: models of al-Ḥusayn's tomb that are peculiar to South Asia). Earlier ones had been built in the Deccan, although it is unclear whether there is a direct link between the Deccan structures and those in Lucknow. Āṣaf al-Dawla's Bara (large) Imāmbāra (also known as the Asafi Imāmbāra) was constructed as a famine-relief project, giving the workers employment and thus money for purchasing food, which had been made expensive by the famine. The colossal complex, consisting of three courtyards, was once attached to the Macchi Bhavan palace, which no longer survives. The *imāmbāra* was entered through gateways on the east and west; only the western one, known as the Rumi Darwaza (Turkish, i.e., west-facing, gate), survives [Illustration 4]. This enormous gate's triple-arched entrance is surmounted by large finials that give it an air and a sense of dynamic articulation never seen in the more harmoniously balanced structures of the Mughals. A huge free-standing mosque and a deep step-well were also part of the complex. At the time of its construction, the *imāmbāra* had one of the largest pre-modern vaulted halls with an uninterrupted span. The space under the

Illustration 4. The Rumi Darwaza (west-facing gate), commissioned in 1198/1784, Lucknow. Photograph courtesy of Catherine Asher.

roof incorporated a support system forming a complex maze that attracts tourists today but was probably used by servants as passages for lighting oil lamps for night gatherings *(majālis)*. These lamps, set on the parapet along the *imāmbāra*'s interior walls, are depicted by Sita Ram (active 1813–23), an Indian artist who worked for Lord Hastings (d. 1818), the governor general of the East India Company's holdings in India. The *imāmbāra*'s façade is embellished with pairs of curved fish, the royal emblem of the house of Awadh, and inflated floral motifs rendered in stucco. Intended for Shīʿī ritual, the complex also flaunted the nawab's wealth, which was now greater than that of the Mughals.

After the Bara Imāmbāra, at least twenty-one *imāmbāra*s were constructed in the city, ten of them royal constructions and the rest built by the elite. The Shāh Najaf Imāmbāra, built by Nawāb Ghāzī al-Dīn Ḥaydar (r. 1814–27), was intended as a replica of Imām ʿAlī's burial site and was used as the nawab's own tomb. While the exterior is austere, its interior is embellished with European glass chandeliers and a profusion of stucco adornment. The Ḥusaynābād *imāmbāra*, built by Nawāb Muḥammad ʿAlī Shāh (r. 1837–42) in about 1837 and often called the Chhoṭī Imāmbāra (small *imāmbāra*), is part of a large complex. In addition to the domed *imāmbāra*, it includes elaborate stucco-covered entrances, a garden with a pool,

Illustration 5. The tomb of Zīnat Āsiyā, the daughter of Nawāb Muḥammad ʿAlī Shāh (r. 1837–42), at the Chhoṭī Imāmbāra (small *imāmbāra*), built in c.1837. Photograph courtesy of Karishma under the creative commons licence.

and a tomb modelled on the Taj Mahal, although its spatial tensions—that is, the uneven relationships amongst the various shapes of the building—and emphasis on height recall the aesthetics of late Mughal architecture [Illustration 5].

5. Claude Martin

While the exterior of most religious buildings, notably mosques, reflected little European influence, the interiors of many *imāmbāras*, especially those of the nineteenth century, were filled with European fixtures including coloured glass lamps and crystal chandeliers. Some of this enthusiasm for European décor may have been encouraged by the Frenchman Claude Martin (d. 1800), who had a close personal relationship—as friend, architect, and money-lender—with several of the Awadhi nawabs. Martin's vast European-style mansion, Constantia, now a boys' school known as La Martinère, was begun just before his death and influenced many of the nineteenth-century royal buildings of Lucknow. Constantia was built as an enormous single structure with multiple rooms and stories, unlike the multiple pavilions situated in the courtyards of *nawābī* palaces. Its exterior, particularly its roof line, appears as the outline of a dome in silhouette. This was later emulated in some of the pavilions of the Qaysar Bagh palace built in the mid-nineteenth century by Wājid ʿAlī Shāh (r. 1847–56). The roof parapet of Constantia is embellished with multiple stucco sculptures, including lions, a reference to Martin's birthplace of Lyon.

6. Western-style architecture

The Awadhi nawabs constructed Western-style pavilions, most of which are in ruins today, largely for the use of their European residents and guests. The original appearance of Dil Kusha ("heart pleasing"), gutted in the Indian Uprising of 1857–8, is known from early photographs. Designed about 1805 by Gore Ouseley (d. 1844), a self-made English architect, this country house was modelled on an eighteenth-century English one; its extended porch, for example, featured classical Corinthian columns.

In addition to pavilions built in the European style, often at a distance from the nawab's administrative headquarters were palace complexes that combined European-style portico, windows, and other features with Indian-style domes and typical *nawābī* stucco ornament. The Chattar Manzil (Umbrella Palace), begun about 1803, was originally part of a large multi-pavilion complex. Its sole surviving structure has been greatly altered over the years and is today the Central Drug Research Institute. The palace's throne room, with its cusped arches and painted ceiling, conformed closely to Mughal style and was then adapted to Lucknow taste under the rulers of Awadh. The last ruler of Awadh, Wājid ʿAlī Shāh, built his own palace complex known as the Qaysar Bagh, near the Chattar Manzil. Little remains of what was once a vast complex, which was largely destroyed in the Uprising of 1857–8. European photographers documented this ruin in detail, possibly a statement of European superiority over what was seen as a symbol of *nawābī* decadence.

Amongst Lucknow's most famous European-style complexes is the British Residency, where, during the six-month siege in 1857–8, British men, women, and children were trapped, most of whom died before the Residency's liberation. It was begun about 1146/1733, when Nawab Shujāʿ al-Dawla agreed to have a British resident in Awadh, and was added to over time. While it was photographed frequently after it had been largely destroyed in 1857–8, there were few recorded images of it from before that time. A watercolour by the Indian artist Sita Ram shows that the residence consisted of sedate buildings constructed in a Georgian style, a far cry from the exuberance of much contemporary *nawābī* architecture.

7. Western-style painting

Before the Uprising and the deposition of the rulers of Awadh a year earlier, many Europeans resided in Lucknow, including some with an interest in painting. Notable amongst them was Richard Johnson (active in India 1770–90) who amassed sixty-seven albums of multiple styles of Indian paintings, including some from Lucknow, and sold them to the East India Company upon his return to England; they are now held by the British Library. The names of seven Indian artists who worked for Johnson are known, but there were many more. During this period artists began to depict scenes with figures and buildings set in landscapes using aerial perspectives creating distant panoramic views.

The presence in eastern India of well-known European artists, such as Johan Zoffany (d. 1810), created a hitherto unknown demand for Europeanised art, and "company painting," art created for European patrons by Indian artists, became fashionable. While the subject matter of company painting varied, it often focused on groups of Indians or Europeans in native dress and/or with Indians, as well as depictions of flora and fauna. Wājid ʿAlī Shāh had his own British court artist, Robert Home (d. 1834), but the nawab also revived an interest in manuscript painting. Wājid ʿAlī Shāh commissioned at least two of his own poetic compositions, his *Dīwān* ("Collection of poetry") and *ʿIshq-nāma* ("Book of love"), and he is depicted in both.

8. The contribution of non-Muslims

Literature on the art and architecture of Awadh largely neglects the region's large non-Muslim population. Lucknow's most visible architecture was provided by royalty and the Shīʿī elite, but Awadh's non-Muslims also built in both the city and the surrounding countryside. The Hindu and Jain temples tend to be smaller than *imāmbāra* complexes. This is not an indication of these communities' relationship with the elite but rather a reflection of eighteenth- and nineteenth-century North Indian temples, including those in Varanasi, one of the holiest Hindu sites. Begum Rābiʿa, the Muslim wife of Nawāb Muḥammad ʿAlī Shāh, is credited with building a temple in Lucknow dedicated to the Hindu monkey god, Hanuman, after she had a dream revealing a buried image of the god and her subsequent delivery of a long-awaited child thanks to the deity's blessing. Tikait Rai, a Hindu minister to Nawāb Āṣaf al-Dawla, and other wealthy Hindus in *nawābī* service founded market towns in agriculturally rich Awadh and provided them with public works and temples. These temples were embellished with stucco motifs similar to those on *nawābī* architecture, as well as images of deities.

9. The destruction of *nawābī* Lucknow

After 1858 much of *nawābī* Lucknow that had not been destroyed in the Uprising was now razed, as colonial authorities reconfigured the city by using mosques as temporary housing for the military and adding wide streets, a cantonment, and a railway system. These additions were intended not to serve a local population but to promote the colonialist agenda. The University of Lucknow was built in 1867 in the Indo-Saracenic style, that is, with buildings planned by European architects for Indian clients using features associated with Indo-Muslim architecture. The Char Bagh Railway Station, built between 1914 and 1923, on the site of a former orchard, linked Lucknow and Kanpur, a major industrial centre. Designed by J. H. Hornimen, the train station too was constructed in the Indo-Saracenic style. Both buildings have domes atop towers, those on the University mimicking the pointed tops of those on Awadhi structures, and arches.

Bibliography

Molly Emma Aitken, Parataxis and the practice of reuse, from Mughal margins to Mir Kalan Khan, *Archives of Asian Art* 59 (2009), 81–103; Catherine B. Asher, Lucknow's architectural heritage, in Stephen Markel and Tushara Bindu Gude (eds.), *India's fabled city. The art of courtly Lucknow* (Los Angeles 2010), 121–43; Rosemary Crill, Textiles and dress in Lucknow in the eighteenth and nineteenth centuries, in Stephen Markel and Tushara Bindu Gude (eds.), *India's fabled city. The art of courtly Lucknow* (Los Angeles 2010), 227–42; Neeta Das, The "country houses" of Lucknow, in Rosie Llewellyn-Jones (ed.),

Lucknow, city of Illusion (Munich 2006), 180–91; Hussein Keshani, Architecture and the Twelver Shiʿi tradition. The great Imambara complex of Lucknow, *Muqarnas* 23 (2006), 219–50; J. P. Losty, *Sita Ram's painted views of India. Lord Hastings's journey from Calcutta to the Punjab, 1814–15*, London 2015; Rosie Llewellyn-Jones, *Engaging scoundrels. True tales of old Lucknow*, New Delhi 2000; Rosie Llewellyn-Jones (ed.), *Lucknow, city of illusion*, Munich 2006; Rosie Llewellyn-Jones, *A very ingenious man. Claude Martin in early colonial India*, Delhi 1992; Stephen Markle, "This blaze of wealth and magnificence." The luxury arts of Lucknow, in Stephen Markel and Tushara Bindu Gude (eds.), *India's fabled city. The art of courtly Lucknow* (Los Angeles 2010), 119–226; Veena Talwar Oldenberg, *The making of colonial Lucknow 1856–77*, Princeton 1984, repr. Delhi 1989; Stephen Markel and Tushara Bindu Gude (eds.), *India's fabled city. The art of courtly Lucknow*, Los Angeles 2010; Malani Roy, Origins of the late Mughal painting tradition in Awadh, in Stephen Markel and Tushara Bindu Gude (eds.), *India's fabled city. The art of courtly Lucknow* (Los Angeles 2010), 165–86; Banmali Tandan, *The architecture of Lucknow and its dependencies, 1722–1856*, New Delhi 2001.

Catherine B. Asher

M

Majlis Ugama Islam Singapura

The **Majlis Ugama Islam Singapura** (MUIS, Islamic Religious Council of Singapore) is a statutory board responsible for administering Muslim affairs and representing the interests of Singapore's Muslim community, comprising fourteen percent of the population (2015), the majority of whom are ethnic Malays. Notwithstanding a general policy of equal treatment of religious and ethnic groups, Malays enjoy a "special status" as "indigenous people," and the government is mandated "to protect…and promote their…religious…interests" (Constitution of the Republic of Singapore, art. 152). MUIS was founded in 1968 under the Administration of Muslim Law Act (AMLA), which came into force in 1966, replacing a regulatory framework established under British colonial rule. The Mohammedan Advisory Board, formed in 1915, followed by the Muslim Advisory Board, were the predecessors of MUIS.

MUIS advises the president of Singapore on matters related to the Muslim community. The president appoints all members of the MUIS Council (Majlis Tertinggi MUIS), its highest authority. MUIS administers Islamic alms (Ar. *zakāt*) and other financial aid for needy Muslims, endowments *(waqf)*, pilgrimage *(ḥajj)* matters, *ḥalāl* certification, mosque building and maintenance, Islamic education and schools, and Islamic legal opinions. MUIS operates under the Ministry of Culture, Community and Youth and is overseen by a minister of Muslim affairs, a post first filled in 1977.

The MUIS Council comprises the MUIS president, the *muftī*, a chief executive, and at least fourteen appointed individuals, a maximum of seven of whom are appointed on the recommendation of the minister in charge to the president of Singapore, while the others are appointed following recommendations by "such Muslim societies as are prescribed for the purpose by the Majlis (Council)" (AMLA, pt. II, chap. 3). Another influential MUIS institution is the Fatwa (Legal) Committee, which issues Islamic legal opinions and engages in Islamic reasoning, in cooperation with external experts, including scientists from non-religious backgrounds. In 2018, the MUIS Council members included four women; below the Council are several female directors. This reflects increasing female representation on Singapore's state-linked Muslim organisations and amongst the *sharīʿa* judiciary, up to the leadership level. The MUIS president, CEO, and *muftī* were, however, all men.

MUIS promotes interpretations of Islam compatible with and contributing to the Singaporean nation state. Singapore's semi-authoritarian government pursues guided multi-culturalism and considers itself secular, albeit not non-religious. Since 2005, MUIS's educational mission of promoting a state brand of Islam is subsumed under the Singapore Muslim Identity (SMI), defining ten desirable characteristics of Singaporean Muslimness, including being "progressive," "inclusive," "adaptive," and "contributive" to Singapore's multicultural, multireligious society under conditions of secular modernity, while insisting firmly on Islamic principles. Singaporean Muslims should promote "universal values," be "good citizens," and have a "good understanding" of current affairs, all of which MUIS justifies on religious grounds. The flagship research institution of MUIS, the MUIS Academy, aims to foster knowledge and leadership skills amongst the Muslim community.

MUIS serves as a mediator between the government and local Muslim communities. The latter can bring up concerns to the government via MUIS, and MUIS communicates government policies to them. Concerning Islamic reasoning, MUIS emphasises its intellectual independence, in the face of occasional accusations of serving as an instrument of government control. MUIS engages in intense exchanges with non-state Muslim actors, including critics and Muslim minority groups that are marginalised and sometimes banned for alleged "deviance" *(sesat)* in neighbouring Malay-speaking countries. MUIS engages extensively in government-supported interfaith projects.

MUIS oversees an accreditation system for Islamic teachers *(asatizah)*, that is, anyone providing Islamic instruction outside the family. The Asatizah Recognition Scheme is overseen by the Asatizah Recognition Board. Following a revision of AMLA in 2017, individuals and institutions offering Islamic education must register with MUIS. Education providers and Qurʾānic teachers must fulfil specific requirements to receive "certificates of recognition."

Although MUIS is a state institution, some activities are community-funded. Since 1975, Muslims can support a Mosque Building Fund through voluntary salary deductions. Today, MUIS-led mosques are largely independent of state funding, but the state provides infrastructure assistance for collecting those funds.

For the administration of its endowments *(wakaf*, Ar. *waqf)*, MUIS has created Warees (acronym of Wakaf Real Estate; Malay *waris* also means heritage/beneficiary), an endowment-portfolio management company, to manage assets worth more than SGD$711 million, as of 2015. Warees also manages community real estate. It aims at regeneration and enhancement, while preserving community heritage, under its Wakaf Revitalisation Scheme (WRS) and through a financing instrument, the Institutional Investments Initiative.

The headquarters of MUIS is located at the Singapore Islamic Hub, which also houses a mosque (Masjid Muhajirin) and an Islamic school (Madrasah Irsyad Zuhri al-Islamiah). Its architecture, blending symbols of Islam and urban modernity, aims to express the adaptive and progressive orientation of MUIS.

Bibliography

Walid Jumblatt Abdullah, Religious representation in secular Singapore. A case study of MUIS and Pergas, *Asian Survey* 53/6 (2013), 1182–1204; Johan Fischer, In the halal zones of Malaysia and Singapore, in Johan Fischer (ed.), *Islam, standards, and technoscience in global halal zones*, Abingdon UK 2016; Tim Lindsey and Kerstin Steiner, *Islam, law and the state in Southeast Asia*, vol. 2, *Singapore* (London 2012), 28–77; Tuty R. Mostarom, The Singapore *ulama*. Religious agency in the context of a strong state, *Asian Journal of Social Science* 42/5 (2014), 561–83; Dominik M. Müller, The bureaucratization of Islam and its socio-legal dimensions in Southeast Asia, *Max Planck Institute for Social Anthropology Working Paper* 187 (2017), www.eth.mpg.de/cms/de/publications/working papers/wp0187; Nazirudin Mohd Nazir and Majlis Ugama Islam Singapura, *Fatwas of Singapore. Science, medicine and health*, Singapore 2017; Afif Pasuni, Negotiating statist Islam. Fatwa and state policy in Singapore, *Journal of Current Southeast Asian Affairs* (special Issue, *The bureaucratization of Islam in Southeast Asia. Transdisciplinary perspectives*, ed. Dominik Müller and Kerstin Steiner) 37/1 (2018), 57–88; Kerstin Steiner, Governing Islam. The state, the Administration of Muslim Law Act (AMLA) and Islam in Singapore, *Australian Journal of Asian Law* 16/1 (2015), art. 6, https://ssrn.com/abstract=2627501; Bryan S. Turner, Soft authoritarianism, social diversity and legal pluralism. The case of Singapore, in Adam Possamai, James T. Richardson, and Bryan S. Turner (eds.), *The sociology of shariʿa. Case studies from around the world* (New York 2014), 69–81.

Dominik M. Müller

Mardam Bik, Khalīl

Khalīl Mardam Bik (Khalil Mardam Bey, 1895–1959) was a Syrian poet and littérateur, who in 1939 penned the Syrian national anthem. Born and raised in Damascus to an aristocratic and educated family of Turkish origins, he lost both parents during his teenage years, which had a profound effect on his psyche and left him with a sadness that he channelled into his poetry and literary studies. Despite becoming an orphan, he remained committed to his education, and, when he could no longer afford a private education, he studied *ḥadīth* (prophetic tradition), *fiqh* (Islamic law), and grammar with notable Damascene *ʿulamāʾ* (religious scholars). He started writing poetry at the age of fifteen.

Mardam Bik was an early advocate of Arab nationalism, signing a declaration calling for emancipation from the Ottoman Empire that was presented to the Arab Congress in Paris. In 1914 he was arrested for his support of and association with the Arab nationalist ʿAbd al-Ghanī al-ʿArīsī. In 1918, after the departure of the Ottomans from Syria, he began working as a civil servant with the new Arab government in Damascus. In 1921, he founded al-Rābiṭa al-Adabiyya ("the Literary League"), a salon modelled after the Mahjar ("exiled") writers' al-Rābiṭa al-Qalamiyya ("the Pen League") in New York.

He began writing nationalist poetry at an early age. When the French bombed Damascus in 1918, he penned his classic poem *Yawm al-fazaʿ al-kabīr* ("The day of great terror"). His anti-French activism led him to flee Syria. From 1926 to 1929 he lived in exile in Lebanon, Alexandria, and finally London, where he studied English literature for three years. Upon his return to Syria, he taught Arabic literature at al-Kulliyya al-ʿIlmiyya al-Waṭaniyya ("the National Science College") in Damascus until 1938. During that time he wrote the first five volumes of his literary series Aʾimmat al-adab al-ʿArabī ("Masters of Arabic literature"), comprising studies of al-Jāḥiẓ (d. 255/868–9), Ibn al-Muqaffaʿ (d. c.139/756), Ibn al-ʿAmīd (d. 360/970), al-Ṣāḥib Ibn ʿAbbād (d. 385/995), and al-Farazdaq (d. 114/732).

In 1933, along with the educator Jamīl Ṣalībā, he co-founded the journal *al-Thaqāfa* ("Culture"), although it lasted for only one year. He served as minister of education under three governments, in 1942, 1943, and 1949. All the while, he continued to follow his major passions, editing volumes of both major and lesser Arab littérateurs and writing his own poetry. As his fame spread, he was appointed to numerous memberships in literary and academic associations throughout the region. Before becoming president of al-Majmaʿ al-ʿIlmī al-ʿArabī bi-Dimashq ("the Arab Academy of Damascus") in 1953, following the death of its founder, Muḥammad Kurd ʿAlī, he served for three years as deputy minister at the Syrian embassy in Baghdad.

Twenty-three volumes of poetry and critical editions of the work of Arab littérateurs through the ages are attributed to him. In addition, a number of unpublished manuscripts were collected, edited, and published by his son, ʿAdnān, after his death, when he was officially named *shāʿir al-Shām* ("the poet of Damascus").

Bibliography

Sāmī Kayyālī, *al-Adab al-ʿArabī al-muʿāṣir fī Sūriyya, 1850–1950*, Cairo 1959; Khalīl Mardam, *Dīwān Khalīl Mardam Bik, 1895–1959*, ed. ʿAdnān Mardam, Damascus 1960; Khalīl Mardam, *Taqārīr al-Khalīl al-diblūmāsiyya*, ed. ʿAdnān Mardam, Beirut 1982; Muḥammad Fuʾād Naʿnāʿ, *Khalīl Mardam Bik. Ḥayātuhu wa-shiʿruhu*, Damascus 2001; Fādiyah ʿAbd al-Laṭīf Malīḥ, *Khalīl Mardam Bik. Raʾīs al-Majmaʿ al-ʿIlmī al-ʿArabī bi-Dimashq. Dirāsa adabiyya fī ḥayātihi wa-shiʿrihi wa-muʾallafātih*, Damascus 1991.

Alexa Firat

al-Marjānī, Shihāb al-Dīn

Shihāb al-Dīn Ibn Bahāʾ al-Dīn b. Subḥān **al-Marjānī** al-Ḥanafī al-Bulghārī al-Qazānī (1818–89) was the most important Islamic scholar and religious leader of the Volga-Ural region of Russia [Illustration 1]. Born in the village of Yapançı (Russ., Epanchino), near Kazan in present-day Tatarstan, al-Marjānī hailed from a scholarly family of repute—his father and grandfather were both learned *ʿulamāʾ* (religious scholars)—and he was educated locally before travelling in 1838 to Central Asia to continue his studies. He spent the next eleven years in Bukhara and Samarqand, immersing himself in the study of Ḥanafī *fiqh* (Islamic law) and Māturīdī *kalām* (theology) and being initiated into the Naqshbandī-Mujaddidī Ṣūfī order. Returning to Russia in 1849, he became *imām* at Kazan's First Mosque (now the Marjānī Mosque (Tatar, Märcani Mäçete)) [Illustration 2]—perhaps the most prominent position amongst the *ʿulamāʾ* of the Russian Empire—and a leading religious scholar, teacher, and author.

In Samarqand, al-Marjānī became acquainted with the works of Abū l-Naṣr al-Qūrṣāwī (d. 1812), a controversial scholar from the Volga region who had been condemned for heresy in Bukhara in 1808. Al-Qūrṣāwī had criticised the dominant position on the divine attributes *(ṣifāt)*, that is, that there are seven or eight attributes superadded to the divine essence *(dhāt)* and possible of existence *(mumkinat al-wujūd)* in themselves. He argued that positing number, superaddition, and possibility to the attributes rendered them too distinct from the divine essence, thereby undermining God's transcendence *(tanzīh)*. In making this critique, al-Qūrṣāwī focused on the work of the theologian Saʿd al-Dīn

Illustration 1. A portrait of Shihāb al-Dīn al-Marjānī from the mid-nineteenth century. Source: *Istoriya Tatarskoy ASSR*, Kazan 1980 (public domain).

Illustration 2. The Marjānī Mosque (Tatar, Märcani Mäçete) in Kazan, Russia. It was built in 1766–70 on the authority of Catherine the Great (r. 1762–96), funded by the donations of the city's population. Photograph courtesy of A. Savin, 2016 (public domain).

al-Taftāzānī (d. 791/1389), especially his famous commentary on Najm al-Dīn ʿUmar al-Nasafī's (d. 537/1142) creed (*ʿaqāʾid*). Al-Qūrṣāwī's opponents, in turn, condemned him for denying the attributes' distinct existence (*taʿṭīl*) and thus verging on the theological position of the Muʿtazilī school (al-Marjānī, *Mustafād*, 2:172–3). Al-Marjānī found these charges baseless, and he defended al-Qūrṣāwī in his first work, the *Risālat tanbīh abnāʾ al-ʿaṣr ʿalā tanzīh anbāʾ Abī l-Naṣr* ("Epistle informing contemporaries about transcendence in reports of Abū l-Naṣr," composed in 1849, publ. 2000).

Al-Qūrṣāwī was the most important inspiration for al-Marjānī, who refined and furthered his ideas. Al-Marjānī saw earlier Ashʿarī scholars, notably Fakhr al-Dīn al-Rāzī (d. 606/1210), as responsible for the flawed view of the attributes, and he argued that the emphasis on the attributes' possible existence was based on a misunderstanding of post-Avicennian ontology. He articulated this stance in commentaries on al-Nasafī's creed (bypassing al-Taftāzānī's commentary) and Jalāl al-Dīn al-Dawānī's (d. 908/1502) *Sharḥ al-ʿAqāʾid al-ʿAḍudiyya* ("Commentary on the creed of ʿAḍud [al-Dīn al-Ījī]," d. 756/1356), which were the two most important texts of the Central Asian theological tradition.

Michael Kemper has shown that theological disputes were an important part of Volga-Ural Islamic discourse, which was characterised by debates over religious belief, ritual, and authority. Chief amongst them was the question of the *ʿishāʾ* (night) prayer, that is, whether it should be performed during summer when its appointed time—the disappearance of dusk *(ghaybūbat al-shafaq)*—does not occur in the far north. Al-Marjānī rejected the prevailing position that it should not be performed. In his *Nāẓūrat al-ḥaqq fī farḍiyyat al-ʿishāʾ wa-in lam yaghib al-shafaq* ("View of the truth on the obligation of *ʿishāʾ*, even if dusk does not disappear," 1870), he—like al-Qūrṣāwī—linked his stance on the prayer with *ijtihād* (independent legal interpretation), which he saw, controversially, as a religious necessity, essential for addressing such questions in reference to the specific context. He argued that *ijtihād* was thus open to legal scholars capable of using the jurisprudence *(uṣūl al-fiqh)* of their legal school *(madhhab)*. (Al-Marjānī himself composed multiple works on Ḥanafī *fiqh*, some published in his lifetime, which remain largely unstudied).

Al-Marjānī's reformist posture extended to issues of education and the practical import of Islamic scholarship. He was open to Russian society and advances in Russian academia and argued that Muslims should learn Russian and adopt some European scholarly approaches for their own benefit. One of his earliest students, Khusain Faizkhanov (d. 1866), followed this path, joining the Oriental Faculty at Kazan University after completing his studies with al-Marjānī. A major figure in Russian orientalism, Faizkhanov corresponded frequently with al-Marjānī about the transformation of Islamic education along European lines. Al-Marjānī was also an early supporter of the Crimean journalist and intellectual Ismail Gasprinski's (Gaspirali, d. 1914) famed reform of Islamic pedagogy, the *uṣūl-i jadīd* (new method), from which Jadidism, the Muslim modernist movement that flourished in the early twentieth-century Russian Empire, takes its name.

Al-Marjānī's most significant link with Russian academia was in the realm of history. He wrote several historical works, mostly on local or regional subjects. In addition to Islamic sources he used Russian and European sources and approaches, and he frequently criticised Islamic sacred historiography on empiricist grounds, raising doubts about the histories attached to local religious shrines and sites, including assertions that some Prophetic companions had travelled to, and were buried in, the Volga region. Most prominently, he questioned the authenticity of the Samarqand codex of the Qurʾān widely attributed to the caliph ʿUthmān (r. 23–35/644–56). He was rewarded for such work with membership in the Russian Archaeological Society (Sharaf, 128). Amongst his works, the *Wafiyyat al-aslāf wa-taḥiyyat al-akhlāf* ("The faithfulness of the ancestors and praising the successors"), a six-volume biographical dictionary of the entirety of Islamic history, is perhaps his magnum opus (so far unpublished), and the *Mustafād al-akhbār fī aḥwāl Qazān wa-Bulghār* ("Beneficial reports on the circumstances of Kazan and Bulghar"), a work on the history and *ʿulamāʾ* of the Volga-Ural region, is the most influential. The latter is considered one of the first works of Tatar historiography, "Tatar" being an ethnonym championed by al-Marjānī (e.g., *Mustafād*, 1:4), which he preferred to "Bulghārī," the previously customary self-identifier for Volga-Ural Muslims that fell out of use around 1900.

Soviet-era secondary literature presented al-Marjānī as a nationalist intellectual, misrepresenting his advocacy of *ijtihād* as a call for secular rationalism and freethinking and ignoring his theological writings. Post-Soviet scholarship, beginning largely with Kemper, has re-established the religious content of his thought, although the older historiographical portrayal remains widespread.

Bibliography

Works by al-Marjānī

Ḥāshiya ʿalā sharḥ Jalāl al-Dīn Dawānī ʿalā l-ʿAqāʾid al-ʿAḍudiyya, printed alongside Ismāʿīl b. Muṣṭafā l-Kalanbawī, *Ḥāshiyat al-Kalanbawī ʿalā sharḥ al-Dawānī*, Istanbul 1316/1898; *al-Ḥikma al-bāligha al-janiyya fī sharḥ al-ʿAqāʾid al-Ḥanafiyya*, Kazan 1888; *Mustafād al-akhbār fī aḥwāl Qazān wa-Bulghār*, 2 vols., 1897–1900 Kazan, repr. Ankara 1997; *Nāẓūrat al-ḥaqq fī farḍiyyat alʿishāʾ wa-in lam yaghib al-shafaq*, Kazan 1870; *Wafiyyat al-aslāf wa-taḥiyyat al-akhlāf*, 6 vols., Kazanskiĭ Gosudarstvennyĭ Universitet, MSS A 609–15.

Other sources

Riḍāʾ al-Dīn Fakhr al-Dīn, *Āthār*, pt. 1, Kazan 1900, pts. 2–15, Orenburg 1901–8; Riḍāʾ al-Dīn Fakhr al-Dīn (Rizaéddin Fäxreddin), *Asar. Öchenche häm dürtenche tomnar*, Kazan 2010; Michael Kemper, Šihabaddin al-Marğani über Abu n-Nasr al-Qursawis Konflikt mit den Gelehrten Bucharas, in Anke von Kügelgen, Aširbek Muminov, and Michael Kemper (eds.), *Muslim culture in Russia and Central Asia*, vol. 3, *Arabic, Persian and Turkic manuscripts (15th–19th centuries)* (Berlin 2000), 353–83; *Marjānī*, ed. Ṣāliḥ b. Thābit ʿUbaydallīn, Kazan 1333/1915; Muḥammad Murād Ramzī, *Talfīq al-akhbār wa-talqīḥ al-āthār fī waqāʾiʿ Qazān wa-Bulghār wa-mulūk al-Tatār*, ed. Ibrāhīm Shams al-Dīn, 2 vols., Beirut 2002; Shahr Sharaf, Marjānīnīñ tarjima-yi ḥālī, *Marjānī*, ed. Ṣāliḥ b. Thābit ʿUbaydallīn (Kazan 1333/1915), 2–193.

Studies

Ia. G. Abdullin, *Tatarskaia prosvetitelʹskaia myslʹ*, Kazan 1976; M. Kh. Iusupov, *Shigabutdin Mardzhani kak istorik*, Kazan 1981; Michael Kemper, *Sufis und Gelehrte in Tatarien und Baschkirien, 1789–1889. Der islamische Diskurs unter russischer Herrschaft*, Berlin 1998; Azade-Ayşe Rorlich, *The Volga Tatars. A profile in national resilience*, Stanford 1986; Uli Schamiloglu, The formation of a Tatar historical consciousness. Şihabäddin Märcani and the image of the Golden Horde, *Central Asian Survey* 9 (1990), 39–49; Nathan Spannaus, *Preserving Islamic tradition. Abu Nasr Qursawi and the beginnings of modern reformism*, Oxford 2019; Nathan Spannaus, Šihab al-Din al-Marğani on the divine attributes. A study in *kalam* in the 19th century, *Arabica* 62 (2015), 74–98; Nathan Spannaus, The Ur-text of Jadidism. Abu Nasr Qursawi's *Irshad* and the historiography of Muslim modernism in Russia, *JESHO* 59 (2016), 93–125; Mirkasym Usmanov, Istochniki knigi Sh. Mardzhani *Mustafad al-akhbar fi akhval Kazan va Bulgar*, in A. L. Litvin (ed.), *Ocherki istorii povolzhʹia i priuralʹia*, vols. 2 and 3 in one (Kazan 1969), 144–54.

Nathan Spannaus

Meteorology

Meteorology in Islam was part of the natural sciences. The knowledge of meteorological phenomena contributed to weather forecasting. The principles and causes of the phenomena required scientific proofs, which overcame the controversies of astrologers, as well as incorrect opinions based on tradition. A statement to this effect by the philosopher al-Kindī (d. between 247/861 and 259/873) (Brentjes, 19f.) is based on his knowledge of Aristotle's methodology and meteorology, as known to the Arabs as early as the third/ninth century.

1. The Aristotelian tradition

At that time, Aristotle's (d. 322 B.C.E.) *Meteorology* had been translated into Arabic by the Christian Yaḥyā b. al-Biṭrīq (d. c.215/830) on the basis of a late Greek revision, with the title *Kitāb al-āthār al-ʿulwiyya* ("Book of the upper/celestial effects"; ed. Schoonheim, *Aristotle's Meteorology;* cf. Lettinck *Aristotle's Meteorology*, 7f.). This translation became the main source for later authors for their information about meteorological phenomena. The earliest texts quoting the translation are the medical encyclopaedia *Firdaws al-ḥikma* by the Persian physician ʿAlī b. Rabban al-Ṭabarī (third/ninth century) (Daiber, *Kompendium*, 74, 94; *GAS*, 7:237–40) and, presumably at the same time, writings attributed to Jābir b. Ḥayyān (*GAS*, 7:233–6). Later, in the fifth/eleventh century, Ibn al-Biṭrīq's translation appears to have been adapted in Abū Ḥātim al-Isfizārī's (d. 504/1110) *Risāla-yi āthār-i ʿulviyya kāʾināt-i javv* ("Treatise on the upper/celestial effects existing in the air"), the oldest work on meteorology written in Persian and used by later Persian authors, partly with additions from the Arabic *Meteorology* of Ibn Sīnā (Avicenna, d. 428/1037) (Zakeri). Perhaps in the seventh/thirteenth century, the *Kitāb al-ḥikma* (Istanbul, MS Esad Efendi 1933, fols. 82r–94v), an anonymous compendium of metaphysics, meteorology, and biology, integrated parts of Ibn al-al-Biṭrīq's translation (Wakelnig 87f.).

Another Arabic version of Aristotle's *Meteorology* is a "compendium" *(jawāmiʿ)*, which, according to the manuscripts, was translated by Ḥunayn b. Isḥāq (d. 262/876), perhaps from a lost Syriac version also by Ḥunayn (ed. Daiber, *Kompendium;* cf. Daiber, Nestorians, and Baffioni, Elaboration). There is a long excerpt in the anonymous *Kitāb fīhi ārāʾ al-ḥukamāʾ fī l-ṭabīʿiyyāt wa-l-ārāʾ wa-l-kalimāt al-rūḥāniyya* ("Book on the opinions of the philosophers about physics and on the spiritual opinions and sayings") in Istanbul Aya Sofya MS 2450 (perhaps eighth/fourteenth century), fols. 79r–88v (*GAS*, 7:268). There are shorter excerpts in the *Kitāb al-manfaʿa* ("The useful book") by the Christian scholar ʿAbdallāh b. al-Faḍl (fifth/eleventh century) (Daiber, Graeco-arabica christiana, nos. 24–5). Ḥunayn's "compendium" is shorter than the translation by Yaḥyā b. al-Biṭrīq but shares with it certain late Greek interpretations.

In some cases, other Greek-Arabic sources, based partly on Syriac versions, became influential in later Syriac meteorological texts, beginning in the late third/ninth century (Takahashi, *Aristotelian meteorology*, esp. 37–41); they were translations of commentaries on Aristotle's *Meteorology* by the following authors:

1) Alexander of Aphrodisias (fl. second-third century C.E.): the Arabic version is lost, although fragments are available in Samuel b. Ṭibbon's (d. 1230 C.E.) Hebrew

version of Ibn al-Biṭrīq's text (Fontaine, x et seq. and xxxix–lxxi), and it is used by, amongst others, Ibn al-Khammār (d. after 407/1017) in his *Maqāla fī l-āthār al-mutakhayyila fī l-jaww* ("Treatise on meteorological effects appearing in the air"; ed. and trans. Lettinck, *Aristotle's Meteorology*, 313–79). Ibn Rushd (Averroës, d. 595/1198) used Alexander's commentary whenever he found discrepancies between this text and Aristotle's *Meteorology* in the version of Ibn al-Biṭrīq (Lettinck, *Aristotle's Meteorology*, 29).

2) Olympiodorus of Alexandria (fl. sixth century C.E.): the Arabic version is lost, but was known to several Arabic authors (Lettinck, *Aristotle's Meteorology*, index).

3) Olympiodorus of Alexandria: a Syriac version combines the meteorological part of Nicolaus of Damascus's (b. c. 64 B.C.E.) *Compendium* of Aristotle's philosophy (lost in the Greek original) with scholia taken from Olympiodorus' *Commentary* and is said to have been translated into Arabic by Ḥunayn b. Isḥāq (d. 260/873) and revised by his son Isḥāq b. Ḥunayn (d. 289/910) and titled a commentary, said to be written by Olympiodorus (= Ps.-Olympiodorus), to Aristotle's *Meteorology* (ed. Badawī; cf. Takahashi, *Aristotelian meteorology*, 38f.; Takahashi, Syriac version). Amongst others, it was known to Ibn Sīnā (Lettinck, *Aristotle's Meteorology*, index 491f. and 493f.) and to the Nestorian Ibn al-Khammār in his *Maqāla* (313–79).

4) Theophrastus (d. 288–5 B.C.E.): of considerable influence was his *Meteorology* and its aetiology of meteorological effects (Taub, 115–24). It is lost in the Greek original but was translated into Syriac, perhaps by the Nestorian Job of Edessa (d. c.220/835) and from Syriac into Arabic by Ibn al-Khammār. The Arabic version by Bar Bahlūl (fourth/tenth century) is an independent abbreviated and often simplifying translation of the same Syriac text (ed. and trans. Daiber, *Meteorology* of Theophrastus).

2. Theophrastian meteorology

Theophrastus's *Meteorology* is quoted by Ibn al-Khammār in his *Maqāla* (Lettinck, *Aristotle's Meteorology*, 336f.). Fragments of Theophrastian meteorology appear in several Arabic sources, and it is unclear whether they derive from a common source combining Aristotle and Theophrastus, as well as Arabic meteorological texts (e.g., al-Kindī, below). This might be the case with the fourth/tenth-century *Rasāʾil Ikhwān al-Ṣafāʾ* ("Encyclopaedia of the Brethren of Purity") (natural sciences including meteorology, ed. and trans. by Carmela Baffioni, *Epistles*) and with the cosmography by al-Qazwīnī (d. 682/1283), the *ʿAjāʾib al-makhlūqāt wa-gharāʾib al-mawjūdāt* ("The marvels of creatures and strange things existing," trans. Daiber, *Meteorology* of Theophrastus, 222–5).

Theophrastian ideas reached the Arabs also through translations of the Greek commentaries or compendia mentioned above. In addition, the Syriac and Arabic translations of ps.-Aristotle's *De mundo* transmitted Theophrastian ideas to Syriac Christians and the Arabic world (Daiber, *Meteorology* of Theophrastus, 292; *GAS* 7:215, 219; Takahashi, Syriac and Arabic transmission; Daiber, Possible echoes), and the meteorological section (bk. 4) of Qusṭā b. Lūqā's (d. 300/912) Arabic translation of Aëtius's (d. c.366 C.E.) *Placita philosophorum* (ed. and trans. Daiber, *Aetius Arabus)*, which perhaps used Theophrastus's *Physikōn doxai* (Daiber, *Meteorology* of Theophrastus, 287f.).

3. The tradition of al-Kindī

The Arabic title for "Meteorology"—*al-Āthār al-ʿulwiyya* (or *al-ʿalawiyya*), "The upper/celestial effects"—became the usual name for an Aristotelian branch of science that was, in the early third/ninth century, already well-known to al-Kindī, who mentions variant titles (Adamson and Pormann, 326, n. 15): *Aḥdāth al-jaww wa-l-arḍ* ("Phenomena of heaven and earth"), *al-ʿUlwī/al-ʿAlawī* ("What belongs to the heavens"), and *al-Nihāyāt* ("The limitations [of what is below the upper eternal, unlimited motions]"); cf. Aristotle, *Meteor.* I 2. 338 b 20ff.). In his short description of Aristotle's *Meteorology*, al-Kindī (Adamson and Pormann, 294; cf. 283) is followed by his younger contemporary, the historian al-Yaʿqūbī (late third/ninth century) in his *Taʾrīkh* (Klamroth, 429). In early Islam, meteorology was dominated by astrometeorology and its assumption of an influence of the stars on phenomena in the sky, therefore called *āthār* (effects). We find an echo of this in al-Kindī, who writes in his meteorological treatises of "celestial causes" (*asbāb ʿulwiyya/al-ʿalawiyya; Rasāʾil*, 2:80) or of "influence" (*taʾthīr; Rasāʾil*, 2:75, 121). His younger contemporary Qusṭā b. Lūqā—who translated in his Arabic version of Aëtius's *Placita philosophorum* the Greek phrase τὰ μετάρσια with *al-āthār allatī tazharu fī aʿlā l-jaww* (the effects that appear in the upper air) and τὰ μετάρσια πάθη with *al-āthār allatī takūnu fī l-jaww* ("the effects that arise in the air") (Daiber, *Aetius Arabus*, 522)—consequently assumed a tripartition of the principles of the natural sciences into astronomy *(al-ʿilm bi-l-falak wa-l-kawākib)*, meteorology *(al-ʿilm bi-l-āthār al-kāʾina fī l-jaww)*, and geology *(al-ʿilm bi-l-āthār al-kāʾina fī l-arḍ)* (Daiber, Qosṭā Ibn Lūqā, 109–10). The background of this tripartition is an Aristotelian and Neoplatonising doctrine of al-Kindī and his contemporary, the astrologer Abū Maʿshar al-Balkhī (d. 272/886). Both assume an influence of the divine celestial bodies upon the sublunar world, which reaches from the earth to the moon and which consists of the natural elements of earth, water, air, and fire. The sun becomes the all-permeating divine light and determines, through mediating causes, the seasons, meteorological phenomena, and the fate of people and countries. The heavenly bodies replace the old Arabic *anwāʾ* ("Stars going down [forecasting a gale])" (Fahd, 412–6) and become the causes for meteorological phenomena and no longer mere indications. An example of mediating causes between sun and earth is, according to al-Kindī, the friction of air. This creates heat, which leads to various meteorological phenomena (Daiber, Erkenntnistheoretische Grundlagen, 151ff., 156ff.).

Al-Kindī knew Aristotle's *Meteorology* in Ibn al-Biṭrīq's translation (Lettinck, *Aristotle's Meteorology*, 111, 234), and he knew Aristotle's concept of the sun as a source of heat causing meteorological phenomena, which have their origin in dry and humid exhalations, which cause wind, precipitation, and lightning and thunder (al-Kindī, *Rasāʾil*, 2:90–100; Lettinck, *Aristotle's Meteorology*, 50–3). He added, however, the influence of the heavenly bodies, their motion, and their friction with the air. In the explanation of peculiarities of winds (cf. Lettinck, *Aristotle's Meteorology*, 176), rain (al-Kindī, *Rasāʾil*, 2:70–5), mist (al-Kindī, *Rasāʾil*, 2:76–8), snow, hail, lightning, thunder, and *zamharīr* (snow in the shape of a needle) (al-Kindī, *Rasāʾil*, 2:80–5), he sometimes differs from Aristotle (cf. Lettinck, *Aristotle's Meteorology*, 107–11, 233f.). Many of these differences are shared by the scholar and *wazīr* Abū l-Faḍl Ibn al-ʿAmīd (d. 360/970) in his letters to the Būyid ruler ʿAḍud al-Dawla (r. 367–72/978–83). These letters demonstrate a thorough knowledge of al-Kindī's meteorology, to which Ibn al-ʿAmīd added new details and other examples (Daiber, *Naturwissenschaft*, 121–5, 136–43). Another witness of al-Kindī's meteorology is the *Rasāʾil* of the Ikhwān al-Ṣafāʾ (Lettinck, *Aristotle's Meteorology*, 9f., 53f., 111, 176f.), which may have used a source that combined al-Kindī's meteorological concepts with ideas taken from Theophrastus and Aristotle, a combination later used by al-Qazwīnī (see above).

4. Ibn Sīnā, Olympiodorus, Nicolaus of Damascus

The Kindian tradition is not continued by Ibn Sīnā, who, instead, in the meteorological part of his *Kitāb al-shifāʾ* (*al-Ṭabīʿiyyāt*, 5) follows a tradition that often deviates from Aristotle's *Meteorology*, mixing it with the commentary by Olympiodorus in a version that is a combination of Olympiodorus with Nicolaus of Damascus's compendium of Aristotle's philosophy, in the section on meteorology (= Ps.-Olympiodorus, see above). Nicolaus and Olympiodorus themselves appear to have used Theophrastus's *Meteorology* in some of their work. This is apparent in Ibn Sīnā's discussion of the double exhalation (i.e., vapour and smoke), which causes all the meteorological phenomena under heating by the reflected rays of the sun. Contrary to al-Kindī, who maintained an astrometeorological orientation, the heating motion of celestial bodies plays no role for Ibn Sīnā, who describes shooting stars, comets, and other phenomena, while excluding, contrary to Aristotle, the Milky Way, which he considered, in accordance with Ibn al-Biṭrīq and Ps.-Olympiodorus, a phenomenon of the celestial world (Lettinck, *Aristotle's Meteorology*, 80–2). Other phenomena treated are the formation of clouds, dew, hail, and mist (Lettinck, *Aristotle's Meteorology*, 111–3); the formation of mountains, rivers, and the sea and its saltiness (Lettinck, *Aristotle's Meteorology*, 141–5); winds (Lettinck, *Aristotle's Meteorology*, 177–82); the reason for inhabitable and uninhabitable areas of the world (Lettinck *Aristotle's Meteorology*, 195–9); earthquakes (Lettinck *Aristotle's Meteorology*, 218–21; Baffioni), lightning and thunder (Lettinck, *Aristotle's Meteorology*, 234–7); and haloes, rainbows, mock suns, and rods that appear beside the sun, especially at sunset (Lettinck, *Aristotle's Meteorology*, 277–83).

Ibn Sīnā's *Meteorology* became the main reference work for interested educated people who sought information in belletristic works (Lettinck, Science), encyclopaedias, books on cosmography and geography (Lettinck, *Aristotle's Meteorology*, 1f.), and monographs on meteorology, such as that of Muḥammad b. Mūsā l-Ṭālishī from the ninth/fifteenth century (Takahashi, Treatise on meteorology). It was widely used, even in the Syriac encyclopaedia *Butyrum sapientiae* by Barhebraeus (d. 685/1286), and in works by Abū l-Barakāt al-Baghdādī (d. after 560/1164–5), Fakhr al-Dīn al-Rāzī (d. 607/1210), and others (Takahashi, *Aristotelian meteorology*, 48–59).

Ibn Sīnā's *Meteorology* met with differing responses from members of his "school": Bahmanyār b. al-Marzubān (d. 458/1066–7) followed his master's work slavishly. After him, Abū l-Barakāt al-Baghdādī and, to a lesser degree, Fakhr al-Dīn al-Rāzī differ from him to some extent in their formulations and explanations (Lettinck, *Aristotle's Meteorology*, sections on the

"School of Ibn Sīnā"), and they return to the Kindian astrometeorological thesis of the celestial influence on meteorological phenomena, which arise not only from terrestrial causes (Lettinck, *Aristotle's Meteorology*, 11). The same compromise is found in the commentary on Aristotle's *Meteorology* by the Andalusī philosopher Ibn Bājja (d. 532–3/1138–9). This book is, in fact, a collection of supplementary notes, which do not cover all topics. The only complete discussion is that of the Milky Way, which is, according to him, a sublunar phenomenon, as in Aristotle, but also a phenomenon in the celestial region as in the version of Ibn al-Biṭrīq, which is quoted by him, and as proven by Olympiodorus and Ps.-Olympiodorus (Lettinck, *Aristotle's Meteorology*, 58–61, 86–8). With regard to the mentioned compromise, Ibn Rushd, in his *Short commentary*, followed Ibn Bājja. In his *Middle commentary*, however, he renounced this view and left the question open. The arguments pro and con and the compromise by Ibn Bājja seemed to Ibn Rushd unsatisfactory (Lettinck, *Aristotle's Meteorology*, 12–14, 88–96). In his discussions of meteorological phenomena (Lettinck, *Aristotle's Meteorology*, 117–9, 149–55, 187–93, 205–8, 222–4, 239–42), however, Ibn Rushd left questions mostly unanswered and presented contradictory explanations, which he found in Ibn al-Biṭrīq, the commentary by Alexander of Aphrodisias, Ps.-Olympiodorus, and Ibn Sīnā. Remarkably, in his discussion of haloes and rainbows, he used the works of Ibn al-Haytham (d. 430/1039) and was able to give a clear picture of these phenomena (Lettinck, *Aristotle's Meteorology*, 287–298), which impressed the German philosopher Dietrich of Freiberg (d. c.1310 C.E.) (Lettinck, *Aristotle's Meteorology*, 298–300).

5. Arabic meteorology in mediaeval Europe

Arabic works on meteorology became known in mediaeval Europe through Latin translations of: 1) Ibn al-Biṭrīq's version of Aristotle's *Meteorology*, translated by Gerard of Cremona (d. 1187 C.E.) (ed. Schoonheim, *Aristotle's Meteorology*), whose translation was commented by Alfred of Sareshel (eleventh-twelfth century C.E.) and is said to have been known to Albertus Magnus (d. c.1280 C.E.) in his *Meteorum tractatus quattuor* (Besnier 322; Schoonheim, Météorologiques, 327; Mandosio, 173–81; Ducos); 2) Ibn Sīnā, *Kitāb al-shifāʾ, al-Ṭabīʿiyyāt* 5 = *Meteorology* (Mandosio and Di Martino; Di Martino; Di Donato); 3) Ibn Rushd, *Short commentary* and *Middle commentary* on Aristotle's *Meteorology*, parts of which are available in a late Latin translation, in a print of 1562 C.E. in Venice (Lettinck, *Aristotle's Meteorology*, 483f.; Daiber, *Islamic thought*, 142, n. 229; cf. Hasse 77, n. 17); 4) al-Kindī's astrometeorological treatises, preserved, in part, only in Latin and Hebrew translation (ed. Bos and Burnett; cf. Daiber, Erkenntnistheoretische Grundlagen, 158f.; Hasse 336). The influence of these Latin versions on the intensive discussions in Europe since the Middle Ages is still little known in detail (Hellmann 5ff.; Heninger; Ducos; Martin). There is a unique example of an Arabic meteorological work written before 1569 C.E. by a Christian scholar from the Antioch region. He perhaps had contacts with Italy, as he quotes Seneca's *Quaestiones naturales* and, amongst others, the Greek version of Aristotle's *Meteorology*. He quotes Ibn Sīnā, with whom he agrees, he knew Ibn Rushd's concept of "intelligible forms," and he had some affinity for astrometeorology. Numerous references to the Bible make the text a "Christian" meteorology written by a philosophically minded scholar who had mastered Arabic, Greek, and Latin (Daiber, Christan Arabic meteorological treatise).

Bibliography

Sources

Aristotle, *Aristotle's Meteorology in the Arabico-Latin tradition. A critical edition*, ed. Pieter L. Schoonheim, Leiden 2000; ʿAbd al-Raḥmān Badawī (ed.), Tafsīr Ulimfīdūrūs li-*Kitāb Arisṭāṭālīs fī l-āthār al-ʿulwiyya*. Tarjamat Ḥunayn b. Isḥāq, in ʿAbd al-Raḥmān Badawī (ed.), *Shurūḥ ʿalā Arisṭū mafqūda fī l-Yūnāniyya, wa-rasāʾil ukhrā = Commentaires sur Aristote perdus en grec et autres épîtres*, Beirut 1971; Brethren of Purity, *Epistles of the Brethren of Purity. On the natural sciences. An Arabic critical edition and English translation of epistles 15–21*, ed. and trans. Carmela Baffioni, Oxford 2013; Samuel Ibn Tibbon, *Otot ha-shamayim. Samuel Ibn Tibbon's Hebrew version of Aristotle's Meteorology*, trans. Resianne Fontaine, Leiden 1995; al-Kindī, *Rasāʾil al-Kindī al-falsafiyya*, ed. Muḥammad ʿAbd al-Hādī Abū Rīda, vol. 2, Cairo 1953; al-Yaʿqūbī, *Taʾrīkh*, in *The works of Ibn Wāḍiḥ al-Yaʿqūbī*, vol. 2, ed. Matthew S. Gordon, Chase F. Robinson, Everett K. Rowson, and Michael Fishbein, Leiden 2018, trans. Martin Klamroth, Ueber die Auszüge aus griechischen Schriftstellern bei al-Jaʿqûbî, *ZDMG* 41 (1887), 415–42.

Studies

Peter Adamson and Peter E. Pormann, *The philosophical works of al-Kindī*, Oxford 2012; Carmela Baffioni, The elaboration of ancient theories on earthquakes. Avicenna and Faḫr al-Dîn al-Râzî in relation to their Greek and Arabic sources, in Agostino Cilardo (ed.), *Islam and globalisation. Historical and contemporary perspectives* (Leuven 2013), 435–62; Bernard Besnier, *Météorologiques.* Tradition grecque, in Richard Goulet, Jean-Marie Flamand, and Maroun Aouad (eds.), *Dictionnaire des philosophes antiques. Supplément* (Paris 2003), 315–23; Gerrit Bos and Charles Burnett, *Scientific weather forecasting in the Middle Ages. The writings of al-Kindi. Studies, editions and translations of the Arabic, Hebrew and Latin texts*, London and New York 2000; Sonja Brentjes, Teaching the sciences in ninth-century Baghdad as a question in the history of the book. The case of Abū Yūsuf Yaʿqūb b. Isḥāq al-Kindī (d. after 256/870), *Intellectual History of the Islamicate World* 5 (2017), 1–27; Hans Daiber, *Ein Kompendium der aristotelischen Meteorologie in der Fassung des Ḥunain Ibn Isḥāq*, Amsterdam and Oxford 1975, and *Verhandelingen der Koninklijke Nederlandse Akademie van Wetenschappen*, Literature Sect., n.s., 89 (1975); Hans Daiber, *Aetius Arabus. Die Vorsokratiker in arabischer Überlieferung*, Wiesbaden 1980; Hans Daiber, A Christan Arabic meteorological treatise attributed to ʿAbdallāh Ibn al-Faḍl (11th c.) or to Bonaventura de Lude (17th c.). Its Greek, Arabic and Latin sources. Prolegomena to a critical edition, in Aafke M. I. van Oppenraay and Resianne Fontaine (eds.), *The letter before the spirit. The importance of text editions for the study of the reception of Aristotle* (Leiden 2012), 73–94; Hans Daiber, Erkenntnistheoretische Grundlagen der Wetterprognose bei den Arabern. Das Beispiel von Kindī, dem "Philosophen der Araber" (9. Jh. n. Chr.), in Alexander Fidora and Katrin Bauer (eds.), *Die mantischen Künste und die Epistemologie prognostischer Wissenschaften im Mittelalter* (Cologne 2013), 151–65; Hans Daiber, Graeco-arabica christiana. The Christian scholar ʿAbd Allāh Ibn al-Faḍl from Antiochia (11th c. A.D.) as transmitter of Greek works, in Felicitas Opwis and David Reisman (eds.), *Islamic philosophy, science, culture, and religion. Studies in honor of Dimitri Gutas* (Leiden 2011), 3–9; Hans Daiber, *Islamic thought in the dialogue of cultures. A historical and bibliographical survey*, Leiden 2012; Hans Daiber, The *Meteorology* of Theophrastus in Syriac and Arabic translation, in William W. Fortenbaugh and Dimitri Gutas (eds.), *Theophrastus. His psychological, doxographical, and scientific writings* (New Brunswick NJ and London 1992), 166–293; Hans Daiber, *Naturwissenschaft bei den Arabern im 10. Jahrhundert n. Chr. Briefe des Abū l-Faḍl Ibn al-ʿAmīd (gest. 360/970) an ʿAḍudaddaula*, Leiden 1993; Hans Daiber, Nestorians of 9th century Iraq as a source of Greek, Syriac and Arabic. A survey of some unexploited sources, *ARAM* 3 (1991), 45–52; Hans Daiber, Possible echoes of *De mundo* in the Arabic-Islamic world. Christian, Islamic and Jewish thinkers, in Johan C. Thom (ed.), *Cosmic order and divine power. Pseudo-Aristotle, On the cosmos* (Tübingen 2014), 169–80; Hans Daiber, Qosṭā Ibn Lūqā (9. Jh.) über die Einteilung der Wissenschaften, *ZGAIW* 6 (1990 [1991]), 94–129; Silvia Di Donato, Les trois traductions latines de la *Météorologie* d'Avicenne. Notes pour l'histoire du texte, in *Documenti e studi sulla tradizione filosofica medievale* 28 (2017), 331–49; Carla Di Martino, I "Meteorologica" di Avicenna, in Concetto Martello et al. (eds.), *Cosmogonie e cosmologie nel medioevo. Atti del convegno della Società Italiana per lo Studio del Pensiero Medievale (S.I.S.P.M.), Catania, 22–24 settembre 2006* (Louvain-la-Neuve 2008), 35–46; Joëlle Ducos, *La météorologie en français au Moyen Age (XIIIe–XIVe siècles)*, Paris 1998; Toufic Fahd, *La divination arabe*, Leiden 1966; Dag Nikolaus Hasse, *Success and suppression. Arabic sciences and philosophy in the Renaissance*, Cambridge MA 2016; G. Hellmann, *Beiträge zur Geschichte der Meteorologie*, vol. 2 (nos. 6–10) (Berlin 1917), 1–341; S. K. Heninger, *A handbook of Renaissance meteorology, with particular reference to Elizabethan and Jacobean literature*, Durham NC 1960; Paul Lettinck, *Aristotle's Meteorology and its reception in the Arab world*, Leiden 1999; Paul Lettinck, Science in *adab* literature, *ASP* 21 (2011), 149–63, and in Wan Mohd. Nor Wan Daud and Muhammad Zainiy Uthman (eds.), *Knowledge, language, thought and the civilization of Islam. Essays in honor of Syed Muhammad Naquib al-Attas* (Skudai, Malaysia 2010), 267–82 (a preliminary version appeared in Emilia Calvo, Mercè Comes, Roser Puig, and Mònica Rius, eds., *A shared legacy. Islamic science East and West. Homage to Professor J. M. Millàs Vallicrosa*, Barcelona 2008, 237–45); Jean-Marc Mandosio, Meteorology and weather forecasting in the Middle Ages, in Alexander Fidora and Katrin Bauer (eds.), *Die mantischen Künste und die Epistemologie prognostischer Wissenschaften im Mittelalter* (Cologne 2013), 167–81; Jean-Marc Mandosio and Carla Di Martino, La "Météorologie" d'Avicenne (*Kitāb al-Šifā'* V) et sa diffusion dans le monde latin, in Andreas Speer and Lydia Wegener (eds.), *Wissen über Grenzen. Arabisches Wissen und lateinisches Mittelalter* (Berlin 2006), 406–24; Craig Martin, *Renaissance meteorology. Pomponazzi to Descartes*, Baltimore 2011; Pieter L. Schoonheim, Météorologiques. Tradition syriaque, arabe et latin, in Richard Goulet, Jean-Marie Flamand, and Maroun Aouad (eds.), *Dictionnaire des philosophes antiques. Supplément* (Paris 2003), 324–8; Hidemi Takahashi, *Aristotelian meteorology in Syriac. Barhebraeus, Butyrum sapientiae. Books of mineralogy and meteorology*, Leiden 2004; Hidemi Takahashi, Syriac and Arabic transmission of *On the cosmos*, in Johan C. Thom (ed.), *Cosmic order and divine power. Pseudo-Aristotle, On the cosmos* (Tübingen 2014), 153–67; Hidemi Takahashi, Syriac fragments of Theophrastean meteorology and mineralogy. Fragments in the Syriac version of Nicolaus Damascenus, *Compendium of Aristotelian philosophy* and the accompanying scholia, in William W. Fortenbaugh and Georg Wöhrle (eds.), *On the Opuscula of Theophrastus, Akten der 3. Tagung der Karl-und-Gertrud-Abel-Stiftung vom 19.-23. Juli 1999 in Trier* (Stuttgart 2002), 189–225; Hidemi Takahashi, Syriac version by Ḥunain (?) of Nicolaus Damascenus' compendium of Aristotelian philosophy and accompanying scholia, *Journal of the Canadian Society for Syriac Studies* 5 (2005), 18–34; Hidemi Takahashi, A treatise on meteorology by Muḥammad Ibn Mūsā al-Ṭālishī (MS Daiber Collection II, 82), in Anna Akasoy and Wim Raven (eds.), *Islamic thought in the Middle Ages. Studies in text, transmission and translation, in honour of Hans Daiber* (Leiden 2008), 363–401; Liba Taub, *Ancient meteorology*, London and New York 2003; Elvira Wakelnig, A new version of Miskawayh's *Book of triumph*. An alternative recension of *al-Fawz al-aṣghar* or the lost *Fawz al-akbar?*, *ASP* 19 (2009), 83–119; Mohsen Zakeri, The reception of Aristotle's *Meteorologia* in the Persian world. Isfizārī's *Meteorology*, in Emilia Calvo, Mercè Comes, Roser Puig, and Mònica Rius (eds.), *A shared legacy. Islamic science east and west. Homage to Professor J. M. Millàs Vallicrosa* (Barcelona 2008), 309–20; *GAS* 7.

Hans Daiber

Missionaries, Christian, in the Islamic world

Christian missionaries in the Islamic world, from the sixteenth century to the twentieth centuries, built upon mediaeval patterns, attempting primarily to convert local Eastern Christians. While most considered the conversion of Muslims their ultimate aim, this effort was largely postponed because of political and social constraints. Missions in the Middle East were motivated by generic ideas about converting the heathen but also by a certain type of piety in which the "Land of the Bible" or the "Holy Land" represented both the place of Christianity's origins (i.e., Holy Places) and the canvas upon which the "end of times" would be painted (i.e., the location of the Second Coming of Jesus Christ).

1. Early missions after the Crusades

Christian missionaries in the Islamic world had their origins in the seventh/thirteenth century, when, following up on the Crusades, the recently established Dominican and the Franciscan orders considered the conversion of Muslims a main priority.

Many of the missionaries travelled the Silk Routes, often under the protection of Mongol rulers. Most early Catholic mission centres were established outside what is usually seen as the Middle East, in Armenia, Tabriz, Samarkand. Missionaries worked mainly for and with local Christians rather than with Muslims. Meanwhile, the Franciscans in Jerusalem guarded many of the Christian holy places that had been appropriated during the Crusader period, supporting Christian pilgrims from Europe. While they left the conversion of Muslims to their brethren elsewhere, the Franciscans from the Custody of the Holy Land came to play a crucial role in attempts to bring Eastern Christians into the Roman Catholic fold. From the beginning, conversionist missions in the Islamic world were thus practically and ideologically connected with missions that worked amongst Eastern Christians and had a broader Christian interest in, and claims on, the Christian holy places.

2. Catholic missions under Ottoman and Ṣafavid rule

Roman Catholic missions to the Middle East took a new turn in the tenth/sixteenth century, after the Ottoman Empire had conquered and largely unified most of the region. Especially after the Council of Trent (1545–63), the Catholic Church was motivated to compensate for the losses it had suffered in northern and central Europe by strengthening its missions in the Americas and by working to "re-unite" wayward Eastern Christians with the Mother Church from which they had ostensibly separated. From 977/1569 onwards, capitulations granted by Ottoman sultans to Christian nations allowed French Catholic priests to work in the Ottoman Empire, even if their activities had officially to be restricted to Catholic Christians. In Ṣafavid Iran, missionaries were cautiously allowed to establish missions. The fledgling Uniate (Eastern Catholic) churches were supported by Rome-educated local clergy and by newly printed missals in which their liturgies were adapted (usually lightly) to Catholic theological standards. The missionaries, both the older Franciscan, Dominican, and Carmelite orders and the newly established Jesuit congregation focused, in addition to catechism and pastoral care, on education and medicine which benefited the Christian populations in particular. While the Ottoman government tended to support the Eastern prelates in their struggle against Catholic influence over their flock, propagandists for union were found amongst all Eastern churches. Reasons for conversion to Catholicism ranged from attraction to a new, more individualistic kind of religious belief and practice to the hope of prosperity by profiting from tax exemptions enacted for Western Christians. For bishops and patriarchs who initiated unions with Rome, conversion was motivated as much by long-standing ideas about the Roman See being the principal patriarchate of the global Christian church as by seeking ways to ensure foreign protection against local discrimination and oppression of their flock.

3. The advent of Protestants and millennialism

During the late eighteenth century, culminating in the French Revolution, many Catholic missions were prevented from continuing their work. In the same period Protestant missionaries, who had until then hardly been active in the Middle East, entered the region. One of the larger Protestant organisations was the interdenominational American Board of Commissioners to Foreign Missions. By the 1840s it was funnelling almost half of its funds into the region. The ABCFM's earliest mission was focused on Jerusalem and its Jewish communities. Strong local resistance soon caused them to give up this project, but the conversion of the Jews as an essential stage in the millennialist choreography that was to play out at the "end of times" in the Holy Land would time and again motivate missionaries, whether as part of large, well funded organisations such as the Anglican Church Mission Society (CMS) or as small, nearly private missions supported by a few donors in America, England, or mainland Europe. The Anglo-Prussian bishopric of Jerusalem, an Anglican-Lutheran cooperation established in 1841—which later separated into the Anglican bishopric and the Lutheran Church of Jerusalem—originated in similar millennialist ideologies. Its later phases were focused mostly on Arabic-speaking Eastern Christians, although its original focus on Jewish Christianity has been preserved in Christ Church (Jerusalem), founded in 1848.

Instead of Jews, however, the ABCFM hoped to convert Muslims, although it soon became clear that the Ottoman and Persian governments would permit no proselytism amongst Muslims. From the beginning, therefore, their missions were focused mostly on Eastern Christians. Initially, the Protestants aimed not for individual conversions to Protestantism but for setting in motion a reform movement like that of Luther, renewing the Eastern churches from within. True to the sixteenth-century model, however, individual conversions to Protestantism and opposition from the leadership of the Eastern churches soon led to the formation of separate Protestant communities. In the 1840s, the first Protestant churches were established in Jerusalem, Beirut, and Istanbul, with most converts coming from the Eastern churches. Like the Catholics before them, Protestant missionaries invested much of their time and resources in education, printing, and medical support. In doing so, they often changed social dynamics, by educating a part of the population that had little access to it, translating reading materials from around the world that would change how people looked at society and their role in it, and establishing a model of modernity that was copied by many. To the missionaries' disappointment, they proved to be considerably more successful in modernising than in conversion, the number of converts remaining very small in comparison to those of the Catholic and traditional churches.

4. The revival of Catholic missions

By the 1840s, Catholic missions had recovered from the setbacks that resulted from the French revolution and other European developments, such as the temporary suppression of the Jesuit order (1773). Challenged by Protestant successes and support by new European rulers, Catholic missionaries returned to the Middle East. They established new congregations and renewed their methods, and benefitted from the recently re-established patriarchate of Jerusalem (1847). Education was taken on more systematically, and, while earlier Catholic missionaries had considerable success amongst the female Christian population, female congregations newly established in the nineteenth century, such as the Sisters of Charity, emulated the Protestants in providing education, health care, and social services especially for women.

5. The arrival of Russian Orthodox missions

In the second half of the nineteenth century, the Russian Orthodox Church became more active in the Middle East. While they had been in touch with Middle Eastern Churches as part of intra-Orthodox concerns and converging interests in the holy places, it was during this period that they aimed to strengthen the Orthodox churches against what they saw as the assault of the Catholics and Protestants. While this did not lead to an Orthodox version of Uniatism, it did support the Orthodox churches of Palestine and Syria in setting up rival educational and health care systems serving their own populations.

6. Revived focus on the conversion of Muslims

In the final decades of the nineteenth century, the conversion of Muslims to Christianity again became the explicit aim of several missionary organisations. The reasons for this shift in emphasis included a new wave of missionaries from Europe and the United States who were inspired by evangelical spirituality and had little patience for working with what they thought were the "nominal" and "ritualistic" Christians of the Middle East. These younger generations no longer believed, like their predecessors, that "regenerated" local Christians would make the best missionaries to Muslims. The Ottoman Empire, Egypt, and Iran increasingly came under Western colonial influence and were discouraged from prohibiting such missionary activities, even if local resistance remained as strong as ever. While some of these young missionaries would gradually adopt the practices of their predecessors and focus increasingly on education (including universities) and health care, others remained committed to the work of conversion. In hindsight, although conversionist aims remained part of the missions, the most important effect of the mid- and late-nineteenth-century missions was their contribution to the emergence of new kinds of communal identities in a Middle East that was very much in flux. Most importantly, they provided some of the building blocks for ethno-cultural revivals such as the Arab *nahḍa* and the Armenian and Syriac/Assyrian literary revivals, which not only constituted non-denominational and civic Republics of Letters but also propagated models of self and nation that allowed ethno-national interpretations to replace religiously based communitarianism.

7. Twentieth and twenty-first centuries

The First World War put on hold much of the more traditional missionary work, with the remaining missionaries focusing on emergency aid and foster care for the numerous orphans who survived the Syriac-Armenian genocides in Anatolia and the famines in Syria. After the war, some of the earlier work was resumed, but the combination of emergency work and changing theologies that preferred inter-religious and inter-denominational dialogue and cooperation to conversion changed the intentions and activities of the older organisations. Many of them left or became ecumenical humanitarian organisations that supported the churches of the Middle East and Middle Eastern societies more generally. Simultaneously, new organisations focused on the conversion of Muslims continued to send missionaries to the Middle East, even after post-colonial independent governments had usually forbidden all missionary work. Such evangelistic work, which continues mostly covertly into the twenty-first century, has led, in most countries, to the emergence of modest but growing communities of what often are called "believers with Muslim-background" (BMBs), often of the more evangelical or Pentecostal type, and often sharing millennialist readings of the Middle East not very different from those of the early Catholics and Protestants.

Bibliography

Adam Becker, *Revival and awakening. Christian mission, orientalism, and the American evangelical roots of Assyrian nationalism (1834–1906)*, Chicago 2015; J. F. Coakley, *The Church of the East and Church of England. A history of the archbishop of Canterbury's Assyrian mission*, Oxford 1992; Bernard Heyberger, *Les chrétiens du Proche Orient au temps de la réforme catholique*, Rome 1994; Benjamin Z. Kedar, *Crusade and mission. European approaches toward the Muslims*, Princeton 1984; Akram Fouad Khater, *Embracing the divine. Passion and politics in the Christian Middle East*, Syracuse 2011; Ussama Makdisi, *Artillery of heaven. American missionaries and the failed conversion of the Middle East*, Ithaca 2008; Heleen Murre-van den Berg (ed.), *New faith in ancient lands. Western missions in the Middle East in the nineteenth and early twentieth centuries*, Leiden 2006; Thomas S. R. O'Flynn, *The western Christian presence in the Russias and Qājār Persia, c.1760–c.1870*, Leiden 2017; Inger Marie Okkenhaug, *The quality of heroic living, of high endeavour and adventure. Anglican mission, women and education in Palestine, 1888–1948*, Leiden 2002; K. A. Panchenko, *Arab Orthodox Christians under the Ottomans, 1516–1831*, Jordanville NY 2016; Jean Richard, *La papauté et les missions d'Orient au Moyen Âge (XIIIe–XVe siècles)*, Rome 1977, 1998²; Kenneth R. Ross, Mariz Tadros, and Todd M. Johnson (eds.), *Christianity in North Africa and West Asia*, Edinburgh 2018; Heather J. Sharkey, *American evangelicals in Egypt. Missionary encounters in an age of empire*, Princeton 2008; Theofanis G. Stavrou, *Russian interests in Palestine, 1882–1914. A study of religious and educational enterprise*, Thessaloniki 1963; Martin Tamcke and Michael Marten (eds.), *Christian witness between continuity and new beginnings*, Berlin 2006; Eleanor Harvey Tejirian and Reeva Spector Simon, *Conflict, conquest and conversion. Two thousand years of Christian missions in the Middle East*, New York 2012; Chantal Verdeil (ed.), *Mission chrétiennes en terre d'Islam. Moyen-Orient, Afrique du Nord (XVIIe–XXe siècles)*, Turnhout 2013; Keith David Watenpaugh, *Bread from stones. The Middle East and the making of modern humanitarianism*, Berkeley 2015.

Heleen Murre-van den Berg

Moriscos

In modern historical terminology, the term **Moriscos** refers to Muslims in the Spanish kingdoms who, under various degrees of duress, were converted to Christianity between 1499 and 1526, and to their descendants who continued to live in Spain until the Expulsion of 1609–14 and—in small numbers, even after 1614—who lived mostly as Christians but, in some cases, especially in Granada, as crypto-Muslims (Soria Mesa). In Spain, the Moriscos were the subject of a long public debate (especially after the forced migration of the Granadan Moriscos to Castile in 1570) about the sincerity of their conversions, but no such discussions took place in Portugal, where the Mouriscos were more often migrants from outside Portugal (such as prisoners of war and African Muslims) rather than descendants of the Muslim population. The Muslims of Portugal were offered the choice between conversion and expulsion in 1496, and many migrated to Castile, which probably indicates that most Muslims had left Portugal. The Portuguese Mouriscos were expelled in 1614 (Barros, 74). In Spain, there were about 280,000 Moriscos in 1609. Spanish authors referred to them at first as *nuevos convertidos de moros* (new Moorish converts), and it is not until the second half of the seventeenth century that the term "Morisco" came into use in the specific historical sense (it always had the general sense of "Moorish," as in *traje morisco* "Moorish dress"). The term "Morisco" is also often applied to refugees after their arrival in North Africa and other Islamic lands, where they almost always resumed an Islamic life and long retained—up to the present in some areas of Tunisia, Algeria, and Morocco—a distinct social and ethnic identity. In Arabic sources these people were described collectively as Andalus (sic) and, as individuals, often as Andalusian (Andalusī); the term Muriskiyyūn is a modern borrowing from "Morisco."

1. Prelude to Expulsion

The scholarly debate about the reasons for the expulsion of 1609–14 and its significance has continued to the present. New elements in the discussions are the role played by the Morisco elites, the continued Morisco presence in Spain after the official expulsions, and local variations in Morisco life. During the conquest of the kingdom of Granada, some members of the Muslim elites began to serve the Castilian authorities and collaborate with them, often as soldiers in the Castilian armies but also as servants in the administration (Galán Sánchez). These groups claimed special privileges, and some converted voluntarily. The first forced conversions occurred some years after the fall of the city. As had happened during capitulations with several other Naṣrid cities upon their rendition, a capitulation seemed to guarantee the continued existence of a stable minority of *mudejars* (Muslims who remained after the Christian reconquest) (Ladero Quesada), but this was not to be. Political and religious pressures increased. First, the Jews were expelled from Spain in 1492 (Amelang). In the first years under the first archbishop of Granada, Hernando de Talavera (d. 1507), the capitulation settlement was generally respected, although some capitulations were violated: the bearing of arms was prohibited, for example, and a new fiscal policy made it possible for converted Granadan Muslims to inherit from their Muslim parents, a clear infringement of the capitulation. A rapid, large-scale emigration to North Africa followed. The arrival in 1499 of the archbishop of Toledo, Francisco Jiménez de Cisneros (d. 1517), marked the abandonment of

Talavera's gradual conversion campaign. Converts to Islam from Christianity and their descendants *(elches)* had had their rights guaranteed in the capitulations, but it was apparently Cisneros's method to secure their return to Christianity; in December 1499, this led to a revolt in the Muslim quarter, the Albaicín, which spread to the Alpujarras (a mountainous area south-east of Granada) and was put down by military force in 1501. Large-scale conversions followed, while more Muslims took the continuing opportunity to emigrate to Islamic lands. In February 1502 the *mudejar*s of Castile (including Granada) were offered the choice amongst conversion, emigration, and death (Ladero Quesada, doc. 148). In their diplomatic efforts in Egypt and the Ottoman Empire to justify the events, the Catholic kings argued that the rebellion had nullified the capitulations, thus justifying forced conversion (Harvey, 45ff.).

We may conclude from the difficulties imposed on those who opted for emigration—they could leave only via harbours in the Bay of Biscay and had to abandon most of their possessions—that conversion was, in fact, the aim of the Castilian authorities. In 1515 the new Castilian legislation was made applicable to Navarre when it was incorporated into the Spanish crown. Many Navarrese *mudejar* communities took refuge in Aragonese territory, but the lands of the crown of Aragon (Aragon and Valencia) were not to remain a refuge for long.

In 1521–2, during the disorders of the Germanía (lit., the brotherhood, a revolutionary movement) in Aragon and Valencia, the mob turned against *mudejar* vassals who had remained loyal to their Christian lords and subjected them to forcible baptism. The validity of such baptisms was contested, but a conference of theologians confirmed it in 1525. In 1526 the general conversion of all Muslims in Aragon and Valencia was decreed. Islam as a public religion ceased to exist (Poutrin).

Conversion was pursued by means of evangelisation, legislation, and ecclesiastical organisation. Until 1568, efforts were concentrated on the kingdom of Granada, where Moriscos constituted about forty percent of the population. The possession of Islamic books was prohibited, and customs that were supposed to be connected with Islam, such as bathing, were banned. Many Moriscos, as they were called soon after their conversion, were able to negotiate postponement of interference from the Inquisition for several decades. It is not clear how far the state or the church backed the policy of assimilation and acculturation that apparently prevailed at this stage; in any case, the implementation of the policy was, for various reasons, circumscribed [Illustration 1].

Many Moriscos, especially those in the service of lords, remained subject to taxes that they had already paid as *mudejar*s. To these were added taxes corresponding to their new status. This fiscal inequality turned these lords eventually into protectors of Morisco Islam and the Moriscos into their dependants. In Granada a new tax, the *farḍa*, which was to be paid only by the New Christians, was introduced before 1510. By the second half of the sixteenth century, Christianisation had made little progress in Granada.

In 1567 new legislation in Granada was directed not only against Islam as a religion but against all manifestations of traditional culture, such as the oral and written use of Arabic and the performance of traditional dance *(zambra)* [Illustration 2]. At the same time a crisis in the silk industry

Illustration 1. "Morisco and Morisca on their way to Carmen," in Christoph Weiditz, *Trachtenbuch* (1530–40), 105–106. Image courtesy of the Germanisches Nationalmuseum—Digitale Bibliothek.

Illustration 2. "Morisco dance," in Christoph Weiditz, *Trachtenbuch* (30–1540), 107–108. Image courtesy of the Germanisches Nationalmuseum—Digitale Bibliothek.

(made worse by the crown's fiscal policy) harmed many Granadan Moriscos, as voiced in the protest by Fernando Nuñez Muley (a Granadan Morisco nobleman, former servant to the Granadan archbishop Hernando de Talavera). At the end of 1568 a second revolt broke out in the Alpujarras and spread throughout the kingdom of Granada.

After the revolt's suppression in 1570 about 84,000 Granadan Moriscos were deported and scattered throughout Castile, although some succeeded in returning clandestinely. Others, often members of the converted Granadan elites, escaped deportation. As a consequence, tensions between the Morisco and Old Christian communities, tensions hitherto virtually unknown in Castile, became a cause for concern. Fear, warranted or not, of contacts between Moriscos and foreign powers such as Morocco, France, the Ottoman Empire, and North African pirates, led to a ban on Moriscos residing near the coasts.

2. Expulsion

From 1570 onwards several radical repressive solutions were advanced, and, by 1582, there was already in government circles a preference for expulsion, although the economic consequences of such a drastic measure were feared. Even some members of the clergy, such as the Valencian archbishop Juan de Ribera (d. 1611), favoured (partial) expulsion. Other important elements of the ecclesiastical leadership, however, such as the Valencian bishops in their meeting of 1608–9, refused to declare the Moriscos collectively apostates and opted for a renewed effort to convert them (Benítez Sánchez Blanco). The Vatican never approved this collective punishment (Pastore). When the final decision to expel all 300,000 known descendants of Moriscos was taken in 1609 by the Spanish authorities, it was justified on grounds of state interest (alleging *crimen de lesa patria*, lit., crime against the nation), namely, alleged Morisco conspiracies with foreign (Muslim and Protestant) powers (Lomas; Benítez Sánchez Blanco). In official propaganda, King Philip III (r. 1598–1621) was pictured as the Christian sovereign who had finally purged Spain of all heretics. It immediately became a very controversial measure. Not all Moriscos were Muslims in secret nor had they all been plotting against Spain, and Christianisation and integration did take place. Nevertheless, the Moriscos were expelled in phases between 1609 and 1614 [Illustration 3]. Some communities were transported through harbours in the south to North Africa, and others crossed to France, and went, sometimes via Italy, to the Ottoman Empire, Egypt, Algeria, and, especially, Morocco and Tunisia. Rumours about the imminent expulsion led Morisco refugees to begin migrating clandestinely already before 1609. Some Moriscos—those who succeeded in arguing that they had lived as Christians—were able to evade expulsion, and some returned secretly. Both things happened in the case of the Moriscos of Villarubia de los Ojos, one of the so-called five villages of the Campo de Calatrava, the inhabitants of which were all able to remain; their offspring have continued to live there until today (Dadson). The same may have happened elsewhere, for example, Blanca, in the Valle de Ricote (Westerveld) and Granada (Soria Mesa). Many presented documents, often forged (Soria Mesa), that demonstrated their Old Christian background. The inhabitants of Hornachos

Illustration 3. Vicente Carducho, *The expulsion of the Moricos*, c.1627. Bluish gouache, feather, and pencil on paper, 380 × 504 mm. © Museo Nacional del Prado, Madrid, Spain.

(Extremadura) left as a collective and settled in Rabat (Morocco), then tried to negotiate their return (as Muslims), and, in the end, decided to remain (Bouzineb). This shows that a large variety of local circumstances and various types of lived religion existed. Cultural transformations often accompanied Christianisation. In Granada, for example, about 250 Moriscos of the (perhaps) thousands who continued to live there were tried by the Inquisition for secret Islamic practices in 1729, probably in relation to the veneration of the "Lead Tablets" (Wiegers, Lead Tablets; Soria Mesa). Recent research suggests that such groups may have existed elsewhere in Spain as well and consisted of Moriscos who had become indistinguishable from other Spaniards.

3. Religious life

Many Muslims expected the effects of baptism to be temporary and hoped to be able again to practise Islam openly. Abū l-ʿAbbās Aḥmad b. Abī Jumʿa al-Maghrāwī al-Wahrānī (d. 917/1511), a *muftī* at Fez (Stewart), wrote circa 1504 a *fatwā* for Muslims living in "strange lands" (Ar. *ghurabāʾ*) and forced to express unbelief and dissimulate. His advice, soon translated into Spanish (in Arabic script, *aljamiado*), was that they may, if forced, practice dissimulation *(taqiyya)*: they are allowed to express unbelief and dispense with the obligations connected with ritual ablutions and prayer. Nawaz found passages aiming to instruct the Moriscos how to dissimulate Islam in *aljamiado* manuscripts found in the Aragonese village of Almonacid de la Sierra (the manuscripts are now held at the Consejo Superior de Investigaciones Científicas, as Tomás Navarro Tomás, no. 32). Recent research has clarified the various local forms of religion, although it is impossible to do justice to all of these. Being a Morisco in urban areas such as Ávila (Tapia Sánchez) and Arévalo (El Mancebo de Arévalo) in Castile was, for example, very different from being a Morisco in rural areas in Valencia or Aragon. These local forms of Muslim life were at times surprisingly vital. Recent research shows the extent to which the New Converts had been integrated into Iberian society. In 1491 *mudejars* still went on the *ḥajj* and returned to their native cities, as was the case with ʿOmar Paṭōn from Ávila. It is clear that Moriscos, in spite of barriers, succeeded in integrating themselves into the middle and upper classes. While Moriscos continued, in general, to copy older Islamic Arabic manuscripts and few new Arabic texts were written, new Islamic writings in Spanish, often written in *aljamiado*, were produced (such as those by El Mancebo de Arévalo, lit., the young man of Arévalo, fl. sixteenth century), whose work evinces the influence of Thomas à Kempis, d. 1471) (López Baralt; López Morillas; Narvaez; Van Koningsveld; Wiegers, *Islamic literature*). The (oral) use of Arabic was concentrated in Valencia and Granada (see, e.g., Barceló and Labarta, who studied Arabic documents preserved in Inquisition records), and the use of Castilian, in *aljamiado* and Latin script, was focused in Aragon and Castile (*Memoria de los Moriscos*; the *aljamiado* sources published in CLEAM; López Baralt; Barletta; Harvey). An important corpus of new texts is the *Libros plúmbeos del Sacromonte* ("Lead books of Sacromonte," a series of Lead Books secretly written by Moriscos authors, discovered around 1595 on the slopes of the Valparaíso hillock in Granada, see Wiegers, Lead Tablets). Some educated Granadan Moriscos, such as the Jesuit priest Ignacio de las Casas (d. 1608) and the Granadan Morisco physician Miguel de Luna (d. 1615) and others contributed to Spanish literary and scholarly culture (Bernabé Pons). Testaments drawn up by Moriscos in Spain provide important evidence of the influence of Christian ideas (García Pedraza), including a remarkable adherence to the figure of Mary as immaculate. The Moriscos of Villarubia were good and faithful Christians in 1609 (Dadson), as was the case in other areas (Tueller). Inquisition records, although biased, are important sources of the lived religion of Moriscos under trial (Cardaillac, *Morisques et Chrétiens*; García-Arenal; Amelang).

After the Expulsion, Moriscos wrote several anti-Christian texts in Castilian in Latin script (Cardaillac, *Morisques et Chrétiens*). Important authors of Arabic writings in the diaspora include Muḥammad Ibn ʿAbd al-Rafīʿ, who wrote about genealogy and noble descent amongst the Moriscos, and Aḥmad b. Qāsim al-Ḥajarī (d. after 1050/1640), who wrote in Egypt in 1637 about the polemics with Christians and Jews in which he had been involved during his travels. The Spanish-language works of Muhammad Alguazir (d. 1610) and Juan Alonso Aragonés were particularly influential in Morisco circles in the diaspora (Wiegers).

Bibliography

The following printed publications and websites provide an introduction to Morisco sources:

For manuscripts in the Biblioteca Nacional de España, see *Memoria de los Moriscos. Escritos y relatos de una diáspora cultural*, Madrid 2010. In the Consejo Superior de Investigaciones Científicas (CSIC, Madrid), *aljamiado* and Arabic manuscripts from Almonacid de la Sierra are held in the Biblioteca Tomás Navarro Tomás (http://manuscripta.bibliotecas.cchs.csic.es). A recent study of Arabic documents is Carmen Barceló and Ana Labarta, *Cancionero morisco. Poesía árabe del siglo XV y XVI*, Valencia 2016. For editions of Spanish Islamic texts, see the *Colección de literatura española aljamiado y morisca* (CLEAM) (16 vols. so far); *Corpus de textos aljamiado-moriscos* (COTEAM, Universidad de Oviedo), http://www.arabicaetromanica.com/coteam/; Álvaro Galmés de Fuentes, *Los manuscritos aljamiado-moriscos de la biblioteca de la Real Academia de la Historia*, Madrid 1998. On Francisco Núñez Muley, see Vincent Barletta (ed. and trans.), *A memorandum for the president of the Royal Audiencia and Chancery Court of the city and kingdom of Granada by Francisco Núñez Muley*, Chicago 2007. On El Mancebo de Arévalo, see María Teresa Narváez Córdova (ed.), *Tratado = Tafsira*, Madrid 2003; Omar Patún, *De Ávila a la Meca. El relato del viaje de Omar Patún 1491–1495*, ed. Xavier Casassas Canals et al., Valladolid 2017. For some Arabic texts written after the Expulsion, see Houssem Eddine Chachia et al. (eds.), *Entre las orillas de dos mundos. El itinerario del jerife Morisco Ibn ʿAbd al-Rafīʿ de Murcia a Túnez*, Murcia 2017; Aḥmad Ibn Qāsim al-Ḥajarī, *Kitāb Nāṣir al-Dīn ʿalā l-qawm al-kāfirīn = The supporter of religion against the infidel*, ed. P. S. van Koningsveld, Q. al-Samarrai, and Gerard A. Wiegers, Madrid 1997, rev. ed. Madrid 2015.

Studies

James S. Amelang, *Parallel histories. Muslims and Jews in inquisitorial Spain*, Baton Rouge 2013; Luis F. Bernabé Pons, Estudio preliminar, in Miguel de Luna, *Historia verdadera del Rey Don Rodrigo* (facs. ed.), ed. Luis F. Bernabé Pons, Granada 2001; Vincent Barletta, *Covert gestures. Crypto-Islamic literature as cultural practice in early modern Spain*, Minneapolis 2005; H. Bouzineb, *La alcazaba del Buregreg. Hornacheros, andaluces y medio siglo de designios españoles frustrados*, Rabat 2007; Rafael Benítez Sánchez Blanco, *Heroicas decisiones. La monarqúia católica y los moriscos valencianos*, Valencia 2001; Louis Cardaillac, *Morisques et chrétiens. Un affrontement polémique*, 1492–1640, Paris 1977; Louis Cardaillac (ed.), *Les morisques et l'Inquisition*, Paris 1990; Julio Caro Baroja, *Los moriscos del reino de Granada. Ensayo de historia social*, Madrid 1957, 1976²; Brian A. Catlos, *Muslims of medieval Latin Christendom, c. 1050–1614*, Cambridge 2014; Trevor J. Dadson, *Tolerancia y convivencia en la España de los Austrias. Cristianos y moriscos en el Campo de Calatrava*, Madrid 2017; Antonio Domínguez Ortiz and Bernard Vincent, *Historia de los moriscos. Vida y tragedia de una minoría*, Madrid 1978; Ángel Galán Sánchez, *Una sociedad en transición. Los granadinos de mudéjares a moriscos*, Granada 2010; Mercedes García-Arenal, *Inquisición y moriscos. Los procesos del Tribunal de Cuenca*, Madrid 1978, 1983²; Mercedes García-Arenal and Béatrice Leroy, *Moros y judíos en Navarra en la baja Edad Media*, Madrid 1984; Mercedes García-Arenal and Gerard Wiegers (eds.), *The expulsion of the Moriscos from Spain. A Mediterranean diaspora*, Leiden 2014; Amalia García Pedraza, El otro morisco. Algunas reflexiones sobre el estudio de la religiosidad morisca a través de fuentes notariales, *Sharq al-Andalus* 12 (1995), 223–34; Leonard Patrick Harvey, *Muslims in Spain 1500–1614*, Chicago 2005; Henri Lapeyre, *Geografía de la España morisca*, Valencia 2009; P. S. van Koningsveld, Andalusian-Arabic manuscripts. A comparative, intercultural approach, *IOS* 12 (1992), 75–110; Miguel Angel Ladero Quesada, *Los mudéjares de Castilla en tiempos de Isabel I*, Madrid 1969; Manuel Lomas Cortés, *El proceso de expulsión de los moriscos de España (1609–1614)*, Valencia 2011; María Filomena Lopes de Barros, Muslims in the Portuguese kingdom. Between permanence and diaspora, in José Alberto R. Silva Tavim et al. (eds.), *In the Iberian Peninsula and beyond. A history of Muslims and Jews (15th–17th centuries)* (Cambridge 2015), 1:64–85; Luce López Baralt, *La literatura secreta de los últimos musulmanes de España*, Madrid 2009; Consuelo López Morillas, *El Corán de Toledo. Edición y estudio del manuscrito 235 de la Biblioteca de Castilla-La Mancha*, Gijón 2011; Francisco Márquez Villanueva, El morisco Ricote y la hispana razón de estado, in Francisco Márquez Villanueva, *Personajes y temas del Quijote*, Madrid 1975; Francisco Márquez Villanueva, *El problema morisco (desde otras laderas)*, Madrid 1991; Amina Nawaz, *Sixteenth century Morisco devotional manuscripts in their Mediterranean contexts*, Ph.D. diss., University of Cambridge 2015; Muḥammad Razzūq (Muhammad Razouq), *al-Andalusiyyūn wa-hijratuhum ilā al-Maghrib khilāla l-qarnayn 16–17*, Casablanca 1989, 1991²; Stefania Pastore, Rome and the Expulsion, in Mercedes García-Arenal and Gerard Wiegers (eds.), *The expulsion of the Moriscos from Spain. A Mediterranean diaspora* (Leiden 2014), 132–55; José Maria Perceval, *Todos son uno. Arquetipos, xenofobia y racismo. La imagen del morisco en la monarquía española durante los siglos XVI y XVII*, Almería 1997; Isabelle Poutrin, *Convertir les musulmans. Espagne 1491–1609*, Paris 2012; Pablo Roza Candás (ed.), *Memorial de ida y venida hasta Makka. La peregrinación de ʿOmar Paṭōn*, Oviedo 2018; Enrique Soria Mesa, *Los últimos moriscos. Pervivencias de la población de origen islámico en el reino de Granada (siglos XVII-XVIII)*, Valencia 2014; Devin Stewart, Dissimulation in Sunni Islam and Morisco *taqiyya*, *Al-Qantara* 34/2 (2013), 439–90; Serafín de Tapia Sánchez, *La comunidad morisca de Ávila*, Salamanca 1991; James B. Tueller, The Moriscos who stayed behind or returned, post-1609, in Mercedes García-Arenal and Gerard A. Wiegers (eds.), *The expulsion of the Moriscos from Spain. A Mediterranean diaspora* (Leiden 2014), 197–215; Bernard Vincent, *L'Islam d'Espagne au XVIᵉ siècle. Résistances identitaires des morisques*, Saint-Denis 2017; Govert Westerveld, *Blanca, "El Ricote" de Don Quijote. Expulsión y regreso de los moriscos del último enclave islámico más grande de España, años 1613–1654*, 2 vols., Blanca, Murcia 2001–14; Gerard Wiegers, *Islamic literature in Spanish and Aljamiado. Yça of Segovia (fl. 1450), his antecedents and successors*, Leiden 1994; Gerard Wiegers, Lead Tablets, Granadan, *EI3*; Gerard Wiegers, Muhamad Alguazir, in David Thomas, John Chesworth et al. (eds.), *Christian-Muslim relations. A bibliographical history. Volume 9. Western and Southern Europe (1600–1700)* (Leiden 2017), 133–42; Gerard Wiegers, Muḥammad as the Messiah. A comparison of the polemical works of Juan Alonso with the *Gospel of Barnabas*, *BO* 52/3–4 (1995), 245–91.

Gerard A. Wiegers

Mughniyya, Muḥammad Jawād

Muḥammad Jawād Mughniyya (1904–79) was a prominent Lebanese *mujtahid* (a scholar qualified to give legal opinions) from Jabal ʿĀmil, in southern Lebanon, known for his works on Twelver Shīʿī law and jurisprudence, as well as for his support for educational reform in Najaf, Shīʿī-Sunnī unity, and the demands of peasants and workers in Lebanon's disadvantaged south.

Mughniyya was born in Ṭayr Dibbā, in Jabal ʿĀmil, in 1904, to a family of Shīʿī *ʿulamāʾ* (Muslim religious scholars); his brother ʿAbd al-Karīm Mughniyya (d. 1936) was the *imām* (prayer leader) in the adjacent town of Maʿraka. Mughniyya left his home town around 1925 to pursue his studies at Najaf's Shīʿī seminary *(ḥawza)* amid political turmoil and economic hardship. Having reached the rank of *mujtahid*, he returned to Lebanon in 1936. In 1948, he served as a *qāḍī* (judge) at the Jaʿfarī (Twelver Shīʿī) court in Beirut. In 1949 he was appointed legal adviser *(mustashār)* to Lebanon's Highest Jaʿfarī Court (al-Maḥkama al-Sharʿiyya al-Jaʿfariyya al-ʿUlyā), and in 1951 he became its president. However, when he refused to bend to the efforts of influential politicians to interfere in court rulings, he lost his position as president in 1956. He remained the court's legal adviser until retiring from this position in 1968.

In Najaf, Mughniyya espoused educational reform, involving a reorganisation of the curriculum, the introduction of new fields and books, and the modernisation of methods of teaching. He studied with prominent Shīʿī jurists such as Muḥammad Saʿīd Faḍlallāh (d. 1955), Āghā Jamāl Gulpayigānī (d. 1957), and Abū l-Qāsim al-Khūʾī (d. 1992). He adopted some of the juristic views of Shaykh Murtaḍā al-Anṣārī (d. 1864) on *ijmāʿ* (consensus of the jurists) (Mughniyya, *ʿIlm uṣūl al-fiqh*, intro.). He also admired Mirza Ḥusayn al-Nāʾīnī (d. 1927), who had argued that the jurist was morally obligated to play an active role in society and not merely implement the *sharīʿa* (Mughniyya, *Tajārib*, 44–5; Mughniyya, *al-Khumaynī*, 71). Creative in legal issues such as testament *(waṣiyya)*, Mughniyya pursued no such effort in resolving women's grievances in the areas of divorce and child custody (Mughniyya, Min al-fiqh al-Jaʿfarī, 37–40; Mughniyya, *Tajārib*, 123).

A prolific writer, Mughniyya produced over 60 works in law, jurisprudence, Islamic doctrine, Qurʾānic exegesis, ethics, political philosophy, rational theology, and devotional literature. His concise and lucid writings in the areas of Shīʿī jurisprudence won him wide acclaim. He also cultivated close ties with leading Sunnī scholars, especially Shaykh Maḥmūd Shaltūt (d. 1963) at al-Azhar in Egypt, and strove to achieve unity among Arab Muslim scholars, especially jurists, whose expertise in law would be the cornerstone of a viable unity. This quest for unity rests on Mughniyya's view that the doctrinal differences among Muslims can be overcome in the area of law, where commonalities exist. At the same time, he refuted several aspects of Wahhābī law and doctrine (Mughniyya, *Hādhihi hiya al-Wahhābiyya*, 131–44; Mughniyya, *Tajārib*, 318–9, 374).

Mughniyya was one of the earliest Shīʿī scholars to refute Khomeini's political theory of *wilāyat al-faqīh* (deputyship of the jurist). Temporal authority, in his view, belonged exclusively to the infallible Imām, and no *mujtahid*, however qualified, possessed the right to demand political allegiance from believers (Mughniyya, *al-Khumaynī*, 59, 71). At the same time, he called upon the *ʿulamāʾ* to support the peasants and workers in southern Lebanon and supported the actions of leftists and unionists against the Lebanese government and large landholders (Mughniyya, *Tajārib*, 96–7, 103–7, 114–7). Mughniyya's enemies accused him of Communist sympathies, but he insisted that it was Islam, not Communism, that inspired his commitment to social justice (Mughniyya, *Abū Dharr*, 52–6, 70–8, 345; Mughniyya, *Tajārib*, 175–6, 184–5). Mughniyya did not take up teaching positions, and devoted himself to writing new works. He died in Beirut in 1979.

Bibliography

Works

Abū Dharr al-Ghifārī. Ramz al-yaqẓa fī l-ḍamīr al-insānī (Beirut 1990), 52–6, 70–8, 345; *Hādhihi hiya al-Wahhābiyya*, ed. Sāmī al-Ghurayrī (al-Gharrāwī) (Qum 2006), 131–44; *ʿIlm uṣūl al-fiqh* (Beirut 1975), intro; *al-Khumaynī wa-l-dawla al-Islāmiyya*, Beirut 1979; Min al-fiqh al-Jaʿfarī wa-l-fiqh al-Ḥanafī, *al-ʿIrfān* 36/1 (1368/1949), 37–40; *Tajārib Muḥammad Jawād Mughniyya*, ed. Riyāḍ al-Dabbāgh (Beirut 1980), 31–46, 89–90, 108–9, 111–4.

Sources

Aḥmad al-ʿAlāwina, *Dhayl al-aʿlām. Qāmūs tarājim li-ashhar al-rijāl wa-l-nisāʾ min al-ʿArab wa-l-mustaʿribīn wa-l-mustashriqīn* (Jidda 1998), 173; Ḥasan al-Amīn, *Mustadrakāt aʿyān al-Shīʿa* (Beirut 1987), 9:205; Muḥsin al-Amīn al-ʿĀmilī, *Aʿyān al-Shīʿa*, ed. Ḥasan al-Amīn (Beirut 1986), 10:68–9, 110; Muḥammad Hādī al-Amīnī, *Muʿjam rijāl al-fikr wa-l-adab fī l-Najaf khilāl alf ʿām* (Beirut 1999), 423; ʿAlī al-Khāqānī, *Shuʿarāʾ al-Ghurī* (Najaf 1954), 7:433–5.

Studies

ʿIṣām ʿAytāwī, *al-Shaykh Muḥammad Jawād Mughniyya wa-mashrūʿuhu al-iṣlāḥī*, Beirut 2008; H. E. Chehabi and Hasan I. Mneimneh, Five centuries of Lebanese-Iranian encounters, in H. E. Chehabi (ed.), *Distant relations. Iran and Lebanon in the last 500 years* (London

2006), 40; Hādī Faḍlallah, *Muḥammad Jawād Mughniyya. Fikr wa-iṣlāḥ* (Beirut 1993), 180, 182, 184, 227, 316, 323, 329; Karl-Heinrich Göbel, *Moderne schiitische Politik und Staatsidee* (Opladen 1984), 65–139; ʿAlī Maḥraqī, Muḥammad Jawād Mughniyya. *Maʿārikuhu wa-musājalātuhu al-ʿilmiyya*, Beirut 2011; ʿAlī Maḥraqī, *Muḥammad Jawād Mughniyya. Sīratuhu wa-ʿaṭāʾuhu*, Manama 1997; Chibli Mallat, *Shiʿi thought from the south of Lebanon* (Oxford 1988), 16–25; Max Weiss, *In the shadow of sectarianism. Law, Shiʿism and the making of modern Lebanon* (Cambridge 2010), 216–7.

Rula J. Abisaab

Muḥammad Kāẓim

Muḥammad Kāẓim (d. 1092/1681) was born into an intellectual family, where he was introduced to historiographical writing at an early age. His father, Muḥammad Amīn (d. after 1056/1646), composed the *Pādshāh-nāma* ("Book of the emperor"), the history of the first ten years of the reign (1037–68/1628–58) of the Mughal emperor Shāh Jahān. Kāẓim began his career as a *munshī* (secretary) at the Mughal court under the emperor Awrangzīb ʿĀlamgīr (r. 1068–1118/1658–1707) and was given access to the state library and archives. His early interest in historiographical writings apparently brought success, as the recently crowned emperor became aware of Kāẓim's talents and ordered him to record all important events of his rule from the first year of his reign: the only condition the ruler imposed was that the newly appointed official chronicler should read to him regularly from his text so that he could dictate any needed corrections.

But, after Kāẓim had completed the first ten years and presented his thousand-page account titled *ʿĀlamgīr-nāma* ("Book of the World Conqueror")—with each of the ten years corresponding to a chapter about one hundred pages in length—Awrangzīb abolished the traditional office of the court chronicler in the eleventh year of his reign (1078/1668) and rejected Kāẓim's chronicle as official. After the rejection of his work, however, Kāẓim remained closely associated with the royal secretariat *(dār al-inshāʾ)*.

The reasons for the sudden closing of the office of the court chronicler are the subject of controversy: "Aurangzeb's reasons for hardening his heart against his court chronicler (Muḥammad Kāẓim) remain unclear. Numerous scholars have tried to solve the riddle of Aurangzeb's sudden distaste, hypothesizing that he elected to focus on esoteric rather than external things, the king became too pious to fund non-theological texts, or the royal treasury was strapped. All of these theories are unlikely given subsequent events at the royal court" (Truschke , 42).

In any case, after the "Kāẓim affair," Awrangzīb never again hired an official court historian, in sharp contrast to his predecessors Akbar (r. 963–1014/1556–1605) and Shāh Jahān, but that does not mean that Mughal historiographical production slackened. On the contrary, Awrangzīb's reign is the richest period in Mughal history in terms of the number of histories written (Husain, 15). Furthermore, Awrangzīb expressly allowed the posthumous publication in 1096/1685 of Muḥammad Bakhtāvar Khān's (d. 1096/1685) *Mirʾāt al-ʿālam* ("Mirror of the world"). It is striking that the emperor appointed Kāẓim, after the rejection of his chronicle, to such prestigious and well paid posts as those at the *dār al-inshāʾ* and as *dārūgha-yi ibtiyāʿ khāna*, (superintendant of the purchases required for the royal household), which we also observe by recently fired musicians which, too, received higher posts "at enhanced salaries, curiously" (Truschke, 43) after their rejection.

Despite his dismissal as official court chronicler, Kāẓim's death in 1090/1679 in Delhi remains a turning point in the intellectual, cultural, and political life of Mughal India, as he was one of the last chroniclers to have been appointed directly by a Mughal emperor to this highly respected office. The importance of Kāẓim's work and intellectual life is further clarified by the fact that his text would later serve as the main reference for the first ten years of the *Ma'āthir-i ʿĀlamgīrī* ("Heroic deeds of ʿĀlamgīr"). In it, the author, Mustaʿidd Khān (d. 1136/1724), praises Kāẓim's detailed descriptions and intellectual reputation and advises the reader to read Kāẓim's entire *ʿĀlamgīr-nāma*.

Bibliography

Sources

Musta'idd Khān, *Ma'āthir-i ʿĀlamgīrī*, ed. Āghā Aḥmad ʿAlī, 2 vols., Calcutta 1870–3; Muḥammad Kāẓim, *ʿĀlamgīr-nāma*, ed. Khādim Ḥusayn and ʿAbd al-Ḥayy, 2 vols., Calcutta, 1865–73.

Studies

Muzaffar Alam and Sanjay Subrahmanyam, The making of a *munshi*, *Comparative Studies of South Asia, Africa and the Middle East* 24/2 (2004), 61–72; Sajida Alvi, The historians of Awrangzeb. A comparative study of three primary sources, in Donald P. Little (ed.), *Essays on Islamic civilization presented to Niyazi Berkes* (Leiden 1976), 57–73; Katherine Butler Brown, Did Aurangzeb ban music? Questions for the historiography of his reign, *Modern Asian Studies* 41/1 (2007), 77–120; Stephan Conerman, *Historiographie als Sinnstiftung. Indo-persische Geschichtsschreibung während der Mogulzeit (932–1118/1516–1707)*, Wiesbaden 2002; Munis D. Faruqui, Awrangzīb, *EI3*; S. M. Azizuddin Husain, Aurangzeb and the court historians. A case study of Mirza Muhammad Kazim's *Alamgir Nama*, in Shah Mohammad Waseem (ed.), *Development of Persian historiography in India. From the second half of the 17th century to the first half of the 18th century* (New Delhi 2003), 4–18; Rajeev Kinra, *Writing self, writing empire. Chandar Bhan Brahman and the cultural world of the Indo-Persian state secretary*, Oakland 2015; Tilmann Kulke, *A Mughal munšī at work. Conflicts and emotions in Mustaʿidd Ḫān's Ma'āsir-i ʿĀlamgīrī. A narratological investigation*, Ph.D. diss., European University Institute, Florence 2016; Audrey Truschke, *Aurangzeb. The life and legacy of India's most controversial king*, Stanford, 2017.

Tilmann Kulke

Mustafa Çelebi

Şehzade **Mustafa** (Şehzāde Muṣṭafā) **Çelebi** (921–60/1515–53), the son of Süleyman I (Süleymān, r. 926–74/1520–66) and his concubine Mahidevran (Māh-i Devrān, d. 988/1581), lived his life in competition with his half-brothers, his rivals as heirs to the dynasty; he died, executed by order of his father, on suspicion of rebellion and treason. He was born in Manisa, in Western Anatolia, during Süleyman's tenure as provincial governor of Saruhan. Shortly after Süleyman became sultan in 926/1520, Mustafa moved to Istanbul with his mother. After the death of two elder brothers in early childhood, Mustafa became Süleyman's eldest child, and appears to have enjoyed the attention given to an eldest son within a patriarchal court society. He was taught the fundamentals of religion and belles-lettres and received training in martial arts and horsemanship. His education continued, but the foundations of his eventual demise were already established. Süleyman's relationship with his concubine Hürrem (Khürrem,

d. 965/1558) intensified, and their sons, Mehmed (Meḥmed, d. 950/1543), Bayezid (Bāyezīd, d. 969/1561), Selim (Selīm II, r. 974–82/1566–74), and Cihangir (Cihāngīr, d. 960/1553), were born between the late 920s/early 1520s and the early 930s/late 1520s. In Ottoman dynastic practice, all male members of the dynasty were eligible to become sultan, but only one of them could inherit the undivided domain. Every succession involved armed conflict among princes and resulted in the death of all dynastic males except the victor and his children. This was the eventuality for which Mustafa, his half-brothers, and their associates had to prepare.

The maturation of Mustafa, Mehmed, and Selim as potential heirs to the throne was celebrated during a lavish ceremony in 936/1530, on the occasion of their circumcision. In 940/1534, Mustafa moved to Manisa as provincial governor of Saruhan. His appointment to his father's old gubernatorial seat would have been interpreted as a sign of sultanic favour. However, the death of Süleyman's mother, Hafsa (Ḥafṣa, d. 940/1534), and the execution of the grand vizier İbrahim (İbrāhīm, d. 942/1536) removed two of Mustafa's potential supporters in the struggles ahead. Moreover, Süleyman's unyielding affection for Hürrem and their children, which culminated in his formal marriage to Hürrem shortly after Hafsa's death, did not bode well for Mustafa. In 948/1541, Mustafa's governorship was changed from Saruhan to Amasya, farther from Istanbul. Saruhan was given to his younger half-brother Mehmed in 949/1542 and, following Mehmed's unexpected death in 950/1543, to Selim in 951/1544. Mustafa's growing isolation and the continued rise of Hürrem's sons became ever more apparent.

Between 951/1544 and his execution in 960/1553, pro-Hürrem circles increasingly considered Mustafa a threat to her sons and to Süleyman himself. Groups of dissenters, such as low-ranking military men whose land grants had been revoked and peasants who had fled their lands to escape taxes, saw Mustafa as their candidate to the throne, whose rise to power would redress unjust policies. Mustafa himself may not have desired to play either role, but he clearly believed that succeeding his father was his right, even if he refrained from open rebellion. The grand vizier Rüstem (d. 968/1561), son-in-law of Hürrem and Süleyman, eventually devised the plan that would lead to Mustafa's death. In early 960/1553, Rüstem traveled east, apparently to prepare for a campaign against the Ṣafavids). He contacted Süleyman soon after, to inform him of Mustafa's plans to rebel, take command of the forces under Rüstem, march to the capital, and depose the sultan. His accusations were supported by a purported letter from Mustafa to the Ṣafavid shah, Ṭahmāsp (r. 930–84/1524–76), fabricated by Rüstem, and the shah's genuine answer.

Süleyman was thus compelled to attack his eldest son. Leaving Istanbul, he marched east and invited Mustafa to his army camp near Konya Ereğlisi, in south-central Anatolia. On 27 Şevval (Shawwāl) 960/6 October 1553, Mustafa entered his father's tent for an audience. There, he was strangled by executioners. Mustafa's corpse was displayed in front of Süleyman's tent as a warning to his supporters. Some members of his retinue were also executed. Mustafa's properties were sequestered and Mahidevran, who had accompanied her son since his move to Saruhan in 940/1534, was sent to Bursa, where Mustafa's corpse was dispatched for burial. Mustafa's young son Mehmed (Meḥmed, d. 961/1554), another potential heir, was strangled shortly after his father's execution.

Rüstem was identified by many as the figure behind the plot, and Süleyman dismissed him from the grand vizierate to allay tensions. Despite this, repercussions continued. Poems that decried the prince's demise circulated widely. A year after the execution, a pretender claiming to be Mustafa rebelled in the Rumelian provinces. The biggest personal cost to Süleyman was the loss of his youngest son with Hürrem, Cihangir, whose sudden death shortly after the execution was widely attributed to a state of distress brought about by Mustafa's demise.

Bibliography

Mecmūʿa, aka *Dizfūlī Münşe'ātı*, Istanbul, Beyazıt Devlet Kütüphanesi, MS Veliyyüddin Efendi 2735; *Rūznāmçe Defteri*, Istanbul, Başbakanlık Osmanlı Arşivi, MS Kamil Kepeci 1766; Mustafa Ali, *Künhü'l-aḫbār. Dördüncü Rükn. Osmanlı tarihi*, ed. Ahmet Uğur and Ali Çavuşoğlu, vol. 1, Ankara 2009; Zahit Atçıl, Why did Sultan Süleyman execute his son Şehzade Mustafa in 1553?, *JOS* 48 (2016), 67–103; Ogier Ghiselin de Busbecq, *Les lettres turques*, trans. Dominique Arrighi, Paris 2010; Mehmed Çavuşoğlu, Şehzâde Mustafa Mersiyeleri, *İstanbul Üniversitesi Edebiyat Fakültesi Tarih Enstitüsü Dergisi* 12 (1982), 641–86; M. Tayyib Gökbilgin, Rüstem Paşa ve hakkındaki ithamlar, *Tarih Dergisi* 8 (1955), 11–12:11–50; Colin Imber, The dynasty, in *The Ottoman Empire, 1300–1650. The structure of power* (Basingstoke 2002), 87–127; Celālzāde Muṣṭafā, *Geschichte Sultan Süleymān Ḳānūnīs von 1520 bis 1557, oder, Ṭabaḳāt ül-Memālik ve Derecāt ül-Mesālik von Celālzāde Muṣṭafā genannt Ḳoca Nişāncı*, ed. Petra Kappert, Wiesbaden 1981; Bernado Navagero, Relazione dell'Impero ottomano del clarissimo Bernardo Navagero, stato bailo a Costantinopoli, fatta in Pregadi nel mese di febbraio del 1553, in Eugenio Albèri (ed.), *Relazioni degli ambasciatori veneti al Senato*, series 3 (Florence 1840), 1:33–110; Relazione anonima della guerra di Persia dell'anno 1553, e di molti altri particolari, relative alle cose di Solimano in quell'epoca, in Eugenio Albèri (ed.), *Relazioni degli ambasciatori veneti al Senato*, series 3 (Florence 1840), 1:193–269; Leslie Peirce, *The imperial harem. Women and sovereignty in the Ottoman Empire*, Oxford and New York 1993; Leslie Peirce, *Empress of the east. How a European slave girl became queen of the Ottoman Empire*, New York 2017; Marino Sanuto, *I diarii di Marino Sanuto*, vol. 53, ed. Guglielmo Berchet et al., Venice 1899; Kaya Şahin, *Süleyman the Magnificent. Renaissance prince, Muslim emperor*, Oxford and New York, forthcoming; Domenico Trevisano, Relazione dell'Impero ottomano del clarissimo Domenico Trevisano, tornato bailo da Costantinopoli sulla fine del 1554, in Eugenio Albèri (ed.), *Relazioni degli ambasciatori veneti al Senato*, series 3 (Florence 1840), 1:111–92; Şerafettin Turan, Mustafa Çelebi, *TDVİA* 31 (2006), 290–2; Çağatay Uluçay, Kanunî Sultan Süleyman ve ailesi ile ilgili bazı notlar ve vesikalar (3 fotokopi ile birlikte), in *Kanunî Armağanı* (Ankara 1970), 227–57.

Kaya Şahin

Mustaʿidd Khān

Mustaʿidd Khān (b. c.1060/1650, d. 1136/1724) was born in Aḥmadnagar (Deccan) and died in Delhi. He was raised by his foster father Muḥammad Bakhtāvar Khān (d. 1096/1685), author of the *Mir'āt al-ʿālam* ("The mirror of the world"). From 1096/1685 onwards, Mustaʿidd Khān worked successively as overseer *(mushrif)* of the royal painting atelier *(naqqāsh-khāna)* and of the royal carpet-weaving workshop *(jānamāz-khāna)*, as a writer *(vāqiʿ-nigār)*, as guardian of the private royal treasury *(khavāṣṣān)*, and, from 1702/1114, as "*munshī* of *the nudhūrāt*" (Mustaʿidd Khān, 275), superintendent of royal gifts. At the end of his career, he was named vizier.

After the death of the Mughal emperor Awrangzīb (r. 1068–1118/1658–1707), ʿInāyat Allāh Khān b. Mīrzā Shukr (d. 1139/1726–7), one of Awrangzīb's closest advisers, urged Mustaʿidd Khān to write a chronicle of Awranzīb's entire reign. In 1122/1710, the author presented to his patron the *Maʾāthir-i ʿĀlamgīrī* ("Heroic deeds of (Awrangzīb) ʿĀlamgīr"). The first part, according to Mustaʿidd Khān, is a summary of Muḥammad Kāẓim's (d. 1092/1679) court history of Awranzīb's first ten years of rule (*ʿĀlamgīr-nāma*, " The book of the world conqueror"). He also refers frequently to the *Mirʾāt al-ʿālam* ("Mirror of the world") by his foster father Muḥammad Bakhtāvar Khān, a text to which he himself contributed and which he published posthumously in 1096/1685, at the command of Awrangzīb. The second part of the *Maʾāthir-i ʿĀlamgīrī* is based on Mustaʿidd Khān's own observations, his intensive questioning of many contemporary witnesses, and his free access to the state archives. From the latter, the author quotes numerous decrees, orders, chancery letters, and other correspondence of royal reporters scattered throughout the empire. The result is a concise and typical Mughal chronicle, noteworthy for its pragmatic and sober tone.

Research has labelled the *Maʾāthir-i ʿĀlamgīrī* a "much abridged" history in comparison with other Mughal *nāmas*, which lost its "flowers of rhetoric" and was filled with "trite reflections and moralizations" (Sarkar, ed. *Maāsir-i ʿĀlamgīrī*, vi) and whose author often wrote carelessly and sloppily, without naming his sources (Alvi, *Historians of Awrangzeb*, 78). The *Maʾāthir-i-ʿĀlamgīrī* has often been used to demonstrate the religious polarisation in Awrangzīb's period and his destruction of temples and to portray its author as a representative of the Muslim intelligentsia of the time, who allegedly celebrated and supported the so-called anti-Hindu campaigns of Awrangzīb (Kulke, 10–5).

Many important aspects have, however, been overlooked in the research, and the *Maʾāthir-i ʿĀlamgīrī* appears rather as a complex and multifarious narrative, "as much a rhetorical masterpiece as a history" (Truschke, 84). In his chronicle, Mustaʿidd Khān skilfully suggests advice for the new ruler Shāh ʿĀlam Bahādur (r. 1118–24/1707–12) and his government, including the intensification of collaboration with loyal Hindus. Mustaʿidd Khān's *Maʾāthir-i ʿĀlamgīrī* is thus not only a chronicle reporting the past and glorifying an emperor who destroyed temples but also a programme calling for new forms of government after Awrangzīb's death (Kulke, 23).

Bibliography

Sources

Bakhtāvar Khān, *Mirʾāt al-ʿālam*, ed. Sajida S. Alvi, *Mirʾat al-ʿalam. History of emperor Awangzeb ʿAlamgir*, 2 vols., Lahore 1979; Muḥammad Sāqī Mustaʿidd Khān, *Maʾāthir-i ʿĀlamgīrī*, ed. Āghā Aḥmad ʿAlī, 2 vols., Calcutta 1870–3, trans. Jadunath Sarkar, *Maāsir-i-ʿĀlamgiri. A history of the emperor Aurangzib-ʿĀlamgir (reign 1658–1707 A.D.)*, Calcutta 1947.

Studies

Sajida S. Alvi, The historians of Awrangzeb. A comparative study of three primary sources, in Donald P. Little (ed.), *Essays on Islamic civilization presented to Niyazi Berkes* (Leiden 1976), 57–73; Stephan Conerman, *Historiographie als Sinnstiftung. Indo-persische Geschichtsschreibung während der Mogulzeit (932–1118/1516–1707)*, Wiesbaden 2002; Henry M. Elliot and John Dowson (trans.), *The history of India as told by its own historians*, 8 vols., London 1867–77, repr. Cambridge 2013; S. M. Azizuddin Husain, *Kalimat-i-taiyibat (Collection of Aurangzeb's orders)*, Delhi 1982; Tilmann Kulke, *A Mughal munšī at work. Conflicts and emotions in Mustaʿidd Ḫān's Maʾāṯir-i ʿĀlamgīrī. A narratological investigation*, Ph.D. diss., European University Institute, Florence 2016; Audrey Truschke, *Aurangzeb. The life and legacy of India's most controversial king*, Stanford 2017.

Tilmann Kulke

N

Naima

Mustafa **Naima** (Muṣṭafā Naʿīmā, 1065–1128/1655–1716), known by his pen name *(mahlas, makhlaṣ)* Naima, was the author of one of the most highly regarded histories of the Ottoman state, the first in a series of state-sponsored histories that would continue until the end of the empire.

He was born in Aleppo, probably around 1065/1655, the son and grandson of Janissary commanders resident in the city. He arrived in Istanbul around 1091/1680, where he entered the *baltacılar* (*bālṭacīlar*, halberdiers), one of the corps of palace guards, and was trained for the scribal service. He displayed particular aptitudes for literature, history, and astrology; the highs and lows of his professional career have been attributed, to some extent, to his skills in the latter field. On completing his education, he was given an apprenticeship as secretary (*katib, kātib*) to a member of the Imperial Divan *(dīvān)* in 1097/1686 (Afyoncu, 84) , and thus initiated a lifetime career in administration.

During these early years, he enjoyed the support of several highly placed officials, among them the *reisülküttab* (*raʾīs al-kuttāb*, head of the secretaries) Rami (Rāmī) Paşa, who secured him a salary of 120 *akçe (aqçe)* per day from the Istanbul customs. By far the most important support came from the Köprülü Grand Vizier Amcazade Hüseyin Paşa (ʿAmūjazāde Ḥüseyin, in office 1109–14/1697–1702), who had in his possession manuscripts of a draft history by Şarih ül-Menarzade Ahmed Efendi (Shārih al-Manārzāde Aḥmed, d. 1067/1657). Around 1110/1698–9, Amcazade Hüseyin Paşa commissioned Naima to make a fair copy of this manuscript, which formed the basis of the work for which he is known: the *Rawḍat al-Ḥusayn fī khulāṣat akhbār al-khāfiqayn (Ravzatü-l-Hüseyn fī hulāsati ahbāri'l-hāfikayn*, "Garden of Husayn, in summary of the histories of East and West").

Şarih ül-Menarzade was a member of the *ulema* (*ʿulamāʾ*, religious scholars), an established *müderris* (professor), and a protégé of the powerful *ulema* family of descendants of Hoca Sadeddin Efendi (Khōca Saʿduddīn, d. 1008/1599). As a result, he was close to such events as the deposition and execution of Sultan İbrahim (Ibrāhīm, r. 1049–58/1640–8). No copies survive of his history, which ran to 1065/1655. In addition to incorporating almost all of Şarih ül-Menarzade's work, Naima drew on other historians and eyewitnesses of the period, such as Tuği (d. after 1032/1623), Hasan Beyzade (Ḥasan Beyzāde, d. 1046/1636–7), Peçevi (Peçevī, d. 1059/1649?), and, in particular, on the *Fezleke* of Katib Çelebi (d.1067/1657). His contribution has been characterised thus: "He took what was bequeathed to him, material and form. He improved upon both, increasing and evaluating the material, rationalizing and simplifying the form" (Thomas, 159).

After several adjustments, Naima's text, as published, runs from 1000/1591 to 1070/1660. It comprises two prefaces containing Naima's ideas on history and government, and a year-by-year account of the period. It is regarded as the first in a series of Ottoman state histories written by a designated office-holder, the *vak'anüvis (waqʿa-nūwīs)*. It is debated whether Naima formally held that title, with one view suggesting that the *vak'anüvis* post was not instituted until 1126/1714 for his immediate successor, Raşid (Rāşid, d. 1148/1735).

The work has been published three times: first—and perhaps indicative of the regard in which it was held—as one of the earliest Ottoman printed books, published by İbrahim Müteferrika (Ibrāhīm Müteferriqa, d. 1160/1747) in two volumes in Istanbul in 1147/1734–5 (the first volume reprinted in 1259/1843); two later printed editions, each of six volumes, were published, also in Istanbul, in 1280/1863–4 and 1281–3/1864–7 respectively. These publications are not properly edited, and each is—to a greater or lesser extent—imperfect. There are also two complete romanised texts: *Naîmâ târihi*, edited by Zuhuri Danışman; and *Târih-i Na'îmâ (Ravzatü-l-Hüseyn fî hulâsati ahbâri'l-hâfikayn)*, edited by Mehmed İpşirli.

It is not known when Naima completed the *Ravzat* but he may well have done so at or about the time he received an appointment as *Anadolu mühasebecisi* (Accountant for Anatolia) with the senior secretariat rank of *hacegan* (*khwājegān*, "bureau chief") in Zilhicce (Dhū l-Ḥijja) 1115/April 1704 (Afyoncu, 84). He then seems to have abandoned writing history and turned entirely to a somewhat chequered civil service career. He was dismissed from his post in Ramazan (Ramaḍān) 1117/December 1705 (Afyoncu, 84), and before long, early in Çorlulu Ali Paşa's term as Grand Vizier (Çorlulu ʿAlī, Grand Vezir for four years from 19 Muharrem (Muḥarram) 1118/3 May 1706), he was banished from Istanbul (see the order in Baysun, 45a, dated early Safer (Ṣafar) 1118/15–25 May 1706), apparently on the grounds that his horoscopes had caused offense to important men. In the event he was exiled to Hanya (Khania) in Crete and spent six months there. He was finally allowed to return to Istanbul in Receb (Rajab) 1119/October 1707 where he reentered service in the Divan. He then held a variety of administrative posts, serving two further tenures as *Anadolu mühasebecisi* and one as *baş* (*bāş*) *mühasebecisi* (Chief Accountant) before being demoted in 1127/1715 to the office of provincial *defter emini* (*emīni*, Custodian of the Registers) in the Morea. He died in that post in Şaban (Shaʿbān) 1128/August 1716 and was buried in Patras.

Bibliography

Erhan Afyoncu, Osmanlı Müelliflerine Dair Tevcihat Kayıtları, TTK Belgeler XX/24, Ankara 2000; Cavid Baysun, Naima, *İA*; Katib Çelebi, *Fezleke*, Istanbul 1286–7/1869–71; Mehmed İpşirli, Naîmâ, *TDVİA*;

Mustafa Naima, *Târih-i Na'îmâ* (*Ravzatü-l-Hüseyn fî hulâsati ahbâri'l-hâfikayn*), Istanbul 1281/1864–6; Mustafa Naima, *Naîmâ târihi*, ed. Zuhuri Danışman, Istanbul 1967–9; Gabriel Piterberg, *An Ottoman tragedy. History and historiography at play*, Berkeley 2003; Lewis Victor Thomas, *A study of Naima*, ed. Norman Itzkowitz, (New York 1972), 159; Christine Woodhead, Naʿīmā, *EI2*.

Richard C. Repp

Najīb al-Dīn al-Samarqandī

Najīb al-Dīn Abū Ḥāmid (or Abū l-Muḥāmid or Abū l-Fatḥ) Muḥammad b. ʿAlī b. ʿUmar **al-Samarqandī** (d. 619/1222) was a physician and author of several books on medicine. Little is known about his life other than that he suffered a violent death during the Mongol conquest of Herat in 619/1222 (Ibn Abī Uṣaybiʿa, 2:31; cf. *GAL*, 1:490–1; Iskandar, 451; Ullmann, 170). He started writing medical texts before 594/1197–8, as can be deduced from the oldest known dated copy of one of his works (a Mosul manuscript described in *GAL*, 1:491; cf. Müller, 313). Al-Samarqandī either worked or studied at a hospital in Baghdad before writing a pharmacopeia that mentions the hospital (Levey and al-Khaledy, 170; Müller, 313). He had a nephew by the name of Aṣīl al-Dīn whom he trained as a doctor (Iskandar, 451–57; Müller, 314).

Al-Samarqandī wrote at least six comprehensive books on pathology, dietetics, pharmacognosy, and pharmacy, as well as several shorter treatises on other medical fields, including cardiology, ophthalmology, and gynaecology (*GAL*, 1:491 and *GALS*, 1:895–6; Iskandar, 451, 458–62; 470–3; Müller, 314–21; Ullmann, 170, 201–2, 278, 308). His books were often copied together and referred to as *al-Najībiyyāt* ("The [books] of Najīb") or *al-Khamsa al-Najībiyya* ("The five [books] of Najīb"), with the five books varying in different manuscripts. This indicates that al-Samarqandī's books might not necessarily have been perceived as autonomous monographs, but rather as interrelated parts within his corpus of writings. Since the collective titles of *al-Najībiyyāt* and *al-Khamsa al-Najībiyya* only appear in several later manuscripts, they were probably not used by al-Samarqandī himself (Müller, 321–8).

Al-Samarqandī's most famous and comprehensive work is the *Kitāb al-asbāb wa-l-ʿalāmāt* ("On causes and symptoms"; see editions of Bābāpūr et al. and Chaabane). It was commented upon by Nafīs b. ʿIwaḍ al-Kirmānī in 827/1424 in his *Sharḥ al-Asbāb wa-l-ʿalāmāt*, which served as a source for the Persian *Ṭibb-i Akbarī* by the physician Muḥammad Akbar Arzānī in 1112/1700 (*GAL*, 1:491; *GALS*, 1:895–6; Iskandar, 459; Müller, 316; Ullmann, 170). Another commentary on the *Asbāb* was written by the Damascene ʿIzz al-Dīn Ibrāhīm b. Suwaydī (d. 690/1292). The *Kitāb al-asbāb wa-l-ʿalāmāt* was also translated into Turkish and—at least partially—into Hebrew (Müller, 316). Al-Samarqandī composed two dietetic books: *Kitāb aṭʿimat al-marḍā* ("The foods of the sick") and *Kitāb al-aghdhiya wa-l-ashriba* ("On foods and drinks"; see edition by Müller and *GAL*, 1:491; *GALS*, 1:896; Iskandar, 451; Müller, 315–7; Ullmann, 201–2)—the latter being an encyclopaedia of food items and their medical effects and the former an encyclopaedia of illnesses and the appropriate foods for their cure. Both were translated into Byzantine Greek (Cronier). For the *Kitāb al-aghdhiya wa-l-ashriba*, manuscript evidence shows that the book was widespread throughout the Islamic East, including India and Central Asia, but did not reach the Maghreb until recently (Müller, 444). There are also notes of the *Kitāb al-aghdhiya wa-l-ashriba* having been copied in hospitals in Cairo and Khwārazm, which might imply that al-Samarqandī's writings were part of the inventory of medical reference works in hospital libraries in various parts of the Islamic East (Müller, 445). In the tenth/sixteenth century, the physician Luṭfallāh b. Saʿd al-Dīn al-Fārūqī used the *Kitāb al-aghdhiya wa-l-ashriba* as a source for his medical encyclopaedia *Kitāb tarwīḥ al-arwāḥ fī ʿilal al-ashbāḥ* ("Spirits' relief on persons' diseases"; Müller, 447–8). In the field of pharmacology and pharmacy, al-Samarqandī wrote a book on simples—*Kitāb al-adwiya al-mufrada* ("On simple drugs"; *GAL*, 1:491, *GALS*, 1:895–6; Iskandar, 458; Müller, 315; Ullmann, 278)—and two pharmacopeias on composed drugs: *Kitāb al-qarābādhīn ʿalā tartīb al-ʿilal* ("Pharmacopeia arranged according to Illnesses"; see the uncritical edition by Tohmé) and *Kitāb uṣūl tarkīb al-adwiya* ("The principles of the composition of drugs"; see the editions by ʿAbbās and Levey/al-Khaledy; *GAL*, 1:491; *GALS*, 1:895; Iskandar, 459–60; Müller, 317; Ullmann, 308). There are abbreviated versions of both pharmacopeias, as well as translations of the *Uṣūl* into Byzantine Greek, Hebrew and probably also Persian (Cronier; Müller, 317–8).

Among al-Samarqandī's short treatises are *Adwiyat al-qalb wa-mā yataʿallaq bihī* ("Drugs for the heart and what relates to it"), *Maqāla fī kayfiyyat tarkīb ṭabaqāt al-ʿayn* ("On the structure of the layers of the eye"), *Risāla fī mudāwāt wajaʿ al-mafāṣil* ("On the medication of joint pain"), and *Fī tafsīr al-raḥim* ("Explanation of the uterus"; the title of the latter probably should be emended to: *Fī tafsīr al-waḥam*, "Explanation of the pregnancy cravings," cf. Müller, 319). None of these treatises has been edited so far (*GAL*, 1:491; Iskandar, 458, 460; Müller, 318–19; Ullmann, 170). There are several other treatises for which the authorship of al-Samarqandī is doubtful, among them a Persian text called *al-Manhaj* ("The method"), attributed to "the physician Najīb al-Dīn," which is extant in two manuscripts in its Arabic translation titled *Kitāb ghāyat al-gharaḍ fī muʿālajat al-maraḍ* ("The ultimate goal in the therapy of disease") by al-Sharīf Manṣūr al-Ḥusaynī al-Ḥasanī (fl. thirteenth/nineteenth cent.; cf. *GAL*, 1:491; Müller, 320).

Bibliography

Works

Najlāʾ Qāsim ʿAbbās (ed.), *Najīb al-Dīn al-Samarqandī. Uṣūl tarkīb al-adwiya*, Baghdad 1989; Yūsuf Bēg Bābāpūr et al. (eds.), *al-Asbāb wa-l-ʿalāmāt. Najīb al-Dīn al-Samarqandī*, Tehran 1391sh/2012; Zouhour Chaabane (ed.), *Les causes et les symptômes (al-Asbāb wa-l-ʿalāmāt) d'al-Samarqandī. Édition critique avec présentation et annotations*, Ph.D. diss., University of Paris IV 2013; Martin Levey and Nuri al-Khaledy (eds.), *The medical formulary of al-Samarqandī and the relation of early Arabic simples to those found in the indigenous medicine of the Near East and India*, Philadelphia 1967; Juliane Müller (ed.), *Nahrungsmittel in der arabischen Medizin. Das Kitāb al-Aġḏiya wa-l-ašriba des Naǧīb ad-Dīn as-Samarqandī. Edition, Übersetzung und Kontext*, Leiden and Boston 2017; Georges Tohmé (ed.), *Pharmacopée sur la classification des causes par Néjibeddine Assamarkandi*, Beirut 1994.

Source

Ibn Abī Uṣaybiʿa, *ʿUyūn al-anbāʾ fī ṭabaqāt al-aṭibbāʾ*, ed. A. Müller, Cairo and Königsberg 1884.

Studies

GAL, 1:490–1; *GALS*, 1:895–6; Tarabein Chérif, *Contribution à l'histoire de la pharmacie arabe. Étude particulière du manuscrit intitulé: Al-Nadjibiate al-Samarkandiate*, Ph.D. diss., Strasbourg University 1952; Marie Cronier, *Des traductions grecques inédites de traités médicaux arabes*, in P. Athanasopoulos (ed.), *Translation activity in late Byzantium. Contexts, authors and texts*, Berlin forthcoming; Albert Zaki Iskandar, A study of al-Samarqandī's medical writings, *Le Muséon* 85 (1972), 451–79; Emilie Savage-Smith, *A new catalogue of Arabic manuscripts in the Bodleian Library, University of Oxford. Vol. I: Medicine*, Oxford 2011; Manfred Ullmann, *Die Medizin im Islam*, Leiden and Cologne 1970.

Juliane Müller

CUMULATIVE LIST OF ENTRIES 2020-4

Aaron 2007-2 : 1
Aaron ben Elija of Nicomedia 2008-1 : 1
ʿAbābda 2008-2 : 1
Abaginskiy 2017-1 : 1
Abān b. ʿUthmān b. ʿAffān 2007-3 : 1
Abān al-Lāḥiqī 2007-2 : 2
Abangan 2007-2 : 3
Abāqā 2010-2 : 1
Abarqubādh 2009-1 : 1
Abarqūh 2009-3 : 1
Abarshahr 2011-2 : 1
ʿAbāṭa, Muḥammad Ḥasan 2010-2 : 9
Abay Qunanbayulı 2007-2 : 6
ʿAbbād b. Salmān 2009-3 : 2
ʿAbbād b. Ziyād b. Abī Sufyān 2009-2 : 1
ʿAbbādān (Ābādān) 2010-1 : 1
al-ʿAbbādī 2014-1 : 1
ʿAbbādids 2011-4 : 1
ʿAbbās I 2016-1 : 1
ʿAbbās II 2008-2 : 2
ʿAbbās III 2009-3 : 3
al-ʿAbbās b. ʿAbd al-Muṭṭalib 2009-2 : 2
ʿAbbās b. Abī l-Futūḥ 2007-2 : 7
al-ʿAbbās b. al-Aḥnaf 2009-1 : 2
al-ʿAbbās b. ʿAmr al-Ghanawī 2011-1 : 1
ʿAbbās b. al-Ḥusayn al-Shīrāzī 2014-2 : 1
al-ʿAbbās b. al-Maʾmūn 2013-4 : 1
al-ʿAbbās b. Mirdās 2008-1 : 2
al-ʿAbbās b. Muḥammad b. ʿAlī 2013-3 : 1
al-ʿAbbās b. al-Walīd b. ʿAbd al-Malik 2008-1 : 3
ʿAbbās Efendī 2008-2 : 5
ʿAbbās Ḥilmī I 2014-2 : 2
ʿAbbās Ḥilmī II 2007-1 : 1
ʿAbbās, Iḥsān 2010-2 : 10
ʿAbbās Mīrzā 2012-1 : 1
ʿAbbās Sarwānī 2007-2 : 9
ʿAbbāsa bt al-Mahdī 2008-1 : 4
al-ʿAbbāsī 2008-1 : 6
ʿAbbāsī 2009-3 : 4
ʿAbbāsī, Shaykh 2011-4 : 5
ʿAbbāsid Revolution 2007-1 : 2
ʿAbbāsid art and architecture 2012-1 : 4
ʿAbbāsid music 2019-4 : 1
Abbasquluağa Bakıxanov 2015-1 : 1
ʿAbbūd, Mārūn 2007-2 : 10
ʿAbd al-Aḥad Nūrī Sīvāsī 2009-3 : 6
ʿAbd al-ʿAzīz al-Amawī 2007-2 : 10
ʿAbd al-ʿAzīz b. al-Ḥajjāj b. ʿAbd al-Malik 2008-1 : 6
ʿAbd al-ʿAzīz b. Marwān 2009-2 : 3
ʿAbd al-ʿAzīz b. Mūsā b. Nuṣayr 2013-4 : 2
ʿAbd al-ʿAzīz b. al-Walīd b. ʿAbd al-Malik 2008-1 : 7

ʿAbd al-ʿAzīz Dihlawī	2010-1 : 3
ʿAbd al-ʿAzīz al-Mahdawī	2016-2 : 1
ʿAbd al-Bāqī, Shaykh	2011-1 : 2
ʿAbd al-Bārī	2007-2 : 11
ʿAbd al-Bāsiṭ ʿAbd al-Ṣamad	2018-6 : 1
ʿAbd al-Ghaffār Khān	2015-1 : 2
ʿAbd al-Ghafūr of Swāt	2015-1 : 4
ʿAbd al-Ghanī al-Nābulusī	2012-1 : 20
ʿAbd al-Hādī, ʿAwnī	2009-1 : 4
ʿAbd al-Hādī Shīrāzī	2015-4 : 1
ʿAbd al-Ḥafīẓ b. al-Ḥasan	2016-3 : 1
ʿAbd al-Ḥakīm	2013-3 : 2
ʿAbd al-Ḥakīm, Khalīfa	2008-1 : 8
ʿAbd al-Ḥamīd b. Yaḥyā al-Kātib	2009-1 : 4
ʿAbd al-Ḥamīd-i Lāhawrī	2012-3 : 1
ʿAbd al-Ḥaqq Bāba-yi Urdū	2009-1 : 8
ʿAbd al-Ḥaqq Dihlavī	2016-2 : 3
ʿAbd al-Ḥayy Ḥasanī	2012-3 : 2
ʿAbd al-Ḥayy al-Laknawī	2011-1 : 3
ʿAbd al-Ḥayy, Ṣāliḥ	2007-2 : 12
ʿAbd al-Ḥusayn Mūnis ʿAlī Shāh	2015-4 : 2
ʿAbd al-Ilāh	2007-2 : 13
ʿAbd al-Jabbār b. ʿAbd al-Qādir al-Jīlānī	2009-1 : 9
ʿAbd al-Jabbār b. ʿAbd al-Raḥmān	2009-4 : 1
ʿAbd al-Jabbār b. Aḥmad al-Hamadhānī	2007-3 : 9
ʿAbd al-Karīm	2012-1 : 28
ʿAbd al-Karīm Kashmīrī	2015-3 : 1
ʿAbd al-Karīm Wāʿiẓ Emīr Efendī	2013-4 : 3
ʿAbd al-Khāliq al-Ghijduwānī	2010-1 : 9
ʿAbd al-Laṭīf	2013-4 : 4
ʿAbd al-Laṭīf al-Baghdādī	2018-6 : 2
ʿAbd al-Laṭīf, Bahādur	2016-2 : 7
ʿAbd al-Majīd al-Khānī	2011-1 : 4
ʿAbd al-Malik b. Ḥabīb	2009-4 : 2
ʿAbd al-Malik b. Qaṭan al-Fihrī	2009-1 : 10
ʿAbd al-Malik b. Ṣāliḥ	2007-3 : 18
ʿAbd al-Malik al-Muẓaffar	2009-2 : 4
ʿAbd al-Muʾmin al-Dimyāṭī	2013-4 : 8
ʿAbd al-Muqtadir	2010-1 : 12
ʿAbd al-Muṭṭalib b. Hāshim	2007-2 : 13
ʿAbd al-Nabī	2012-3 : 3
ʿAbd al-Nabī Qazvīnī	2014-2 : 3
ʿAbd al-Qādir, Amīr	2014-2 : 5
ʿAbd al-Qādir b. ʿAlī b. Yūsuf al-Fāsī	2009-2 : 6
ʿAbd al-Qadir b. ʿUthman Gidado	2019-5 : 1
ʿAbd al-Qādir al-Baghdādī	2007-3 : 19
ʿAbd al-Qādir Dihlawī	2011-2 : 2
ʿAbd al-Qādir al-Jīlānī	2009-1 : 11
ʿAbd al-Qādir al-Marāghī, b. Ghaybī	2007-3 : 21
ʿAbd al-Quddūs Gangohī	2012-2 : 1
ʿAbd al-Quddūs, Iḥsān	2007-2 : 15
ʿAbd al-Raḥīm Dihlawī	2016-3 : 3
ʿAbd al-Raḥīm Khān	2009-3 : 7
ʿAbd al-Raḥīm al-Qināʾī	2012-3 : 3
ʿAbd al-Raḥmān (Sanchuelo)	2010-1 : 13
ʿAbd al-Raḥmān, ʿĀʾisha	2007-2 : 16
ʿAbd al-Raḥmān b. ʿAbdallāh al-Ghāfiqī	2010-2 : 12
ʿAbd al-Raḥmān b. ʿAwf	2015-3 : 2
ʿAbd al-Raḥmān b. Ḥabīb al-Fihrī	2016-4 : 1
ʿAbd al-Raḥmān b. Khālid b. al-Walīd	2013-1 : 1
ʿAbd al-Raḥmān b. Muʿāwiya	2009-2 : 7
ʿAbd al-Raḥmān b. Rustam	2011-3 : 1
ʿAbd al-Raḥmān b. Samura	2017-4 : 1
ʿAbd al-Raḥmān al-Ifrīqī	2009-3 : 9
ʿAbd al-Raḥmān Katkhudā	2013-1 : 1
ʿAbd al-Raḥmān Khān	2010-2 : 13
ʿAbd al-Raḥmān Sirrī	2009-2 : 10
ʿAbd al-Raḥmān al-Ṣūfī	2008-1 : 9

ʿAbd al-Raḥmān al-Thughūrī 2011-1 : 6
ʿAbd al-Raḥmān al-Zaylaʿī 2013-4 : 9
ʿAbd al-Rashīd b. ʿAbd al-Ghafūr 2010-1 : 14
ʿAbd al-Rashīd Jawnpūrī 2011-4 : 6
ʿAbd al-Rashīd al-Tattawī 2007-2 : 18
ʿAbd al-Rāziq, ʿAlī 2009-1 : 14
ʿAbd al-Rāziq, Muṣṭafā 2008-1 : 12
ʿAbd al-Razzāq b. ʿAbd al-Qādir al-Jīlānī 2010-2 : 13
ʿAbd al-Razzāq Beg Dunbulī 2008-2 : 6
ʿAbd al-Razzāq al-Kāshānī 2009-3 : 10
ʿAbd al-Razzāq Samarqandī 2014-1 : 2
ʿAbd al-Razzāq al-Ṣanānī 2007-1 : 7
ʿAbd al-Riḍā Khān Ibrāhīmī 2013-3 : 3
ʿAbd al-Ṣabūr, Ṣalāḥ 2007-2 : 20
ʿAbd al-Salām b. Muḥammad 2010-1 : 16
ʿAbd al-Ṣamad Hamadhānī 2012-3 : 8
ʿAbd al-Ṣamad al-Palimbānī 2007-2 : 25
ʿAbd al-Sattār Lāhawrī 2015-1 : 6
ʿAbd al-Wādids 2009-2 : 11
ʿAbd al-Wahhāb Ilḥāmī 2010-2 : 15
ʿAbd al-Wahhāb, Muḥammad 2009-4 : 4
ʿAbd al-Wāḥid b. Zayd 2011-2 : 3
ʿAbd al-Wāḥid Bilgrāmī 2014-3 : 1
ʿAbd al-Wāḥid al-Marrākushī 2009-2 : 14
ʿAbd al-Waḥīd Turkistānī 2013-4 : 11
Abdalan-ı Rum, historical 2012-4 : 1
Abdalan-ı Rum, literature 2015-3 : 4
ʿAbdalī 2008-1 : 14
ʿAbdallāh b. ʿAbbās 2012-1 : 30
ʿAbdallāh b. ʿAbd al-Malik b. Marwān 2013-4 : 13
ʿAbdallāh b. ʿAbd al-Muṭṭalib 2010-2 : 16
ʿAbdallāh b. ʿAlawī al-Ḥaddād 2012-1 : 43
ʿAbdallāh b. ʿAlī 2010-1 : 17
ʿAbdallāh b. ʿĀmir 2008-1 : 15
ʿAbdallāh b. ʿAwn 2008-1 : 16
ʿAbdallāh b. Ḥanẓala 2008-2 : 7
ʿAbdallāh b. al-Ḥasan 2009-2 : 15
ʿAbdallāh b. al-Ḥusayn 2007-2 : 21
ʿAbdallāh b. Jaʿfar b. Abī Ṭālib 2010-2 : 18
ʿAbdallāh b. Jaḥsh 2011-2 : 5
ʿAbdallāh b. Judʿān 2010-1 : 18
ʿAbdallāh b. Khāzim 2015-2 : 1
ʿAbdallāh b. Maymūn 2013-3 : 4
ʿAbdallāh b. Muʿāwiya 2013-4 : 14
ʿAbdallāh b. Muḥammad b. ʿAbd al-Raḥmān 2011-2 : 5
ʿAbdallāh b. Mūsā b. Nuṣayr 2014-1 : 3
ʿAbdallāh b. Muṭīʿ 2009-2 : 16
ʿAbdallāh b. Rawāḥa 2009-2 : 17
ʿAbdallāh b. Sabaʾ 2016-1 : 6
ʿAbdallāh b. Salām 2013-4 : 16
ʿAbdallāh b. Ṭāhir 2007-3 : 21
ʿAbdallāh b. Ubayy 2009-2 : 18
ʿAbdallāh b. ʿUmar b. ʿAbd al-ʿAzīz 2009-2 : 19
ʿAbdallāh b. ʿUmar b. al-Khaṭṭāb 2009-2 : 20
ʿAbdallāh b. Wahb 2016-1 : 8
ʿAbdallāh b. al-Zubayr 2009-2 : 22
ʿAbdallāh Bihbihānī 2011-1 : 8
ʿAbdallāh, Mirzā 2007-3 : 23
ʿAbdallāh, Muḥammad ʿAbd al-Ḥalīm 2008-1 : 17
ʿAbdallāh Pasha 2007-2 : 22
ʿAbdallāh Shaṭṭār 2013-4 : 17
ʿAbdallāh Ṣūfī Shaṭṭārī 2010-2 : 19
ʿAbdallāh al-Taʿīshī 2009-1 : 17
ʿAbdallāh al-Tulanbi 2007-3 : 23
ʿAbdallāh, Yaḥyā l-Ṭāhir 2010-2 : 20
ʿAbdān, Abū Muḥammad 2007-2 : 23
ʿAbdī 2012-1 : 47
ʿAbdī Bābā 2011-3 : 2
ʿAbdī Bukhārī 2007-3 : 24
ʿAbdī Shīrāzī 2008-2 : 8
ʿAbdorauf Fitrat 2007-2 : 19
Abduction 2011-4 : 8
ʿAbduh, Muḥammad 2007-3 : 25
Abdul Kadir Semarang 2008-1 : 18
Abdul Karim Amrullah (Haji Rasul) 2007-1 : 9
Abdul Rahman, Tunku 2007-1 : 10
Abdülhalim Memduh 2014-2 : 8
Abdülhamid I 2010-1 : 7
Abdülhamid II 2007-3 : 4
Abdulla Şaiq (Talıbzadə) 2015-1 : 8

Abdullah b. Abdul Kadir Munsyi 2007-2 : 26
Abdullah Cevdet 2017-1 : 2
ʿAbdullāh Frères 2007-1 : 11
Abdullah Kaşgari 2014-4 : 1
Abdullah Paşa Kölemen 2014-1 : 4
Abdülmecid Firişteoğlu 2018-6 : 8
Abdülmecid I 2017-5 : 1
Abdulmuhyi 2007-3 : 32
Abdurrahman Hibri 2017-4 : 2
Abdürrahman Nureddin Paşa 2008-1 : 9
Abdurrahman Şeref 2014-2 : 9
Abdurrahman Wahid 2013-1 : 4
Abdurrauf Singkili 2007-2 : 27
Abdürreşid İbrahim Efendi 2018-5 : 1
Abhā 2008-2 : 11
al-Abharī, Athīr al-Dīn 2008-2 : 11
ʿĀbid 2015-1 : 9
ʿAbīd b. al-Abraṣ 2007-3 : 32
Abid Husain 2007-3 : 34
Abidjan 2009-3 : 14
Abikoesno Tjokrosoejoso 2007-2 : 30
al-Abīwardī 2007-2 : 31
Abkhaz 2013-4 : 19
Ablution 2007-2 : 32
Abnāʾ 2009-2 : 26
Abortion 2007-3 : 35
Abraha 2009-2 : 27
Abraham 2008-1 : 18
Abraham b. Dāwūd 2012-2 : 3
Abraham bar Ḥiyya 2007-3 : 38
Abraham de Balmes 2009-1 : 19
Abraham Ibn Ezra 2019-2 : 1
Abrek 2008-1 : 29
Abrogation 2007-3 : 40
Absence and presence 2009-3 : 16
Abū ʿAbdallāh al-Baṣrī 2011-3 : 3
Abū ʿAbdallāh al-Shīʿī 2008-1 : 30
Abū ʿAbdallāh Yaʿqūb b. Dāʾūd 2016-3 : 4
Abū l-ʿĀliya al-Riyāḥī 2007-1 : 12
Abū ʿAlqama al-Naḥwī 2007-2 : 38
Abū l-ʿAmaythal 2007-2 : 39
Abū ʿAmmār ʿAbd al-Kāfī b. Abī Yaʿqūb 2008-1 : 34
Abū ʿAmr b. al-ʿAlāʾ 2009-1 : 20
Abū ʿAmr al-Shaybānī 2015-4 : 5
Abū ʿAmr al-Ṭabarī 2008-2 : 13
Abū l-Aswad al-Duʾalī 2012-3 : 9
Abū ʿAṭāʾ al-Sindī 2008-2 : 14
Abū l-ʿAtāhiya 2009-1 : 23
Abū l-Aʿwar al-Sulamī 2009-4 : 5
Abū ʿAwn Abd al-Malik b. Yazīd 2010-1 : 19
Abū Ayyūb al-Anṣārī 2013-3 : 7
Abū l-ʿAẓm, Maḥmūd 2008-2 : 15
Abū Bakr 2015-2 : 2
Abū Bakr al-ʿAtīq 2014-1 : 6
Abū Bakr b. Sālim 2010-1 : 25
Abū Bakr Bā Kathīr 2013-3 : 8
Abū l-Barakāt Munīr Lāhawrī 2009-4 : 6
Abū Bayhas 2008-1 : 36
Abū Bishr Ḥawshab al-Thaqafī 2007-3 : 48
Abū Dahbal al-Jumaḥī 2015-2 : 7
Abū l-Dardāʾ 2009-1 : 26
Abū Dāwūd al-Sijistānī 2007-3 : 49
Abu Dhabi 2013-4 : 22
Abū l-Dhahab, Muḥammad Bey 2008-1 : 37
Abū Dharr al-Ghifārī 2016-1 : 9
Abū Dhuʾayb 2007-1 : 13
Abū Duʾād al-Iyādī 2007-2 : 40
Abū Dulāma 2007-2 : 40
Abū l-Faḍl-i ʿAllāmī 2009-1 : 26
Abū l-Faraj al-Iṣfahānī 2007-3 : 51
Abū l-Fatḥ b. ʿAbd al-Ḥayy b. ʿAbd al-Muqtadir 2009-1 : 30
Abū l-Fatḥ Khān Zand 2011-2 : 6
Abū l-Fatḥ Mirzā, Sālār al-Dawla 2008-2 : 16
Abū l-Fidāʾ 2008-1 : 39
Abū Fudayk 2007-2 : 41
Abū l-Futūḥ al-Rāzī 2007-3 : 55
Abū Ghānim Bishr b. Ghānim al-Khurāsānī 2007-1 : 14
Abū l-Ghayth b. Jāmil 2008-2 : 17
Abū Ḥafṣ al-Ballūṭī 2015-4 : 7
Abū Ḥafṣ al-Ḥaddād 2009-3 : 18
Abū Ḥafṣ al-Miṣrī 2007-2 : 42
Abū Ḥafṣ al-Shiṭranjī 2007-2 : 43
Abū Ḥafṣ Sughdī 2009-1 : 31
Abū Ḥafṣ ʿUmar b. Jamīʿ 2007-3 : 57

Abū Ḥafṣ ʿUmar al-Hintātī 2009-2 : 32
Abū l-Ḥajjāj Yūsuf al-Uqṣurī 2012-3 : 11
Abū Ḥāmid al-Qudsī 2013-4 : 25
Abū Ḥanīfa 2007-2 : 43
Abū l-Ḥasan Gulistāna 2009-4 : 7
Abū l-Ḥasan Khān Ghaffārī 2009-4 : 8
Abū l-Ḥasan Zayd Fārūqī 2014-1 : 8
Abū Hāshim 2009-2 : 33
Abū Hāshim al-Ṣūfī 2011-2 : 8
Abū Ḥātim al-Malzūzī 2011-3 : 5
Abū Ḥātim al-Rāzī 2011-3 : 7
Abū Ḥātim al-Sijistānī 2007-2 : 52
Abū l-Haytham al-Jurjānī 2014-3 : 3
Abū Ḥayya al-Numayrī 2007-3 : 58
Abū Ḥayyān al-Gharnāṭī 2008-1 : 40
Abū l-Hindī 2008-1 : 41
Abū l-Hudā al-Ṣayyādī 2007-3 : 58
Abū l-Hudhayl 2008-1 : 43
Abū Hurayra 2007-2 : 53
Abū l-Ḥusayn al-Baṣrī 2007-1 : 16
Abū Ḥuzāba 2008-2 : 19
Abū l-ʿIbar 2007-2 : 55
Abū ʿĪsā al-Iṣfahānī 2009-2 : 35
Abū ʿĪsā l-Warrāq 2008-1 : 45
Abū Isḥāq al-Ilbīrī 2007-2 : 56
Abū Isḥāq al-Isfarāyīnī 2008-2 : 19
Abū Jahl 2007-3 : 59
Abū Kāmil Shujāʿ b. Aslam al-Miṣrī 2007-3 : 62
Abū l-Khaṭṭār al-Ḥusām b. Ḍirār al-Kalbī 2009-1 : 32
Abū l-Khayr al-Ishbīlī 2008-2 : 21
Abū Māḍī, Īliyā 2007-3 : 63
Abū Madyan 2016-1 : 10
Abū Maḥallī 2015-2 : 8
Abū Manṣūr Ilyās al-Nafūsī 2012-2 : 4
Abū Manṣūr al-Iṣfahānī 2008-1 : 47
Abū Maʿshar 2007-3 : 64
Abū Maʿshar al-Sindī 2015-2 : 10
Abū l-Mawāhib al-Shādhilī 2009-2 : 37
Abū Mikhnaf 2009-3 : 20
Abū Misḥal 2007-2 : 57
Abū Muḥammad Ṣāliḥ 2013-3 : 9
Abū Muslim al-Khurāsānī 2015-4 : 9
Abū l-Muʾthir al-Bahlawī 2017-2 : 1
Abū l-Najm al-ʿIjlī 2007-2 : 58
Abū Naṣr al-ʿIyāḍī 2009-3 : 25
Abū Nuʿaym al-Iṣfahānī 2011-1 : 10
Abū Nukhayla 2008-2 : 21
Abū Nuwās 2007-1 : 19
Abū l-Qāsim Khān Kirmānī Ibrāhīmī 2009-4 : 10
Abū l-Qāsim Lāhutī 2018-5 : 4
Abū Qubays 2008-1 : 50
Abū Rīda, Muḥammad ʿAbd al-Hādī 2007-3 : 67
Abū Righāl 2007-2 : 59
Abū Riyāsh 2008-1 : 52
Abū Saʿd al-Makhzūmī 2008-2 : 22
Abū Safyān 2009-3 : 25
Abū Saʿīd b. Abī l-Khayr 2009-3 : 26
Abū Saʿīd b. Sulṭān Muḥammad 2013-2 : 1
Abū Saʿīd Bahādur Khān 2018-3 : 1
Abū Saʿīd Shāh 2009-3 : 30
Abū l-Sāj 2009-1 : 33
Abū Salama Ḥafṣ b. Sulaymān al-Khallāl 2009-2 : 38
Abū Salama al-Samarqandī 2008-1 : 53
Abū l-Ṣalt al-Harawī 2009-3 : 31
Abū l-Ṣalt Umayya b. ʿAbd al-ʿAzīz 2009-1 : 35
Abū l-Sarāyā al-Shaybānī 2011-4 : 10
Abū Shabaka, Ilyās 2008-1 : 54
Abū Shādī, Aḥmad Zakī 2007-1 : 23
Abū Shakūr al-Sālimī 2009-3 : 32
Abū Shāma Shihāb al-Dīn al-Maqdisī 2009-2 : 40
Abū Shujāʿ 2016-2 : 9
Abū Sufyān 2009-2 : 41
Abū l-Suʿūd 2009-3 : 33
Abū Ṭāhir Ṭarsūsī 2007-3 : 68
Abū Ṭālib 2009-2 : 42
Abū Ṭālib al-Makkī 2010-1 : 27
Abū Ṭālib Tabrīzī 2009-4 : 12
Abū l-Ṭamaḥān al-Qaynī 2009-1 : 38
Abū Tammām 2007-3 : 70
Abū Tāshufīn I 2011-1 : 14
Abū Tāshufīn II 2011-1 : 14
Abū l-Ṭayyib al-Lughawī 2007-2 : 60
Abū Thawr 2012-1 : 49
Abū Turāb 2008-1 : 55
Abū Turāb al-Nakhshabī 2009-4 : 12

Abū ʿUbayd al-Qāsim b. Sallām 2008-1 : 55
Abū ʿUbayda 2007-1 : 24
Abū ʿUbayda b. al-Jarrāḥ 2007-3 : 75
Abū ʿUthmān al-Dimashqī 2008-1 : 58
Abū l-Wafāʾ al-Būzjānī 2008-2 : 22
Abū l-Walīd al-Ḥimyarī 2007-3 : 77
Abū Yaʿqūb al-Khuraymī 2008-1 : 60
Abū Yaʿqūb al-Sijistānī 2007-1 : 25
Abū Yaʿqūb Yūsuf b. ʿAbd al-Muʾmin 2008-2 : 25
Abū Yaʿqūb Yūsuf al-Hamadānī 2010-1 : 30
Abū Yaʿzā 2016-3 : 5
Abū Yazīd al-Nukkārī 2013-1 : 9
Abū Yūsuf 2011-4 : 11
Abū Yūsuf Yaʿqūb al-Manṣūr 2007-2 : 61
Abū Zahra, Muḥammad 2008-2 : 28
Abū Zakariyyāʾ al-Warjlānī 2012-2 : 5
Abū Zayd al-Anṣārī 2010-2 : 21
Abū Zayd, Naṣr Ḥāmid 2012-4 : 4
Abū Zayd al-Qurashī 2007-2 : 63
Abū Ziyād al-Kilābī 2007-2 : 64
Abū Zurʿa al-Dimashqī 2007-2 : 65
Abū Zurʿa al-Rāzī 2010-1 : 33
Abubakar Gumi 2014-1 : 10
Abūqīr 2009-1 : 39
Abyaḍ, Jūrj 2008-2 : 30
Abyan 2007-3 : 78
Aceh 2007-1 : 26
Acknowledgement 2008-1 : 61
Acquisition 2008-2 : 30
Acre 2007-2 : 66
Action in Ṣūfism 2009-2 : 44
ʿĀd 2008-2 : 33
al-Ādāb 2007-1 : 32
Adab a) Arabic, early developments 2014-3 : 4
Adab b) and Islamic scholarship in the ʿAbbāsid period 2013-4 : 34
Adab c) and Islamic scholarship after the “Sunnī revival” 2013-4 : 38
Adab d) in Ṣūfism 2009-1 : 40
Adab e) modern usage 2014-2 : 10
Adab al-muftī 2008-2 : 33
Adab al-qāḍī 2007-3 : 79
Adabiyah school 2007-2 : 68
Adakale 2009-3 : 37
Adalet Partisi 2017-4 : 3
Adam 2008-1 : 64
Adana 2012-4 : 7
Adapazarı 2010-1 : 35
Adarrāq 2011-3 : 8
Aḍḍāḍ 2012-4 : 10
Adelard of Bath 2008-2 : 37
Aden 2007-2 : 69
Ādhar, Ḥājjī Luṭf ʿAlī Beg 2011-3 : 10
Adhruḥ 2013-4 : 43
ʿAdī b. Ḥātim 2007-3 : 83
ʿAdī b. Musāfir 2011-1 : 15
ʿAdī b. al-Riqāʿ 2009-1 : 43
ʿAdī b. Zayd 2009-2 : 46
Adīb Naṭanzī 2010-1 : 37
Adīb Nīshāpūrī 2016-3 : 9
al-ʿĀḍid li-Dīn Allāh 2009-1 : 44
al-ʿĀdil b. al-Sallār 2015-2 : 14
ʿĀḍil Shāh 2009-4 : 14
ʿĀdil Shāhīs 2010-2 : 23
Adile Sultan 2008-1 : 68
Adıvar, Abdülhak Adnan 2008-1 : 70
Adıyaman 2008-1 : 71
ʿAdliyya courts 2007-2 : 70
Administrative law 2008-2 : 38
ʿAdnān 2016-3 : 10
Adni, Recep Dede 2017-5 : 3
Adoption 2008-1 : 72
Adrār of Ifoghas 2011-2 : 10
Adrar of Mauritania 2008-1 : 76
ʿAḍud al-Dawla 2011-2 : 12
ʿAḍud al-Dawla 2009-3 : 138
ʿAḍud al-Dīn Muḥammad b. ʿAbdallāh 2009-2 : 47
ʿAḍud al-Mulk, ʿAlī Riḍā Qājār 2008-1 : 78
Advice and advice literature 2007-1 : 34
Aesthetics 2010-2 : 25
Aetius 2008-1 : 80
Āfāq, Khwāja and the Āfāqiyya 2011-3 : 11
ʿAfar 2017-5 : 5
ʿAfar and Issa 2008-2 : 43
al-Afḍal b. Badr al-Jamālī 2007-2 : 73
Afḍal al-Dīn Turka 2008-1 : 80
Afḍal al-Ḥusaynī 2014-2 : 14
al-Afḍal, Kutayfāt 2015-2 : 16
al-Afḍalī, Yaḥyā b. Ṣāliḥ 2020-3 : 1
Afdeeling B 2007-2 : 75
Afghanistan until 1747 2020-3 : 2
Afghanistan since 1747 2020-3 : 10
Afghanistan, art and architecture 2007-3 : 85
Afghāns in India 2007-1 : 59

Aflaḥ b. ʿAbd al-Wahhāb 2014-1 : 11
Aflākī ʿĀrifī 2017-1 : 4
ʿAflaq, Michel 2009-1 : 46
Afrāsiyābids 2015-2 : 18
Africa Muslims Agency 2013-3 : 15
Afshār 2010-1 : 38
Afshārids 2012-1 : 50
Afshīn 2011-3 : 14
Afṭasids 2011-2 : 15
Afterlife 2009-3 : 39
al-Afwah al-Awdī 2007-2 : 76
Afyonkarahisar 2011-1 : 16
Agadez 2018-2 : 1
Agadir 2007-2 : 77
Āgahī (Muḥammad Riḍā) 2015-1 : 9
Aganafat 2008-2 : 45
Ağaoğlu, Samet 2016-2 : 11
Agathodaimon 2008-1 : 82
Agehi 2014-1 : 13
Ageng Tirtayasa, Sultan 2007-1 : 62
Āghā Muḥammad Qājār 2012-1 : 53
al-Aghlab al-ʿIjlī 2009-3 : 46
Ağıt 2014-1 : 14
Agnosticism 2009-2 : 47
Agolli, Vehbi 2008-1 : 82
Agop, Güllü 2007-1 : 64
Agra 2011-3 : 15
Ağrı 2010-1 : 42
Agung, Sultan 2007-2 : 78
Agus Salim 2007-2 : 80
al-Aharī, ʿAbd al-Qādir 2009-3 : 46
al-Aḥbāsh 2010-2 : 35
Aḥbāsh movement in Subsaharan Africa 2014-2 : 15
al-Aḥdab, Muḥammad b. Wāṣil 2019-5 : 2
al-Ahdal, ʿAbd al-Raḥmān b. Sulaymān 2007-1 : 64
al-Ahdal family 2010-1 : 43
Aḥdāth 2010-2 : 37
Ahdi 2017-5 : 7
Ahi 2013-2 : 4
Aḥidus 2009-1 : 47
Ahl-i Ḥadīth 2007-3 : 92
Ahl al-ḥall wa-l-ʿaqd 2007-1 : 65
Ahl-i Ḥaqq 2009-2 : 51
Ahl al-Kisāʾ 2008-1 : 83
Ahl al-raʾy 2009-2 : 50
Ahl al-Ṣuffa 2009-1 : 48
Ahl Sunna in Niger 2018-1 : 1
Ahlī-yi Shīrāzī 2008-2 : 45
Aḥmad, name of the Prophet 2007-3 : 97
Aḥmad b. Abī Duʾad 2007-1 : 68
Aḥmad b. Abī l-Ḥawārī 2010-1 : 45
Aḥmad b. ʿAlī Manṣab 2013-3 : 17
Aḥmad b. ʿAliwa 2011-2 : 18
Aḥmad b. ʿAlwān 2008-2 : 47
Aḥmad b. ʿĀṣim al-Anṭākī 2010-1 : 47
Aḥmad b. Ḥābiṭ 2009-2 : 58
Aḥmad b. Ḥanbal 2009-4 : 15
Aḥmad b. Idrīs 2012-2 : 7
Aḥmad b. Muḥammad b. ʿAbd al-Ṣamad 2009-2 : 60
Aḥmad b. Muḥammad b. Sālim 2008-1 : 84
Aḥmad b. Sahl 2009-2 : 60
Aḥmad b. Sumayṭ 2009-2 : 61
Aḥmad b. Ṭūlūn 2011-1 : 18
Aḥmad b. Yaḥyā, Hamīd al-Dīn 2008-1 : 85
Aḥmad Bābā al-Tinbuktī 2011-3 : 39
Aḥmad Bey 2007-3 : 98
Aḥmad-i Bukhārī 2013-1 : 23
Aḥmad Grāñ 2011-3 : 42
Aḥmad-i Jām 2009-1 : 51
Aḥmad al-Kabīr 2010-1 : 48
Aḥmad Khān, Sayyid 2010-1 : 50
Aḥmad Khaṭīb of Minangkabau 2007-3 : 102
Aḥmad Khaṭīb Sambas 2007-1 : 69
Aḥmad Lamīn al-Shinqīṭī 2009-1 : 50
Aḥmad Lobbo 2017-5 : 9
Aḥmad al-Nāṣirī al-Salāwī 2008-1 : 86
Ahmad Rifaʾi (or Ripangi) 2007-2 : 81
Aḥmad Rizā Khān Barelwī 2007-1 : 71
Ahmad Sanusi bin Abdurrahim of Sukabumi 2007-2 : 83
Aḥmad Shāh Durrānī 2015-2 : 21
Aḥmad Shāh Qājār 2020-2 : 1
Ahmad Siddiq 2007-1 : 75
Aḥmad al-Ṭayyib b. al-Bashīr 2010-2 : 40
Aḥmad Yār 2007-3 : 104
Aḥmad, Zakariyyā 2007-1 : 76
Aḥmadābād 2007-1 : 76
Aḥmadī 2015-1 : 10
al-Aḥmadī al-Yāfiʿī, Ṣalāḥ 2007-1 : 79
Aḥmadīlīs 2011-4 : 13
Aḥmadiyya 2007-1 : 80
Aḥmadiyya (Badawiyya) 2016-1 : 26
Aḥmadiyya-Idrīsiyya 2010-2 : 42

Aḥmadiyya-Rashīdiyya 2013-3 : 19
Aḥmadnagar 2017-5 : 10
Aḥmadpūrī, Gul Muḥammad 2015-2 : 23
al-Aḥmar, Abū l-Ḥasan 2008-1 : 87
Aḥmed I 2009-3 : 47
Aḥmed II 2009-4 : 23
Aḥmed III 2012-1 : 55
Ahmed Arifi Paşa 2008-1 : 87
Ahmed Azmi Efendi 2007-1 : 86
Ahmed Cevad Paşa, Kabaağaçzade 2008-2 : 49
Ahmed Cevdet Paşa 2009-2 : 62
Ahmed Esad Paşa 2008-2 : 49
Ahmed Hamdi Paşa 2008-2 : 50
Ahmed Haşim 2017-5 : 17
Ahmed İzzet Bey 2016-2 : 12
Ahmed Lütfü Efendi 2007-1 : 87
Ahmed Midhat Efendi 2012-2 : 10
Ahmed Midhat Şefik Paşa 2008-1 : 88
Ahmed Muhtar Paşa, Katırcıoğlu Gazi 2008-2 : 50
Ahmed Paşa 2014-1 : 15
Ahmed Paşa, Bonneval 2012-2 : 11
Ahmed Paşa, Bursalı 2007-1 : 87
Ahmed Paşa, Gedik 2009-3 : 49
Ahmed Paşa, Hersekzade 2011-2 : 20
Ahmed Paşa, Melek 2008-2 : 51
Ahmed Paşa, Şehla 2010-1 : 55
Aḥmed Pasha, al-Khāʾin 2010-1 : 54
Ahmed Rasim 2013-1 : 24
Ahmed Resmi 2009-2 : 64
Ahmed Rıza 2009-4 : 25
Ahmed Şemseddin Marmaravi 2013-4 : 43
Ahmed Şuayb 2010-1 : 56
Ahmed Tevfik Paşa, Okday 2008-1 : 89
Ahmed Vefik Paşa 2009-1 : 54
Aḥmedī 2012-3 : 18
al-Ahrām 2007-1 : 88
Aḥrār Movement 2009-4 : 27
Aḥrār, ʿUbaydallāh 2015-1 : 11
al-Aḥsāʾ 2008-1 : 89
al-Aḥsāʾī, Aḥmad 2008-1 : 90
Ahteri 2018-1 : 3
al-Aḥwal 2019-4 : 8
al-Ahwānī, Aḥmad Fuʾād 2008-2 : 51
Aḥwash 2009-1 : 54
al-Ahwāz 2009-2 : 65
ʿĀʾisha al-Bāʿūniyya 2007-1 : 89
ʿĀʾisha bt. Abī Bakr 2011-2 : 22
ʿĀʾisha bt. Aḥmad al-Qurṭubiyya 2009-3 : 50
ʿĀʾisha bt. Ṭalḥa 2010-1 : 57
ʿĀʾisha Qandīsha 2007-2 : 85
Aïssaouas (ʿĪsāwa) 2009-2 : 67
Ajal 2008-2 : 52
ʿAjārida 2007-3 : 106
Ajem-Turkic 2014-1 : 15
al-ʿAjjāj 2007-1 : 89
ʿAjlūn 2007-1 : 90
Ajmal Khān, Ḥakīm 2009-1 : 56
ʿAjmān 2007-2 : 85
Ajmer 2009-3 : 51
Ajnādayn 2014-1 : 16
Ajūdānbāshī 2009-3 : 54
Ajvatovica 2012-4 : 12
Ak Kirman 2010-2 : 72
Aka Gündüz 2015-3 : 6
al-ʿAkawwak, ʿAlī b. Jabala 2008-1 : 92
Akbar 2011-2 : 27
Akçe 2007-1 : 91
Akçura, Yusuf 2020-3 : 20
Akhavān Thālith, Mahdī 2015-1 : 16
Akhbāriyya and Uṣūliyya 2007-1 : 92
al-Akhḍarī, ʿAbd al-Raḥmān 2019-2 : 5
al-Akhfash 2009-2 : 68
Akhījūq 2009-3 : 56
Akhī-Qādiriyya 2011-4 : 21
Akhisar 2010-1 : 58
Akhlāṭ 2011-4 : 22
Akhmīm 2009-1 : 56
Akhsīkath 2009-2 : 70
al-Akhṭal 2007-2 : 86
al-Akhṭal al-Ṣaghīr 2009-1 : 58
Ākhūnd al-Khurāsānī 2010-2 : 45
Akif Mehmed Paşa 2011-2 : 36
Akıncı 2014-3 : 14
ʿAkkāsbāshī, Ibrāhīm 2009-3 : 57
Aksaray 2011-1 : 20
Akşehir 2011-1 : 21
Aksel, Malik 2014-2 : 16
Aktham b. Ṣayfī 2014-4 : 2
al-Akwaʿ, Muḥammad 2007-2 : 87
Āl-i Aḥmad, Jalāl 2013-2 : 7
Āl al-Shaykh 2009-1 : 58
ʿAlāʾ al-Dawla, Aḥmad Khān 2009-3 : 59
ʿAlāʾ al-Dīn al-Samarqandī 2008-2 : 54
ʿAlāʾ al-Mulk, Maḥmūd Khān 2009-3 : 60
Alaca Ḥiṣār (Kruševac) 2010-1 : 59
Alagözoghlu, Savvas S. 2014-2 : 18
ʿAlāʾī, Shaykh 2009-1 : 60

ʿĀlam ārā-yi ʿAbbāsī 2008-2 : 56
ʿĀlam-i Nisvān 2010-1 : 60
ʿAlamī family 2008-2 : 58
Alamūt 2007-2 : 88
Alāns 2009-2 : 71
Alanya 2009-4 : 29
Ālāol 2013-3 : 22
Alaşehir 2010-1 : 61
Alauddin Riayat Syah al-Kahar (of Aceh) 2007-2 : 90
Alauddin Tumenanga ri Gaukanna, Sultan 2007-2 : 91
ʿAlawī dynasty 2007-1 : 96
al-ʿAlawī, Jamāl al-Dīn 2009-2 : 73
ʿAlawī, Muḥammad b. ʿAlī 2007-1 : 99
ʿAlawī, Wajīh al-Dīn 2010-1 : 62
ʿAlawīs, classical doctrines 2010-1 : 64
ʿAlawīs, contemporary developments 2010-1 : 69
ʿAlawiyya (in Ḥaḍramawt) 2010-2 : 47
ʿAlawiyya (in Syria and Palestine) 2009-2 : 75
ʿAlawiyya (in the Maghrib) 2009-3 : 62
ʿAlawiyya in East Africa 2013-3 : 24
Alay 2016-1 : 27
al-Albānī, Nāṣir al-Dīn 2019-5 : 4
Albania 2010-1 : 72
Alborz College 2010-1 : 76
Album 2015-4 : 17
Alchemy 2016-2 : 15
Alembic 2007-2 : 92
Aleppo (pre-Ottoman) 2013-4 : 45
Aleppo, Ottoman 2014-1 : 18
Aleppo, architecture 2011-2 : 37
Alevi music 2013-3 : 25
Alevīs 2008-1 : 93
Alexandria (early period) 2011-4 : 23
Alexandria (modern period) 2011-4 : 36
Alexandria, School of 2016-4 : 2
Alexandropol, Treaty of 2015-1 : 18
Alfā 2008-2 : 59
Alfā Hāshim 2010-1 : 77
Alfonso the Wise 2008-2 : 60
Algebra 2007-1 : 101
Algerian Literature 2007-2 : 93
Algiers 2007-1 : 104
Algorithm 2007-2 : 96
Alhambra 2008-1 : 121
Ali Aziz Efendi 2009-4 : 89
ʿAlī b. al-ʿAbbās al-Majūsī 2009-2 : 76
ʿAlī b. ʿAbdallāh b. ʿAbbās 2009-2 : 77
ʿAlī b. Abī Ṭālib 2008-2 : 62
ʿAlī b. Ḥanẓala b. Abī Sālim 2008-1 : 135
ʿAlī b. al-Ḥusayn 2013-3 : 26
ʿAlī b. al-Ḥusayn b. al-Ḥusayn b. ʿAlī al-Qurashī 2008-2 : 71
ʿAlī b. Ḥusayn Wāʿiẓ Kāshifī 2009-1 : 60
ʿAlī b. Ibrāhīm al-Qummī 2008-1 : 136
ʿAlī b. ʿĪsā 2009-3 : 64
ʿAlī b. ʿĪsā b. Dāʾūd b. al-Jarrāḥ 2013-2 : 10
ʿAlī b. Khalaf al-Kātib 2007-2 : 97
ʿAlī b. Muḥammad al-Wafāʾ 2007-2 : 98
ʿAlī b. Muḥammad al-Zanjī 2010-1 : 79
ʿAlī b. Muqātil 2020-1 : 1
ʿAlī b. Sulaymān al-Muqaddasī 2012-3 : 19
ʿAlī b. ʿUbayda al-Rayḥānī 2009-1 : 61
ʿAlī b. al-Walīd 2009-3 : 66
ʿAlī Bey al-Kabīr 2007-2 : 100
ʿAlī Dede al-Sigetvārī 2011-4 : 40
ʿAlī Dīnār 2015-1 : 19
Ali Ekber Hıtai 2013-3 : 26
Ali Ekrem Bolayir 2014-1 : 24
ʿAlī Emīrī 2010-2 : 50
ʿAlī l-Hādī 2017-2 : 2
Ali Haji, Raja 2007-2 : 102
Ali Hasjmy 2016-3 : 12
ʿAlī Ḥaydar 2007-2 : 105
ʿAlī Hormova 2009-4 : 33
Ali İhsan Sabis 2015-2 : 24
ʿAlī Kurdī Maqtūl 2011-2 : 46
ʿAlī Mardān Khān 2019-6 : 1
ʿAlī Mardān Khān Bakhtiyārī 2008-2 : 72
ʿAlī Mubārak 2007-3 : 108
ʿAlī Murād Khān Zand 2012-1 : 58
ʿAlī Muttaqī 2009-1 : 63
Ali Paşa Çorlulu 2009-3 : 65
Ali Paşa, Damat (Şehit) 2012-2 : 14
Ali Paşa, Hadım 2010-2 : 51
Ali Paşa Hekimoğlu 2008-1 : 138
Ali Paşa, Mehmed Emin 2008-2 : 73
Ali Paşa, Sürmeli 2009-3 : 66
Ali Paşa Tepedelenli 2014-3 : 16
ʿĀlī Qāpū 2008-2 : 74
ʿAlī al-Qārī 2014-3 : 18

ʿAlī Qulī Jadīd al-Islām 2009-3 : 68
ʿAlī Qulī Khān 2007-2 : 106
ʿAlī al-Riḍā 2009-3 : 69
Ali Rıza Paşa 2016-3 : 12
ʿAlī Shīr Navāʾī 2011-1 : 22
ʿAlī Suʿāvī 2012-1 : 59
ʿAlī al-Zaybaq, Romance of 2007-2 : 107
ʿAlids 2008-2 : 78
Alimuddin, Sultan (of Sulu) 2007-1 : 107
Aliran 2007-2 : 109
ʿAlīzāda, Ghazāla 2013-2 : 14
Allāh Virdī Khān 2015-1 : 20
Allāh Virdī Khān b. Khusraw Khān 2009-4 : 36
Allāh-Naẓar 2012-1 : 61
Allahu akbar 2007-3 : 110
Allāhumma 2009-3 : 74
Allusion (in Ṣūfism) 2012-2 : 15
ʿAllūya 2019-4 : 9
ʿAlma 2014-3 : 21
al-Almālī, Maḥmūd 2011-1 : 29
Almāmī 2008-2 : 81
Almamy ʿAbd al-Qādir 2012-1 : 62
Almaty 2010-1 : 81
Almaẓ 2013-3 : 28
Almería art and architecture 2019-6 : 4
Almohads 2014-1 : 25
Almoravids 2009-3 : 75
Almucantar 2009-1 : 66
Alp Arslan 2013-2 : 15
Alpago, Andrea 2008-2 : 82
Alptekin 2011-2 : 47
ʿAlqama 2009-1 : 66
Alqās Mīrzā 2015-4 : 21
Altai 2010-2 : 52
Altai, region, culture and language 2010-2 : 54
Altaians 2010-2 : 55
Altınay, Ahmed Refik 2014-4 : 3
Altruism 2010-2 : 56
Altūntāsh al-Ḥājib 2016-1 : 29
Aludel 2011-2 : 48
Alus, Sermet Muhtar 2016-3 : 14
al-Ālūsī family 2009-1 : 68
al-ʿAlwānī, Ṭāhā Jābir 2019-6 : 6
al-Aʿmā al-Tuṭīlī 2009-1 : 72
Amal 2008-2 : 83
ʿAmal (judicial practice) 2007-2 : 112
ʿAmālīq 2009-2 : 81
Amān 2007-3 : 111
Amānallāh Pānīpatī 2011-2 : 49
Amānallāh Shāh 2010-1 : 82
Amangkurat I, Susunan 2007-2 : 117
al-ʿAmāra 2007-2 : 119
al-Aʿmash 2009-1 : 73
Amasya 2012-2 : 16
Amasya, Treaty of 2015-4 : 23
Amber 2007-2 : 119
Ambiguity 2013-4 : 50
Ambon 2007-1 : 109
Amen 2009-3 : 80
Amghar 2007-3 : 113
ʿAmīd 2009-4 : 37
al-Āmidī, Abū l-Qāsim 2010-1 : 84
al-ʿAmīdī, Abū Saʿīd 2008-1 : 138
al-ʿAmīdī, Rukn al-Dīn 2008-2 : 84
al-Āmidī, Sayf al-Dīn 2012-3 : 20
ʿĀmil, Jabal 2009-3 : 81
ʿĀmila 2010-1 : 87
al-ʿĀmilī Iṣfahānī, Abū l-Ḥasan 2009-1 : 78
Amīn, Aḥmad 2008-2 : 85
Amīn al-Ḍarb 2010-2 : 59
Amīn al-Ḍarb II 2008-2 : 86
Amīn al-Dawla 2008-1 : 139
Amīn al-Dīn Abū l-Qāsim Ḥājjī Bula 2011-1 : 31
al-Amīn, Muḥammad 2010-2 : 61
al-Amīn, Muḥsin 2008-2 : 87
Amīn, Qāsim 2007-2 : 120
Amīn, ʿUthmān 2008-2 : 88
Amīna 2010-2 : 64
Āmina 2007-3 : 114
Amīna-yi Aqdas 2010-2 : 65
Amīnjī b. Jalāl b. Ḥasan 2009-1 : 80
Aminu Kano 2013-2 : 18
ʿĀmir I and II 2007-1 : 110
Amīr-ākhūr-bāshī 2010-2 : 67
Amīr ʿAlī, Sayyid 2009-2 : 81
Amīr al-ʿArab, 1204-1517 2020-1 : 2
al-Āmir bi-Aḥkām Allāh 2011-2 : 51
Amīr al-ḥajj 2015-1 : 22
Amīr Kabīr 2015-4 : 24
Amīr Khurd 2015-2 : 27
Amīr Khusraw Dihlavī 2017-3 : 1
Amīr-i Lashkar 2011-1 : 35
Amīr majlis 2009-3 : 84
al-Amīr, Muḥammad b. Ismāʿīl 2007-1 : 111
Amīr Niẓām Garrūsī, Ḥasan ʿAlī Khān 2008-2 : 89
Amīr Silāḥ 2009-4 : 38
Amīr al-umarāʾ 2011-1 : 33
ʿĀmirids 2013-4 : 54
Amjad Ḥaydarābādī 2019-3 : 1
al-ʿĀmm wa-l-khāṣṣ 2007-3 : 115
Amma Aççıgıya 2018-1 : 4
Amman 2007-2 : 122
Amman, Mīr 2014-1 : 32

ʿAmmār b. ʿAlī al-Mawṣilī 2008-2 : 92
ʿAmmār b. Yāsir 2011-2 : 53
ʿAmmār, Banū (Libya) 2015-3 : 8
ʿAmmār, Banū (Syria) 2014-3 : 24
ʿAmmār al-Baṣrī 2009-4 : 39
Ammonius (Ps.) son of Hermias 2007-1 : 111
ʿAmmūriyya 2007-1 : 112
Ampel, Sunan 2007-2 : 122
Amputation 2010-1 : 89
Amr (theology) 2011-3 : 45
ʿAmr b. ʿAdī 2010-1 : 90
ʿAmr b. al-ʿĀṣ 2010-2 : 68
ʿAmr b. Bāna 2019-4 : 72
ʿAmr b. Dīnār 2009-3 : 84
ʿAmr b. Hind 2010-2 : 69
ʿAmr b. Kirkira 2009-3 : 86
ʿAmr b. Kulthūm 2008-2 : 93
ʿAmr b. al-Layth 2010-1 : 91
ʿAmr b. Luḥayy 2008-1 : 141
ʿAmr b. Maʿdīkarib 2009-2 : 83
ʿAmr b. Masʿada 2010-1 : 92
ʿAmr b. Qamīʾa 2007-2 : 123
ʿAmr b. ʿUbayd 2008-2 : 94
Amrī Shīrāzī 2008-2 : 96
Āmū Daryā 2018-3 : 3
Amulet 2007-2 : 124
ʿAmwās, plague of 2016-2 : 28
Ana Bacı 2016-1 : 30
Anabolu 2008-1 : 142
Anadolu Ḥisārı 2008-2 : 97
Analogy 2013-1 : 25
Anamur 2008-2 : 97
ʿĀnāniyya 2011-3 : 48
ʿAnāq 2009-1 : 81
Anarchism 2012-2 : 19
Anas b. Mālik 2011-4 : 41
Anastasiades, Leontinos 2013-3 : 28
Anatomy 2007-2 : 126
ʿAnaza 2012-1 : 63
ʿAnbar Ānā 2010-1 : 93
al-Anbārī, Abū Bakr 2009-1 : 82
al-Anbārī, Abū Muḥammad 2009-1 : 83
al-ʿAnbarī, ʿUbaydallāh b. al-Ḥasan 2015-3 : 9
Anbiya, Sĕrat 2007-1 : 113
Ancients and Moderns 2007-1 : 113
ʿAndalīb, Khvāja Muḥammad 2014-1 : 33
al-Andalus, etymology and name 2017-5 : 18
al-Andalus, political history 2017-5 : 25
Andalusian art and architecture 2007-3 : 118
Andalusian music 2009-2 : 84
Andelib, Mehmet Esat 2016-3 : 15
Andijān uprising 2012-2 : 20
Angāre 2009-1 : 84
Angels 2009-3 : 86
Angels in art and architecture 2007-1 : 114
Angkatan Belia Islam Malaysia 2007-1 : 11
Anglo-Muhammadan law 2009-1 : 84
Animals 2014-3 : 25
Animals, in law 2008-1 : 144
Animism 2007-1 : 116
Anīs 2017-2 : 3
Anīs al-Dawla 2009-1 : 91
Anjuman-i Khuddām-i Kaʿba 2008-2 : 98
Anjuman-i Khuddām al-Ṣūfiyya 2013-3 : 29
Anjuman-i Maʿārif 2010-1 : 95
Ankara, Treaty of 2015-2 : 29
ʿAnnāzids 2014-3 : 32
Annihilation and abiding in God 2008-1 : 148
Anniyya 2009-2 : 92
al-ʿAnqāʾ, Muḥammad 2014-2 : 20
Anqaravī, Ismāʿīl 2009-3 : 99
al-Anṣār (Sudan) 2009-3 : 101
ʿAnṣara 2015-4 : 28
al-Anṣārī, ʿAbdallāh 2019-3 : 4
al-Anṣārī, Abū l-Ḥasan 2009-1 : 92
al-Anṣārī, Abū l-Qāsim 2009-2 : 94
Anṣārī, Mukhtār Aḥmad 2007-3 : 133
al-Anṣārī, Murtaḍā b. Muḥammad 2008-2 : 100
al-Anṣārī, Zakariyyāʾ 2012-2 : 24
Ansor 2007-2 : 131
Antakya 2019-1 : 1
Antalya 2007-1 : 117
al-Antāqī, Yaḥyā b. Saʿīd 2009-3 : 103
ʿAntar, Sīrat 2007-2 : 133
ʿAntara 2008-2 : 101
Antemoro 2013-2 : 19
Anthologies, Arabic literature (pre-Mongol period) 2007-1 : 118
Anthologies, Arabic Literature (post-Mongol period) 2007-1 : 124
Anthologies, Ottoman 2014-3 : 35
Anthropology of Islam 2016-3 : 16
Anthropomorphism 2011-4 : 46
Antimony 2014-2 : 21
Antinomianism 2014-2 : 22
Anti-Ṣūfī polemics 2012-2 : 26
Anṭūn, Faraḥ 2010-2 : 70
Anūshirwān b. Khālid 2009-2 : 96

Anvarī, Awḥad al-Dīn 2017-5 : 35
Anwāʾ 2007-2 : 137
Apendi 2013-4 : 55
Aphorism 2009-1 : 93
Apocalypse 2007-1 : 128
Apollo Group 2007-3 : 135
Apollonius of Perge 2011-1 : 35
Apollonius of Tyana 2009-4 : 39
Apology 2007-2 : 138
Apostasy 2007-1 : 131
Apostle 2009-3 : 104
Appeal 2007-2 : 139
Aq Shams al-Dīn 2013-1 : 29
Āq-Sunqur al-Bursuqī 2010-1 : 96
Āqā Najafī Iṣfahānī 2011-3 : 49
Āqā Najafī Qūchānī 2010-2 : 72
al-ʿAqaba 2007-2 : 143
ʿAqīl b. Abī Ṭālib 2009-3 : 105
ʿĀqil Khān Rāzī 2013-4 : 55
ʿĀqila 2008-2 : 102
Aqın 2013-2 : 23
ʿAqīqa 2007-3 : 136
ʿAql, Saʿīd 2017-5 : 39
al-ʿAqqād, ʿAbbās Maḥmūd 2007-1 : 134
Aqrābādhīn 2009-1 : 97
al-Aqṣā mosque 2009-1 : 97
al-Aqṣā mosque, art and architecture 2007-1 : 136
al-Aqsarāyī, Karīm al-Dīn 2008-2 : 104
Aqueduct 2007-2 : 144
Arab Higher Committee 2018-4 : 1
Arab League 2011-2 : 55
Arab Revolt 2016-1 : 32
ʿAraba, Wādī 2010-1 : 97
Arabacı Ali Paşa 2017-1 : 6
Arabesk 2013-3 : 31
Arabesque 2010-1 : 97
al-Aʿrābī, Abū Saʿīd 2010-1 : 100
al-ʿArabī, Muḥammad Nūr al-Dīn 2015-3 : 11
Arabian Nights 2007-1 : 137
Arabian Peninsula 2008-2 : 105
Arabian Peninsula, art and architecture 2009-1 : 102
Arabic language: pre-classical 2016-5 : 1
Arabic language: the dialects 2008-2 : 118
Arabic literature 2007-1 : 145
Arabism, Arabists 2008-2 : 125
Arabs (anthropology) 2013-3 : 32
Arabs (historical) 2010-2 : 73
al-ʿArabshāhī, Mīr Abū l-Fatḥ 2019-1 : 3
Arad 2008-1 : 150
al-Aʿrāf 2017-4 : 4
ʿArafāt 2009-3 : 107
ʿArafāt, Yāsir 2008-1 : 151
Arakan 2009-4 : 42
Aral (sea) 2014-4 : 5
Arapkir 2009-1 : 114
Ararat 2012-4 : 14
Arawān 2011-4 : 55
Araz, Nezihe 2016-3 : 23
Arbitration 2014-3 : 37
Archaeology 2009-4 : 47
Archery 2007-1 : 155
Archimedes 2007-3 : 137
Architecture 2007-3 : 139
Archives and chanceries: pre-1500, in Arabic 2013-2 : 24
Archives and chanceries: Arab world 2012-4 : 17
Archives and chanceries: Ottoman Empire and Turkey 2012-3 : 23
Archives: Central Asia 2016-5 : 6
Archives and Chanceries: Ethiopia 2019-2 : 7
Arcot 2010-2 : 78
Ardabīl 2007-2 : 146
Ardahan 2011-1 : 37
Arghūn b. Abāqā 2009-3 : 109
Argot, Turkish 2013-2 : 32
Argots 2007-2 : 150
ʿArīb 2013-3 : 35
ʿArīb b. Saʿīd al-Qurṭūbī 2007-1 : 160
ʿArīḍa, Nasīb 2008-2 : 125
ʿArīf 2007-1 : 161
Arif Çelebi 2018-2 : 3
ʿArīf Chelebī 2007-3 : 170
ʿĀrif Qazvīnī 2014-2 : 27
ʿĀrifī Harawī, Mawlānā Maḥmūd 2009-1 : 114
Aristotle and Aristotelianism 2008-1 : 153
Arithmetic 2009-2 : 96
al-ʿArjī 2009-2 : 101
Arkoun, Mohammed 2015-1 : 24
Arkush 2010-1 : 101
Armenia (topography) 2014-1 : 36
Armenia, Armenians: 1100-1895 2016-3 : 24
Arms and armour 2007-2 : 151
Army, Ottoman (1300-1700) 2016-1 : 33
Army, Ottoman (1700-1923) 2018-6 : 10
Army of Iran, since 1800 2015-1 : 32
Army, India (c. 1200-1947) 2015-1 : 27
al-Arnāʾūṭ, Maʿrūf Aḥmad 2008-2 : 126
Arpalık 2010-1 : 103
al-Arrajānī 2007-2 : 158
al-ʿArrāqiyya 2016-2 : 29
Arrogance 2008-2 : 127

Arşi Tireli	2016-4 : 6
Arşi Yenipazarlı	2017-1 : 8
Arslān Arghun	2014-4 : 5
Arslān al-Dimashqī	2009-4 : 66
Arslan, Shakīb	2007-3 : 171
Arslān-bāb	2014-4 : 6
Arsūf, battle of	2007-3 : 172
al-Arsūzī, Zakī	2009-1 : 115
Artemidorus of Ephesus	2007-1 : 162
Artificial insemination	2007-2 : 158
Artisans, Iran	2011-3 : 56
Artisans, Ottoman and post-Ottoman	2011-3 : 65
Artisans (pre-1500)	2012-2 : 29
Artist, status of	2009-2 : 102
Artvin	2011-1 : 38
ʿArūbī	2018-6 : 18
Arung Palakka	2007-2 : 160
Arūr	2009-3 : 111
Arzan	2019-4 : 10
Arzew	2009-2 : 110
Ārzū	2019-2 : 10
ʿAṣabiyya	2016-3 : 31
Asad b. ʿAbdallāh	2009-3 : 112
Asad b. al-Furāt	2008-1 : 169
Asad Beg Qazvīnī	2015-2 : 29
al-Asad, Ḥāfiẓ	2013-2 : 34
Asad, Muḥammad	2009-1 : 116
Asadābādh	2014-3 : 41
Asadī Ṭūsī	2015-3 : 12
Āṣaf b. Barakhyā	2009-2 : 110
Āṣaf al-Dawla	2007-3 : 173
Āṣaf Jāh	2009-2 : 111
Āṣaf Khān	2008-2 : 135
Āṣaf al-lughāt	2010-1 : 104
Āṣafī Harawī	2009-2 : 115
al-Aṣamm	2011-3 : 71
al-Aṣamm, Sufyān b. Abrad al-Kalbī	2014-4 : 7
Aṣbagh b. al-Faraj	2009-1 : 117
Asceticism	2007-1 : 163
Asclepius	2011-1 : 38
al-Aṣfar	2007-1 : 170
Asfār b. Shīrawayhī	2019-3 : 7
al-Aʿshā	2010-1 : 106
Aʿshā Bāhila	2009-2 : 115
Aʿshā Hamdān	2007-2 : 162
Ashanti	2007-3 : 174
al-Ashʿarī, Abū Burda	2010-2 : 81
al-Ashʿarī, Abū Mūsā	2016-2 : 31
al-Ashʿath b. Qays	2009-3 : 113
Ashgabat	2010-1 : 108
Ashhab	2009-3 : 115
ʿĀshiq Iṣfahānī	2014-3 : 43
Ashīr	2009-4 : 67
Ashjaʿ al-Sulamī	2009-3 : 117
Ashkivarī, Quṭb al-Dīn	2011-1 : 39
al-Ashqar, ʿUmar Sulaymān	2020-4 : 1
Ashraf ʿAlī Thānavī	2015-3 : 14
Ashraf Ghilzay	2009-4 : 68
Ashraf Jahāngīr al-Simnānī	2012-2 : 36
Ashraf Māzandarānī	2011-1 : 41
Ashrafī	2013-2 : 35
al-Ashtar, Mālik b. al-Ḥārith	2014-3 : 44
al-Āshtiyānī, Ḥasan	2008-2 : 136
Ashugh	2015-2 : 31
ʿĀshūr, Nuʿmān	2009-2 : 116
ʿĀshūrāʾ (Shīʿism)	2013-3 : 36
ʿĀshūrāʾ (Sunnism)	2011-1 : 43
Âşık	2007-1 : 170
Âşık Çelebi	2017-2 : 5
Aşık Mehmed	2014-2 : 28
Âşık Ömer	2016-2 : 33
Aşık Veysel	2007-3 : 177
Aşıkpaşazade	2012-1 : 67
Aṣīla	2010-1 : 108
ʿĀṣim	2013-1 : 30
Aşıq Pəri	2016-1 : 44
Asīr-i Iṣfahānī	2009-4 : 69
Asirgarh	2019-5 : 6
Āsiya	2009-2 : 117
ʿAskar Mukram	2015-3 : 17
al-ʿAskarī, Abū Aḥmad	2009-1 : 118
al-ʿAskarī, Abū Hilāl	2007-2 : 162
ʿAskarī Mīrzā	2020-3 : 22
Aşki İlyas	2018-3 : 5
Askiyā Muḥammad	2018-2 : 6
Asmāʾ bt. Abī Bakr	2009-3 : 118
Asmahān	2017-5 : 41
al-Aṣmaʿī	2009-3 : 119
al-Asmar al-Faytūrī	2011-4 : 56
ʿAsqalān	2009-3 : 122
Assassins	2007-3 : 178
Association Musulmane des Etudiants d'Afrique Noire	2015-4 : 30
Assyrian Christians	2013-1 : 31
Astana	2008-1 : 171
Astarābādh	2017-4 : 5
al-Astarābādhī, Raḍī al-Dīn	2009-2 : 118
Astarābādī, Faḍlallāh	2015-1 : 35
Astrakhan	2010-1 : 109
Astrolabes, quadrants, and calculating devices	2007-1 : 171
Astrology	2007-2 : 165
Astronomy	2009-1 : 120
al-Aswad b. Yaʿfur	2009-2 : 118
Aswan	2007-1 : 175
Asyūṭ	2009-1 : 150
ʿAṭāʾ b. Abī Rabāḥ	2009-1 : 153
Ata, Üsküplü	2018-3 : 6
ʿAtābā	2014-4 : 9
Atābak (Atabeg)	2010-2 : 84
Atai	2013-2 : 36
Ātashī, Manūchihr	2016-2 : 34

Atatürk, Mustafa Kemal 2010-1 : 112
Aṭfayyash, Muḥammad b. Yūsuf 2016-3 : 35
Athanasius of Balad 2009-1 : 155
al-Āthārī 2009-2 : 119
Atheism (premodern) 2009-4 : 70
Atheism (modern) 2015-3 : 17
Athens 2008-2 : 138
Athīr al-Dīn Ākhsīkatī 2016-4 : 7
Athos 2009-3 : 124
Atıf Efendi 2007-3 : 180
ʿĀtika bint Shuhda 2013-2 : 39
Atil 2009-2 : 120
ʿAtīra 2010-1 : 116
Ātish, Ḥaydar ʿAlī 2015-4 : 32
Atomism 2013-1 : 32
al-Aṭrash, Farīd 2008-2 : 141
al-Aṭrash, Sulṭān 2008-1 : 172
Atsız b. Muḥammad 2015-1 : 43
ʿAttāb b. Asīd 2020-4 : 3
al-ʿAttābī 2009-3 : 127
ʿAṭṭār, ʿAlāʾ al-Dīn-i 2011-3 : 74
ʿAṭṭār, Farīd al-Dīn 2016-2 : 36
al-ʿAṭṭās, Aḥmad b. Ḥasan 2007-2 : 176
al-Aṭṭās family 2010-1 : 117
Attorney 2009-2 : 121
Attributes of God 2007-2 : 176
Australia 2007-1 : 176
Authority, judicial 2018-3 : 7
Authority, religious 2011-2 : 57
Autobiography in Arabic literature (since 1900) 2010-1 : 121
Autobiography, Urdu 2015-1 : 45
Automata 2009-4 : 74
Avarice, in premodern Arabic literature 2016-1 : 44
Avarız 2009-3 : 135
Avars 2009-3 : 129
Āvāz 2007-2 : 182
Averroism 2011-1 : 48
Avlonya 2013-4 : 56
Avni (Mehmed II) 2017-1 : 9
ʿAwaḍ, Luwīs 2011-3 : 75
Awadh 2008-2 : 143
Awāʾil 2014-2 : 29
ʿAwāna b. al-Ḥakam al-Kalbī 2015-4 : 33
al-ʿAwāzim 2007-2 : 183
Awdaghost 2009-4 : 80
ʿAwfī, Sadīd al-Dīn 2015-3 : 20
Awḥad al-Dīn al-Rāzī 2009-2 : 122
Awḥadī Marāghaʾī 2011-1 : 59
Awlād al-Nās 2007-2 : 184
Awlād al-Shaykh 2012-4 : 22
ʿAwlaqī 2007-2 : 185
Awrangzīb 2011-1 : 64
al-Aws 2014-4 : 10
Aws b. Ḥajar 2007-2 : 187
ʿAwwād, Tawfīq Yūsuf 2009-2 : 123
al-Awzāʿī 2009-3 : 136
Axundzadə, Mirzə Fətəi 2015-2 : 32
Āya 2008-1 : 172
Aya Mavra (Lefkas) 2012-4 : 24
Aya Stefanos, Treaty of 2017-5 : 42
Ayas Mehmed Paşa 2017-1 : 10
Ayaşlı, Münevver 2014-2 : 35
Aybak, al-Muʿizz ʿIzz al-Dīn 2009-4 : 82
al-ʿAydarūs 2011-1 : 76
Aydede 2013-1 : 39
ʿAydhāb 2015-3 : 22
ʿAydīd, ʿAbdallāh b. Abī Bakr 2007-1 : 178
Aydın 2009-4 : 85
Ayin 2009-4 : 86
Ayisyiyah 2007-2 : 188
Ayla 2015-4 : 35
ʿAyn Jālūt 2007-1 : 178
ʿAyn Mūsā 2007-3 : 181
ʿAyn al-Quḍāt al-Hamadhānī (life and work) 2008-2 : 145
ʿAyn al-Quḍāt al-Hamadhānī (intellectual legacy) 2008-2 : 149
Aynabakhtı 2009-4 : 87
al-ʿAynī, Badr al-Dīn 2014-3 : 45
ʿAynī, Ṣadr al-Dīn 2014-4 : 14
ʿĀyşe Ṣıddīqa 2009-4 : 88
Ayvalık 2010-1 : 124
Ayvaz Dede 2011-3 : 76
Ayverdi, Samiha 2016-3 : 37
Ayyām al-ʿArab 2007-3 : 182
ʿAyyār 2014-1 : 38
Ayyūb, Dhū l-Nūn 2007-2 : 189
Ayyūb, Rashīd 2007-2 : 190
Ayyūbid art and architecture 2007-1 : 179
Ayyūbids 2007-2 : 191
ʿAyyūqī 2015-4 : 37
Āzād, Abū l-Kalām 2009-2 : 124
Āzād Bilgrāmī, Ghulām ʿAlī 2013-2 : 40
Āzād Khān Afghān 2012-1 : 68
Azalay 2011-2 : 62
Āzar 2009-1 : 155
Azāriqa 2008-1 : 174
al-Azdī, Abū l-Muṭahhar 2011-4 : 60
al-Azdī, Abū l-Walīd 2009-1 : 156
al-Azdī, Abū Zakariyyāʾ 2010-1 : 125

Azep 2013-1 : 41
Azerbaijani literature 2015-2 : 34
al-Azhar, modern period 2007-3 : 185
al-Azharī, Abū Manṣūr 2007-3 : 188
al-Azharī, Khālid b. ʿAbdallāh 2008-1 : 176
ʿAzīma and rukhsa 2007-3 : 188
al-ʿAẓīmī 2020-4 : 4
Azimuth 2009-1 : 157
al-ʿAzīz bi'llāh 2009-1 : 158
ʿAzīz al-Dīn al-Nasafī 2012-1 : 69
ʿAzīz Koka 2008-2 : 151
ʿAzīz Maḥmūd, Shaykh of Urūmiyya 2012-4 : 27
ʿAzīz Miṣr 2009-4 : 90
al-ʿAẓm family 2007-3 : 190
al-ʿAẓm, Ṣādiq Jalāl 2019-5 : 7
Azov (Azak) 2010-1 : 128
Āzurda 2013-4 : 59
ʿAzza al-Maylāʾ 2013-2 : 41
ʿAzzām, ʿAbdallāh 2009-3 : 138
ʿAzzām, Samīra 2007-3 : 191
Bā ʿAbbād 2014-1 : 41
Bā ʿAlawī 2011-1 : 80
Bā Kathīr, ʿAlī Aḥmad 2011-1 : 81
Bā Makhrama, ʿUmar 2010-2 : 88
Ba, Tijani 2014-1 : 43
Bā Wazīr 2014-1 : 44
Baabullah 2009-3 : 141
Baal 2013-3 : 40
Baalbek 2020-4 : 6
Bāb (in Shīʿism) 2010-2 : 90
Baba 2014-3 : 48
Bābā Faraj 2013-3 : 41
Baba İlyas-i Horasani 2015-1 : 48
Bābā Sammāsī 2015-3 : 25
Bābā Ṭāhir (ʿUryān) 2009-4 : 92
Babaeski 2013-1 : 43
Babai 2015-1 : 51
Bābak 2011-1 : 82
Bābur 2008-2 : 153
Bachetarzi, Mahieddine 2018-2 : 9
Badāʾ 2015-4 : 39
Badajoz 2018-3 : 14
Badakhshī, Nūr al-Dīn Jaʿfar 2016-3 : 39
Badar ud-Din 2009-3 : 141
Badawī al-Jabal 2010-1 : 130
al-Badawī, al-Sayyid 2016-1 : 47
Bādghīs 2010-1 : 132
Badīʿ 2009-3 : 142
al-Badīʿ al-Asṭurlābī 2009-2 : 128
Badīʿ al-Dīn 2009-3 : 144
Badía y Leblich, Domingo 2017-1 : 12
al-Badīʿī, Yūsuf 2009-3 : 147
Badīʿiyya 2009-4 : 94
Badr 2011-3 : 78
Badr al-Dīn al-Ḥasanī 2013-1 : 44
Badr al-Dīn Ibn Mālik 2009-1 : 161
Badr al-Dīn Tabrīzī 2016-4 : 9
al-Badr al-Ḥabashī 2011-1 : 84
Badr al-Jamālī 2010-1 : 133
Badr Shīrvānī 2009-4 : 96
al-Badrī, Abū l-Tuqā 2009-3 : 147
Badrī Kashmīrī 2009-4 : 97
Bādūsbānids 2018-5 : 5
Baeza 2015-2 : 38
Bağçasaray 2015-1 : 55
Baggara 2013-3 : 43
al-Baghawī Abū Muḥammad 2011-1 : 86
Baghdād until 1100 2019-6 : 10
Baghdad, 1500-1932 2016-3 : 41
al-Baghdādī, Majd al-Dīn 2019-5 : 11
Bāghnawī, Ḥabīballāh 2012-3 : 28
Bagirmi 2011-4 : 62
Bahāʾ al-Dawla 2015-1 : 55
Bahāʾ al-Dīn Zuhayr 2010-1 : 134
Baha Tevfik 2012-1 : 72
Bahaeddin Şakir 2014-2 : 37
Bahāʾī Meḥmed Efendi 2016-1 : 48
Bahari 2017-2 : 7
Bahāwalpūr 2017-1 : 13
Bahcat Muṣṭafā Efendi 2009-3 : 148
Bahdīnān 2019-6 : 16
al-Bāhilī, ʿAbd al-Raḥmān b. Rabīʿa 2014-3 : 49
Baḥīrā 2011-3 : 82
Bahmanī dynasty 2016-5 : 8
Bahmanyār b. al-Marzubān 2009-1 : 163
Baḥr al-ʿUlūm, ʿAbd al-ʿĀlī 2015-2 : 40
Baḥr al-ʿUlūm, Muḥammad Mahdī 2009-3 : 149
Bahrain 2017-5 : 44
Bahrām 2011-4 : 63
Bahrām Mīrzā 2012-1 : 73
Bahrām Shāh 2010-1 : 135
Bahrām Shāh b. Ṭughril Shāh 2011-1 : 88
al-Baḥrānī, Aḥmad b. Muḥammad 2009-3 : 150
al-Baḥrānī, ʿAlī b. Sulaymān 2009-3 : 151
al-Baḥrānī, Yūsuf b. Aḥmad 2012-1 : 75
Baḥya b. Paqūda 2012-3 : 30
Bai Shouyi 2015-4 : 41

Baikal 2012-1 : 76
Bāj 2011-3 : 83
Bāja 2012-4 : 30
al-Bajalī 2014-2 : 38
al-Bājī, Abū l-Walīd 2011-1 : 89
Bajkam, Abū l-Ḥusayn 2014-4 : 16
al-Bājūrī, Ibrāhīm b. Muḥammad 2009-2 : 130
Bākharzī, Yaḥyā 2014-1 : 47
Bakhīt al-Muṭīʿī, Muḥammad 2010-2 : 92
Bakhshī (Central Asia) 2018-4 : 3
Bakhshī (Mughal) 2014-4 : 17
Bakht Khān 2009-3 : 152
Bakhtāvar Khān 2015-3 : 26
Bakhtiyār-nāma 2010-1 : 137
Baki 2013-2 : 41
Bakīl 2019-5 : 13
al-Bakkāʾī, Aḥmad 2013-3 : 44
Bakr al-Mawṣilī 2010-2 : 92
al-Bakrī, Abū l-Ḥasan 2019-4 : 12
al-Bakrī, Abū ʿUbayd 2011-4 : 64
al-Bakrī, Ibn Abī l-Surūr 2019-6 : 17
al-Bakrī, Muḥammad b. Abī l-Ḥasan 2019-4 : 14
al-Bakrī, Muḥammad Tawfīq 2019-6 : 19
al-Bakrī, Muṣṭafā Kamāl al-Dīn 2014-2 : 39
Bakriyya 2015-3 : 29
Baku architecture 2014-3 : 50
Balaban, Ghiyāth al-Dīn 2011-3 : 84
al-Balafīqī 2010-2 : 93
al-Balāghī, Muḥammad Jawād 2013-1 : 45
Balambangan 2009-3 : 153
al-Balʿamī 2016-2 : 41
Balāsāghūn 2010-2 : 95
al-Balawī 2015-3 : 31
Baldırzade Mehmed Efendi 2015-1 : 57
Bale 2013-3 : 46
Balıkesir 2015-2 : 41
Balım Sultan 2020-3 : 24
Bālis 2010-2 : 96
Balj b. Bishr 2011-2 : 63
Balkan Wars 2018-1 : 5
Balkans 2015-3 : 32
Balkar 2013-1 : 46
Balkh 2010-1 : 138
Balkhash 2012-1 : 77
al-Balkhī, Abū Muṭīʿ 2009-3 : 154
al-Balkhī, Abū Zayd 2009-4 : 32
al-Ballanūbī 2019-4 : 16
Balta Limanı Commercial Treaty 2018-1 : 8
Baltacıoğlu, İsmail Hakkı 2013-2 : 45
Baluchistan and the Baluch people 2019-3 : 10
Balyan, family of architects 2014-3 : 52
al-Balyānī, Amīn al-Dīn 2018-6 : 25
Bamba, Ahmadu 2013-4 : 63
Bāmiyān 2012-2 : 39
Bānat Suʿād 2016-1 : 49
al-Bandanījī 2019-1 : 6
Bandar ʿAbbās 2012-1 : 78
Bangladesh Awami League 2015-4 : 45
Bāniyās (Buluniyas) 2010-1 : 141
Bāniyās (Paneas) 2010-1 : 142
Banja Luka 2014-1 : 48
Banjārās 2020-4 : 9
al-Banjārī, Muḥammad Arshad 2012-1 : 81
Banjarmasin 2009-3 : 156
Banks and banking, historical 2015-1 : 58
Banks and banking, modern 2015-1 : 62
al-Bannānī family 2009-3 : 158
Banquet 2011-1 : 92
Banten 2010-1 : 143
Banūrī, Muʿizz al-Dīn 2015-3 : 41
Baqī b. Makhlad 2013-4 : 66
Baqīʿ al-Gharqad 2010-1 : 146
Baqliyya 2011-2 : 64
Baqqāl-bāzī 2013-2 : 46
Baqṭ 2010-1 : 147
al-Barāʾ b. ʿĀzib 2011-1 : 93
al-Barāʾ b. Maʿrūr 2010-2 : 97
Barābra 2012-4 : 32
Barāhima 2009-1 : 165
al-Barānis 2016-2 : 48
Baraq Baba 2013-1 : 49
Barāq Ḥājib 2017-3 : 6
Barāq Khān Chaghatay 2015-2 : 42
al-Barbahārī 2009-3 : 160
Barbaros Hayreddin 2011-2 : 65
Barbaṭ 2010-1 : 149
al-Barbīr, Aḥmad 2009-3 : 162
Barcelona 2014-1 : 50
Barelwī, Sayyid Aḥmad 2013-1 : 50
Barelwīs 2011-1 : 94
Barghash 2009-4 : 99
Barhebraeus 2014-2 : 40
Bari, Seh 2008-2 : 160
Barīd 2010-1 : 151
Barīd Shāhīs 2020-1 : 7
al-Barīdī 2010-1 : 153
Barīra 2010-2 : 98
Barjawān 2009-4 : 100
Barlaam and Josaphat 2012-1 : 83
Barmakids 2012-3 : 32
Barnāvī ʿAlāʾ al-Dīn Chishtī 2019-4 : 18

Barqūq, al-Malik al-Ẓāhir 2011-4 : 67
al-Barrādī, Abū l-Qāsim 2015-3 : 43
Barrī Imām 2012-1 : 86
Barsbāy, al-Malik al-Ashraf 2013-4 : 67
Barṣīṣā 2013-3 : 47
al-Bārūdī, Maḥmūd Sāmī 2009-1 : 168
Barus 2011-2 : 67
Barzakh 2011-2 : 67
Barzakh, Ṣūfī understanding 2012-1 : 88
Barzinjīs 2012-2 : 41
Barzū-nāma 2010-1 : 155
Başgil, Ali Fuat 2011-4 : 69
Bashīr b. Saʿd 2011-3 : 87
Bashīr, Munīr 2018-1 : 9
Bashīr Shihāb II 2016-4 : 10
Bashīr, Vaikam Muḥammad 2013-2 : 47
Bashkir 2012-4 : 33
al-Baṣīr, Abū ʿAlī 2009-3 : 162
Basiret 2013-3 : 48
Basiretçi Ali Efendi 2019-6 : 21
Basīsū, Muʿīn 2009-3 : 163
Basmala 2010-1 : 156
Basra until the Mongol conquest 2015-1 : 67
Basra since the Mongol conquest 2015-1 : 68
al-Baṭāʾiḥī, Abū ʿAbdallāh 2014-3 : 53
Batak 2010-1 : 161
Batal Hajji Belkhoroev 2010-1 : 164
Baʿth Party 2011-2 : 71
Baths, art and architecture 2012-3 : 38
Bāṭiniyya 2009-1 : 170
Batriyya 2014-2 : 44
al-Baṭsh, ʿUmar 2018-3 : 15
al-Baṭṭāl, ʿAbdallāh 2011-3 : 89
Bātū b. Jochī 2015-4 : 47
Batu, Selahattin 2016-1 : 50
Batuah, Datuk 2009-4 : 102
Bāul 2018-2 : 11
al-Bāʿūnī 2014-3 : 55
Bayʿa 2014-4 : 18
Bayān b. Samʿān 2011-2 : 74
Bayān in Persian 2015-4 : 49
Bayana 2017-5 : 47
Bayansirullah 2009-3 : 164
Bayar, Mahmut Celal 2011-1 : 99
Bayat, Sunan 2009-3 : 165
al-Bayātī, ʿAbd al-Wahhāb 2007-3 : 192
Baybars I, al-Malik al-Ẓāhir 2010-2 : 98
Baybars II, al-Malik al-Muẓaffar 2012-4 : 34
Baybars al-Manṣūrī 2011-3 : 91
Baybarsiyya 2015-3 : 44
Baydas, Khalīl 2009-3 : 166
al-Bayḍāwī 2017-5 : 53
Bāydū 2015-4 : 52
Baye Fall movement 2014-2 : 46
Bayezid I 2015-1 : 70
Bayezid Paşa 2015-1 : 73
al-Bayhaqī, Abū Bakr 2011-1 : 100
al-Bayhaqī, Ibrāhīm b. Muḥammad 2009-2 : 132
Bayrām Khān 2012-3 : 44
Bayram Paşa 2013-1 : 55
Bayramiyye 2016-3 : 46
Bāysunghur, Ghiyāth al-Dīn 2011-4 : 70
Bayt al-Ḥikma 2009-2 : 133
Bayt al-ṭāʿa 2009-3 : 166
Bayur, Yusuf Hikmet 2012-3 : 46
al-Bayyumī, ʿAlī b. Ḥijāzī 2012-3 : 46
al-Bayyūmiyya 2012-4 : 35
Bazaar, Arab lands 2011-3 : 92
Bazaar, Iran and Central Asia 2011-3 : 98
Bazaar, Anatolia and the Balkans 2011-3 : 96
Bazaar, Indian subcontinent 2013-2 : 49
Bāzargān, Mahdī 2011-2 : 75
Bazīgh b. Mūsā 2013-1 : 56
al-Bazzī 2020-4 : 11
Beautiful names of God 2015-4 : 54
Bedil, Qādir Bakhsh 2013-1 : 58
Bedreddin Simavnalı 2013-4 : 61
Behazin 2017-5 : 57
Beirut 2019-4 : 19
Beja (in Portugal) 2012-3 : 47
Béjaïa 2011-4 : 71
Bektaş, Hacı 2012-4 : 36
Bektaşiyye 2014-4 : 21
Belgium, Islam in 2017-1 : 16
Belgrade 2012-3 : 49
Belief and unbelief in classical Sunnī theology 2010-2 : 101
Belief and unbelief in Shīʿī thought 2017-2 : 8
Bello, Ahmadu 2011-3 : 104
Ben Achour, Abderrahmane 2018-5 : 9
Ben Bādīs 2016-1 : 51
Ben Barka, Mehdi 2018-5 : 10
Benavert 2014-3 : 56
Bengal 2020-1 : 9
Bengal architecture 2011-1 : 101
Bengali literature 2011-1 : 118
Benin 2014-2 : 49
Benjamin 2013-3 : 49
Bennabi, Malek 2018-6 : 27
Bequest 2009-1 : 174

Berār 2020-1 : 19
Berat 2016-2 : 50
Beratlı 2009-1 : 178
Berber music 2019-6 : 23
Berberā 2011-4 : 73
Berkand, Muazzez Tahsin 2016-3 : 48
Berke b. Jochi Khān 2015-2 : 44
Berkyaruq 2013-4 : 69
Berlin, Congress of 2020-2 : 4
Besermyans 2011-3 : 107
Beşir Çelebi 2014-1 : 51
Beşīr Fuʾād 2012-4 : 39
Beste 2013-2 : 52
Beta Israel 2015-3 : 45
Beyani 2017-1 : 21
Beyatlı, Yahya Kemal 2013-1 : 59
Beyoğlu 2012-2 : 45
Beyşehir 2013-2 : 53
Bezm-i Alem 2015-2 : 47
Bhadreshwar 2015-4 : 57
al-Bharūchī, Ḥasan b. Nuḥ 2013-4 : 71
Bhopāl 2011-1 : 123
Bībī Jamāl Khātūn 2010-1 : 165
Bibliographies, Arabic 2015-2 : 48
Bīdil, ʿAbd al-Qādir 2015-4 : 59
Bidlīsī, ʿAmmār 2011-1 : 132
Bihāfarīd b. Farwardīn 2010-2 : 111
Bihārī calligraphy 2020-2 : 7
al-Bihbahānī, Āyatallāh Muḥammad 2009-3 : 170
al-Bihbahānī, Muḥammad ʿAlī 2009-3 : 169
al-Bihbahānī, Muḥammad Bāqir 2009-3 : 172
Bījāpūr 2012-1 : 91
Bilāl b. Jarīr al-Muḥammadī 2017-4 : 7
Bilbaşar, Kemal 2016-3 : 49
al-Bilbaysī 2010-1 : 165
Bilecik 2019-1 : 8
Bilgrāmī brothers 2019-1 : 10
Bilma 2013-4 : 72
Bilqīs 2011-2 : 77
Bin Bāz 2011-2 : 79
Bin Laden, Usama 2017-4 : 8
Bioethics 2009-4 : 102
Biography of the Prophet 2011-3 : 108
al-Biqāʿī 2010-2 : 113
Biʾr Maʿūna 2011-4 : 75
Birecik 2012-2 : 47
Birgi 2013-2 : 55
Birgivī Meḥmed 2017-3 : 7
al-Bīrjandī 2020-1 : 20
Birth control 2009-4 : 108
Birthday of the Prophet 2017-5 : 58
al-Bīrūnī 2013-3 : 50
Birzāl, Banū 2013-1 : 60
al-Birzālī, ʿAlam al-Dīn 2011-1 : 133
al-Bishr 2011-1 : 134
Bishr b. al-Barāʾ 2011-2 : 83
Bishr b. al-Muʿtamir 2018-1 : 10
Bishr b. al-Walīd 2011-1 : 136
Bishr al-Ḥāfī 2011-2 : 83
Bisṭāmī, Abd al-Raḥmān 2010-2 : 115
Bisṭāmī Bāyazīd 2012-3 : 51
Bisṭāmī Shihāb al-Dīn 2013-3 : 56
al-Bīṭār, ʿAbd al-Razzāq 2010-1 : 167
al-Bīṭār, Ṣalāḥ al-Dīn 2017-5 : 62
Bitlis 2014-1 : 52
Bitola 2014-1 : 54
al-Biṭrūjī 2009-3 : 173
Bıyıklı Mehmed Paşa 2019-3 : 16
Bizerta 2011-4 : 77
Black Death 2014-3 : 57
Black Sea 2013-4 : 73
Bloodletting and cupping 2019-2 : 13
Boabdil 2013-4 : 81
Body, in law 2012-2 : 48
Bohras 2013-2 : 56
Bonang, Sunan 2009-3 : 175
Bonjol, Imam 2011-3 : 116
Book 2013-2 : 66
Bookbinding 2009-2 : 137
Boon companion 2011-1 : 137
Booty 2015-4 : 62
Boran, Behice 2013-4 : 83
Boratav, Pertev Naili 2016-4 : 12
Börekçi, Mehmed Rifat 2015-2 : 52
Bornu 2015-4 : 65
Bosnia and Herzegovina 2013-2 : 73
Bostancıbaşı 2018-5 : 12
Botany 2012-1 : 98
Bouaké 2014-2 : 51
Boumedienne, Houari 2013-2 : 81
Bourguiba 2011-2 : 85
Boy Scout 2019-4 : 25
Boyaciyan, Arşag Agop 2013-1 : 61
Boz Ulus 2012-2 : 51
Bozcaada 2012-2 : 53
Bozkurt, Mahmut Esat 2016-1 : 54
Brakna 2014-2 : 52
Breath and breathing 2011-3 : 118
Brethren of Purity 2013-4 : 84
Bridge 2011-3 : 120
Brunei 2009-4 : 113
Bryson 2015-3 : 47

Buʿāth 2011-4 : 77
Bucharest 2018-6 : 30
Bucharest, Treaty of 2019-1 : 15
Buda 2014-2 : 53
Budayl b. Warqāʾ 2010-1 : 169
Bughā al-Kabīr 2010-2 : 117
Bughā al-Saghīr 2010-2 : 118
al-Bughṭūrī, Maqrīn 2013-3 : 57
Bugis 2009-4 : 117
Buhlūl 2009-4 : 120
Built environment, in law 2009-3 : 176
Buisan of Maguindanao 2009-4 : 121
Bukayr b. Māhān 2011-2 : 88
Bukayr b. Wishāḥ 2011-2 : 90
Bukhara art and architecture 2019-4 : 27
al-Bukhārī 2012-2 : 54
al-Bukhārī, ʿAlāʾ al-Dīn 2013-1 : 63
Bukhārlıq 2011-3 : 130
Bukovina 2013-1 : 64
Būlāq 2014-3 : 60
al-Bulaydī, Muḥammad al-Ḥasanī 2013-1 : 65
Bulgaria 2012-2 : 58
Bulghārs 2011-2 : 92
Bullhe Shāh 2009-3 : 179
al-Bulqīnī family 2013-4 : 90
Buluggīn b. Zīrī 2011-4 : 79
Bumiputera 2009-4 : 122
al-Būnasī, Abū Isḥāq 2016-2 : 51
Bundār 2015-3 : 49
al-Bundārī, al-Fatḥ b. ʿAlī 2013-4 : 91
Bundu 2014-2 : 55
Bungsu, Raja 2009-4 : 122
al-Būnī 2011-1 : 140
Būrān 2010-2 : 118
al-Burāq 2012-4 : 40
Burayda b. al-Ḥuṣayb 2011-4 : 80
Burdur 2013-4 : 93
Burhān al-Amawī 2015-3 : 50
Burhān al-Mulk, Mīr Muḥammad 2011-1 : 143
Burhān-i qāṭiʿ 2015-1 : 75
Burhāniyya 2015-3 : 51
Būrids 2015-2 : 53
Burkina Faso 2012-3 : 54
Burma (Myanmar), Muslims in 2009-4 : 123
Bursa 2015-1 : 76
Bursa, art and architecture 2012-3 : 55
Bursalı Mehmed Tahir 2017-5 : 64
Burṭās 2011-2 : 98
al-Burzulī 2010-2 : 119
Busḥāq Aṭʿima 2014-4 : 30
Bushire 2017-1 : 23
al-Būṣīrī 2010-1 : 171
Busr b. Abī Arṭāt 2011-4 : 81
Bust 2017-2 : 16
al-Bustānī family 2018-6 : 30
al-Bustī, Abū l-Qāsim 2014-3 : 61
al-Būṭī, Muḥammad Saʿīd Ramaḍān 2015-3 : 54
al-Butr 2016-3 : 50
Būyid art and architecture 2009-4 : 132
Buzurg-Ummīd, Kiyā 2016-2 : 52
Byzantium 2010-2 : 122
Cabolek 2009-4 : 139
Cadiz 2013-2 : 85
Caesarea 2011-4 : 83
Cafer Çelebi, Tacizade 2016-4 : 14
Cafer Efendi 2016-3 : 52
Cain and Abel 2011-4 : 87
Cairo, Ottoman 2018-2 : 14
Cairo, modern period 2017-2 : 22
Çaka Bey 2013-4 : 94
Çakeri 2017-4 : 13
Çakmak, Fevzi 2013-4 : 95
Calatayud 2011-2 : 102
Calatrava 2011-4 : 90
Calendar of Córdoba 2011-1 : 145
Caliph and caliphate up to 1517 2016-5 : 17
Call to prayer 2015-2 : 56
Camel, Battle of the 2014-2 : 57
Cameroon 2018-1 : 13
Çamlıbel, Faruk Nafiz 2015-1 : 80
Çandarlı family 2015-1 : 81
Çandarlızade Ali Paşa 2018-1 : 15
Caniklizade family 2016-5 : 32
Çankırı 2013-1 : 67
Canon and canonisation, in classical Arabic literature 2011-1 : 146
Canon and canonisation of ḥadīth 2017-4 : 14
Canon and canonisation of the Qurʾān 2013-3 : 59
Cantemir, Dimitrie 2012-4 : 47
Capacity, legal 2011-4 : 92
Çapanoğulları 2013-1 : 68
Cape Town 2014-2 : 58
Capital punishment 2011-2 : 104
Capitalism, Islam and 2015-1 : 82
Caravanserai, Iranian 2012-3 : 62
Çar-ender-çar 2018-2 : 20

Carita Sultan Iskandar, Carita Nabi Yusuf, and Kitab Usulbiyah	2017-5 : 66
Carpets	2011-4 : 95
Cartography	2016-4 : 15
Caspian Sea	2018-4 : 5
Castile	2012-4 : 56
Cat	2015-2 : 58
Caucasus, pre-1500	2014-4 : 32
Caucasus, post-1500	2016-4 : 29
Cautery	2019-2 : 17
Cavid Bey, Mehmed	2017-5 : 68
Cavid Paşa	2018-1 : 17
Cek Ko-po	2009-4 : 140
Celal Sahir Erozan	2016-4 : 33
Celalzade Mustafa Çelebi	2018-1 : 18
Çelebizade İsmail Asım	2018-1 : 19
Celibacy	2013-3 : 68
Cem	2011-2 : 111
Cem Sadisi	2016-3 : 53
Cemal Paşa	2016-4 : 33
Cemal Süreya	2017-5 : 69
Cemaleddin Aksarayi	2014-2 : 61
Cenap Şahabettin	2014-2 : 64
Cenotaph	2010-2 : 129
Centhini, Serat	2011-1 : 149
Cerrahi-Halveti order	2019-2 : 19
Çeşme	2012-2 : 70
Cetinje	2013-3 : 69
Cevri	2019-1 : 17
Chad	2011-2 : 113
Chaghatay Khān	2015-3 : 58
Chaghatay literature	2018-5 : 13
Chaldean Christians	2016-4 : 37
Chams	2010-1 : 173
Chanak Crisis	2015-2 : 60
Chancery manuals	2014-3 : 63
Chanderi	2011-2 : 117
Chāndnī Chawk	2011-3 : 132
Chapar b. Qaidu	2016-3 : 54
Charity since 1900	2016-3 : 56
Charkhī, Yaʿqūb-i	2019-1 : 18
Chechnya	2012-2 : 73
Chen Keli	2011-2 : 119
Chihil Sutūn	2011-2 : 122
Children of Israel	2011-2 : 124
China, Islam in, contemporary period	2012-2 : 84
China, Islamic architecture in	2015-4 : 69
Chinese Muslim literature	2014-2 : 65
Chinggis Khān	2017-4 : 24
Chinggisids	2015-3 : 60
Chios	2015-2 : 60
Chirāgh ʿAlī Khān, Maulvī	2011-2 : 128
Chishtī Muʿīn al-Dīn	2015-2 : 61
Chishtiyya	2016-1 : 56
Chittor	2011-3 : 133
Christian religion (premodern Muslim positions)	2017-2 : 26
Christian-Muslim relations in modern sub-Saharan Africa	2017-2 : 32
Christian-Muslim relations in the Indian subcontinent	2017-2 : 34
Chronogram, Persian	2015-1 : 88
Chronogram, Ottoman	2016-1 : 61
Chronogram, Muslim Southeast Asia	2016-5 : 34
Chūbak, Ṣādiq	2018-1 : 21
Chūbānids	2016-3 : 59
Churās, Shāh Maḥmūd	2017-5 : 70
Chuvash	2013-1 : 69
Chyhyryn campaign	2016-4 : 40
Cigalazade Sinan Paşa	2018-5 : 15
Cik di Tiro	2011-4 : 109
Çırāghān	2011-3 : 135
Circassians, Mamlūk	2012-3 : 69
Circassians, modern	2016-4 : 43
Circle of Justice	2012-1 : 104
Circumambulation	2011-4 : 110
Cirebon	2009-4 : 140
City panegyric, in classical Arabic	2011-2 : 130
Çivizade	2018-6 : 36
Claims of God and claims of men	2011-3 : 136
Client	2017-2 : 37
Codicology	2017-1 : 26
Coffee and coffeehouses, Iran	2015-4 : 95
Coffee and coffeehouses, Ottoman	2012-1 : 110
Command, in Islamic law	2015-3 : 65
Commander of the Faithful	2011-4 : 112
Commitment, in modern Arabic literature	2010-2 : 140
Committee of Union and Progress	2015-1 : 90
Communauté Musulmane du Burkina Faso	2014-3 : 66
Communism	2014-4 : 38
Communism in Indonesia	2018-1 : 22

Comoros 2012-2 : 90
Companionship 2016-3 : 62
Compass 2015-3 : 67
Conakry 2020-4 : 13
Concubinage, in Islamic law 2014-4 : 42
Confession 2017-2 : 40
Congo 2020-2 : 11
Congratulations, Arabic 2014-2 : 73
Congress of Arab Music 1932 2018-3 : 17
Constantinus Africanus 2011-2 : 131
Constitution of Medina 2012-2 : 100
Constitutional Revolution in Iran 2016-1 : 61
Consul 2011-2 : 133
Contagion 2010-1 : 180
Contract law 2013-3 : 70
Córdoba 2014-1 : 58
Córdoba, architecture 2019-2 : 20
Correspondence, philosophical 2015-2 : 63
Corruption 2014-1 : 60
Çorum 2013-4 : 96
Cossack Brigade 2016-4 : 46
Costume albums 2018-1 : 25
Côte d'Ivoire 2018-4 : 8
Cotonou 2019-2 : 28
Courts of law, historical 2017-1 : 39
Courts of law, Ottoman 2016-2 : 54
Courts of law, Mughal 2020-1 : 22
Covenant (religious) pre-eternal 2014-2 : 74
Createdness of the Qurʾān 2015-3 : 70
Creed 2014-3 : 67
Crescent (symbol of Islam) 2014-4 : 47
Crete 2014-2 : 78
Crimea 2012-1 : 113
Crown 2011-4 : 114
Crusades 2014-4 : 49
Çukurova 2013-1 : 70
Cumalı, Necati 2014-2 : 81
Cumhuriyet 2011-2 : 135
Cursing, ritual 2018-3 : 22
Custody, child 2014-3 : 73
Custom as a source of law 2014-3 : 76
Customs dues, historical 2015-3 : 72
Cyprus 2011-4 : 118
al-Dabbāgh, ʿAbd al-ʿAzīz 2011-3 : 141
al-Ḍabbī, Abū Jaʿfar 2016-2 : 58
Dabīr, Mirzā Salāmat ʿAlī 2011-3 : 143
Dabistān-i madhāhib 2013-1 : 72
al-Dabūsī, Abū Zayd 2014-1 : 64
Dadanitic 2019-3 : 18
Dāgh Dihlavī 2014-1 : 66
Daghestan 2013-1 : 73
Dahbīdiyya 2016-2 : 59
Dahira 2017-5 : 73
Dahiratoul Moustarchidina wal Moustarchidaty 2014-1 : 70
Dahlak Islands 2015-1 : 92
Daḥlān, Aḥmad b. Zaynī 2016-5 : 36
Dahlan, Haji Ahmad 2014-1 : 73
Daḥlān, Iḥsān Jampes 2019-4 : 43
Dahrīs 2012-4 : 59
Dāʿī (in Ismāʿīlī Islam) 2012-4 : 66
Dajjāl 2012-2 : 105
Dakanī, Maʿṣūm ʿAlī Shāh 2019-2 : 138
Dakanī, Riḍā ʿAlī Shāh 2020-2 : 15
Dakar 2014-3 : 82
Dakhinī Urdū 2015-2 : 71
al-Dakhwār 2019-1 : 21
Dāmād 2013-1 : 90
Damad İbrahim Paşa 2016-1 : 65
al-Dāmaghānī, Abū ʿAbdallāh 2017-1 : 48
al-Damanhūrī, Aḥmad 2013-4 : 98
Damascus, Ottoman 2014-1 : 75
Damietta 2018-3 : 25
Damirdāshiyya 2016-1 : 67
Danākil 2014-4 : 65
Dandanakan, battle of 2013-3 : 81
Dandarāwiyya 2013-4 : 100
al-Dānī 2014-1 : 89
Daniel 2012-3 : 72
Daniel al-Qūmisī 2013-2 : 87
Danişi 2019-6 : 28
Danişmendname 2015-4 : 102
Danubian Principalities 2014-3 : 85
Daqāyiqī Marvazī 2014-3 : 89
al-Daqqāq, Abū ʿAbdallāh 2018-5 : 18
al-Daqqāq, Abū ʿAlī 2016-1 : 69
Dār al-ʿadl (premodern) 2012-4 : 70
Dār ʿadl (modern) 2012-2 : 106
Dār al-Funūn (Iran) 2013-2 : 90
Dār al-Ḥikma 2014-3 : 91
Dār al-Islām and dār al-ḥarb 2016-5 : 37
Dār al-Nadwa 2016-3 : 65
Dār al-ʿUlūm 2012-2 : 109
Dārā Shikūh 2018-1 : 28

al-Dārānī, Abū Sulaymān 2013-2 : 91
al-Dāraquṭnī 2012-3 : 74
Darb al-Arbaʿīn 2015-3 : 74
Dardanelles 2013-1 : 91
Dardic and Nūristānī languages 2013-4 : 101
al-Dardīr, Aḥmad, and Dardīriyya 2011-4 : 125
al-Dārimī 2012-4 : 74
al-Dārimī, Abū Saʿīd 2015-3 : 74
al-Darjīnī, Aḥmad 2012-4 : 75
Darphane 2019-4 : 45
Darqāwa 2018-1 : 30
Dars-i Niẓāmī 2015-2 : 74
Darul Arqam 2017-2 : 45
Darü'l-Hikmeti'l İslamiye 2016-1 : 70
Darul Islam 2014-2 : 82
Darülfünun, Ottoman 2013-1 : 92
Darüşşafaka 2015-2 : 77
Darzī, Muḥammad b. Ismāʿīl 2012-3 : 77
Dātā Ganj Bakhsh, shrine of 2014-4 : 66
Dāʾūd al-Anṭākī 2010-1 : 183
Daud Beureu'eh 2016-5 : 48
Daura 2014-3 : 92
David 2012-3 : 78
Daʿwa, modern practices 2017-1 : 50
Dawlat Khān Lodī 2015-1 : 93
Dawlatshāh Samarqandī 2015-4 : 103
Dawlatshāh Samarqandī 2017-2 : 46
Dāwūd b. Jirjīs 2012-2 : 112
Dāwūd b. Khalaf 2011-4 : 127
Dāwūd al-Faṭṭānī 2016-1 : 72
Dāwūd al-Qayṣarī 2015-1 : 94
Dāwūd al-Ṭāʾī 2012-2 : 113
Dāya Rāzī 2012-3 : 81
al-Daybulī, Abū Mūsā 2014-4 : 68
Ḍayf, Shawqī 2012-2 : 115
Dayı 2015-2 : 78
al-Daylamī, Muḥammad b. al-Ḥasan 2013-2 : 92
Dayṣanīs 2012-2 : 116
Death in Islamic law 2014-1 : 91
Dede 2012-1 : 119
Dede Korkut 2014-4 : 69
Deedat, Ahmed 2018-2 : 23
Definition 2014-2 : 85
Dehhani 2016-3 : 66
Delhi, architecture 2014-3 : 93
Delhi Sultanate architecture 2020-2 : 17
Deli Birader, Gazali 2014-2 : 89
Deli Orman 2014-4 : 72
Demak 2011-2 : 136
Demir Baba Tekke 2015-1 : 96
Democritus 2015-2 : 79
Demokrat Parti 2016-2 : 67
Denmark, Muslims in 2014-2 : 91
Deobandīs in Africa 2015-4 : 104
Deposit 2013-4 : 103
Dermagandhul, Serat 2013-1 : 94
Dervish 2011-4 : 129
Devil (Satan) 2018-5 : 19
Dewan Dakwah Islamiyah Indonesia 2017-2 : 48
al-Dhahabī 2016-1 : 73
Dhahabiyya 2012-2 : 118
Dhawq 2015-1 : 97
Dhawq, Ibrāhīm 2011-3 : 145
Dhimma 2012-3 : 87
Dhow 2016-5 : 50
Dhū l-Faqār 2012-4 : 77
Dhū l-Kifl 2012-2 : 121
Dhū l-Nūn al-Miṣrī 2012-4 : 79
Dhū l-Rumma 2011-3 : 147
Didactic poetry, Arabic 2011-4 : 135
Dietary law 2012-1 : 121
Dihkhudā, ʿAlī-Akbar 2018-6 : 38
al-Dihlawī, Shāh Walī Allāh 2015-4 : 106
Dihqān 2015-1 : 104
Dīk al-Jinn 2011-4 : 137
Dilāʾ 2019-4 : 46
Dilmaçoğulları beyliği 2014-3 : 101
al-Dimyāṭī, Nūr al-Dīn 2015-2 : 80
Dīn-i ilāhī 2015-2 : 81
al-Dīnawarī, Abū Saʿd 2016-2 : 68
Diogenes 2012-2 : 123
Dioscorides 2014-4 : 73
Dipanagara 2012-2 : 126
Dire Dawa 2014-1 : 94
Ḍirghām b. ʿĀmir 2014-4 : 75
Disciple in Ṣūfism 2018-2 : 24
Dīwān Group 2012-4 : 81
Ḍiyāʾ al-Dīn al-Makkī 2016-2 : 69
Diyāb, Maḥmūd 2012-1 : 126
al-Diyārbakrī, al-Ḥusayn 2015-3 : 75
Diyarbekri, Abdussamed 2013-2 : 93
Djambek, Djamil 2014-3 : 102
Djenné 2015-3 : 78
Djibouti 2017-1 : 54
Djula 2016-2 : 70
Dobhāshī 2014-4 : 77
Döger (Ghuzz) 2018-1 : 33
Dogon 2018-4 : 13
Dome 2017-5 : 74
Dome of the Rock 2014-4 : 78
Dongola 2015-3 : 80

Donkey (eschatological aspects) 2013-3 : 82
Dönme 2012-3 : 92
Doughty, Charles Montagu 2018-1 : 34
Doxography 2015-2 : 83
Drama, Urdu 2014-1 : 95
Drawing 2019-5 : 14
Dreams 2012-3 : 96
Druzes 2013-4 : 104
al-Duʿājī, ʿAlī 2012-1 : 126
Dualism 2012-1 : 127
Dūbayt in Arabic 2014-1 : 96
al-Dukālī,ʿAbd al-Wāḥid 2018-5 : 27
Dukayn al-Rājiz 2011-4 : 138
Dulkadir 2017-2 : 49
Dunqul, Amal 2012-2 : 129
al-Duwayhī, Ibrāhīm al-Rashīd 2011-4 : 139
Düzme Mustafa 2019-6 : 29
East Africa 2016-2 : 74
əbdürrəhim bəy Haqverdiyev 2015-1 : 109
Ebubekir Kani 2020-1 : 28
Ebubekir Ratib Efendi 2016-4 : 50
Ebüziyya Mehmed Tevfik 2015-3 : 83
Ecevit, Bülent 2019-5 : 27
Edebiyat-ı Cedide 2017-5 : 82
Edhem Paşa 2016-3 : 70
Edirne 2018-3 : 28
Edirne, Treaty of 2016-2 : 79
Education, general (up to 1500) 2017-4 : 29
Education, early Ottoman 2016-2 : 80
Education, later Ottoman 2018-3 : 35
Education in the Indian subcontinent 2017-4 : 48
Education in Muslim Southeast Asia 2017-1 : 58
Education in West Africa 2020-1 : 30
Efendi 2017-5 : 84
Eger 2016-4 : 52
Egypt until 1517 2016-3 : 72
Egypt, art and architecture 2018-1 : 36
Əhməd Cavad Axundzadə 2015-2 : 88
Elements 2014-2 : 93
Əli bəy Hüseynzadə 2015-2 : 89
Elias of Nisibis 2014-4 : 85
Elijah 2012-2 : 131
Elisha 2012-4 : 84
Elixir 2013-4 : 109
Elvān Çelebi 2019-4 : 48
Emanation 2016-1 : 81
Emin Nihad 2017-1 : 62
Empedocles 2011-4 : 142
Emrullah Efendi 2018-1 : 41
Encümen-i şuara 2017-1 : 63
Encyclopaedias, Arabic 2015-2 : 90
Enderun Mektebi 2017-1 : 64
Enderuni Fazıl 2015-2 : 94
Entente Liberale 2017-3 : 12
Epics, Persian 2020-4 : 15
Epicureanism 2013-4 : 112
Epigram, classical Arabic 2012-1 : 131
Epigram, Persian 2016-2 : 83
Epistemology in philosophy 2018-4 : 17
Equator 2016-4 : 53
Erakalın, Ülkü 2019-6 : 31
Erbakan, Necmettin 2016-3 : 78
Erbervelt, Pieter 2012-2 : 132
Ergenekon 2020-2 : 27
Eritrea 2015-4 : 112
Erotica, Ottoman 2018-4 : 28
Erucakra 2015-4 : 117
Erzincan 2018-5 : 32
Erzurum 2016-2 : 85
Esendal, Memduh Şevket 2018-2 : 27
Esotericism and exotericism 2015-2 : 96
Eşrefoğlu Rumi 2016-4 : 55
Essence and existence 2015-4 : 118
Esztergom 2016-1 : 90
Eternity 2014-3 : 104
Ethics in philosophy 2015-1 : 110
Ethics in Sufism 2016-1 : 92
Ethiopia, Islam and Muslims in 2014-4 : 88
Euboea 2015-4 : 124
Euclid 2013-4 : 114
Eunuchs 2015-3 : 84
Euthanasia 2015-1 : 117
Eutychius of Alexandria 2013-3 : 83
Eve 2018-1 : 42
Evidence 2016-2 : 87
Evliya Celebi 2016-1 : 95
Evren, Kenan 2018-1 : 44
Existence in philosophy and theology 2017-4 : 52
Exorcism 2014-4 : 93
Expiation 2011-2 : 138
Eyüboğlu, Bedri Rahmi 2019-6 : 32
Eyüp 2016-3 : 79
Ezekiel 2012-4 : 85
Fable 2016-1 : 100
Fable, animal, in Muslim Southeast Asia 2019-4 : 50
Faculties of the soul 2018-6 : 41
Faḍāʾil 2018-3 : 40
Fadak 2018-3 : 45
Faḍal Shāh 2012-2 : 134

al-Fāḍil al-Hindī 2013-1 : 97
al-Faḍl b. Dukayn 2020-4 : 23
al-Faḍl b. al-Ḥubāb 2015-3 : 93
al-Faḍl b. Marwān 2013-1 : 98
al-Faḍl b. al-Rabīʿ 2016-3 : 84
al-Faḍl b. Sahl 2013-1 : 99
al-Faḍl b. Shādhān 2012-3 : 104
Faḍl-i Ḥaqq Khayrābādī 2015-2 : 104
Faḍl-i Imām Khayrābādī 2015-2 : 106
Faḍl al-Shāʿira 2012-4 : 88
Faḍlallāh al-Burhānpūrī 2012-3 : 106
Faḍlī Namangānī 2017-1 : 66
Fahri 2014-4 : 96
Fahri of Bursa 2013-4 : 121
Fakhkh 2016-3 : 85
Fakhr al-Dīn Dihlavī 2018-6 : 48
Fakhr al-Din Maʿn 2015-4 : 127
Fakhr-i Mudabbir 2012-4 : 89
Fakhruddin, H. A. R. 2014-4 : 97
al-Fākhūrī, Arsānyūs 2016-4 : 56
Fākhūrī, ʿUmar 2012-3 : 108
Fakih Usman 2013-2 : 95
Fakiri (Kalkandelenli) 2013-4 : 122
Fallata 2016-2 : 94
Fānī Badāyūnī 2017-3 : 14
Fānī Kashmīrī 2012-3 : 109
Fansuri, Hamzah 2016-1 : 106
Faqīh, Bā 2012-4 : 91
Faqīr, Faqīr Muḥammad 2012-3 : 111
al-Fārābī 2015-2 : 108
al-Fārābī, music 2015-4 : 129
Farāhānī, Adīb al-Mamālik 2013-4 : 123
Farāhī, Ḥamīd al-Dīn 2019-3 : 20
Faraj, Alfrīd 2012-4 : 93
Faraj, al-Malik al-Nāṣir 2015-3 : 94
Farangī Maḥall 2013-1 : 102
Farāz, Aḥmad 2012-2 : 135
al-Farazdaq 2012-4 : 94
Farghana Valley 2014-2 : 96
al-Farghānī 2013-1 : 107
al-Farghānī, Saʿīd al-Dīn 2016-2 : 96
Farḥat Allāh Beg 2020-2 : 30
Farḥāt, Ilyās 2012-4 : 98
Farīd 2012-2 : 137
Farīd al-Dīn Masʿūd 2018-1 : 46
Farīdī, Shahīdallāh 2017-4 : 62
Farīghūnids 2015-4 : 132
Fāris, Bishr 2013-1 : 109
al-Fārisī, Abū ʿAlī 2012-3 : 113
al-Fārisī, Kamāl al-Dīn 2014-3 : 114
Farmān, Ghāʾib Ṭuʿma 2012-4 : 100
Farqad al-Sabakhī 2012-1 : 134
al-Farrāʾ 2012-3 : 115
Farrukh Ḥusayn 2017-1 : 67
Farrūkh, ʿUmar 2013-1 : 110
Farrukhābād 2015-3 : 97
Farrukhī Sīstānī 2012-3 : 118
Farrukhzād, Furūgh 2020-1 : 34
al-Fārūq 2012-4 : 101
al-Fārūqī, ʿAbd al-Bāqī 2016-5 : 53
Fārūqīs 2016-2 : 98
al-Fārūthī, ʿIzz al-Dīn 2012-1 : 135
Fasānjus, Banū 2016-5 : 55
al-Fasawī, Yaʿqūb 2016-2 : 102
al-Fāshir 2019-2 : 32
Fashoda Incident 2013-1 : 111
al-Fāsī family 2018-5 : 35
al-Fāsī, Taqī l-Dīn 2015-2 : 127
al-Fāsiyya 2015-4 : 134
Faskyu (Ithaca) 2017-1 : 78
Fatahillah 2012-2 : 138
al-Faṭānī, Aḥmad b. Muḥammad Zayn 2016-5 : 56
al-Fatāt 2012-2 : 139
al-Fatāwā l-ʿĀlamgīriyya 2012-3 : 120
Fatayat Nahdlatul Ulama 2018-5 : 39
Fatehpur Sikri 2018-4 : 39
al-Fatḥ 2015-4 : 136
al-Fatḥ b. Khāqān 2013-1 : 112
al-Fatḥ al-Mawṣilī 2013-3 : 85
Fatḥallāh Shīrāzī 2015-2 : 128
Fatḥī, Ḥasan 2015-2 : 129
al-Fātiḥa 2013-2 : 96
Fatiḥpurī, Niyāz 2012-2 : 140
Fāṭima bt. Muḥammad 2014-2 : 100
Fāṭima al-Yashruṭiyya 2020-3 : 28
Fāṭimid art and architecture 2012-3 : 123
Fatimids 2014-1 : 98
Fatma Aliye 2018-1 : 50
Fatwā, premodern 2017-4 : 63
Fatwā, modern 2017-4 : 69
Fatwa, modern media 2017-4 : 74
Favour (divine) 2013-2 : 100
Fawwāz, Zaynab 2012-3 : 132
Fayʾ 2013-2 : 102
Fayḍ, Fayḍ Aḥmad 2012-3 : 133
Fayḍī, Abū l-Fayḍ 2016-3 : 86
Fayḍiyya 2016-4 : 57
Fayṣal b. ʿAbd al-ʿAzīz 2016-3 : 89
al-Faytūrī, Muḥammad 2017-2 : 65
Fayyāḍ, Ilyās 2013-1 : 113
al-Fayyūm 2019-6 : 35
al-Fazārī 2016-3 : 91
al-Fazārī, ʿAbdallāh b. Yazīd 2016-5 : 57
Fazli 2015-1 : 119
Fazzān 2019-2 : 33

Fear of God and hope (in Ṣūfism) 2012-4 : 102
Federation of Arab Republics 2012-1 : 136
Fehim Süleyman 2016-3 : 93
Fenarizade 2014-1 : 110
Fener 2013-1 : 114
Feraizcizade Mehmed Şakir 2015-1 : 120
Ferhad Paşa 2017-5 : 85
Ferhad u Şirin (in Turkic literatures) 2016-1 : 109
Feridun Bey 2014-2 : 108
Ferman 2016-2 : 103
Ferraguto, Pietro 2014-3 : 115
Fetihname 2014-3 : 116
Feyzullah Efendi 2018-4 : 45
Fez 2013-2 : 104
Fibonacci, Leonardo 2016-4 : 58
Fiction, Arabic, modern 2014-4 : 98
Fiction, Persian 2013-1 : 115
Fiction, Urdu 2012-3 : 137
Fidāʾiyyān-i Islām 2013-1 : 119
Figani 2014-4 : 103
Fighānī Shīrāzī, Bābā 2012-3 : 141
Fijār 2012-4 : 104
Fikrī, ʿAbdallāh 2013-4 : 125
Finance 2014-4 : 104
Fındıkoğlu, Ziyaeddin Fahri 2015-4 : 140
Fines 2013-1 : 120
Fiqh, faqīh, fuqahāʾ 2015-2 : 130
Firḍa 2020-2 : 32
Firdawsī, Abū l-Qāsim, and the Shāhnāma 2017-2 : 66
Firdawsiyya 2012-4 : 105
Firdevsi-yi Rumi 2016-4 : 61
Fīrūz Shāh Tughluq 2017-5 : 87
Fitna in early Islamic history 2012-4 : 107
Fiṭra 2016-2 : 104
Flagellation 2015-2 : 133
Flags 2014-3 : 119
Flood 2013-3 : 86
Flores 2013-2 : 110
Fodi Kabba Dumbuya 2013-2 : 112
Fondaco 2013-2 : 113
Forgery in ḥadīth 2018-5 : 41
Fort William College 2013-1 : 122
Fortress, in the Middle East 2015-2 : 134
Forty Traditions 2016-2 : 107
Foundling 2013-1 : 124
Fountain 2013-4 : 126
Franks 2013-2 : 114
Free verse, Arabic 2013-3 : 89
Freemasonry 2014-4 : 112
Friday prayer 2016-5 : 60
Friend of God 2013-3 : 90
al-Fuḍayl b. ʿIyāḍ 2013-3 : 92
Fūdī, ʿAbdallāh 2016-2 : 111
Fūdī, ʿUthmān 2016-2 : 112
Fulbe, Fulfulde 2019-5 : 30
Fūmanī, ʿAbd al-Fattāḥ 2018-2 : 29
Funerary practices 2013-2 : 116
Funj 2015-4 : 141
al-Fūrakī, Abū Bakr 2013-4 : 128
Furāt b. Furāt al-Kūfī 2012-4 : 108
Futa Toro 2015-2 : 139
Futūḥ 2012-2 : 141
Futuwwa (in Ṣūfism) 2012-3 : 143
Fuuta Jalon 2017-4 : 76
al-Fuwaṭī, Hishām b. ʿAmr 2016-1 : 110
Fuzuli, Mehmed b. Süleyman 2014-3 : 124
Gabriel 2014-3 : 126
Gagauz (language and literature) 2013-3 : 95
Gagauz people 2015-1 : 122
Galatasarayı 2015-2 : 141
Galen 2013-4 : 130
Galip Şeyh 2020-2 : 35
Ganizade Nadiri 2016-5 : 64
Garami 2018-6 : 51
Gardens 2014-2 : 112
Gardīzī 2013-2 : 127
Garebeg 2019-5 : 34
Gasprinski, İsmail 2015-3 : 101
Gatholoco, Suluk 2013-1 : 127
Gaur 2014-2 : 122
Gaza 2014-4 : 116
Gaza, art and architecture 2014-4 : 120
Gazel (Qəzəl) in Azerbaijani literature 2016-4 : 64
Gazi Hüsrev Bey 2018-1 : 52
Gecekondu 2013-4 : 134
Gedik 2014-4 : 126
Gelenbevi, İsmail 2015-1 : 123
Gelibolulu Mustafa Ali 2015-1 : 125
Genç Kalemler 2013-4 : 137
Gender and law 2017-1 : 81
General average 2014-3 : 129
Generation and corruption 2016-2 : 114
Genetic testing 2013-3 : 96
Gentry in South Asia 2020-2 : 37
Geography in Arabic 2020-3 : 30
Geomancy 2013-3 : 98
Georgius de Hungaria 2017-5 : 92
Gerakan Aceh Merdeka 2017-3 : 16
Gerard of Cremona 2014-1 : 112
Germany, Islam in 2014-3 : 138
Geuffroy, Antoine 2013-3 : 101
Ghadames 2019-5 : 35
Ghadīr Khumm 2014-2 : 123

al-Ghāfiqī, Abū Jaʿfar 2016-2 : 119
al-Ghāfiqī, Muḥammad 2013-3 : 102
Ghallāb, ʿAbd al-Karīm 2020-1 : 37
Ghamkolvī, Ṣūfī Ṣāḥib 2013-3 : 103
Ghana, Muslims in contemporary 2013-1 : 128
Ghanī Kashmīrī 2014-3 : 138
Ghānim, Fatḥī 2013-3 : 105
Ghawwāṣī 2014-2 : 128
Ghaylān al-Dimashqī 2013-4 : 139
Ghazal in Persian 2016-2 : 121
Ghazālī Mashhadī 2014-3 : 140
al-Ghazālī, Muḥammad 2015-1 : 127
Ghāzān Khān Maḥmūd 2019-2 : 37
Ghāzī al-Dīn Ḥaydar 2013-3 : 106
al-Ghāzī Ghumūqī 2018-2 : 31
Ghāzī Miyāṇ, Sālār Masʿūd 2013-4 : 141
Ghaznavid art and architecture 2015-3 : 103
Ghaznavids 2016-3 : 95
Ghazw 2013-4 : 143
Ghiyāth al-Dīn Tughluq Shāh I 2018-2 : 34
Ghiyāth al-Dīn Tughluq Shāh II 2016-4 : 65
al-Ghubrīnī, Abū l-ʿAbbās 2016-2 : 127
al-Ghubrīnī, Abū Mahdī 2016-2 : 128
Ghūl 2013-4 : 144
Ghulām Aḥmad, Mīrzā 2013-3 : 107
Ghulām ʿAlī Shāh 2013-3 : 110
Ghulām Farīd 2013-1 : 132
Ghulām Khalīl 2015-4 : 145
Ghulām Rasūl 2013-1 : 135
Ghulāt (extremist Shīʿīs) 2018-2 : 37
al-Ghumārī, ʿAlī b. Maymūn 2013-2 : 128
Ghurāb, Banū 2017-4 : 79
Ghurābiyya 2013-1 : 137
Ghūrid art and architecture 2014-2 : 129
Ghūrids 2015-3 : 109
al-Ghuzūlī 2016-3 : 105
Gifts 2013-3 : 111
Girāy Khāns 2012-1 : 138
Giri, Sunan/Panĕmbahan 2012-4 : 111
Girona 2014-1 : 113
Gīsū Darāz, Bandanavāz 2014-2 : 132
Gıyaseddin Keyhüsrev I 2018-1 : 53
Glass 2018-5 : 44
Globalisation and Muslim societies 2014-3 : 141
Globes (celestial and terrestrial) 2016-2 : 129
Gnāwa 2019-1 : 23
Gnosticism 2017-4 : 82
Gobind Singh 2014-1 : 114
Goddess of the Southern Ocean (Ratu Kidul) 2013-1 : 138
Gog and Magog 2013-3 : 113
Golconda art and architecture 2014-2 : 133
Golconda, history 2016-2 : 132
Gold 2014-3 : 145
Golden Horde 2016-3 : 106
Goliath 2014-1 : 115
Gondwāna 2013-3 : 114
Gontor, Pondok Modern 2014-4 : 129
Gospel, Muslim conception of 2014-4 : 130
Gospel of Barnabas 2014-1 : 116
Goyā, Faqīr Muḥammad Khān 2013-1 : 139
Grammar and law 2015-3 : 129
Granada 2014-4 : 135
Granada art and architecture 2013-3 : 116
Grand National Assembly Turkey 2018-2 : 47
Grand vizier 2019-4 : 53
Gratitude and ingratitude 2014-1 : 121
Grave visitation/worship 2016-1 : 112
Greece, Muslims in 2014-1 : 124
Greek fire 2013-4 : 146
Greek into Arabic 2016-1 : 116
Gregory Thaumaturgus 2013-3 : 127
Gresik 2013-2 : 130
Gritti, Alvise 2016-4 : 66
Guarantee 2013-3 : 128
Guild 2015-1 : 130
Gūjars 2015-2 : 143
Gulbadan Begam 2010-1 : 185
Gulbarga 2020-1 : 38
Gulbargā, art and architecture 2014-2 : 138
Gülhane, Edict of 2015-3 : 133
Gulkhanī Muḥammad Sharīf 2015-3 : 135
Gulshaniyya 2018-6 : 52
Gulshīrī, Hūshang 2013-2 : 131
Gümülcineli Ahmed Asım Efendi 2014-4 : 141
Gümüşhanevi, Ahmed Ziyaeddin 2016-1 : 134
Gunābādiyya 2013-4 : 148
Günaltay, Mehmet Şemsettin 2015-1 : 134
Gunung Jati, Sunan 2014-3 : 148
Gürsel, Cemal 2016-2 : 137
Gürses, Müslüm 2016-4 : 67
Guruş 2019-4 : 55

Güzelce Ali Paşa	2014-1 : 129
Gwalior	2018-3 : 49
Gwalior Fort, art and architecture	2015-1 : 136
Ḥabā'ib Southeast Asia	2018-1 : 56
Ḥabash al-Ḥāsib al-Marwazī	2017-4 : 87
Ḥabīb b. Maslama al-Fihrī	2016-4 : 70
Ḥabīballāh Khān	2017-2 : 87
Habsi	2017-4 : 90
Ḥaddād, Fu'ād	2016-2 : 139
Hadice Turhan Sultan	2017-3 : 19
Hadım Süleyman Paşa	2019-2 : 40
Ḥadīth	2018-4 : 48
Ḥadīth commentary	2018-4 : 61
Ḥadīth criticism	2019-5 : 39
Ḥadīth, Ibāḍism	2016-2 : 140
Ḥadīth qudsī	2017-4 : 91
Hadiyya (Ethiopia)	2016-3 : 113
Ḥaḍra in Ṣūfism	2016-4 : 72
Ḥaḍramī diaspora Southeast Asia	2018-3 : 51
Ḥāfiẓ	2018-5 : 52
Hafiz İsmail Paşa	2018-6 : 63
al-Ḥāfiẓ li-Dīn Allāh	2017-2 : 89
Hafiz Post	2016-5 : 66
Ḥafṣ al-Fard	2017-1 : 95
Hafsa Sultan	2017-5 : 94
Hagar	2017-3 : 21
Hagiography, Persian and Turkish	2018-6 : 65
Hagiography in South Asia	2019-4 : 57
Haji, Sultan	2017-4 : 97
Ḥājib	2018-1 : 59
al-Hajiri, Ḥusām al-Dīn	2020-2 : 41
al-Ḥājj, Unsī	2016-4 : 74
al-Ḥajjāj b. Yūsuf b. Maṭar	2016-4 : 75
Ḥājjī l-Dabīr	2016-4 : 77
Ḥājjī Pasha	2017-3 : 22
al-Ḥakam b. 'Abdal	2016-4 : 78
al-Ḥakam b. Qanbar	2016-4 : 79
al-Ḥākim bi-Amr Allāh	2017-3 : 24
al-Ḥakīm, Tawfīq	2016-1 : 137
al-Ḥakīm al-Tirmidhī	2018-5 : 58
Ḥākimiyya	2017-3 : 30
Ḥāl (theory of "states" in theology)	2016-5 : 67
Halay	2018-6 : 69
Halevi, Judah	2018-1 : 63
al-Ḥalīmī, Abū 'Abdallāh	2010-1 : 189
Halkevleri	2018-1 : 68
Ham	2017-4 : 99
Ḥamā	2017-2 : 91
Ḥamā, art and architecture	2017-2 : 93
Hamadānī, 'Alī	2015-2 : 147
al-Hamadhānī, Badī' al-Zamān	2019-2 : 41
Ḥamādisha	2011-4 : 145
Ḥamallāh	2017-3 : 32
Hāmān	2017-4 : 100
Ḥamās	2017-1 : 97
al-Ḥamawī, 'Alwān	2016-5 : 71
Ḥamdān b. Abān al-Lāḥiqī	2019-3 : 25
Ḥamdān Qarmaṭ	2016-5 : 73
al-Ḥamdawī	2020-1 : 42
Hamdullah Efendi	2017-1 : 99
Hamengkubuwana I	2016-4 : 80
Ḥamīd al-Dīn Qāḍī Nāgawrī	2016-5 : 74
Ḥamīd al-Dīn Ṣūfī Nāgawrī	2016-5 : 76
Ḥamīd Qalandar	2017-3 : 35
Hamidullah, Muhammad	2017-2 : 96
Hamka (Haji Abdul Malik Karim Amrullah)	2017-2 : 98
al-Ḥammāmī	2016-2 : 144
Hamon, Moses	2016-4 : 81
Hampī	2018-6 : 70
al-Ḥāmūlī, 'Abduh	2018-2 : 49
Ḥamza b. 'Abd al-Muṭṭalib	2016-3 : 114
Ḥamza b. 'Alī	2017-2 : 102
Ḥamza b. Bīḍ	2016-2 : 145
Ḥamza Makhdūm	2017-4 : 101
Ḥamza, Romance of	2018-1 : 70
Ḥamzat-Bek al-Dāghistānī	2017-2 : 104
al-Ḥanafī, Aḥmad b. Abī Bakr	2016-4 : 82
Hang Tuah, Hikayat	2016-4 : 83
Hānsavī, Jamāl al-Dīn	2018-6 : 73
Ḥanẓala b. Ṣafwān (prophet)	2016-4 : 86
Ḥaqqānī, 'Abd al-Ḥaqq	2018-2 : 50
Ḥaqqī, Yaḥyā	2017-3 : 36
Ḥarāfīsh	2017-4 : 103
Harakada al-Islah	2019-1 : 28
Harakada Mujahidinta al-Shabab	2019-1 : 30
Harar	2016-5 : 77
al-Hararī, 'Abdallāh	2013-2 : 133
Ḥarāṭīn in Mauretania	2017-2 : 105
Haravī, Amīr Ḥusaynī	2011-4 : 147
Hareket Ordusu	2017-4 : 104
Harem, in the Middle East	2018-6 : 74
al-Ḥarīrī	2016-5 : 80

al-Ḥārith b. Ḥilliza 2017-3 : 39
al-Ḥārith b. Kalada 2017-2 : 109
Ḥāritha b. Badr al-Ghudānī 2017-4 : 105
Haron, Abdullah 2017-1 : 102
Harthama b. Aʿyan 2018-3 : 53
Hārūt and Mārūt 2017-5 : 95
Hasaitic 2016-4 : 88
Ḥasan b. ʿĀmir 2016-5 : 85
al-Ḥasan b. Ṣāliḥ 2016-4 : 90
al-Ḥasan al-Baṣrī 2017-1 : 103
Hasan Beyzade 2018-2 : 53
Ḥasan Ghaznavī 2012-3 : 149
Ḥasan II 2017-3 : 40
Ḥasan, Mīr Ghulām 2020-1 : 43
Hasan Mustapa 2017-3 : 42
Ḥasan Niẓāmī 2017-1 : 107
Ḥasan-i Ṣabbāḥ 2016-4 : 91
Hasankeyf 2018-6 : 80
Hasbi Ash Shiddieqy 2017-5 : 97
Hasbihal 2020-1 : 47
Ḥasdāy b. Shaprūṭ 2019-3 : 26
Ḥāshid 2020-4 : 25
Ḥashwiyya 2016-5 : 86
Haşimi Emir Osman Efendi 2019-6 : 38
Ḥasrat Mohānī 2016-4 : 97
Hassan, A. 2017-3 : 44
Hasyim Asy'ari 2017-5 : 98
Hātif Iṣfahānī 2018-1 : 72
Ḥātim al-Aṣamm 2019-4 : 59
Hatt-ı hümayun 2018-6 : 82
Hatta, Mohammad 2016-4 : 99
Ḥaṭṭīn 2017-3 : 45
Hausaland 2017-3 : 47
Ḥawāla, money transfer 2016-5 : 87
Hawāwīr 2018-6 : 83
Ḥawḍ 2016-4 : 101
Ḥāwī, Khalīl 2017-3 : 49
al-Ḥawrānī, Akram 2019-2 : 44
Ḥayāt al-Dīn b. Saʿīd 2016-4 : 102
Ḥayāt Maḥmūd 2015-1 : 140
Ḥaydar ʿAlī 2017-1 : 109
Ḥaydar Ḥasan Mirzā, Āghā 2019-1 : 32
Ḥaydar, Qurrat al-ʿAyn 2017-3 : 50
Ḥaydariyya 2020-2 : 43
Hayduk 2019-6 : 39
Ḥayṣa Bayṣa 2017-1 : 111
Ḥayy b. Yaqẓān 2018-1 : 74
Hazairin 2016-5 : 91
Hazāras 2017-4 : 106
al-Ḥaẓīrī 2020-2 : 45
Heart in Ṣūfism 2018-1 : 76
Hebron since 1516 2019-5 : 51
Hekimbaşı 2016-4 : 104
Hell 2010-2 : 143
Henna 2016-4 : 105
Heraklion 2017-5 : 100
Herat art and architecture 2019-6 : 42
Hermann of Carinthia 2018-1 : 79
Hermes and Hermetica 2009-3 : 182
Hero of Alexandria 2017-2 : 111
Hibatallāh b. Muḥammad 2018-3 : 54
Hidāyat, Riḍā Qulī Khān 2018-3 : 56
Hidāyat, Sādiq 2016-3 : 116
Ḥifnī al-Mahdī 2018-5 : 71
Highway robbery 2016-5 : 92
Hijāʾ 2017-3 : 52
Hijar 2017-4 : 112
Ḥijāz Railway 2017-5 : 102
Hijra 2018-2 : 54
Hilāl al-Ṣābiʾ 2017-4 : 113
al-Hilālī, Taqī al-Dīn 2018-4 : 68
Ḥilm 2017-3 : 55
Hind bt. al-Khuss 2016-4 : 107
Hind bt. ʿUtba 2018-5 : 72
Hindāl Mīrzā 2020-3 : 45
Hindi 2018-5 : 74
Hindustani 2019-6 : 52
Hippocrates 2017-3 : 59
al-Ḥīra 2016-5 : 94
al-Ḥīrī, Abū ʿUthmān 2018-4 : 69
Ḥiṣār-i Fīrūza 2016-5 : 95
Ḥisba (modern times) 2017-3 : 63
Hishām b. al-Ḥakam 2020-1 : 48
Ḥiṣn al-Akrād 2017-3 : 65
Historiography, Ottoman 2018-2 : 58
Ḥizb al-Daʿwa al-Islāmiyya 2016-4 : 107
Hizbullah, Barisan 2018-3 : 58
Homicide and murder 2016-5 : 98
Homs 2017-2 : 112
Homs, art and architecture 2017-2 : 114
Horoscope 2020-1 : 50
Hotin 2012-1 : 144
Ḥourī 2016-4 : 109
Household 2016-4 : 111
Ḥubaysh b. al-Ḥasan al-Dimashqī 2017-4 : 115
Hūd 2017-3 : 70
Hudhayl, Banū 2017-3 : 73
Hudood Ordinances 2017-1 : 112
Ḥujr b. ʿAdī l-Kindī 2016-4 : 113
Hülegü b. Toluy b. Chinggis Khān 2018-3 : 59
Ḥulmāniyya 2018-2 : 73
Humā 2018-4 : 71
Humām al-Dīn al-Tabrīzī 2016-3 : 119
Ḥumayd al-Arqaṭ 2018-2 : 74
Ḥumayd b. Thawr al-Hilālī 2016-3 : 121
al-Ḥumaydī, ʿAbd al-Raḥmān 2020-2 : 47

Ḥumaynī 2017-3 : 75
Humāyūn, Nāṣir al-Dīn 2017-4 : 117
Ḥums 2017-5 : 103
Ḥunayn b. Isḥāq 2017-3 : 76
Hünkar İskelesi, Treaty of 2017-4 : 119
Hürrem Sultan 2017-3 : 83
Ḥurūfiyya 2016-1 : 139
al-Ḥuṣarī, Maḥmūd Khalīl 2018-6 : 84
Ḥusayn, Aḥmad 2016-3 : 123
al-Ḥusayn b. ʿAlī b. Abī Ṭālib 2016-3 : 124
al-Ḥusayn al-Mahdī 2019-5 : 57
Ḥusayn, Muḥammad Kāmil 2019-4 : 61
Ḥusayn, Shaykh 2016-5 : 102
Ḥusayn, Ṭāhā 2017-3 : 84
Ḥusayn Vāʿiẓ Kāshifī 2017-3 : 88
al-Ḥusaynī, Amīn 2019-5 : 60
al-Ḥusaynī, Ṣadr al-Dīn 2017-2 : 117
Hüseyin Hilmi Paşa 2016-5 : 105
Ḥusnī, Dāwūd 2017-5 : 104
al-Ḥuṣrī, Abū Isḥāq 2017-4 : 121
al-Ḥuṣrī al-Ḍarīr 2018-2 : 75
al-Ḥuṭayʾa 2016-2 : 146
Iamblichus 2017-2 : 120
ʿIbādat-khāna 2017-3 : 97
Ibdāl 2016-5 : 106
Ibn al-Abbār, Abū Jaʿfar 2018-1 : 81
Ibn al-Abbār, al-Quḍāʿī 2016-4 : 116
Ibn ʿAbd al-Barr 2019-3 : 27
Ibn ʿAbd al-Ḥakam, ʿAbdallāh 2019-1 : 34
Ibn ʿAbd al-Ḥakam family 2017-4 : 125
Ibn ʿAbd al-Malik al-Marrākushī 2018-5 : 83
Ibn ʿAbd Rabbih 2017-2 : 121
Ibn ʿAbd Rabbihi, Abū ʿUthmān 2018-1 : 82
Ibn ʿAbd al-Ṣamad 2016-5 : 107
Ibn ʿAbd al-Ẓāhir 2017-4 : 125
Ibn ʿAbdūn 2017-1 : 116
Ibn ʿAbdūn al-Jabalī 2018-3 : 62
Ibn Abī l-Ashʿath 2017-4 : 128
Ibn Abī l-Bayān 2018-1 : 83
Ibn Abī l-Ḍiyāf 2020-4 : 27
Ibn Abī l-Dunyā 2018-5 : 85
Ibn Abī l-Ḥadīd 2018-2 : 78
Ibn Abī Ḥātim al-Rāzī 2019-5 : 62
Ibn Abī l-Iṣbaʿ 2017-3 : 100
Ibn Abī l-Rijāl, ʿAlī 2018-4 : 74
Ibn Abī Shayba 2020-4 : 28
Ibn Abī Ṭayyiʾ 2017-4 : 130
Ibn Abī Uṣaybiʿa 2019-2 : 47
Ibn Abī Zamanīn 2016-4 : 118
Ibn Abī Zarʿ 2017-1 : 118
Ibn Abī Zayd al-Qayrawānī 2017-3 : 101
Ibn Abī l-Zinād 2019-1 : 36
Ibn al-ʿAdīm 2017-5 : 106
Ibn ʿAjība 2016-4 : 119
Ibn ʿAmīra al-Makhzūmī 2017-3 : 104
Ibn ʿAmmār, Abū Bakr 2016-5 : 108
Ibn ʿAqīl, Abū l-Wafāʾ 2017-3 : 105
Ibn al-Aʿrābī, Abū ʿAbdallāh 2016-5 : 111
Ibn al-ʿArabī, Abū Bakr 2018-3 : 63
Ibn ʿArafa al-Warghammī 2020-3 : 47
Ibn ʿArūs 2018-4 : 76
Ibn ʿAsākir family 2017-3 : 108
Ibn al-Ashtarkūnī 2018-1 : 84
Ibn ʿĀṣim al-Gharnāṭī 2018-2 : 82
Ibn ʿAskar 2018-4 : 79
Ibn ʿAṭāʾ Aḥmad 2017-3 : 111
Ibn ʿAṭāʾallāh al-Iskandarī 2019-4 : 64
Ibn Aʿtham al-Kūfī 2019-1 : 36
Ibn al-Athīr, Majd al-Dīn 2017-1 : 119
Ibn ʿAṭṭāsh, ʿAbd al-Malik 2017-4 : 132
Ibn ʿAṭṭāsh, Aḥmad 2017-4 : 133
Ibn al-Baladī 2017-2 : 123
Ibn al-Bannāʾ, Abū ʿAlī 2017-4 : 133
Ibn al-Bannāʾ al-Marrākushī 2018-1 : 85
Ibn Baqī 2017-3 : 113
Ibn Baraka al-Bahlawī 2016-2 : 148
Ibn Barrajān 2017-3 : 115
Ibn Barrī, Abū l-Ḥasan 2019-5 : 65
Ibn Bashkuwāl 2018-1 : 87
Ibn Bassām al-ʿAbartāʾī 2018-1 : 90
Ibn Bassām al-Shantarīnī 2018-2 : 85
Ibn Baṭṭūṭa 2016-5 : 112
Ibn Baydakīn 2019-5 : 66
Ibn al-Bazzāz al-Ardabīlī 2018-6 : 86
Ibn al-Buhlūl 2018-3 : 65
Ibn Dādhurmuz, Saʿīd 2020-3 : 49
Ibn Daftarkhwān 2017-5 : 109
Ibn Dāniyāl 2016-3 : 131
Ibn Darrāj al-Qasṭallī 2016-5 : 117
Ibn al-Dawādārī 2016-4 : 122
Ibn Dāwūd al-Iṣfahānī 2017-2 : 124
Ibn Dhakwān, Aḥmad 2018-3 : 66

Ibn Dhakwān, Sālim 2020-3 : 51
Ibn al-Dubaythī 2017-2 : 126
Ibn al-Dumayna 2019-1 : 38
Ibn Duqmāq 2017-1 : 121
Ibn Durayd 2018-1 : 92
Ibn Faḍlallāh al-ʿUmarī 2020-4 : 30
Ibn Faḍlān 2017-3 : 121
Ibn Fahd 2017-2 : 127
Ibn al-Faḥḥām 2018-5 : 87
Ibn al-Faqīh 2019-5 : 67
Ibn al-Faraḍī 2016-5 : 118
Ibn Faraj al-Jayyānī 2020-3 : 52
Ibn Farḥūn 2018-2 : 88
Ibn al-Fāriḍ 2016-5 : 121
Ibn Farīghūn 2017-1 : 123
Ibn Fūrak 2017-2 : 130
Ibn al-Furāt 2020-4 : 33
Ibn Gabirol 2016-4 : 123
Ibn Ghālib al-Gharnāṭī 2017-2 : 132
Ibn Habal 2016-5 : 124
Ibn al-Habbāriyya 2015-3 : 137
Ibn Ḥamdīn 2019-4 : 73
Ibn Ḥamdīs 2019-4 : 75
Ibn Ḥamdūn 2018-1 : 94
Ibn Ḥāmid 2016-4 : 125
Ibn al-Ḥannāṭ 2017-5 : 110
Ibn Harma 2018-1 : 95
Ibn Ḥasday, Abraham 2019-2 : 50
Ibn Ḥasdāy, Abū l-Faḍl 2018-2 : 90
Ibn Ḥasdāy, Abū Jaʿfar 2018-2 : 91
Ibn Ḥawqal 2017-1 : 125
Ibn al-Ḥawwās 2018-2 : 92
Ibn al-Haytham, ʿAbd al-Raḥmān 2019-2 : 52
Ibn Ḥayyūs 2016-4 : 129
Ibn Ḥibbān al-Bustī 2018-3 : 68
Ibn Ḥijjī 2016-4 : 127
Ibn Hindū 2016-5 : 125
Ibn Hubayra 2018-3 : 69
Ibn Hūd, Badr al-Dīn 2017-5 : 111
Ibn Hūd al-Muʾtaman 2018-4 : 81
Ibn Hudhayl al-Fazārī 2018-1 : 97
Ibn ʿIdhārī al-Marrākushī 2016-4 : 128
Ibn al-Imām al-Shilbī 2017-3 : 128
Ibn ʿInaba 2017-4 : 135
Ibn Isḥāq 2019-4 : 76
Ibn Isrāʾīl al-Dimashqī 2017-5 : 114
Ibn al-Jadd 2019-5 : 69
Ibn Jaʿfar 2017-4 : 137
Ibn Jāmiʿ 2019-4 : 79
Ibn al-Jazarī 2018-5 : 89
Ibn al-Jillīqī 2016-5 : 127
Ibn Jubayr 2017-3 : 129
Ibn Jumayʿ 2017-4 : 138
Ibn Jurayj 2016-2 : 149
Ibn Juzayy, Abū ʿAbdallāh 2020-2 : 50
Ibn Kabar 2017-5 : 116
Ibn Kammūna 2016-4 : 130
Ibn Kathīr, ʿImād al-Dīn 2016-5 : 128
Ibn Khafīf 2016-5 : 137
Ibn Khaldūn, ʿAbd al-Raḥmān 2018-4 : 83
Ibn Khaldūn, Yaḥyā 2016-4 : 134
Ibn al-Khallāl al-Baṣrī 2018-3 : 70
Ibn Khallikān 2018-5 : 91
Ibn al-Khammār 2018-6 : 88
Ibn al-Khashshāb 2017-4 : 139
Ibn al-Khaṣīb, Abū ʿAlī 2017-2 : 134
Ibn al-Khaṭīb, Lisān al-Dīn 2017-5 : 116
Ibn Khurdādhbih 2018-6 : 92
Ibn Khuzayma 2018-3 : 71
Ibn Killis 2017-4 : 140
Ibn Kunāsa 2017-2 : 135
Ibn al-Labbāna 2018-1 : 100
Ibn Lajaʾ 2017-5 : 123
Ibn Luyūn 2017-3 : 133
Ibn al-Maḥrūma 2016-4 : 136
Ibn Māja 2016-3 : 134
Ibn Makkī 2017-1 : 128
Ibn Manda family 2019-5 : 70
Ibn Manẓūr 2016-3 : 135
Ibn Mardanīsh 2017-3 : 135
Ibn Marzūq 2016-4 : 136
Ibn Maṣāl 2018-5 : 100
Ibn Masarra 2016-5 : 143
Ibn Mashīsh, ʿAbd al-Salām 2016-5 : 145
Ibn al-Māshiṭa 2019-4 : 80
Ibn Masʿūd, ʿAbdallāh 2018-3 : 73
Ibn Maʿṣūm 2018-1 : 102
Ibn Maṭrūḥ 2017-2 : 136
Ibn Mattawayh 2012-1 : 147
Ibn Mawlāhum Khayālī 2018-1 : 104
Ibn Maymūn 2017-1 : 129
Ibn Mayyāda 2018-1 : 105
Ibn Melek Firişteoğlu 2020-1 : 57
Ibn Misjaḥ 2018-1 : 106
Ibn Mītham 2019-2 : 53
Ibn Muʿādh al-Jayyānī 2017-3 : 137
Ibn Mufliḥ 2017-3 : 139
Ibn Muḥriz 2018-2 : 93
Ibn Mujāhid 2017-5 : 124
Ibn al-Mulaqqin 2018-2 : 93
Ibn Muljam 2016-2 : 151
Ibn al-Mundhir al-Naysābūrī 2018-2 : 96
Ibn Munīr al-Ṭarābulusī 2019-2 : 54
Ibn Muqbil 2018-1 : 107
Ibn al-Murābiʿ 2018-2 : 98

Ibn Muʿṭī al-Zawāwī 2020-3 : 54
Ibn Muyassar 2017-5 : 125
Ibn al-Muzawwiq 2018-3 : 77
Ibn al-Nabīh 2017-2 : 137
Ibn al-Naḥḥās 2020-2 : 51
Ibn Nāʿima al-Ḥimṣī 2018-1 : 109
Ibn Nājī 2019-5 : 78
Ibn al-Najjār, Muḥibb al-Dīn 2017-3 : 140
Ibn Nawbakht, Mūsā 2019-1 : 39
Ibn Nujayd 2018-4 : 101
Ibn Nujaym 2018-2 : 99
Ibn Nuṣayr 2010-1 : 192
Ibn al-Qalānisī 2019-1 : 40
Ibn Qalāqis 2018-1 : 110
Ibn Qāniʿ 2020-2 : 53
Ibn Qasī family 2018-4 : 102
Ibn al-Qaṭṭāʿ al-Ṣiqillī 2020-1 : 59
Ibn al-Qaṭṭāʿ, al-Yaḥṣubī 2018-5 : 101
Ibn al-Qaysarānī, Abū ʿAbdallāh 2017-2 : 139
Ibn al-Qaysarānī, Abū l-Faḍl 2020-4 : 35
Ibn Qiba 2019-2 : 56
Ibn Qunfudh 2019-2 : 58
Ibn al-Qūṭiyya 2018-6 : 97
Ibn Quzmān 2019-2 : 60
Ibn al-Rāhib 2019-1 : 41
Ibn Rajab 2019-6 : 55
Ibn al-Raqqām 2019-1 : 44
Ibn Rashīq 2018-2 : 101
Ibn Riḍwān al-Mālaqī 2018-6 : 99
Ibn Rushayd 2019-1 : 46
Ibn Rushd, Abū Muḥammad 2009-1 : 181
Ibn al-Sāʿātī, Bahāʾ al-Dīn 2018-1 : 113
Ibn al-Sāʿātī, Fakhr al-Dīn 2019-2 : 63
Ibn Saʿd 2019-5 : 83
Ibn Saddiq 2017-4 : 142
Ibn al-Ṣaffār 2019-1 : 49
Ibn al-Ṣaghīr 2018-4 : 103
Ibn Sahl al-Ishbīlī 2020-3 : 55
Ibn al-Ṣāʾigh al-ʿAntarī 2018-1 : 114
Ibn al-Ṣalāḥ, Najm al-Dīn 2019-6 : 57
Ibn al-Samḥ, Abū ʿAlī 2019-2 : 64
Ibn Sarābiyūn, Yūḥannā 2020-1 : 62
Ibn Saʿūd, ʿAbd al-Azīz 2018-4 : 105
Ibn Sawdakīn 2017-5 : 127
Ibn al-Ṣayrafī, Tāj al-Riʾāsa 2018-5 : 102
Ibn Sayyid al-Nās 2019-5 : 85
Ibn Shaddād, Bahāʾ al-Dīn 2019-1 : 51
Ibn Shaddād, ʿIzz al-Dīn 2018-5 : 104
Ibn Shāhīn al-Ẓāhirī 2019-3 : 29
Ibn Shahrāshūb 2019-1 : 53
Ibn al-Shajarī 2020-4 : 39
Ibn Sharaf al-Qayrawānī 2019-2 : 66
Ibn Sharīf al-Rundī 2020-4 : 40
Ibn al-Shāṭir 2019-2 : 67
Ibn Sīda 2020-1 : 63
Ibn Siqlāb 2019-5 : 87
Ibn Sūdūn 2019-6 : 58
Ibn al-Sulaym al-Aswānī 2018-1 : 116
Ibn Surayj, ʿUbayd 2018-5 : 105
Ibn al-Ṣūrī 2019-1 : 55
Ibn Tāfrājīn 2014-1 : 132
Ibn al-Thumna 2018-2 : 103
Ibn Ṭufayl 2018-1 : 116
Ibn Ṭumlūs 2018-1 : 122
Ibn al-Ukhuwwa 2019-3 : 31
Ibn Uṣfūr 2019-1 : 56
Ibn Wāfid al-Lakhmī 2019-1 : 58
Ibn Wahb, Isḥāq b. Ibrāhīm 2018-1 : 124
Ibn Wahbūn al-Mursī 2018-2 : 103
Ibn Waḥshiyya 2019-1 : 61
Ibn Wakīʿ al-Tinnīsī 2018-3 : 78
Ibn al-Walīd, al-Ḥusayn b. ʿAlī 2018-3 : 79
Ibn Wallād 2019-2 : 72
Ibn Wāṣil 2016-4 : 139
Ibn Yasīr al-Riyāshī 2020-1 : 65
Ibn al-Zarqālluh 2018-3 : 80
Ibn Zaydūn 2020-1 : 66
Ibn al-Zayyāt al-Tādilī 2019-1 : 65
Ibn al-Zibaʿrā, ʿAbdallāh 2020-4 : 42
Ibn al-Zubayr al-Gharnāṭī 2019-1 : 69
Ibrāhīm ʿĀdil Shāh II 2018-4 : 106
Ibrāhīm b. al-Ashtar 2018-3 : 84
Ibrāhīm b. Isḥāq al-Ḥarbī 2018-3 : 87
Ibrāhīm b. al-Mahdī 2018-3 : 88
Ibrāhīm b. al-Mahdī (music) 2018-3 : 90
Ibrāhīm b. Shīrkūh 2019-1 : 72
Ibrāhīm b. al-Walīd 2019-3 : 33
Ibrāhīm Bey 2018-5 : 106
Ibrāhīm Bey Abū Shanab 2018-5 : 108
İbrahim Edhem Paşa 2018-1 : 125
Ibrāhīm, Ḥāfiẓ 2017-4 : 143
İbrahim Hakkı Paşa 2018-1 : 126

Ibrahim (Mansur Syah) 2018-4 : 107
Ibrāhīm al-Mawṣilī 2018-6 : 100
İbrahim Müteferrika 2016-5 : 147
Ibrāhīm Sulṭān b. Shāh Rukh 2018-5 : 109
Ibrail 2018-4 : 108
al-Ibshīhī, Bahāʾ al-Dīn 2018-2 : 105
Icehouses 2019-5 : 89
Iconoclasm 2019-3 : 34
al-Idkāwī al-Muʾadhdhin 2019-2 : 74
Idrīs ʿImād al-Dīn 2018-4 : 111
Idrīs, Suhayl 2019-3 : 40
Idrīs, Yūsuf 2014-1 : 137
al-Idrīsī, Abū ʿAbdallāh 2018-3 : 91
Idrīsids 2018-5 : 110
Idrīsiyya, in Indonesia 2018-2 : 107
Ifrīqiyā 2019-5 : 93
ʿIfrīt 2018-3 : 99
Ijāra (protection) 2020-4 : 43
al-Ījāz wa-l-iṭnāb 2020-1 : 69
Ikhwān, Saudi Arabia 2018-4 : 114
Ilgaz, Rıfat 2019-5 : 95
İlhan, Attila 2019-3 : 42
Īlkhānids 2019-4 : 81
İlmiye 2020-3 : 57
Iltutmish 2018-2 : 109
ʿImād al-Mulk 2018-3 : 100
Imagination in philosophy 2018-3 : 103
al-Imām 2017-2 : 141
İmam Hatip schools 2018-1 : 127
Imām (technical term) 2020-4 : 46
Imāmate in Khārijism and Ibāḍism 2017-4 : 145
Imāmbāra 2018-2 : 112
İmamzade Mehmed Esad 2016-3 : 138
Immolation 2017-4 : 149
Imperial Arsenal 2015-1 : 142
Impetus, in philosophy 2019-1 : 74
Īnāl al-Ajrūd, al-Malik al-Ashraf 2018-1 : 129
Īnālids 2018-1 : 133
ʿInāyat Allāh Khān 2020-4 : 47
ʿInāyat Khān 2018-5 : 118
Independence Courts 2018-3 : 105
India (Hind) 2007-1 : 185
Indian diaspora in Africa 2018-2 : 115
Indian Ocean early-modern 2019-3 : 44
Indonesia: Java from the coming of Islam to 1942 2019-4 : 97
Indonesia: Islam and politics since 1942 2019-4 : 106
Indonesia: social ecology and ethno-cultural diversity 2019-2 : 75
Initiation in Ṣūfism 2018-6 : 101
Inshāʾ Allāh Khān 2019-1 : 77
Institut Agama Islam Negeri 2017-3 : 142
Institut Kefahaman Islam Malaysia 2019-5 : 97
İntizami 2018-6 : 105
Intoxication in Ṣūfism 2019-1 : 80
Iqrītish dynasty 2016-3 : 140
Iqtibās 2019-1 : 83
Īraj Mīrzā 2018-2 : 120
Iram 2019-4 : 117
al-Īrānshahrī, Abū l-ʿAbbās 2019-1 : 85
ʿIrāqī, Fakr al-Dīn 2017-5 : 129
al-Irjānī, Abū Yaḥyā Zakariyyāʾ 2018-4 : 115
al-Irsyad 2018-6 : 106
ʿĪsā b. ʿUmar 2020-4 : 48
ʿĪsā al-Kurdī 2019-4 : 121
Isaac 2018-1 : 135
al-Isfarāyīnī, Abū Ḥāmid 2009-4 : 34
al-Isfarāyīnī, ʿIṣām al-Dīn 2018-6 : 108
İsfendiyaroğulları (Candaroğulları) 2019-2 : 79
al-Isfizārī, Abū Ḥāmid 2018-4 : 116
İshaki, Ayaz 2019-6 : 60
Isḥāq b. Ḥunayn 2020-1 : 72
Isḥāq b. Ibrāhīm al-Mawṣilī 2018-6 : 109
Isḥāq Efendi, Başhoca 2009-1 : 182
Ishmael 2018-1 : 137
Iskandar Beg Munshī 2018-4 : 118
Islamic Foundation 2017-5 : 132
Islamic Movement in Nigeria 2019-2 : 83
Ismāʿīl b. Yasār 2020-4 : 50
İsmail Beliğ 2014-1 : 140
Ismāʿīl Bey 2018-5 : 119
İsmail Dede Efendi 2018-2 : 121
İsmail Ferruh Efendi 2018-1 : 140
İsmail Hakkı (Eldem) 2020-1 : 75
Ismāʿīl, ʿIzz al-Dīn 2019-6 : 62
Ismāʿīl Minangkabau 2019-3 : 48
Ismāʿīl, Muṣṭafā 2018-6 : 110
Ismāʿīl Pasha 2019-6 : 63
İsmeti 2018-6 : 111
Isnād 2018-5 : 120
Isrāfīl 2018-3 : 106
Isrāʾīliyyāt 2019-3 : 49
Istanbul, Treaty of 2018-5 : 124

Istiqlal Mosque 2019-5 : 98
Istiqlāl Party 2018-6 : 113
al-Itihad al-Islamiya 2019-1 : 87
Iʿtiṣām al-Dīn 2017-5 : 133
Iʿtiṣāmī, Parvīn 2017-5 : 135
Izetbegović, Alija 2018-6 : 114
Izmir 2017-2 : 142
ʿIzrāʾīl (ʿAzrāʾīl) 2018-3 : 108
ʿIzz al-Dawla 2019-1 : 88
ʿIzz al-Dīn Kāshānī 2018-2 : 123
ʿIzz al-Dīn al-Mawṣilī 2018-3 : 110
İzzet Mehmed Paşa, Safranbolulu 2018-3 : 111
İzzet Paşa, Ahmed 2019-5 : 99
Jabarti 2015-1 : 146
Jābir b. Ḥayyān 2019-1 : 91
Jābir b. Zayd 2019-1 : 97
al-Jābirī, Muḥammad ʿĀbid 2020-3 : 60
al-Jābirī, Muḥammad Ṣāliḥ 2018-3 : 113
Jabrā, Jabrā Ibrāhīm 2014-1 : 141
Jacob bar Shakkō 2019-2 : 86
Jacob of Edessa 2019-1 : 98
Jaʿd b. Dirham 2016-5 : 150
Jadidism 2018-5 : 126
Jaʿfar b. Abī Yaḥyā 2019-6 : 67
al-Jaghmīnī 2020-4 : 51
Jahān Sūz 2018-5 : 129
Jahāngīr 2011-2 : 144
Jāhīn, Ṣalāḥ 2019-6 : 70
Jainism and Jains 2020-1 : 77
Jaipur 2019-3 : 54
Jakarta Charter 2019-4 : 124
Jakhanke 2016-1 : 145
Jalāl al-Dīn Aḥsan 2018-2 : 126
Jalāl al-Dīn Mangburnī 2018-1 : 142
Jalāl al-Dīn Yazdī 2018-6 : 115
Jālib, Ḥabīb 2018-3 : 114
Jamāhīriyya 2019-1 : 99
Jamāl al-Dīn Iṣfahānī 2018-3 : 116
Jamālzada, Muḥammad ʿAlī 2018-2 : 128
Jamiat Kheir 2020-1 : 84
Jān-i Jānān, Maẓhar 2019-4 : 125
al-Janbīhī, Muḥammad 2018-4 : 124
Janissaries 2017-2 : 146
Janjīrā 2018-2 : 131
al-Jannābī, Abū Saʿīd 2018-3 : 117
al-Jannābī, Abū Ṭāhir 2018-3 : 119
al-Jannāwunī, Abū Zakariyyāʾ 2008-2 : 161
Japan, relations with the Islamic world 2020-1 : 85
Japheth 2020-4 : 55
Jassin, Hans Bague 2018-4 : 125
Jassy, Treaty of 2019-4 : 127
Javanese Wars of Succession 2017-5 : 137
al-Jawālīqī, Abū Manṣūr 2020-1 : 89
al-Jawharī, Ismāʿīl b. Ḥammād 2018-2 : 133
al-Jawnpūrī, Maḥmūd 2012-4 : 113
al-Jawwānī 2019-1 : 101
Jāyasī, Muḥammad 2019-5 : 102
al-Jazarī, Badīʿ al-Zamān 2019-4 : 128
al-Jazarī, Shams al-Dīn 2018-5 : 130
al-Jazūlī, Abū Mūsā 2019-3 : 59
al-Jazzār, Abū l-Ḥusayn 2016-4 : 141
al-Jazzār, Aḥmad Pasha 2020-2 : 56
Jerusalem since 1516 2018-4 : 127
Jidda 2018-6 : 118
Jigar Murādābādī 2018-2 : 136
al-Jildakī 2020-1 : 92
Jimma 2018-2 : 138
al-Jinān 2019-4 : 131
Jinnah, Mohammad Ali 2019-1 : 103
Jirga 2019-6 : 71
al-Jisr family 2019-1 : 105
al-Jisrī, ʿAlī b. ʿĪsā 2009-1 : 184
Jīvan, Aḥmad 2018-5 : 132
al-Jīzī 2019-4 : 133
Jochi b. Chinggis Khān 2018-5 : 134
John of Damascus 2018-3 : 120
Jombang 2019-5 : 104
Josh Malīḥābādī 2020-2 : 58
Jubrān, Jubrān Khalīl 2014-2 : 142
Juḥā 2017-5 : 139
Jumadil Kubra 2018-2 : 139
al-Junbulānī, Abū Muḥammad 2008-2 : 162
al-Jundī, Anwar 2018-4 : 140
Jundīshāpur 2015-3 : 139
al-Jurāwī 2018-1 : 146
Jurayj 2019-1 : 108
Jurayrī, ʿAbdallāh 2019-2 : 87
al-Jurjānī, ʿAbd al-Qāhir 2020-1 : 93
Jurnal 2017-5 : 141
Kaarta 2019-3 : 62
Kaʿba 2019-6 : 74
Kabābīsh 2018-3 : 123
Kabul art and architecture 2020-4 : 57
Kachchh 2019-3 : 63
Kadın 2018-3 : 124
Kadınlar Dünyası 2018-5 : 137
Kaftārū, Aḥmad 2020-4 : 63
Kāfūr, Malik 2019-3 : 67
Kāhī 2019-1 : 110
Kajoran, Raden 2017-5 : 143

Kākatīya dynasty 2018-2 : 142
al-Kalābādhī 2018-3 : 125
Kalāt, khānate of 2019-3 : 69
Kalatidha, Serat 2018-4 : 142
Kalbāsī, Muḥammad Ibrāhīm 2019-6 : 79
Kalgay 2019-6 : 80
Kalijaga, Sunan 2018-6 : 125
Kalīm Kāshānī 2019-2 : 89
Kalīmallāh Shāhjahānābādī 2018-3 : 127
al-Kalwadhānī, Abū l-Khaṭṭāb 2019-2 : 91
Kalyana 2019-2 : 92
Kamāl al-Dīn Iṣfahānī 2018-3 : 129
Kamālī, Ḥaydar ʿAlī 2018-3 : 132
Kamaniçe 2013-1 : 141
al-Kāmiliyya 2020-4 : 65
Kāmrān Shāh Durrānī 2019-5 : 106
Kān wa-kān 2020-1 : 99
Kanafānī, Ghassān 2018-1 : 148
al-Kānimī 2018-3 : 133
Kano 2018-6 : 126
Kār Kiyā dynasty 2020-3 : 65
Karabakh, Nagorno 2018-6 : 128
al-Karābīsī, Aḥmad 2019-2 : 95
Karaçelebizade Abdülaziz Efendi 2020-2 : 62
Karachay-Cherkessia 2019-4 : 134
Karachi 2019-1 : 111
Karadjordje 2020-4 : 66
Karaferye (Veroia) 2019-1 : 115
Karaim (language) 2017-5 : 144
Karak 2018-5 : 138
Karakhanid art and architecture 2019-6 : 82
Karakhanid literature 2019-6 : 86
Karakol Cemiyeti 2018-4 : 143
Karamani Mehmed Paşa 2018-1 : 150
Karaosmanoğlu, Yakup Kadri 2018-4 : 143
Karaosmanoğulları 2018-4 : 145
Karavezir Seyyid Mehmed Paşa 2020-1 : 100
Kārkhāna 2018-5 : 143
al-Karkhī, Maʿrūf 2019-3 : 73
Karlowitz (Karlofça) 2018-5 : 146
al-Karrāmiyya 2020-4 : 68
Kars, Treaty of 2018-2 : 144
Kartid dynasty 2017-5 : 146
Kartini, Raden Ajeng 2018-2 : 145
Kartosuwiryo, Sekarmaji Marjan 2018-4 : 147
Kāshānī, Abū l-Qāsim 2019-6 : 90
Kashgar 2020-1 : 101
Kashmīrī 2020-2 : 64
Kasravī, Aḥmad 2018-5 : 149
Kasrāyī, Siyāvash 2018-6 : 131
Katanov Nikolay 2018-6 : 133
al-Kātibī al-Qazwīnī 2019-1 : 117
Katsina 2019-1 : 122
Kauman 2018-4 : 148
Kawāhla 2018-3 : 134
al-Kawākibī, ʿAbd al-Raḥmān 2019-6 : 92
Kawār 2018-2 : 147
Kay Kāʾūs b. Iskandar 2018-2 : 148
Kayalpatnam 2018-3 : 135
Kaygılı, Osman Cemal 2019-6 : 95
Kayserili Halil Paşa 2020-1 : 105
al-Kayyāl 2018-3 : 143
Kazakhstan 2018-6 : 133
Kāzarūnī 2020-1 : 106
Kazārūniyya 2019-5 : 107
Kebatinan 2019-5 : 111
Keçiboynuzu İbrahim Hilmi Paşa 2019-5 : 112
Kedhiri, Babad 2013-1 : 142
Kelantan 2020-4 : 73
Kemal Ümmi 2019-2 : 97
Kemankeş Ali Paşa 2014-4 : 143
al-Khabbāz, Yaḥyā 2019-3 : 75
al-Khāl, Yūsuf 2020-1 : 111
Khalafallāh, Muḥammad Aḥmad 2019-6 : 96
Khālid b. Ṣafwān 2019-2 : 98
Khalwatiyya in Indonesia 2019-3 : 76
Khambāyat 2019-3 : 78
Khān, Ṣiddīq Ḥasan 2020-2 : 66
Khānaqāh 2020-3 : 74
Khandesh 2019-3 : 79
Kharāj in South Asia 2020-1 : 112
Khārijīs 2020-3 : 83
Khārṣīnī 2019-2 : 100
al-Khaṣāṣī, Abū l-Faḍl 2019-6 : 98
al-Khaṣībī, Abū ʿAbbās 2016-3 : 144
al-Khaṣībī, Abū ʿAbdallāh 2016-5 : 152
Khāṣṣ Beg b. Palang-Eri 2020-2 : 69
Khat'ak 2019-2 : 101
al-Khaṭībī, ʿAbd al-Kabīr 2019-5 : 113
al-Khawlānī, Abū Idrīs 2019-6 : 99
al-Khawlānī, Abū Muslim 2019-6 : 100
Khāyrbak 2018-6 : 142
Khāzindār 2020-1 : 114
Khedive 2020-2 : 70
Khilāfat movement 2019-2 : 103
Khiṭaṭ 2019-3 : 81

Khodjaev	2019-6 : 102
Khoiriyah, Nyai	2020-2 : 72
Kholil Bangkalan	2020-3 : 96
Khoqand	2018-6 : 143
Khudā Bakhsh, Mawlvī	2019-5 : 115
al-Khujandī	2019-6 : 103
al-Khuldī, Jaʿfar	2019-3 : 84
al-Khūnajī, Afḍal al-Dīn	2010-2 : 149
Khusraw Malik	2019-5 : 116
Khusraw Shāh	2019-5 : 118
Khuṭba, premodern	2020-2 : 73
Khvāja-yi Jahān	2019-3 : 87
Khvājū Kirmānī	2019-1 : 124
al-Khvānsārī, Muḥammad Bāqir	2020-3 : 97
Khwushḥāl Khān Khat'ak	2019-2 : 105
Kiai	2019-5 : 119
Kıbrıslı Mehmed Emin Paşa	2019-1 : 128
al-Kibsī family	2020-3 : 99
Kılıç Ali Paşa	2014-4 : 145
Kilwa	2019-2 : 108
Kimeks	2019-3 : 88
Kınalızade Hasan Çelebi	2019-5 : 120
Kipchak	2019-3 : 89
Kirmānī, Āqā Khān	2019-5 : 123
Kirmānī, Awḥād al-Dīn	2020-1 : 115
al-Kirmānī, Ḥamīd al-Dīn	2017-1 : 131
Kisve bahası	2019-4 : 135
Kitab kuning	2020-3 : 104
Kizimkazi	2019-2 : 113
Kızlar Ağası	2019-2 : 114
Koca Mustafa Paşa	2019-3 : 93
Kochi	2019-2 : 116
Kong	2019-3 : 94
Köprülü, Mehmed Fuad	2019-1 : 129
Korkud (şehzade)	2019-1 : 131
Köse Dağı, battle of	2019-2 : 122
Kösem Sultan	2019-3 : 96
Kosovo Polje, First Battle of	2019-2 : 124
Kozanoğulları	2020-3 : 105
Kozhikode	2019-1 : 132
Kritoboulos of Imbros	2019-2 : 125
Kubrā, Najm al-Dīn	2019-3 : 97
Kubraviyya	2019-3 : 101
Küçük Hüseyin Paşa	2017-5 : 149
Küçük Kaynarca	2019-3 : 108
Kūh-i Nūr	2018-4 : 149
Kuloğlu	2018-4 : 151
Kumasi	2019-1 : 138
Kumyks	2019-4 : 137
Kunta-Ḥājjī	2020-1 : 118
Kurr	2020-2 : 76
Kūshyār b. Labbān	2020-2 : 77
Ladākh	2019-5 : 126
Lakhm	2020-4 : 77
Laks	2019-4 : 141
Laʾl	2019-5 : 130
Lala Mustafa Paşa	2018-6 : 148
Lala Şahin Paşa	2019-3 : 110
Lālla Awīsh al-Majdhūba	2019-6 : 107
al-Lamkī, Aḥmad	2015-4 : 150
Larbi Ben Sari	2019-6 : 108
Lawu, Sunan	2018-6 : 149
Layennes	2020-2 : 81
Laz	2018-3 : 145
Lembaga Dakwah Islam Indonesia	2019-4 : 143
Lembaga Kajian Islam dan Sosial	2018-6 : 150
Leo Africanus	2019-3 : 111
Leran	2019-2 : 127
Levant Company	2019-1 : 140
Lexicography, Arabic	2020-4 : 78
Lexicography, Persian	2019-3 : 114
Lexicography, Urdu	2020-1 : 122
Libraries of Arabic and Persian texts in late imperial China	2020-4 : 90
Lidj Iyasu	2019-3 : 120
Liḥyān	2019-5 : 131
Lisān al-ḥāl	2019-6 : 110
Literacy, in Arabic and Persian, in late imperial China	2020-4 : 92
Literary criticism, Urdu	2020-4 : 95
Liyāqat ʿAlī Khān	2019-2 : 127
Louis IX	2020-4 : 99
Lucknow until 1856	2020-1 : 125
Lucknow art and architecture	2020-4 : 103
Lū<u>dh</u>iāṅā	2019-2 : 131
Luqmānjī b. Ḥabīballāh	2019-2 : 132
Luṭf ʿAlī Khān	2020-3 : 108
Luṭfallāh, Muḥammad	2019-2 : 134
Lütfi Paşa	2019-3 : 122
Luṭfī al-Sayyid, Aḥmad	2019-6 : 111
Ma families of warlords	2020-3 : 111
Ma Fulong	2019-6 : 115
Ma Hualong	2020-3 : 114
Ma Zhu	2019-6 : 116
Maʿbad b. ʿAbdallāh al-Juhanī	2019-3 : 124
Macaronic Turkic poetry	2019-6 : 119
Madagascar	2019-3 : 125
Madanī, Ḥusayn Aḥmad	2019-1 : 143

Madjid, Nurcholish 2019-5 : 135
Madrasa in South Asia 2019-3 : 131
Madrasa in Southeast Asia 2019-5 : 137
Madura 2019-2 : 136
Madurai 2019-3 : 138
Maghrib since 1830 2020-2 : 84
Maghribī, Aḥmad Khattū 2020-1 : 132
Maḥbūb b. al-Raḥīl, Abū Sufyān 2019-1 : 145
Mahfudz Tremas 2020-3 : 115
Maḥfūẓ, Najīb 2008-2 : 164
Māhlaqā Bāʾī Chandā 2020-2 : 88
Maḥmūd, ʿAbd al-Ḥalīm 2014-4 : 148
Maḥmūd Gāvān 2015-3 : 142
Maḥmūdābād family 2020-1 : 133
al-Majdhūb, ʿAbd al-Raḥmān 2014-2 : 146
Majdhūb, Muḥammad 2020-1 : 137
Majelis Permusyawaratan Ulama 2019-5 : 140
al-Mājishūn 2009-2 : 151
Majlis Ugama Islam Singapura 2020-4 : 113
Makal, Mahmut 2019-6 : 121
Makhdūm-i Aʿẓam, Aḥmad 2012-1 : 150
Makhlūf, Muḥammad Ḥasanayn 2013-3 : 130
Makouria 2020-2 : 91
Malang 2020-3 : 117
Malawi 2020-3 : 120
Malay and other languages of insular Southeast Asia 2019-1 : 147
al-Malībārī, Zayn al-Dīn 2019-3 : 146
Malik Ayāz 2020-3 : 122
al-Mālikī, Abū Bakr 2017-5 : 152
Maltese 2020-3 : 123
Maʿmar b. Rāshid 2019-6 : 122
Mamlūks, Ottoman period 2019-6 : 124
Maʿn b. Aws 2020-2 : 92
Manāṣīr 2020-2 : 94
Manastırlı İsmail Hakkı 2019-6 : 129
Mande (Mandingo) 2020-1 : 138
Mandūr, Muḥammad 2020-2 : 95
Manghit tribal groups 2020-2 : 97
Mangkunagara I 2019-4 : 145
al-Mannūbiyya, ʿĀʾisha 2013-4 : 153
Mantʾo, Sāʿadat Ḥasan 2020-2 : 102
Mardam Bik, Khalīl 2020-4 : 115
Mardāvīj b. Ziyār 2018-6 : 152
al-Marjānī, Shihāb al-Dīn 2020-4 : 116
Maryam al-Adhraʿiyya 2020-1 : 139
Maşizade Fikri Çelebi 2014-3 : 151
Masʿūd-i Saʿd-i Salmān 2011-2 : 152
Masyumi 2020-3 : 127
Mataram 2019-4 : 146
Maybudī, Qāḍī Mīr Ḥusayn 2020-2 : 106
Mecca, 1000-1500 2020-2 : 107
Medina since 1918 2019-6 : 130
Megiser, Hieronymus 2017-2 : 151
Mehdizadə (Abbas Səhhət) 2015-2 : 152
Mehmed Esad, Sahaflar Şeyhizade 2016-2 : 153
Mehmed Halife 2019-5 : 141
Mehmed Zaim 2019-5 : 142
Meteorology 2020-4 : 121
Mezzomorto Hüseyin Paşa 2017-1 : 136
Minaret 2019-6 : 132
Mīr ʿAlī Tabrīzī 2020-2 : 110
Mīr Jaʿfar 2020-1 : 141
Mīr Sayyid Aḥmad 2020-2 : 112
Mīrak al-Bukhārī 2018-2 : 153
Missionaries, Christian, in the Islamic world 2020-4 : 127
Montenegro 2020-2 : 114
Moriscos 2020-4 : 131
Moses Ibn Ezra 2020-2 : 118
al-Muʾayyad al-Shīrāzī 2020-2 : 121
Mudanya Armistice 2020-2 : 127
Mudros, Armistice of 2020-2 : 128
al-Mufaḍḍal b. Abī l-Faḍāʾil 2020-2 : 129
Mughal architecture 2020-3 : 129
Mughniyya, Muḥammad Jawād 2020-4 : 139
Mughulṭāy b. Qilīj 2020-1 : 144
Muhājirūn 2019-6 : 142
Muḥammad b. ʿAbd al-Karīm al-Sammān 2020-2 : 131
Muḥammad b. Zayd 2020-2 : 132
Muḥammad Bakhsh 2020-1 : 145
Muḥammad al-Bāqir 2020-2 : 135
Muḥammad Kāẓim 2020-4 : 141
Muḥammad Qulī Quṭb Shāh 2020-2 : 139
Muḥammad Shāh Qājār 2020-1 : 149
Muḥammad al-Wālī 2019-4 : 147

Muhammadiyah 2019-6 : 145
Muhsinzade Mehmed Paşa 2020-2 : 140
al-Munajjim, Banū 2019-3 : 148
al-Murādī, Muḥammad Khalīl 2015-3 : 147
al-Mushattā 2020-3 : 141
Mushfiq-i Kāẓimī, Murtaḍā 2019-2 : 141
Mustafa Çelebi 2020-4 : 142
Mustaʿidd Khān 2020-4 : 144
Muways b. ʿImrān 2016-1 : 152
Muzakkar, Abdul Kahar 2018-2 : 154
al-Naḥḥās, Abū Jaʿfar 2019-4 : 149
Naima 2020-4 : 146
Nāʾīn 2019-5 : 144
Najīb al-Dīn al-Samarqandī 2020-4 : 148
Naon, Avram 2013-4 : 155
Nigm, Aḥmad Fuʾād 2019-5 : 146
Niẓām Shāhīs 2017-3 : 146
Novel, Arabic 2014-1 : 152
Oghuz 2020-2 : 143
Oromo 2014-2 : 148
Osman Hamdi Paşa 2019-6 : 149
Paşa 2014-2 : 151
Persian grammar 2018-3 : 148
Pir Sultan Abdal 2013-2 : 135
Reşid Rahmeti Arat 2016-3 : 146
Ṣabrī, Ismāʿīl 2019-4 : 151
al-Ṣaffār al-Bukhārī 2012-2 : 144
al-Samarqandī, Abū Ṭāhir 2013-2 : 137
Sarāy Malik Khānum 2013-2 : 139
Sayyid Baraka 2017-1 : 138
Sayyid Sulṭān 2014-3 : 153
Shāmlū, Aḥmad 2020-3 : 146
Shaqīq al-Balkhī 2016-2 : 155
Shawqī, Aḥmad 2015-3 : 150
al-Shaykh Imām 2019-5 : 149
Sri Lanka 2015-1 : 148
Sub-Saharan African literature, ʿAjamī 2012-2 : 145
Suhrāb 2019-1 : 152
Sulṭān Ḥusayn Bāyqarā 2017-1 : 143
Sylhet Nagari 2015-1 : 152
Ṭalḥa b. ʿUbaydallāh 2014-4 : 150
Tamīm b. al-Muʿizz 2012-4 : 116
Tayyarzade Ata Bey 2015-4 : 151
al-Thamīnī, ʿAbd al-ʿAzīz 2010-1 : 194
Tokgöz, Aḥmed İḥsān 2013-1 : 144
Tūrsūn-zāda, Mīrzā 2018-6 : 155
Uluboy, Abdülbaki Fevzi 2016-3 : 149
ʿUmar b. Hubayra 2019-5 : 151
United Kingdom, Muslims in the 2017-1 : 146
al-ʿUthaymīn, Muḥammad b. Ṣāliḥ 2020-3 : 149
Vasi Alisi 2016-3 : 151
Wahab Chasbullah 2017-5 : 155
Yazīd b. ʿUmar b. Hubayra 2019-5 : 153
Yusuf Amiri 2016-4 : 144
Zarrūq, Aḥmad 2013-3 : 132
Zuhr, Banū 2019-2 : 145

Printed in the United States
By Bookmasters

THE ENCYCLOPAEDIA OF ISLAM
THREE

THE ENCYCLOPAEDIA OF ISLAM

THREE

Edited by

Kate Fleet, Gudrun Krämer, Denis Matringe,
John Nawas, and Everett Rowson

With

Roger ALLEN, Edith AMBROS, Thomas BAUER, Johann BÜSSOW,
Ruth DAVIS, Ahmed EL SHAMSY, Maribel FIERRO, Najam HAIDER, Konrad
HIRSCHLER, Nico KAPTEIN, Alexander KNYSH, Corinne LEFÈVRE, Scott
LEVI, Roman LOIMEIER, Daniela MENEGHINI, M'hamed OUALDI,
D. Fairchild RUGGLES, Emilie SAVAGE-SMITH, and Ayman SHIHADEH

BRILL

LEIDEN • BOSTON
2020

Library of Congress Cataloging-in-Publication Data

A C.I.P. record for this book is available from the Library of Congress.

EI3 is published under the patronage of the international union of academies.

ISSN: 1873-9830
ISBN: 978-90-04-41343-6

This book is printed on acid-free paper and produced in a sustainable manner.

LIST OF ABBREVIATIONS

A. PERIODICALS

AI = *Annales Islamologiques*
AIUON = *Annali dell' Istituto Universitario Orientale di Napoli*
AKM = *Abhandlungen für die Kunde des Morgenlandes*
AMEL = *Arabic and Middle Eastern Literatures*
AO = *Acta Orientalia*
AO Hung. = *Acta Orientalia (Academiae Scientiarum Hungaricae)*
ArO = *Archiv Orientální*
AS = *Asiatische Studien*
ASJ = *Arab Studies Journal*
ASP = *Arabic Sciences and Philosophy*
ASQ = *Arab Studies Quarterly*
BASOR = *Bulletin of the American Schools of Oriental Research*
BEA = *Bulletin des Études Arabes*
BEFEO = *Bulletin de l'Ecole Française d'Extrême-Orient*
BEO = *Bulletin d'Études Orientales de l'Institut Français de Damas*
BIE = *Bulletin de l'Institut d'Égypte*
BIFAO = *Bulletin de l'Institut Français d'Archéologie Orientale du Caire*
BKI = *Bijdragen tot de Taal-, Land- en Volkenkunde*
BMGS = *Byzantine and Modern Greek Studies*
BO = *Bibliotheca Orientalis*
BrisMES = *British Journal of Middle Eastern Studies*
BSOAS = *Bulletin of the School of Oriental and African Studies*
BZ = *Byzantinische Zeitschrift*
CAJ = *Central Asiatic Journal*
DOP = *Dumbarton Oaks Papers*
EW = *East and West*
IBLA = *Revue de l'Institut des Belles Lettres Arabes, Tunis*
IC = *Islamic Culture*
IHQ = *Indian Historical Quarterly*
IJAHS = *International Journal of African Historical Studies*
IJMES = *International Journal of Middle East Studies*

ILS = *Islamic Law and Society*
IOS = *Israel Oriental Studies*
IQ = *The Islamic Quarterly*
JA = *Journal Asiatique*
JAIS = *Journal of Arabic and Islamic Studies*
JAL = *Journal of Arabic Literature*
JAOS = *Journal of the American Oriental Society*
JARCE = *Journal of the American Research Center in Egypt*
JAS = *Journal of Asian Studies*
JESHO = *Journal of the Economic and Social History of the Orient*
JIS = *Journal of Islamic Studies*
JMBRAS = *Journal of the Malaysian Branch of the Royal Asiatic Society*
JNES = *Journal of Near Eastern Studies*
JOS = *Journal of Ottoman Studies*
JQR = *Jewish Quarterly Review*
JRAS = *Journal of the Royal Asiatic Society*
JSAI = *Jerusalem Studies in Arabic and Islam*
JSEAH = *Journal of Southeast Asian History*
JSS = *Journal of Semitic Studies*
MEA = *Middle Eastern Affairs*
MEJ = *Middle East Journal*
MEL = *Middle Eastern Literatures*
MES = *Middle East Studies*
MFOB = *Mélanges de la Faculté Orientale de l'Université St. Joseph de Beyrouth*
MIDEO = *Mélanges de l'Institut Dominicain d'Études Orientales du Caire*
MME = *Manuscripts of the Middle East*
MMIA = *Majallat al-Majmaʿ al-ʿIlmi al-ʿArabi, Damascus*
MO = *Le Monde Oriental*
MOG = *Mitteilungen zur Osmanischen Geschichte*
MSR = *Mamluk Studies Review*
MW = *The Muslim World*
OC = *Oriens Christianus*
OLZ = *Orientalistische Literaturzeitung*
OM = *Oriente Moderno*
QSA = *Quaderni di Studi Arabi*
REI = *Revue des Études Islamiques*
REJ = *Revue des Études Juives*
REMMM = *Revue des Mondes Musulmans et de la Méditerranée*
RHR = *Revue de l'Histoire des Religions*
RIMA = *Revue de l'Institut des Manuscrits Arabes*
RMM = *Revue du Monde Musulman*
RO = *Rocznik Orientalistyczny*
ROC = *Revue de l'Orient Chrétien*
RSO = *Rivista degli Studi Orientali*
SI = *Studia Islamica (France)*
SIk = *Studia Islamika (Indonesia)*
SIr = *Studia Iranica*

TBG = *Tijdschrift voor Indische Taal-, Land- en Volkenkunde* (of the Bataviaasch Genootschap van Kunsten en Wetenschappen)
VKI = *Verhandelingen van het Koninklijk Instituut voor Taal-, Land en Volkenkunde*
WI = *Die Welt des Islams*
WO = *Welt des Orients*
WZKM = *Wiener Zeitschrift für die Kunde des Morgenlandes*
ZAL = *Zeitschrift für Arabische Linguistik*
ZDMG = *Zeitschrift der Deutschen Morgenländischen Gesellschaft*
ZGAIW = *Zeitschrift für Geschichte der Arabisch-Islamischen Wissenschaften*
ZS = *Zeitschrift für Semitistik*

b. Other

ANRW = *Aufstieg und Niedergang der Römischen Welt*
BGA = *Bibliotheca Geographorum Arabicorum*
BNF = Bibliothèque nationale de France
CERMOC = Centre d'Études et de Recherches sur le Moyen-Orient Contemporain
CHAL = *Cambridge History of Arabic Literature*
CHE = *Cambridge History of Egypt*
CHIn = *Cambridge History of India*
CHIr = *Cambridge History of Iran*
Dozy = R. Dozy, *Supplément aux dictionnaires arabes*, Leiden 1881 (repr. Leiden and Paris 1927)
EAL = *Encyclopedia of Arabic Literature*
EI1 = *Encyclopaedia of Islam*, 1st ed., Leiden 1913–38
EI2 = *Encyclopaedia of Islam*, 2nd ed., Leiden 1954–2004
EI3 = *Encyclopaedia of Islam Three*, Leiden 2007–
EIr = *Encyclopaedia Iranica*
EJ1= *Encyclopaedia Judaica*, 1st ed., Jerusalem [New York 1971–92]
EQ = *Encyclopaedia of the Qurʾān*
ERE = *Encyclopaedia of Religion and Ethics*
GAL = C. Brockelmann, *Geschichte der Arabischen Litteratur*, 2nd ed., Leiden 1943–49
GALS = C. Brockelmann, *Geschichte der Arabischen Litteratur, Supplementbände I–III*, Leiden 1937–42
GAP = *Grundriss der Arabischen Philologie*, Wiesbaden 1982–
GAS = F. Sezgin, *Geschichte des Arabischen Schrifttums*, Leiden 1967–
GMS = *Gibb Memorial Series*
GOW = F. Babinger, *Die Geschichtsschreiber der Osmanen und ihre Werke*, Leipzig 1927
HO = *Handbuch der Orientalistik*
IA = *Islâm Ansiklopedisi*
IFAO = Institut Français d'Archeologie Orientale
JE = *Jewish Encyclopaedia*
Lane = E. W. Lane, *Arabic-English Lexicon*
RCEA = *Répertoire Chronologique d'Épigraphie Arabe*
TAVO = *Tübinger Atlas des Vorderen Orients*
TDVIA = *Türkiye Diyanet Vakfi Islâm Ansiklopedisi*
UEAI = Union Européenne des Arabisants et Islamisants
van Ess, *TG* = J. van Ess, *Theologie und Gesellschaft*
WKAS = *Wörterbuch der Klassischen Arabischen Sprache*, Wiesbaden 1957–

A

ʿAlī b. Muqātil

ʿAlī (or ʿAlāʾ al-Dīn) **b. Muqātil** b. ʿAbd al-Khāliq al-Ḥamawī al-Tājir ("the merchant," d. 761/1359) was one of the most influential *zajal* poets of the eighth/ fourteenth century. His *zajal*s (stanzaic poems in dialect) count among the most cited of the genre and he is accorded a preponderant place in works specifically relating to *zajal*s such as the *Bulūgh al-amal fī fann al-zajal* ("The fulfillment of hope in the technique of composing *zajal*s") by Ibn Ḥijja al-Ḥamawī (d. 837/1434). He is also held in such esteem in anthologies such as the *ʿUqūd al-laʾāl fī l-muwashshaḥāt wa-l-azjāl* ("The pearl necklaces of *muwashshaḥa*s and *zajal*s") by al-Nawājī (d. 788/1386), the *al-Durr al-maknūn fī sabʿat funūn* ("The hidden pearls of seven modes of poetry") by Ibn Iyās al-Ḥanafī (d. c.926/1520), and the *Rawḍ al-ādāb* ("The garden of literature") by al-Ḥijāzī (d. 875/1471). ʿAlī b. Muqātil's *zajal*s were emulated by prominent poets such as his contemporary and rival from Damascus, al-Amshāṭī (d. 725/1325), as well as al-Ṣafadī (d. 764/ 1363), and Ibn Ḥijja.

Almost nothing is known about the early life of ʿAlī b. Muqātil. According to Ibn Ḥajar al-ʿAsqalānī's (d. 852/1449) *al-Durar al-kāmina* he was born in Hama, hence his *nisba* al-Ḥamawī; a second *nisba*, al-Dimashqī, indicates either that his family originated from Damascus or that he lived there. Acknowledging his mastery in composing *zajal* poetry, al-Ṣafadī notes that ʿAlī b. Muqātil became famous only relatively late in his life. It was most probably during this period that he was granted access to the court of the Ayyūbid ruler of Hama, ʿImād al-Dīn Abū l-Fidāʾ al-Malik al-Muʾayyad (d. 732/1331; see Ibn Faḍlallāh al-ʿUmarī, 177). Al-Ṣafadī met ʿAlī b. Muqātil twice, once in Damascus and once in Hama. ʿAlī b. Muqātil recited some of his *zajal*s to him. In one meeting al-Ṣafadī presented his own *muʿāraḍa* (emulative poem) to one of ʿAlī b. Muqātil's most acclaimed *zajal*s, namely, *Qalbī yiḥibb tayyāh* ("My heart loves a homeless wanderer"; al-Ṣafadī, *Aʿyān*, 3:556). According to several biographers, ʿAlī b. Muqātil gathered his *zajal*s in a dedicated *zajal*-only *dīwān* that consisted of two volumes, which are not extant.

ʿAlī b. Muqātil was recognised as one of the most eminent *zajal* poets even during his own lifetime, as attested by an incident that took place in Syria during the reign of the Mamlūk sultan al-Malik al-Nāṣir Muḥammad (r. 693–4/1293–4, 698–708/1299–1309, 709–41/1310–41). The cities of Hama and Damascus were both particularly renowned for their fondness for *zajals*, yet they disagreed as to who composed the best *zajals*. Hama took the view that their son, ʿAlī b. Muqātil, was superior, whereas Damascus supported their own son, al-Amshāṭī. Al-Nāṣir, himself a passionate *zajal* poet, decided to settle the dispute by appointing a jury consisting of three of the most illustrious men of letters of that time: Ibn Nubāta (d. 768/1366), Ibn Sayyid al-Nās (d. 734/1334), and Abū Ḥayyān al-Gharnāṭī (d. 745/1345). The jury decided in favour of ʿAlī b. Muqātil (Ibn Ḥijja, *Bulūgh*, 129).

Bibliography

Sources

Ibn Ḥabīb, *Tadhkirat al-nabīh fī ayyām al-Manṣūr wa-banīh*, ed. Muḥammad Muḥammad Amīn (Cairo 1986), 3:239; Ibn Ḥajar al-ʿAsqalānī, *al-Durar al-kāmina fī aʿyān al-miʾa al-thāmina*, ed. ʿAdnān Darwīsh (Beirut 1993), 3:133–4; al-Ḥijāzī, *Rawḍ al-ādāb*, Istanbul, Ayasofya, MS Ar. 4018, fol. 155a; Ibn Ḥijja al-Ḥamawī, *Bulūgh al-amal fī fann al-zajal*, ed. Riḍā Muḥsin al-Qurayshī (Damascus 1974), 70–1, 79, 81–3, 87, 89, 104–5, 115–17, 129; Ibn Ḥijja al-Ḥamawī, *Khizānat al-adab wa-ghāyat al-arab*, ed. ʿIṣām Shaʿītū (Beirut 1987), 1:94–5, 153, 313, 353; Ibn Iyās al-Ḥanafī, *al-Durr al-maknūn fī sabʿat funūn*, Cairo, Shiʿr Taymūr, MS Ar. 724, fols. 173b–177b; Ibn Mubārakshāh, *Safīna*, Istanbul, Feyzullah Efendi, MS Ar. 1612, fols. 3a–9a; al-Nawājī, *ʿUqūd al-laʾāl fī l-muwashshaḥāt wa-l-azjāl*, ed. Muḥammad ʿAṭā (Cairo 1999), 274–85, 295–302; Ibn Qāḍī Shuhba, *Taʾrīkh Ibn Qāḍī Shuhba*, ed. ʿAdnān Darwīsh (Damascus 1994), 2:173–4; al-Ṣafadī, *Aʿyān al-ʿaṣr wa-aʿwān al-naṣr*, ed. ʿAlī Abū Zayd et al. (Damascus 1998), 5:556–66; al-Ṣafadī, *al-Wāfī bi-l-wafayāt*, ed. Ramzī al-Baʿalbakī (Beirut 1983), 22:218–21; Ibn Taghrībirdī, *al-Manhal al-ṣāfī wa-l-mustawfī baʿd al-Wāfī*, ed. Muḥammad Muḥammad Amīn (Cairo 1984), 8:223–6; Ibn Faḍlallāh al-ʿUmarī, *Dhahabiyyāt al-ʿaṣr*, ed. Ibrāhīm Ṣāliḥ (Beirut 1983), 177.

Studies

Samir Haykal, *The eastern muwashshaḥ and zajal. A first study including edition of the ʿUqūd al-laʾālī of al-Nawājī*, Ph.D. diss., University of Oxford 1983; Wilhelm Hoenerbach, *Die vulgärarabische Poetik al-Kitāb al-ʿĀṭil al-Ḥālī wal-Muraḫḫaṣ al-Ġālī des Ṣafīyaddīn Ḥillī* (Wiesbaden 1956), 49; Riḍā Muḥsin al-Qurayshī, *Al-Funūn al-shiʿriyya ghayr al-muʿraba* (Baghdad 1977), 61.

Hakan Özkan

Amīr al-ʿArab, 1204–1517

The ***amīr al-ʿarab*** ("Bedouin representative") is the highest Bedouin rank within the framework of *imrat al-ʿarab* ("Bedouin representation"). This institution was inaugurated by the Ayyūbids around 600/**1204** to gain control over the Bedouin population in Syria and Egypt. The Mamlūks, when they gained power in Egypt and in Syria in 648/1250–1, adopted the institution, which then partly continued into the Ottoman era (cf. Winter, Holt). As the term "*amīr*" (pl., *umarāʾ*, "commander") implies, the *amīr al-ʿarab* was a member of the military elite and, as such, he had to fulfil certain tasks in return for which he was granted a number of privileges. The literal meaning of "*imrat al-ʿarab*" is "authority over the Bedouin." In the sources, the *amīr* is also occasionally called *amīr al-ʿurbān* (using a post-classic Arabic plural form of *ʿarab*, cf. Leder) and also *malik al-ʿarab* ("King of the

Bedouin"). The latter title seems to suggest a firmly rooted position of power among the respective Bedouin groups. However, an *amīr al-ʿarab* was appointed by the sultan and not by the Bedouin groups, who from time to time refused to accept the appointed *amīr al-ʿarab.* Accordingly, the term should be translated as "Bedouin representative" rather than as "Bedouin *amīr*," which is an imprecise term since the sultan also appointed other Bedouin notables as *amīr*s without connection to the institution of the *imrat al-ʿarab*.

The relationship between Bedouin tribes and the ruling dynasties was always subject to negotiation. Bedouin, especially the camel breeding groups, were important providers of auxiliary military forces, but at the same time, they were feared for their occasional attacks on the pilgrimage *(ḥajj)* and trade routes. Furthermore, nomadic groups were generally hard to control due to their mobility. There were different arrangements such as payments to the tribes to prevent them from attacking the *ḥajj* route or the appointment of a specialised Mamlūk *amīr* to deal with Bedouin affairs, be it as arbitrator in intertribal conflicts or as distributor of money and collector of taxes on their animals. However, it was not before the Ayyūbid ruler al-Malik al-ʿĀdil I (596–615/1200–18), that the relationship between ruler and tribes was officially institutionalised by a legal document *(taqlīd)*. For the first time, there was the ideal of having only one representative to the government for all Bedouin groups. This was practiced in the Syrian part of the Empire, whereas in Egypt there was always more than one Bedouin representative. However, also in the Syria region, some appointed Bedouin representatives were contested, leading to situations in which there were multiple Bedouin representatives also in this part of the Empire.

As for Syria during the Ayyūbid and Mamlūk periods, the *amīr al-ʿarab* was always appointed from among the Banū Rabīʿa, the dominant tribal group of the Syrian steppe from the sixth/twelfth century onwards. The most famous *amīr al-ʿarab* was Muhannā b. ʿĪsā (d. 735/1335) from the Banū Rabīʿa lineage of the Āl Faḍl (Banū Faḍl). He was in close contact with Sulṭān al-Nāṣir Muḥammad (684–741/1285–1341) and was one of al-Nāṣir Muḥammad's allies when the latter gained back the throne for the third time (709–41/1310–41). The fame of Muhannā is reflected in biographical anecdotes provided in Mamlūk writings, especially in the *Masālik al-abṣār fī mamālik al-amṣār* of al-ʿUmarī (d. 749/1349).

By appointing an *amīr al-ʿarab*, the Ayyūbids and especially the Mamlūks helped to construct aristocratic Bedouin dynasties, since the office of the *amīr al-ʿarab* was often transferred within one family. Whereas in Syria the *amīr al-ʿarab* was appointed from the dominant Banū Rabīʿa, in Egypt things were different. In the course of the eighth/fourteenth century, the numbers of Egyptian Bedouin representatives increased, as we can learn from the report of al-Qalqashandī (d. 821/1418) on the local *umarāʾ al-ʿarab* in his *Ṣubḥ al-aʿshā fī ṣināʿat al-inshāʾ*.

It is especially the case that in Egypt two aspects of the relationship between the sultan and his *amīr*s can be observed. First, while appointing a "Bedouin representative" was the sultan's prerogative, at least some Bedouin strongly lobbied for the position. The *Kitāb al-sulūk li-maʿrifat duwal al-mulūk* of al-Maqrīzī (d. 845/1442) provides us with a comparatively well-documented example of a campaign to have a specific individual appointed as representative, namely, the Bedouin leader al-Aḥdab from the ʿArak tribe in Upper Egypt. After instigating a Bedouin uprising in Upper Egypt and even proclaiming his own sultanate in 754/1353, al-Aḥdab managed to be appointed *amīr al-ʿarab* in the context of peace negotiations. His descendants served as *amīrs* at least up to the Ottoman conquest of Egypt in 1517.

Second, at least some Mamlūk sultans seem to have used effective tactics in dealing with dominant local Bedouin groups, as can be studied in the case of Sulṭān Barqūq in the 780s/1380s. In order to achieve a balance of Bedouin power, he separated a part of the Hawwāra Bedouin in Lower Egypt after inter-tribal quarrels and placed them around Girga in Upper Egypt, where he granted them extensive *iqṭāʿāt* (administrative grants) that lead to some prosperity. The most interesting point is, however, that Barqūq divided this newly arrived group into two parts, whom he placed in such a way that they encircled the ʿArak Bedouin, who, since the expulsion of the Awlād al-Kanz (Banū Kanz) in 766/1365 by the Mamlūks, probably were the strongest Bedouin group in Upper Egypt. With this measure, Barqūq created a new Bedouin force that soon became the most influential group in Upper Egypt and whose leaders were bearing the title of the *amīr al-ʿarab* for Upper Egypt (Garcin, 469–71; Büssow-Schmitz, *Beduinen*, 105–6). Their predominant role continued after the conquest of the Ottomans until 983/1576, when they were formally dismissed by the new rulers (Holt). In the eastern province of al-Sharqiyya, the *imrat al-ʿarab* seems to have been allocated interchangeably by different Bedouin groups. The strategically important position of Sharqiyya as the land bridge to Sinai, Ḥijāz, and Syria probably motivated the Mamlūks to want to control the appointment of the local Bedouin representative. This is especially the case given that Sharqiyya is home to the Darb al-Badriyya, an important smuggling route.

The appointment of an *amīr al-ʿarab* was fixed by the handover of a diploma *(taqlīd)* and robe of honour *(khilʿa, tashrīf)* for the appointed Bedouin representative, in return for his rendering an oath of loyalty to the sultan. It was common for an *amīr al-ʿarab* to visit the sultanic court regularly to attend upon the sultan, paying him tribute and asserting loyalty. Likewise, it often happened, especially with the powerful Syrian Bedouin *amīrs*, that the Bedouin representative "stepped out of the bounds of loyalty" *(kharaja ʿan al-ṭāʿa)*, as the sources have it, in order to re-negotiate a given arrangement, such as an increase in his *iqṭāʿāt*.

By appointing Bedouin representatives, the Ayyūbids and Mamlūks fostered a Bedouin hierarchy within their empires. A hierarchy existed also within the group of Bedouin representatives, as can be inferred from the *Ṣubḥ al-aʿshā*, which lists different forms of addresses for different Bedouin *amīrs*. It also transpires from this work that Bedouin *amīrs* from Egypt did not enjoy the same hierarchical status as the Syrian Bedouin *amīr*.

The sources at hand allow only limited insight into the administrative routines involving an *amīr al-ʿarab*. In his *al-Taʿrīf bi-l-muṣṭalaḥ al-sharīf*, al-ʿUmarī transmits an "instruction for a Bedouin representative" *(waṣiyyat amīr al-ʿarab)*, which forms part of an idealised model text for a letter of appointment *(taqlīd)*. According to this text, the Bedouin representative first and foremost is the link between the government and the Bedouin groups he represents. Ideally, every communication between Mamlūks and Bedouin should run via the *amīr al-ʿarab*. He has to be a good insider knowing how to deal with the different groups and individuals according to their social status, be it a notable, *kabīr*, or a commoner, *ṣaghīr*. He is responsible for the Bedouin's obedience towards the sultan and is prompted "to judge justly" between the Bedouin he represents, obviously, according to customary law. Concerning the military aspect, an appointed *amīr al-ʿarab* had to provide military support, which included the provision of horses and intelligence. He also had to secure the frontiers of the empire against enemies as well as against tribal groups who made their livestock graze in the empire without permission. Furthermore, an *amīr al-ʿarab* was responsible for safeguarding economic livelihoods as well as for preventing any crime falling under *ḥudūd* punishments, especially highway robbery *(qaṭʿ al-ṭarīq)*. Another task transmitted in the *waṣiyyat amīr al-ʿarab* was the prompt to give asylum and protection to people in need, a prompt that touched upon the Bedouin custom of *dakhāla*, "grant of protection" (Büssow-Schmitz, *Beduinen*, 133). Other tasks, not included in the *waṣiyyat amīr al-ʿarab*, but reported elsewhere, were tax collection from Bedouin groups as well as the provision of auxiliary forces for the Mamlūks in battles, and the payment of tributes, often in horses. In return, the government granted *iqṭaʿāt* that could considerably contribute to the *amīr al-ʿarab*'s wealth. Another important privilege was access to the ruling elite, which could help in cases of need, for example, if intercession *(shafāʿa)* was needed in a conflict between the Bedouin and the sultan (Büssow-Schmitz, Rules of Communication).

Some networks of Bedouin representatives not only included high-ranking Mamlūk *amīrs*, but also members of the cultural and intellectual elite. For example, one important source for the historian al-ʿUmarī was the intellectual and Ṣūfī shaykh Maḥmūd ibn ʿAbd al-Raḥmān al-Iṣbahānī (d. 749/1349), who was in good contact with Muhannā and his family, and who provided him with information about the famous *amīr*'s life (al-ʿUmarī, *Masālik*, 118, 120). Al-Maqrīzī writes that when the well-known jurist Ibn Taymiyya (d. 728/1328) was arrested in 1306 on the charge of heresy, it was Muhannā who successfully intervened on the former's behalf (al-Maqrīzī, 2: 87–8). One year later, Ibn Taymiyya wrote a work titled *al-ʿAqīda al-Tadmuriyya* (also *al-Risāla al-Tadmuriyya*, named after the famous Syrian oasis) which he dedicated to this prominent Syrian *amīr al-ʿarab* (Laoust). Muhannā's nephew Sayf al-Dīn b. Faḍl chaired a reconciliation between Ibn Taymiyya's disciple Ibn Qayyim al-Jawziyya (d. 751/1350) and his rival Taqī al-Dīn al-Subkī (d. 756/1355), thereby ending a controversy on the topic of divorce (Holtzman, 221). Also, with regard to Egypt, we read about good contacts between Bedouin *amīrs* and members of the local intellectual and cultural scene. Thus, the rebellious al-Aḥdab chose a Ṣūfī shaykh as intermediary between him and the sultan, and also for the fifteenth century, the sources report close connections between some Bedouin *amīrs* and Islamic scholars in Egypt (Shwartz, 213).

Bibliography

Sources

Al-Maqrīzī, *Kitāb al-sulūk li-maʿrifat duwal al-mulūk*, 3 vols., ed. Muḥammad Muṣṭafa Ziyāda and Saʿīd ʿAbd al-Fattāḥ ʿĀshūr,

Cairo 1956–73 (reprinted 2007); Abū l-ʿAbbās Aḥmad b. ʿAlī al-Qalqashandī, *Ṣubḥ al-aʿshā fī ṣināʿat al-inshāʾ*, 14 vols., Cairo 1963; Ibn Faḍl Allāh al-ʿUmarī, *Masālik al-abṣār fī mamālik al-amṣār. Qabāʾil al-ʿarab fī l-qarnayn l-sābiʿ wa-l-thāmin al-hijriyyayn*, ed. Dorothea Krawulsky, Beirut 1985; Ibn Faḍl Allāh al-ʿUmarī, *al-Taʿrīf bi-l-muṣṭalaḥ al-sharīf*, ed. Samīr al-Drūbī, Karak 1992.

Studies

Sarah Büssow-Schmitz, *Die Beduinen der Mamluken. Beduinen im politischen Leben Ägyptens im 8./14. Jahrhundert*, Wiesbaden 2016; Sarah Büssow-Schmitz, Rules of communication and politics between Bedouin and Mamluk elites in Egypt. The case of the al-Aḥdab revolt, *Eurasian Studies* 9/1–2 (2011), 67–104; Kurt Franz, Bedouin and States. Framing the Mongol-Mamlūk wars in long-term history, in Kurt Franz and Wolfgang Holzwarth (eds.), *Nomad military power in Iran and adjacent areas in the Islamic period* (Wiesbaden 2015), 29–105; Jean-Claude Garcin, *Un centre musulman de la Haute-Egypte médiévale. Qus*, Cairo 1976; M. A., Hiyari, The origins and development of the amīrate of the Arabs during the seventh/thirteenth and eighth/fourteenth centuries, *BSOAS* 38 (1975), 509–24; Peter Holt, Hawwāra, *EI2*; Livnat Holtzman, Ibn Qayyim al-Jawziyyah, in Joseph E. Lowry and Devin J. Stewart, *Essays in Arabic literary biography* (Wiesbaden 2009), 203–23; Henri Laoust, Ibn Taymiyya, *EI2*; Stefan Leder, Towards a historical semantic of the Bedouin, 7th to 15th centuries. A survey, in *Der Islam* 92 (2015), 85–123; Igal Shwartz, *Ha-Beduim be-Mitzrayim ba-tequfa ha-mamlukit*, Ph.D. diss., University of Tel Aviv 1987; Stefan Winter, Aufstieg und Niedergang des osmanischen Wüstenemirats (1536–1741). Die Mawali-Beduinen zwischen Tribalisierung und Nomadenaristokratie, *Saeculum* 63 (2013), 249–263.

Sarah Büssow-Schmitz

B

Barīd Shāhīs

The **Barīd Shāhīs** ruled the previously Bahmanī city of Bīdar from the end of the ninth/fifteenth century until 1028/1619. With the disintegration of the Bahmanī sultanate (ruled in the northern Deccan, 748–934/1347–1528), its military commanders—mostly *gharībān* (foreigners from western and eastern Islamic lands)—rose to prominence. Relations between these contenders for power were complex, with no clear loyalties upon which to rely.

Qāsim Barīdī, a Sunnī Turk in the service of Maḥmūd Shāh Bahmān (r. 887–924/1482–1518), engaged in both war and political intrigue. He was not always successful in those efforts, but he managed to solidify his position as the effective ruler of Bīdar and its surrounding area early in the final years of the last decade of the ninth/fifteenth century. The Barīdīs would rule Bīdar until 1028/1619, when the ʿĀdil Shāhīs of the neighbouring sultanate of Bījāpūr (r. 895–1097/1490–1686) gained control of the city under Ibrāhīm II (r. 987–1035/1579–1626), expanding their kingdom to the frontier lands of the Quṭb Shāhīs of Golconda (r. 901–1098/1496–1687).

Qāsim Barīdī's victorious campaigns against the Marathas (Marāṯ'ẖās), a warrior group from present day Maharashtra, western Deccan, contributed to his prestige. He married his son Amīr (r. 910–50/1504–43) to the daughter of the Maratha chief Sabājī whom he had defeated. He died in 909/1503–4 and was succeeded by Amīr, whose wars against the ʿĀdil Shāhīs intensified, with serious territorial losses to the Barīdīs. Amīr died in Dawlatābād in 950/1543 and was succeeded by ʿAlī (r. 950–87/1543–79), politically the most astute and culturally the most gifted Barīdī ruler and the first to adopt the title of Shāh. During ʿAlī's reign, Bīdar was attacked by Murtaḍā Niẓām Shāh (r. 972–97/1565–89) of Aḥmadnagar, with the help of Ibrāhīm Quṭb Shāh (r. 957–88/1550–80) of Golconda Muḥammadnagar. The city was saved with the help of the ʿĀdil Shāhīs and the troubles brought by the contemporaneous rebellion of Murtaḍā's son in Aḥmadnagar.

Despite these seemingly never-ending quarrels between the leaders of most of the Deccanī sultanates, the ʿĀdil Shāhīs, the Niẓām Shāhīs, and the Quṭb Shāhīs allied themselves with the Barīdīs in order to conquer Vijayanagara. This wealthy Hindu kingdom had ruled the regions south of the Tungabhadra and Krishna rivers since 736/1336. Following the celebrated battle of Talikota (972/1565), the sultanates, profiting from the plunder amassed from Vijayanagara, embarked on a series of impressive building projects. Amongst those of ʿAlī Barīdī were the remodelling of the Rangīnī Maḥal (coloured palace) in the southwestern group of palaces inside the royal enclosure of Bīdar fort, his majestic sepulchre, west of Bīdar city; and the development of Deccanī artillery.

The Rangīnī Maḥal boasts basalt colonettes inlaid with mother-of-pearl and arched spandrels decorated with exquisite mother-of-pearl inlays of spiralling scrolls and amorous spiritual verses, architectural and decorative features unique to Bīdar. This inlaid work parallels the carved patterns on the renowned Barīdī cannons in Bīdar fort: Ṭūp-i Ilāhī (divine cannon), dated 977/1569–70; Fatḥ-i Lashkar (victory of the army), dated 988/1580; and Ṭūp-i Ḥaydarī (lion cannon), begun during the reign of Qāsim Barīdī II (995–99/1587–91 ?) and completed under the usurper Amīr Barīdī in 1004/1596. These patterns were originally inlaid in silver or gold and must have stood out against the dark iron body of the cannon as forceful reminders of the Barīdīs' wealth and power.

The mausoleum of ʿAlī Barīdī deviated from Bahmanī funerary models, as did that of his son, Ibrāhīm (r. 987–97/1579–89), whose tomb, a humbler copy, is close to that of his father, west of Bīdar city and close to the royal polo ground. Set on a platform, ʿAlī Barīdī's tomb imitated a garden pavilion framed on all sides by majestic arches and crowned by an onion-shaped dome. Beneath this dome lies the sultan's beautifully carved cenotaph, with the Islamic confession of faith together with the date of his death and the completion of his tomb (984/1576–7) three years ealier. Painted tiles with polychrome underglaze decorate the interior walls with Qurʾānic inscriptions and verses of the famous Persian poet ʿAṭṭār (d. 618/1221), signed by the calligrapher Khᵛājaʾī, from Shīrvān in the eastern Caucasus.

Ibrāhīm's death (997/1589) was followed by turbulent years for the Barīdīs, with short reigns, the nominal successions of relatives, and takeovers of the throne. The Persian-language narrative of the Indian historian Muḥammad Qāsim Firishta (d. c.1029/1620) concludes in 1018/1609, that is, ten years before Bīdar was annexed to the ʿĀdil Shāhī sultanate and the last Barīdīs ended their lives as captives in Bījāpūr.

Bibliography

Source

Muḥammad Qāsim Firishta, *Tārīkh-i Firishta* (lithog.), 2 vols., Lucknow 1864–5, trans. John Briggs, *History of the rise of the Mahomedan rule in India till the year AD 1612*, 4 vols., London 1829, repr. Calcutta 1908, 1966, New Delhi 1981.

Studies

Jean Deloche, *Studies on fortification in India*, Pondicherry 2007; Richard M. Eaton and Phillip B. Wagoner, *Power, memory, architecture. Contested sites on India's Deccan plateau, 1300–1600*, Delhi 2014; James Stewart King, *The history of the Bahmani dynasty founded on the Burhân-i Maʾâṣir*, London 1900; George Michell and Helen Philon, *Islamic architecture of the Deccan. Forts, palaces, mosques and tombs*, London 2018; George Michell and Mark Zebrowski, *Architecture and art of the Deccan sultanates*, Cambridge 1999; Helen Philon, *Gulbarga, Bidar, Bijapur*, Mumbai 2012; Helen Philon (ed.), *Silent splendour. Palaces of the Deccan, 14th–19th centuries*, Mumbai 2010; Venetia Porter, *Islamic tiles*, London 1995; Klaus Rötzer, Deccani guns. Features and ornamentations, in Laura E. Parodi (ed.), *The visual world of Muslim India. The art, culture and society of the Deccan in the early modern era* (London 2014), 123–42; H. K. Sherwani and P. M. Joshi, *History of medieval Deccan, 1295–1724*, 2 vols., Hyderabad 1974; Ghulam Yazdani, *Bidar. Its history and monuments*, London 1947, repr. Delhi 1995.

Helen Philon

Bengal

Islam, brought by conquerors, adventurers, and mystics, entered **Bengal** (including the Indian province of West Bengal in the west and the present nation state of Bangladesh in the east) from the early seventh/thirteenth century.

1. Before Islam

Like the setting in which Islam emerged as a cultural, literary, and political-economic force in nearby Southeast Asian kingdoms, Bengal was home, in the centuries before the rise of Islam, to various religious practices, including an expanding Sanskritic Brahmanic culture, Theravada Buddhist monastic communities, Jain mendicants, and the worship of deities indigenous to the region that pre-date Sanskritic culture, amongst them Monosha *(mānasā)*, who protects against snakebites, and Chondi *(caṇḍī)*, goddess of forest life (Eaton, *Rise of Islam*; Tony Stewart, In search; Sufia Uddin; Van Schendel).

2. The advent of Islam

Into a social and cultural environment incorporating multiple religious references and communities came Islam, via the conquests of the Turkic Khaljī tribesman Muḥammad Bakhtiyār (r. 594–603/1198–1206) and his cavalry, who raided parts of eastern India, beginning with attacks on Buddhist monasteries in Bihar in the late sixth/twelfth century, and, from 599–600/1203–4, conquered Nabadwip, a centre of ancient learning, and Gaur (Gaud'), the erstwhile capital of the Sena dynasty that had ruled most of Bengal since the late fifth/eleventh century. At Gaur, Muslims in the early seventh/thirteenth century began to enter the contested terrain of northeastern India, which for centuries had been ruled by the Buddhist Pala kingdom established in the second/eighth century, and which lasted until the rise of a southern migrant Hindu force, and the Brahmanic Sena dynasty in the mid-590s/late 1190s. This Hindu dynasty conquered Bengal and ruled from Gaur in the late fifth/eleventh century. The setting for the rise of Islam in northeastern India was the confrontation between an insurgent Brahmanic force contesting the pre-existing Buddhist political order and the many challenges to Sanskritic culture posed by local religious traditions and practices, informed by the various forms of Buddhism practised in eastern India.

3. Under the Bengal sultanate, and others

Bengal remained nominally under the rule of the Delhi Sultanate—governed by Turkic Bakhtiyārs and, later, by rulers of the line of the Delhi sultan Balban (r. 664–86/1266–87)—until 743/1342, when Sulṭān Shams al-Dīn Ilyās Shāh (r. 740–59/1339–58) established an independent Bengal sultanate. From the mid-eighth/fourteenth century to the late tenth/

sixteenth century, Bengal (with capitals primarily in northern and northwestern Bengal, the seats of previous Pala and Sena rulers) was transformed into an independent political entity and developed localised literature, architecture, and religious practice and local memorialisation of saints arriving from various parts of the Muslim world. For nearly two hundred fifty years, until the rise of Mughal power in the region from the late tenth/sixteenth century to the early eleventh/seventeenth, Bengal's crossroads of Brahmanic, Buddhist, and Jaina cultures in South Asia was governed by a diverse set of rulers from various parts of the expanding Muslim world. These included 1) members of the Ilyās Shāhī dynasty until 892/1487, with 2) the interlude, between 817/1414 and 840/1437, of the rules of the Hindu noble, Rāja Ganesh (r. 819–21/1416–8), who converted to Islam, and of his descendants), 3) Abyssinian Ḥabashīs, former military slaves (r. 892–8/1487–93), and 4) sultans of the line of the Arab ʿAlāʾ al-Dīn Ḥusayn Shāh (r. 898–925/1493–1519) from 898/1493 to 944/1537. From 944/1537, Bengal was overrun by Afghan conquerors and ruled by members of the Afghan Sūrī (944–71/1537–64) and Karrānī (971–84/1564–76) dynasties.

4. Under the Mughal Empire

In 984/1576, at the battle of Rajmahal, the expanding Mughal forces under Emperor Akbar (r. 963–1014/1556–1605) defeated the independent Bengal sultanate. Mughal forces gradually took over all of Bengal, which became a province *(ṣūba)* of the Mughal Empire.

5. Architecture

During two and a half centuries of Bengal's sultanate, a distinctive type of Bengali Muslim architecture emerged, consisting primarily of mosques but including also mausoleums, palaces, caravanserais, and *madrasas*, which combined Muslim forms from elsewhere with local material and styles. One such style is *tughrā* calligraphy, which, although known in the Ottoman world as a signature and monogram decorative piece, is considered in Bengal an independent calligraphy, typical of the local Muslim culture. The first Muslim inscription dates to 639/1241, during the reign of the Delhi Mamlūk sultan Naṣīr al-Dīn Maḥmūd Shāh (r. 644–64/1246–66). From the late seventh/thirteenth century, mosques were built in Gaur, Hooghly, and Pandua (in present-day West Bengal, India), and in Dhaka, Rajshahi, and Khulna, amongst other places (in present-day Bangladesh). The earliest existing Muslim monuments in Bengal are the mausoleum of Zafar Khān Ghāzī (d. 697/1298), a general of the Delhi Sultan ʿAlāʾ al-Dīn Khaljī (r. 695–715/1296–1316) and the attached mosque, located in Hooghly and dating to 697/1298.

Bengal mosque architecture is characterised by its distinctive curvilinear roof, carved cornice above a range of arches, panels on walls, doorways, and spandrels ornamented by terracotta. The Bengal tradition began with the Adina mosque, the largest at the time in India, built in what is now Pandua in 774/1373 by Sikandar Shāh (r. 759–92/1358–90), son of Ilyās Shāh. The mosque conforms to the style and standards of the great mosques of Córdoba, Damascus, Baghdad, and Cairo, by including a courtyard and cloisters. The inclusion of terracotta decorations above the *miḥrāb* began a trend of terracotta decorative arts in Bengali-styled Muslim architecture, which would be imitated later.

The Eklakhi mausoleum of Jalāl al-Dīn Shāh (r. 821–36/1418–33), son of Rāja Ganesh, built soon after his death, begins the trend of appropriating Hindu forms, such as pointed arches with lintels, marked by carvings of deities such as Vishnu, and a hemispherical dome in Stupa style, as in Sanchi and Manikyala. The Bengali elements include the cornice carved downward, recalling Bengali huts, and a single domed structure, which came to be used in later Bengali architecture. The curved cornice is found also in the mosque of Bābā Ādam, built in 888/1483 in Munshiganj, and the Tantipara Mosque, built in 880/1475, in Gaur, in present-day Western Bengal.

The Adina mosque of Pandua holds the only known example of Kufic calligraphy in Bengal, in an undated inscription on the *miḥrāb*, probably from about 797/1395. This inscription includes the *bismilla* and a series of Qurʾānic verses mingling Kufic and *thuluth* calligraphic styles on a single panel. Although many types of calligraphy were used in Bengal, such as *naskh* and *tawqīʿ*, the style most associated with the local culture of Bengal is *tughrā*. As an abstract form of calligraphic representation, *tughrā* in Bengal was used to represent boats, oars, bows, arrows, lines of Muslims at prayer, pelicans, swans, and it was undoubtedly influenced by the culture of the Bengal delta, as evidenced by the *dargāh* (shrine) at Hazrat Pandua, built in 898/1493, and the Gaumalti mosque in Gaur, as well as numerous tombs and inscriptions on basalt from the ninth/fifteenth and early tenth/sixteenth centuries.

6. Holy places of Bengal

In the era of the Bengal sultanate, folklore of holy men and women arriving into Bengal from Central Asia, Arabia, Iran, and Anatolia began to appear in the legends of Bengali Muslim communities and in the inscriptions and legends around tombs of saints such as Shāh Jalāl Mujarrad (d. 747/1346), Bāyazīd Bisṭāmī (d. 261/874–5 or 234/848–9), and Khān Jahān ʿAlī (d. 863/1459). According to one legend, the venerated saint Shāh Jalāl (d. 747/1346), born in Konya, was sent with a clump of earth in hand by a spiritual guide to settle in a region with similar soil, which turned out to be Sylhet, in northern Bengal (Sufia Uddin, 36–7; Van Schendel 28–30). Shāh Jalāl's reputation as a Ṣūfī saint and the large number of his followers attracted the famous Moroccan traveller and writer Ibn Baṭṭūṭa (d. 770 or 779/1368 or 1377), who journeyed by boat on the rivers of Bengal and noted places such as Habiganj and Sonargaon, en route to his meeting with the saint in the early eighth/fourteenth century (Ibn Baṭṭūṭa, *Rihlat*). Another account of Shāh Jalāl presents him as a disciple of the Central Asian Ṣūfī *shaykh* Sayyid Aḥmad Yasawī, successfully pursuing *jihād* in Sirhat (i.e., Sylhet) (in the hagiographical work *Gulzār-i abrār*, 1021/1612–3, cited in Eaton, *Rise of Islam*, 74).

7. The land under the Mughals

From the rise of formal Mughal power until the establishment of the English East India Company dominion in 1178/1764, the region witnessed an expansion in Muslim population and a change in geopolitical centres, as the new capital of Mughal Bengal became Jahangirnagar (Dhaka), east of the Padma river, distant from earlier centres of power such as Gaur, in the north, home of the Pala, Sena, and Bengal sultans. The Mughal Empire also oversaw the clearing of forests and establishment of wet-rice plough cultivation, in a manner unprecedented in Bengal's history. As the empire expanded to the north and east, it issued land grants *(jāgīr)* to enterprising individuals, often Ṣūfīs, who drew increasing numbers of adherents to Islam: Panjāb and Bengal are, for the same reasons, the only two regions of India where Ṣūfīs played a decisive role in conversions to Islam (Eaton, *Rise of Islam*). As the Bengal delta moved east, dense forest regions were cut down by emergent cultivators, and large Muslim populations began to grow amongst the cultivators and fisherfolk settling the land. It was primarily the middlemen, brokers between *zamīndār*s (elite local landholders) and the Mughal state, who did the actual work, such as *shaykh*s and *ḥājjī*s who had contact with rural populations excluded from Sanskritic Brahmanic culture. Such people who became Muslims largely followed localised non-Brahmanic religious practices: "Those areas east of the Ganga tended to yield more readily to Muslim development because of certain explicit restrictions on Brahmana settlement and the more general fact that much of that land was insufficiently domesticated for Hindu habitation of a kind favored elsewhere" (Stewart, In search, 261).

8. Literature

Tied to this process of Islamisation was the growth of literature in Bengali intended as instruction for readers about proper forms of religious practice. Such works as *naṣīḥat-nāma*s (books of advice), were composed from the tenth/sixteenth century to the thirteenth/nineteenth and used Arabic terms such as *nabī* (prophet) and *kalima* (word of God), as well as indigenous terms such as *punya* (merit), a Sanskrit term referring to the Hindu doctrine of *karma* and rebirth. Literature that preached Islam within Bengali linguistic, literary, and philosophical registers began to emerge in the late tenth/sixteenth century. One of the most prolific authors of the eleventh/seventeenth century was Ālāol (fl. 1061–82/1651–71). A talented musician proficient in Sanskrit, Bengali, Persian, and Hindi, Ālāol was patronised by Muslim dignitaries of the Buddhist kingdom of Arakan and produced treatises on music and many translations of Indian stories into Bengali. In about 1060/1650, he translated the romantic poem *Padmāvat*, as well as many Persian stories, into Bengali.

The paradigmatic text that defines Bengali Islam in the pre-modern period is Sayyid Sulṭān's *Nabīvaṃśa*. Dating to between the 990s/1580s and the 1040s/1630s, this work is the first biography of the prophet Muḥammad written in Bengali. It is at once a universal history, modelled after existing Islamic histories, and an Indian *purāṇa*, including cosmogony and cosmology, Hindu mythology, hagiography, genealogy, asceticism, and devotional praxis. The book also first describes how the Vedas were divinely revealed texts that foreshadow the coming of the Prophet, who becomes a paradigmatic Ṣūfī *pīr* (Pers., lit., old, hence spiritual master), a common figure of the Bengali landscape of the eleventh/seventeenth century embodying God's beloved, the *faqīr* and intercessor.

During the early eleventh/seventeenth century under Mughal rule, the region saw the rise of Hindu *zamīndār*s and of landed Hindus as private secretaries, accountants, and generals. Concurrently, Bengal underwent Persianisation on the one hand, via elite literary and bureaucratic culture, evidenced by the rise of clerics and financiers associated with the Mughal regime, working in Persian, and, on the other hand, through the development of literary writing in Persian, including by Bengali Brahmins. Bengal also saw the rise of Persian writers such as Sayyid Mīr, Mukhliṣ Ḥusayn Tabrīzī, and Ḥasan Beg Grāmī, as recounted in works of the period, such as Mīrzā Muḥammad Ṣādiq's *Ṣubḥ-i Ṣādiq* ("Ṣādiq's morning," composed between 1038/1629 and the author's death, in 1060/1650). Works by Hindus such as Jayānanda's (fl. tenth/sixteenth century) *Chaitanya Mangala*—a poem on the life of Chaitanya (d. 939/1533), the famous intiator and figurehead of the theist Hindu movement *(bhakti)* that developed into Gaud'īya Vaishnavism—attest that a knowledge of Persian was common amongst Bengali Brahmins. Islam in Bengal began to develop a set of new cultures of religiosity associated with deities worshipped by both Hindus and Muslims, such as Satyanarāyaṇa/Satya Pīr, Dakshin Roy, and Bon Bībī, while stories about the exploits of *pīr*s and love stories of both Indian and Persian or Arabic origin were intended for Hindu and Muslim audiences (Tony Stewart, In search, and *Fabulous females*).

9. The ascendancy of the East India Company and the British Empire

Geopolitical fortunes began to shift again with the decline of central Mughal power in the early decades of the twelfth/eighteenth century, as the English East India Company, based in Calcutta, began to gain power in coastal settlements established in Madras, Calcutta, and Bombay. Simultaneously, nawabs (originally, delegates of the Mughal emperor) began to assume autonomous power in Bengal; Murshid Qulī Khān (d. 1139/1727), for instance, in 1129/1717 established a new capital in Murshidabad, in northern Bengal, on the eastern banks of the Bhagirathi river. The heir of Murshid Qulī Khān, Alīvardī Khān (d. 1169/1756), assumed power after the deposition of Murshid Qulī Khān by his son-in-law, Sarfarāz Khān, in 1153/1740. This moment marked a departure in the governance of Bengal, as Alīvardī Khān combined the posts of *ṣūbadār* (governor) and *dīwān* (finance officer), which had, to this point, been distinct appointments by the Mughal emperor. Autonomous nawabs began to rule Bengal from this period through the conquest of Bengal by the East India Company. The growing number of military fortifications built by its agents and its political alliance with powerful banking families such as those of Amīrchand and the house of Jagat Set'h, made it possible for the Company to defeat the nawabs of Bengal in 1170/1757 and take revenue from the land in Bengal, Bihar, and Orissa in 1179/1765–6.

10. Popular movements

During the period of Company (1764–1858) and imperial rule (1858–1947), Bengal was home to a series of reformist movements and a reorientation to Islam in line with the modern forms of religiosity and politics ushered in by Company and imperial rule. Men such as Ḥājī Sharīʿatallāh (d. 1840), from Faridpur, in eastern Bengal, studied in Mecca and al-Azhar (in Cairo) between 1798 and 1818 and began to critique allegedly Hindu practices such as praying and worshipping at *dargāh*s and observing Hindu customs such as Dīpāvalī (the festival of lights) as "accretions" antithetical to Islam. He began a movement called Farāʾiḍī (from *farāʾiḍ*, obligations to Islam). Sharīʿatallāh's son, nicknamed Dūdū Miyāṇ (d. 1862) continued this movement in the eastern countryside in the 1830s, transforming it into an explicitly political peasant movement, aimed at exposing and curtailing abuses of Muslim riots against land tenants as well as at establishing a system of justice alternative to British courts. Linking the material and economic worlds of the peasantry with an awareness of Islam in rural east Bengal, the movement politicised significant numbers of the peasantry in rural eastern Bengal and instigated the creation of a Muslim identity in those communities (Iqbal). The formal movement withered away after Dūdū Miyāṇ's death. Other contemporaneous movements in Bengal include the Ṭarīqa-yi Muḥammadiyya (lit., way of Muḥammad) led by Sayyid Aḥmad Barelwī (d. 1831), who aimed to purge Islam of innovations and waged *jihād* against the Sikhs and the British Empire in the Northwest Frontier; the movement came to an end with Sayyid Aḥmad's death in a battle against the Sikhs in 1831 (Gaborieau).

The movement that resonated most powerfully with Bengali peasants was the Taʿayyunī (lit., identity) movement, led by Karāmat ʿAlī (d. 1873) from Jawnpur (present-day Uttar Pradesh), who migrated to Bengal in 1835 and lived and preached there until his death. His movement, heir to that launched by Sayyid Aḥmad Barelwī, aimed to purge traces of Hindu activities such as attending Hindu festivals, visiting tombs of saints, and consulting astrologers (Ali). Revivalists such as Karāmat ʿAlī declared that India was *dār al-Islām* (the land of Islam) and not *dār al-ḥarb* (the land of war), sheltered, at least theoretically, by the British empire (Ghose). Soon after the rise of revivalist movements in rural Bengal, the viceroy of India, Lord Curzon (in office 1899–1905), implemented the controversial partition of the province of Bengal into Bengal (including Western Bengal, Bihar, and Orissa), with a Hindu majority, and eastern Bengal and Assam, ruled from the provincial capital of Dhaka, with a Muslim majority. The official reason was administrative efficiency, given the large population of undivided Bengal and the lack of infrastructure and personnel to manage the eastern half. This event resulted in a wide variety of political and sociocultural changes for the peoples of Bengal. Officials also claimed that the creation of a Muslim majority province with Dhaka as capital would revive glories of the Mughal Empire. Powerful Muslim landlords, such as Nawāb Salīmallāh of Dhaka, on whose estate the Muslim League was born in 1906, supported the partition plan as well as the prospect of new administrative jobs and government services for the primarily Muslim population in eastern Bengal and Assam. The partition faced opposition from much of the population—Hindu and Muslim—and comprised one of the targets of the *swadeshi* (Sanskrit *svadeśī*, lit., one's own country) movement of anti-colonial boycott and protest in India. As protests and pressures rose to a fever pitch from 1905 onwards, the partition plan was reversed in 1911 by then viceroy Charles Hardinge (in office 1910–6), and the capital of British India was moved to Delhi from Calcutta. Results of this event included heightened passionate nationalist agitation and the Bengal government's establishment of Dhaka University, intended for the residents of eastern Bengal, which opened in 1921. The opening of Dhaka University encouraged Bengali

Muslim populations to identify with the newly created Muslim-majority province and develop a political identity as a Muslim community (Sharifuddin Ahmed; Saxena).

In the early twentieth century, as a small but increasingly visible Muslim middle class developed in Bengal, Muslims began to take new jobs available in the public sphere, in business, universities, and the government. Muslims also began to produce new journals and newspapers in Bengali, suggesting proper Muslim practices, criticising Christian missionary practices, and creating a space for discussion of the Muslim community in the popular press. While certain Bengali Muslim authors were beginning, in the colonial context, to write texts influenced by European literature, others, such as Naʿīm al-Dīn (d. 1908), undertook to translate the entire Qurʾān into Bengali and to contribute to *tafsīr* (Qurʾānic commentary). Even a non-Muslim writer such as the Hindu reformist Girish Chandra Sen (d. 1910) took part in this enterprise. During the inter-war period, this rising Muslim middle class increasingly joined the ranks of the Bengal Provincial Muslim League, a political branch of the All-India Muslim League.

11. The idea of Pakistan

Beginning with the All-India Muslim League's 1940 Lahore Resolution, which announced the proclamation by the Muslim League to promote a federation of new Muslim majority states in an independent India, notions of Pakistan as a potential homeland for Indian Muslims began to dominate political discourse in colonial India. In the 1940s, Bengali Muslim literary critics and modern poets such as Abū l-Manṣūr Aḥmad (d. 1979) and Abū l-Kalām Shams al-Dīn (d. 1978) began to write in Bengali about the idea of Pakistan in Bengal, supported by such societies as the Purba (eastern) Pakistan Renaissance Society of Calcutta. Bengali support for the idea of Pakistan was also expressed in poetry and literary prose in Bengali-language periodicals and newspapers aimed at the Muslim communities. There were, however, also Muslims in Bengal who opposed the idea of Pakistan, including Riḍā al-Karīm (d. 1993), a Congress politician who opposed the partition of Bengal and supported a united India. Nonetheless, the idea of Pakistan promoted by the majority of Bengali Muslim intellectuals conceived of the entire province of Bengal as included in a putative state of Pakistan (Bose). From 1945 to 1947, negotiations between the Bengal Provincial Muslim League and All-India Muslim League led to a merger of those organisations in Bengal, through the rise of Muḥammad ʿAlī Jinnāḥ (d. 1948) amongst Bengali Muslim politicians in 1946 and 1947, during the height of the debate in late colonial India about a future Pakistan. The rise of Jinnāḥ led to the victory of the Muslim League in the 1946 elections, the first time the Muslim League had won a provincial election. Concomitantly, the premier of Bengal, Ḥusayn Shahīd Suhrawardī (d. 1963), became associated with Muslim communal politics in the Bengali public sphere and generated great opposition to Muslims in the organised Hindu political sphere, strengthening a public split between Muslim and Hindu communities in Bengal politics. Although a United Bengal Movement, including Hindus and Muslims, opposed a partition of colonial Bengal as a part of the partition of colonial India, colonial India was divided, in the summer of 1947, into independent India (including West Bengal and Calcutta) and a divided Pakistan consisting of West Pakistan (Panjāb, Baluchistan, the Northwest Frontier Province, and Sind), and East Pakistan (Bengal, with its capital in Dhaka).The partition caused confusion, fear, violence, and streams of refugees in both directions across the new border between India and East Pakistan.

12. The period of East Pakistan

During the East Pakistan period (1947–71), the state declared itself an Islamic republic in 1956. In the 1950s and 1960s, Bengali Muslim intellectuals and critics began to write about Islam in new ways. Abū l-Hāshim (d. 1974), a Bengali Muslim politician, supporter of United Bengal, and intellectual, published *Creed of Islam* in 1950. Composed during the tumultuous end of the British Empire, this book defined Islam as the source of a revolutionary consciousness and politics in the new moment of decolonisation. A key activist in support of creating Pakistan, Hāshim pushed for the redefinition of Islam in light of the new political moment facing Bengal and the rest of South Asia. At the same time, Mawlānā Bhasani (d. 1976), a charismatic *pīr* and political activist, supported the rise of East Pakistan and endured as one of its most prominent adherents, in the service of a nation state based on economic justice and transformation, developing a religio-political philosophy defined loosely as "Islamic socialism": "There is only one path to the freedom of all people from all forms of oppression—"socialism" and I will, till my last breath, work to establish it. I will participate in the volunteer corps of *Krishak Samiti* to eradicate the foundations of capitalism, feudalism, bribery, corruption and all other social ills from the country" (cited in Layli Uddin, 238). The state of Pakistan founded the Bait-ul Mukarram mosque in Dhaka, in 1959, and the Islamic Academy in 1960, as well as the Asiatic Society of Pakistan, which funded research throughout the 1960s into the broader history, culture, and anthropology of Islam in Eastern Bengal.

13. The imposition of Urdu

From the early years of the new Pakistan state in 1947 and 1948, the central government began to impose Urdu on the entire population as a means of Islamicising the Bengali Muslim population and creating a unified nation state. Bengali Muslim activists rejected the imposition of Urdu through demonstrations, strikes, and mass political actions, leading to a *bhāṣā āndolan* (language movement), bringing together politicians, students, and activists to protest the government's Urdu-only policy. A general strike called on 21 February 1952, comprising mostly students and youth leaders, led to state forces firing on the crowd, injuring many and killing five. From that date, marked today by UNESCO as Mother Language Day, the language movement sought to protest the central government's policies of preference for Urdu speakers as well as economic and social privileges granted to West Pakistan. This imposition of Urdu fit into broader tensions between East and West Pakistan. From the beginning of the state's history, the majority of personnel in the military and government positions were flown in from the West, the majority of funding for development was reserved for the West, and little support arrived to aid East Pakistanis during the famine of 1947–51.

14. The birth of Bangladesh

With roots in the broader resistance to the growing colonial relationship between West and East Pakistan, eastern Bengali rebel forces, called *mukti bahini* (freedom fighters), including the future prime minister of Bangladesh Sheikh Mujibur Rahman (d. 1975), declared war against the Pakistani state on 26 March 1971. This war, led primarily by peasants, lasted until December of that year. On 16 December 1971, after thirteen days of formal war between Indian forces in an alliance with rebel forces against the Pakistani state, the new state of Bangladesh was created in December 1971. The state of Bangladesh preserved and protected the Bengali language, spoken by the vast majority of inhabitants of then East Pakistan. Although not the only language spoken in East Bengal, Bengali was the primary mode of communication for most East Bengali inhabitants.

Today, the nation state of Bangladesh includes nearly 150 million Muslims, the fourth-largest Muslim population in the world. The Muslim population of the Indian state of Bengal—the state with the second largest largest population of Muslims in India, after the northern Indian state of Uttar Pradesh—is approximately twenty-four million. Bangladesh is one of the world's youngest independent nation states and contains, in addition to its Muslim population, numerous historic non-Muslim communities, including Hindus, Buddhists, and various indigenous groups. Islam in all of Bengal stretches back more than eight hundred years and has shaped indelibly art, architecture, and language, at the same time being transformed by the cultural, linguistic, and religious lives of the local population.

Bibliography

Sources

Abū l-Faḍl ʿAllāmī, *Āʾīn-i Akbarī*, ed. Henry Blochmann, Calcutta 1867–77, 1927–49² (vol. 1 trans. Henry Blochman and rev. Douglas C. Phillot, vols. 2–3 trans. Henry S. Jarrett, rev. J. Sarkar), repr. New Delhi 1977–8; Abū l-Faḍl-i ʿAllāmī, *Akbar-nāma*, ed. ʿAbd al-Raḥīm (Abdur Rahim), 3 vols. in 2, Calcutta 1873–87, trans. Henry Beveridge, 3 vols., Calcutta 1897–1921, repr. New Delhi 1979; Ālāol (trans.), *Padmāvat*, ed. Syed Ali Ahsan, Dhaka 2000 (translated between 1061/1651 and 1082/1671); ʿAlī Rāja, *Āgama*, c. 1700, in *Bāṅalāra sūphī sāhitya. Alocana o Nayakhani grantha samvalita*, ed. Ahmed Sharif, Dhaka 1969; Ḍiyāʾ al-Dīn Baranī, *Tārīkh-i Fīrūz Shāhī*, ed. W. Nassau Lees, Kabir al-Din, and Saiyid Ahmad Khan, *The Táríkh-i Feroz-sháhí of Ziaa al-Din Barni*, Calcutta 1862; F. B. Bradley-Birt, *Twelve men of Bengal in the nineteenth century*, Calcutta 1910; Ghulām Ḥusayn "Salīm," *Riyāḍ al-salāṭīn*, ed. Maulavi Abdul Haq Abid, Calcutta 1890–1, trans. Maulavi Abdus Salam, Calcutta 1902–4; Ibn Baṭṭūṭā, *Riḥlat*, ed. ʿAbd al-Hādī al-Tāzī, 5 vols., Rabat 1997, trans. H. A. R. Gibb, *The travels of Ibn Baṭṭūṭa AD 1325–1354*, 3 vols., New Delhi repr. 2004; Victor Jacquemont, *Letters from India, 1829–1832, being a selection from the correspondence of Victor Jacquemont*, trans. Catherine Alison Phillips, ed. John Sidney Lethbridge and K. G. Lethbridge, London 1936; Mīr Musharraf Ḥusayn, *Bishad-Sindhu*, Calcutta c. 1888; Muhammad Akram Khan, *Mustafā Charit*, Calcutta 1926; Mohammed Naimuddin, *Koran śariph*, Mymensingh, Bangladesh 1891; Mirzā Nathan, *Bahāristān-i-ghaybī. A history of the Mughal wars in Assam, Cooch Behar, Bengal, Bihar and Orissa during the reigns of Jahāngīr and Shāhjahān*, trans. Moayyidul Islam Borah, 2 vols., Gauhati, Assam 1936; Mukunda, *Caṇḍīmaṅgal* (composed 1006/1589), in *Caṇḍīmaṅgala. Dhanapati upākyāna*, ed. Bijanibihari Bhattacarya, Kolkata 1966; L. S. S. (Lewis Sydney Stewart) O'Malley, *Census of India, 1911*, vol. 5, *Bengal, Bihar, Orissa, and Sikkim*, Calcutta 1913; Fanny Parkes, *Wanderings of a pilgrim in search of the picturesque during four and twenty years in the East with revelations of life in the Zenana*, London 1850; Khondkar

Fuzli Rubbee, *The origin of the Musalmans of Bengal*, Calcutta 1895; Muhammad Sagir, *Iusuph-Jolekha*, ed. Muhammad Enamul Hak, in Mansur Musa (ed.), *Muhammad Enamul Hak. Racanabali*, 2 vols. (Ḍhaka 1993), 495–886; Sayyid Sulṭān, *Nabīvaṃśa*, ed. Ahmed Sharif, 2 vols., Dhaka 1978; Abul Hashim, *Creed of Islam, or the revolutionary character of Kalima*, Dhaka 1950; Rokeya Sakhawat Hossain, *Sultana's dream*, Madras 1905; Mohammed Mozammel Huq, *Islam Saṅgit*, Calcutta 1923; Rezaul Karim, *Pakistan examined*, Calcutta 1941; *Report on the administration of East Bengal and Assam*, 1910–1, Shillong 1912; Girish Chandra Sen, *Korān sharīph*, Calcutta 1881; Henry Vansittart, *A narrative of the transactions in Bengal from the year 1760, to the year 1764*, London 1766.

Studies

Rafiuddin Ahmed, *The Bengal Muslims, 1871–1906. A quest for identity*, Delhi 1981; Sharifuddin Ahmed, *Dhaka. A study in urban history and development*, Dhaka 2003; Wakil Ahmed, *Unish satake Bangālī Mussalmaner chinta chetanar dhara* ("Bengali Muslim thought and consciousness in the nineteenth century"), Dhaka 1983; Khondkar Alamgir, *Sultanate architecture of Bengal. An analysis of architectural and decorative programs*, Delhi 2011; A. Yusuf Ali, Karāmat ʿAlī, *EI2*; Anisuzzaman, *Muslim manas o Bangla sahitya (1757–1918)*, Dhaka 1983; Gautam Bhadrā, *Imān o nishān. Banglar krishak chaitanyer ek adhyay* ("Faith and the flag. An aspect of peasant consciousness"), Calcutta 1994; Neilesh Bose, *Recasting the region. Language, culture, and Islam in colonial Bengal*, New Delhi 2014; Kumkum Chatterjee, *The cultures of history in early modern India. Persianization and Mughal culture in Bengal*, New Delhi 2009; David L. Curley, *Poetry and history. Bengali Maṅgal-kābya and social change in precolonial Bengal*, New Delhi 2008; Richard M. Eaton, Approaches to the study of conversion to Islam in India, in Richard C. Martin (ed.), *Approaches to Islam in religious studies* (Tucson 1985), 106–23; Richard M. Eaton, *The rise of Islam and the Bengal frontier, 1204–1760*, Berkeley 1993; Marc Gaborieau, *Le mahdi incompris. Sayyid Ahmad Barelwî (1786–1831) et le millénarisme en Inde*, Paris 2010; Rajarshi Ghose, Islamic law and imperial space. British India as a "domain of Islam" circa 1803–1870, *Journal of Colonialism and Colonial History* 15/1 (2014), 141–87; Perween Hasan, *Sultans and mosques. The early Muslim architecture of Bangladesh*, London 2007; Thibaut d'Hubert, *In the shade of the Golden Palace. Alaol and Middle Bengali poetics in Arakan*, New York 2018; Muhammed Enamul Huq, *Muslim Bengali literature*, Karachi 1957; Iftekhar Iqbal, *The Bengal Delta. Ecology, state, and social change, 1840–1943*, Basingstoke 2010; Ayesha Irani, Mystical love, prophetic compassion, and ethics. An ascension narrative in the medieval Bengali *Nabīvaṃśa* of Saiyad Sultān, in Christiane Gruber and Frederick Colby (eds.), *The Prophet's ascension. Cross-cultural encounters with the Islamic miʿraj tales* (Bloomington 2010), 225–51; Narahari Kaviraj, *Wahabi and Faraizi rebels of Bengal*, New Delhi 1982; Muin-ud-din Ahmed Khan, *History of the Faraʾidi movement in Bengal, 1818–1906*, Karachi 1965; Muhammad Mojlum Khan, *The Muslim heritage of Bengal. The lives, thoughts, and great achievements of great Muslim scholars, writers, and reformers of Bangladesh and West Bengal*, Markfield, Leicestershire 2013; Azizur Rahman Mallick, *British policy and the Muslims in Bengal, 1757–1856*, Dhaka 1977; Peter J. Marshall, *Bengal. The British bridgehead. Eastern India, 1740–1928*, Cambridge 1987; Ralph Nicholas, Vaishnavism and Islam in rural Bengal, in David Kopf (ed.), *Bengal regional identity* (East Lansing 1969), 33–47; Asim Roy, *The Islamic syncretistic tradition in Bengal*, Princeton 1984; Jadunath Sarkar (ed.), *The history of Bengal. Muslim period, 1200–1757*, Patna 1973; Jagdish Narayan Sarkar, *Islam in Bengal (thirteenth to nineteenth century)*, Calcutta 1972; Vinod Kumar Saxena, *The partition of Bengal, 1905–11. Select documents*, Delhi 1987; Tony K. Stewart, In search of equivalence. Conceiving Muslim-Hindu encounter through translation theory, *History of Religions* 40/3 (2001), 260–87; Tony K. Stewart, *Fabulous females and peerless pirs. Tales of mad adventure in old Bengal*, New York 2004; Mohammad Yusuf Siddiq, An epigraphical journey to an eastern Islamic land, *Muqarnas* 7 (1990), 83–108; Layli Uddin, *In the land of eternal Eid. Maulana Bhashani and the political mobilisation of peasants and lower class urban workers in East Pakistan, c. 1930s–1971*, Ph.D. diss., University of London 2015; Sufia M. Uddin, *Constructing Bangladesh. Religion, ethnicity, and language in an Islamic nation*, Chapel Hill 2006; Willem Van Schendel, *A history of Bangladesh*, Cambridge 2009.

Neilesh Bose

Berar

Berar (Berār) is a region in the Deccan, located south of the Vindhya mountains and paralleled by the Satpura range, where the Tapti River originates. A tributary of the Tapti, the Purna, divides Berar into a northern region, containing Gawilgarh and Narnala, two of the Deccan's most impressive mountain forts, and a southwestern region bordered by the Ajanta range, east of which was the mighty fort of Mahur.

Rich in fertile black soil suited to the cultivation of cotton and lying at a trading crossroads, Berar was contested by the Malwa rulers to the north, Gujarat to the west, various semi-independent princedoms, and the Bahmanīs (r. 748–934/1347–1528 in the northern Deccan). These polities rose to power following the disintegration of the Tughluq sultanate (r. 720–815/1320–1412), the final blow to Tughluq sovereign power being the Mongol Tīmūr's (r. 771–807/1370–1405, from Samarkand) conquest of Delhi, in 800/1398.

The Fārūqī *khān*s (warlords) of Khandesh started out as Tughluq governors. Malik Rāja (r. c.784–801/c.1382–99) declared his independence a few decades after the Bahmanīs did and retained control of western Berar until the arrival, in 1009/1601, of the Mughal emperor Akbar (r. 963–1014/1556–1605). Malik Rāja chose as his capital Thalner, the site of a once important but now crumbling fort overlooking the Tapti River that retained its importance as the location of the royal necropolis of the Fārūqīs (r. c.784–1009/c.1382–1601 in northwestern Deccan). Its monumental tombs with stone-carved motifs and inscriptions are associated with the grave of Ḥaḍrat Shāh Rāja, a disciple of ʿAyn al-Mulk of Delhi (two ahistorical figures). Malik Rāja's son and successor, Nāṣir Khān (r. 801–41/1399–1437), expanded his father's profitable cultivation by moving the capital to Burhānpūr, 150 kilometres further up the Tapti River, in a prime cotton-growing zone. Burhānpūr would develop into a wealthy textile-producing centre, thereby attracting the interest of the Mughals.

Aḥmad I Shāh Bahmanī (r. 825–39/1422–36) realised the importance of Berar, both for its economic possibilities and as a buffer zone between the Deccan and the Malwa and Gujarat kingdoms. He conquered Kherla, a fort east of Khandesh of which little survives, and, in 828/1425, Mahur, in northeastern Berar. Kherla remained under Bahmanī control until 873/1469, when it returned to the Khaljī sultans of Malwa (r. 839–937/1436–1531), along with Ellichpur (Achalpur), in the northeast. Mahur, where an impressive Bahmanī gatehouse and granaries survive, came under the control of the Niẓām Shāhīs of Ahmadnagar during the second decade of the tenth/sixteenth century.

The mountain forts of Gawilgarh and Narnala in Berar's forested hinterland, in the northeastern Deccan, had been outposts of the later Bahmanī sultans of Bidar but were really under the control of local commanders such as Fatḥallāh ʿImād al-Mulk (r. 890/1485), a Hindu convert to Islam, who founded the independent ʿImād Shāhī sultanate (r. 896–982/1491–1574, in Berar) but continued to use Gawilgarh and Narnala as his headquarters. Besieged on several occasions by the armies of Ahmadnagar and Golconda, both forts succumbed in 1007/1599 to Akbar's forces, by which time the ʿImād Shāhīs had shifted their capital to Achalpur, on the plains below. By the end of the twelfth/eighteenth century, Berar had come under the sway of the Marathas, from whom it passed to the Niẓāms of Hyderabad, in 982/1574.

Bibliography

John Burton-Page, Gawilgarh, Narnala, and Thalner (three articles), in George Michell (ed.), *Indian Islamic architecture. Forms and typologies, sites and monuments* (Leiden 2008), 136–8, 168–9, and 170–6; George Michell and Helen Philon, *Islamic architecture of Deccan India. Forts, palaces, mosques and tombs*, London 2018; Radhey Shyam, The Nizam Shahis and the Imad Shahis, in *History of medieval Deccan, 1295–1724*, ed. Haroon Khan Sherwani and Purushottam Mahadev Joshi (Hyderabad 1974), 1:223–89, 491–517.

Helen Philon

al-Bīrjandī

Niẓām al-Dīn ʿAbd al-ʿAlī b. Muḥammad b. Ḥusayn **al-Bīrjandī** (d. 934/1527–8), known as ʿAbd al-ʿAlī Bīrjandī, was a renowned Persian polymath. He was born in the second half of the ninth/fifteenth century in the area of Bīrjand, the capital city of South Khurāsān province in present-day Iran. During the early years of his life he lived in and was educated in Bīrjand and Herat. There is no detailed and reliable record of his specific scientific activities and involvement in the ninth/fifteenth century. However, there are reliable sources that indicate that he was engaged in scientific work at the court of the Ṣafavid *shāh* Ismāʿīl I (r. 907–30/1501–24) in Isfahan. He died in the Bīrjand area, and was buried in a cemetery in Bujd, a village southeast of Bīrjand, where twenty members of his family are buried, including his wife and daughter.

Al-Bīrjandī wrote some of his works in his native Persian, but he wrote mostly in Arabic, in order to make his work more accessible to a wider readership. While he was known for his contributions to the fields of astronomy and mathematics, he also wrote treatises, commentaries, and books on astrology, logic, cosmology, agriculture, physics, geography, and religion. Even more impressive are his commentaries in Arabic on the Qurʾān. While some of his works are original, most of his contributions are commentaries and improvements on existing works written by others.

A total of twenty-two books, treatises, and commentaries are attributed to al-Bīrjandī, including the following:

1. *Sharḥ-i Zīj-i Khāqānī* ("Commentary on Khāqānī's Zīj"), completed in Persian in 816/1413–4. *Zīj-i Khāqānī* (by Jamshīd al-Kāshī), in Persian, is the revised version of Naṣīr al-Dīn al-Ṭūsī's (d. 672/1274) *Zīj-i Īlkhānī*, completed in Persian in 671/1272–3.

2. *Ḥāshiya dar sharḥ-i Mulakhkhaṣ* ("Supercommentary [Marginal notes] on the Commentary on the Compendium"), in Persian. The original *al-Mulakhkhaṣ fī ʿilm al-hayʾa al-basīṭa* ("Compendium on theoretical astronomy") was by Maḥmūd Chaghmīnī, completed in Arabic in 808/1405–6, with a commentary by Ṣalāḥ al-Dīn Mūsā Qāḍīzāde al-Rūmī, *Sharḥ al-Mulakhkhaṣ fī ʿilm al-hayʾa al-basīṭa* ("Commentary on the Compendium of theoretical astronomy," better known as *Mulakhkhaṣ*), completed in Arabic in 813/1410–1.

3. *Bīst bāb dar taqvīm* ("Twenty chapters on the calendar"), completed in Persian in 883/1478.

4. *Sharḥ al-Tadhkira*, completed in Arabic in 913/1507–8, a commentary on *al-Tadhkira fī ʿilm al-hayʾa* ("Memoir on astronomy") by Naṣīr al-Dīn al-Ṭūsī, completed in Arabic in 657/1258–9. Chapter 11 of the second book of al-Bīrjandī's *Sharḥ al-Tadhkira* was translated from Arabic into Sanskrit by Nayanasukhopādhyāya and Muḥammad ʿĀbida in 1729. An English translation of the Sanskrit translation, with extensive commentary, was published by Takanori Kusuba and David Pingree.

5. *Sharḥ taḥrīr al-Majisṭī* ("Commentary on the exposition of Almagest"), completed in Arabic in 921/1515–6.

6. *Sharḥ-i Zīj-i Ulugh Beg* ("Commentary on Ulugh Beg's Astronomical tables"), completed in Persian in 929/1522–3.

7. *Ābād va-ajrām* ("Distances and sizes [of celestial bodies]"), completed in Persian in 930/1523–4.

It must be noted that the authenticity of some of the works attributed to al-Bīrjandī is still in dispute and requires further study.

Bibliography

Mohammad K. Azarian, A study of Risāla al-watar waʾl jaib ("The treatise on the chord and sine"), *Forum Geometricorum* 15 (2015), 229–42, available at http://forumgeom.fau.edu/FG2015volume15/FG201523.pdf; Mohammad K. Azarian, A study of Risāla al-watar waʾl jaib ("The treatise on the chord and sine"). Revisited, *Forum Geometricorum* 18 (2018), 219–22, available at http://forumgeom.fau.edu/FG2018volume18/FG201828.pdf; Takanori Kusuba and David Pingree, *Arabic astronomy in Sanskrit. Al-Birjandī on Tadhkira II, Chapter 11 and its Sanskrit translation*, Leiden 2002; Takanori Kusuba, Bīrjandī, ʿAbd al-ʿAlī ibn Muhammad ibn Husain al-Bīrjandī, in Thomas Hockey, Virginia Trimble, Thomas R. Williams, Katherine Bracher, Richard Jarrell, Jordan D. Marché, and F. Jamil Ragep (eds.), *The biographical encyclopedia of astronomers* (New York 2007), 127; David Pingree, ʿAbd al-ʿAlī Bīrjandī, *EIr*; Mahmood Rafīʿī, *Proceedings of the International Congress in Commemoration of Bīrjandī*, Bīrjand 2002; Boris A. Rosenfeld and Ekmeleddin Ihsanoğlu, *Mathematicians, astronomers, and other scholars of Islamic civilization and their works (7th–19th c.)*, Istanbul 2003; Charles Ambrose Storey, *Persian literature. A bio-bibliographical survey* (London 1972), 2/1:80–2, no. 121.

Mohammad K. Azarian

C

Courts of law, Mughal

Mughal courts of law included various tribunals, from the court of the classical Islamic judge, the *qāḍī*, to Brahmin assemblies, merchant associations, village councils, and the courts of nobles, princes, and emperors. Evidence regarding legal institutions and practice is prolific but scattered and varies by region and period. As in Central Asia and Iran, there is no evidence of systematic registers of *qāḍī*-court decisions from the **Mughal** Empire in the manner of Ottoman *sijilāt* (Repp). Instead, source materials consist of programmatic statements in official surveys and royal chronicles, *waqāʾiʿ* (official newsletters), treatises of Islamic jurisprudence, administrative and accounting manuals, books of Persian belles-lettres (*inshāʾ*) with sections on legal formularies, and numerous collections of legal deeds belonging to propertied families and institutions and deposited in various archives and libraries across South Asia. The amount of material increases immensely from the eleventh/seventeenth century onwards. There are also two large collections of archival material related to Mughal military and revenue administration, with occasional reports of legal cases, held in archives at New Delhi and Hyderabad, respectively. Finally, there is ample, but anecdotal, evidence available in personal and collective memoirs, European travel accounts, and the records of European trading companies.

1. *Qāḍīs*' Courts

The Mughal emperors of India were Ḥanafī Sunnīs, in the tradition of several other Muslim dynasties in India. Consequently, the basic institutions of Islamic law, such as the seminary or *madrasa*, positions and offices of the judge and juriconsult (*qāḍī* and *muftī*), and the occasional censor and market supevisor (*muḥtāsib*), were well established and evident throughout the empire. All this was tempered by a Persianate imperial ideology, which insisted on the supreme authority of the ruler and his delegates, and by the predominantly non-Muslim context. In his *Āʾīn-i Akbarī* ("Rules of Akbar"), an encyclopaedic survey of the Mughal Empire completed in about 1011/1602, Abū l-Faḍl Allāmī (d. 1011/1602), a close adviser, confidant, and historiographer of the emperor Akbar (r. 963–1014/1556–1605), began the brief entry on the *qāḍī* by asserting that "the supreme authority and the redress of grievances rests with the sovereign monarchs," although, because the monarch could achieve nothing by himself, he appointed judicial delegates. The *qāḍīs*, as those delegates, were instructed to investigate cases of "oppression" thoroughly, in order to arrive at the truth. The *Āʾīn-i Akbarī* proposed splitting the office into two, *qāḍī* and *mīr ʿadl* (lit., chief of justice). It is not clear whether this was an effective proposal, but the post of *mīr ʿadl* was referred to at least once by Akbar's successor, Jahāngīr (r. 1014–37/1605–27), in his memoirs (Jahāngīr, 61). Another important office was that of the *ṣadr*, or the director of charities, which, amongst other things, supported families of Muslim religious scholars from which *qāḍīs* were appointed. During Akbar's reign, the chief *ṣadr* and the chief *qāḍī* of the empire were the same person; in subsequent reigns, these offices were separated, the *ṣadr* becoming a significant *manṣabdār* (imperial rank-holder) with considerable power over the appointment of *qāḍīs*.

The post of a *qāḍī* ranged from the prestigious positions of the *qāḍī al-quḍḍāt* (judge of judges) and *qāḍī-yi lashkar* (judge of the army) down to the practically hereditary *pargana* (district) *qāḍīs*. All *qāḍīs* were appointed by the emperor or the *ṣadr* and held office at the emperor's will. While it is not clear whether the appointment of every *qāḍī* merited an imperial order (*farmān*), many district *qāḍīs* were appointed with one (Mohiuddin, 77–8). There was no formal appellate hierarchy amongst Mughal *qāḍīs*, but special importance attached to the *qāḍī* who accompanied the mobile imperial camp, whose title as *qāḍī al-quḍḍāt*, developed in the eleventh/seventeenth century, during Jahangir's reign. Appointees to this post appear regularly in imperial chronicles. It is more difficult to form a fuller view of lower-ranking *qāḍīs*, although their ubiquity is attested to not just by the occasional appointment orders but by their notes and seals, which abound in the thousands of Persian legal documents that have survived from the Mughal era.

The *Khātima* ("Supplement") to the twelfth/eighteenth-century *Mirʾāt-i Aḥmadī* ("Mirror of Aḥmad") produced by ʿAlī Muḥammad Khān (in office 1158–1168/1746–1755), the last Mughal *dīvān* (revenue minister) of Gujarat province, is the only text that approaches the *Āʾīn-i Akbarī* in its scope. This work has a similarly short section on the role of the district *qāḍī*, noting mainly that *qāḍīs* were appointed by the *ṣadr;* that they were paid (small) cash salaries as well as land grants and that there was an associated office of *muftī* (juriconsult). The *Mirʾāt* also reproduces a *farmān* of Emperor Awrangzīb (r. 1068–1118/1658–1707), clarifying the procedural rules of *qāḍīs'* courts, mainly in relation to trials for crimes; these propose a conjoint role for the *ṣūbadār* and the *qāḍī* (Khān, *Mirʾāt*, 1:277–83). Other sources for reconstructing the role of the Mughal *qāḍī* are the prolific but unevenly comprehensive *dastūr al-ʿamals* (manuals of administration) and glossaries, many produced for the British in the twelfth/eighteenth century. These usually offer bare definitions; for example, Khᵛāja Yāsīn's dictionary, produced in the late twelfth/eighteenth century, states that the *qāḍī* is he who applies the rules of *sharīʿa*, a term he translated into English simply as "justice."

Surviving imperial and sub-imperial orders (*farmāns* and *parvānas*) from the mid-eleventh/seventeenth to the mid-twelfth/eighteenth centuries, appointing district *qāḍīs*, directed them to settle disputes, judge people for crimes, officiate at marriages, deal with inheritances and orphans, and issue legal deeds. Extant collections of documents, especially those pertaining to propertied families or religious institutions, demonstrate the importance, to both Muslims and non-Muslims, of the notarial functions of the Mughal *qāḍī*. Regardless of their religious affiliation, people found it necessary to have deeds of lease, sale, and gift (including gifts to religious institutions) endorsed and sealed by the *qāḍī*. Accountancy manuals such as the *Khulāṣat al-siyāq* ("The quintessence of accountancy"), composed in 1115/1703, possibly by Indar Sen, mention that the seal of the *qāḍī* was necessary to validate tax records forwarded from the districts to the imperial centres. European travellers noted that the *qāḍīs* of important commercial centres were charged with the evaluation of goods for the calculation of transit duties.

2. Noble and Imperial Courts

The *qāḍī*'s court was, however, only one of several tribunals available to Mughal subjects and not necessarily the most effective one. The *ṣūbadār* (provincial governor) had enormous powers, and below him, the *fawjdār* (lit., holder of troops) was an important Mughal official controlling one or more districts, who had hundreds of armed soldiers under his command to deal with tax default, rebellion, banditry, and all kinds of violent crime. There was also the *kūtvāl*, a lower-ranking officer with similar policing power. Accounts written by civilians such as the eleventh/seventeenth-century Jain merchant Banārasīdāsa suggest that such officers used rough investigatory methods, in which local connections and reputations constituted the most crucial evidence. They were able to impose harsh punishments, possibly as deterrents, with little or no reference to trained jurists.

In matters involving significant amounts of property, wealthy and powerful disputing parties, Muslims and Hindus, did take their disputes to the local *qāḍī*, but they also regularly approached the current *jāgīrdār*, the Mughal official who held the temporary rights to collect taxes in the area as his salary. In resolving the dispute, the *jāgīrdār* would naturally be concerned with maintaining the flow of revenue. He might consult the *qāḍī* but also various other administrative officials, such as the *fawjdār*, *amīn* (imperial tax-collector), and *qānūngū* (district-level keeper of revenue records). There does not appear to be a clear-cut separation of jurisdictions in these matters, but a pattern of overlaps. This is reflected in the multiple documents that record the outcome of a dispute: typical are a *parvāna* from the *jāgīrdār* and a *rāḍī-nāma* (deed of agreement) of the parties, sealed by the *qāḍī*. The best-connected individuals and entities sought to secure imperial *farmāns* confirming their rights to property and privileges. This included the European trading companies. In 1111/1699, the imperial court imposed a *muchalka* (written bond/agreement) on Dutch, English, and French merchants confirming their shared responsibility to protect shipping against and compensate for piracy in the Indian Ocean. When a prominent Indian merchant's ship was attacked in 1113/1701, the Dutch refused to pay compensation but were compelled to do so by the imperial court.

The Mughal emperors involved themselves in the dispensation of justice in various ways. A set of *farmāns* issued by Emperor Akbar, discovered and published by Irfan Habib, shows how a Hindu *rangrīz* (cloth dyer) appealed to the emperor when a Muslim debtor attempted to evade payment by accusing the *rangrīz* of insanity. The emperor ordered the *shiqdār* (police official) to ensure that the debtor was brought to the *qāḍī*'s court and not allowed to impede the course of justice. Emperor Jahāngīr installed a golden "chain of justice" for the "oppressed" who could not get justice because of the "hypocrisy" of those charged with dispensing it (Jahāngīr, 7). The aim here seems to be the same as with Akbar: to activate and supplement the existing judicial machinery rather than replace it. It was, however, a political matter where nobles were concerned; when a certain noble killed one of his guests in a wine-party, the emperor Jahāngīr ordered the noble's rank and payments to be lowered rather than any of the punishments/compensatory processes one would expect in cases of homicide (Jahāngīr, 421).

3. The Law of Mughal Courts

The law applied in all these courts was a context-specific amalgam of Islamic *fiqh* (jurisprudence), administrative rules, local custom (*dastūr*), and political expedience. Emperor Awrangzīb ʿĀlamgīr, who cultivated a reputation of piety, is also well known for having compelled the *qāḍī l-quḍāt* to find legal solutions that matched politically pre-determined outcomes, such as the execution of his brother and rival Dārā Shikūh (d. 1069/1659), the conquest of Muslim sultanates of the south, and the execution of Muslim prisoners of war. He also patronised the compilation of the largest work of Islamic jurisprudence (*fiqh*) produced in India, *al-Fatāwā l-ʿĀlamgīriyya*. Despite this conspicuous deference to Islamic legal standards, imperial nobles, even under Awrangzīb, remained contemptuous of *qāḍī*s and the justice they offered. For example, a biographical dictionary of Mughal nobles, the *Maʾāthir al-umarā*, pointed out how even eminent Muslim scholars were helpless against the pressure of emperors and nobles and that, for the hereditary village *qāḍī*s, "the registers of the *deśpāṅḍ'yā*s (village accountants) and the words of *zāmīndār*s (landlords) are their law and holy books" (Khān, *Maʾāthir al-umarāʾ*, 1:78). Such reports may, however, simply indicate that the judges of Mughal India, from *qāḍī*s to emperors, saw Islamic *fiqh* as collocated with imperial regulations and local custom, and all of this united by shared practices of documentation.

4. Community Tribunals and Assemblies

Although a commonplace, there is only limited substantial evidence for the functioning of community or profession-based self-regulatory bodies from the Mughal period. The community-based tribunals of the Julfan Armenian merchants, present in several cities of the Mughal Empire, are the best recorded. The *jumiat* (Armen., local assembly) of Armenian merchants attempted to settle disputes and, when they failed to do so, sent the details of the proceedings and any documented evidence to the assembly of merchants in New Julfa, in Isfahan, Iran. It is unclear how these assemblies enforced their decisions and any sanctions, other than through boycott. Documents preserved by a family of wealthy and well-connected Gujarati Jain merchants demonstrate how heterodox subsects of this community complained to the Mughal emperor Shāh Jahān (r. 1037–68/1628–58) about the refusal of other Jains to eat with and intermarry with them. The emperor assumed a stance of neutrality, in effect favouring the majority side; the imperial *farmān* declared that, according to *sharīʿa*, marriages and co-dining should take place only with the consent of all parties (Commissariat, 36–7).

There are very few sources available to show whether and how village level councils or *pancāyat*s, so popular in colonial and post-colonial times, may have functioned in the Mughal era, but we do have documents recording the role of village heads (*muqaddams*, *pātils*) in resolving border disputes between villages. Rosalind O'Hanlon has shown how, at least from the early seventeenth century, assemblies of Brahmins based in Banaras adjudicated disputes related to caste status and ritual rules, but their decisions applied mainly to individuals and families resident in the Marathi-speaking areas beyond the Mughal realm. The Marathi-writing areas ruled by the Bījāpūr sultanate also had a long tradition of decision-making by twinned tribunals, the *got* (community, lit., paternal lineage) assembly paired with the *majlis*, involving state officials, including the *qāḍī*. There is, however, insufficient evidence to show whether and how this system continued to function during the short period of Mughal rule in the region (1097–1136/1686–1724), after which the region came under the growing Maratha empire.

Bibliography

Published sources

Abū l-Faḍl ʿAllāmī, *Āʾīn-i Akbarī*, ed. Henry Blochman, 3 vols., Calcutta 1876[1], Calcutta 1927–49[2] (vol. 1 trans. Henry Blochman and rev. Douglas C. Phillot, vols. 2–3 trans. Henry S. Jarrett, rev. Jadunath Sarkar), repr. New Delhi 1977–8; Banārasīdāsa, *Ardhakathānaka*, ed. and trans. Mukund Lath, *Half a tale. A study in the interrelationship between autobiography and history. The Ardhakathanaka*, Jaipur 1981; M. S. (Manekshah Sorabshah) Commissariat, Imperial Mughal farmans in Gujarat, *Journal of the University of Bombay* 9 (1940), 1–56; B. N. Goswamy and J. S. Grewal (eds.), *The Mughals and the Jogis of Jakhbar. Some madad-i-maʿāsh and other documents*, Simla 1967; Brijinder Nath Goswamy and Jaswant Singh Grewal (eds.), *The Mughals and Sikh rulers and the Vaishnavas of Pindori*, Simla, 1968; Warren Hastings, *Selections from the state papers of the governors general of India*, ed. G. W. Forrest, vol. 2, Oxford 1910; Jahāngīr, *Tūzuk-i Jahāngīrī*, trans. Alexander Rogers and Henry Beveridge, 2 vols., London 1909–14; ʿAlī Muḥammad Khān, *Mirʾāt-i Aḥmadī*, ed. Syed Nawab Ali, 2 vols., Baroda 1927–8, and Supplement, 2 vols., ed. Syed Nawab Ali, Baroda 1928–30; Shāh Nawāz Khān, *Maʾāthir al-umarāʾ*, trans. Henry Beveridge and B. Prashad, Calcutta 1911–52, New Delhi 1979[2]; Francisco Pelsaert, *Remonstrantie*, trans. William Harrison Moreland and Pieter Geyl, *Jahangir's India*, Cambridge 1925; M. Z. A. Shakeb, *A descriptive catalogue of the Batala collection of Mughal documents, 1527–1757*, London 1990; N. Ahmed Siddiqui, Khulasat-us-Siyaq, *Proceedings of the Indian History Congress* 22 (1959), 282–7; Sayyid Akbarali Ibrahimali Tirmizi, *Mughal documents, 1526–1627*, New Delhi 1989.

Unpublished sources

Thomas Metcalfe, album, London, British Library, Add. Or. 5475; Batala collection of Mughal documents, London, British Library, MS I.O. (India Office) Islamic 4720; Awrangzīb's Farmān, London, British Library, MS Or 11698; *Khulāṣat al-siyāq*, London, British Library, MS Add. 6588, fols. 64–94; Khᵛāja Yāsīn's dictionary, London, British Library, MS Add. 6603, fols. 40–84; Acquired (Persian) documents, New Delhi, National Archives of India; Surat documents, Paris, BNF, MS Supplément persan 482.

Studies

Sebouh David Aslanian, *From the Indian Ocean to the Mediterranean. The global trade networks of Armenian merchants from New Julfa*, Berkeley 2011; M. L. Bhatia, *The ulama, Islamic ethics and courts under the Mughals. Aurangzeb revisited*, New Delhi 2006; Rafat M. Bilgrami, *Religious and quasi-religious departments of the Mughal period, 1556–1707*, New Delhi 1984; Nandini Chatterjee, Reflections on religious difference and permissive inclusion in Mughal law, *Journal of Law and Religion* 29/3 (2014), 396–415; Sumit Guha, The *qazi, dharmadhikari* and the judge. Political authority and legal diversity in pre-modern India, in Gijs Kruitjtzer and Thomas Ertl (eds.), *Law addressing diversity. Pre-modern Europe and India in comparison (13th–18th centuries)* (Berlin 2017), 97–115; Irfan Habib, Three early *Farmāns* of Akbar, in favour of Rāmdās, the master dyer, in Irfan Habib (ed.), *Akbar and his India* (New Delhi 1997), 270–87; Farhat Hasan, *State and locality in Mughal India. Power relations in western India, c. 1572–1730*, Cambridge 2004; Ibn Hasan, *Central structure of the Mughal Empire*, Oxford 1936, repr. Delhi 1980; Corinne Lefèvre, Beyond diversity. Mughal legal ideology and politics, in Gijs Kruitjtzer and Thomas Ertl (eds.), *Law addressing diversity. Pre-modern Europe and India in comparison (13th–18th centuries)* (Berlin 2017), 116–41; Momin Mohiuddin, *The chancellery and Persian epistolography under the Mughals*, Calcutta 1971; Rosalind O'Hanlon, Speaking from Siva's temple. Banaras scholar households and the Brahman "ecumene" of Mughal India, *South Asian History and Culture* 2/2 (2011), 253–77; Rosalind O'Hanlon, Letters home. Banaras pandits and the Maratha regions in early modern India, *Modern Asian Studies* 44/2 (2010), 201–40; M. Reza Pirbhai, A historiography of Islamic law in the Mughal Empire, in Anver M. Emon and Rumee Ahmed (eds.), *The Oxford handbook of Islamic law*, Oxford 2016, http://www.oxfordhandbooks.com/view/10.1093/oxfordhb/9780199679010.001.0001/oxfordhb-9780199679010-e-65; Om Prakash, *European commercial enterprise in pre-colonial India*, Cambridge 1998; Richard C. Repp, Courts of law, Ottoman, *EI3*; John F. Richards, *Mughal administration in Golconda*, Oxford 1975; Zameeruddin Siddiqi, The institution of *qazi* under the Mughals, *Medieval India. A Miscellany* 1 (1969), 240–59.

Nandini Chatterjee

E

Ebubekir Kani

Ebubekir Kani (Abū Bakr Kānī, also known as "Tokatlı Kani," 1124–1206/1712–91), an Ottoman poet, prose writer, and master satirist, is a leading figure in twelfth/eighteenth-century Turkish literature. He was born in Tokat, in north-central Anatolia, where he also received his elementary education. He developed an interest in poetry at an early age and made a name for himself for his wittiness in both prose and verse. Depression in his youth compelled him to become a follower of the Mevlevi (Mevlevī) *shaykh* Abdülahad (ʿAbd al-Aḥad) Dede (d. 1179/1766) and affiliate himself with the Mevlevi lodge in Tokat. He achieved recognition as a poet after he arrived in Istanbul in 1168/1755 with Hekimoğlu Ali (Ḥekīm-oghlu ʿAlī) Paşa (1100–71/1689–1758).

In Istanbul, Kani was trained in the clerical section of the *divan-ı hümayun* (*dīvān-ı hümāyūn*, imperial council) and attained the rank of *hacegan-ı divan-ı hümayun* (*khʷācegān-ı dīvān-ı hümāyūn*, senior scribe of the imperial chancery). In 1168/1755, he accompanied Ali Paşa to Silistre (Silistra, Bulgaria), after the latter was removed from the post of grand vizier. While travelling in Eflak (Wallachia), Rusçuk (Ruse, Bulgaria), and neighbouring districts, Kani met Ulah (Vlach) *beys*, for whom he performed scribal duties. He also served as the private secretary of the voivode (*voyvoda*, ruler of a province) of Wallachia İskerletzade Constantine, in Bucharest, where he wrote the work *Be-nām-ı ḥavāriyyūn-ı bürūc-ı fünūn* ("In the name of the twelve apostles of the towers of the sciences") to teach Turkish to the voivode's nephew, Alexander. In 1196/1782, at the invitation of the grand vizier Yeğen Seyyid Mehmed (Meḥmed) Paşa (d. 1202/1787), he returned to Istanbul and became the grand vizier's secretary. After being sentenced to death for disclosing secrets connected to his official duties, he was saved from execution by the *reisülküttab* (*reʾīsü l-küttāb*, head of chancery of the *divan-ı hümayun*) Hayri (Khayrī) Efendi (d. 1203/1789) and exiled to the Aegean island of Lemnos. Kani's personal correspondence from this period reveals that his life in exile was spent in hardship and poverty. After being pardoned in his later years, he returned to Istanbul where he died in 1206/1791. His grave is in

Istanbul's Eyüp cemetery, on the right side of the tomb of Feridun Paşa. Upon Kani's death, Süruri (Sürūrī, d. 1229/1814) and Sünbülzade Vehbi (Sünbül-zāde Vehbī, d. 1224/1809) composed chronograms: translated, respectively, as "Every word of his was a mine of jewels. Kani has gone" and "He has gone; he was as if a jewel, that learned Kani." Kani's works include a *divan* (*dīvān*, collection of a poet's poems), *münşeat* (*münşe'āt*, collection of letters, written by the author in a humorous style), *letaifname* (*leṭā'if-nāme*, a collection of poems of humour and *hezel*, known as *Letaif/Leṭā'if* and *Hezliyat/Hezlīyāt*), and the *Be-nām-ı ḥavāriyyūn-ı bürūc-ı fünūn*.

Various views have been advanced about Kani's association with the Mevlevis. Though he lived as a Mevlevi in Tokat, he distanced himself completely from the Mevlevi line after he came to Istanbul. His ties to the Mevlevis remained that of a *muhip* (*muḥibb*, sympathizer). His absence from the *Tedhkire-i şu'arā-yı Mevleviyye* ("Biographies of Mevlevi poets") of Esrar (Esrār) Dede (d. 1211/1797), written in 1210/1796, after Kani's death, demonstrates that he was not considered a Mevlevi poet.

Kani's prose works are more interesting and worthy of consideration than his poetry. He was the most notable humorous and satiric writer of the era, and his witty personality was always in the foreground. Shortly before his death, he remarked to friends, "Don't write *Fātiḥa* on my gravestone; I'm not a *Fātiḥa* beggar," demonstrating that his humour, which he never abandoned, pushed the limits. He was a powerful observer, looked at life through the lens of humour, and expressed his views with irony. A letter, known as *Hirrenāme*, written under the name *Tekir bint-i Pamuk* ("Tabby, daughter of Cotton"), particularly reflects his approach to humour and satire. Besides his letter to Yeğen Seyyid Mehmed Paşa, Kani's work titled *Leṭā'if* ("Witty anecdotes") offers an example of the genre of satire. In his satiric pieces he touches on important Turkish humorous characters such as Karagöz, Hacivat, Nasreddin (Naṣreddīn) Hoca, and İncili Çavuş. However, he was criticised for using slang and obscenities in his satire and witty anecdotes.

Whereas Kani's *letaifname* pushes the bounds of wit and facetiae *(hezel/hezl)* and is entirely humorous, his *divan* represents the classic tradition of Turkish poetry. He used various genres of verse in his *divan* and diverged from traditional poets, preferring to write the *tevhid* (*tevhīd*, pronouncement of God's unity), *münacat* (*münācāt*, intimate prayers to God), *naat* (*na't*, poem praising the prophet Muḥammad), and *medhiye* (*medḥīye*, eulogies) composed in *kaside (qaṣīde)* format in the form of *gazel*s (*ghazels*). Kani was a powerful observer and critic in his *kaside*s, but took great pains with his style, and was more moderate in his criticisms than the harsh, aggressive Nefi (Nef'ī, d. 1044/1635). His *gazel*s exhibit wisdom, freethinking, and a tender (loving) manner of speech. Besides social topics, his poems revolve around themes of humankind's futile struggles, destiny's unchanging nature, the world's insignificance, transitoriness, material pleasures, the beloved, alcohol, and grievances about fate.

Bibliography

Faṭīn, *Hātimetü'l-eş'ār* (Istanbul 1271/1855), 352 ff.; Mu'allim Nācī, *Esāmī* (Istanbul 1308/1892), 261–2; Ebüzziya Tevfik, *Nümune-i edebiyat-ı Osmaniye* (Istanbul 1308/1892), 43–61; Mehmet Süreyya, *Sicill-i Osmani* (Istanbul 1311/1895), 4:74; Şemseddīn

Sāmī, *Qamūsü'l-a'lām* (Istanbul 1314/1898), 5:3819; Şehābeddīn Süleymān, *Tārīkh-i edebiyāt-ı Osmāniye* (Istanbul 1328/1912), 231–9; Ahmed Rifat, *Lügat-ı tarihiyye ve coğrafiye* (Istanbul 1330/1914), 6:70; Bursalı Mehmet Tahir, *Osmanlı müellifleri* (Istanbul 1333/1917), 2:392–3; Sadettin Nüzhet Ergun, *Tanzimata kadar muhtasar Türk edebiyatı tarihi ve nümuneleri*, Istanbul 1931; Yusuf Atılgan, *Tokatlı Kânî, sanatı, şahsiyet ve psikolojisi*, master's thesis, Istanbul University 1944; E. J. W. Gibb, *A history of Otoman poetry*, (London 1967), 4:159–74; Vasfi Mahir Kocatürk, *Türk edebiyatı tarihi*, Ankara 1970; Sırrı Akıncı, Hekimoğlu Ali Paşa ve Kâni Efendi, *Hayat-Tarih Mecmuası* 2/9 (1971), 14–17; Nihat Sami Banarlı, *Resimli Türk edebiyatı tarihi* (Istanbul 1971), 2:751–2; Faruk Kadri Timurtaş, *Tarih içinde Türk edebiyatı* (Istanbul 1981), 254–5; Sabahattin Küçük, Divan edebiyatında sosyal tenkid. Ebû Bekir Kâni Efendi'nin hasbihâli, *Türk Kültürü* 262 (1985): 21–128; Haluk İpekten et al., *Başlangıcından günümüze büyük Türk klâsikleri* (Istanbul 1988), 7:21–3; Önder Göçgün, *Türk edebiyatı araştırmaları* (Konya 1991), 1:153–60; Muhittin Eliaçık, *Tokatlı Kânî divanının tenkitli metni, hayatı, kişiliği, vazifeleri, eserleri, dili, sanatı ve üslubu*, master's thesis, Istanbul University 1992; Cemal Kurnaz (ed.), *Osmanlı şâirleri* (Istanbul 1995), 256–9; H. Dilek Batislam, *Kâni'nin mensur letâifnâmesi ve hezliyyâtı*, Ph.D. diss., Çukurova University, Adana 1997; Bilal Elbir, *Kani divanı üzerine bir inceleme*, master's thesis, Dokuz Eylül University, Izmir 1997; Erdoğan Erbay, *Eskiler ve yeniler*, Erzurum 1997; Dilek Batislam, Kâni'nin mensur letaifnamesi ve hezliyatı, *Çukurova Üniversitesi Sosyal Bilimler Dergisi* 5/5 (1998), 181–5; Durmuş Ali Çıraklı, *Kânî'nin manzum letâifnâmesi. İnceleme-metin*, master's thesis, Çukurova University, Adana 1998; Hakkı Süha Gezgin and Beşir Ayvazoğlu (eds.), *Edebi portreler*, Istanbul 1999; Cemal Kurnaz and Mustafa Tatçı (eds.), *Tuhfe-i Nâilî* (Ankara 2001), 2:848–9; Ahmet Atilla Şentürk and Ahmet Kartal, *Eski Türk edebiyatı tarihi*, Istanbul 2004; Osman Horata, Son klâsik dönem, in Talât Sait Halman, *Türk edebiyatı tarihi* (Istanbul 2007), 2:476–8; İlyas Yazar, *Kâni dîvânı tenkidli metin ve tahlil*, Istanbul 2010; Fevziye Abdullah Tansel, Kânî, *Türk ansiklopedisi* (Ankara 1974), 21:204; Atilla Özkırımlı, Kânî, *Türk edebiyatı ansiklopedisi* (Istanbul 1984), 3:715–6; *Ana Britanica*, Kânî, (Istanbul 1988), 12:515; *Türk dili ve edebiyatı ansiklopedisi*, Kânî, (Istanbul 1988), 5:145–6; Th. Menzel, Kānī, *EI1*; J.R. Walsh, Kānī, *EI2*; Kânî, *İA* 6:158–9; İsa Kayaalp, Kânî, *TDVİA* 24:306–7.

İlyas Yazar

Education in West Africa

Islamic **education** has been an essential component of Islam in **West Africa** since its introduction by the fourth/tenth century. The celebrated Moroccan traveller Ibn Baṭṭūṭa (d. 770 or 779/1368 or 1377), who visited the empire of Mali in the eighth/fourteenth century, noted with approval the Malian emphasis on memorisation of the Qurʾān. He observed children shackled in chains until they had committed to memory the passages from the Qurʾān that their teacher had assigned. Teachers since then have refrained from such extreme measures, but classical Qurʾānic education in West Africa has remained focused on the proper recitation and, ideally, the memorisation of the Qurʾān.

1. Before colonialism

Before the colonial period, Islam was the religion of a minority in most of West Africa. Even in Muslim communities, Islamic education was often restricted to children (in many cases to boys) from clerical lineages, and only a few in any given location were actually specialised in advanced Islamic learning. For most pupils, the aim of this education was to teach them proper modes of prayer and ablutions and the ability to recite accurately from a written text in Arabic and presumably to understand its meaning in general terms. The teacher would write a text in black ink on a wooden writing tablet for the pupil to learn. When the pupil demonstrated the ability to recite the text with absolute accuracy, the ink was washed off and the text replaced by a new one. Pupils did not take the writing boards home with them but left them with their teacher. Each pupil proceeded at his own pace. A group of pupils would simultaneously study different texts. Pupils would continue until they had recited the entire Qurʾān (or sometimes only half). If a pupil wished to proceed, he would repeat the process of reciting the Qurʾān several times, acquiring increasing familiarity not only with the text but also with the Arabic language. There was never a fee for instruction, but parents generally gave gifts to the teacher, which, if the instructors were powerful and prosperous, might be very generous. Pupils, especially those who boarded with a teacher, were often expected to perform household chores or to work in the teacher's fields. Such expectations were hardly exploitative, as they would have performed similar tasks had they remained at home. Teachers were not expected to feed boarders, who begged for food in the evening, relying on the charity of community members.

2. Advanced studies

Few students proceeded beyond this level. Those who chose to pursue their studies further were, for the most part, from specialised clerical lineages and generally began their studies with their father or some other learned senior kinsman. Mālikī *fiqh* (jurisprudence) was the first and, in many cases, the primary focus of study. The most common elementary text was *Mukhtaṣar fī l-ʿibādāt* ("The précis on adoration"), a manual of ritual duties by the Algerian author al-Akhḍarī (d. 953/1546). The *Risāla* ("Treatise") by al-Qayrawānī (d. 386/996), a leading scholar of the Mālikī law school in fourth/tenth-century North Africa, was a more comprehensive survey, while the *Mukhtaṣar* ("Précis") of Khalīl b. Isḥāq (d. c.776/1374–5) was more difficult. In Qurʾānic exegesis, the most fundamental text was the *Tafsīr al-Jalālayn* ("The Qurʾānic commentary by the two Jalāls") by Jalāl al-Dīn al-Maḥallī (from Cairo, d. 864/1459) and Jalāl al-Dīn al-Suyūṭī (born in Cairo, but of Persian origin, d. 911/1505). Other subjects included Arabic syntax, devotional poetry, *tawḥīd* (theology) and, primarily beginning in the twelfth/eighteenth century, *taṣawwuf* (Ṣūfism). Although the various works studied in West Africa, as evidenced by the contents of libraries throughout the region, tended to constitute a common core, there was no fixed order in which these books were studied, and students proceeded at their own pace. The most ambitious and advanced students would travel, often long distances, to study particular works with specific teachers. Centres of learning tended to be in large trading towns. Alongside the more formal curriculum, there was a large corpus of esoteric knowledge, such as talismans and techniques of divination, that constituted a more secret fund of knowledge transmitted from teacher to student.

At all levels, from Qurʾānic education to advanced learning, the personal bond between teacher and student was permanent and fundamental. Teachers exercised quasi-parental authority over their students, not only during their studies but in later life. A student would be awarded a chain of transmission *(isnād)* at the end of his studies. The identity of his teacher, and of his teacher's teacher, guaranteed the quality of his knowledge. The very nature of instruction ensured the thorough personalisation of Islamic knowledge.

3. Under colonial rule

The advent of colonial rule led to sweeping changes in Islamic education. Initially, the political and economic transformation of West African society under colonialism actually favoured widespread Islamisation and brought an increasing number of children into Qurʾānic schools, but the French and English colonial schools constituted a rival system of education underpinned by a radically different epistemology of learning. There were important differences between the colonial powers. The French administration was aggressively secularist and suspicious of all forms of religious education, especially Islamic education. Early on, they did create a few hybrid French-Islamic schools, but their attempts were half-hearted and generally unsuccessful. The British relied extensively on Christian missionaries as teachers, creating a different set of problems, but were, for that very reason, less averse to religious education in principle. Most notably, in northern Nigeria, the British created the Northern Provinces Law School (later the School for Arabic Studies) to train Islamic notables such as *qāḍīs* (judges). Even so, many Muslims perceived colonial schools as either Christian or, at best, secular, and ideologically hostile to Islam, and they preferred to continue sending their children to Qurʾānic schools.

In the late colonial period, after the Second World War, the Qurʾānic schools began to face opposition from within the Muslim community. In particular in francophone colonies, young men who had returned from study at al-Azhar (in Cairo), influenced by new styles of Islamic reform, found the Qurʾānic schools ideologically and pedagogically inadequate. They created a new form of religious school, structured much like colonial schools, with classrooms and curricula but with a strictly Islamic content. These schools challenged the authority not only of the colonial powers but also of established Islamic (particularly Ṣūfī) leadership, and they aroused considerable hostility.

4. After independence

Immediately following independence, positions at all levels of the government bureaucracy suddenly became open to Africans educated in colonial schools, and government schooling became an increasingly attractive option, even for Muslim parents who had heretofore expressed reservations about this sort of education. African governments easily obtained loans from the World Bank along with other major international banks, alongside development aid from European and North American governments, which they used, in part, to expand the educational sector. In the 1980s, however, it became increasingly clear that such expansion was unsustainable, and international donors subjected African countries to programmes of structural adjustment that radically downsized the government sector, including education. Government schools declined rapidly in quality, and there were, in any case, few government jobs available to those leaving school. Private Islamic schools became an increasingly attractive alternative. Many of these were hybrid, offering education both in Arabic and in either English or French. They were modelled after Western schools, with grades, classrooms, textbooks, and blackboards and were quite unlike Qurʾānic schools, even though they taught Islamic values and religious knowledge. In some instances, they received financial assistance from Saudi Arabia or the Gulf States. Some of the graduates went on to study in Saudi Arabia, particularly at the University of Medina, after which they might return to these same schools as teachers. Until recently, African governments were reluctant to recognise diplomas from these schools, and graduates were prevented from pursuing their education at higher levels in their own country. Even so, the French or English literacy and numeracy taught in the schools was useful to graduates, even in the informal sector.

In 1987, an Islamic university, offering instruction exclusively in Arabic, was opened in Say, in Niger. At last, Islamic education in West Africa was not limited to primary and (more rarely) secondary schooling. Even so, the costs of such modernised forms of Islamic education, while they remain modest, are still out of the reach of many poorer families, especially in rural areas. For such pupils, Qurʾānic schools remain a viable option. As a result, the kind of education children receive is increasingly aligned with class. Elite students, Muslim and otherwise, are most likely to attend exclusive Western-style private schools. Middle-class Islamic students are more likely to attend modernised Franco-Arabic or Anglo-Arabic schools, which are increasingly achieving recognition from African governments, while the poorest Muslim students are educated in Qurʾānic schools.

Bibliography

Louis Brenner, *Controlling knowledge. Religion, power and schooling in a West African Muslim society*, Bloomington 2001; Bruce S. Hall and Charles C. Stewart, The historic "core curriculum" and the book market in Islamic West Africa, in Graziano Krätli and Ghislaine Lydon (eds.), *The trans-Saharan book trade* (Leiden 2011), 109–74; Hannah Hoechner, *Quranic schools in northern Nigeria. Everyday experiences of youth, faith, and poverty*, Cambridge 2018; Ousmane Oumar Kane, *Beyond Timbuktu. An intellectual history of Muslim West Africa*, Cambridge MA and London 2016; Robert Launay (ed.), *Islamic education in Africa. Writing boards and blackboards*, Bloomington 2016; Renaud Santerre, *Pédagogie musulmane d'Afrique noire*, Montreal 1973; Rudolph T. Ware III, *The walking Qurʾān. Islamic education, embodied knowledge, and history in West Africa*, Chapel Hill 2014.

Robert Launay

F

Farrukhzād, Furūgh

Furūgh Zamān **Farrukhzād** (1313–45sh/1935–67), among the greatest Iranian poets of the twentieth century, was born in Tehran to a family that valued art and literature. She attended school in Tehran and was married in 1951 at the age of sixteen, becoming a mother in the following year. Renouncing family life, she divorced her husband in 1954, considering marital life an obstacle to her literary passions.

Farrukhzād began to compose verse in a classical style while still a teenager. Her first poetic collection, titled *Asīr* ("The captive") was published in 1955. The collection contained forty-four poems, mainly focussed on the sense of oppression and imprisonment of a woman's life. In these first poems Farrukhzād describes the most intimate sensations of the female body, she desires and demands, but at the same time she implicitly expresses the frustrations and social limitations suffered by women. Already in this period Farrukhzād distanced herself from contemporary female poets who continued to express themselves using language and themes shared with male poets (Milani, Love and sexuality, 117–28). Her poetry had an often negative response in the society of the time, something which, together with other personal reasons, caused her a crisis and contributed in 1955 to her hospitalisation in a psychiatric clinic (Jalālī, Introduction, 15–8).

With two subsequent poetic collections, *Dīvār* ("The wall," 1956), containing twenty-five compositions, and *ʿIsyān* ("Rebellion," 1958), with seventeen poems, Farrukhzād found a well-defined place in the intellectual and literary circles of Tehran. Her individual rebellion almost involuntarily took on social forms and embodied a collective rebellion that in those years penetrated into the consciousness and identity of Iranian society (Karimi-Hakkak, 18–20; Kadkanī, 69–77). In the poems of these collections Farrukhzād presented herself to be unscrupulous, sometimes even "sinning" without hesitation, her intention being to deal with entrenched prejudices: *Gunāh kardam gunāh-ī pur zi lidhdhat | dar āghūsh-ī ki garm-u ātashīn būd* (I sinned, a sin full of enjoyment | in the arms of a warm and fiery man, *Majmūʿa*, 121).

Travel contributed to the maturation of Farrukhzād's poetic language, along with activity in other artistic fields (such as painting, theatre, and cinema) and the political vicissitudes of her country. A close acquaintance with Ibrāhīm Gulistān (1922–), a well-known director and writer, led to collaboration in productions such as *Khāna siyāh ast* ("The house is black," 1963), a successful blend of poetry and cinema that documented the raw everyday life of Tabriz's lepers. The film won the first prize at the Überhausen International Film Festival (Karāchī, 45–59).

In the 1960s Farrukhzād published *Tavallud-ī dīgar* ("Another birth," 1964), with thirty-five poems. According to critics, this was her best collection, truly representing the birth of an autonomous and original female voice in twentieth-century Persian poetry (Barāhinī, 405–8). In this more mature phase Farrukhzād welcomed principles of "new poetry" *(shiʿr-i naw)*, a style that significantly differed from classical Persian poetry in both form and content. Indeed, Farrukhzād abandoned the traditional prosodic rules in favour of a certain strophic fluidity and a much freer structure of verse, even though she did not reject rhythmic research (Lazard, 223–9; Kadkanī, 76–7). She adopted fresher and more colloquial language, often of nostalgic but sometimes of satirical tone, and a style characterised by abundant symbolism. The content of her poems in this period is closely connected with everyday life, the various angles of which are carefully and intimately explored. Her verses often have an autobiographical character but through her personal explorations she broaches themes and motives—such as love, death, night, vision, eternity, and loneliness—which concern all.

In her poems Farrukhzād perceives anxiety for the evanescence of things, the transience of time, ephemeral happiness, but also a certain feeling of self-identification with nature. Poetry was for her like a "window" that opened onto a utopian world, and is an instrument capable of defeating death because, in the end, as stated by the title of one of her poems, *Tanhā ṣidā-st ki mīmānad* (Only voice remains, *Majmūʿa*, 411).

Farrukhzād died in Tehran in a road accident on 13 February 1967 at the age of 32. After her death a collection titled *Īmān biyāvarīm bi āghāz-i faṣl-i sard* ("Let us believe in the coming of the cold season") was published in 1974. Containing seven compositions, this posthumously published collection did not, from a formal perspective, differ much from her previous collection.

Bibliography

Main Works

Furūgh Farrukhzād, *Asīr*, Tehran 1334sh/1955; Furūgh Farrukhzād, *Dīvār*, Tehran 1335sh/1956; Furūgh Farrukhzād, *ʿIṣyān*, Tehran 1337sh/1958; Furūgh Farrukhzād, *Tavallud-ī dīgar*, Tehran 1343sh/1964; Furūgh Farrukhzād, *Īmān biyāvarīm bi āghāz-i faṣl-i sard*, Tehran 1353sh/1974; Furūgh Farrukhzād, *Majmūʿa-yi kāmil-i shiʿrhā*, Frankfurt 2003.

Studies

Riḍā Barāhinī, *Ṭalā dar mis. Dar shiʿr va shāʿirī* (Tehran 1358sh/1979[3]), 2:390–412; Dominic P. Brookshaw and Nasrin Rahimieh, *Forugh Farrokhzad. Poet of modern Iran. Iconic women and feminine pioneer of new Persian poetry*, London 2010; Abd al-ʿAlī Dastghayb, *Parī-yi kūchak-i daryā. Naqd va taḥlīl-i shiʿr-i Furūgh Farrukhzād*, Tehran 1385sh/2006; Michael C. Hillmann, *A lonely woman. Forugh Farrokhzad and her poetry*, Washington D.C. 1987; Muḥammad Huqūqī, *Shiʿr-i zamān-i mā. Furūgh Farrukhzād*, Tehran 1372sh/1993; Amīr Ismāʿīlī and Abū l-Qāsim Ṣidārat, *Jāvidāna Furūgh Farrukhzād*, Tehran 1347sh/

1968; Bihrūz Jalālī (ed.), Introduction, in *Dīvān-i ashʿār-i Furūgh Farrukhzād*, Tehran 1371sh/1992; Bihrūz Jalālī, *Furūgh Farrukhzād. Jāvidāna zīstan dar awj māndan*, Tehran 1375sh/1996[2]; Muḥammad Riḍā Shafīʿī Kadkanī, *Advār-i shiʿr-i Fārsī. Az mashrūṭiyyat tā suqūṭ-i salṭanat*, Tehran 1383sh/2004[2]; Rūḥangīz Karāchī, *Furūgh. Yāghī-yi maghmūm*, Tehran 1376sh/1997; Rūḥangīz Karāchī, *Furūgh Farrukhzād. Hamrāh bā kitābshināsī*, Shiraz 1383sh/2004; Ahmad Karimi-Hakkak, *An anthology of modern Persian poetry* (Boulder 1978), 18–20,137–59; Gilbert Lazard, La versification de Foruq Farroxzād, *SIr* 12/2 (1983), 223–9; Farzaneh Milani, Love and sexuality in the poetry of Forugh Farrokhzād. A reconsideration, *Iranian Studies* 15/1–4 (1982), 117–28; Farzaneh Milani, *Veils and words. The emerging voices of Iranian women writers* (Syracuse 1992), 127–52; Farzāna Mīlānī, *Furūgh Farrukhzad. Zindigī-nāma-yi adabī hamrāh bā nāmahā-yi chāp nashuda*, Toronto 2016; Sīrūs Shamīsā, *Nigāh-ī bi-Furūgh Farrukhzād*, Tehran 1376/1997[3].

Nahid Norozi

G

Ghallāb, ʿAbd al-Karīm

ʿAbd al-Karīm Ghallāb (1919–2017), a Moroccan writer, intellectual, and journalist, was born in Fez. He pursued his studies at the Qarawiyyīn University in Fez before travelling in 1937 to Cairo, where he stayed until 1948, completing graduate studies. It was in Egypt that Ghallāb interacted with major Arab writers and critics, such as Ṭāhā Ḥusayn (1889–1973), Tawfīq al-Ḥakīm (1898–1987), ʿAbbās Maḥmūd al-ʿAqqād (1889–1969), and Muḥammad Mandūr (1907–65), among others. Because of his realistic style and representation of the transformation of Moroccan society in the twentieth century, he has been described as both "the Moroccan debtor of [the Egyptian Najīb] Maḥfūẓ, founder of the Moroccan novel tradition" (Parrilla, 79) and the representative author of the Moroccan novel in its fundamental form (al-Allam, 45).

One of the most prolific and academically influential Moroccan writers in Arabic, as well as a prominent journalist of the twentieth and early twenty-first centuries, he wrote more than seventy books, both fiction and non-fiction, on a variety of subjects, including social criticism, national history, Islam, Moroccan politics, and democracy.

As an important Moroccan intellectual, his political affiliations and vision informed his career; his work traces the growth of nationalist ideology and the trajectory of the Istiqlāl party—the political party of independence that grew out of the resistance movement in the 1940s and 1950s. He served as a member of its central committee and was editor-in-chief of its newspaper *al-ʿAlam* until 2004. He was also one of the founding members of the Moroccan Writers Union and served as its president (1958–76). As an ardent nationalist, he often saw himself as a defender of both Arab identity and Islamic values; his works serve as illustrations of the thought of the Istiqlāl party and of its ideologue, ʿAllāl al-Fāsī (1910–74).

Most of Ghallāb's literary work fictionalises historical events that trace the transformation of Moroccan society and politics from the colonial period to independence—especially from the 1930s to the 1950s. While in his first novel, *Sabʿat abwāb* ("Seven gates," 1965), Ghallāb explores the experience of political imprisonment under the French colonial regime, in his two most famous novels, *Dafannā l-Māḍī* ("We have buried the past," 1963) and *al-Muʿallim ʿAlī* ("Master ʿAli," 1971), he focuses on concepts of political commitment and the promotion of the Istiqlāl nationalist ideology. In *Dafannā l-Māḍī*, his most famous novel, the transition from protectorate to independence is explored through the drama of al-Ḥājj al-Tahāmī's bourgeois household in Fez. Through the transformation of one of the family's sons, ʿAbd al-Raḥmān, the narrative brings to life the emergence of nationalist consciousness. The novel ends with the return of King Muḥammad V from exile and the death of the family patriarch. In the sequel, *al-Muʿallim ʿAlī*, Ghallāb focuses on the struggle of the lower social classes. The central character, ʿAli, initially suffers hardships as an apprentice in various crafts, but is then employed at a French factory and becomes involved in the intrigues of unionism—a struggle that reflects the growth of his political and nationalist consciousness and parallels the nation's collective march towards political action and maturation.

Ghallāb's other novels include *Ṣabāḥ wa-yazḥaf al-layl: riwāya* ("Morning and crawl of the night: a novel," 1984), in which he explores the alienation faced by two young Moroccans, Qāsim and Rāqiya, during the independence era and the lure of western values. This theme resurfaces in his last novel, *Sharqiyya fī Pārīs: riwāya* ("An oriental woman in Paris: a novel," 2006), where the cultural clash between East and West is resolved through the successful marriage of Sāmiya, a Syrian student in Paris, to her French professor, François.

When viewed together, these novels, studies, and memoirs provide varied depictions of socio-cultural and political trends in Morocco and illustrate the ideology of Moroccan nationalism as represented by the Istiqlāl party.

Bibliography

Works by ʿAbd al-Karīm Ghallāb

ʿAbd al-Karīm Ghallāb, *Sabʿat abwāb*, Cairo 1965; ʿAbd al-Karīm Ghallāb, *Dafannā al-māḍī*, Beirut 1966; ʿAbd al-Karīm Ghallāb, *al-Muʿallim ʿAlī*, Beirut 1971; ʿAbd al-Karīm Ghallāb, *Taʾrīkh al-ḥaraka al-waṭaniyya al-Maghribiyya*, Casablanca 1976; ʿAbd al-Karīm Ghallāb, *Ṣabāḥ wa-yazḥaf al-layl. Riwāyah*, Beirut 1984; ʿAbd al-Karīm Ghallāb, *Sharqiyya fī bārīs. Riwāya*, Rabāṭ 2006; ʿAbd al-Karīm Ghallāb, *al-Aʿmāl al-kāmila*, Rabat 2001.

Studies

ʿAbd al-Raḥīm al-ʿAllām, *Bibliyūghrāfiyā l-riwāya al-Maghribiyya al-maktūbah bi-l-ʿArabiyya, 1942–1999*, Rabat 2000; ʿAbd al-Raḥīm al-ʿAllām (ed.), *Suʾāl al-ḥadātha fī l-riwāya al-Maghribiyya*, Casablanca 1999; Ahmed Idrissi Alami, Moroccan nation-building and the bildungsroman in ʿAbdelkarīm Ghallāb's *Dafannā al-Māḍī* and *al-Muʿallim ʿAli*, *MEL* 16/2 (2013), 1–16; Ian Campbell, The cell and the ward. Imprisonment, servitude and nationalist identity in two novels by ʿAbdalkarīm Ghallāb, *MEL*, 11/3 (2008), 303–15; Ḥamīd Laḥmidānī, *Min ajl taḥlīl ṣūsyū-bināʾī lil-riwāya. Riwāyat* al-Muʿallim ʿAlī *numūdhajan*, Morocco 1984; Gonzalo Fernández Parrilla, Breaking the canon. Zafzaf, Laroui and the Moroccan novel, in Stephan Guth and Gail Ramsay (eds.), *From new values to new aesthetics. Turning points in modern Arabic literature*, vol. 2: *Postmodernism and thereafter* (Wiesbaden 2011), 75–84; Said Graiouid, We have not buried the simple past. The public sphere and post-colonial literature in Morocco, *Journal of African Cultural Studies*, 20/2 (2008), 145–58.

Ahmed Idrissi Alami

Gulbarga

Gulbarga was selected by ʿAlāʾ al-Dīn Bahman Shāh (r. 748–59/1347–58), the founder of the Bahmanī dynasty (r. 748–

934/1347–1527 in the northern Deccan), as the second capital of his kingdom, after the short-lived initial choice of Dawlatābād. Gulbarga is in present-day northern Karnataka and straddles the boundary between the Indo-Aryan Marathi (Marāt'hī) and Dravidian Kannada languages. Its fertile black soils of basaltic origin, rich in crops such as sugarcane, sunflower, gram (whole pulses), and *bajra* (a type of millet), and its many water sources, both natural and engineered, account, in part, for its choice as the Bahmanī capital.

1. Historical background

Gulbarga owes its built landscape and continuing importance to Fīrūz Shāh Bahmanī (r. 800–25/1397–1422). His invitation to the Chishtī scholar and exegete Sayyid Muḥammad Gīsū Darāz (d. 825/1422) to settle in Gulbarga made it the Bahmanīs' most sacred city. Thanks to the presence of Gīsū Darāz's *dargāh* (shrine), this distinction persisted even after the transfer of the capital to Bīdar in about 834/1431 (the Chishtiyya probably originated in Chisht, near Herat, towards the end of the sixth/twelfth century, and was introduced into India by Chishtī Muʿīn al-Dīn Ḥasan Sijzī, commonly known as Muʿīn al-Dīn Chishtī, d. 633/1236).

Gulbarga was the capital of the rising political and economic Bahmanī power following Tīmūr's (r. 771–807/1370–1405) invasion of India in 800/1398 and was a venerated spiritual centre, thanks to its various *khānaqā*s (Ṣūfī convents) and *dargāhs*, founded by charismatic spiritual leaders. Gulbarga attracted settlers from across the Islamic world, as well as from Hindustan. Together, these diverse communities promulgated a hybrid architectural style, indebted to local vernacular, Persian, and other traditions and contributing to the creation of an architectural matrix impregnated with sacrality. This style was first formulated in the visual emblems of the Bahmanīs and in styles that continued to inspire their successors in Gulbarga, the ʿĀdil Shāhīs (r. from Bījāpūr 895–1097/1490–1686). Their indebtedness to local traditions is conveyed clearly in several monuments; the new architectural forms they devised remained particular to Gulbarga and its neighbourhood.

2. Architecture

Gulbarga consists of a walled fort and two open urban areas that evolved organically northwest and southeast of Gulbarga Fort. Originally oval in plan, a rectangular section was added to the fort on its northwestern, northern, and northeastern sides, probably during the reign of Fīrūz Shāh and when the eastern section of the Hāthī Darwāza (Elephant Gate) was built and the East Gate added. The ʿĀdil Shāhīs extended the Hāthī Darwāza, giving it an impressive protective horn-shaped profile for its defence.

Stone revetments were affixed to the Fort's wall probably during the ʿĀdil Shāhī period and at the time the fortified embrace known as Bālā Ḥiṣār was constructed around the *ivān* audience hall of the early Bahmanīs (the Pers. *īvān*/Ar. *īwān* is a vaulted hall open on one side). This was a two-level edifice with monumental transverse arches, indebted to Tughluq courtly structures (the Tughluqs ruled over the Delhi sultanate from 720/1320 to 815/1412). It was aligned with the South Gate of the fort, suggesting the existence of a ceremonial avenue connecting this gate to the first Bahmanī audience hall. The dome of this gate has been blocked by a bastion and, being situated at the lowest level of the fort, has been partly buried under runoff sedimentation. The gate opened onto a pre-Islamic water reservoir on its southeast and a ceremonial avenue framed by two columned platforms within the fort, suggesting the existence of a ceremonial avenue connecting this gate to the first Bahmanī audience hall.

Southwest of the *iwān* audience hall stands the Great Mosque, which probably began as the Hazār Sutūn (Thousand Pillar) Palace of Fīrūz Shāh Bahmanī in about 809/1407, soon after his marriage to the daughter of the raja of the Hindu kingdom of Vijayanagar (736–972/1336–1565). Thanks to its directional orientation, this audience hall could function also as a mosque, even though it has none of the attributes that distinguish Deccani mosques.

Missing are the projecting vertical shaft on the façade of its western or *qibla* wall found in all other Deccani examples that marks the presence of the main *miḥrāb* on the inside, the courtyard and the *mulūk khāna* (royal enclosure) found in all congregational mosques. Exemplifying a mixture of spiritual and royal traditions associated with the abode of Solomon and Jamshid—in mediaeval Persian lore Jamshid was the greatest ruler of Iran and was analogous to the sagacious biblical king Solomon—which was, according to Persian lore, located in the Apadana of Persepolis, the royal audience hall of the Achaemenid kings of Iran (550–330 C.E.), this emblematic edifice also employed decorative schemes seen in the Elephant Stables of Vijayanagar. The architectural evidence indicates that this palace/audience hall was probably converted to a mosque during the Mughal (932–1274/1526–1858) or ʿĀsaf Jāhī (1724–1948, Hyderabad, Deccan) occupation of the Deccan from about the middle of the eleventh/seventeenth century.

The influence of local traditions became more pronounced during the reign of Fīrūz Shāh, perhaps to counterbalance the growing influence of gifted immigrants from Central Asia, Iran, the Arab world, and Anatolia. The latter were invited and encouraged to settle in peninsular India by Bahmanī and later sultans. Westerners were known as *āfāqī* or *gharbī*. Also part of the socio-political order in peninsular India were the Dakhinīs (Muslims from Hindustan, Deccani converts, and Abyssinian slaves), who joined a local Hindu majority and would be responsible for perennial problems, including the division into essentially two opposing socio-political groups that contributed to the disintegration of the Bahmanī kingdom.

There are two other mosques in the fort. The Ladies' Mosque dates from the early ninth/fifteenth century, and the *masjid* on the northwestern side of the bazaar is from the ʿĀdil Shāhī era. Begun by Fīrūz Shāh, the bazaar street started north of the Bālā Ḥiṣār and ended a few metres east of the Hāthī Gate. Northwest of and outside the Hāthī Gate another commercial avenue connected the Fort to the Shāh Bāzār *jāmiʿ*, the only congregational mosque in Gulbarga. Its closest parallel is found in the royal foundation of Fīrūzābād, a few kilometres southwest of Gulbarga.

Near the Shāh Bāzār mosque is the *dargāh* of Shaykh Sirāj al-Dīn Junaydī (d. 781/1380), the spiritual adviser of the kingdom's founder and his immediate successors. In the same funerary garden, denoting the commitment of the ʿĀdil Shāhīs to the Gulbarga *dargāhs*, is the tomb of Nāṣir al-Dīn Uways, a descendant of Sirāj al-Dīn (and his fourth spiritual successor) and a spiritual adviser of Yūsuf ʿĀdil Khān (r. 895–916/1490–1510).

It is the architectural and ornamental styles and themes of Bahmanī Gulbarga that inspired the decorative repertoire of Uways's sepulchre. These archaising visual expressions are also found in the tomb of his venerated ancestor implying that work was also undertaken in his tomb during the late 9th/15th–early 10th/16th century. For the monumental two-storeyed gateway to this *dargāh*—distinguished by its lofty minarets inspired by those in the *madrasa* of Maḥmud Gāvān, the first minister of the Bahmanī sultanate (in office 862–86/1468–81) and completed in 876/1472 in Bīdar—the ʿĀdil Shāhīs devised a new architectural model that remained particular to Gulbarga.

East of the Fort, a similar gateway stands outside the entrance to the *dargāh* of Gīsū Darāz, along the northwestern shore of a reservoir, built or restored by Fīrūz Shāh Bahmanī. A devotee of this *dargāh* and the person responsible for the majestic single-arched gate that opened onto Fīrūz Shāh's reservoir was Afḍal Khān (fl. eleventh/seventeenth century), the minister of Bījāpūr's last two sultans. Below it was built a pavilion covered by a Bangla type of roof (refers to the paddy-roofed buildings of rural Bengal). East of this *dargāh* is the presumed tomb of Chand Bībī (d. 1008/1599–1600), the widowed wife of ʿAlī I (r. 965–87/1558–79) who purposefully fought the Mughals.

On the western shore of this reservoir is the Haft Gumbad (Seven Domes), the second royal necropolis of the Bahmanīs and the burial place of Fīrūz Shāh. His two-chambered tomb has Tīmūrid associations, but, in its decorative repertory of Qurʾānic texts against lotus scrolls and iconographic themes harking back to local traditions, he inaugurated a new visual vocabulary. On the eastern side of this reservoir is the *dargāh* of Shaykh Mujarrad, an otherwise obscure saint. These are the earliest datable sepulchres built on the shores of a body of water, called in local traditions a *tīrtha* (Skr., a crossing or ford), introduced the veneration of water into the cult of saints and tombs.

Bibliography

Sources

Muḥammad Qāsim Firishta (Mahomed Kasim Ferishta), *History of the rise of the Mahomedan power in India till the year AD 1612*, ed. and trans. John Briggs, vols. 2–3, London 1829, repr. Cambridge 2013; James Stewart King, *The history of the Bahmanî dynasty. Founded on the Burhân-i Maʾâsir*, 4 vols., London 1900.

Studies

Richard Maxwell Eaton, *A social history of the Deccan, 1300–1761. Eight Indian lives* (Cambridge 2005), 33–58; Richard Maxwell Eaton, *Sufis of Bijapur*, Princeton 1978; Carl Ernst, *Eternal garden. Mysticism, history, and politics at a South Asian Sufi center*, Minneapolis 2003; Elizabeth Schotten Merklinger, *Sultanate architecture of pre-Mughal India*, Delhi 2005; George Michell and Richard Eaton, *Palace city of the Deccan*, Oxford 1997; George Michell and Helen Philon, *Islamic architecture of the Deccan. Forts, palaces, mosques and tombs*, London 2018; George Michell and Mark Zebrowski, *Architecture and art of the Deccan*, Cambridge 1999; Helen Philon, Daulatabad, Gulbarga, Firuzabad and Sagar under the early Bahmanis (1347–1422), in Helen Philon (ed.), *Silent splendour. Palaces of the Deccan, 14th–19th centuries* (Mumbai 2010), 34–43; Helen Philon, *Gulbarga, Bidar, Bijapur*, Mumbai 2012; Helen Philon, The Great Mosque of Gulbarga reinterpreted as the Hazar Sutun of Firuz Shah Bahmani (r.1396–1422), in Laura E. Parodi (ed.), *The visual world of Muslim India. The art, culture and society of the Deccan in the early modern era* (London 2014), 97–122; H. K. Sherwani and P. M. Joshi, *History of medieval Deccan, 1295–1724*, 2 vols., Hyderabad 1973–4; Muhammad Suleman Siddiqi, *The Bahmani Sufis*, Delhi 1989; Anna Suvorova, *Muslim saints of South Asia, The eleventh to fifteenth centuries*, New York 2004.

Helen Philon

H

al-Ḥamdawī

Abū ʿAlī Ismāʿīl b. Ibrāhīm b. Ḥamdawayh (c. 200–70/816–84), known as **al-Ḥamdawī** (or al-Ḥamdūnī, an incorrect version of his patronymic often found in the sources), was a Basran secretary poet, who mainly composed satiric epigrams. Hailing from nearby Maysān, he spent most of his life in Basra, employed presumably in the local administration. He socialised with local notables and entertained good relations with several contemporary poets and philologists.

His fame rests on two series of witty epigrams. The first thematises the used, supposedly threadbare *ṭaylasān* (hooded cloak) that he received as a gift from Ibn Ḥarb, a patron of his (33 epigrams, 2–6 verses long). The second is about a lean, allegedly bony and starved ewe that was donated to him by a certain Saʿīd for the *ʿĪd al-Aḍḥā* (Feast of Sacrifice) (8 epigrams, 4–6 verses long). The two series enjoyed great popularity throughout the premodern era and inspired several poets to similar compositions. Both series explore various aspects of the sordidness and frailty of the gifts, which they humorously magnify. The cloak was supposedly so old that it had witnessed Noah; it had been patched so many times that it became mere patches and could alone find its way to the darner's shop; the mildest breeze, a cough, or even a glance could tear it asunder; and so on. The starved ewe, a paragon of boniness and sickliness, hallucinated and mistook green clothes for fodder, dreamed of fodder, or wept and sang love songs whenever she passed by the fodder-seller. Hyperbole and the use of *taḍmīn* (insertion of verses by other poets) in the punchlines were masterfully exploited to increase the humour of the pieces.

Al-Ḥamdawī also composed a few pieces in which he complained about his circumstances (on wanting a mount, on being neglected and unappreciated, on his bad luck and unprosperousness), contributing to the growth of complaint poetry on the misery of littérateurs. He also composed epigrams satirising stingy hosts, bores, paupers, and fellow poets. Rather than offending, his witty poetry aimed at entertaining and raising a laugh. His poetic remains (87 pieces, 14 of which are also attributed to other poets, amounting to 360 verses) have been collected and edited twice.

Bibliography

Editions
Aḥmad al-Najdī, Dīwān al-Ḥamdawī, *al-Mawrid* 2/3 (1973), 73–90; Muḥammad Jabbār al-Muʿaybid, *Shuʿarāʾ Baṣriyyūn min al-qarn al-thālith al-hijrī* (Baghdad 1977), 111–82.

Reference Works and Studies
A. Arazi, al-Ḥamdawī, *EI2*; Albert Arazi, Thèmes et style d'al-Ḥamdawī. Un poète chansonnier du IIIe/IXe s., *JA* 267 (1979), 261–307; Joseph van Ess, *Der Ṭailasān des Ibn Ḥarb. "Mantelgedichte," in arabischer Sprache*, Heidelberg 1979; Tilman Seidensticker, Die Gattungszugehörigkeit der "Mantelgedichte" des Ḥamdawī, *AS* 48 (1994), 959–71; *GAS* 9:296.

Nefeli Papoutsakis

Ḥasan, Mīr Ghulām

Mīr Ghulām Ḥasan, known by his pen name Ḥasan (Mīr Ḥasan, d. 1200/1786) was a biographer, critic, and poet remembered chiefly for a romantic Urdu *mathnavī* later named *Siḥr al-bayān* ("The enchantment of speech").

1. Life

The details of Mīr Ḥasan's life come to us mainly from his own writings (*Gulzār-i Iram* and *Tadhkira-yi shuʿarā*). Estimates of the year of his birth range from 1140/1727–8 to 1155/1742 (Qurayshī, *Mīr Ḥasan*, 179–89). He was born in the Sayyidwāŕa area of Delhi to a family that, as his name Mīr (Pers., from. Ar. *amīr*, lit., prince, chief, used as an equivalent of Ar. *sayyid*) suggests, traced its lineage to the Prophet. In India, the family traced its descent to a scholar, poet, and administrator named Mīr Imāmī, who came to Delhi from Herat during the reign of the emperor Shāh Jahān (r. 1037–68/1628–57). Mīr Ḥasan's father, Mīr Ghulām Ḥusayn Ḍāḥik (d. 1195/1781) is remembered as a poet of humorous Urdu verse who was himself famously lampooned by the celebrated Urdu satirist Mirzā Rafīʿ Sawdā (d. 1195/1781). As a young man, Mīr Ḥasan attended literary salons at the home of the celebrated Urdu poet Mīr Taqī Mīr (d. 1810), who wrote that Mīr Ḥasan practised poetry under Sawdā (Mīr, 145). Mīr Ḥasan himself wrote that he studied with—but did not emulate the style of—Mīr Ḍiyāʾ al-Dīn Ḍiyāʾ (fl. twelfth/eighteenth century; moved from his native city of Delhi to Faizabad/Fayḍābād), an associate of Mīr Taqī Mīr renowned for his presentation of themes of various types) (Saksena, *Muraqqaʿ*, 20; Mīr, 152).

In his youth, Mīr Ḥasan left Delhi with his father for Awadh. Passing through Lucknow, he eventually settled at Faizabad, where he was patronised by the nawab Sālār Jang—a descendant of Mughal court officials in Delhi, uncle by marriage of the nawab of Awadh Āṣaf al-Dawla (r. 1189–1212/1775–97), and a major patron of Urdu poets and writers—and his son, Navāzish ʿAlī Khān (d. c.1818–27; Qurayshī, *Mīr Ḥasan*, 261). Sālār Jang had moved to Faizabad from Delhi in about 1167/1754 (Āzād, 775–6). Some scholars claim that Mīr Ḥasan eventually found patronage in Lucknow, at the court of the nawab Āṣaf al-Dawla (whom Mīr Ḥasan mentions in his last and most famous *mathnavī*), but this claim is contested. Most scholars follow the celebrated Urdu poet from Amroha (120 kilometres east of Delhi) Muṣḥafī (c. 1750–1824), who knew Mīr Ḥasan, in fixing the date of Mīr Ḥasan's death in 1–10 Muḥarram 1201/24 October-2 November 1786 (Muṣḥafī 69). Luṭf (118) suggests 1205/1790–1, but scholars consider Luṭf unreliable.

Mīr Ḥasan's descendants are also an important part of his literary legacy in Urdu. His son Mīr Mustaḥsan Khalīq (d. 1844, Naqvī, 116, and Fārūqī, 238; or d. 1804, Schimmel, 200) is remembered for developing the Urdu *marthiya* (elegy) genre; his other sons Mīr Aḥsan Khulq (fl. 1845–6; Naqvī, 100–1) and Mīr Iḥsān Makhlūq were also poets of some distinction. Biographers write that he had a fourth son, Mīr Muḥsin Muḥsin, although family accounts do not mention him (Zaidi, *Mir Anis*, 27; Naqvī 100–1; Fārūqī 47–8). His grandson by Khalīq, Mīr Babar ʿAlī Anīs (d. 1874), is amongst the most celebrated poets in Urdu literature and, like his father, is remembered especially for his Urdu *marthiyas* commemorating the martyrdom of Ḥusayn b. ʿAlī at Karbalāʾ (61/680).

2. Prose

Mīr Ḥasan's *Tadhkira-yi shuʿarāʾ* ("Biographical dictionary of poets," completed 1192/1777–8) is an anthology of Urdu poets. As was typical at the time, the introduction and entries are in Persian. First edited and published in 1922, it was eventually translated into Urdu and published in 1971.

3. Poetry

The *Dīvān* (collected poems) of Mīr Ḥasan appears to have been compiled by 1192/1778–9. A selection from it was first published in 1912 by Naval Kishor as *Dīvān-i Mīr Ḥasan*. Another selection, by the Indian poet and politician Ḥasrat Mohānī (d. 1951), was published in 1944. Several collections of Mīr Ḥasan's *ghazals* exist in manuscripts and printed critical editions (al-Ḥaqq, ed., *Ghazaliyāt-i Mīr Ḥasan*, 1–4). In *Tadhkira-yi shuʿarāʾ*, Mīr Ḥasan writes that he composed *marthiyas* on the martyrdom of the Imām, a reference to Ḥusayn b. ʿAlī (Ḥasan, 85), and Ḍamīr Akhtar Naqvī (103–13) copies a selection of *marthiya* poetry attributed to him. A collection of poetry and prose for Ḥusayn has been published as *Yāzda majlis-i Mīr Ḥasan* ("Eleven assemblies of Mīr Ḥasan") and attributed to Mīr Ḥasan, but the authorship is contested (see discussion of the critical edition by Hamdānī in *Yāzda majlis*, 65–70 (see below) and Khān, *Siḥr al-bayān*, 25).

Twelve *mathnavīs* (narrative verse of rhyming couplets) of varying length written between 1183/1769 and 1199/1785 have been attributed to Mīr Ḥasan. The collection *Mathnaviyāt-i Mīr Ḥasan* (ed. Qurayshī) begins with several short, humorous but expurgated *mathnavīs*, followed by a *mathnavī* on the wedding in 1183/1769 of the nawab of Awadh Āṣaf al-Dawla. *Rumūz al-ʿārifīn* ("Secrets of the gnostics") (1188/1774–5) is a mystical poem in Urdu and Persian comprising short didactic tales about famous mystics—including the prominent early ascetic from Balkh Ibrāhīm b. Adham (d. 161/777–8), the famous mystical poet from Nīshāpūr Farīd al-Dīn ʿAṭṭār (d. 618/1221), the Ṣūfī poet from Awadh Malik Muḥammad Jāʾisī (d. c.949/1542), the celebrated Baghdādī mystic of Persian origin, author, and Shāfiʿī legal scholar Junayd (d. 297/910), Junayd's associate Abū l-Ḥasan Nūrī (d. 295/907–8), and the Persian Bāyazīd Bisṭāmī (d. 261/875)—and the Mughal emperor Akbar (r. 963–1014/1556–1605). The poem includes quotations from the mystical Persian *Mathnavī* by Jalāl al-Dīn Rūmī (d. 672/1273).

Gulzār-i Iram ("The rose garden of Iram," 1192/1778–9) is an autobiographical *mathnavī* that recounts Mīr Ḥasan's departure from Delhi and his journey to Awadh, famously lampooning the city of Lucknow and praising Faizabad (then the location of the court of the nawabs of Awadh). It contains valuable descriptions of the procession, festival, and practices of the Madārī Ṣūfīs (the Madāriyya was founded by Badīʿ al-Dīn Shāh Madār, d. 838/1434), an Aleppo-born Ṣūfī who emigrated to India. The French orientalist Garcin de Tassy (d. 1878) translated parts of the *mathnavī* into French (de Tassy, 534–40).

Two other *mathnavī*s in the *Mathnaviyāt* are dedicated to Jawāhir ʿAlī Khan, an employee of the royal court at Faizabad. The *mathnavī* *Khʷān-i niʿmat* ("Table of blessing") describes the cuisine at the court of Āṣaf al-Dawla. In another *mathnavī*, *Hajv* ("Lampoon"), Mīr Ḥasan describes the decrepit state of his own home, a common topic of *hajv* poetry at the time.

4. The *mathnavī* of Mīr Ḥasan (known as *Siḥr al-bayān*)

Mīr Ḥasan's most celebrated poem is his *mathnavī* called variously *Mathnavī-yi Mīr Ḥasan* ("The *mathnavī* of Mīr Ḥasan"), *Mathnavī-yi Bīnaẓīr-u Badr-i munīr* ("The *mathnavī* of Benaẓīr and Badr-i Munīr," the names of its protagonists), and *Siḥr al-bayān* ("Enchantment of description"). Mīr Ḥasan himself appears not to have named the poem. Scholars generally follow a chronogram (not found in all early manuscripts) that gives the date of the text as 1199/1784–5. Comprising more than two thousand couplets, it tells the story of the capture of Prince Benaẓīr by a fairy, his encounter with Princess Badr-i Munīr, and their love affair, separation, and, after a series of adventures, their eventual reunion and marriage (Russell and Islam, 70–90, give a detailed summary).

The *mathnavī* was first edited and published by the College of Fort William, founded in 1800 in Calcutta under British patronage (see Ḥasan, *Sihr ool buyan* 1805). This edition included a preface by an anonymous author generally believed to be Fort William *munshī* (lit., scribe or secretary, hence a native language teacher or secretary in colonial India) Sher ʿAlī Afsos (d. 1809), who had spent ten years with Mīr Ḥasan under the patronage of the nawab Navāzish ʿAlī Khān. The preface has been an important source of both historical information about Mīr Ḥasan and critical evaluation of the *mathnavī*. Indeed, Garcin de Tassy appears to have relied heavily on it in his influential study of Urdu literature (Akhtar, 195–6). There are many later editions of the *mathnavī*. The critical edition compiled by Rashīd Ḥasan Khān is based on eleven manuscripts and two printed editions.

Under the supervision of John Gilchrist (d. 1841), philologist and professor of Hindustani at Fort William College at Calcutta from 1800 to 1804, the *mathnavī* was rendered into Urdu prose (interwoven with verse) by Meer Buhadoor Ulee (Mīr Bahādur ʿAlī Ḥusaynī) and published, as *Nusri Benuzeer*, by Fort William College in 1803. This version, which omits parts of the original, was used as a textbook at the college and eventually became part of the proficiency examinations administered by the British. Cyril William Bowdler Bell and Major Henry Court later published English translations of this prose version.

5. Critical reception

The Austrian orientalist Aloys Sprenger (d. 1893) wrote that the *mathnavī* was "considered the best poem in the Hindústány language" (609). In Urdu, early critical opinion of the poem ranged from positive to lukewarm (Khān, 58–9). Later, the Urdu literary critic and historian Ghulām Ḥusayn Āzād (d. 1910), in his influential work *Āb-i ḥayāt* ("The water of life"), praised the *mathnavī* for its fluid, conversational language and its realistic descriptions of Indian court life in the twelfth/eighteenth century. Following Āzād, Urdu critics often compare the *mathnavī* with the *mathnavī* called *Gulzār-i Nasīm* (1838) by Pandit Dayā Shankar Nasīm (d. 1843), which similarly tells the story of a prince's adventures in a land of fairies (Āzād, 243–5). Although the plot of Mīr Ḥasan's *mathnavī* is original, elements of the story may have been borrowed from Arabic, Persian, and Deccani Urdu literature (Jayn, 304–7). Literary historians argue that the *mathnavī* not only set the standard for later Urdu *mathnavī*s but also inspired many Urdu poets to write long-form *mathnavī*s (Jayn, 268; Sarwarī, 111). The popularity and influence of the poem are evinced by the fact that many of its lines have passed as quotable sayings into common use in Urdu (Akhtar, 193–4).

Bibliography

Selected published collections

Mīr Ḥasan, *Dīvān-i Mīr Ḥasan*, Lucknow 1912; Mīr Ḥasan, *Ghazaliyāt-i Mīr Ḥasan*, ed. Muḥammad Dhakī al-Ḥaqq, Patna 1999; Mīr Ḥasan (Dihlavī), *Mathnavī Rumūz al-ʿārifīn*, ed. Aḥmadallāh Qādirī, Hyderabad 1934; Mīr Ḥasan, *Mathnaviyāt-i Ḥasan*, ed. Waḥīd Qurayshī, Lahore 1966; Mīr Ḥasan, *Siḥr al-bayān*, ed. Rashīd Ḥasan Khān, New Delhi 2000; Mīr Ḥasan, *Tadhkira-yi shuʿarā-yi urdū*, trans. Shāh ʿAṭā al-Raḥmān ʿAṭā Kākwī, Patna 1971 (in Urdu); Mīr Ḥasan, *Tadhkira-yi shuʿarā-yi urdū*, ed. Ḥabīb al-Raḥmān Shirwānī, Aligarh 1922; Mīr Ḥasan (?), *Yāzda majlis-i Mīr Ḥasan maʿrūf ba akhbār al-aʾimma*, Aligarh 1994 (authorship contested).

The *Mathnavī* in Urdu prose

Meer Buhadoor Ulee (Mīr Bahādur ʿAlī), *Nusri Benuzeer or A prose version by Meer Buhadoor Ulee of the Sihr ool buyan. An enchanting fairy-tale in Hindoostanee verse by Meer Husun composed for the use of the Hindoostanee students, in the College of Fort William; under the superintendence of John Gilchrist*, Calcutta 1803.

Translations (based on the Urdu prose version by Meer Buhadoor Ulee cited above)

Cyril William Bowdler Bell, *Nasr i Be-Nazīr (or Story of Prince Be-Nazīr). An eastern fairy tale translated from the Urdū*, Calcutta 1871; Henry Court, *Nusr-i-Benazeer, or, The incomparable prose of Meer Hasan, literally translated into English*, Simla 1871, rev. ed. Calcutta 1889.

Studies

Salīm Akhtar, *Urdu adab kīmukhtaṣartarīn tārīkh. Aghāz se 2000 tak* (Delhi and Lahore 2000), 193–6; Ahmad Ali, *The golden tradition* (New York 1973), 191–9; Ghulām Ḥusayn Āzād, *Āb-e Ḥayāt. Shaping the canon of Urdu poetry*, ed. and trans. Frances Pritchett and Shamsur Rahman Faruqi (New Delhi 2001), 217–21; Ghulām Ḥusayn Āzād, *Āb-i ḥayāt* (Lahore 1907), 241–6; T. Grahame Bailey, *A history of Urdu literature* (Calcutta 1932), 52–3, 61–2, 81; Maḥmūd Fārūqī, *Mīr Ḥasan awr khāndān ke dūsre shuʿarā*, Lahore 1956; Najm al-Hudā, *Mathnavī kā fann awr Urdū mathnaviyāṇ* (Patna 1976), 92–3; Gyān Chand Jayn (Giān Chand Jain), *Urdū mathnavī shumālī hind meṇ* (Aligarh 1969), 295–324; Rashīd Ḥasan Khān, Tamhīd, in Mīr Ḥasan, *Siḥr al-bayān* (New Delhi 2000), 11–142; Shāh Nawāz Khān, *Maʾāthir al-umarā*, vol. 3, Calcutta 1891 (for information on his patrons); Mirzā ʿAlī Luṭf, *Tadhkira-yi Gulzār-i Ibrāhīm* (Aligarh 1934), 118–24; Mīr Taqī Mīr, *Tadhkira-yi Nikāt al-shuʿarā*, Lucknow 1984; Ghulām Hamadānī Muṣḥafī, *Tadhkira-yi Hindī* (Delhi 1933), 68–71; Ḍamīr Akhtar Naqvī, *Khāndān-i Mīr Anīs ke nāmvar shuʿarā* (Karachi 1994), 80–253; Ḥāmid Ḥasan Qādirī, *Dāstān-i tārīkh-i Urdū* (Delhi 1938, repr. 2007), 132; Waḥīd Qurayshī, *Mīr Ḥasan awr un kā zamāna*, Lahore 1959; Waḥīd Qurayshī, Muqaddama, in Mīr Ḥasan, *Mathnaviyāt-i Ḥasan* (Lahore 1966), 9–38; Ralph Russell and Khurshidul Islam, *Three Mughal poets. Mir, Sauda, Mir Hasan* (Cambridge MA 1968), 69–94; Mohammed Sadiq, *A history of Urdu literature* (London 1964, Delhi 1984[2]), 150–3; Ram Babu Saksena, *A history of Urdu literature* (Allahabad 1927, 1940[2]), 67–70; Rām Bābū Saksena (ed.), *Muraqqaʿ-i shuʿarā*, Delhi 1956 (for information on Mīr Ḥasan's milieu); ʿAbd al-Qādir Sarvarī, *Urdū mathnavī kā irtiqā* (Hyderabad 1940), 108–15; Annemarie Schimmel, *Classical Urdu literature from the beginning to Iqbal* (Wiesbaden 1975), 184–5; Anna Aronova Suvorova, *Masnavi. A study of Urdu romance* (Oxford 2000), 101–64; Aloys Sprenger, *A catalogue of the Arabic, Persian and Hindústány manuscripts of the libraries of the king of Oudh* (Calcutta 1854), 1:609; Joseph Héliodore Garcin de Tassy, *Histoire de la littérature hindouie et hindoustanie* (Paris 1870[2]), 1:528–40; Ali Jawad Zaidi, *A history of Urdu literature* (Delhi 1993), 109–13, 117–9; Ali Jawad Zaidi, *Mir Anis*, New Delhi 1986 (Eng., with Urdu passages).

Gregory Maxwell Bruce

Hasbihal

Hasbihal *(Ḥasb-i ḥāl)* is the name of a genre of Ottoman Turkish literature derived from the combination of the Arabic *ḥasb* ("calculation" [in Turkish "requirement, quality"]) and *ḥāl* ("condition"). The equivalent term in Persian is widely used to mean "an event experienced" or "events that happen to someone." In Turkish it means "to share troubles in a heart-to-heart talk," or "to chat." In poetry it is also used to denote a condition experienced personally by the poet (Dihkhudā, 8948). In Ottoman literature, different poetic genres are described by the term *hasbihal*. For example, *hasbihal* (or sometimes *arz-ı hal/ʿarḍ-i ḥāl*) can appear in the heading of poems in *divans* (*dīvān*, collection of a poet's poems) that are written in the *kaside (qaṣīde)*, *kıta (qiṭʿa)*, short *mesnevi (methnevī)*, and other poetical forms. These are generally short poems that express material difficulties in which the poet finds himself and the bleak psychological condition occasioned by these difficulties, requests for positions or rewards from high authorities, or various complaints. The writers of *tezkires* (*tedhkire*, poets' biographies) also use the term *hasbihal* to define all couplets that express the psychological condition of the poets.

Love stories in verse, which are written in the *mesnevi* form with fictitious unity and enriched by fictional elements, can also be described as *hasbihals* because one of the most important shared characteristics of these *mesnevis* is the attribution to the poet, either directly or indirectly, of the love story and hence the use of the first person narrative. In all the examples apart from one (*Heves-nāme*, "Book of desire," see below) the beloved is a young man and the events take place in towns within the Ottoman Empire. Therefore, *hasbihals* undoubtedly contain elements of truth and represent a realist, local, and original counterpart to *mesnevis* on love such as *Khusrev u Şīrīn* ("Khusrev and Şīrīn"), *Leylā vü Mecnūn* ("Leylā and Mecnūn"), or *Yūsuf u Züleykhā* ("Yūsuf and Züleykhā"). In general, emphasis on originality is mentioned as the reason for composition *(sebebi telif/ sebeb-i teʾlīf)* in these works.

While the first example of this genre in Ottoman Turkish literature is Halili's (Khalīlī, d. c.890/1485–6) *Fürqat-nāme* ("Book of separation," completed in 876/1471–2), it was Tacizade Cafer Çelebi's (Tācīzāde Caʿfer Çelebi, d. 921/ 1515) *Heves-nāme* ("Book of passion," completed in 899/1493–4) and Taşlıcalı Yahya's (Taşlıcalı Yaḥyā, d. 990/1582–3) *Şāh u Gedā* ("The shah and the beggar," completed roughly 943/1536–7) which popularised the form. Many works were written under the influence of this trend, particularly in the tenth/sixteenth century. As Nev'i's (Nevʿī, d. 1007/1599) *Ḥasb-i ḥāl* (completed in 962/1554–5) was composed within the context of Ṣūfism, it can be seen as a sub-genre of the *hasbihal* genre. Although *hasbihals* may be accepted as ego-documents containing autobiographical details, they cannot be regarded in the same category as the *sergüzeştname* (*sergüdheştnāme*, "book of adventure"), *seyahatname* (*seyāḥatnāme*, "book of travel"), *gazavatname* (*ghazavātnāme*, "book of military campaign in furtherance of Islam"), or other similar genres of literature that comprise stories of events that actually occurred and in which the fictional elements remain secondary.

The term *hasbihal* can also be applied to works written in a critical or satirical style based on the poet's observations of various professional or social groups. The most famous example of this type of *hasbihal*, which is also called *tarifat* (*taʿrīfāt*, "description"), is *Hasbihal* of Safi, completed in 995/1586–7.

Bibliography

Dilek Batislam, Tarih ve kültür kaynaği olarak Hasb-i Hâller, *Türklük bilimi araştırmaları* XXII (2007), 29–42; Ali Akbar Dihkhudā, *Lughatnāma*, ed. Jaʿfar Shahīdī (Tehran 1998), 6:8948; Halûk Gökalp, *Eski Türk edebiyatında manzum sergüzeştnâmeler*, Istanbul 2009; Selim Sırrı Kuru, Mesnevi biçiminde aşk hali. Birinci tekil şahıs anlatılar olarak Fürkat-nâme, Heves-nâme üzerinden bir değerlendirme, in Hatice Aynur, Müjgân Çakır, Hanife Koncu, Selim S. Kuru, and Ali Emre Özyıldırım (eds.), *Nazımdan nesire edebî türler* (Istanbul 2009), 168–83; Agâh Sırrı Levend, *Türk edebiyatı tarihi*, Ankara 1973; Ali Emre Özyıldırım, Sergüzeştnâmeler üzerine hasbihal veya hasbihâlin sergüzeşti, in Hatice Aynur, Müjgân Çakır, Hanife Koncu, Selim S. Kuru, and Ali Emre Özyıldırım (eds.), *Nazımdan nesire edebî türler* (Istanbul 2009), 134–66; Sâfî, *Hasbihâl-i Sâfî*, trans. Dilek Batislam, Istanbul 2003.

Ali Emre Özyıldırım

Hishām b. al-Ḥakam

Hishām b. al-Ḥakam (d. c.179/795 or 796) was one of the most notorious theologians of the late second/eighth century. Usually classed by Sunnī heresiographers among the "Rāfiḍī" (Shīʿī) theologians (those who "rejected" the legitimacy of the caliphs Abū Bakr, ʿUmar, and ʿUthmān), he participated in the theological disputations of the early Muʿtazilīs. His physical theory was apparently especially influential for al-Naẓẓām (d. c.230/845), a prominent early Muʿtazilī. He is remembered chiefly for his unorthodox position on the corporeality of God and for his contributions to Imāmī Shīʿī thought. Born in Kufa, he became a client (*mawlā*) of the Banū Shaybān, an important Arab tribe, and was associated with the Shīʿī Imāms Jaʿfar al-Ṣādiq and Mūsā l-Kāẓim (d. 148/765 and 183/799 respectively). He was occasionally involved in the intellectual circles of the early ʿAbbāsid court in Baghdad during the reign of Hārūn al-Rashīd (r. 170–93/786–809). It seems that he died in the aftermath of the imprisonment of Imām Mūsā l-Kāẓim and the fall of the Barmakids, the family of *wazīrs* in Hārūn's court who promoted theological discussions and aesthetic pursuits (that is, after c.179/795), although biographical sources offer later dates as well. None of his thirty or so attested works survive, but his doctrines have been preserved in the major doxographies. Hishām is the most frequently cited Imāmī thinker in the *Maqālāt* of al-Ashʿarī (d. 324/936); throughout that work his positions appear alongside those of later Muʿtazilīs. Other heresiographers (see bibliography) devote substantial space to his doctrines. Among Imāmī theorists, Hishām was apparently the first to articulate explicitly the doctrine of *ʿiṣma*, the infallibility of the Imām. Although Imāmī writers acknowledge his importance, celebrating him as the earliest great Shīʿī practitioner of *kalām* (discursive theology), his association with the Barmakid circle seems to have damaged his reputation. Van Ess and Madelung (see bibliography) have provided the most up-to-date studies of Hishām; van Ess's account exhaustively covers the available sources.

Hishām infamously professed the corporeality of God. This was not merely an assertion of *tashbīh* (anthropomorphism) but rather a set of propositions derived from or substantiating Hishām's physical theory. He held that God is three-dimensional, limited in size, with no dimension greater than another. Hishām frequently described God using light imagery: for example, he reportedly claimed that God is "a radiant light of a certain size, in a particular location, like a pure ingot shining brightly, like a perfectly round pearl" (al-Ashʿarī, 32). Hishām's unusual depiction of God is the theoretical centre around which his ideas about the natural world and the human person are arranged: the most significant of these ideas concern attribution, perception, and human (and divine) acts.

Hishām defined the "attribute" (*ṣifa*) as a momentary instance of motion or action, that is, as a conceptual entity (*maʿnā*) distinct from bodies. Like al-Naẓẓām after him, but against the general trend among practitioners of *kalām*, he denied that physical properties, such as colour, taste, scent, and so forth, were "accidents" distinct from but inhering in material substrates. Rather, according to Hishām and al-Naẓẓām, such properties were discrete, subtle bodies themselves: indeed, they were the sole physical constituents of the world. Thus, as opposed to the substance/accident or atom/accident arrangement propounded by his contemporaries, Hishām posited a world of conceptual entities (motions and modes or states of being) and subtle property-bodies only. It seems that Hishām inaugurated the use of Naẓẓāmian concepts such as latency and interpenetration to illustrate this view, which was also perhaps influenced by contemporary dualist physical theory (exemplified by the followers of Abū Shākir al-Dayṣānī, about whom little is known; various sources accuse Hishām of association with this figure, but Hishām is also credited with writing tracts against the Dualists). Thus, physical properties were regarded as subtle bodies latent in one another, and interpenetrating one another: physical change involved the manifestation of properties (such as "redness" or "heat") where they had previously been latent, or hidden, without any persisting substrate (as in Aristotelian philosophy). On the other hand, his classification of psychological attributes allowed Hishām to assert that the acts, motions, and will of God were conceptually separate from His essence, while requiring God's corporeality as a ground for those *ṣifāt*. Although Hishām was at pains to point out that God is a "body unlike other bodies," the divine body is uniquely unified with His bodily properties (His colour, etc.), precluding any ontological schism in His nature resulting from diverse physical properties.

On perception, Hishām held that God "sees" by means of rays interpenetrating their objects. Hishām seems to have conflated contemporary theories of (human) vision by extramission with a more conceptual epistemology, whereby the reality of objects is perceived in the heart by means of acts of imagination and estimation (these were to be treated as faculties of the soul in the philosophy of Ibn Sīnā [Avicenna, d. 428/1037]; estimation, *wahm*, in particular, became a crucial faculty for the apprehension of non-sensible *maʿnā*s in objects of knowledge). Thus, as van Ess noted (1:365–7), he anticipated the Greek-inspired optical theory of al-Kindī (d. c.252/870) and was apparently the first to articulate in Arabic some of the epistemological issues in facultative psychology, the dominant model of the following centuries. Although Hishām's ontology of subtle property-bodies and momentary *ṣifāt* was decidedly materialist, discounting abiding psychological realities, his anthropology skewed dualist: he is consistently reported to have asserted that the human body and the spirit (*rūḥ*) are two distinct conceptual entities (*maʿnā*). "The human body is inanimate, whereas the spirit is the agent and perceiver of things; it is a light among lights" (ʿAbd al-Jabbār, 11:310).

Hishām's claims regarding human and divine acts reflect many of the early technical concerns of the Muʿtazilīs. As a class, human and divine acts are *ṣifāt*, neither the same as nor different from the bodies with which they are associated. His analysis of acts emphasises the ambiguity inherent in the assertion of human choice; acts belong to their (human) agent, but are necessitated by virtue of God's having supplied an impetus (*sabab*, that is, an immediate cause; see al-Ashʿarī, 41–3).

It is not clear whether Hishām's theology determined his physical theory or vice versa, but he seems to have been the first Islamic thinker to thoroughly integrate the two. His positions were clearly influential in the development of Muʿtazilī thought, and at several points—for example, with respect to the apperception of the true nature of objects through mental faculties, and the definition of body as an existent, self-subsistent thing—that is, a substance—he could almost be considered a forerunner of Arabic Aristotelianism.

Bibliography

Sources

ʿAbd al-Jabbār, *al-Mughnī fī abwāb al-tawḥīd*, vol. 11, ed. ʿAlī al-Najjār and ʿAbd al-Ḥalīm al-Najjār, Cairo 1965; al-Ashʿarī, *Maqālāt al-Islāmiyyīn*, ed. Helmut Ritter, Beirut 2005[4]; al-Baghdādī, *al-Farq bayna l-firaq*, ed. Muḥammad Muḥyī l-Dīn ʿAbd al-Ḥamīd (Cairo 1964), 65–8; al-Shahrastānī, *Kitāb al-milal wa-l-niḥal*, ed. William Cureton (London 1842–6), 1:141–2; al-Khayyāṭ, *Kitāb al-intiṣār*, ed. Albīr Naṣrī Nādir, Beirut 1957; al-Maqdisī, *Kitāb al-badʾ wa-l-taʾrīkh*, 6 vols., ed. Clément Huart, Paris 1899–1919.

Studies

Wilferd Madelung, The Shiite and Khārijite contribution to pre-Ashʿarite *kalām*, in Parviz Morewedge (ed.), *Islamic philosophical theology* (Albany 1979), 120–39; van Ess, *TG* 1:349–79 (see also the English trans. by John O'Kane, *Theology and society in the second and third century of the Hijra*, Leiden 2017, 1:410–48) and 5.70–100 (for testimony).

David Bennett

Horoscope

A **horoscope** is a diagram of the positions of various elements considered astrologically significant on the celestial sphere. Horoscopes are calculated for a particular moment and place and casting them is the main practice of astrology and the basis for astrological predictions.

Despite the fact that some scientific authorities and Islamic theologians strongly condemned astrology, its practitioners found reasoned that it is compatible with the Islamic religion, based mainly on the idea that the stars do not really exert influences on the world but are indicators that make it possible to adopt preventive measures to avoid future misadventure. Thus, predictions based on the interpretation of the positions of the celestial bodies were broadly used in a variety of fields and for many purposes, including the promotion of political ideas, economic forecasts, medical prognostication, decision making on important affairs, the divination of future events, and the location of hidden objects.

One of the most relevant functions of astrology in Islamic societies was connected to politics. Prominent astrologers often enjoyed the patronage of caliphs and other political leaders. They were highly appreciated as court astrologers and were responsible for casting and interpreting the horoscopes related to world astrology. This branch of astrology, based on the theory of cyclical conjunctions of the upper planets and the horoscope of the "revolution of the world-year" *(taḥāwīl sinī l-ʿālam)*, was devoted to the historical and political affairs of civilisations, nations, religions, and dynasties. In the political milieu, horoscopes were also cast on the occasions of the coronations of kings, the birth of important people, and anniversaries, and before making important decisions, such as the foundation of a city or embarking on military action. These political horoscopes were sometimes made retrospectively and were often reproduced in historical annals. They functioned largely as an instrument to promote and legitimate political ideas and events, such as the authority of a ruler or the supremacy of a dynasty, presented as indicated by the stars and, ultimately, by God. The Arabs inherited from the Persian astrological tradition this model of political astrology as a system for predicting religious and political change. It was much later transmitted to Europe through the Latin translation of Arabic astrological texts and became very popular during the early Renaissance as an instrument of political governance (Burnett; Samsó, Astrology in Morocco; Forcada; Díaz-Fajardo; Gutas; Pingree; Pingree and Madelung; Kennedy and Pingree).

The dimension of astrology concerned with natural phenomena uses horoscopes to deal with floods, droughts, plagues, and other natural disasters, but also to forecast the weather, the yield of crops, and the oscillation of prices of agricultural produce in the economy. The interest in this category of predictions produced a large number of astrological texts in agronomical treatises (Burnett; Samsó, Astrology in Morocco; Forcada).

In astrological medicine, techniques based on the positions of the elements of the horoscope were used to estimate the moment of a foetus' conception and the exact duration of a woman's pregnancy. A suitable celestial configuration was to be observed for the election of an appropriate day for therapeutic treatment, and a theory of connections of plant medicines with the seven planets and parts of the body determined the propitious moments for gathering herbs and their clinical use (Burnett; Samsó, *Ciencias*, 117–8, 321; Vernet).

Many other applications of horoscopes derived from the use of the astrological doctrines of "elections" *(ikhtiyārāt)* and "interrogations" *(masāʾil)*. Elections are used to determine the most appropriate moment to start an activity or for an important event, for example, to start a journey, to get married, to have sexual intercourse, to make a talisman, or to build a new house. With the system of interrogations the astrologer evaluates the convenience of performing an activity itself, or determines the location or the condition of hidden things. Examples of the use of interrogations concern divination of future events, treasure hunting, the determination of the gender of the foetus, or the location of lost cattle (Burnett; Samsó, *Ciencias*, 50–2; Schmidl).

The astronomers and mathematicians of medieval Islamic society, who were responsible for supplying the information that astrologers needed, brought together the Greek, Persian, and Indian astrological traditions (Burnett), dealt with the geometric definitions involved in the horoscope, and developed new computational procedures that clearly shaped the subsequent practice of astrology.

For casting a horoscope, astrologers needed to know the day and the hour, and the latitude of the place for which the horoscope is cast. Then they used astronomical tables, ephemerides, almanacs, or instruments to determine on the zodiacal belt the positions of the Sun, the Moon, the lunar nodes (intersections of the ecliptic with the lunar orbit), and the planets.

The connection of the celestial objects to the local horizon is determined by the operation of dividing or "equating" the astrological "houses" *(taswiyat al-buyūt)*. These houses are twelve divisions of the ecliptic around the local horizon [Illustration 1] and each one represents a particular aspect of life. During one apparent daily revolution of the celestial sphere, any celestial body will pass through all twelve houses. Therefore, the influence of a particular element on the different aspects of life represented by the houses will depend on the moment of the day.

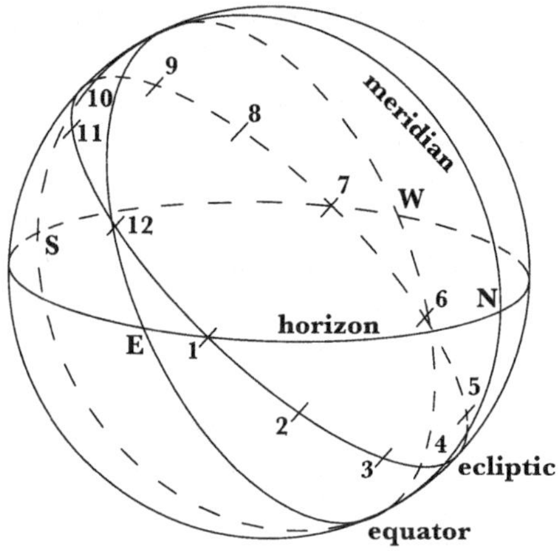

Illustration 1. The cusps of the twelve astrological houses.

The houses are numbered counterclockwise, starting from the ecliptic point that is rising on the eastern horizon, which is called the "ascendant" *(al-ṭāliʿ)*, or beginning of the first house. The ecliptic point diametrically opposed is the beginning of the seventh house, the "descendant" *(al-ghārib)*. In general, the system of the houses also includes the two intersections of the ecliptic and the local meridian, called the upper midheaven, beginning of the tenth house *(watad al-samāʾ* or *watad al-ʿāshir)*, and the lower midheaven, beginning of the fourth house *(watad al-arḍ)*. These four ecliptic points define the four angular or cardinal houses *(al-awtād al-arbaʿa)*.

The definition and computation of the eight non-cardinal houses led to the development of a variety of procedures that, yielding different results, involved a varying degree of mathematical complexity. Some of the most common systems for the division of houses used by modern astrologers either originated or have an important background in medieval Islamic society (Casulleras and Hogendijk; Kennedy; North).

The most popular method for the division of houses in the Middle Ages was the one that modern historians call the Standard Method. With this method, the houses are defined on the ecliptic by meridians crossing equal divisions of the equatorial arcs lying between the local meridian and the meridians that pass through the ascendant and the descendant points of the ecliptic. Illustration 2 shows the houses of the Eastern hemisphere using this procedure. This system is attested to in a Greek horoscope of the fifth century C.E. Modern astrologers attach to this method the name of Alcabitius, the Latin form of al-Qabīṣī (d. 356/967), the court astrologer of Sayf al-Dawla (r. 333–56/944–67, Ḥamdānid dynasty, Aleppo).

Another popular procedure for the division of the houses was the Hour Lines Method. According to this system, the cusps of the houses are the intersections of the ecliptic with the lines of the even seasonal hours [Illustration 3]. This method is reported to have been known in late second/early ninth-century Baghdad by Māshā'allāh (d. 199/815) and Ḥabash al-Ḥāsib (d. after 255/869), and it is mentioned by many Eastern and Western medieval authors. Modern astrologers attribute this system to Placidus, a seventeenth-century Perugian monk.

Two other common methods for the houses are called the Prime Vertical Method and the Equatorial Method.

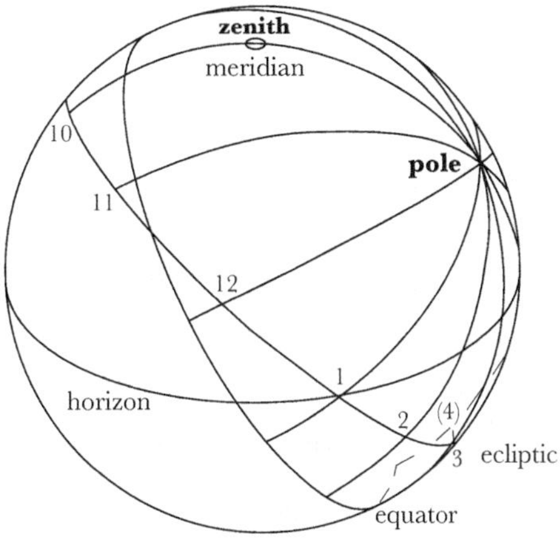

Illustration 2. The Standard Method for the division of the houses.

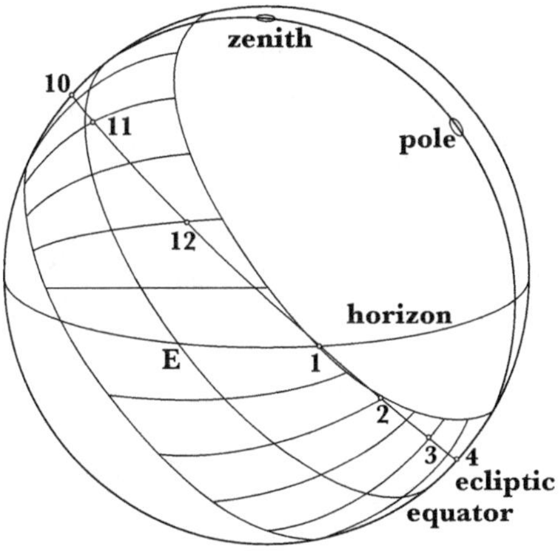

Illustration 3. The Hour Lines Method for the division of the houses.

They define the houses as the intersections of the ecliptic with the great circles on the celestial sphere passing through the North and South points of the local horizon, which are called position circles.

For the first method [Illustration 4], these position circles cross equal divisions of the Prime Vertical, which is the great circle passing through the local zenith and

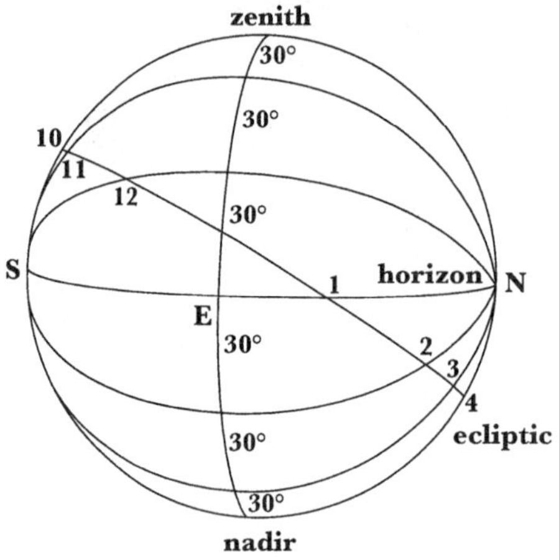

Illustration 4. The Prime Vertical Method for the division of the houses.

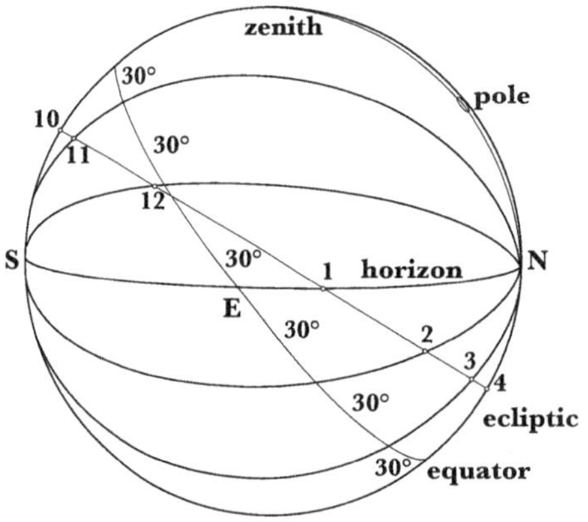

Illustration 5. The Equatorial Method for the division of the houses.

the East and West points on the local horizon. For the Equatorial method, they cross the celestial Equator [Illustration 5].

The Prime Vertical Method is attributed to the thirteenth-century C.E. Italian author Campanus of Novara in the Latin West, but it is mentioned for the first time in the Islamic world by al-Bīrūnī (d. c.440/1048) in Iran or Afghanistan and, almost simultaneously, by Ibn al-Samḥ (d. 426/1035) in al-Andalus. The Andalusī mathematician and astronomer Ibn Muʿādh al-Jayyānī (d. 485/1093) formulated the first correct computation for the Equatorial Method but modern astrologers call it the system of Regiomontanus, a fifteenth-century author who was seemingly the owner of a Latin translation of the astronomical tables of Ibn Muʿādh, in which the method is described.

All the mentioned systems for the division of the houses were performed using standard or special astrolabe plates (Casulleras, 519–22; Calvo). Alternatively, the astrologers used specific tables giving the beginnings of the houses as a function of the latitude of the place and the ascendant degree of the ecliptic.

After establishing the positions of the relevant celestial objects and their connection to the houses, the doctrine of the "projection of rays" *(maṭraḥ al-shuʿāʿāt)* or astrological aspects furnishes the horoscope with another interpretational package. This theory considers the astrological significance of certain angular distances (60°, 90°, 120°, and 180°) defined between the objects on the celestial sphere. Illustration 6 is a schematic representation of the different rays of a planet *P* on the ecliptic circle: the "rays" *PP*1, *PP*2, and *PP*3 are called the left "sextile" *(tasdīs)*, "quartile" *(tarbīʿ)* and "trine" *(tathlīth)* rays, respectively. Similarly, *PP*7, *PP*6, and *PP*5 are called the right "sextile" *(tasdīs)*, "quartile" *(tarbīʿ)* and "trine" *(tathlīth)* rays, respectively. *P*4 is called "the opposition" *(al-muqābala)*.

The horoscope is also the groundwork for the astrological system of the "progressions" *(tasyīr)*. This theory establishes a relationship between angular distances and periods of time as a basis for astrological predictions. A typical application of the *tasyīr* is the attempt to find the moment of death, by giving a value of

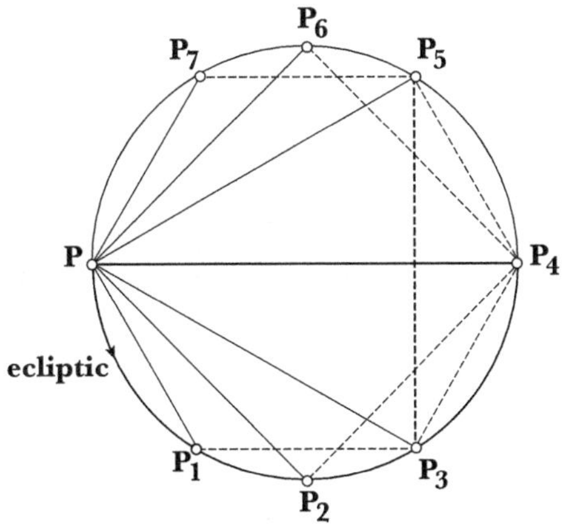

Illustration 6. The astrological aspects or rays.

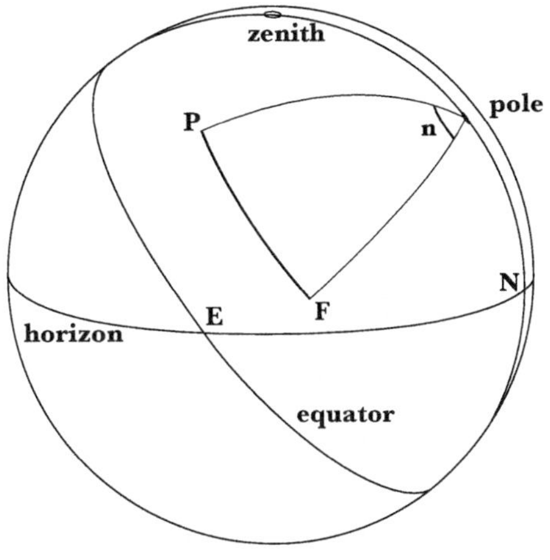

Illustration 7. The *tasyīr* or system of progressions.

one year of life per degree of the angle between two significant objects selected in the celestial configuration at the moment of the individual's birth. One of these objects is thought of as emitting life-force, and the other is seen as destroying life. In Illustration 7, the point *F* represents the destructive point that will reach the initial position of the emitting point *P* after rotation over *n* degrees around the celestial axis. According to this theory, the angle *n* corresponds to the arc of *tasyīr* and the individual will live *n* solar years.

The computations for the projection of rays and the progressions also led to a variety of procedures, often based on the same geometrical approaches of the methods for the houses (Casulleras and Hogendijk). However, modern astrologers ignore these medieval methods and simply obtain the arcs for the aspects and the *tasyīr* on the ecliptic.

Bibliography

Charles Burnett, Astrology, *EI3*; Emilia Calvo, La resolution graphique des questions astrologiques à al-Andalus, *Histoire des mathématiques arabes. Actes du 3me colloque Maghrébin sur l'histoire des mathématiques arabes, Tipaza, 1–3 Décembre 1990* (Algiers 1998), 31–44; Josep Casulleras, The instruments and the exercise of astrology in the medieval Arabic tradition, *Archives Internationales d'Histoire des Sciences* 63/170–1 (2013), 518–40; Josep Casulleras and Jan P. Hogendijk, Progressions, rays and houses in medieval Islamic astrology. A mathematical classification, *Suhayl. International Journal for the History of the Exact and Natural Sciences in Islamic Civilisation* 11 (2012), 33–102; Montse Díaz-Fajardo, The transformation of the "world periods" in the Islamic west. From Abū Maʿshar to al-Baqqār, in Agostino Cilardo (ed.), *Islam and globalisation. Historical and contemporary perspectives. Proceedings of the 25th Congress of L'Union Européenne des Arabisants et Islamisants = Orientalia Lovaniensia Analecta* 226 (Leuven, Paris, and Walpole MA 2013), 483–93; Miquel Forcada, Astrology in al-Andalus during the eleventh and twelfth centuries. Between religion and philosophy, in Charles Burnett and Dorian Gieseler Greenbaum (eds.), *From Māshā'allāh to Kepler. Theory and practice in medieval and renaissance astrology* (Ceredigion 2015), 149–76; Dimitri Gutas, *Greek Thought, Arabic Culture. The Graeco-Arabic translation movement in Baghdad and early ʿAbbasid society (2nd–4th/8th–10th centuries)* (London and New York 1998), 45–6; Jan P. Hogendijk, The mathematical structure of two Islamic astronomical tables for "casting the rays," *Centaurus* 32 (1989), 171–202; Jan

P. Hogendijk, Al-Bīrūnī on the computation of primary progression *(tasyīr)*, in Charles Burnett and Dorian Gieseler Greenbaum (eds.), *From Māshāʾallāh to Kepler. Theory and practice in medieval and renaissance astrology* (Ceredigion 2015), 279–308; Edward S. Kennedy, The astrological houses as defined by Medieval Islamic astronomers, in Josep Casulleras and Julio Samsó (eds.), *From Baghdad to Barcelona. Studies in the Islamic exact sciences in honour of Prof. Juan Vernet* (Barcelona 1996), 535–78 (reprinted as Edward S. Kennedy, *Astronomy and astrology in the medieval Islamic world* (Aldershot 1998), no. XIX); Edward S. Kennedy and Haiganoush Krikorian-Preisler, The astrological doctrine of "projecting the rays," *Al-Abḥāth* 25 (1972), 3–15 (reprinted in Edward S. Kennedy, colleagues, and former students, *Studies in the Islamic exact sciences* (Beirut 1983), 372–84); Edward S. Kennedy and David Pingree (eds. and trans.), *The astrological history of Māshāʾallāh*, Cambridge MA 1971; John D. North, *Horoscopes and history*, London 1986; David Pingree, Ḳirān, *EI2*; David Pingree and Wilferd Madelung, Political horoscopes relating to late ninth-century ʿAlids, *JNES* 36/4 (1977), 247–75; Julio Samsó, *Islamic astronomy and medieval Spain* (Aldershot 1994), nos. II–IV; Julio Samsó, *Astronomy and astrology in al-Andalus and the Maghrib* (Aldershot 2007), nos. V, VI, and X; Julio Samsó, *Astrometeorología y astrología medievales* (Barcelona 2008), nos. VIII–XIV; Julio Samsó, *Las ciencias de los antiguos en al-Andalus* (Almería 2011), 50–2, 117–8, and 321; Julio Samsó, Astrology in Morocco towards the end of the fourteenth century and beginning of the fifteenth century, in Charles Burnett and Dorian Gieseler Greenbaum (eds.), *From Māshāʾallāh to Kepler. Theory and practice in medieval and renaissance astrology* (Ceredigion 2015), 407–24; Petra G. Schmidl, Lunar elections in Ibn Raḥīq's folk-astronomical treatise, in Charles Burnett and Dorian Gieseler Greenbaum (eds.), *From Māshāʾallāh to Kepler. Theory and practice in medieval and renaissance astrology* (Ceredigion 2015), 425–53; Joan Vernet, Un tractat d'obstetrícia astrològica, *Boletín de la Real Academia de Buenas Letras de Barcelona*, 22 (1949), 69–96 (reprinted in Juan Vernet, *Estudios sobre historia de la ciencia medieval* (Barcelona-Bellaterra 1979), 273–300).

Josep Casulleras

I

Ibn Melek Firişteoğlu

Ibn Melek Firişteoğlu (Firişteoghlu, d. after 821/1418), a scholar of Ḥanafī jurisprudence and a glossarist, lived in the city of Tire (in the Aegean region of present-day Turkey) during the period of the Aydınoğulları *beylik* (708–92/1308–90; 803–29/1401–25). While he is well known as İbn Melek Firişteoğlu he uses different names in his books such as Abdülaziz b. Abdüllatif (ʿAbdülazīz b. ʿAbdüllaṭīf) b. Melek (*Mabāriq al-azhār*); Mehmed b. Abdüllatif b. Ferişte (*Sharḥ Manār*), and sources differ about the origin of his patronymic "Firişteoğlu." Ibn Baṭṭūṭa states that during his journey to Anatolia in 732 (1332) he encountered Firişteoğlu's father, Kadi İzzeddin Firişte (Qāḍī ʿİzzeddīn Firişte, d. after 732/1332), in Birgi (a town in today's western Turkey, in the Ödemiş district of the province of Izmir), and that he was known by the pseudonym Firişte ("Angel") because of his piety and virtue. This may explain why later sources use the patronymic Firişteoğlu to refer to his sons. According to Mehmed Seyyid Beg (d. 1343/1924) (*Uṣūl-ı fıkh. Medḫal* (Istanbul 1333/1917), 55), Kadı İzzeddin Firişte (one of Seyyid Beg's forebears) was from Turkistan and came to Anatolia on the invitation of the Aydınoğulları.

Ibn Melek taught for many years at the *medrese (madrasa)* in Tire that was built by Aydınoğlu Mehmed (Aydınoghlu Meḥmed, d. 733/1334), and he came to be called "Firişteoğlu." According to Evliya (Evliyā) Çelebi, he also taught Mehmed Bey's sons, namely İsa (ʿĪsā) Çelebi (d. before 802/1400), Selim (Selīm) Çelebi, and Hızır Şah (Khıḍr Şāh, d. 761/1360?). While Ibn Melek is known to have taken lessons from his father (Kadı İzzeddin), Evliya Çelebi relates that he was educated at Manisa's Saruhan Medrese, where he had a cell that the public could visit. Ibn Melek's death date is disputed; however, the autograph copy of his work (in Arabic) *Sharḥ Manār al-anwār*, in the collection of the Necip Paşa Library (manuscript no. 200) in Tire, in the province of Izmir, is dated 821/1418, which indicates that he died after this date.

Ibn Melek was a prominent scholar in his period, particularly in the sciences of *fiqh*, *uṣūl al-fiqh*, and *ḥadīth*. Upon Timur's (d. 807/1405) arrival in Tire, Ibn Melek met the famous scholar of the

Arabic language, *kalām*, and *fiqh* Sayyid Sharīf al-Jurjānī (d. 816/1413), who was in Timur's entourage and gained Ibn Melek's respect because of his knowledge and manners. Ibn Melek constructed a *bedesten* (covered market) in Tire. He had a brother, Abdülmecid (ʿAbd al-Mecīd) Firişteoğlu (d. after 864/1459–60), known for his works on Hurufism (Ḥurūfīsm), and two sons. One of his sons, Muhammed b. Abdüllatif (Muḥammad b. ʿAbd al-Laṭīf, d. after 868/1463), also known by the patronymic Ibn Melek, likewise wrote books. According to Katip (Kātib) Çelebi, his other son was named Cafer (Caʿfer).

Six works by Ibn Melek have been located, all of which were well known in the Ottoman realm, although his son's use of the same patronymic has temporarily confused research.

1. *Sharḥ Manār al-anwār*, a commentary in Arabic on the brief text by Abū l-Barakāt al-Nasafī (d. 710/1310) entitled *Manār al-anwār*, which treats theoretical jurisprudence. Ottoman *medrese*s used this work as a textbook, and it survives in the form of several manuscripts located at libraries, as well as in many printed editions. Some of the printed copies include supercommentaries in their margins, written by scholars such as Şerefeddin Yahya b. Karaca al-Ruhavi (Sharaf al-Dīn Yaḥyā b. Qaraca al-Ruhāvī, d. 1000/1591) and Azmizade Mustafa Haleti (ʿAzmīzāde Muṣṭafā Ḥāletī, d. 1040/1631).

2. *Mabāriq al-azhār fī sharḥ Mashāriq al-anwār*, a commentary in Arabic on the *ḥadīth* work *Mashāriq al-anwār al-nabawiyya* by Raḍiyy al-Dīn al-Ṣāghānī (d. 650/1252), who was a glossarist, linguist, and a scholar of jurisprudence and *ḥadīth*. It includes explanations of 2,250 prophetic traditions and survives in a large number of manuscripts and several printed editions.

3. *Sharḥ Majmaʿ al-Baḥrayn*, a commentary in Arabic on the work on Islamic jurisprudence by the Ḥanafī jurist Muẓaffar al-Dīn Ibn al-Sāʿātī (d. 694/1295). There are a large number of extant manuscripts of this work, which served as a source for future works on jurisprudence, and on which Qāsım b. Qutlubugha (d. 879/1474) composed a super-commentary.

4. *Firişteoghlu lughatı*, the oldest Arabic-Turkish dictionary, composed by Ibn Melek in 795/1392 as a textbook to help his grandson Abdurrahman (ʿAbd al-Raḥmān) memorise the Arabic words in the Qurʾān. Written in verse, this work includes the Turkish equivalents of 1,528 Arabic words, and it served as a model for future glossaries. When Evliya Çelebi visited the Firişteoğlu Medrese and Ibn Melek's tomb in Tire, he remembered with nostalgia the *Firişteoghlu lughatı*, which he had studied as a child. He quoted the beginning of the dictionary's first verse and stated playfully that he had learned his first Arabic words from Firişteoğlu's work. There are a large number of extant manuscripts of the dictionary. It was also printed several times and was the subject of a commentary.

5. *Sharḥ al-Wiqāya*, one of the most reputed commentaries (in Arabic) on one of the four major texts of Ḥanafī jurisprudence, *Wiqāya al-riwāya*, by Burhān al-Sharīʿa Maḥmūd b. Ṣadr al-Sharīʿa (d. 673/1274), brother of Tāj al-Sharīʿa (d. 709/1309), the author of *al-Hidāya*. Ibn Melek composed this work towards the end of his life, and it was lost after his death. His son Muhammed rewrote it subsequently from his father's rough drafts and included some additions of his own.

6. *Sharḥ Tuḥfat al-mulūk*, a commentary in Arabic on a work that treats religious services according to Ḥanafī jurisprudence, written by the scholar of Arabic language and literature and commentator of the Qurʾān *(mufassir)* Zayn al-Dīn Muḥammad b. Abū Bakr al-Rāzī (d. after 666/1268). It was published in 1428/2007, in Riyad.

A seventh work, in Arabic, of which there is no extant copy, is *Badr al-wāʿiẓīn wa-ẓuhr al-ʿābidīn*, consisting of twenty chapters on topics related to faith and religious service. It is mentioned by Katib Çelebi (1:231) and *Hadiyyat al-ʿārifīn* (1:618).

Four other books are also attributed to Ibn Melek, but none appear to be extant.

1. *al-Shāfī fī l-ṭibb*, a book on medicine attributed to Ibn Melek by Katib Çelebi (2:1023).
2. *Qaṣīdat al-munfarij* (According to Katib Çelebi (2:1346) Ibn Melek added 5 lines to this poem by Ibn al-Naḥwī (d. 513/1119), and it reached thirty-five couplets).
3. *Sharḥ al-Muqaddimāt fī l-ṣalāt*, according to Bursalı Meḥmed Ṭāhir (1:220), a commentary on Abū l-Layth al-Samarqandī's (d. 373/983) *al-Muqaddima fī l-ṣalāt*.
4. An unnamed book on *tasavvuf ("risāla laṭīfa fī al-taṣawwuf")* mentioned by Taşköprülüzāde, who added that it was a perfect example of Ibn Melek's knowledge of *sharīʿa-minded taṣawwuf*.

Bibliography

Katib Çelebi, *Keshfü'z-ẓünūn*, ed. M. Şerefettin Yaltkaya and Kilisli Rıfat Bilge, 2 vols. (Istanbul 1941/1360 and 1943/1362), 1:231, 374–5, 2:1601, 1689, 1825; Bağdatlı İsmail Paşa, *Hadiyyat al-ʿārifīn. Asmāʾ al-muʾallifīn wa-athār al-muṣannifīn*, ed. Kilisli Rifat Bilge and İbnülemin Mahmud Kemal İnal, vol. 1, Istanbul 1951; Cemal Muhtar, *Ferişteoğulları'nın Arapça-Türkçe lügatları üzerine araştırma*, Ph.D. diss., Ankara University 1981; Ṭāshkubrīzāda (Ṭāşköprüzade), *al-Shaqāʾiq al-nuʿmāniyya fī ʿulamāʾ al-Dawlat al-ʿUthmāniyya*, ed. Aḥmad Ṣubḥī Furāt (Istanbul 1985), 45; Mecdî Mehmed Efendi, *Hadaiku'ş-şakaik*, ed. Abdülkadir Özcan (Istanbul 1989), 66–7; Mustafa Baktır, Tireli İbn Melek. Hayatı, eserleri ve Menâr şerhi, *AÜ İlâhiyat Fakültesi Dergisi* 9 (1991), 40–66, and 10 (1991), 51–8; Cemal Muhtar, *İki Kur'ân sözlüğü. Luğat-ı Ferişteoğlu (Abdullatîf İbn Melek) ve Luğat-ı kânûn-ı ilâhî*, Istanbul 1993; Mustafa Baktır, Tireli İbn Melek ve ilmî muhiti hakkında bazı tesbitler, in Mehmet Şeker (ed.), *Türk kültüründe Tire* (Ankara 1994), 32–42; Ebû Abdullah Muhammed İbn Battûta Tancî, *İbn Battûta seyahatnâmesi*, trans. A. Sait Aykut (Istanbul 2004), 419; Evliyā Çelebi, *Seyâhatnâme* (Istanbul 2005), 9:81b; Fatih Sarıkaya, İbn Melek ve ailesi, *MCBÜ Sosyal Bilimler Dergisi* 15/1 (2017): 639–56; Ömer Faruk Akün, Firishte-oghlu, *EI2*; Mustafa Baktır, İbn Melek, *TDVIA* 22:175–6.

Hatice Aynur

Ibn al-Qaṭṭāʿ al-Ṣiqillī

Abū l-Qāsim ʿAlī b. Jaʿfar b. ʿAlī b. Muḥammad al-Saʿdī, widely known as **Ibn al-Qaṭṭāʿ al-Ṣiqillī** (433–515/1041–1121), was a distinguished Arab philologist and anthologist. He was born in Sicily on 10 Ṣafar 433 (9 October 1041) and was descended from the Aghlabids, a dynasty which ruled Ifrīqiya (Eastern Maghreb) in the third/ninth century and that seized Sicily from the Byzantines. His great-grandfather, grandfather, and father were all known littérateurs. Ibn al-Qaṭṭāʿ studied under several scholars in his homeland and specialised in literature and philology, disciplines that he studied under Ibn al-Birr al-Ṣiqillī (d. 460/1068), the leading linguist of his time in Sicily.

He presumably left the island sometime between 463/1071 and 483/1091 and before the Norman Conquest was completed. He seems to have initially sought refuge in Muslim Spain, most probably at the court of the Hūdids of Saragossa. Eventually, however, he settled in Cairo, around 500/1106. His fame as a scholar having preceded him there, he was well received and honoured by the Egyptian authorities and scholarly circles. Besides tutoring the children of the Fāṭimid *wazīr* al-Afḍal b. Badr al-Jamālī (d. 515/1121), the de facto ruler of Egypt at that time, he attracted numerous students interested in philology, being widely recognised as an authority in linguistic studies. The most distinguished among his pupils was the then very young Ibn Barrī (499–582/1106–87). Ibn al-Qaṭṭāʿ died at al-Fusṭāṭ in Ṣafar 515/April–May 1121 (or 514/1120) and was buried close to the tomb of al-Shāfiʿī (d. 204/820), the Sunnī jurist and eponym of one of the canonical Sunnī jurisprudential schools.

The most famous lexicographical work of Ibn al-Qaṭṭāʿ is the *Kitāb al-afʿāl* ("Book of verbs"), which aimed at complementing and improving upon Ibn al-Qūṭiyya's (d. 367/977) book bearing the same title. Both are dictionaries of verbs of the first and fourth verbal forms *(faʿala*, etc., and *afʿala)*, which were widely confused in daily usage in the local dialects. Besides making considerable additions to Ibn al-Qūṭiyya's material, thanks to its basically alphabetical arrangement Ibn al-Qaṭṭāʿ's book is easier to use. Likewise, in *Abniyat al-asmāʾ wa-l-afʿāl wa-l-maṣādir* ("The word-patterns of nouns, verbs, and verbal nouns"), a work on morphology rather than a lexicon, he succeeded in systematising and supplementing the work of several earlier grammarians. Besides simplifying the presentation of the various word-patterns, he also discusses particles.

A group of short lexicographical treatises by Ibn al-Qaṭṭāʿ survive in a Topkapı manuscript (Koğuşlar 1096). The treatises include six collections of synonymous words for marriage *(Kitāb al-nikāḥ)*, swords *(Kitāb al-sayf ṣifātuhū wa-asmāʾuhū)*, short people *(Kitāb al-qiṣār)*, tall people *(Kitāb al-ṭiwāl)*, walking and travelling *(Kitāb al-mashy wa-l-sayr)*, and various sounds *(Kitāb al-aṣwāt)*. Also included are the additions *(ziyādāt)* of Ibn al-Qaṭṭāʿ to similar collections of synonyms and special vocabulary by other authors, namely, the *Kitāb al-dawāhī* ("Book of calamities") of Abū ʿUbayda (d. 210/825), the *Kitāb al-aḥjār* ("Book of stones") of al-Ṣāḥib Ibn ʿAbbād (d. 385/995), the *Kitāb al-ḥayāt wa-l-mawt* ("Book of life and death") of Ibn Durustawayh (347/958), and *al-Khamr wa-asmāʾuhā* ("Wine and words for it") by Ibn al-Muʿtazz (d. 296/908) (which is not known through any other sources).

Ibn al-Qaṭṭāʿ's marginal notes *(ḥawāshī)* on al-Jawharī's (d. c.398/1008) comprehensive dictionary, *al-Ṣiḥāḥ*, a work which he transmitted on the authority of his teacher Ibn al-Birr, have been integrated into Ibn Barrī's improvements *(Kitāb al-tanbīh wa-l-īḍāḥ ʿammā waqaʿa fī l-Ṣiḥāḥ)* to that lexicon.

Ibn al-Qaṭṭāʿ's *Kitāb al-bāriʿ fī ʿilm al-ʿarūḍ* ("The outstanding book on metrics") is a systematic treatise of prosody, whereas *al-Shāfī fī l-qawāfī* ("The healer concerning rhymes") deals with rhyme. Another three short treatises on metrics and a work on *tajwīd* (Qurʾān recitation) have also survived (Weipert, *"Ein Unglück,"* 14).

Ibn al-Qaṭṭāʿ's anthology of Sicilian poets, *al-Durra al-khaṭīra fī shuʿarāʾ al-Jazīra*, which is said to have included 170 poets and around 20,000 verses, survives only partly in the form of two abridgments and several quotations in later works. A further anthology on Andalusian poets titled *Lumaḥ al-mulaḥ* (or *al-Mulaḥ al-ʿaṣriyya*) has not survived; in his *Masālik al-abṣār* (ed. al-Jubūrī, 17:346–58) Ibn Faḍlallāh's (700–49/1301–49) drew from it material concerning twenty-three poets.

Ibn al-Qaṭṭāʿ also composed a commentary on difficult verses by al-Mutanabbī (303–54/915–65). His *Taʾrīkh Ṣiqilliyya* ("History of Sicily") has been lost. Some seventy verses of his survive in various sources.

Bibliography

Edited Works

Ibn al-Qaṭṭāʿ, *Kitāb al-afʿāl*, 3 vols., Hyderabad 1360–1 (1941–2); Fritz Krenkow, *Fihris Kitāb al-afʿāl*, Hyderabad 1364 (1945); Ibn al-Qaṭṭāʿ, *Kitāb al-bāriʿ fī ʿilm al-ʿarūḍ*, ed. Aḥmad Muḥammad ʿAbd al-Dāyim, Mecca 1985[2]; Reinhard Weipert, Ibn al-Qaṭṭāʿs *Kitāb al-Qiṣār.* Ein lexikographischer Traktat aus dem frühen 6./12. Jh., in Regine Schulz and Manfred Görg (eds.), *Lingua restituta orientalis. Festgabe für Julius Assfalg* (Wiesbaden 1990), 388–404; Ibn al-Qaṭṭāʿ, *al-Durra al-khaṭīra fī shuʿarāʾ al-Jazīra*, ed. Bashīr al-Bakkūsh, Beirut 1995; ʿAbd al-Majīd Aḥmad al-Isdāwī, Mā tabaqqā min shiʿr Ibn al-Qaṭṭāʿ al-lughawī, *ʿĀlam al-kutub* 17/3 (1416/1996), 241–7 (on the remaining poems of Ibn al-Qaṭṭāʿ); Ibn al-Qaṭṭāʿ, *al-Shāfī fī l-qawāfī*, ed. Ṣāliḥ Ḥusayn ʿĀʾid, Riyadh 1998; Ibn al-Qaṭṭāʿ, *Abniyat al-asmāʾ wa-l-afʿāl wa-l-maṣādir*, ed. Aḥmad Muḥammad ʿAbd al-Dāyim, Cairo 1999; Ibn al-Qaṭṭāʿ, Sharḥ al-mushkil min shiʿr al-Mutanabbī, in Muḥsin Ghayyāḍ (ed.), *Shurūḥ shiʿr al-Mutanabbī* (Baghdad 2000), 153–208.

Reference Works

GAL 1:308; *GALS* 1:540; *GAS* 2:441, 494; Umberto Rizzitano, Ibn al-Qaṭṭāʿ, *EI2;* Khayr al-Dīn Ziriklī, *al-Aʿlām*, 12 vols. (Beirut 1969–70[3]), 4:269; Ramzi Baalbaki, *The Arabic lexicographical tradition. From the 2nd/8th to the 12th/18th century* (Leiden 2014), 258–60, 264–5, 333.

Select sources

Ibn Barrī al-Miṣrī, *Kitāb al-tanbīh wa-l-īḍāḥ ʿammā waqaʿa fī l-Ṣiḥāḥ*, ed. Muṣṭafā Ḥijāzī et al., 2 vols., Cairo 1980–1; al-Silafī, *Muʿjam al-safar*, ed. ʿAbdallāh ʿUmar al-Bārūdī (Beirut 1993), index; ʿImād al-Dīn al-Iṣfahānī, *Kharīdat al-qaṣr. Qism shuʿarāʾ al-Maghrib wa-l-Andalus*, ed. Muḥammad al-Marzūqī et al. (Tunis 1986[3]), 1:51–5; Yāqūt al-Rūmī, *Irshād al-arīb*, ed. Iḥsān ʿAbbās (Beirut 1993), 4:1669–70 and index; Ibn Khallikān, *Wafayāt al-aʿyān*, ed. Iḥsān ʿAbbās (Beirut 1977), 3:322–4; al-Qifṭī, *Inbāh al-ruwāt*, ed. Muḥammad Abū l-Faḍl Ibrāhīm (Cairo and Beirut 1987), 2:236–9; al-Ṣafadī, *al-Wāfī bi-l-wafayāt*, ed. Aḥmad Ḥuṭayṭ (Beirut 2007), 20:476–9; al-Dhahabī, *Taʾrīkh al-Islām*, ed. ʿUmar ʿAbd al-Salām Tadmurī (Beirut 1987–2000), 35:390–2; al-Dhahabī, *Siyar aʿlām al-nubalāʾ*, ed. Shuʿayb al-Arnaʾūṭ et al. (Beirut 1996[11]), 19:433–5; Ibn Ḥajar al-ʿAsqalānī, *Lisān al-mīzan*, ed. Salmān ʿAbd al-Fattāḥ Abū Ghadda (Beirut 2002), 5:506–7; al-Suyūṭī, *Bughyat al-wuʿāt*, ed. Muḥammad Abū l-Faḍl Ibrāhīm (Cairo 1964–5), 2:153–4.

Studies

Umberto Rizzitano, Notizie bio-bibliografiche su Ibn al-Qaṭṭāʿ "il siciliano" (433–515 Eg.), in *Atti della Accademia Nazionale dei Lincei. Rendiconti morali*, 8/9 (1954), 260–94; Aḥmad Muḥammad ʿAbd al-Dāyim, *Ibn al-Qaṭṭāʿ al-Ṣiqillī wa-juhūduhū l-ʿilmiyya*, Cairo 1997; Reinhard Weipert, *"Ein Unglück kommt selten allein." Vier arabische Synonymensammlungen zum Wortfeld* dāhiya (Munich 2004), 10–7, 19–20, 131–47; Oriana Capezio, Il trattato di metrica *Kitāb al-bāriʿ fī ʿilm al-ʿarūḍ* di Ibn al-Qaṭṭāʿ, *QSA* 10 (2015), 139–56; Oriana Capezio, Ibn al-Qaṭṭāʿ et la métrique arabe en Sicile entre le XIe et le XIIe siècle, *JAIS* 17 (2017), 79–96; Francesco Grande, Originality of the semantic approach in Arabic linguistic thought with particular reference to Ibn al-Qaṭṭāʿ's work, *JAIS* 17 (2017), 97–113; Cristina La Rosa, The *Maǧmūʿa min šiʿr al-Mutanabbī wa-ġawāmiḍihī* by Ibn al-Qaṭṭāʿ aṣ-Ṣiqillī. A morphological and lexical analysis, *JAIS* 17 (2017), 114–35.

Nefeli Papoutsakis

Ibn Sarābiyūn, Yūḥannā

Yūḥannā b. Sarābiyūn (third/ninth century), known in the Latin West as Serapion Senior, was the Christian author of a medical compendium (*kunnāsh*) composed in Syriac in two distinct versions, the smaller of which consisted of seven chapters (*maqālāt*), and the larger, twelve or thirteen. The bio-bibliographer Ibn Abī Uṣaybiʿa (d. 668/1269–70; 158) relates that Yūḥannā's father, who hailed from Bājarmā, in northern Iraq, and his brother Dāwūd b. Sarābiyūn were also physicians. Notwithstanding this testimony, Dāwūd is unlikely to be the younger brother of Yūḥannā because he appears to have lived in the late second/eighth century (al-Qifṭī, 431; Ibn Abī Uṣaybiʿa, 242). Mediaeval Latin sources attribute a work on simple medicines, *Liber aggregatus in medicinis simplicibus*, to a "Serapion Junior"; this author, however, has no relation to Yūḥannā, as the Latin text derives from the *Kitāb al-adwiya al-mufrada* ("The book of simple medicines") by the Andalusī physician Ibn Wāfid al-Lakhmī (d. 467/1075).

Of the two compendia, the *Small compendium* (*al-Kunnāsh al-ṣaghīr*) had a more profound influence on mediaeval medicine through its Arabic, Hebrew, and Latin translations. A few fragments of the original Syriac text of this composition survive in the lexicon of the Christian scholar Bar Bahlūl (fourth/tenth century). About half of the Arabic version of the *Small compendium* is extant. Ibn Abī Usaybiʿa and evidence from the manuscript tradition indicate that Yūḥannā's text was translated into Arabic several times. Abū Bishr Mattā b. Yūnus al-Qunnāʾī (d. 328/940) appears to have rendered the *Small compendium* into Arabic first, and the secretary Mūsā b. Ibrāhīm al-Ḥadīthī produced a translation that was more refined (or "of better expression," *aḥsan ʿibāratan*) in 318/930 for the physician Abū l-Ḥasan Ibn Nafīs. In his *al-Kitāb al-ḥāwī*, Abū Bakr al-Rāzī (known in the West as Rhazes; d. 313/925 or 323/935) draws on the former translation. Although Ibn Abī Usaybiʿa writes that Bar Bahlūl translated Yūḥannā's work into Arabic afresh, an analysis of his version suggests that he revised al-Ḥadīthī's copy (Pormann, 253–6). It is unclear on which Arabic translation Gerard of Cremona (d. 1187) based his fully extant Latin rendering of the *Small compendium*, which circulated under the titles *Brevarium medicinae* and *Practica*. The Italian physician and Arabist Andrea Alpago (d. c.1521–2) reworked Gerard's translation and added an index of drug names; his version was published posthumously in Venice in 1550. Moshe ben Maẓliaḥ also utilised Gerard's Latin text to make his Hebrew copy of the *Small compendium*, which survives in one manuscript produced in Rome in 1413.

Similar to most medical compilations from the mediaeval period, the *Small compendium* covers diseases in a head-to-toe arrangement and includes final chapters on fevers and *materia medica*. The *Large compendium* (*al-Kunnāsh al-kabīr*), which is lost in Syriac and extremely fragmentary in Arabic, seems to have followed this layout as well. Quotations of the *Large compendium* in the notebook of the fourth/tenth-century doctor al-Kaskarī show influence from the late antique Alexandrian medical tradition, in that Yūḥannā appeals to Aristotle's four causes (material, efficient, formal, and final) to explain diseases (Pormann, 258–60).

Bibliography

Sources
Ibn Abī Uṣaybiʿa, *Kitāb ʿuyūn al-anbāʾ fī ṭabaqāt al-aṭibbāʾ*, ed. Nizār Riḍā, Beirut 1965; al-Qifṭī, *Taʾrīkh al-ḥukamāʾ*, ed. J. Lippert, Leipzig 1903.

Studies
Peter E. Pormann, Yūḥannā Ibn Sarābiyūn: Further Studies Into the Transmission of His Works, *ASP* 14 (2004), 233–62; Lutz Richter-Bernburg, Pseudo-Ṯābit, Pseudo-Rāzī, Yūḥannā ibn Sarābiyūn, *Der Islam* 60 (1983), 48–77; Gérard Troupeau, Du syriaque au latin par l'intermédiaire de l'arabe. Le Kunnaš de Yuhanna ibn Sarabiyun, *ASP* 4/2 (1994), 267–77; Manfred Ullmann, *Die Medizin im Islam* (Leiden and Cologne 1970), 102–3; Manfred Ullmann, Yuḥanna ibn Sarabiyun. Untersuchungen zur Überlieferung seiner Werke, *Medizinhistorisches Journal* 6/4 (1971), 278–96; *GAS* 3:240–2.

Aileen R. Das

Ibn Sīda

Abū l-Ḥasan ʿAlī b. Ismāʿīl (or b. Aḥmad) **Ibn Sīda** al-Andalusī al-Mursī al-Ḍarīr (c.398–458/c.1008–66) was a prolific Andalusian lexicographer and philologist born in Murcia. He was blind, probably from birth, as was his father. Among his teachers were his father and Ṣāʿid b. al-Ḥasan al-Baghdādī (d. 417/1026). The biographer Ibn Ṣāʿid (d. 462/1070) mentions that, in addition to philology, Ibn Sīda also studied logic, making written contributions to the field.

Ibn Sīda must have been gifted with an excellent memory, for it is frequently related that he knew the entire *Gharīb al-muṣannaf* of Abū ʿUbayd al-Qāsim b. Sallām (d. 224/838) by heart. The ruler of Dénia, Mujāhid al-Muwaffaq (r. c.403–36/1012–44–5), who was eager to present himself as a promoter of science and the arts, acted as a patron of Ibn Sīda. It was under Mujāhid's patronage that he wrote his two major lexicographical works, *al-Muḥkam* and *al-Mukhaṣṣaṣ*. But tensions with Mujāhid's son and successor, ʿAlī Iqbāl al-Dawla (r. 436–68/1044–76), forced Ibn Sīda to leave Dénia. He returned only after he reconciled himself with the heir of his former patron by presenting to him a long *qaṣīda* (ode) composed in his honour. Ibn Sīda died rather suddenly in 458/1066 (or, according to some, in 448/1056) after suffering a stroke.

Ibn Sīda's first major work was the lexicon *Kitāb al-muḥkam wa-l-muḥīṭ al-aʿẓam*, arranged according to the phonetic-permutative principle that was applied for the first time in the *Kitāb al-ʿayn* of al-Khalīl b. Aḥmad (d. c.175/791), the first Arabic dictionary. Ibn Sīda's dictionary, then, was not arranged by the conventional Arabic alphabet, but rather according to places of articulation *(makhārij)*: for each consonant in the triliteral or quadriliteral root of a word all possible articulations would be registered before proceeding to the next combination. Among the sources of the *Muḥkam* are Abū ʿUbayd's (d. 224/838) *Gharīb al-muṣannaf*, Ibn al-Sikkīt's (d. c.243/857) *Tahdhīb al-alfāẓ* and *Iṣlāḥ al-manṭiq*, and Ibn Durayd's (d. 321/933) *Jamharat al-lugha*. Within the lemmata, Ibn Sīda cites his sources by name only rarely. The *Muḥkam* in turn became one of the five sources of Ibn Manẓūr's (d. 711/1311) *Lisān al-ʿArab* ("The tongue of the Arabs"), one of the great Arabic lexica.

The other lexicographical work that made Ibn Sīda famous was his *Kitāb al-mukhaṣṣaṣ*, a lexicon of the *mubawwab* type, that is, not being arranged alphabetically but rather semantically. Its arrangement follows largely the arrangement of

Abū ʿUbayd's *Gharīb al-muṣannaf* (the earliest lexicon with semantic arrangement), but also includes chapters on grammar. The *Gharīb al-muṣannaf* is also the major source of the *Mukhaṣṣaṣ*—being not just cited on virtually every page but also subsumed in its entirety. Contrary to his methodology in *al-Muḥkam*, Ibn Sīda cites here his sources meticulously by name, thus creating a much more scholarly work than the *Muḥkam*.

Another extant work of Ibn Sīda is his commentary on the poetry of al-Mutanabbī (d. 354/965), *Sharḥ al-mushkil min shiʿr al-Mutanabbī*, in which the difficult verses of al-Mutanabbī's *Dīwān* are selected for discussion. Other books whose titles are mentioned in biographies, but which are no longer extant, are *Sharḥ Iṣlāḥ al-manṭiq* (a commentary on a philological work by Ibn al-Sikkīt), *al-Anīq fī sharḥ al-Ḥamāsa* (a commentary on the anthology of poetry by Abū Tammām, d. 231/845), *al-ʿĀlam fī l-lugha ʿalā l-ajnās* (probably a work on homonyms, said to be "a very large work"), *al-ʿĀlim wa-l-mutaʿallim ʿalā l-masʾala wa-l-jawāb* (probably wrongly attributed to Ibn Sīda, cf. *GAS* 9:223), *al-Wāfī fī ʿilm aḥkām al-qawāfī* (on the principles of rhyme), *Shādhdh al-lugha* (on irregular phenomena in the language), *Sharḥ kitāb al-Akhfash* (also known as *al-Akhfash al-awsaṭ*, d. 215/830, but probably wrongly attributed to Ibn Sīda, cf. *GAS* 9:223), and *Sharḥ abyāt al-Jumal lil-Zajjājī* (a commentary on the verses quoted in the book on syntax by al-Zajjājī, d. 337/949).

Bibliography

Works by Ibn Sīda

Kitāb al-muḥkam wa-l-muḥīṭ al-aʿẓam, ed. Muṣṭafā l-Saqqāʾ et al., 12 vols., Cairo 1958–99; *Kitāb al-mukhaṣṣaṣ*, 17 vols., Cairo 1898–1903; *Sharḥ al-mushkil min shiʿr al-Mutanabbī*, ed. Muṣṭafā l-Saqqāʾ and Ḥāmid ʿAbd al-Majīd, 2 vols., Cairo 1976.

Sources

Ṣāʿid al-Andalusī, *Ṭabaqāt al-umam*, ed. Louis Cheikho (Beirut 1912), 77, trans. Régis Blachère (Paris 1935), 2:141–2; al-Ḥumaydī, *Jadhwat al-muqtabis fī taʾrīkh ʿulamāʾ al-Andalus*, ed. Ibrāhīm al-Ibyārī (Cairo and Beirut 1984), 493–4; Ibn Khāqān, *Maṭmaḥ al-anfus wa-masraḥ al-taʾannus*, ed. Muḥammad ʿAlī Shawābika (Beirut 1983), 291–3; Ibn Bashkuwāl, *al-Ṣila*, ed. Francisco Codera y Zaidín (Madrid 1883), 410–11, no. 889; Ibn Khayr, *Fahrasat mā rawāhu ʿan shuyūkhihī*, ed. Francisco Codera and Julián Ribera Tarrago (Beirut 1963), 356–7; al-Ḍabbī, *Bughyat al-multamis fī taʾrīkh rijāl al-Andalus*, ed. Francisco Codera y Zaidín (Madrid 1885), 405–7, no. 1205; Yāqūt, *Muʿjam al-udabāʾ*, ed. Iḥsān ʿAbbās (Beirut 1993), 4:1648–50; al-Qifṭī, *Inbāh al-ruwāt*, ed. Muḥammad Abū l-Faḍl Ibrāhīm (Cairo 1952), 2:225–7; Ibn Khallikān, *Wafayāt al-aʿyān*, ed. Iḥsān ʿAbbās (Beirut n.d. [1985]), 3:330–1; al-Ṣafadī, *al-Wāfī bi-l-wafayāt* (Beirut 2007), 20:339–42; al-Ṣafadī, *Nakt al-himyān fī nukat al-ʿumyān* (Cairo 1911), 204–5; al-Suyūṭī, *Bughyat al-wuʿāt fī ṭabaqāt al-lughawiyyīn wa-l-nuḥāt* (Cairo 1326), 327.

Studies

GAL 1:308–9; *GALS* 1:542; Ramadan Abdel-Tawab, *Das Kitāb al-Ġarīb al-muṣannaf von Abū ʿUbaid und seine Bedeutung für die nationalarabische Lexikographie* (Münich 1962), 178–81, 216–20; Stefan Wild, *Das Kitāb al-ʿAin und die arabische Lexikographie* (Münich 1965), 81–4; Ramzi Baalbaki, *The Arabic lexicographical tradition. From the 2nd/8th to the 12th/18th century* (Leiden 2014), 274–8, 322–9; Muḥammad al-Ṭālibī, *al-Mukhaṣṣaṣ l-Ibn Sīda*, 2 vols., Tunis 1956; Dolores Serrano-Niza, *El proyecto lexicográfico de Ibn Sīdah, un sabio en la Taifa de Denia*, Onda 1999; Dario Cabanelas Rodríguez, *Ibn Sida de Murcia, el mayor lexicógrafo de al-Andalus*, Murcia 1986[2]; John A. Haywood, Ibn Sīda (d. 458/1066). The greatest Andalusian lexicographer, in *Primer Congreso de Estudios Arabes e Islámicos. Córdoba 1962. Actas* (Madrid 1964), 309–16; ʿAbd al-Karīm Shadīd Muḥammad al-Nuʿaymī, *Ibn Sīda. Āthāruhū wa-juhūduhū fī l-lugha*, Baghdad 1984; Dolores Serrano-Niza, Una fuente de Ibn Sīdah (s. XI). El Garīb al-muṣannaf de Abū ʿUbayd (s. IX), *Boletin de la Asociacion Española de Orientalistas* 33 (1997), 57–67; Dolores Serrano-Niza, *Glossario árabe español de indumentaria según el Kitāb al-Mujaṣṣaṣ de Ibn Sīda* (Madrid 2005); Gérard Troupeau, Le vocabulaire chrétien dans le *Kitāb al-muḫaṣṣaṣ* d'Ibn Sīdah, *Zeitschrift für arabische Linguistik* 25 (1993), 289–301; Rafael Muñoz Jiménez, El léxico agrícola y alimentario en el Mujaṣṣaṣ de Ibn Sīda, *Ciencias de la naturaleza en al-Andalus* 3 (1994), 121–42; Georges Douillet, Essai d'analyse du chapitre du Muḫaṣṣaṣ d'Ibn Sidoh consacré aux autruches, *REI* 61–2 (1993–4), 109–22.

Stefan Weninger

Ibn Yasīr al-Riyāshī

Muḥammad **Ibn Yasīr al-Riyāshī** was an early ʿAbbāsid poet of Basra who died sometime after 198/814. He was a member of the Riyāsh clan of the Khathʿam tribe and reportedly never left his native Basra to seek the patronage of wealthy grandees in Baghdad or elsewhere. Nevertheless, Ibn Yasīr maintained good relations with local notables, the governors of Basra, and several Hāshimites and members of the ʿAbbāsid family that lived in the city, regularly attending their drinking parties. Even though on several occasions he petitioned them for—or received from them—gifts and money, it is unclear to what extent they maintained him, as he seemingly did not compose any praise poetry for them. Very occasionally Ibn Yasīr alludes to his straitened circumstances (such as his tattered shoes, his inability to entertain guests lavishly, and his wanting a mount) or urges himself to be content with his lot, but he never really complains about it. Several of his poems refer to the drinking parties he frequented and to various ensuing incidents, his drunkenness, the jokes he exchanged with the hosts or drinking companions, and so forth. Other poems relate to his scholarly activities: he boasts about his love of learning, intelligence, and good memory (he did not need to bring paper and pen to the study sessions he attended); he praises books for all the knowledge they preserve and for being better and safer company than men; he laments the theft of his writing-tablets.

Ibn Yasīr's fame rests primarily on two long poems. On the one hand, there is a 51-verse ode in which he curses the ewe *(shāt)* of Manīʿ, his neighbour, which had crossed into his garden, devoured his plants, then entered his house and munched on his notebooks too. On the other hand, there is a 35-line poem in which he curses the pigeons of al-Madanī—a pigeon-breeder who had deceitfully sold him ordinary pigeons, passing them off as pedigree pigeons—wishing them to fall prey to falcons, hawks, cats, and hunters. His corpus also includes mild lampoons of some of his acquaintances. The two most recent collections of his extant poetry contain some seventy items, at least twenty of which are also attributed to other poets, altogether amounting to around 400 verses.

In some sources (al-Marzubānī and al-Ṣafadī) the name of Ibn Yasīr's father is misspelled as Bashīr. His poetry is sometimes muddled with that of the Umayyad poet Muḥammad b. Bashīr al-Khārijī.

Bibliography

Editions

Charles Pellat, Muḥammad b. Yasīr al-Riyāshī wa-ashʿāruhū, *al-Mashriq* 49 (May-June 1955), 289–338; Muẓhar al-Ḥajjī, *Dīwān Muḥammad b. Yasīr al-Riyāshī*, Homs 1996; Muḥammad Jabbār al-Muʿaybid and Muzhir al-Sūdānī, Shiʿr Muḥammad b.

Yasīr al-Riyāshī, *al-Dhakhāʾir* 2 (1420/2000), 55–138.

Reference works

GAS 2:506–7, 9:295; Charles Pellat, Muḥammad b. Yasīr al-Riyāshī, *EI2*; Khayr al-Dīn al-Ziriklī, *al-Aʿlām* (Beirut 1969–70³), 7:144.

Sources

al-Jāḥiẓ, *Kitāb al-ḥayawān*, ed. ʿAbd al-Salām Muḥammad Hārūn, 8 vols. (Cairo 1965–9²), index; al-Jāḥiẓ, *al-Bayān wa-l-tabyīn*, ed. ʿAbd al-Salām Muḥammad Hārūn, 4 vols. (Cairo 1998⁷), index; Ibn Qutayba, *al-Shiʿr wa-l-shuʿarāʾ*, ed. Aḥmad Muḥammad Shākir (Cairo, 1966–7), 2:879–80; al-Iṣfahānī, *Kitāb al-aghānī*, ed. Iḥsān ʿAbbās et al. (Beirut 2008³), 14:13–32; al-Marzubānī, *Muʿjam al-shuʿarāʾ*, ed. Fritz Krenkow (Beirut 1982²), 418; Yāqūt al-Rūmī, *Irshād al-arīb*, ed. Iḥsān ʿAbbās (Beirut 1993), 3:1279–80, 4:1492–3 (attributing to him a three-line poem on the Barmakids not found in his collected poetry); al-Ṣafadī, *al-Wāfī bi-l-wafayāt*, ed. Aḥmad Arnāʾūṭ and Turkī Muṣṭafā (Beirut 1420/2000), 2:182–3.

Nefeli Papoutsakis

Ibn Zaydūn

Abū l-Walīd Aḥmad b. ʿAbdallāh **Ibn Zaydūn** al-Makhzūmī (born in Córdoba in 394/1003, died in Seville in 463/1070) was the most famous poet of al-Andalus and is especially remembered for his love poems addressed to the Umayyad princess and poet Wallāda (d. 484/1091), daughter of the caliph al-Mustakfī (r. 414–6/1024–5). Ibn Zaydūn was also a fine prose writer, greatly appreciated in Syria and Egypt in particular, with his epistles being the subject of commentaries and included in anthologies as samples of literary craftsmanship. Besides his literary activity, Ibn Zaydūn was also active in the political sphere, serving as *wazīr* and ambassador for the rulers of Córdoba and Seville.

The sources for Ibn Zaydūn's biography are essentially Ibn Bassām (d. 543/1147), who cites the historian Ibn Ḥayyān (d. 469/1076), Ibn Khāqān (d. 529/1134), and Ibn al-Abbār (d. 658/1260). All other authors only repeat their information, trying sometimes to construct a consistent account of Ibn Zaydūn's love life and politics.

Ibn Zaydūn belonged to an aristocratic family of Córdoba. After his father's death in 405/1014–5, his maternal grandfather, a specialist in Islamic law and the Islamic sciences, oversaw his formation. Later in his life he probably played some part in the abolition of the Umayyad caliphate in al-Andalus (422/1031), given that he subsequently found himself serving the ruling elite of Córdoba, led by Abū l-Ḥazm Ibn Jahwar (r. 422–35/1031–43), as *wazīr* and ambassador to the petty kings of al-Andalus following the dynastic change, his eloquence and savoir-faire being fundamental to his success. Around 432–5/1040–3 Ibn Zaydūn was imprisoned for a charge ambiguously reported in Arabic sources as a political or economic crime or as political intrigue. His poems and epistles to Ibn Jahwar pleading for mercy or to his friends asking for their intercession with the ruler were of no avail (see, for example, his *al-Risāla al-jiddiyya*, "Epistle on serious matters"). After many months in jail he was freed, and when his friend Abū l-Walīd succeeded his father, Abū l-Ḥazm, as Córdoba's ruler (r. 435–55/1043–63), Ibn Zaydūn was restored to office, although his close relation with other Ṭāʾifa rulers sometimes aroused the suspicion of his Córdoban master. Finally, in 441/1049, Ibn Zaydūn left Córdoba for Seville, where he spent the rest of his life as *wazīr* of the ʿAbbādid rulers al-Muʿtaḍid (r. 433–

61/1042–69) and al-Muʿtamid (r. 461–84/1069–91). He returned to Córdoba when al-Muʿtamid conquered the city in 462/1070. Ibn Zaydūn died the following year in Seville, where he had been sent in order to subdue a social disturbance. His son Abū Bakr Muḥammad b. Abī l-Walīd Ibn Zaydūn (d. 484/1091) succeeded him as one of al-Muʿtamid's *wazīrs*.

As a court poet, Ibn Zaydūn composed many poems both praising his patrons and extending condolences to them, as well as occasional descriptive poems composed for the literary meetings presided over by the Sevillian rulers. But he was also a ferocious satirist (al-Ḥumaydī; Ibn Saʿīd). The poems of Ibn Zaydūn inspired by princess Wallāda are among the best Arabic love poems because he succeeds in expressing a vivid experience, sometimes not at all conventional, in which literary tropes, rhythm, and emotion are merged to great effect. The most celebrated of Ibn Zaydūn's love poems, his *Nūniyya* (rhyming in *n*), has been frequently imitated by later Arab poets, from the mediaeval period until the twentieth century. Ghazāl reproduces fifty-two such poems *(muʿāraḍāt)*, the most famous of which is a neo-classical poem by the Egyptian poet Aḥmad Shawqī (d. 1932). Some of these imitations are composed in a strophic form, such as a *muwashshaḥa* by Ibn Wakīl (d. 716/1316; al-Maqqarī, 1:632–4; Ghazāl, *Muʿāraḍāt*, 251–2). Other strophic imitations have been composed as *muṣammaṭ*, usually *mukhammasāt*, that is, strophic poems having five lines per stanza (Ghazāl, *Muʿāraḍāt*, 87–94, 130–5, 170–4, 236), but sometimes six (al-Maqqarī 3:278; Ghazāl, *Muʿāraḍāt*, 75–86).

It is not known when Ibn Zaydūn met Wallāda, perhaps in her literary salon where men of letters were welcomed, but it was probably in the last years of the Umayyad Caliphate, although no dates are recorded. The first time Ibn Bassām mentions her name is in connection with a violent satire by Ibn Zaydūn against a Córdoban *wazīr*, Abū ʿĀmir Ibn ʿAbdūs, who was a protector of Wallāda in her old age, but appears in later sources as Ibn Zaydūn's rival for Wallāda's love but also as the man who instigated his imprisonment. Ibn ʿAbdūs is also the addressee of another satire by Ibn Zaydūn, *al-Risāla al-hazliyya* ("The jocular epistle"), in which Wallāda is depicted as deriding Ibn ʿAbdūs. The end of this love affair seems to have been some furious satires by Wallāda against Ibn Zaydūn (al-Maqqarī 4:205–6). Ibn Khāqān, however, extends Ibn Zaydūn's affection for the princess over a longer period of time; even in 446/1054 Wallāda is the feminine figure evoked in the amorous prelude of a eulogy composed in honour of Seville's ruler al-Muʿtaḍid.

Ibn Zaydūn was a successful prose writer, greatly appreciated in his time. It is said that his chancery epistles to other petty kings of al-Andalus were so beautifully written that they were appreciated almost as poetry, but they have not been preserved (*Dhakhīra*, 1:337; also quoted by Ibn al-Abbār, *Iʿtāb*, 213). Those that have been preserved are linked to his adventurous life, his imprisonment, and his tempestuous love for princess Wallāda. The most famous epistles by Ibn Zaydūn are *al-Risāla al-jiddiyya* (partially preserved in Ibn Bassām's *Dhakhīra*, 1:340–6) and *al-Risāla al-hazliyya*. Both epistles were reproduced and commented by Eastern authors writing in the eighth/fourteenth century. Al-Nuwayrī (d. 733/1332) included both epistles in his encyclopaedic work, *Nihāyat al-arab fī funūn al-adab*. The titles of both epistles, echoing each other, were added by later authors in order to highlight their contents.

Ibn Zaydūn's *al-Risāla al-jiddiyya*, written in jail in an attempt to justify himself to Abū l-Ḥazm Ibn Jahwar, was commented upon by al-Ṣafadī (d. Damascus 764/1363) in *Tamām al-mutūn fī sharḥ Risālat Ibn Zaydūn*. Ibn Zaydūn's *al-Risāla al-hazliyya* also received critical attention by another Egyptian author, Ibn Nubāta (d. 768/1366) in *Sarḥ al-ʿuyūn fī sharḥ Risālat Ibn Zaydūn*. Composed in the style of the *Kitāb al-tarbīʿ wa-l-tadwīr* by the famous ʿAbbāsid prose writer al-Jāḥiẓ (d. 255/868), *al-Risāla al-hazliyya* is a display of erudition and forceful argument written with the aim of debasing Ibn ʿAbdūs.

Al-Maqqarī (d. 1041/1632), citing Ibn Saʿīd (d. 685/1286), says that Ibn Zaydūn composed a history of the Umayyad caliphs (al-Maqqarī, 3:182) titled *Kitāb al-tabyīn fī khulafāʾ Banī Umayya bi-l-Andalus* ("A book elucidating the Umayyad caliphs of al-Andalus"). He asserts that this history follows the model of *al-Taʿyīn fī khulafāʾ al-mashriq* ("On the caliphs of the orient") by the Baghdadi historian al-Masʿūdī (d. 345/956)—a work occasionally referred to by al-Maqqarī (1:332; 3:46) but which is no longer extant. Perhaps, as suggested by Iḥsān ʿAbbās (the editor of al-Maqqarī's *Nafḥ al-ṭīb*), *Kitāb al-tabyīn* was not written by Ibn Zaydūn but rather by his son Abū Bakr.

Ibn Zaydūn's love for princess Wallāda has inspired some interesting modern Arab plays, including *Riwāyat Abī l-Walīd Ibn Zaydūn maʿa Wallāda bint al-Mustakfī*, written by Ibrāhīm al-Aḥdab (1826–91); *Gharām Wallāda* by Ḥusayn Sirāj (1912–2007); and *al-Wazīr al-ʿāshiq* by Farūq Juwayda (Farouk Gouida; b. 1946). Similarly, a number of novels that evoke the tale of Ibn Zaydūn and Wallāda have also been penned, including *Hātif min al-Andalus* by Alī al-Jārim (1881–1949).

Bibliography

Works by and about Ibn Zaydūn are too numerous to mention here. These include a number of works arising out of two conferences focussed on exploring Ibn Zaydūn's life and legacy. The first was held in Rabat in 1975 to commemorate one thousand years since the birth of Ibn Zaydūn. The proceedings of this conference were published in *al-Dhikrā l-alfiyya li-mīlād Ibn Zaydūn*, Rabat 1975. The second conference, held in Córdoba in 2004, was sponsored by the Albabtain Poetic Prize and encouraged the printing (and re-printing) of Ibn Zaydūn's oeuvre and works that seek to elucidate the context in which he lived.

Editions and Translations

Ibn Zaydūn, *Dīwān Ibn Zaydūn wa-rasāʾiluh*, ed. ʿAlī ʿAbd al-ʿAẓīm, Cairo 1376/1957 and Kuwait 2004[3]; Ibn Zaydūn, *Dīwān, Maʿah rasāʾiluh wa-akhbāruh*, ed. Muḥammad Sayyid Kīlānī, Cairo 1956; Ibn Zaydūn, *Dīwān Ibn Zaydūn*, ed. Karam Bustānī, Beirut 1975; Ibn Zaydūn, *Dīwān Ibn Zaydūn*, ed. Yūsuf Farḥāt, Beirut 1410/1994[2]; *Casidas de amor profano y místico. Ibn Zaydun, Ibn Arabi*, ed. and trans. Vicente Cantarino, Mexico City 1977; Ibn Zaydūn, Epístola burlesca, in *Epístolas árabes del siglo XI*, trans. Julio Samsó and Leonor Martínez (Barcelona 1999), 177–91; Ibn Zaydūn, *Poesías*, ed. and trans. Mahmud Sobh, Madrid 1985; Ibn Zaydūn, *Casidas selectas*, ed. Mahmud Sobh, Madrid 2005; ʿAbdallāh Sanda, *Dīwān Ibn Zaydūn. Dirāsa wa-tahdhīb*, Beirut 2005.

Sources

Ibn al-Abbār, *Iʿtāb al-kuttāb*, ed. Ṣāliḥ al-Ashtar, Damascus 1380/1961, 207–13 (no. 64); Ibn Bassām, *al-Dhakhīra fī maḥāsin ahl al-jazīra*, ed. Iḥsān ʿAbbās (Beirut 1978), 1:336–428; al-Ḥumaydī, *Jadhwat al-muqtabis fī dhikr wulāt al-Andalus* (Cairo 1966), 130–1 (no. 224); Ibn Khāqān, *Qalāʾid al-ʿiqyān*, ed. Muḥammad b. ʿĀshūr (Tunis 1990), 175–99 (no. 7); Ibn Saʿīd al-Maghribī, *al-Mughrib fī ḥulā l-Maghrib*, ed. Shawqī Ḍayf (Cairo n.d.), 1:63–9; al-Maqqarī, *Nafḥ al-ṭīb*, ed. Iḥsān ʿAbbās (Beirut 1388/1968), index; al-Ṣafadī, *Tamām al-mutūn fī sharḥ Risālat Ibn Zaydūn*, ed. Muḥammad Abū l-Faḍl Ibrāhīm,

1389/1969; Ibn Nubāta, *Sarḥ al-ʿuyūn fī sharḥ Risālat Ibn Zaydūn*, ed. Muḥammad Abū l-Faḍl Ibrāhīm, Beirut 1406/1986; al-Nuwayrī, *Nihāyat al-arab fī funūn al-adab* (Cairo 1923), 7:271–302.

Studies

L. Alvarez, Ibn Zaydun, *EAL*, 1:384–5; Rachel Arié, Ibn Zaydūn wa-Banū l-Afṭas, *Awrāq jadīda* 7–8 (1985), 69–73; Auguste Cour, *Un poète arabe d'Andalousie, Ibn Zaïdoûn. Étude d'après le Dîwân de ce poète et les principales sources arabes*, Constantine 1920; Terri DeYoung, Aḥmad ibn ʿAbd Allāh Ibn Zaydūn, in Terri DeYoung and Mary St. Germain (eds.), *Essays in Arabic literary biography. 925–1350* (Wiesbaden 2011), 204–15; Raymond K. Farrin, The *nūniyya* of Ibn Zaydūn. A structural and thematic analysis, *JAL* 34/1–2 (2003), 82–106; Teresa Garulo, La biografía de Wallāda, toda problemas, *Anaquel de estudios árabes* 20 (2009), 97–116; ʿAdnān Muḥammad Ghazāl, *Muʿāraḍāt qaṣāʾid Ibn Zaydūn*, Kuwait 2004; ʿAdnān Muḥammad Ghazāl, *Maṣādir dirāsat Ibn Zaydūn*, Kuwait 2004; Salma Khadra Jayyusi, Andalusī poetry. The golden period, in Salma Khadra Jayyusi (ed.), *The legacy of Muslim Spain* (Leiden 1992), 1:317–66; Abū l-Qāsim Karrū, *Shawqī wa-Ibn Zaydūn fī nūniyyatayhimā*, Tunis 2004[3] (originally published Tunis 1956); G. Lecomte, Ibn Zaydūn, *EI2*; Sieglinde Lug, *Poetic techniques and conceptual elements in Ibn Zaydūn's love poetry*, Washington 1982; Fedwa Malti-Douglas, Ibn Zaydūn. Towards a thematic analysis, *Arabica* 23/1 (1976), 63–76; Bruno Marchand, Un *muwaššaḥ* d'Ibn Zaydūn, *Arabica* 25 (1978), 10–17; Jaime Sánchez Ratia, Ibn Zaydūn, Abū l-Walīd, *Biblioteca de al-Andalus* (Almería 2009), 6:287–304; Devin J. Stewart, Ibn Zaydūn, in *The literature of al-Andalus, CHAL*, 306–17.

Teresa Garulo

al-Ījāz wa-l-iṭnāb

Al-ījāz wa-l-iṭnāb form a conceptual pair in Arabic literary theory and rhetoric, denoting respectively conciseness and prolixity.

Since both *ījāz* and *iṭnāb* are relative values marking the poles of a continuum, a third concept, *al-musāwāt*, referring to the standard expression, that is, the wording that an average speaker would use to express an intended meaning, is usually taken as a given, although not always explicitly mentioned. If the intended meaning is adequately (*bi-l-muṭābaqa*) conveyed by a more succinct expression than what might be considered the standard, straightforward wording, it is termed *ījāz*. If the supposed balance between words (*lafẓ*) and meaning (*maʿnā*) is altered towards a more verbose style, it is an instance of *iṭnāb*. Most theorists regard *musāwāt* as a class of its own, a style that might be used intentionally in certain situations, while others see it as a feature of conciseness. Occasionally, it is replaced as a point of reference by the concept of basic intention (*aṣl al-murād*; al-Qazwīnī, 281).

While *ījāz* is highly appreciated, to the extent that it is sometimes identified with eloquence itself (al-Jāḥiẓ, 1:96), theorists state that *ījāz* per se is not necessarily a virtue of speech but becomes such only when used in the right place. Both *ījāz* and *iṭnāb* are related to their corresponding communicative purposes according to the principle that an expression must match a given context (*li-kulli maqām maqāl*). If brevity is not adequate to the situation, it is seen as a deficiency (*taqṣīr*). But in many contexts, conciseness is highly valued, as in poetry, where conciseness is often required for formal reasons and because of the constraints of metre. Brevity is associated with the Bedouins and their purported mastery of Arabic, and with the social elite. Secretaries and poets are expected to have command of a succinct style (Ibn al-Athīr, 2:268), and edicts and verdicts of rulers that are phrased in a terse and original way are viewed as exemplifying the ideal of brevity in eloquence (Gruendler, 102). A good ellipsis, it is claimed, can be more indicative of an intended meaning than the explicit words would be (Ibn al-Athīr, 2:277). On the other hand, even figures of semantic redundancy (*ḥashw, taṭwīl*) may be pleasing. Prolixity is the style of choice for formal orations, sermons, praise and glorification, and accounts of battles and the like. When, in the seventh/thirteenth century, the formation of a standard theory of Arabic rhetoric turned into scholasticism, handbooks present numerous subcategories of both *ījāz* and *iṭnāb*, which are sometimes listed as figures of speech in their own right, the designations of which often reveal the purpose for which they are used.

Impulses for the theoretical and terminological elaboration of both concepts have their origins in the fields of grammar, the education of secretaries (*kuttāb*), literary theory, and the philologically based interpretation of the Qurʾān.

Omission of a word or group of words is also a subject of early grammatical writing. The famed grammarian Sībawayh (d. c.180/796) categorises cases exemplified by phrases such as *isʾal al-qarya*, "ask the village" (Q 12:82), rather than the more explicit *isʾal ahl al-qarya*, "ask the people of the village," as instances of *ījāz* and *ikhtiṣār* (brevity; Versteegh 281). In a work of early philological exegesis, Abū ʿUbayda (d. 210/825) cites the same verse as an example of *ḥadhf* (ellipsis) and also mentions the category of *ikhtiṣār* among the variety of linguistic patterns found in the Qurʾān (Abū ʿUbayda, 1:8f.). In both categories, a hidden element is involved: while *ḥadhf* refers to a smaller unit that can be easily inferred, *ikhtiṣār* can pertain to an entire sequence or phrase that may require more effort to understand. Clearly drawing from the work of his predecessors, al-Rummānī (d. 384/994), one of the key figures among those who brought the study of rhetoric to bear on the idea of the inimitability of the Qurʾān (*iʿjāz al-Qurʾān*), posited what was henceforth a canonical classification of *ījāz* into *ḥadhf* and *qiṣar*. With *ḥadhf*, one dispenses with a word because something in the situation or in the text hints at it, and the word itself then becomes unnecessary. Other instances in which dimensions of meaning are added to a basic meaning while the number of words is reduced, but without recourse to ellipsis, are termed *qiṣar*, the standard example of which is Q 2:179, *lakum fī l-qiṣāṣi ḥayātun* "in retaliation there is life for you" (al-Rummānī, 70f.). Theorists detect a number of rhetorical qualities that make this wording more concise and eloquent than other phrases with the same intended meaning, ranging from its potential to evoke multiple associations to the formal aspects of the words used. Compared to the semantically similar saying of the Bedouins, *al-qatlu anfā lil-qatli* "killing best prevents killing," for its part also an example of succinctness, the Qurʾānic sequence (a) encompasses a wider meaning by evoking the idea of justice and mentioning life as the desired purpose, (b) is more concise because *fī l-qiṣāṣi ḥayātun* as the equivalent of the Bedouin saying consists of fewer Arabic letters, (c) is free of repetition, and (d) has a more harmonious flow of sounds and is easier to pronounce.

From the fourth/tenth century onwards, the concept of *iʿjāz* was considered by many scholars unsurpassable in terms of rhetorical superiority, with brevity seen to be the heart of eloquence and conciseness a key element of Qurʾānic inimitability. Making use of the writings of al-Jāḥiẓ

(d. 255/868), Ibn Qutayba (d. 276/889), and al-Rummānī, Abū Hilāl al-ʿAskarī (d. 395–400/1005–1010) applied the analytical tools of literary criticism available in his time to both poetry and prose. His influence can be found especially in Ḍiyāʾ al-Dīn Ibn al-Athīr's (d. 637/1239) work *al-Mathal al-sāʾir*, dedicated to the education of secretaries and men of letters, which includes a detailed section on *ījāz* and *iṭnāb*. With the exceptions of Ibn al-Athīr and Ibn Abī l-Iṣbaʿ (d. 654/1256), the theorists' analyses are usually restricted to the sentence level.

Already Sībawayh does not treat a case such as Q 12:82 as merely an ordinary elision of a word, but as a challenge for the hearer to join the surface meaning of the expression to the intended meaning. In order to be brief, the speaker deviates from the normal use of speech, thus demanding a mental operation on the part of the hearer to infer what is meant. Commentators later employ the terms *ḥaqīqa* and *majāz* for these instances (Versteegh, 281). For Ibn Abī l-Iṣbaʿ (180), *ījāz* is of two kinds, one forming a trope (*majāzī*) and one based on literal meaning (*ḥaqīqī*), with each trope implying *ījāz*, even though not every succinct mode of expression is a trope.

Since the days of al-Sakkākī (d. 626/1229) and up to the present, *al-ījāz wa-l-iṭnāb* have been treated by most theorists as part of the *ʿilm al-maʿānī*, the study of the relationship between syntactical patterns and speech acts, which builds a bridge between grammar and the study of tropes. In manuals of a less systematic type dedicated to rhetorical devices, conciseness and prolixity are classified with the other figures and embellishments of speech under the heading of *badīʿ* (figures of speech).

Bibliography

Sources

Abū ʿUbayda, *Majāz al-Qurʾān*, ed. Fuat Sezgin, 2 vols., Beirut 1981; Abū Hilāl al-ʿAskarī, *Kitāb al-ṣināʿatayn*, ed. Mufīd Qumayḥa, Beirut 1984[2]; Ibn Abī l-Iṣbaʿ, *Badīʿ al-Qurʾān*, ed. Ḥifnī Muḥammad Sharaf, Cairo 1957; Ḍiyāʾ al-Dīn Ibn al-Athīr, *al-Mathal al-sāʾir fī adab al-kātib wa-l-shāʿir*, 2 vols., ed. Aḥmad al-Ḥūfī and Badawī Ṭabāna, Cairo 1960; Ibn Qutayba, *Taʾwīl mushkil al-Qurʾān*, ed. al-Sayyid Aḥmad Ṣaqr, Cairo 2006; al-Jāḥiẓ, *al-Bayān wa-l-tabyīn*, ed. ʿAbd al-Salām M. Hārūn, 4 vols. in 2, Cairo 1968[3]; al-Khaṭṭābī, al-Rummānī, and ʿAbd al-Qāhir al-Jurjānī, *Three treatises on the* Iʿjāz *of the Qurʾān. Qurʾanic studies and literary criticism*, ed. Muhammad Khalaf-Allāh Aḥmad and Muḥammad Zaghlūl Sallām, trans. Issa J. Boullata, reviewed by Terri L. DeYoung, Reading 2014; Jalāl al-Dīn al-Qazwīnī, *al-Īḍāḥ fī ʿulūm al-balāgha*, ed. Muḥammad al-Khafājī, Beirut 1985; al-Rummānī, *al-Nukat fī iʿjāz al-Qurʾān*, in Muḥammad Khalafallāh (ed.), *Thalāth rasāʾil fī iʿjāz al-Qurʾān* (Cairo 1955), 67–104.

Studies

Lale Behzadi, *Sprache und Sprachverstehen. Al-Ǧaḥiẓ über die Vollkommenheit des Ausdrucks*, Wiesbaden 2009; Geert Jan van Gelder, Brevity. The long and the short of it in classical Arabic literary theory, in Rudolph Peters (ed.), *Proceedings of the Ninth Congress of the Union Européenne des Arabisants et Islamisants* (Leiden 1981), 78–88; Beatrice Gruendler, *Tawqīʿ* (Apostille). Royal brevity in the pre-modern Islamic appeals court, in Lale Behzadi and Vahid Behmardi (eds.), *The weaving of words. Approaches to classical Arabic prose* (Beirut 2009), 101–29; George J. Kanazi, *Studies in the Kitāb aṣ-ṣināʿatayn of Abū Hilāl al-ʿAskarī*, Leiden 1989; Udo Simon, *Mittelalterliche arabische Sprachbetrachtung zwischen Grammatik und Rhetorik*. ʿIlm al-maʿānī *bei as-Sakkākī*, Heidelberg 1993; Kees Versteegh, Freedom of the speaker? The term *ittisāʿ* and related notions in Arabic grammar, in Michael G. Carter and Kees Versteegh (eds.), *Studies in the history of Arabic grammar* (Amsterdam 1990), 2:281–93.

Udo Simon

Isḥāq b. Ḥunayn

Abū Yaʿqūb **Isḥāq b. Ḥunayn** b. Isḥāq al-ʿIbādī (d. 298/910) was, like his father Ḥunayn b. Isḥāq (d. 260/873–4), a leading translator of ancient Greek texts, well versed in the Arabic, Syriac, and Greek languages. Ḥunayn's *nisba* al-ʿIbādī indicates that Isḥāq was of Arab Christian descent. He followed the medical profession of his father, who dedicated to him some of his translations of Galen (d. c.216 C.E.). These translations were from Greek into Syriac, not into Arabic, as Syriac was then still the language of the medical profession in Baghdad. Isḥāq was one of the team of translators working under the guidance of Ḥunayn. Isḥāq translated into either Syriac or Arabic, as requested by his clients. In some cases he corrected the Arabic translations made by Ḥunayn's other collaborators, who had no command of Greek and relied on Ḥunayn's Syriac versions. It is wrong, however, to assume that Isḥāq himself used Ḥunayn's Syriac when translating into Arabic; he preferred the Greek original whenever this was available. Of Isḥāq's own writings, mainly on medicine and pharmacology, only the brief tract *Taʾrīkh al-aṭibbāʾ* ("History of the physicians") is extant. It is the earliest known, if unsatisfactory, attempt to write about the origins of medicine in the context of the history of philosophy and religion. An interesting piece about the use of styrax in divine service is quoted in al-Bīrūnī's (d. 440/1048) *Kitāb al-ṣaydana fī l-ṭibb* ("Pharmacognosy"), a voluminous list of names of materia medica in various languages (see Karimov's translation no. 936 for the passage that is missing from Hakim Mohammed Said's edition).

As a translator, Isḥāq was less concerned with medicine; he left the numerous works of Galen to the other members of his father's school and rendered only two of them into Syriac and nine into Arabic—for example, Galen's treatise on the parts of medicine *Περὶ τῶν τῆς ἰατρικῆς μερῶν (De partibus artis medicativae)*, which Isḥāq translated as *Kitāb ajzāʾ al-ṭibb*, completing the version that Ḥunayn had left unfinished at his death (Lyons, ed.). He was interested mainly in philosophy, as is evident from his many translations in this field. A talk between Ḥunayn and Isḥāq about the beginnings of philosophy is included in the *Ṣiwān al-ḥikma* ("Receptacle of wisdom") incorrectly attributed to Abū Sulaymān al-Sijistānī (d. c.375/985).

It was by his translations of nearly all texts of the Aristotelian corpus that Isḥāq rendered his greatest service. Other philosophers with whom he was concerned are Alexander of Aphrodisias (fl. c.200 C.E.), Nemesius of Emesa (fl. c.390 C.E.), Nicolaus of Damascus (b. c.64 B.C.E.), Porphyry (d. c.305 C.E.), Olympiodorus (d. after 565 C.E.), Themistius (d. 385 C.E.), and Theophrastus (d. c.287 B.C.E.). From works associated with Plato (d. c.348 B.C.E.) Isḥāq translated a pseudonymous tract about the education of young men *(Waṣiyyat Aflāṭūn fī taʾdīb al-aḥdāth)*.

He translated also the two most important standard Greek works on mathematics and astronomy, the *Elements* of Euclid (fl. third century B.C.E.) and the *Almagest* of Ptolemy (d. c.168 C.E.). These versions were revised by Thābit b. Qurra (d. 288/901), who was a greater expert in those subject areas. The fragment of a letter on astronomical problems sent to Isḥāq by Thābit testifies to the friendly cooperation of the two men (Carmody, 45–6). This was also a sign of the liberal spirit of the ʿAbbāsid age, in which scientists from various religions could cooperate in their pursuit of knowledge, in this case, a Christian with a pagan Ṣābian from Ḥarrān.

Isḥāq also translated scientific texts by Apollonius of Perge (d. c.192 B.C.E.), Archimedes (d. 212 B.C.E.), Autolycus of Pitane (d. c.290 B.C.E.), and Menelaus of Alexandria (d. 140 C.E.). Isḥāq's translations testify to greater linguistic skills and a higher intellectual standard than those evinced by the attempts of earlier translators. This may be studied in Kunitzsch's parallel edition of Ptolemy's star catalogue in the *Almagest*, which lays out the versions of both al-Ḥajjāj b. Yūsuf b. Maṭar (fl. 169–218/786–833) and Isḥāq. Isḥāq's better translation did not, however, displace the earlier one from the book market, the result being a cross-contamination between the old text and the new. This is especially obvious in the case of the manuscripts used by Gerard of Cremona (d. 1187 C.E.) for his Latin translation.

Isḥāq followed his father's footsteps as physician to the caliphs and other members of the ruling class. He was apparently integrated fully into educated society in Baghdad, but the claim of ʿAlī b. Zayd al-Bayhaqī (d. 565/1169) that Isḥāq was a boon companion and astrological adviser to the caliph al-Muktafī (r. 289–95/902–8) and was a good Muslim must be questioned (al-Bayhaqī, ed. M. Shafīʿ, fasc. 1, pp. 4–5). Isḥāq distinguished himself in that he could write Arabic poetry, and the bibliographers attest that his Arabic style was superior to that of his father.

In addition to his role as a physician he was able, in one instance, to offer help with his knowledge of the Greek language. In 293/906 a diplomatic letter from Italy arrived in Sāmarrāʾ, where al-Muktafī was hunting. The sender was Bertha, countess of Tuscany (d. 925 C.E.), and the letter was written, on white silk, in Latin, which no one understood. In the end, a Frank in charge of the wardrobe was found, who knew Latin and Greek and rendered the letter into Greek, whereupon Isḥāq was called to translate it from Greek into Arabic (Levi Della Vida).

Isḥāq was on familiar terms with al-Muktafī's *wazīr* al-Qāsim b. ʿUbaydallāh (in office 289–91/902–4), with whom he exchanged witty epigrams. In 290/903 Isḥāq composed, at the request of al-Qāsim, his *Taʾrīkh al-aṭibbāʾ* ("History of the physicians"). This little tract is the earliest known, if unsatisfactory, attempt to write about the origins of medicine in the context of the history of philosophy and religion. After suffering partial paralysis of one side of his body *(al-fālij)*, he died in Baghdad, in Rabīʿ II 298/December 910.

Bibliography

Work by Isḥāq b. Ḥunayn

Taʾrīkh al-aṭibbāʾ, ed. Franz Rosenthal, Isḥâq b. Ḥunayn's *Taʾrīḫ al-aṭibbâʾ*, *Oriens* 7 (1954), 55–80, repr. in Franz Rosenthal, *Science and medicine in Islam. A collection of essays* (Aldershot 1990), no. II.

Translations by Isḥāq b. Ḥunayn

Apollonius of Perge, *Apollonius de Perge, Coniques*, vol. 1/1, *Livre I* (Arabic text), ed. Roshdi Rashed, Berlin, New York 2008; Aristotle, *The Arabic version of the Nicomachean ethics*, ed. Anna A. Akasoy and Alexander Fidora, trans. Douglas M. Dunlop, Leiden 2005 (cf. the remarks by Ernst A. Schmidt and Manfred Ullmann in *Aristoteles in Fes. Zum Wert der arabischen Überlieferung der Nikomachischen Ethik für die Kritik des griechischen Textes*, Heidelberg 2012); Aristotle, *ʾArisṭūṭālīs. Fī l-nafs*, ed. Abd al-Raḥmān Badawī, Cairo 1954, repr. Kuwait and Beirut 1980; Aristotle, *Arisṭūṭālīs. Fī l-samāʾ wa-l-āthār al-ʿulwiyya*, ed. ʿAbd al-Raḥmān Badawī, Cairo 1961; Aristotle, *Arisṭūṭālīs. Al-ṭabīʿa*, ed. ʿAbd al-Raḥmān Badawī, 2 vols., Cairo 1964–5; Aristotle, *Manṭiq Arisṭū*, ed. ʿAbd al-Raḥmān

Badawī, 3 vols., Kuwait and Beirut 1980; ʿAbd al-Raḥmān Badawī (ed.), *Arisṭū ʿinda l-ʿarab*, Cairo 1947, Kuwait 1978²; ʿAbd al-Raḥmān Badawī (ed.), *Shurūḥ ʿalā Arisṭū mafqūda fī l-Yūnāniyya wa-rasāʾil ukhrā = Commentaires sur Aristote perdus en grec et autres épîtres* (Beirut 1971), 31–42; L. Cheikho (ed.), *Waṣiyyat Aflāṭūn fī taʾdīb al-aḥdāth, al-Mashriq* 9 (1906), 677–83; Galen, *Galeni De partibus artis medicativae libelli versio arabica*, ed. Malcolm C. Lyons (Berlin 1969), 22–49; Khalil Georr (ed.), *Les catégories d'Aristote dans leurs versions syro-arabes*, Beirut 1948; Ibn Rushd (Averroes), *Tafsīr mā baʿd al-ṭabīʿa*, ed. Maurice Bouyges (ed.), 3 vols. in 4, Beirut 1948 (see Aristotle's lemmata); W. Kutsch and Khalil al-Jurr (Georr) (eds.), *al-Maqāla al-ūlā* min *Kitāb al-samāʿ al-ṭabīʿī* li-Aristūṭālīs, in *MFOB* 39 (1964), 266–312; Nicolaus Damascenus, *De plantis. Five translations*, ed. Hendrik Joan Drossaart Lulofs and E. L. J. Poortman, Amsterdam and New York 1989; Isidor Pollak (ed.), *Die Hermeneutik des Aristoteles in der arabischen Übersetzung des Isḥāk ibn Ḥonain*, Leipzig 1913; Ptolemy, *Der Sternkatalog des Almagest. Die arabisch-mittelalterliche Tradition*, vol. 1, *Die arabischen Übersetzungen*, ed. Paul Kunitzsch, Wiesbaden 1986, vol. 2, *Die lateinische Übersetzung Gerhards von Cremona*, Wiesbaden 1990; Themistius, *An Arabic translation of Themistius Commentary on Aristoteles De anima*, ed. Malcolm C. Lyons, London 1973; Theophrastus, The Arabic version of Theophrastus' *Metaphysica*, ed. Ilai Alon, *JSAI* 6 (1985), 163–217; Theophrastus, *Theophrastus On first principles (known as his Metaphysics). Greek text and medieval Arabic translation*, ed. Dimitri Gutas, Leiden 2010.

Other sources

ʿAlī b. Zayd al-Bayhaqī, *Tatimmat Ṣiwān al-ḥikma*, ed. Muḥammad Shafīʿ (Lahore 1935), fasc. 1 (Ar. text); al-Bīrūnī, *Kitāb al-ṣaydana* (or *al-ṣaydala*) *fī l-ṭibb*, trans. U. I. Karimov, *Farmakognoziya v meditsine*, Tashkent 1973, ed. and trans. Hakim Mohammed Said, *Al-Biruni's book on pharmacy and material medica*, 2 vols., Karachi 1973; Ḥunayn b. Isḥāq, *Risāla ilā ʿAlī b. Yaḥyā fī dhikr mā turjima min kutub Jālīnūs bi-ʿilmihi wa-baʿḍ mā lam yutarjam*, ed. and trans. Gotthelf Bergsträsser, *Ḥunain ibn Ishāq über die syrischen und arabischen Galenübersetzungen*, Leipzig 1925, repr. in Fuat Sezgin (ed.), *Galen in the Arabic tradition. Texts and studies* (Frankfurt am Main 1996), 1:185–306; Ibn Abī Uṣaybiʿa, *ʿUyūn al-anbāʾ fī ṭabaqāt al-aṭibbāʾ*, ed. August Müller (Cairo 1882), 1:200–3; Ibn al-Nadīm, *Kitāb al-fihrist*, ed. Gustav Flügel, 2 vols. in 1 (Leipzig 1871–2), index:272; Ibn al-Qifṭī, *Taʾrīkh al-ḥukamāʾ*, ed. Julius Lippert (Leipzig 1903), 80 and index; *The Muntakhab Ṣiwān al-ḥikma of Abū Sulaimān as-Sijistānī*, ed. D. M. Dunlop (The Hague 1979), § 238; Thābit b. Qurra, *The astronomical works of Thabit b. Qurra*, ed. Francis J. Carmody, Berkeley 1960.

Studies

H. H. Biesterfeldt, Kommunikation durch Übersetzung. Ziele und Methoden der griechisch-arabischen Übersetzungen des 9. Jahrhunderts, in Gerhard Binder and Konrad Ehlich (eds.), *Kommunikation durch Zeichen und Wort* (Trier 1995), 137–92; Cristina D'Ancona, Aristotle and Aristotelianism, *EI3;* Cristina D'Ancona and Giuseppe Serra (eds.), *Aristotele e Alessandro di Afrodisia nella tradizione araba*, Padova 2002 (with contributions on Isḥāq by Gerhard Endress, Cecilia Martini, Carmela Baffioni, Emma Gannagé, Silvia Fazzo, Marc Geoffroy, and Mauro Zonta); Gregg De Young, Isḥāq ibn Ḥunayn, Ḥunayn ibn Isḥāq, and the third Arabic translation of Euclid's *Elements, Historia Mathematica* 19 (1992), 188–99; Gregg De Young and Sonja Brentjes, al-Ḥajjāj b. Yūsuf b. Maṭar, *EI3*; Richard M. Frank, Some fragments of Isḥāq's translation of the de Anima, in *Les Cahiers de Byrsa* 8 (Carthage 1958–9), 231–51, repr. in Richard M. Frank, *Philosophy, theology and mysticism in medieval Islam. Texts and studies on the development and history of kalam*, ed. Dimitri Gutas (Aldershot 2005), article II; Charles Genequand, Vers une nouvelle édition de la *Maqāla fī mabādiʾ al-kull* d'Alexandre d'Aphrodise, in Ahmad Hasnawi, Abdelali Elamrani-Jamal, and Maroun Aouad (eds.), *Perspectives arabes et médiévales sur la tradition scientifique et philosophique grecque* (Leuven and Paris 1997), 271–6; Richard Goulet (ed.), *Dictionnaire des philosophes antiques. Supplément* (Paris 2003), index s.v. Isḥāq b. Ḥunayn al-ʿIbādī; Dimitri Gutas, *Greek thought, Arabic culture. The Graeco-arabic translation movement in Baghdad and early ʿAbbāsid society*, London and New York 1998; Max Krause, Die Sphärik von Menelaos aus Alexandrien in der Verbesserung von Abū Naṣr Manṣūr b. ʿAlī b. ʿIrāq, in *Abhandlungen der Gesellschaft der Wissenschaften zu Göttingen*, phil.-hist. Kl. 3/17, Berlin 1936; Paul Kunitzsch, *Der Almagest.*

Die Syntaxis mathematica des Claudius Ptolemäus in arabisch-lateinischer Überlieferung, Wiesbaden 1974; Paul Lettinck, *Aristotle's Physics and its reception in the Arab world*, Leiden et al. 1994; Giorgio Levi Della Vida, La corrispondenza di Berta di Toscana col califfo Muktafi, *Rivista Storica Italiana* 66 (1954), 21–38, repr. in Giorgio Levi Della Vida, *Aneddoti e svaghi arabi e non arabi* (Milan and Naples 1959), 26–44; J. N. Mattock, The early translations from Greek into Arabic. An experiment in comparative assessment, in Gerhard Endress (ed.), *Symposium Graeco-Arabicum II* (Amsterdam 1989), 73–102; F. E. Peters, *Aristoteles Arabus. The oriental translations and commentaries on the Aristotelian Corpus*, Leiden 1968; Roshdi Rashed (ed.), *Thābit ibn Qurra. Science and philosophy in ninth-century Baghdad*, Berlin and New York 2009 (with information about still unpublished translations by Isḥāq); Franz Rosenthal, Some Pythagorean documents transmitted in Arabic. II. Plato's exhortation concerning the education of young men, *Orientalia* n.s. 10 (1941), 383–95; Gotthard Strohmaier, Der syrische und der arabische Galen, in Wolfgang Haase and Hildegard Temporini (eds.), *ANRW*, 2. *Principat* (Berlin and New York 1994), 37/2:1987–2017, repr. in Gotthard Strohmaier, *Hellas im Islam* (Wiesbaden 2003), 85–106; Manfred Ullmann, *Die Medizin im Islam*, Leiden and Cologne 1970; Manfred Ullmann, *Die Natur- und Geheimwissenschaften im Islam*, Leiden 1972; Manfred Ullmann, *Wörterbuch zu den griechisch-arabischen Übersetzungen des 9. Jahrhunderts. Supplement*, vol. 2, *Π-Ω* (Wiesbaden 2007), 12–7 (on the Arabic translation of Nemesius of Emesa, *De natura hominis*); Richard Walzer, *Greek into Arabic*, Oxford 1962; F. W. Zimmermann, The chronology of Isḥāq Ibn Ḥunayn's *Taʾrīkh al-aṭibbaʾ*, *Arabica* 21 (1974), 324–30; *GAS*, 3:267–8 and index; 4:344; 5:272–3 and index; 6:171 and index; 7:index.

Gotthard Strohmaier

İsmail Hakkı (Eldem)

Alişanzade **İsmail Hakkı** (ʿĀlīşānzāde İsmāʿīl Ḥaqqı) **(Eldem)** (1287–1363/ 1871–1944), a Ottoman Turkish author and diplomat, graduated from the Mekteb-i Mülkiye (School of Civil Service) around 1307/1890. His first published work (1303/1886) was a translation from Voltaire. His *Müntehabat-ı teracim-i meşahir (Müntekhabāt-ı terācim-i meşāhīr*, "Selection of famous biographies"), published in 1307/1890, was followed by his first collection of poems, *Sevda-yı hazan yahud tahassür (Sevdā-yı khazān yākhud taḥassür*, "Autumn love or longing"), and three booklets devoted to three contemporary authors, Ahmed Mithat (Aḥmed Midḥat) Efendi (1260–1331/1844–1912), Ahmed (Aḥmed) Cevdet Paşa (1238–1312/1823–95), and Recaizade Mahmud Ekrem (Recāʾīzāde Maḥmūd Ekrem) Bey (1263–1332/1847–1914).

In 1308/1890, İsmail Hakkı Bey started a bureaucratic career as a clerk in the bureau of consular affairs at the ministry of foreign affairs. He had an uneventful career, punctuated by routine rises and promotions within the bureau. His first assignment abroad came in 1321/1904, as inspector of the Ottoman consulates in Corfu and Italy.

İsmail Hakkı Bey continued to pursue his literary activities in c.1307–16/the 1890s, publishing two more volumes on contemporary authors, namely Muallim Naci (Muʿallim Nācī, 1265?–1310/1850–93) and Şemseddin Sami (Şemseddīn Sāmī, 1266–1322/1850–1904); a small volume on *Muasir şairlerimiz* (*Muʿāṣır şāʿirlerimiz*, "Our contemporary poets"); and an authored work by the name of *İki hakikat (İki haqīqat*, "Two truths"). He also translated Jules Verne's *Un Drame dans les airs*, Octave Feuillet's *Le Roman d'un jeune homme pauvre*, and Alphonse de Lamartine's *Raphaël*.

In 1314/1897, İsmail Hakkı Bey married Azize Hanım (ʿAzīze Khanım, 1297/1880–1957). Azize was the granddaughter of a major Tanzimat statesman,

Edhem Paşa (1233?–1310/1818?–1893); the daughter of the bureaucrat and numismatist İsmail Galib (İsmāʿīl Ghālib) Bey (1263–1313/1847–96); and the niece of the celebrated painter and museum director Osman Hamdi (ʿOthmān Ḥamdī) Bey (1258–1328/1842–1910). In short, İsmail Hakkı Bey had joined a respected and super-Westernised family at the centre of the Ottoman intelligentsia of the time.

İsmail Hakkı Bey was a typical *damat* (*dāmād*, son-in-law), in that he submitted to his family-in-law's authority, as illustrated by the fact that in 1934, he abandoned his own patronym to take on the surname Eldem, invented as a homage to Edhem Paşa. In 1327/1909, his career also took a turn that befitted his in-law family's penchant for the West. He was appointed consul to Marseilles (1909–14), Zurich (1917–1918), and Munich (1918–1919), where the couple lived with their three sons, Vedat (Vedād, 1326/1906–83), Sedad (Sedād, 1326/1908–88), and Sadi (Saʿdī, 1328/1910–95). Although the Munich consulate was closed in 1919, the family remained in the Bavarian capital until 1924.

Back in Istanbul, İsmail Hakkı Bey was commissioned by the government to publish and print the texts relating to the Treaty of Lausanne. He resumed the literary activity he had interrupted some twenty-five years earlier, translating Baudelaire's *Les Fleurs du mal*, Maurois' *Le Cercle de famille*, Loti's *Vers Ispahan*, Tolstoy's *Seméynoye schástiye* (*Семейное счастье*, "Family happiness"), and Mauriac's *Les Anges noirs*.

İsmail Hakkı Bey also proved to be a *damat* worthy of his family-in-law by providing his children with an education and exposure that guaranteed their success in areas consistent with the familial tradition. Vedat (Eldem) became an economist and statistician; Sedad (Hakkı Eldem) turned out to be the most successful architect of Republican Turkey; and Sadi (Eldem) followed his father's career as a diplomat. The couple's oldest child, Galibe (Ghālibe (Okyar), 1315/1898–1981), married a young Macedonian officer, Fethi (Fetḥī) Bey, who became one of the most prominent statesmen of the Kemalist regime, under the name Fethi Okyar (1297/1880–1943).

Bibliography

Works by İsmail Hakkı

Müntehabât-ı terâcim-i meşâhir, Istanbul 1307/1890; *Tahassür*, Istanbul 1308/1891; *Ahmed Midhat Efendi*, Istanbul 1308/1891; *Cevdet Paşa*, Istanbul 1308/1891; *Ekrem Bey*, Istanbul 1308/1891; *Muallim Naci Efendi*, Istanbul 1311/1894; *Şemseddin Sami Bey*, Istanbul 1311/1894; *Muasır şairlerimiz*, Istanbul 1311/1894; *İki hakikat*, Istanbul 1311/1894.

Translations

Jules Verne, *Balonda facia*, Istanbul 1311/1894; Octave Feuillet, *Talihsiz*, Istanbul 1311/1894; Alphonse de Lamartine, *Rafael*, Istanbul 1311/1894; Charles Baudelaire, *Elem çiçekleri*, Istanbul 1927; Émile Salomon Wilhelm Herzog, *Aile çemberi*, Istanbul 1934; Pierre Loti, *İsfahana doğru*, Istanbul 1934; Lev Nikolayeviç Tolstoy, *Samimi saadet*, Istanbul 1934; François Mauriac, *Kara melekler*, Istanbul 1942.

Studies

Hakkı Tarık Us, *Elli yıl* (Istanbul 1943), 50, 84, 88; Edhem Eldem, Sedad Hakkı Eldem olunmaz, doğulur (mu?). Bir aile ve gençlik hikâyesi, in Edhem Eldem, Bülent Tanju, and Uğur Tanyeli (eds.), *Sedad Hakkı Eldem. I. gençlik yılları* (Istanbul 2008), 10–41; Edhem Eldem, İsmail Hakkı [Eldem], in Edhem Eldem (ed.), *Osman Hamdi Bey sözlüğü*, (Istanbul 2010), 303–6.

Edhem Eldem

J

Jainism and Jains

Jainism is a religion that originated in eastern India. Its most recent founder, Mahāvīra (lit., great hero, traditionally dated 599–27 or 582–10 B.C.E. but dated c.497–25 B.C.E. by scholars), was an elder contemporary of the Buddha. Mahāvīra is regarded as the last of twenty-four figures in our age known as *tīrthāṅkaras* (lit., ford makers, that is, those who show the way to liberation from the predicament of death and rebirth, which is thought of as crossing over a vast ocean) or *jinas* (victors) (unless otherwise indicated, all Indo-Aryan words in this entry are in Sanskrit and transliterated accordingly); their followers are known as **Jains**.

1. Jain beliefs

Jainism holds that the universe is uncreated and eternally existent, consisting of matter occupied by a countless and inexhaustible number of *jīvas* (souls) that dwell in everything, from the elements (earth, air, fire, and water) to plants, animals, humans, deities, and Hell beings. Souls go through innumerable rebirths in these various forms of life because they are bound up with *karma*, a subtle form of matter that permeates the soul through one's actions. Karma must be destroyed through ascetic practice and proper conduct to achieve the ultimate goal, liberation *(mokṣa)*. A soul liberated from karma and thus from the cycle of death and rebirth *(saṃsāra)* realises its own inherent omniscience. The *jinas* take the additional step of using their omniscience to teach the correct path, the main tenet of which is a thoroughgoing commitment to non-injury *(ahiṃsā)*, eschewing violence toward other living beings in thought, word, and deed, as it is by doing such harm that one accumulates karma. Upon death, the liberated soul exists in an unending state of bliss, knowledge, power, and understanding, but, because it has overcome all passions, the soul has no desire and thus cannot engage with beings still mired in cyclic existence. Humans are the only beings who can attain liberation, as they are uniquely capable of making ethical choices, responding with detachment to joy and suffering, and practising the asceticism necessary to transcend karma by joining the mendicant order. There are two main denominations of

Jains: the Śvetāmbara (white-clad), whose monks and nuns wear white robes, and the Digambara (sky-clad), whose monks observe their vow of possessionlessness by renouncing clothing. Partly because of the requirement to go naked, Digambaras believe that women cannot attain *mokṣa*.

Observant Jains are vegetarians and avoid overtly violent occupations, having followed mercantile and banking professions. For this reason, they have generally been a highly mobile and well-educated group. They are known today for participating in the international gem trade and for playing significant roles in finance and industry in India—where their cultural centres are in the western and southern parts of the country—and abroad. Even in India, Jains remain one of the smallest religious minorities, with 4.45 million adherents (0.4 percent) as of 2011. Approximately 200,000 live abroad. Significant communities of Jains reside in the United States, Canada, the United Kingdom, Belgium, Kenya, Tanzania, and South Africa. The majority of Jains worship images *(mūrti, pratimā)* of the Jinas in temples *(mandira)*, although there are substantial minorities of non-image-worshipping Jains, including the Śvetāmbara Sthānakavāsī and Terāpanthī traditions, which arose in the ninth/fifteenth century.

Jainism's limited exposure beyond India is due in part to mendicants' highly restrictive monastic vows that hamper travel outside of India. Further, lay Jains living abroad have been disinclined to proselytise or publicise their faith. In recent decades, however, an increasing number of Jain centres have arisen to serve diaspora communities, and new institutional developments in India have led several Jain religious leaders to begin travelling abroad to reach these communities.

2. Jain relations with Hindus and Buddhists

Jains have competed with various Hindu and Buddhist traditions for adherents across India. They have largely coexisted with their neighbours in northern India, despite moments of persecution. In South India, several periods of persecution in the mediaeval era led to the reduction in the size of the Jain communities of Tamilnadu and Karnataka, but it is difficult to assess whether the proportion of Jains relative to the total population of India has changed significantly since mediaeval times.

Mercantile communities arose with the growth of cities in the Gangetic plain in ancient India, many of which were affiliated with Jainism and Buddhism. Jain monks and laymen acted as advisers to Hindu kings in North and South India, a role they continued to play during the Sultanate and Mughal periods. Jain intellectuals engaged in literary competitions and philosophical debates with Buddhists and Hindus and were great collectors of Hindu, Buddhist, and secular literature in Sanskrit and Prakrit. Jains were also at the forefront of the "*bhakti* movement," the rise of devotional religious literatures in emerging vernacular languages from the fifteenth century onwards.

Because of the nature of social organisation in South Asia, Jains also have a caste *(jāti)*-based social order similar to that of Hindus; communities that affiliate with Jainism usually retain a tradition of worshipping clan goddesses *(kuladevīs)* and local deities *(kṣetrapālas)*, who are themselves thought to have "converted" to Jainism by ceasing to accept blood sacrifice, effectively becoming "vegetarian." These deities, such as the goddess *(devī)* Padmāvatī and the *kṣetrapāla* of the Jain temple at Nākoṛā, Bheru, have gained widespread devotional followings, becoming known as protectors of the faith and agents who aid pious Jains in their quotidian affairs.

While Jains maintain that the rulers of the first empires in eastern India were Jain, including the early Mauryan emperor Candragupta (r. c.322–297 B.C.E.), the evidence for this is scant. For brief periods, Jains held political power directly in South India—Karnataka and Tamilnadu—and in western and central India (modern Gujarat, Rajasthan, Madhya Pradesh). Jains have historically also competed for political position and royal patronage with certain Hindu groups, such as the Puṣṭimārg Vaiṣṇavas in western India beginning in the seventeenth century, and even periods of persecution, with the "revival" of Śaivism in seventh-century Tamilnadu, the advent of the Vīraśaiva tradition in thirteenth-century Karnataka, and with the takeover of Jain temples by Śaiva Hindus in eighteenth-century Amer (near Jaipur). Recently, Jains have occasionally been targets of Hindu nationalist and "sons of the soil" political groups, which have, for example, opposed government bans on meat sales on certain Jain holidays. An organisation called the Anup Mandal has allegedly targeted and killed several Jain monks and nuns. On the whole, however, Jains are part of Indian society and often identify themselves as Hindus, despite being granted religious minority status by the Indian government in 2014.

Jains, Hindus, and Buddhists shared ritual practices and spaces in ancient India. Jains built stupas at Mathurā but abandoned them before the mediaeval period. Jain relations with Buddhists have largely been studied as a matter of intellectual and polemical competition, although the Buddhist canonical texts make laudatory references to "Nātaputta," a name for Mahāvīra. Jain canonical scriptures make oblique references to Buddhists and take issue with the emphasis Buddhists place on intention in assessing the moral and karmic impact of a person's actions. Jains regard the philosophers Dignāga (Diṅnāga, fl. fifth-sixth century C.E.) and Haribhadra (fl. eighth century C.E.) as converts from Buddhism to Jainism; they helped to bring philosophical inquiry, already strong in the Buddhist tradition, into Jainism. Jains and Buddhists shared key areas of political influence in eastern India, especially before and during the Mauryan Empire and in western India and the Deccan until Buddhism faded away there before the twelfth century C.E.

3. Early Jain-Muslim history

It can be difficult for historians to distinguish Muslims' interactions with Jains from those with Hindus. Early Persian and Arabic sources rarely distinguish amongst indigenous religious communities. Jains are often called *baniyā* (from Sanskrit *vaṇij*), a western Indian term for several merchant castes that also includes Hindus. Some scholars have argued that Indian merchants historically tended to take pragmatic approaches to their religious affiliations, so a single caste group may have included Jains, Hindus, and Muslims.

Jains' first encounters with Muslims occurred via trade with Arab and Persian merchants, whose presence in South Asia predates Islam. Archaeological evidence suggests that there were Muslim communities in coastal towns in peninsular Gujarat as early as the mid to late first/late seventh to early eighth centuries. Jain merchants held key ministerial posts in the courts of the Hindu Caulukya (Solāṅki) rulers of Gujarat (329–710/941–1310), where they helped their Muslim trading partners, hailing largely from southwestern Iran and North Africa, to settle in major port cities such as Cambay (Khambhāt) by financing the construction of mosques. The seventh/thirteenth-century Jain merchant Jagadeva Shāh (Jagaḍū Śā) paid to rebuild the local mosque after marauders destroyed the Kacchi town of Bhadreśvara. Western Indian mosques use architectural elements similar to those found in Jain and Hindu temples, showing that local guilds were employed to build them.

The 92/711 conquest of Sindh by the Umayyad general Muḥammad b. Qāsim (d. 96/715) gave Jains their earliest experience of being ruled by Muslims. Jains and Hindus were considered *dhimmīs*; various rulers issued decrees that their temples and images were not to be harmed as long as they paid the *jizya* (Friedmann, 180–1) (*dhimmīs*, lit. protected persons, were non-Muslim citizens of an Islamic state who had their rights protected in their communities but, as citizens of an Islamic state, had certain restrictions imposed upon them and had to pay an annual per capita tax, the *jizya*). This policy was generally maintained under Sunnī rulers. New temples were constructed in Muslim-ruled Sindh and Panjāb. Maḥmūd of Ghazni (r. 388–421/998–1030) nevertheless raided several Jain temples in western India during several of his campaigns. A stone image of a *jina* was excavated from the royal palace in Ghazni, suggesting that it was—beyond indicating Maḥmūd's peculiar iconoclastic zeal—an object of fascination and curiosity, which, scholars have argued, was an effort to earn in 416/1025 an investiture *(manshūr)* from the ʿAbbāsid caliph Abū l-ʿAbbās al-Qādir (r. 381–422/991–1031) (Flood, 32).

The Ghūrid incursions into western India led by Muḥammad b. Sām (r. 569–602/1173–1206) in 573/1178 and 593/1197 and military actions by the early sultans of Delhi in the seventh/thirteenth century did not diminish the Jains' prosperity or cultural efflorescence, as the finest works of Jain architecture in western India were built in the fifth/eleventh through seventh/thirteenth centuries, including the famous Delwaḍa temples atop Mt. Abu (southwestern end of the Arāvalī range in Rajasthan). The widespread use of paper for producing manuscripts beginning in the seventh/thirteenth century and expanding in the next encouraged both enormous Jain libraries and the miniature-painting traditions of western India.

4. Under the Delhi sutans

The advent of the Delhi Sultanate (602–932/1206–1526), the first imperial Muslim power to rule a large part of the Indian Subcontinent, forced Jains to reshape their political and economic ties. Jain monks and wealthy laymen helped facilitate this transition by participating in the intellectual life of the courts and the imperial bureaucracy, especially in the Khaljī and Tughluq eras (689–816/1290–1413). Jain lineage histories describe monks and laymen obtaining *farmāns* (edicts) from sultans permitting them to lead large pilgrimage parties across vast portions of Sultanate territory.

Research suggests that temples and images were destroyed or desecrated more often for political than religious reasons. Jain images and temples, both in trading towns and pilgrimage sites, were subject to plunder and desecration during military actions to expand the empire. For example, the original Delhi *masjid-i jāmiʿ* (congregational mosque) known today as the Quwwat al-Islām (strength of Islam) was built from parts of some twenty-seven Hindu and Jain temples, as indicated in its dedicatory inscription. Colonial-era and nationalist historians have frequently taken this mosque's origin as motivated by a putative "Islamic iconoclasm." However, its location, within the confines of the fort of the erstwhile Hindu kingdom of the Tomaras (r. ninth century-1192), indicates instead that its meaning marks more directly the Ghūrids' conquest of Delhi in 588/1192, by Muʿizz al-Dīn Muḥammad of Ghūr (r. 568–602/1173–1206), led by his general, Quṭb al-Dīn Aybak (founder of the Mamlūk dynasty in northern India, r. 602–7/1206–10). Several Jain temples at important pilgrimage sites were damaged in 713/1313 during the extended efforts of the Delhi sultan ʿAlāʾ al-Dīn Khaljī (r. 695–715/1296–1316) to annex Gujarat. However, Alp Khān (d. c.715/1316), the governor appointed to the territory by ʿAlāʾ al-Dīn Khaljī, worked with the Jain merchant Samara Shāh (probably fl. 715–33/1315–33) to restore Śatruñjaya and other sites in 714/1315. The Khaljīs and Tughluqs employed Jains in key positions in their government. Ṭhakkura Pherū (fl. 690–723/1291–1323) was appointed mint master by ʿAlā al-Dīn Khaljī and wrote treatises on gemology, coin billons, and mathematics.

Muḥammad b. Tughluq (r. 724–52/1324–51), regarded by Persian and Arabic sources and modern historiographers as an ambitious but unstable ruler, is remembered well in Jain sources. The monk Jinaprabhasūri (d. c.733/1333) gained several *farmāns* protecting Jain pilgrimage sites and granting both Śvetāmbara and Digambara Jains safe passage throughout the empire. The sultan is also said to have established a Jain quarter in Delhi, and he sponsored a temple to house an image of Mahāvīra returned to the Jains from his treasury. The monk also claims to have become a trusted adviser to the sultan, even accompanying him on a military campaign. Muḥammad's successor, Fīrūz Shāh Tughluq (r. 752–90/1351–88), cast as a religious zealot by modern historiographers, is also remembered positively in Jain sources. He commissioned the Jain monk Mahendrasūri to compose the *Yantrarāja*, the first Sanskrit treatise on the astrolabe, which appears to have required collaboration with intellectuals literate in Arabic and Persian.

Jains remained influential as the Sultanate fragmented into regional polities in the ninth/fifteenth century. The city of Aḥmadābād (Ahmedabad), in Gujarat, founded by Aḥmad Shāh I (r. 814–46/1411–42), became a new commercial centre in western India. The city grew with the help of Jain magnates, who adopted the title of *nagarśeṭh* ((chief) merchant of the city). Between the ninth/fifteenth and thirteenth/nineteenth centuries, the city became a centre for Jain intellectuals and the epicentre of the Sthānakavāsī reform movement that eschews image worship. While some have speculated that Jain iconoclasm arose under the influence of Islam, there have long been debates amongst Jain sects about the validity of the practice (Dundas, 246–54). Islam's role in the burgeoning of iconoclastic Jain sects may have been more social or economic than theological, as the leader of the first group of iconoclasts, Loṅkā Shāh (d. c.880/1475), was employed as a scribe and was therefore well connected with Muslim authorities in Aḥmadābād, which probably gave him the influence needed to advance his message.

5. Under the Mughals

Jain monks and merchants also played significant roles in the Mughal Empire (932–1274/1526–1858), especially after the annexation of Gujarat in 980/1572–3. The monk Hīravijayasūri (d. 1003/1595) forged strong relations with Emperor Akbar (r. 963–1014/1556–1605), leading his sect to become the most powerful Śvetāmbara order. Akbar granted him several *farmān*s: one banned meat sales on Jain holidays and another granted his sect control of the pilgrimage site of Śatruñjaya. Abū l-Faḍl (d. 1011/1602), the historian, military officer, chief secretary, and confidant of Akbar, recognised him in the *Āʾīn-i Akbarī* (Institutions of Akbar) as amongst the twenty-one most learned religious leaders of Akbar's time. The Mughals even became involved in appointing successors to leadership of certain Jain monastic lineages (*gaccha*s), including the Tapā Gaccha, the largest Śvetāmbara monastic order. In Akbar's court, Jains had to answer to the charge of atheism, which caused a major shift in the way Jains write about their theology. The emperor Jahāngīr (r. 1014–37/1605–27) had a Jain monk as a childhood tutor. He issued edicts affirming the right of Jains to worship freely and took a vow not to kill animals, but he also banished Jain monks twice from the empire, only to rescind the order a short time later on both occasions.

The Jain merchant Śāntidās Jhaverī (d. 1069/1659), *nagarśeṭh* of Aḥmadābād, was a court jeweller to the Mughals and lent them large amounts of cash. He was awarded control of the town of Palitāṇa, at the foot of Śatruñjaya Hill in Gujarat, and used his influence to persecute non-image-worshipping Jain sects. His grandson, Khuśālcand (d. 1161/1748), paid a large ransom to the Marathas (Marāṯ'hās) to prevent them from sacking the city, keeping it under Mughal control. Vīrjī Vorā (d. c.1086/1675) worked with Muslim business partners to broker trade with Europeans in the city of Surat, which became the most important port in Gujarat after Cambay became silted and unusable. Digambara Jains were also prominent merchants there.

6. Modern history

Jains continued to reside in significant numbers in Sindh and western Punjab until the Partition of India and Pakistan in 1947. Two Jain temples survive but lie vacant in Lahore. A few members of the Bhabra (or Bhabhra) community, a Jain trading caste once numerous in towns across Panjāb, still reside in the state. Some Jain households remain in Nagarparkar (in Sindh), where a few Jain temples dating as far back as the third/ninth century and renovated as recently as the early twentieth stand in ruins. The only non-Jain shrine atop Śatruñjaya Hill is the *dargāh* (shrine) of Aṅgar Shāh Pīr, who, according to local legend, saved the site from destruction at the hands of a "Mughal" army.

Bibliography

For translations of accounts of Jinaprabhasūri's meetings with Sulṭān Muḥammad b. Tughluq, see Granoff (1992) and Vose (2013).

Sources

Ambadevasūri, Saṅghapati Samarasiṃha Rāsa, in Jinavijaya (ed.), *Jain aitihāsik Gūrjar kāvya-saṃcay* (Bhāvanagara 1926), 238–53 (text), 117–70 (notes); Devavimalagani, *Hīrasaubhāg-yamahākāvya*, ed. Śivadatta and K. Śarmā, Kālandrī 1985; Jinapāla Upādhyāya et al., *Kharataragacchabṛhadgurvāvali*, ed. Muni Jinavijaya, Bombay 1956; Jinaprabhasūri, *Vividhatīrthakalpa*, ed. Jina Vijaya, Śāntiniketan 1934; Kakkasūri, *Nābhinandanajinoddhārapraba ndha*, ed. Bhagavāndās Harakhcaṃd, Ahmedabad 1985 saṃvat/1929; Sarvānandasūri, *Jagaḍūcaritamahākāvya*, ed. Umaṅgavijayagaṇi, Ambālā 1925; Siddhicandragaṇi, *Bhānucandragaṇicarita*, ed. Mohanlal Dalicand Desai, Aḥmadābād and Calcutta 1941.

Studies

Gil Ben-Herut, *Śiva's saints. The origins of devotion in Kannada according to Harihara's Ragaḷegaḷu*, New York 2018; Chronology of Jainism, in *Jainpedia*, www.jainpedia.org/resources/chronology.html; John E. Cort, Twelve chapters from the *Guidebook to various pilgrimage places*, the *Vividhatīrthakalpa* of Jinaprabhasūri, in Phyllis Granoff (ed.), *The clever adulteress and the hungry monk* (Oakville ON and New York 1990), 245–90; Richard H. Davis, The story of the disappearing Jains. Retelling the Śaiva-Jain encounter in medieval South India, in John E. Cort (ed.), *Open boundaries. Jain communities and cultures in Indian history* (Albany 1998), 213–24; Paul Dundas, Jain perceptions of Islam in the early modern period, *Indo-Iranian Journal* 42/1 (1999), 35–46; Paul Dundas, *The Jains*, London and New York 2002[2]; Richard M. Eaton, Temple desecration and Indo-Muslim states, in David Gilmartin and Bruce B. Lawrence (eds.), *Beyond Turk and Hindu. Rethinking religious identities in Islamicate South Asia* (Gainesville 2000), 246–81; Ellison B. Findly, Jahāngīr's vow of non-violence, *JAOS* 107/2 (1987), 245–56; Ellison B. Findly, Jaina ideology and early Mughal trade with Europeans, *International Journal of Hindu Studies* 1/2 (1997), 288–313; Finbarr B. Flood, *Objects of translation. Material culture and "Hindu-Muslim" encounter*, Princeton 2009; Peter Flügel and Ahmad Muzaffar Ahmad, An exploratory survey of the Jaina heritage in Pakistan, *Jaina Studies. The Newsletter of the Centre of Jaina Studies* 13 (2018), 26–32; Yohanan Friedmann, The temple of Multān, in *IOS* 2 (1972), 176–82; Phyllis Granoff, Tales of broken limbs and bleeding wounds. Responses to Muslim iconoclasm in medieval India, *East and West* (ISMEO) 41/1–4 (1991), 189–203; Phyllis Granoff, Jinaprabhasūri and Jinadattasūri. Two studies from the Śvetāmbara Jain tradition, in Phyllis Granoff and Koichi Shinohara (eds.), *Speaking of monks. Religious biography in India and China* (Oakville ON 1992), 1–96; Phyllis Granoff, The Jina bleeds. Threats to the faith and rescue of the faithful in medieval Jain stories, in Richard H. Davis (ed.), *Images, miracles and authority in Asian religious traditions* (Boulder 1998), 121–39; Agha Mahdi Husain, *Tughluq dynasty*, Calcutta 1963; Peter D. Jackson, *The Delhi Sultanate. A political and military history*, Cambridge 1999; Shalin Jain, Interaction of the "Lords." The Jain community and the Mughal royalty under Akbar, *Social Scientist* 40/3–4 (2012), 33–57; Shalin Jain, *Community, identity, and state. The Jains under the Mughals*, Delhi 2017; Shalin Jain, Piety, laity and royalty. Jains under the Mughals in the first half of the seventeenth century, *Indian Historical Review* 40/1 (2013), 67–92; Meat ban protests. MNS attempts to cook chicken outside Jain community program hall in Thane, *DNA (Daily News and Analysis)* (2015), https://www.dnaindia.com/india/report-meat-ban-protests-mns-attempts-to-cook-chicken-outside-jain-community-program-hall-in-thane-2124784; Makrand Mehta, *Indian merchants and entrepreneurs in historical perspective*, Delhi 1991; Alka Patel, *Building communities in Gujarāt. Architecture and society during the twelfth through fourteenth centuries*, Leiden 2004; Pushpa Prasad, *Sanskrit inscriptions of the Delhi Sultanate, 1191–1526*, Delhi 1990; Pushpa Prasad, The Jain community in the Delhi Sultanate, *IC* 70/2 (1996), 49–62; Sreeramula Rajeswara Sarma, *Yantrarāja*. The astrolabe in Sanskrit, *Indian Journal of the History of Science* 34/2 (1999), 145–58; Samira Sheikh, *Forging a region. Sultans, traders, and pilgrims in Gujarat, 1200–1500*, Delhi 2010; Mehrdad Shokoohy, *Bhadreśvar. The oldest Islamic monuments in India*, Leiden 1988; Audrey Truschke, *Culture of encounters. Sanskrit at the Mughal court*, New York 2016; Audrey Truschke, Dangerous debates. Jain responses to theological challenges at the Mughal court, *Modern Asian Studies* 49/5 (2015), 1311–44; Audrey Truschke, Jains and Muslims, *Brill's Encyclopedia of Jainism Online*; Audrey Truschke, Jains and the Mughals, in *Jainpedia*, www.jainpedia.org/themes/places/jainism-and-islam/jains-and-the-mughals.html; Audrey Truschke, A Mughal debate about Jain asceticism, in Hani Khafipour (ed.), *The empires of the Near East and India*

(New York 2019), 107–23; Steven M. Vose, *Reimagining Jainism in Islamic India. Jain intellectual culture in the Delhi Sultanate*, London forthcoming.

Steven M. Vose

Jamiat Kheir

Jamiat Kheir (from Ar. *jamʿiyyat khayr*, benevolent society) was the first modern organisation established by members of the Ḥaḍramī Arab community in Indonesia. Formed in Jakarta in 1901, it was a pioneer of *al-nahḍa al-Ḥaḍramiyya* (Ar., the Ḥaḍramī awakening), which sought to bring progress and education to the Ḥaḍramī community.

Jamiat Kheir was a modern-style organisation with a formal structure, a governing executive elected at annual general meetings, and registered members. It was recognised as a legal body by the Dutch colonial government in July 1905. Jamiat Kheir was inspired, at least in part, by the Tiong Hoa Hwe Koan Batavia (from Chin. Zhōnghuá Huìguǎn, Chinese guildhall of Batavia) formed by Chinese migrants in Jakarta in March 1900.

Jamiat Kheir began with about seventy members. It opened the first modern school for Ḥaḍramīs and other Muslim children in Pekojan, Jakarta in 1906, followed by schools in the Krukut and Tanah Abang districts of Jakarta and the city of Bogor. These schools adopted many features of modern education including graded classes, students seated at desks, illustrated textbooks, and a curriculum that incorporated not only religious subjects and Arabic but also secular subjects, such as arithmetic, geography, and English. Jamiat Kheir inspired the spread of similar organisations and schools amongst the Ḥaḍramī population in Java and served as a precursor for the earliest Indonesian Islamic movements.

Jamiat Kheir brought teachers to the Indies from abroad, the most senior being Ahmad Surkati (d. 1943), a Sudanese scholar who served as inspector of Jamiat Kheir schools. He resigned in 1914, after losing the support of the organisation's more conservative *sayyid* leaders by issuing a *fatwā* stating that it was, contrary to longstanding tradition in Ḥaḍramawt, legal for the daughter of a *sayyid* (descendant of the prophet Muḥammad) to marry a non-*sayyid*. Surkati's departure split Jamiat Kheir, with his supporters leaving to form the rival organisation Al-Irsyad (from Ar. *irshād*, guidance, instruction). The schism provoked a long and bitter division in the Ḥaḍramī community in which Jamiat Kheir was a leading voice defending the status of the *sayyid*s.

Jamiat Kheir continues to operate schools in Jakarta under the name Yayasan Pendidikan Jamiat Kheir (Jamiat Kheir Education Foundation). These include a kindergarten, elementary, middle, and high schools in Tanah Abang, and a second elementary school, SDI Binakheir, in Depok. The foundation also runs an undergraduate teacher training college in Islamic education (Institut Agama Islam Jamiat Kheir) under its auspices in Tanah Abang.

Bibliography

Natalie Mobini-Kesheh, *The Hadrami awakening. Community and identity in the Netherlands East Indies, 1900–1942*, Ithaca 1999; Deliar Noer, *The modernist Muslim movement in Indonesia, 1900–1942*, Kuala Lumpur 1973; Robert Van Niel, *The emergence of the modern Indonesian elite*, The Hague 1960.

Natalie Mobini

Japan, relations with the Islamic world

Japan's **relations with** parts of **the Islamic world** commenced mainly in the nineteenth century, after the 1868 Meiji Restoration initiated a programme of modernisation in Japan that included attempts to establish political and economic ties with Iran and the Ottoman Empire. Prior to the nineteenth century, Japan was barely known to the Islamic world, other than as a distant country in East Asia that sometimes engaged in trade with Muslim states in Southeast Asia, such as the Malacca Sultanate, in the ninth/fifteenth century. Japan was also sometimes associated with the legend of Gog and Magog. However, after the forced "opening" of Japan by Commodore Perry in 1853, followed by the Meiji Restoration of 1868, Japan embarked upon a path of rapid modernisation of state institutions and Japanese society, led by "enlightened" intellectuals and Westernised statesmen who anticipated the nation's acceptance as one of the Great Powers. Meiji Japan's successes in modernising inspired the enthusiasm of many in the Islamic world, who considered Japan a model for their own pursuits of modernity. As an "Eastern" nation, modern Japan was disproving social Darwinist racial hierarchies, which placed non-Western peoples below Europeans on the civilisational ladder. The Crimean Tatar journalist İsmail Gaspıralı (also spelled Gasprinski, d. 1914) was among the early commentators on Japan's rise and achievements, writing in his newspaper *Tercümān* (*Terciman*, "The interpreter"), published in Bahçesaray, Crimea, in the 1890s.

The Ottoman sultan, too, took notice. Various exchanges of presents between the sultan and the Japanese emperor culminated in the decision by the sultan to dispatch an Ottoman frigate, the *Ertuğrul*, to Japan in 1889. This mission was intended not only as a means of reciprocating presents and opening communications as to the possibility of an Ottoman-Japanese alliance, but also as a gesture by the Ottoman sultan to the Islamic world, in his role as the self-proclaimed caliph of all Muslims. The ship stopped along the way in many ports in Muslim territories ruled by Europeans, causing consternation among the colonial powers because of the popular support shown the Ottomans as champions of the colonised local Muslim populations. The frigate endured several crises on the way to Japan, delaying its arrival. Upon its departure from Yokohama in late 1890, although warned by the Japanese navy of impending storms and high seas, the *Ertuğrul* attempted to sail and was struck by a typhoon off the Japanese coast, sinking the ship and killing most of its 609-member crew, including the Ottoman emissary, Admiral Osman Pasha. The survivors (apparently numbering between 69 and 74; the sources vary) were rescued by Japanese locals and eventually transported back to Istanbul via Japanese warships. A monument to commemorate the drowned seamen was erected at Ōshima Island, Japan, and ceremonies have been held there on several occasions.

Japan's dramatic victory over the Russian Empire in 1905 was covered extensively by the press in many places in the Islamic world, including the Ottoman Empire, Egypt, Qajar Iran, India, and Russia, in the Turkic Muslim press. It appeared to have had less effect upon Muslims in Southeast Asia. The war was observed directly by Colonel Pertev Bey (later known by the surname Demirhan; d. 1964), an Ottoman military officer dispatched to Manchuria by the Ottoman sultan Abdülhamid II (ʿAbd al-Ḥamīd II, r. 1876–1909) to report on the war. In the aftermath of the war he published several books in Ottoman Turkish on the conflict. According to him, the Russo-Japanese war symbolised not only the first modern-era victory of an "Eastern" nation over a "Western" one, and of an independent Asian nation-state over the multi-ethnic, multi-religious Russian Empire, but also a victory for constitutional monarchy over Czarist autocracy. These lessons were not lost on political activists, journalists, littérateurs, and statesmen of various ethno-religious backgrounds within the Ottoman Empire (and Muslims elsewhere), many of whom considered empires to be antiquated and instead had turned to nationalism as an alternative organising principle. The Ottoman sultan, fascinated with Japanese modernisation and what he considered to be the Japanese character, commissioned translations of texts that he hoped would unlock the secrets of Japan's progress. Ottoman government publications examined Japanese administrative and military reforms and technology.

Examples of journals analysing the Japanese model abound, including Abdullah Cevdet's (d. 1932) Ottoman Turkish journal *İctihad (Ijtihād)*; Abdürreşid İbrahim's (d. 1944) Arabic journal *al-Tilmīdh*, published in St. Petersburg; the Syrian activist Muḥammad Kurd ʿAlī's (d. 1953) journal *al-Muqtabas*, published in Damascus; the Greek Orthodox Lebanese Jūrjī Zaydān's (d. 1914) *al-Hilāl*, and the Egyptian Muṣṭafa Kāmil's (d. 1908) *al-Liwāʾ*, both published in Cairo; and Sayyid Jalāl al-Dīn Muʾayyid al-Islām Kāshānī's (d. 1930) *Ḥabl al-matīn*, in Persian, published in Calcutta (with an abridged version published by his brother in Tehran). Sātiʿ al-Ḥuṣrī's (Satı Bey, d. 1968) Ottoman Turkish *Japonya ve Japonlılar* (1913) explored Japanese culture and civilisation; others, including the Egyptian poet Ḥāfiẓ Ibrāhīm (d. 1932), who memorialised Japanese war-time patriotism in his poem "Ghādat al-Yābān" ("The Japanese maiden"), and the Egyptian nationalist Muṣṭafā Kāmil, employed Japanese imagery to mobilise Egyptians against the British occupation. British expatriates recounted how people in various locales in the Ottoman Empire—from urban centres such as Cairo and Istanbul, to remote villages in Mt. Lebanon—relished the latest news of Japan's naval victories against the Russian fleet and eagerly awaited information about Japan in coffeehouses, barber shops, and reading salons. For the Ottoman Empire, Czarist Russia was understood to be the greatest enemy.

Revolutionary thinkers and activists in late Qājār Iran (1779–1925) referred to the Japanese model to support their political demands, leading to the constitutional revolution of 1905–11. For anti-colonial nationalists in India, modern Japan was seen as a symbol of the inherent power of the East to overcome Western imperialism (Sevea, 52). In 1905 in Bengal the Indian National Congress initiated the Swadeshi movement as a protest against the British, which included boycotting and burning British-made goods, but Japanese goods were allowed into the country and Japanese machinery was allowed to be used in the manufacture of Indian products. But there were differences of opinion on Japan. The Indian Muslim poet and philosopher Muḥammad Iqbāl (d. 1938) viewed these concessions to Japan as a sign of India's stagnation and "carelessness" (*ghafla*; Iqbāl, 275). Meanwhile Indian exiles such as Mohamed Barakatullah (d. 1927) found a home in Japan among other international political refugees, Muslim and non-Muslim.

While modern Japan was idealised as a progressive Eastern nation in some parts of the Islamic world, official and unofficial encounters with members of the Japanese royal family, Japanese officials, and Japanese businessmen occurred, motivated by attempts to increase trade as well as to create diplomatic alliances that would counter Russian expansion in Asia. These included contacts between Japanese personages—including Emperor Meiji (r. 1868–1912), his representatives abroad, and private Japanese citizens (such as the businessman Yamada Torajirō, d. 1957, and the Japanese agent and convert to Islam, Ömer Yamaoka Kōtarō, d. 1959)—and Muslim figures, such as the Shah of Iran, the Ottoman sultan, Ottoman and Qājār officials, journalists, and travellers, Indian nationalists and political exiles, and Muslim activists in China and the Russian Empire, such as Abdürreşid İbrahim.

The "*Ertuğrul* Incident" of 1890 had sparked a series of official negotiations between the Japanese and Ottoman governments that lasted from the 1890s until roughly 1910. The negotiations were unsuccessful in establishing a political alliance or trade agreement, largely because of the contradictory aims of each party. The Japanese, eager to demonstrate and benefit from their newfound status as a powerful nation embarking upon their own imperialist agenda in Asia, insisted upon being granted capitulatory privileges similar to those previously granted to European powers by the Ottomans. The Ottoman state, having suffered the economic consequences of these capitulations—the detrimental effects of European intervention in domestic production, for example—subtly refused to grant the Japanese such privileges, by delaying or avoiding responding to requests. By 1910 Japan had annexed Korea and seemed to have lost interest in such an alliance altogether. Japan eventually joined the Allies in World War I, and, when the Ottoman government sided with the Central Powers, all Japanese nationals in Ottoman lands were expelled. No official treaties were established until after the demise of the Ottoman Empire; in 1924 Japan ratified the Treaty of Lausanne with the new Turkish Republic.

Japan in the interwar era continued to be viewed by some in the Islamic world as a nation that had been able to modernise without losing its "Eastern essence." But tensions arose between Turkey and Japan in the 1930s, when Japan contemplated establishing a puppet state in Central Asia—perhaps in Chinese Turkestan, it was speculated at the time—with an exiled Ottoman prince, Abdülkerim Efendi (d. 1935), as monarch, and invited him to Japan; however, the plan was soon abandoned. In 1945, as a way of maintaining "active neutrality" during wartime, Turkey, under pressure from the Allies, severed diplomatic and trade relations with Japan, declaring war on Japan and Germany shortly thereafter. Nonetheless diplomatic relations were restored in 1951. Japan opened a legation in Iran in 1929, and Iran reciprocated by opening a legation in Japan in 1930. Diplomatic relations with Iran were suspended in 1942 and resumed in 1953; in 1955 the legations were elevated to the status of embassies. During World War II, in 1941, Japan seized British-controlled Malaya, and in

1942 occupied the Dutch-controlled East Indies, in order to take control of the colony's oil resources. Japan was thus seen initially as a liberator from British and Dutch colonial control. Local awareness of Japan's invasion of China and unwillingness to allow Malayan independence resulted in the British regaining control there, but the Japanese encouraged Indonesian nationalism, promising, and then granting, Indonesian independence in 1945. Some Japanese soldiers assisted Indonesian nationalists in their struggle against Dutch colonial rule from 1945–9.

At the end of World War II, beyond the peoples in East and Southeast Asia who had suffered directly from the brutalities of Japanese imperialism, others, too, such as many of those in the Middle East who had admired Japanese modernity from afar, began to realise that Japan had acted as another imperialist power, much like the Europeans, and had not lived up to the lofty principles it formerly represented. India's status as a British colony during the war, however, had complicated its relationship with Japan. There was still some solidarity with the Japanese after the war, as was demonstrated when India, now independent, boycotted a peace conference in 1951 over the issue of Japan's sovereignty being constrained. India and Japan signed a peace treaty, one of the first of Japan's treaties after World War II, and established diplomatic relations in 1952. Trade relations between Japan and Pakistan from 1948 on were the stimulus for an official diplomatic agreement by 1952. Official ties between Japan and Malaysia were established in 1957; an alliance between Japan and Indonesia was signed in 1958, after a compensation agreement for war reparations was reached.

From the 1960s onwards, Japan was again seen by many in the Middle East as a model of success—as the "Japanese miracle" of rapid economic recovery. Books appeared in Arabic discussing the Japanese work ethic of dedication and self-sacrifice as the key to this economic miracle, similar to earlier views that had seen these traits as the reason for Japan's successful modernisation. Comparisons of Japanese and Turkish modernisation became commonplace. Japan's economy required oil, triggering renewed Japanese interest in the politics of the Middle East and the establishment of relationships with the major natural gas and oil-producing nations in the region, from whom it imports most of its energy needs.

Bibliography

Sources

Cemil Aydin, Japan's pan-Asianism and the legitimacy of imperial world order, 1931–1945, *The Asia-Pacific Journal Japan Focus* 6/3 (2008), 1–33; Pertev Demirhan, *Rus-Japon harbinden alınan mâddî ve manevî dersler ve Japonların esbâb-i muzafferiyeti. Bir milletin tâli'i kendi kuvvetindedir!*, Istanbul 1911; Ali Fuat Erden and Osman Senai, *Musavver Rus-Japon seferi 1904–1905*, Istanbul 1321/1905; Yüzbaşı Aḥmad al-Faḍlī, *Kitāb sirr taqaddum al-Yābān*, Cairo 1911; Hitomi, *Japonya Ahlâk ve Mü'essessâtına Dair Nümûne*, MS 6166, Istanbul University Library, trans. Ahmed Rıza, Istanbul 1901; Sātiʿ al-Ḥusrī, *Büyük Milletlerden Japonlar, Almanlar*, Istanbul 1913; Abdürreşid İbrahim, *Alem-i İslam ve Japonya'da intişar-ı İslamiyet*, 2 vols., Istanbul 1910–11; Muḥammad Ḥāfiẓ Ibrāhīm, *Dīwān Ḥāfiẓ Ibrāhīm*, Cairo 1937; Muṣṭafā Kāmil, *al-Shams al-mushriqa*, Cairo 1904; Süleyman Nutkî, *Ertuğrul firkateyni faciası*, İstanbul 1911; Ahmed Rıza (ed. and publisher), *Meşveret* and *Mechveret supplément français*, Paris, Geneva, Brussels, 1895–1897/8, 1908; Mihran, *Rusya ve Japonya Muhârebesine ait Musavver Resmi Mecmuası—Album de la guerre Russo-Japonaise*, Istanbul 1904.

Studies
J. A. Allan and Kaoru Sugihara (eds.), *Japan and the contemporary Middle East*, New York 1993; Cemil Aydın, *The politics of anti-Westernism in Asia. Visions of world order in pan-Islamic and pan-Asian thought*, New York 2007; R. P. Dua, *The impact of the Russo-Japanese (1905) war on Indian politics*, New Delhi 1966; Selçuk Esenbel, *Japan, Turkey and the world of Islam. The writings of Selçuk Esenbel*, Folkestone 2011; Selçuk Esenbel and Inaba Chiharu (eds.), *The rising sun and the Turkish crescent. New perspectives on the history of Japanese Turkish relations*, Istanbul 2003; Roxane Haag-Higuchi, A topos and its dissolution. Japan in some 20th-century Iranian texts, *Iranian Studies* 29/1–2 (1996), 71–83; M. Şükrü Hanioğlu, *The young Turks in opposition*, New York 1995; Muḥammad Iqbāl, *Bāng-i darā*, Lahore 1924, repr. in *Kulliyāt-i Iqbāl (Urdū)* (Lahore 1973), 1–291; Kaori Komatsu, *Ertuğrul faciası. Bir dostluğun doğuşu*, Ankara 1992; Erol Mütercimler, *Ertuğrul faciası ve 21 yüzyıla doğru Türk-Japon ilişkisi*, İstanbul 1993; San-eki Nakaoka, The Yoshida Masaharu mission to Persia and the Ottoman Empire during the period 1880–1881, *Collected papers of Oriental studies in celebration of seventy years of age of his imperial highness prince Mikasa* (Tokyo 1985), 203–35; Nadir Özbek, İsmail Türkoğlu, Selçuk Esenbel, and Hayrettin Kaya, Özel dosya. Abdürreşid İbrahim (1), *Topumsal Tarih* 4/19 (1995), 6–28; Anja Pistor-Hatam, Progress and civilization in nineteenth-century Japan. The Far Eastern state as a model for modernization, *Iranian Studies* 29/1–2 (1996), 111–26; Paul A. Rodell, Southeast Asian nationalism and the Russo-Japanese war. Reexamining assumptions, *Southeast Review of Asian Studies* 29 (2007), 20–40; Iqbal Singh Sevea, *The political philosophy of Muhammad Iqbal. Islam and nationalism in late colonial India*, Cambridge 2012; Hideaki Sugita, Japan and the Japanese as depicted in modern Arabic literature, *Studies of Comparative Culture* 27 (1989), 21–40; J. D. Thijs, The influence on Asia of the rise of Japan and her victory over Russia, *Acta Historiae Neerlandica* 2 (1967), 142–62; Renée Worringer, "Sick man of Europe" or "Japan of the Near East"?. Constructing Ottoman modernity in the Hamidian and Young Turk eras, *IJMES* 36/2 (2004), 207–30; Renée Worringer (ed.), *The Islamic Middle East and Japan. Perceptions, aspirations, and the birth of intra-Asian modernity*, Princeton 2007; Renée Worringer, Rising sun over bear. The impact of the Russo-Japanese war upon the young Turks, in François Georgeon (ed.), *«L'ivresse de la liberté». La révolution de 1908 dans l'Empire ottoman* (Paris 2012), 454–85; Renée Worringer, *Ottomans imagining Japan. East, Middle East, and non-Western modernity at the turn of the twentieth century*, New York 2014.

Renée Worringer

al-Jawālīqī, Abū Manṣūr

Abū Manṣūr Mawhūb b. Aḥmad **al-Jawālīqī** (466–539/1073–1144), also known as Ibn al-Jawālīqī, was a famous Arab philologist who lived in Baghdad. Growing up in Baghdad, the city in which he was born, al-Jawālīqī studied various subjects. He studied *ḥadīth* under the guidance of tutors such as Abū l-Qāsim Ibn al-Busrī (d. 474/1081), Abū Ṭāhir Ibn Abī l-Ṣaqr al-Anbārī (d. 476/1083), and Abū l-Fawāris Ṭirād b. Muḥammad al-Zaynabī (d. 491/1098). He studied lexicography, grammar, and literature *(adab)* under al-Khaṭīb al-Tibrīzī (d. 502/1109)—whose lessons he followed for seventeen years—and Abū l-Ḥusayn al-Mubārak b. ʿAbd al-Jabbār al-Ṣayrafī (d. 500/1106). Al-Jawālīqī became the successor of al-Tibrīzī in the celebrated Baghdadi *madrasa* al-Niẓāmiyya and inherited his disciples, teaching them *ḥadīth* and Arabic philology. Al-Tibrīzī's disciples were all very promising young scholars and they included al-Samʿānī (d. 562/1166)—who also studied the *Gharīb al-ḥadīth* of Abū ʿUbayd (d. 224/838) and the *Amālī* of al-Ṣūlī (d. 335/947) under al-Jawālīqī—as well as Abū l-Barakāt Ibn al-Anbārī (d. 577/1181), Ibn al-Jawzī (d. 597/1200), Tāj al-Dīn Abū l-Yumn al-Kindī (d. 613/1216), his son Ismāʿīl, his daughter Khadīja, and many others (al-Jawālīqī, *al-Muʿarrab*, ed. Shākir, introduction, 26–33).

Al-Jawālīqī was a trustworthy, reliable transmitter, a competent philologist and an honest and modest man whose pious lifestyle led the caliph al-Muqtafī (r. 530–55/1136–60) to appoint him as his personal *imām* to lead prayers in the caliphal palace. It is reported that al-Jawālīqī copied many books in beautiful handwriting; a fine example of which is preserved in the Escorial manuscript 1705, in which al-Jawālīqī collected eight important old lexicographical works. Sezgin claims that al-Jawālīqī made a redaction of the first text therein, the *Kitāb asmāʾ khayl al-ʿArab wa-fursānihā* ("On the Arabs' horses, their names and their owners") of Ibn al-Aʿrābī (d. 231/846), but since al-Jawālīqī is named transmitter *(rāwī)*, auditor *(sāmiʿ)*, or reader *(qāriʾ)* in connection with the eight works one should see him only as the copyist of the manuscript (*GAS* 8:128, 272).

The following list of edited works contains all books published under al-Jawālīqī's name. Some of them seem to be of disputable authorship, especially no. 9, which is extant in only one manuscript. Here al-Jawālīqī transmits a poem with commentary following the commentary of his teacher al-Tibrīzī, but al-Tibrīzī's own work is different from it; so it remains unclear whether al-Jawālīqī created a new commentary based on other sources or this work is simply attributed to him incorrectly. The same problems are evident in no. 1, al-Jawālīqī's *riwāya* of the *Ḥamāsa*, Abū Tammām's (d. 231/845) iconic anthology of early Arabic poetry. According to the editor (15), it differs from al-Tibrīzi's and al-Marzūqī's (d. 421/1030) versions in many ways; its most remarkable difference is that it contains 122 additional verses. Unfortunately, the editor neither explains from where al-Jawālīqī took these verses nor has he any idea why there are so many variant readings in the version attributed to al-Jawālīqī, even though he knows that the two recensions of the *Ḥamāsa* both stem from Abū Riyāsh Aḥmad b. Ibrāhīm al-Qaysī (d. 339/950). Without both broader research and a comparison with all transmitted versions of the *Ḥamāsa*, no valid conclusion with regard to authorship will be possible. Most of the other works, above all nos. 3, 4, 8, and 10, are mentioned by various biographers and are well known with their attribution raising no doubt.

Edited works

1. *Dīwān al-Ḥamāsa li-Abī Tammām Ḥabīb b. Aws al-Ṭāʾī; riwāyat Abī Manṣūr Mawhūb b. Aḥmad b. Muḥammad b. al-Khaḍir al-Jawālīqī*; ed. ʿAbd al-Munʿim Aḥmad Ṣāliḥ, Baghdad 1980; ed. Aḥmad Ḥasan Bassām, Beirut 1998.

2. *Jawāb masʾala suʾila ʿanhā Abū Manṣūr al-Jawālīqī* ("al-Jawālīqī's reply to a philological question"), ed. Ṭāriq al-Janābī, Baghdad 1975; for another question and his reply see Ibn al-Shajarī, *al-Amālī*, ed. Maḥmūd Muḥammad al-Ṭanāḥī (Cairo 1413/1992), 2:365–6; cf. also no. 7 (below).

3. *Mā jāʾa ʿalā faʿaltu wa-afʿaltu bi-maʿnan wāḥid, muʾallaf ʿalā ḥurūf al-muʿjam* ("On verbs with identical meaning in the first and fourth stem, alphabetically arranged"), ed. Mājid al-Dhahabī, Damascus 1402/1982.

4. *al-Muʿarrab min al-kalām al-aʿjamī ʿalā ḥurūf al-muʿjam* ("The foreign vocabulary in Arabic in alphabetical arrangement"), ed. Eduard Sachau, Leipzig 1867 (incomplete); ed. Aḥmad Muḥammad Shākir, Cairo 1361/1942, reprinted Tehran 1966; ed. F. ʿAbd al-Raḥīm, Damascus

1410/1990 (copies the text of Shākir's edition). Al-Jawālīqī's masterpiece contains more than 730 words with explanations that he mainly culled from the *Jamharat al-lugha* of Ibn Durayd (d. 321/933), the *Tahdhīb al-lugha* of al-Azharī (d. 370/980), and the *Adab al-kātib* of Ibn Qutayba (d. 276/889). See also Ibn Barrī (d. 582/1187), *Ḥāshiya ʿalā Kitāb al-muʿarrab*, ed. Ibrāhīm al-Sāmarrāʾī, Beirut 1405/1985; a critical review of this edition by Ḥātim Ṣāliḥ al-Ḍāmin (*Majallat al-Majmaʿ al-ʿilmī l-ʿIrāqī* 37/2 (Baghdad 1406/1986), 301–50) yields many necessary corrections.

5. *al-Mukhtaṣar fī l-naḥw* ("On syntax"), ed. Muḥammad Abū l-Makārim Qindīl, Cairo 1993.

6. *Mukhtaṣar Sharḥ amthilat Sībawayh li-Abī l-Fatḥ Muḥammad b. ʿĪsā l-ʿAṭṭār* ("Epitome of al-ʿAṭṭār's commentary on the nouns used as examples by Sībawayh in his *Kitāb*"), ed. Ṣābir Bakr Abū l-Suʿūd, Asyūṭ 1399/1979; ed. Dafʿallāh ʿAbdallāh Sulaymān, Riyadh 1410/1990.

7. *al-Radd ʿalā l-Zajjāj fī masāʾil akhadhahā ʿalā Thaʿlab* ("al-Jawālīqī's reply to al-Zajjāj [d. 311/923] concerning disputed philological issues that he held against Thaʿlab [d. 291/904]"), ed. ʿAbd al-Munʿim Aḥmad Ṣāliḥ and Ṣubayḥ Ḥammūd al-Shāṭī, al-Sulaymāniyya 1399/1979.

8. *Sharḥ Adab al-kātib*, a commentary on Ibn Qutayba's work, Cairo 1350; ed. Ṭayyiba Ḥamad Būdī, Kuwait 1415/1995.

9. *Sharḥ Maqṣūrat Ibn Durayd*, a commentary on the famous didactical poem of Ibn Durayd (d. 321/933), ed. Ḥātim Ṣāliḥ al-Ḍāmin and ʿAbd al-Munʿim Aḥmad al-Tikrītī, *al-Mawrid* 16/3 (Baghdad 1987), 103–62.

10. *Takmilat iṣlāḥ mā taghlaṭu fīhi l-ʿāmma*, on language errors and deviations from the classical norm made by common people, with glosses by Ibn Barrī, ed. Hartwig Derenbourg with the title *Khaṭaʾ al-ʿawāmm* in the Festschrift for H. L. Fleischer, *Morgenländische Forschungen* (Leipzig 1875), 107–66; ed. ʿIzz al-Dīn al-Tanūkhī, Damascus 1936, reprinted Tehran 1966; ed. ʿAbd al-Ḥafīẓ Farghalī ʿAlī al-Qaranī, in *Durrat al-ghawwāṣ lil-Qāsim b. ʿAlī b. Muḥammad al-Ḥarīrī* (Beirut and Cairo 1417/1996), 835–911; ed. Ḥātim Ṣāliḥ al-Ḍāmin, Damascus 1428/2007.

Bibliography

Sources

Al-Samʿānī, *al-Ansāb* (Hyderabad 1382–1402/1962–82), 3:370; Ibn al-Anbārī, *Nuzhat al-alibbāʾ*, ed. Ibrāhīm al-Sāmarrāʾī (Baghdad 1970²), 293–5; Ibn al-Jawzī, *al-Muntaẓam fī taʾrīkh al-mulūk wa-l-umam*, ed. Muḥammad ʿAbd al-Qādir ʿAṭā and Muṣṭafā ʿAbd al-Qādir ʿAṭā (Beirut 1415/1995²), 18:46–7; Yāqūt, *Muʿjam al-udabāʾ*, ed. Iḥsān ʿAbbās (Beirut 1993), 6:2735–7; al-Qifṭī, *Inbāh al-ruwāt*, ed. Muḥammad Abū l-Faḍl Ibrāhīm (Cairo 1369–93/1950–73), 3:335–7; Ibn Khallikān, *Wafayāt al-aʿyān*, ed. Iḥsān ʿAbbās (Beirut 1968), 5:342–4; al-Yamānī, *Ishārat al-taʿyīn*, ed. ʿAbd al-Majīd Diyāb (Riyadh 1406/1986), 357–8; al-Ṣafadī, *al-Wāfī bi-l-wafayāt*, ed. Muḥammad al-Ḥujayrī (Beirut 1429/2008), 26:603–6; al-Dhahabī, *al-ʿIbar fī khabar man ghabar*, ed. Abū Hājir Muḥammad al-Saʿīd b. Basyūnī Zaghlūl (Beirut 1405/1985), 2:458–9; al-Dhahabī, *Siyar aʿlām al-nubalāʾ*, ed. Shuʿayb al-Arnaʾūṭ et al. (Beirut 1406/1986⁴), 20:89–91; al-Dhahabī, *Taʾrīkh al-Islām*, ed. ʿUmar ʿAbd al-Salām Tadmurī (Beirut 1415/1995), 36:549–51; al-Fīrūzābādī, *al-Bulgha fī tarājim aʾimmat al-naḥw wa-l-lugha*, ed. Muḥammad al-Miṣrī (Kuwait 1407/1987), 229–30; al-Suyūṭī, *Bughyat al-wuʿāt*, ed. Muḥammad Abū l-Faḍl Ibrāhīm (Cairo 1384/1965), 3:308.

Studies

GAL 1:280; *GALS* 1:492; Michael Casiri, *Bibliotheca Arabico-Hispana escuraliensis*, 2 vols., Madrid 1760–70; Fayṣal al-Ḥafyān, Tawqīʿāt Ibn al-Jawālīqī, *Majallat Maʿhad al-makhṭūṭāt al-ʿarabiyya* 60/1 (1437/2016), 193–220; Ṣabāḥ ʿAbbās al-Sālim, *Awhām al-Jawālīqī fī l-Muʿarrab*, Damascus 2014²; Ṭayyiba

Ṣāliḥ al-Shadhr, *al-Taghayyur al-muʿjamī ʿind al-Jawālīqī*, Cairo 1422/2002; ʿAbd al-Munʿim Aḥmad al-Tikrītī, *Abū Manṣūr al-Jawālīqī wa-āthāruhu fī l-lugha*, Baghdad 1400/1979; Muṣṭafā ʿUwayḍa, *Abū Manṣūr al-Jawālīqī wa-juhūduhu fī l-lugha*, Amman 1414/1994.

Reinhard Weipert

al-Jildakī

ʿIzz al-Dīn Aydamir b. ʿAlī **al-Jildakī** (fl. mid-eighth/fourteenth century) was a prolific author of works mainly on alchemy. Although he is considered "one of the greatest scholars of the Islamic cultural sphere" (Ullmann, *Natur- und Geheimwissenschaften*, 237) and "one of the greatest of the medieval Arab alchemists" (Hill, 339), facts about his life remain scarce, and his works are not yet available in reliable editions. He was probably an Egyptian-born descendant of Turkic *mamlūk*s (Harris, 556), so his name should be given as al-Jildakī rather than the Persian form Jaldakī, as suggested by Henry Corbin (Corbin, 67; Artun, 29, n. 51). He worked in Cairo, Damascus, Alexandria, and Gaza and composed his earliest works in Cairo before 737/1336 (MS Hyderabad, OMLRI, Kīmiyāʾ 53, fols. 1b, 22b). At that time, he had already been studying alchemy for more than seventeen years and travelled to learn from scholars in Iraq, Byzantium, the Maghrib, Egypt, Yemen, the Ḥijāz, and Syria before meeting his principal teacher, whose name he does not mention, and who initiated him in the secrets of alchemy (*GAL*, 2:138–9, *GALS*, 2:171–2; Holmyard, 47). He was strongly influenced by the alchemical corpus attributed to Jābir b. Ḥayyān (fl. second-third/eighth-ninth century?) but also had an interest in the allegorical trend of Arabic alchemy, for example, in the works of Ibn Umayl (Ullmann, *Natur- und Geheimwissenschaften*, 238). His knowledge of practical chemistry should not, however, be underestimated (Holmyard, 48, 51–2).

Most of his works are commentaries on alchemical texts, including excerpts, sometimes long, of previous works (Holmyard, 48, 50–1; *GAS*, 4:45, 49–50, 57, 65, 69–70, 96, 107, 117, 119, 237, 247, 250, 252, 266, 275; Ullmann, *Natur- und Geheimwissenschaften*, 238). He commented on works attributed to Hermes, Apollonius of Tyana (fl. first century C.E.), a certain Biyūn al-Barhamī ("the Brahman"; dates unclear), ʿAlī b. Abī Ṭālib (d. 40/661), and Jābir (fl. second/eighth century?), as well as on works by Dhū l-Nūn al-Miṣrī (d. 246/860), Ibn Umayl (fl. probably first half of the fourth/tenth century), Abū l-Iṣbaʿ Ibn Tammām (fl. end of the fourth/tenth century), and al-Sīmāwī (fl. mid-seventh/thirteenth century). He also wrote no fewer than four commentaries on Ibn Arfaʿ Raʾs's (fl. sixth/twelfth century) *Shudhūr al-dhahab* ("Splinters of gold") or parts thereof (Wiedemann, 22–3; Holmyard, 48–9; Ruska and Hartner, 109–10; Siggel, 1:44–57, 85–9, 3:25–9; Taslimi; *GAS*, 4:118, 165–6, 287, 290; Ullmann, *Natur- und Geheimwissenschaften*, 237–42; Hill, 339–40).

Al-Jildakī often updated and expanded his texts later in his life (cf. Holmyard, 49–50; Ullmann, *Natur- und Geheimwissenschaften*, 238). He refers to five voluminous works as his "five comprehensive books," which he considered his most important (MS Cairo, Dār al-Kutub, al-Maktaba al-Zakiyya 828, pp. 165, 207; MS London, Wellcome, Arabic 29, p. 115): *Nihāyat al-ṭalab fī sharḥ al-Muktasab* ("The end of the search, on the commentary on the *Muktasab*"), *al-Taqrīb fī asrār al-tarkīb* ("The approach, on the secrets of composition"), *Ghāyat al-surūr fī sharḥ al-Shudhūr* ("The summit of joy, on the commentary on the *Shudhūr*"), *al-Burhān fī asrār ʿilm al-mīzān* ("The proof, on the secrets of the science of the balance," partial French trans. Corbin, 29–60, 87–143), and *Kanz al-ikhtiṣāṣ fī ʿilm al-khawāṣṣ* (known also as *Durrat al-ghawwāṣ*, "The diver's pearl," ed. Burjaklī). His late work *al-Miṣbāḥ fī asrār ʿilm al-miftāḥ* ("The lamp, on the secrets of the science of the key," lith. ed. ʿAlī Maḥallatī, ed. in Harris), the first part of which he probably finished in 768/1367, was written as a summary of his previous books and treats the principles and goals of alchemy and gives an overview of its history (cf. MS Leiden University, Or. 1274, fols. 3b, 53a; MS Mashhad, Raḍawī, 10709, not foliated; Harris, 547, n. 59; Ullmann, *Natur- und Geheimwissenschaften*, 240; Wiedemann, 23–4).

Al-Jildakī believed that he would have a successor and heir to his alchemical knowledge in the ninth/fifteenth century, and some of his works were indeed continued by the Ottoman-period author al-Iznīqī (fl. ninth/fifteenth century), who styled himself "the new author" *(al-muʾallif al-jadīd)* (cf. MS Berlin, Staatsbibliothek, Spr. 1916, fol. 292a; Siggel, 1:69–81; Ullmann, *Medizin*, 291–2; Ullmann, *Natur- und Geheimwissenschaften*, 131–2, 413–4).

Bibliography

Works of al-Jildakī

al-Burhān fī asrār ʿilm al-mīzān, pt. 1, London, Wellcome Library, MS Arabic 29; pt. 3, Cairo, Dār al-Kutub, al-Maktaba al-Zakiyya, MS 828; *Kitāb durrat al-ghawwāṣ wa-kanz al-ikhtiṣāṣ fī ʿilm al-khawāṣṣ*, ed. Khiḍr Burjaklī, Beirut 1433/2012; *Kashf al-asrār*, Hyderabad, Oriental Manuscripts Library and Research Institute, MS Kīmiyāʾ 53; *Kitāb al-miṣbāḥ fī asrār ʿilm al-miftāḥ*, ed. ʿAlī Maḥallatī, Cairo and Bombay 1884 (lith. ed.), repr. Jubail, Saudi Arabia 2008 (Leiden University Library, MS Or. 1274, and Mashhad, Kitābkhanā-yi Āstān-i Quds-i Raḍawī, MS 10709).

Studies

Tuna Artun, *Hearts of gold and silver. The production of alchemical knowledge in the early modern Ottoman world*, Ph.D. diss., Princeton University 2013; Henry Corbin, *L'alchimie comme art hiératique*, Paris 1986; Nicholas G. Harris, In search of ʿIzz al-Dīn Aydamir al-Ǧildakī, Mamlūk alchemist, *Arabica* 64 (2017), 531–56; Donald R. Hill, The literature of Arabic alchemy, in M. J. L. Young, J. D. Latham, and R. B. Serjeant (eds.), *Religion, learning, and science in the ʿAbbasid period* (Cambridge 1990), 328–41; Eric John Holmyard, Aidamir al-Jildakī, *Iraq* 4 (1937), 47–53; Julius Ruska and Willy Hartner, *Katalog der orientalischen und lateinischen Originalhandschriften, Abschriften und Photokopien des Instituts für Geschichte der Medizin und der Naturwissenschaften in Berlin*, Berlin 1939; Alfred Siggel, *Katalog der arabischen alchemistischen Handschriften Deutschlands*, 3 vols., Berlin 1949–56; G. Strohmaier, al-Dj̲ildakī, *EI2*; Manuchehr Taslimi, *An examination of the Nihāyat al-ṭalab and the determination of its place and value in the history of Islamic chemistry*, inaugural diss., University College, London 1954; Manfred Ullmann, *Die Medizin im Islam*, Leiden 1970; Manfred Ullmann, *Die Natur- und Geheimwissenschaften im Islam*, Leiden 1972; Eilhard Wiedemann, Zur Alchemie bei den Arabern, Erlangen 1922.

Regula Forster
Juliane Müller

al-Jurjānī, ʿAbd al-Qāhir

Abū Bakr **ʿAbd al-Qāhir** b. ʿAbd al-Raḥmān **al-Jurjānī** (d. 471/1078 or 474/1081) was one of the most important literary theorists of the mediaeval Arab world. While he is often described in biographical dictionaries as "the famous grammarian," his most significant influence stems from his works on eloquence *(Asrār al-balāgha)* and the inimitability of the Qurʾān *(Dalāʾil al-iʿjāz)*. Al-Jurjānī was Persian and, as his Arabicised name reveals, he was from Gurgān, at the south-east corner of the Caspian Sea. He is said to have lived there all his life, not even travelling for the pursuit of knowledge. Nevertheless, he studied with Abū l-Ḥusayn al-Fārisī (d. 421/1030), the nephew and student of the famous grammarian Abū ʿAlī al-Fārisī (d. 377/987). It is also regularly reported that people flocked to him from all directions to learn from him (for example, al-Subkī, 5:149). He was a Shāfiʿī *imām* and an adherent of the Ashʿarī school of theology (al-Subkī, 5:149; al-Kutubī, 2:370). He is not to be confused with other important literary critics and rhetoricians also known as "al-Jurjānī": al-Qāḍī Abū l-Ḥasan ʿAlī b. ʿAbd al-ʿAzīz al-Jurjānī (d. 392/1001), author of *al-Wasāṭa bayn al-Mutanabbī wa-khuṣūmih* ("The mediation between al-Mutanabbī and his opponents"), who is mentioned in one source as having taught ʿAbd al-Qāhir (Yāqūt, 4:1797); al-Qāḍī Abū l-ʿAbbās Aḥmad b. Muḥammad al-Jurjānī (d. 482/1089), author of *Kināyāt al-udabāʾ wa-ishārāt al-bulaghāʾ* ("The allusions of littérateurs and intimations of people of eloquence"); Muḥammad b. ʿAlī al-Jurjānī (d. 729/1329), who wrote *al-Ishārāt wa-l-tanbīhāt fī ʿilm al-balāgha* ("Pointers and reminders on the science of eloquence"); and al-Sayyid al-Sharīf ʿAlī b. Muḥammad al-Jurjānī (d. 816/1413), who wrote, among other works, commentaries on al-Sakkākī's (d. 626/1229) *al-Miftāḥ* ("The Key," itself heavily influenced by ʿAbd al-Qāhir's works on eloquence) and glosses on al-Taftāzānī's (d. between 791/1389 and 797/1395) *al-Muṭawwal*, a supercommentary on *al-Miftāḥ*.

ʿAbd al-Qāhir al-Jurjānī wrote extensively on grammar, including on syntax *(naḥw)* and morphology *(taṣrīf)*, as well as on subfields such as the governing entities *(ʿawāmil)*. His most voluminous work, *al-Mughnī fī sharḥ al-Īḍāḥ* ("The comprehensive explanation of the *Īḍāḥ*"), is said to have been a 30-volume commentary on Abū ʿAlī al-Fārisī's well-known work on syntax, *al-Īḍāḥ* ("The clarification," Ibn al-Anbārī, 265). In the introduction to an abridged version of the work that he consequently wrote, *al-Muqtaṣid fī sharḥ al-Īḍāḥ* ("The sparing in explaining the *Īḍāḥ*"), al-Jurjānī acknowledges that *al-Mughnī* (now lost) was too long and detailed (see 1:67). Al-Jurjānī's other major surviving work on grammar is *al-Muqtaṣid fī sharḥ al-Takmila* ("The sparing in explaining the *Takmila*"), a commentary on al-Fārisī's addendum to *al-Īḍāh*, which focuses on morphology. He wrote two additional short books on morphology, *al-Miftāḥ fī l-ṣarf* ("The key to morphology") and *Kitāb fī l-taṣrīf* ("A book on morphology"). The latter is possibly the same work as *al-ʿUmda fī l-taṣrīf* ("The foundation of morphology"), which is listed in medieval biographical sources among al-Jurjānī's works (see introductions to the two published editions of the work).

Al-Jurjānī's *al-ʿAwāmil al-miʾa* ("The hundred governing entities"), also known as *Miʾat ʿāmil*, is a brief catalogue of grammatical regents (that is, words treated with respect to their grammatical impact on other words in a sentence), which he classifies into one hundred types. It was a popular manual that inspired numerous commentaries (Ḥājjī Khalīfah [Kâtib Çelebi], 2:1179–80, and *al-ʿAwāmil*, 135–43). It is also one of the first studies of Arabic grammar to become known in Europe, as it was translated into Latin in 1617 by the Dutch orientalist Thomas Erpenius (1584–1624), along with Ibn Ājurrūm's (d. 723/1323) *al-Ājurrūmiyya*, another popular Arabic grammar manual. Al-Jurjānī's *Kitāb al-jumal fī l-naḥw* ("The book of clauses on syntax"), also known as *al-Jurjāniyya*, is an elaboration on the *ʿAwāmil* following a different scheme of classification (Ḥājjī Khalīfah [Kâtib Çelebi], 1:602–3, with a list of commentaries). His *Sharḥ al-jumal* is a commentary on this elaboration.

In *Dalāʾil al-iʿjāz* ("The signs of the inimitability of the Qurʾān") al-Jurjānī expands his inquiry from syntax to semantics and pragmatics. He develops the concept of *naẓm* (composition), which considers how the syntactical structure of a sentence affects its meaning. Each grammatical construction of a phrase, he argues, produces a unique "image, or form, of meaning" *(ṣūrat al-maʿnā)*, even when the original unarticulated idea is the same. What is inimitable about the Qurʾān, according to al-Jurjānī, is precisely its *naẓm* (that is, the way its sentences convey their particular meanings). Although the choice of individual words does not form the main basis of the Qurʾān's inimitability, word choice also contributes to eloquence when used to indicate a secondary meaning. He calls this "the meaning of meaning" *(maʿnā l-maʿnā)*, which is achieved through the use of implication *(kināya)* and figurative speech *(majāz)*, including metaphor *(istiʿāra)*.

While the *Dalāʾil* looks at eloquence primarily from the perspective of form, his *Asrār al-balāgha* ("The secrets of eloquence") deals more with aspects relating to poetic meaning and is not premised on proving the inimitability of the Qurʾān. In this work he develops an aesthetic theory of simile *(tashbīh)* and analogy *(tamthīl)*, and a set of rhetorical figures he groups under a rubric he calls "make-believe imagery" *(takhyīl)*. He ends the book with a discussion of borrowing and plagiarism *(akhdh wa-sariqa)* and the question of literal and figurative speech *(al-ḥaqīqa wa-l-majāz)*, including metaphor.

Both works represent major milestones in the development of classical Arabic literary theory. First, he complicates the *lafẓ* (utterance/form)—*maʿnā* (meaning/content) duality by insisting on the impossibility of separating the two at the level of both the word and the sentence (Harb, "Form and content"). Furthermore, he develops a new and sophisticated theory of literary quality, based on the emotional impact poetic speech produces in the listener. This approach has been described as psychological (Khalafallah), anticipating modern Western theories of poetic imagery (Abu Deeb, *al-Jurjānī's theory*) and has been characterised as representing an aesthetic of wonder (Harb, *Poetic marvels*). Finally, the *Dalāʾil* and the *Asrār* form the foundation of what later became a formalised science of eloquence *(ʿilm al-balāgha)*.

Al-Jurjānī's successors organised and added to the material of the *Dalāʾil* and the *Asrār* in a variety of ways. The earliest notable attempt was by Fakhr al-Dīn al-Rāzī (d. 606/1209), in his *Nihāyat al-ījāz fī dirāyat al-iʿjāz* ("The utmost brevity in grasping the inimitability of the Qurʾān"). But it was al-Sakkākī, in his *Miftāḥ al-ʿulūm* ("The key to the sciences"), and al-Khaṭīb al-Qazwīnī (d. 739/1338), in his *Talkhīṣ* ("Summary") and *Īḍāḥ* ("Clarification") of al-Sakkākī's *Miftāḥ*, who cemented the formalisation of the study of eloquence into its three sciences. What became *ʿilm al-maʿānī* (the science of [conveying] meaning), is essentially a study of *naẓm*.

ʿIlm al-bayān (the science of elucidation) is the study of indirect signification *(maʿnā l-maʿnā)* through figurative speech, including metaphor, and implied meaning. It became standard to incorporate the discussion of simile into *ʿilm al-bayān* as the foundation of metaphor, as well as the question of literal versus figurative speech. Thus both al-Jurjānī's major works, the *Asrār* and the *Dalāʾil*, inform *ʿilm al-bayān*. Finally, *ʿilm al-badīʿ* (the science of rhetorical figures), though much expanded, incorporates the remaining rhetorical figures discussed by al-Jurjānī in the *Asrār*. While the final shape of *ʿilm al-balāgha* is quite different from the way al-Jurjānī organised his material, it is based on his two pivotal works. Al-Jurjānī is thus often regarded as the founder of the rhetorical sciences. Outside of the strictly rhetorical disciplines, al-Jurjānī's influence is also evident in al-Zamakhsharī's (d. 538/1144) commentary on the Qurʾān, *al-Kashshāf* ("The Unveiler"), and in al-Muṭarrizī's (d. 610/1213) commentary on al-Ḥarīrī's (d. 516/1122) *Maqāmāt*.

Al-Jurjānī nevertheless was a product of his time, building on and reacting to vibrant discussions on poetry and the inimitability of the Qurʾān that took place in the third/ninth and fourth/tenth centuries. The influence of Aristotelian poetics on his thinking is also debated in modern scholarship (Abu Deeb, al-Jurjānī's classification; Abu Deeb, *al-Jurjānī's theory*; Larkin; Ḥusayn). The role of his Ashʿarī outlook in contrast to the Muʿtazilī views particularly of al-Qāḍī ʿAbd al-Jabbār (d. 415/1025) has also been highlighted (Larkin). Al-Jurjānī's approach, however, had a much greater influence on the trajectory of literary criticism than that of his contemporaries Ibn Sinān al-Khafājī (d. 466/1074) and Ibn Rashīq al-Qayrawānī (d. 456/1063–4 or 463/1070–1).

Besides the *Dalāʾil al-iʿjāz*, additional notes on the inimitability of the Qurʾān by al-Jurjānī are published at the end of Shākir's edition of the work (479–569). In his treatise *al-Risāla al-shāfiya fī wujūh al-iʿjāz* ("The definitive treatise on the aspects of the Qurʾān's inimitability"), he more directly rebuts claims that attribute the inimitability of the Qurʾān to matters other than its eloquence, including the idea of *ṣarfa* (turning away or incapacitation), which identifies the miracle of the Qurʾān as God's rendering humans incapable of producing anything like it. Al-Jurjānī is also believed to have authored *Durj al-durar fī tafsīr al-āy wa-l-suwar* ("The chest of pearls in explaining the Qurʾān's verses and suras"), a work of Qurʾanic exegesis (regarding authorship see *Durj al-durar*, 1:15–21). He has an anthology of selected poetry by the three most contentiously debated poets of the ʿAbbāsid period, al-Buḥturī (d. 284/897), Abū Tammām (d. 231/845 or 232/846), and al-Mutanabbī (d. 354/965) (published in *al-Ṭarāʾif al-adabiyya*). He composed poetry of his own, some of which has survived in biographical dictionaries, and he wrote a mnemonic poem on poetic meters *(bayān al-ʿarūḍ)*. Among his lost works are long and short commentaries on al-Wāsiṭī's (d. 306/918 or 307/919) *Iʿjāz al-Qurʾān*, one of the earliest known (but now lost) treatises on the inimitability of the Qurʾān (Ḥājjī Khalīfah [Kâtib Çelebi], 120).

Bibliography

Works by ʿAbd al-Qāhir al-Jurjānī

On poetics and the inimitability of the Qurʾān: *Asrār al-balāgha*, ed. Hellmut Ritter, Istanbul 1954; *Die Geheimnisse der Wortkunst (Asrār al-balāgha) des ʿAbdalqāhir al-Jurjānī*, German trans. Hellmut Ritter, Wiesbaden 1959; *Asrār al-balāgha*, Persian trans. Jalīl Tajlīl,

Tehran 1366/1987; Vicente Cantarino, *Arabic poetics in the Golden Age* (Leiden 1975), 241–62 [translated excerpts]; Geert Jan Van Gelder and Marlé Hammond (eds.), *Takhyīl. The imaginary in classical Arabic poetics* (Cambridge 2008), 29–69 [translated excerpts]; *Dalāʾil al-iʿjāz*, ed. Maḥmūd Muḥammad Shākir, Cairo 2004; *Les signes d'inimitabilité en grammaire de l'expression*, French trans. Hrazem Rachad, Tangier 2006; *Dalāʾil al-iʿjāz fī l-Qurʾān*, Persian trans. Muḥammad Rādmanish, Mashhad 1368/1989; *Delâilül-İʿcâz. Sözdizimi ve anlambilim*, Turkish trans. Osman Güman, includes in parallel a facsimile of *Dalāʾil*, MS Köprülü, Fazıl Ahmed Paşa 1419, Istanbul 2015; *al-Risāla al-shāfiya fī wujūh al-iʿjāz*, in Maḥmūd Muḥammad Shākir (ed.), *Dalāʾil al-iʿjāz* (Cairo 1984), 573–628; *Thalāth rasāʾil fī iʿjāz al-Qurʾān*, ed. Muḥammad Khalafallah Aḥmad and Muḥammad Zaghlūl Sallām (Cairo 1956), 115–58, trans. as "The peremptory treatise," in *Three treatises on the Iʿjāz of the Qurʾān*, trans. Issa J. Boullata (Reading 2014), 83–114.

On grammar: *al-ʿAwāmil al-miʾa*, ed. al-Shaykhī al-Dāghistānī, Jidda 2009; *The* Miʾut ạmil, *and* Shurḥoo Miʾut ạmil. *Two elementary treatises on Arabic syntax*, trans. A. Lockett, Calcutta 1814; *Kitāb al-jumal*, ed. ʿAlī Ḥaydar, Damascus 1972; *al-Miftāḥ fī l-ṣarf*, ed. ʿAlī Tawfīq Ḥamad, Beirut 1987; *al-Muqtaṣid fī sharḥ al-Īḍāḥ*, ed. Kāẓim Baḥr al-Marjān, 2 vols., Baghdad 1982; *al-Muqtaṣid fī sharḥ al-Takmila*, ed. Aḥmad b. ʿAbdallāh b. Ibrāhīm al-Duwaysh, 3 vols., Riyadh 2007; *Sharḥ al-jumal fī l-naḥw*, ed. Khalīl ʿAbd al-Qādir ʿĪsā, Amman & Beirut 2011; and ed. Khadījā M.Ḥ. Bākistānī, MA Thesis, Umm al-Qurā University, Mecca 1987; [*al-ʿUmud*.] *Kitāb fī l-taṣrīf*, ed. al-Badrāwī Zahrān, Cairo 1987; *Kitāb fī l-taṣrīf*, ed. Muḥsin Sālim al-ʿAmīrī, Mecca 1988.

On Quranic exegesis: *Durj al-durar fī tafsīr al-āy wa-l-suwar*, ed. Ṭalʿat Ṣalāḥ al-Farḥān and Muḥammad Adīb Shakūr, Beirut 2009.

On poetry and prosody: *Bayān al-ʿarūḍ*, in Muḥammad Ḥasan Āl Yāsīn (ed.), *al-Iqnāʿ fī l-ʿarūḍ wa-takhrīj al-qawāfī* (Baghdad 1960), 88–90; *al-Mukhtār min dawāwīn al-Mutanabbī wa-l-Buḥturī wa-Abī Tammām*, in al-Maymanī (ed.), *al-Ṭarāʾif al-adabiyya* (Cairo 1937), 195–305.

Biographical Dictionaries

Al-Bākharzī, *Dumyat al-qaṣr*, ed. Muḥammad al-Tūnjī (Beirut 1993), 578–94; Ḥājjī Khalīfah (Kâtib Çelebi), *Kashf al-ẓunūn ʿan asāmī l-kutub wa-l-funūn*, ed. Muḥammad Sharaf al-Dīn Yāltaqāyā and Rifʿat Bīlkah al-Kilīsī (Istanbul 1941–43), 83, 120, 212, 602–3, 745, 1169–70, 1179, 1621, 1769; Ibn al-Anbārī, *Nuzhat al-alibbāʾ fī ṭabaqāt al-udabāʾ*, ed. Ibrāhīm al-Sāmarrāʾī (Zarqa 1985[3]), 264–5; Ibn al-ʿImād, *Shadharāt al-dhahab fī akhbār man dhahab*, ed. ʿAbd al-Qādir Arnāʾūṭ and Maḥmūd Arnāʾūṭ (Damascus 1986–95), 5:308–9; al-Kutubī, *Fawāt al-wafayāt wa-l-dhayl ʿalayhā*, ed. Iḥsān ʿAbbās (Beirut 1973–7), 2:369–70; al-Qifṭī, *Inbāh al-ruwāt*, ed. Muḥammad Abū l-Faḍl Ibrāhīm (Beirut and Cairo 1986), 2:188–90; al-Subkī, *Ṭabaqāt al-Shāfiʿiyya al-kubrā*, ed. ʿAbd al-Fattāḥ Muḥammad al-Ḥilw and Maḥmūd Muḥammad al-Ṭanāḥī (Cairo 1964–76), 5:149–50; al-Suyūṭī, *Bughyat al-wuʿāt fī ṭabaqāt al-lughawiyyīn wa-l-nuḥāt*, ed. Muḥammad Abū l-Faḍl Ibrāhīm (Cairo 1965), 2:106; al-Yāfiʿī, *Mirʾāt al-jinān wa-ʿibrat al-yaqẓān*, ed. Khalīl al-Manṣūr (Beirut 1997), 3:78.

Studies

Iḥsān ʿAbbās, *Taʾrīkh al-naqd al-adabī ʿinda l-ʿArab* (Beirut 1983[4]), 419–38; Kamal Abu Deeb, al-Jurjānī's classification of *istiʿāra* with special reference to Aristotle's classification of metaphor, *JAL* 2 (1971), 48–75; Kamal Abu Deeb, *al-Jurjānī's theory of poetic imagery*, Warminster 1979; Naṣr Ḥāmid Abū Zayd, Mafhūm al-naẓm ʿinda ʿAbd al-Qāhir al-Jurjānī. Qirāʾa fī ḍawʾ al-uslūbiyya, *Fuṣūl: Journal of Literary Criticism* 5/1 (1984), 11–24; Mohamed Ait el Ferrane, *Die Maʿnā-Theorie bei ʿAbdalqāhir al-Ǧurǧānī (gestorben 471/1079). Versuch einer Analyse der poetischen Sprache*, Frankfurt am Main 1990; Ramzi Baalbaki, The relation between *naḥw* and *balāġa*. A comparative study of the methods of Sībawayhi and Gurgani, *ZAL* 11 (1983), 7–23; Antonella Ghersetti, "Word" in the linguistic thinking of ʿAbd al-Qāhir al-Jurjānī, in Giuliano Lancioni and Lidia Bettini (eds.), *The word in Arabic* (Leiden 2011), 83–108; Antonella Ghersetti, *Per una rilettura in chiave pragmatica di* Dalāʾil al-iʿǧāz *di ʿAbd al-Qāhir al-Ǧurǧānī*, Ph.D. diss., Università degli Studi di Firenze 1998; Lara Harb, *Poetic marvels. Wonder and aesthetic experience in medieval Arabic literary theory*, Ph.D. diss., New York University 2013; Lara Harb, Form, content, and the inimitability of the Qurʾān in ʿAbd al-Qāhir al-Jurjānī's works, *MEL* 18/3 (2015), 301–21; Ṭāhā

Ḥusayn, al-Bayān al-ʿArabī min al-Jāḥiẓ ilā ʿAbd al-Qāhir, in Ṭāhā Ḥusayn and ʿAbd al-Ḥamīd al-ʿAbbādī (eds.), *Naqd al-nathr* (Cairo 1933), 1–32; Alexander Key (ed.), *ʿAbd al-Qāhir al-Jurjānī*, special issue of *Journal of Abbasid Studies* 5 (2018); Muhammad Khalafallah, ʿAbdalqâhir's theory in his "Secrets of eloquence." A psychological approach, *JNES* 14/3 (1955), 164–7; Nejmeddine Khalfallah, *La théorie sémantique de ʿAbd al-Qahir al-Jurjani (m. 471/1078)*, Paris 2014; Margaret Larkin, *The theology of meaning. ʿAbd al-Qāhir al-Jurjānī's theory of discourse*, New Haven 1995; Aḥmad Maṭlūb, *ʿAbd al-Qāhir al-Jurjānī*, Kuwait 1973; Badawī Ṭabāna, *al-Bayān al-ʿArabī* (Cairo 1976[6]), 215–62; Bushrā Tākafrāst, al-Dirāsāt al-ḥadītha wa-naẓariyyat al-naẓm ʿind ʿAbd al-Qāhir al-Jurjānī, *Majallat Jāmiʿat Ibn Yūsuf bi-Marrākish* 4 (2005), 309–38 [an overview of modern scholarship in Arabic on al-Jurjānī]; G. Troupeau, Naḥw, *EI2*; Kees Versteegh, Grammar and rhetoric. Ĝurĝānī on the verbs of admiration, *JSAI* 15 (1992), 113–33; Kees Versteegh, A new semantic approach to linguistics. Al-Jurjânî and as-Sakkâkî on meaning, in Kees Versteegh (ed.), *Landmarks in linguistic thought*, vol. 3, *The Arabic linguistic tradition* (London 1997), 115–26; Yāqūt, *Muʿjam al-udabāʾ*, ed. Iḥsān ʿAbbās (Beirut 1993), 4:1797; Badri Najib Zubir, Departure from communicative norms in the Qur'an. Insights from al-Jurjānī and al-Zamakhsharī, *Journal of Qur'anic Studies* 2/2 (2000), 69–81.

Lara Harb

K

Kān wa-kān

Kān wa-kān is a popular poetic form using vernacular Arabic. Ṣafī al-Dīn al-Ḥillī (d. c.750/1349), the first critic to examine it, counts it among the four non-canonical forms of colloquial poetry. The other three are *zajal*, *mawāliyā*, and *qūmā*. Among these, the *zajal*, strophic poetry in vernacular Arabic, is by far the most popular form. In contrast to the *zajal*, which was invented by Andalusian poets around the end of the fifth/eleventh century, with Eastern poets taking it up later on, the *kān wa-kān* had its origins in the Eastern part of the Arabic-speaking world, probably in Baghdad (al-Ḥillī, 148). The first poets known to have composed *kān wa-kān* are the popular poet Abū Manṣūr Ibn Nuqṭa al-Muzaklish (d. 597/1200), who recited his poems in marketplaces, the Ḥanbalī scholar Abū l-Faraj Ibn al-Jawzī (d. 597/1201), and the Ḥanafī preacher Shams al-Dīn Ibn al-Kūfī al-Wāʿiẓ (d. 675/1276)—all three of them from Baghdad.

A *kān wa-kān* is distinguished by a single rhyme with a long vowel preceding the rhyming consonant throughout the whole poem. Its length ranges from two to fifty verses. One verse consists of two hemistichs of four feet each. The last foot of the second hemistich, however, is shortened by two syllables. A typical verse would be scanned as follows (from left to right):

> ⏓ – ∪ – | ⏓ ∪ – – | ⏓ – ∪ – | ⏓ – ∪ – || ⏓ – ∪ – | ⏓ ∪ – – | ⏓ – ∪ – | ⏓ –. There are two places within this form where scansion may differ: 1) the second foot of both hemistichs may occur as – – – or ∪ ∪ ∪ –. 2) One also encounters ∪ ∪ – ∪ – in the last foot of the first hemistich, and ∪ ∪ – in the shortened foot of the second hemistich.

The very name of this poetic form, which may be rendered literally as "there was and there was," is quite similar to the conventional opening of fairy tales, *kān mā kān fī qadīm al-zamān* (lit. "there was and there wasn't, once upon a time"), and points to a narrated story. Ṣafī al-Dīn al-Ḥillī refers to this feature as being formative for this poetic type. One is therefore not surprised to find many *kān wa-kān*s displaying similar themes and the same setup as typical first-person *zajal* ballads. This may be one of the reasons why some scholars likened the *kān wa-kān* to the *zajal*, other reasons being its length and the convention of breaking one verse into four parts of two feet each, which thus results in one stanza of four separate verses with the last one showing a common rhyme over the whole poem. In some specimens, every stanza has a separate rhyme in the first three verses, which makes it almost impossible to distinguish this form from the *zajal*. Interestingly, *zajal*, *bullayq* (a subtype of the *zajal*), and *kān wa-kān* seem to have a similar *Sitz im Leben*: Ibn Taghrībirdī (d. 874/1470) reports in his chronicle *al-Nujūm* (10:40) how a festive gathering of common people recited *zajals*, *bullayqs*, and *kān wa-kāns*, cheering the arrest and deportation of a disgraced commander of the Mamlūk sultan al-Nāṣir Muḥammad (r. 693–4/1293–4, 698–708/1299–1309, and 709–41/1310–41). Apart from the ballad-like type, an edifying type of *kān wa-kān* gained fame. As was the case with religious *zajals*, this may have resulted from poets such as Ibn al-Jawzī singling out this colloquial poetic form to convey religious messages more easily to the common people.

Bibliography

Sources

Shuʿayb Ḥurayfīsh, *al-Rawḍ al-fāʾiq* (Cairo 1308/[1890–1]), 23, 26, 29, 33, 34, 42, 53, 55, 71, 74, 77, 80, 86, 135, 137, 144, 169, 181, 191, 204, 217; Ibn Ḥijja, *Bulūgh al-amal fī fann al-zajal*, ed. Riḍā Muḥsin al-Qurayshī (Damascus 1974), 139–142; al-Ibshīhī, *al-Mustaṭraf fī kull fann mustaẓraf* (Beirut 1992), 2:286–8; Ṣafī al-Dīn al-Ḥillī, *Die vulgärarabische Poetik. Al-Kitāb al-ʿāṭil al-ḥālī wa-l-muraḫḫaṣ al-ġālī des Ṣafīyaddīn Ḥillī*, ed. Wilhelm Hoenerbach (Wiesbaden 1956), 148–70; Ibn Taghrībirdī, *al-Nujūm al-zāhira fī mulūk Miṣr wa-l-Qāhira*, ed. Muḥammad Ḥusayn Shams al-Dīn (Beirut 1992), 10:39–40.

Studies

Pierre Cachia, *Exploring Arab folk literature* (Edinburgh 2011), 96–101; Riḍā Muḥsin al-Qurayshī, *Kān wa-kān wa-l-qūmā*, Baghdad 1977; Wilhelm Hoenerbach, *Die vulgärarabische Poetik. Al-Kitāb al-ʿāṭil al-ḥālī wa-l-muraḫḫaṣ al-ġālī des Ṣafīyaddīn Ḥillī* (Wiesbaden 1956), 46–7, 72; Margaret Larkin, Popular poetry in the post-classical period, 1150–1850, in Roger Allen and D. S. Richards (eds.), *Arabic literature in the post-classical period*, (Cambridge 2006), 212–3; Muṣṭafā Ṣādiq al-Rāfiʿī, *Taʾrīkh ādāb al-ʿArab* (Cairo 1911), 2:158–9.

Hakan Özkan

Karavezir Seyyid Mehmed Paşa

Karavezir Seyyid Mehmed (Qarāvezīr Seyyid Meḥmed) **Paşa** (1148–95/1735–81), an Ottoman statesman and grand vizier, was born in 1148 (1735–6) in Arapsun (today's Gülşehir, in the province of Nevşehir, in central Turkey). Since his father, Ali (ʿAlī) Efendi, traced his lineage to the Prophet Muḥammad, he was also known as Seyyid (Sayyid, a title of honour for the Prophet's descendants). Under the patronage of his uncle, Süleyman Ağa (Süleymān Āghā), head cook (*Aşçıbaşı*, Āşcībaşī) at Topkapı Sarayı, he entered the palace in 1160 (1747), where he was raised by officers of the janissary corps.

Seyyid Mehmed was accepted into the *teberdaran-ı hassa* (*teberdārān khāṣṣa*, halberdiers corps) in 1173 (1759–60), but due to his calligraphy skills, he was transferred to the treasury bureau (*Hazine odası, Khazīne Odasi*) of the *enderun-i hümayun* (*enderūn-i humāyūn*, inner service of the imperial household) on 13 Şaban (Shaʿbān) 1175 (9 March 1762). Through his brother Mustafa (Muṣṭafā) Ağa, the chief coffee maker (*kahvecibaşı, qahvecibaşī*) of Prince Abdülhamid (ʿAbd al-Ḥamīd), Seyyid Mehmed came into contact with the prince, and when the latter was enthroned as Sultan Abdülhamid I (r. 1187–1203/1774–89), Mehmed entered the *has oda* (*khāṣṣ oda*, privy chamber). On 21 Zilkade (Dhū l-Qaʿda) 1187 (3 February 1774), he became *hazine kethüdası* (*khazīne ketkhüdāsı*, superintendent of the treasury), and on 3 Muharrem (Muḥarram) 1189 (6 March 1775), he was elevated to the post of *silahdar* (*silāḥdār*, the sultan's sword-bearer), a promotion that led to the pinnacle of his career. Upon the dismissal of Grand Vizier Kalafat (Qalafāt) Mehmed Paşa (d. 1207/1793), Seyyid Mehmed was appointed in his place, on 9 Şaban 1193 (22 August 1779).

As grand vizier, Seyyid Mehmed concentrated his efforts mainly on the treasury and military and implemented measures to prevent bribery and collect taxes punctually. Abdülhamid I personally attended the military exercises that took place at Sadabad (Saʿdābād) under his supervision. Seyyid Mehmed died from typhoid on 25 Safer (Ṣafar) 1195 (20 February 1781), and was buried in the graveyard near the tomb of Abdülhamid I (r. 1187–1203/1774–89) in Bahçekapı, Istanbul.

Bibliography

Ahmed Vasıf Efendi, *Mehasinü'l-asar ve hakaikü'l-ahbar*, Istanbul, Topkapı Sarayı Müzesi Kütüphanesi, Hazine, no. 1406; Ahmed Cevdet, *Tarih-i Cevdet*, vol. 2, Istanbul 1308/1890–1; Mehmed Süreyya, *Sicill-i Osmani*, vol. 4, Istanbul 1308/1890–1; Ahmed Cavid, *Verd-i mutarra. Hadikatü'l-vüzera zeyli*, Freiburg 1969; Tayyarzade Ata Bey, *Osmanlı Saray tarihi. Tarih-i enderun*, vol. 2, ed. Mehmet Arslan, Istanbul 2010; Fikret Sarıcaoğlu, Karavezir Mehmed Paşa, *TDVİA* 24: 477–8.

Fatih Yeşil

Kashgar

Kashgar (Chaghatay: Kashghār; Uyghur: Qăshqăr) is an oasis town in the Tarim Basin, or Eastern Turkistan, which has been ruled alternately by various powers, including the Mongols, the Chinese, the Tibetans, and local nobles, among many others. The city's name is often used to refer to the whole oasis in which it is located, or even the entire region of the eastern Tarim Basin. Kashgar is currently regarded as the cultural centre of the Uyghurs, a Turkic-speaking, Muslim ethnic group, though in earlier periods it has sometimes been overshadowed by other Tarim Basin towns, often Yarkand or Khotan. Today the city falls under the administration of the People's Republic of China.

Kashgar is one of the many ancient oasis towns that ring the Taklamakan Desert, watered by rivers that flow from the surrounding mountain ranges. Like most of these oasis towns, Kashgar's earliest records were set down by Chinese historians of the Han dynasty (206 B.C.E.–226 C.E.), which temporarily wrested the Tarim Basin from the control of the nomadic Xiongnu (Hulsewe). These records use the Chinese name for the town, Shu-le; the earliest forms of the name Kashgar were perhaps not used until as late as the sixth century C.E. (Pelliot). While pre-Islamic Kashgar was sometimes an independent kingdom, it was more often incorporated into conquering regimes, including those of the Han, the Xiongnu, the Kushans, the Hephthalites, the Tibetans, the Uighurs, the Tang, and the Qarakhitay.

Kashgar first came to the attention of Muslim societies in the course of the Umayyad conquest of Transoxiana, during which Qutayba b. Muslim (96/715) is said to have planned an attack on the oasis. While Qutayba's attack probably never materialised, some Arab soldiers appear to have participated in one or more minor raids on Kashgar, providing a basis for later legends purporting Qutayba's conquest of the city a few months before his death (Gibb). Whether there were early Muslim raids on Kashgar or not, the religion of Islam did not begin to take root in the city until the middle of the fourth/tenth century when the rulers of Kashgar, the Karakhanids (Qarakhānids) (225–608/840–1212), converted en masse. After losing control of Kashgar to the Buddhist kingdom of Khotan in 970, the Karakhanids reconquered the city sometime around the turn of the fourth/eleventh century, and began striking Kashgar's first Islamic coinage no later than 395/1004–5 (Kochnev 213).

Karakhanid rule brought transformations that remain central to Kashgar's cultural identity down to the present. The Islamisation of Kashgar and its environs proceeded gradually, over the course of many centuries, but the conversion of the Karakhanid ruling class set the direction. Already by the early sixth/twelfth century, ordinary Turkic legal documents were being composed in the Arabic script, which displaced the earlier Uyghur script (Gronke). While Kashgar had seen Turkic rulers in certain earlier periods, Karakhanid rule also entrenched the Turkic language and literary tradition in Kashgar permanently. It was during Kashgar's turn as a Karakhanid capital that the city saw its first literary florescence, which, while modest in the broader context of Central Asian history, produced the world's first Islamic-Turkic literary monument, the Qutadghu Bilig (Dankoff), and nurtured the eleventh-century ethnographer and lexicographer, Maḥmūd Kashgārī. Orally transmitted epics commemorating the Karakhanid wars with the Buddhist Khotanese presumably date to the Karakhanid era itself. By the eighteenth century many of these took written forms as popular hagiographies, and have served as the foundation for the local historiographical imagination ever since (Thum, *Sacred routes*).

As important as the written (as opposed to epic) Karakhanid texts have been to modern scholars, they do not seem to have been widely read in their own time. Indeed, Kashgar made only a modest mark on the medieval intellectual landscape outside of Central Asia, and, aside from world histories and geographies, the town was rarely mentioned by Muslim authors beyond the region. An important exception is the work of the Persian poet, Saʿdī (d. 691/1292), who claimed in his *Gulistān* to have visited Kashgar. Although the chronology of this account suggests it is fictional (Katouzian), the choice of Kashgar suggests that Saʿdī expected his audience to be familiar with the town, even if only as a distant outpost of Islam.

Like all the towns of the Tarim Basin, Kashgar's circumscribed oasis geography made it a poor political power base, and for most of its history it (as well as the rest of the Tarim) has been ruled by empires and kingdoms based elsewhere. Kashgar's military disadvantages were noted explicitly by the sixteenth-century Kashgari nobleman, Mīrzā Ḥaydar Dūghlāt (d. 958/1551), who wrote that, "in Kashgar it is impossible to maintain an army on one harvest" (Dūghlāt 192). But if Kashgar rarely sustained fully independent states, it also benefitted from surrounding geographical barriers that made it costly for distant overlords to govern it closely. So it was that between the Mongol conquest (607–15/1211–9) and the foundation of the Yarkand Khanate (920/1514) the town often enjoyed a measure of autonomy, sometimes even de facto independence, under administrators and Mongol nobles who professed nominal submission to Chingissid Khans, whether the Great Khans, the Chaghatayids, or the Eastern Chaghatayids. Very little is known about this period, from which only one very brief local historical source, Jamāl Qarshī's *Mulḥaqāt al-Ṣurāḥ* ("Addendum to *al-Ṣurāḥ*"), has survived (Sultanov). After Qarshī's work, completed shortly before 705/1305–6, no Kashgari authors are known until Mīrzā Ḥaydar Dūghlāt, who wrote from exile in Kashmir. No known literary texts are thought to have been completed again in the city itself until the 1100s/1690s.

With the foundation of the Yārkand Khanate in 920/1514, Chingissid Khans established a durable, urban court in the Tarim Basin, subduing the local nobility entirely. Although sources for the Yārkand Khanate (r. 920–1090/1514–1679) are few, they reveal several historical transitions of lasting significance for Kashgar. In this period Kashgar was relegated to the status of second city, as the founding ruler, Ṣultān Saʿīd Khān (d. 939/1533), chose Yārkand for his capital; Naqshbandī Sufis of the Khᵛājagān tradition gained a prominent role, claiming disciples among the Khans from the later years of Ṣultān Saʿīd Khān until the end of the dynasty; the Mughals of South Asia wielded strong cultural and economic influence on the Tarim (Thum, *Moghul relations*); and the Persian language came to dominate the intellectual landscape, much as in other parts of Central Asia.

Naqshbandī Sufi leaders (each generally referred to by their honorific title of "*khᵛāja*") played a prominent, perhaps decisive, role in the demise of the Yārkand Khanate. Factional intrigue and civil wars in the eleventh/seventeenth century reached a crescendo around 1090/1679, when one of these *khᵛāja*s, Āfāq (d. 1105/1694), installed a puppet Khan at Kashgar with the aid of Dzungar Mongol armies. Āfāq Khᵛāja's state, sometimes called a theocracy, ushered in eighty years of warfare between Sufi factions, with frequent interventions and overlordship by the Dzungar Mongols. When the China-based Qing Empire conquered the Dzungars in 1757, it claimed control of the Tarim Basin as well, initiating Chinese rule that continues today.

For reasons that are unclear, the chaotic transitions from Khanate to Khᵛāja rule to Dzungar dependency to Qing imperial colony served as a background to Kashgar's second Islamic literary flowering. The end of the Yarkand Khanate (c. 1080/1679) was followed by the rise of the Turki vernacular. After six centuries in which no surviving Tarim Basin text was written in a Turkic language, scholars began to produce vernacular Turki chronicles, poetry collections, hagiographies, and translations in increasing numbers. Older Persian texts continued to be copied, but only a tiny number of elite-oriented texts were newly composed in Persian after the middle of the eighteenth century. At the same time, vernacular texts multiplied, becoming accessible even to the illiterate through public recitations. The most prolific and sophisticated author of this period was Muḥammad Ṣādiq Kashgārī (fl. late twelfth/eighteenth century), who produced history, hagiography, legal commentary, and translations in the late-eighteenth century (Hofman, 20–30). The dominance of the Turki language has continued down to the present day, developing into what is now known as the Uyghur language.

Under China-based rule, Kashgar was frequently a centre of resistance and rebellion. Kashgar also hosted the main Qing garrison in the Tarim Basin, now incorporated into a larger administrative unit called "Xinjiang" ("new territory"), which was governed from Ili. Sufi factionalism persisted under the Qing, with the exiled Āfāqī faction taking advantage of its popular support in Kashgar to launch raids and rebellions from the neighbouring Ferghana Valley (Newby). One such rebellion developed into an independent state, sometimes called the Emirate of Kashgar (1281–94/1865–77), under the leadership of a Khoqandi military officer, Yaʿqūb Beg (d. 1294/1877). When the Qing re-conquered Xinjiang, it instituted an assimilationist policy, designed to sinify the Turkic inhabitants of the region. While these measures largely failed, they signalled the beginning of Chinese interest in not only holding Kashgar and Xinjiang as strategic protectorates, but also in incorporating them into China proper.

In the first half of the twentieth century, intellectuals from Kashgar and its environs played prominent roles in the spread of new ways of thinking, including Jadīdist reform, ethno-nationalism, pan-Turkism, and Islamic fundamentalism. Some of this political and intellectual work was pursued more vigorously by exiles from Xinjiang in the Soviet Union, but Kashgar, along with Ili, provided an important point of reference for the exile community (Brophy, *Uyghur nation*). And Kashgar boasted its own revolutionary initiatives, such as early reformist primary schools and the Tarim Basin's first printing press, created by well-travelled innovators from the city's environs. The city again became a centre of resistance to Chinese rule in the chaos of the 1930s, this time serving as the capital of the short-lived Islamic Republic of Eastern Turkistan (1933–4). This state was also briefly known as the Republic of Uyghuristan, reflecting the growing use of the "Uyghur" ethnonym to describe settled Turks with roots in the Tarim Basin.

The People's Republic of China (PRC) has been more assimilationist than any of Kashgar's previous rulers, and much of Kashgar today looks little different from towns in China's interior. Since 1949, an aggressive settler policy has increased the percentage of Han Chinese in Xinjiang from 5% to 40%. This demographic shift was less dramatic in the city of Kashgar, whose Han population had grown to only 18% as of 1998 (Toops, 245–6, 257). However, during the PRC era, Han settlers began to live not just in the smaller, traditionally Chinese "new city," but also in new developments around the old city. Until the early 2000s, the old city was left largely untouched by Chinese development, and represented one of Central Asia's best preserved pre-modern urban cores, with narrow alleys winding among low, brick and mud-brick courtyard houses. Beginning in 2009 the Chinese state demolished most of the old city and replaced it with replica structures designed to attract tourism and ease authorities' physical access. The Tarim Basin's two most impressive surviving examples of Islamic architecture are located in Kashgar: the Heytgah (ʿĪdgāh) Mosque in the old city and the mausoleum of Āfāq Khʷāja on the city's northern outskirts.

Bibliography

Sources

Anonymous, *Tārīkh-i Kāshgar. Anonimnaia Tiurkskaia khronika vladeteleĭ Vostochnogo Turkestana po konets XVII veka. Faksimile Rukopisi Sankt-Peterburgskogo Filiala Instituta Vostokovedeniia Akademii Nauk Rossii*, ed. O. F. Akimushkin,

St Petersburg 2001; Shāh Maḥmūd Churās, *Khronika*, ed. O. F. Akimushkin, Moscow 1976; Mīrzā Haydar Dūghlāt, *Mirza Haydar Dughlat's Tarikh-i Rashidi. A history of the Khans of Moghulistan*, ed. and trans. W. M. Thackston, Cambridge MA 1996; Anthony François Paulus Hulsewé, *China in Central Asia. The early stage. 125 BC–AD 23. An annotated translation of chapters 61 and 96 of "The history of the former Han dynasty,"* Leiden 1979; Maḥmūd Kāšġarī, *Compendium of the Turkic dialects (Dīwān luġāt at-turk)*, ed. James Kelly and Robert Dankoff, Cambridge MA 1982; Yūsuf Khāṣṣ-Hājib, *Wisdom of royal glory. A Turco-Islamic mirror for princes—Kutadgu Bilig*, trans. Robert Dankoff, Chicago 1983; Muhämmäd Sadiq Qäshqäri, *Täzkirä'i Äzizan*, Kashgar 1988; Mullā Mūsā Sayrāmī, *Tārīkh-i Amaniyya*, Kazan 1905.

Studies

David Brophy, New methods on the new frontier. Islamic reformism in Xinjiang 1898–1917, *JESHO* 59/1–2 (2016), 303–32; David Brophy, *Uyghur nation. Reform and revolution on the Russia-China frontier*, Cambridge MA 2016; H. A. R. Gibb, The Arab invasion of Kashgar in AD 715, *BSOAS* 2/3 (1922), 467–474; Monika Gronke, The Arabic Yārkand documents, *BSOAS* 49/3 (1986), 454–507; H. F. Hofman, *Turkish literature. A biobibliographical Survey. Section III. Moslim Central Asian Turkish literature*, Utrecht 1969; Ildikó Bellér-Hann, *Community matters in Xinjiang 1880–1949. Towards a historical anthropology of the Uyghur*, Leiden 2008; Gunnar Jarring, *Literary texts from Kashghar*, Lund 1980; Homa Katouzian, *Saʿdi. The poet of life, love and compassion.* Oxford 2006; Hodong Kim, *Holy war in China. The Muslim rebellion and state in Chinese Central Asia, 1864–1877*, Stanford 2004; B. D. Kochnev, Svod nadpiseĭ na Karakhanidskikh monetakh. Antroponimy i titylatura. *Vostochnoe istoricheskoe istochnikov edenie i spet͡sial'nye istoricheskie dist͡sipliny*, no. 4 (1995); James Millward, *Eurasian crossroads. A history of Xinjiang*, New York 2009; James Millward, Shinmen Yasushi, and Sugawara Jun (eds.), *Studies on Xinjiang historical sources in 17–20th centuries*, Tokyo 2010; Laura J. Newby, *The empire and the khanate. A political history of Qing relations with Khoqand c.1760–1860*, Leiden 2005; Paul Pelliot, *Notes on Marco Polo*, vol. 1, Paris 1959; T. I. Sultanov, Medieval historiography in manuscripts from East Turkestan, *Manuscripta Orientalia* 2/1 (1996), 25–30; Rian Thum, Moghul relations with the Mughals—economic, political, and cultural, in Onuma Takahiro (ed.), *Xinjiang in the context of Central Eurasian transformations*, Tokyo 2018; Rian Thum, *The sacred routes of Uyghur history*, Cambridge MA 2014; Stanley W. Toops, The demography of Xinjiang, in S. Frederick Starr (ed.), *Xinjiang. China's Muslim borderland* (Armonk NY 2004), 264–75.

Rian Thum

Kayserili Halil Paşa

Kayserili Halil (Qayṣerili Khalīl) **Paşa** (c.977–1038/c. 1570–1629), an Ottoman grand vizier and grand admiral, was born in the village of Zeytun (now Süleymanli), in the province of Kahramanmaraş. He was recruited into the *devşirme* (*devşīrme*, the "collection" of boys from among Balkan and Anatolian Christian subjects) and received his education at the Enderun Mektebi (Enderūn Mektebi, Palace School). In 1014–5/1606, he was appointed *çakırcıbaşı* (chief falconer), a court position for prospective *sancakbeyi*s (*sancaqbeği*, administrator of a sub-district). On 4 Ramazan (Ramaḍān) 1015/ 4 January 1607, he became *ağa* (*āghā*, head) of the Janissaries, and he distinguished himself in the campaigns led by Kuyucu Murad (Murād) Paşa (928–1020/1530–1611) against Kalenderoğlu Mehmed (Meḥmed) Paşa (d. 1019/1610) and Canbolatoğlu Ali (ʿAlī,) Paşa (d. 1020/1611).

On 11 Zilkade (Dhū l-Qaʿda) 1018/16 February 1609, Halil received his first appointment as *kapudan paşa* (*qapūdān paşa*, grand admiral of the Ottoman fleet). After achieving fame by defeating a Maltese naval squadron off Cyprus, he was given the rank of vizier by Sultan Ahmed (Aḥmed) I (r. 1011–26/1603–17), on 27 Şevval (Shawwāl) 1018/25 November

1609. He became grand admiral for the second time on 8 Şevval (Shawwāl) 1022/22 November 1613, after which he refurbished the fleet, accelerated efforts to establish an Ottoman-Dutch-Moroccan alliance against Spain, and battled the Cossacks in the Black Sea. Success in these endeavours led to his appointment as grand vizier on 8 Zilkade (Dhū l-Qaʿda) 1025/17 November 1616.

During his tenure as grand vizier, Halil ended the levying of *haraç* (*kharāj*, the poll-tax for non-Muslims) on members of the Ottoman Empire's four capitulatory nations, which bettered communal relations. After unsuccessful campaigns against Persia around Ardabil (a city located in the northeastern part of Iran's historic Azerbaijan region) on 29 Ramazan 1027/10 September 1618, he was dismissed as grand vizier on 1 Safer (Ṣafar) 1028/18 January 1619 but was appointed grand admiral for a third time on 16 Muharrem (Muḥarram) 1029/23 December 1619. He demonstrated his anti-Spanish policy by advising Osman (ʿOthmān) II (r. 1027–31/1618–22) to invade territory of the kingdom of Spain rather than to attack Venice, which still possessed a formidable navy. In Cemaziyülahır (Jumādā II) 1032/April 1623, the new grand vizier, Mere Hüseyin (Ḥüseyn) (d. 1033/1624), who considered Halil a rival for power, dismissed him from his post and banished him to Malkara (a district in today's Tekirdağ, in European Turkey).

On 13 Rebiülevvel (Rabīʿ I) 1036/2 December 1626, Sultan Murad (Murād) IV (r. 1032–49/1623–40) appointed Halil Paşa as grand vizier and ordered him to subjugate the rebellious Abaza Mehmed (Ābāza Meḥmed) (983–1043/1576–1634). Halil's lack of success on the Persian front as well as his failure to vanquish or negotiate with Abaza Mehmed Paşa resulted in his dismissal from office on 1 Şaban (Shaʿbān) 1037/6 April 1628. He died with the rank of vizier, in Istanbul, on 15 Zilhicce (Dhu l-Ḥijjah) 1038/7 August 1629. During his lifetime, Halil had been linked to various mystical orders, especially the Celvetiye (Celvetiyye), led by Aziz Mahmud Hüdai (ʿAzīz Maḥmūd Hüdāʾī, d. 1038/1628), a famous and influential mystic and religious poet of the period. After his death, Halil was buried in a tomb near the *tekke* (Ṣūfī lodge) and mausoleum of Hüdai in Üsküdar.

Bibliography

Halil Paşa, *Ghazaname-i Khalil Pasha*, Istanbul, Topkapı Sarayı Müzesi Kütüphanesi, Revan Köşkü, no. 1482; Halil Paşa, *Ghazaname-i Khalil Pasha*, Istanbul, Süleymaniye Kütüphanesi, Esad Efendi, no. 2139; A. H. de Groot, A seventeenth century Ottoman statesman. 'Kayseriyeli' Khalil Pasha (1565–1629) and his policy towards European powers, *Der Islam* 54 (1977), 305–8; A. H. de Groot, *The Ottoman Empire and the Dutch Republic* (Leiden and Istanbul 1978), 48–82; Victor Ostapchuk, An Ottoman Ġazānāme on Ḫalīl Paša's naval campaign against the Cossacks (1621), *Harvard Ukrainian Studies* 14 (1990), 482–519; Güneş Alçı, *Üsküdar'da Kayserili Halil Paşa türbesi ve bağlı birimler*, Vakıf Restorasyon Yıllığı 4 (2012), 73–88; Mikail Acıpınar, Osmanlı kronikleri ışığında Kaptan-ı Derya Halil Paşa'nın Akdeniz seferleri (1609–1623), *Tarih İncelemeleri Dergisi* 28 (2013) 5–35; A. H. de Groot, Halil Paşa, Kayserili, *TDVIA* 15: 324–6; A. H. de Groot, Khalīl Pasha Ḳayṣariyyeli, *EI*2.

Tuncay Zorlu

Kāzarūnī

Abū Isḥāq Ibrāhīm b. Shahriyār, called **Kāzarūnī**, the most important successor to Ibn Khafīf (d. 371/982) in Fars, was a militant Ṣūfī and founder of a brotherhood called Kāzarūniyya (also Murshidiyya and

Isḥāqiyya) dedicated to serving the poor. He was born in 352/963, grew up in Kāzarūn, a city west of Shiraz, and died on 8 Dhū l-Qaʿda 426/14 September 1035 (ʿAṭṭār, 766; Meier, 23).

1. Early life

While Farīd al-Dīn ʿAṭṭār (d. c. 618/1221), the Persian poet, theoretician of Ṣūfism, and hagiographer from Nīshāpūr, mentions (763) Kāzarūnī's grandfather, Zādānfarrukh b. Khᵛarshīd, a Zoroastrian, Jāmī (d. 897/1492), the scholar and writer of Ṣūfī literature from Herat, says (254) only that his father had already been born in the era of Islam. The grandfather tried unsuccessfully to prevent the child from attending a Qurʾān school *(maktab)* and encouraged him instead to learn a craft, because the family was poor. At the *maktab*, Kāzarūnī soon proved to be a prodigy far surpassing his classmates. At the age of twelve he was honoured by Abū Bakr Muslim-i Shīrāzī, a disciple of Ibn Khafīf who had settled in Kāzarūn and predicted Kāzarūnī's greatness (Meier, 18; Sobieroj, 653–4).

2. Attachment to Ibn Khafīf

At the age of fifteen (Meier, 18), he wondered which Ṣūfī path *(ṭarīqa)* to follow, and, from amongst three masters (Ibn Khafīf, Muḥāsibī, and Abū ʿAmr b. ʿAlī) he chose—through a supplicatory prayer called *istikhāra*—Ibn Khafīf (ʿAṭṭār, 764). While al-Ḥārith al-Muḥāsibī (d. 243/857) had taught that working to earn one's living is the right interpretation of "trusting God" *(tawakkul)*, Abū ʿAmr (d. 358/969) advocated a general withdrawal from society. Ibn Khafīf, on the other hand, was viewed as the model of a helper of one's contemporaries and, in particular, of the poor (Meier, 61). Kāzarūnī having not yet reached the age of twenty, Akkār al-Fīrūzābādī (d. 391/1001) brought him the books of Ibn Khafīf, and these strengthened his conviction that it was God's will that he adopt Ibn Khafīf's method of serving Him. Akkār invested Kāzarūnī with Ibn Khafīf's *khirqa*, the patched robe of the Ṣūfīs (Zarkūb, 98), and he trained him in Ṣūfī ethics (*taʾaddaba bi-ṣuḥbatihī*, "and he was trained (spiritually) through companionship with him"). According to Junayd-i Shīrāzī (fl. eighth/fourteenth), in his *Shadd* (49–50), composed in 791/1389, Akkār had met Kāzarūnī when the latter was still a child. He was so impressed by his skill in Qurʾān recitation that, enraptured (*tawājada*; Jāmī, 254), he took him to Shiraz, where he met other disciples of Ibn Khafīf as well. Zarkūb-i Shīrāzī (d. 789/1387; 98) makes the chronologically feasible claim that, at that time, he also met Ibn Khafīf (Meier, 13–4).

Besides the *khirqa*, Kāzarūnī received from Ibn Khafīf, through the mediation of Abū ʿAbdallāh Aḥmad b. Ibrāhīm (b.) Bānīk/Mānak of Arrajān (d. c.400/1009–10; Jāmī, *Nafaḥāt*, 266), a disciple of Bundār b. al-Ḥusayn al-Arrajānī (d. 353/964 or 357), the "white shirt of Junayd" (Maḥmūd, *Anwār*, 512–3). Like Junayd (d. 297/910), head of the Ṣūfī school of Baghdad, Kāzarūnī came to be known as a "possessor of sobriety" *(ṣāḥib-i ṣaḥw)*, because, in his mystical method, he shunned "drunkenness and innovation" (Meier, 63).

3. Relations with Zoroastrians

As an adult, Kāzarūnī preached in the great mosque of Kāzarūn-Nūrd but was antagonised by the storytellers *(quṣṣāṣ)*, who viewed him as an unwelcome competitor. When he tried to build his own first mosque, he was opposed by the Zoroastrians, who destroyed the new building repeatedly. At that time, the Kāzarūn region was only thinly islamicised (Lawrence), and the Zoroastrians had influential supporters amongst the higher officials, including the governor, the "Magian of Daylam" (Meier, 21). There were two fire temples in Kāzarūn, and many Zoroastrians preferred paying the poll tax *(jizya)* to converting to Islam (Meier, 40). When, in the first decade of the fifth century/second decade of the twelfth century, the Zoroastrians attempted unsuccessfully to assassinate Kāzarūnī and his disciples sought revenge, the Zoroastrians turned for help to the Būyid *wazīr* Fakhr al-Mulk (d. 407/1016–7; Meier, 21). Once his followers had become sufficiently numerous, Kāzarūnī summoned them to march against the "disbelievers," that is, the Zoroastrians, and he "organised the annual dispatch of *ghāzī*s (Muslim champions in the fight against non-Muslims) to fight the Christians on the Byzantine border" (Algar, Kāzarūnī, Shaykh Abū Isḥāq Ibrāhīm b. Shahriyār). For these activities, Kāzarūnī became known as "Shaykh Ghāzī" (Zarkūb, 106).

4. The *ḥajj* and *ḥadīth* studies

In 388/998 Kāzarūnī made the *ḥajj* (pilgrimage) to Mecca in the company of Akkār (Meier, 22). During this journey, he heard Prophetic traditions in Basra, Mecca, and Medina. The numerous traditions he studied in these places, including Kāzarūn and Shiraz, are quoted in Maḥmūd's *Firdaws* (38–62). When he was learning *ḥadīth* in Shiraz, he was the youngest of all the students but still received, like everyone else, an *ijāza* (licence to transmit the traditions that he had learned) in recognition of his zeal.

After returning from the *ḥajj*, Kāzarūnī wished to settle in Mecca but feared that his virtuousness would be vitiated by the immorality he observed amongst the *mujāwirūn*, the people residing in the holy precinct (Meier, 22). Akkār advised him against staying in the holy city. Amongst the mystics he met in the *ḥaram* area of Mecca, Jāmī (254) mentions the author Ibn Jahḍam al-Hamadhānī (d. 414/1023), from whom Kāzarūnī transmitted a spiritual instruction *(waṣiyya)*, traced to the Nubian Ṣūfī Dhū l-Nūn (d. 245/860, or 248/863; cf. Sulamī, *Ṭabaqāt*, ed. Nūr al-Dīn Shurayba, Aleppo 1986/1406, no. 2), which dealt with the cultivation of contentment.

5. Return to Kāzarūn and his career there

After returning to Kāzarūn, the Ṣūfī devoted himself, for the rest of his life, to spreading Islam and propagating Ṣūfism (Meier, 39). In 426/1034–5, Kāzarūnī fell fatally ill and, on his deathbed, appointed as his successor his companion Khaṭīb Imām Abū l-Qāsim ʿAbd al-Karīm b. ʿAlī b. Saʿd (d. 442/1050; Meier, 23). He stipulated who should wash his corpse, who should say the funeral prayers, and who should dig his grave (Meier, 23). He also ordered that the list of the individuals who repented and became Muslims through his influence be placed in his grave on his breast, next to the arrow shot at him by a would-be assassin; the document *(ṣaḥīfa)* included the names of Jews, Christians, and Zoroastrians (Maḥmūd, 415), who numbered, according to Zarkūb (106), twenty-four thousand converts.

Within his own Muslim community, Kāzarūnī endeavoured to awaken the people's hearts by preaching. After Friday prayers, he would gather his followers, telling them Ṣūfī stories and interpreting the Qurʾān. Maḥmūd's *Firdaws* (215–94) contains a long chapter containing samples of Kāzarūnī's Qurʾānic exegesis on selected verses.

Kāzarūnī also dedicated himself to altruism. Notwithstanding his role in fighting disbelievers, his humanity extended to non-Muslims as well as Muslims. A Jewish traveller who came to Kāzarūnī's hospice incognito expressed his surprise that the *shaykh*, having recognised his identity, fed him as if the Jew were a fellow Muslim. Kāzarūnī explained to him that "there is no one who is not worthy of two loaves of bread" (Maḥmūd, 172). His *futuwwa* (chivalry), along with his readiness to forgive or even love his opponents (Maḥmūd, 123–4), encompassed the animal world as well (Meier, 45).

Kāzarūnī's convent *(buqʿa)* was a lodge *(ribāṭ)* where travellers could stay the night and be fed (Meier, 47). The building in Kāzarūn remained intact until its destruction during the Ṣafavid period, at the beginning of the tenth/sixteenth century (Lawrence). His disciples reproduced this institution in various locations; as many as sixty-five hospices are mentioned by Maḥmūd (cf. Meier, 48). That Kāzarūnī's care for the poor *(faqīr)* included not only Ṣūfīs, who were poor by profession, but also those who were poor due to adverse circumstances explains why his order spread to the periphery of the Islamic world (Meier, 64). Kāzarūnī ordered his followers to serve the poor, but he warned them of the dangers of socialising with certain groups of people, such as unmarried women, boys, and rulers (Meier, 53). Whereas he himself was not married and had no children—meaning that the succession within the order could not be hereditary—Kāzarūnī did not forbid his followers to marry.

6. Kāzarūnī's spirituality and posthumous veneration

Trying to characterise Kāzarūnī's spirituality, ʿAṭṭār highlights, amongst other things, the captivating effect of the *shaykh*'s preaching *(sukhan-i jān-gīr)*, his "burning" *(sūzī)*, his scrupulousness in observing the norms of the divine law *(waraʿ)*, and his clairvoyance *(firāsa)*. As to *waraʿ*, Kāzarūnī is reported to have renounced drinking the water of the river that belonged to the Zoroastrian ruler of Kāzarūn, and he ordered the grain from which his food was prepared to be imported from Jerusalem (ʿAṭṭār, 765). Kāzarūnī's clairvoyance manifested itself in his ability to read the minds of his critics, for example, of a scholar who was convinced of his own superiority while listening to the *shaykh*'s sermon. In response to this thought, Kāzarūnī mentioned the simile of the oil and the water in a lamp, each of which considered itself superior. Comparing himself with the oil, Kāzarūnī explained that, just like the oil, he burned himself in order to enlighten the people (ʿAṭṭār, 766).

While Kāzarūnī believed that God answered his prayers because of the elevated status in which he was held by Him, his contemporaries and succeeding generations of Muslims in Fars and beyond considered the Ṣūfī a great *walī* (saint). His tomb was known as Tiryāk-i Akbar (greatest panacea), as it was observed that people's supplications made there were fulfilled (ʿAṭṭār, 763). Crowds flocked to Kāzarūnī's tomb, asking the saint to intercede with God on their behalf. Kāzarūnī became a revered helper in general and of sailors in distress at sea in particular; the soil from his grave had the reputation of "being able to calm stormy waters when cast into the sea" (Algar, Kāzarūnī, *EI2*).

The posthumous veneration centred on Kāzarūnī's personality was universal and extended to the coast of southeastern China, where sailors from Persia affiliated with his order built convents, as attested by the famous Moroccan travel-writer Ibn Baṭṭūṭa (d. 770/1368–9; 4:271), in the context of a visit made to Zaytūn (Quanzhou, in Fujian province). He mentions a leader of a convent who collected votive offerings *(nudhūr)* that the traders had dedicated to Kāzarūnī as a token of gratitude for the protection they believed they had received from him during their sea journey. Nowadays, however, on the coasts of the South China Sea, thanksgiving for safe arrival in the harbour is usually offered to the goddess Mazu, originally a fisherman's daughter from Fujian who was elevated to divine status for rescuing the shipwrecked.

Kāzarūnī's biography was written in Arabic by the saint's third successor, Khaṭīb Imām Abū Bakr Muḥammad b. ʿAbd al-Karīm (d. 502/1108) (Arberry, 163). Khaṭīb Imām used, amongst other sources, the *Mashyakha* ("The *shaykh*s") by Abū Shujāʿ al-Maqārīḍī (d. 509/1115–6), and both authors knew Kāzarūnī personally (Meier, 2). The Persian translation of the now-lost Arabic text is an encyclopaedic work written in 728/1327 by Maḥmūd b. ʿUthmān, a dervish of Kāzarūn, who also made an abridgement of the *Firdaws* titled *Anwār al-murshidiyya* ("Lights on the Murshadiyya"); he was not a member of Kāzarūnī's order but a disciple of Amīn al-Dīn-i Balyānī (d. 694/1294–5), whose *vita* he also composed. Balyānī traced his lineage back to Abū l-Najīb al-Suhravardī (d. 563/1168), the *shaykh*, scholar, and author from western Iran regarded as the founder of the Suhravardiyya, but also claimed a spiritual connection *(qurbatī bā rūḥ)* with Kāzarūnī (Maḥmūd, *Miftāḥ*, 209). Another eighth/fourteenth-century "inflated" Persian translation of Khaṭīb's Arabic original—that is, one in which additional material (besides the reference text) is incorporated—is *Marṣad al-aḥrār* ("The observation post of the free men") by Rajāʾ Muḥammad b. ʿAbd al-Raḥmān al-Kāzarūnī, surnamed ʿAlāʾ [al-Dīn], who may have been active about 750/1349 (Arberry, 164, 177; Storey, 2:1343).

Bibliography

Sources

Farīd al-Dīn ʿAṭṭār, *Tadhkirat al-awliyāʾ*, ed. Muḥammad Istiʿlāmī (repr. Tehran 1372sh/1993), 763–76; Maḥmūd b. ʿUthmān, *Anwār al-murshidiyya fī asrār al-ṣamadiyya*, in Maḥmūd b. ʿUthmān, *Firdaws*, ed. Īraj Afshar (Tehran 1358sh/1979), 469–753; Maḥmūd b. ʿUthmān, *Firdaws al-murshidiyya fī asrār al-ṣamadiyya*, ed. Fritz Meier, in Fritz Meier (ed.), *Die Vita des Scheich Abū Isḥāq al-Kāzarūnī* (Leipzig 1948), 1–511, ed. Īraj Afshār, new, enlarged edition, Tehran 1358sh/1979; Maḥmūd b. ʿUthmān, *Miftāḥ al-hidāya wa-miṣbāḥ al-ʿināya. Sīrat-nāmayi Sayyid Amīn al-Dīn-i Balyānī*, ed. Manūchihr Muẓaffariyān, Tehran 1380sh/2001; Ibn Baṭṭūṭa, *Riḥla*, ed. Charles F. Defrémery and Beniamino R. Sanguinetti (Paris 1858), 4:271; Junayd-i Shīrāzī, *Shadd al-izār*, ed. Muḥammad Qazvīnī and ʿAbbās Iqbāl, Tehran 1328sh/1949–50; Abū l-ʿAbbās Zarkūb-i Shīrāzī, *Shīrāz-nāma*, ed. Bahman-i Karīmī (Tehran 1310sh/1931), 105–6; Jāmī, *Nafaḥāt*, ed. Mahdī Tawḥīdīpur (Tehran 1336sh/1957), 254–5.

Studies

Arthur J. Arberry, The biography of Shaikh Abū Isḥāq al-Kāzarūnī, *Oriens* 3 (1950), 163–72; Hamid Algar, Kāzarūnī, *TDVIA* 25:145–6; Hamid Algar, Kāzarūnī, *EI2*; Bruce Lawrence, Abū Esḥāq Kāzarūnī, *EIr*; Florian Sobieroj, Mittelsleute zwischen Ibn Ḥafīf und Abū Isḥāq al-Kāzarūnī, *AS* 51/2 (1997), 651–71; Charles A. Storey, *Persian literature. A bio-bibliographical survey*, London 1927–97.

Florian Sobieroj

al-Khāl, Yūsuf

Yūsuf al-Khāl (1917–87) was a Lebanese poet and writer born in Syria. He graduated in 1934 from the American School in Tripoli, where he won first prize for a text titled *Āmālī fī l-mustaqbal* ("My wishes for the future"). In that same year, he left his family home and school in order to commence a journalistic career (mainly at the magazine *al-Makshūf*). Secretly joining the Syrian Social Nationalist Party (SSNP), al-Khāl began writing for its mouthpiece, *al-Nahḍa*, along with Fuʾād Sulaymān (1912–51). Within this same activist context he wrote his first and only novel, *Salmāya*, whose dedication reveals the admiration that he felt for the SSNP leader, Anṭūn Saʿāda (1904–49).

During World War II he returned to his studies, first at the Aleppo American University, then at the Philosophy Department of the American University of Beirut (AUB), where he graduated in 1944 and later taught Arabic literature. His studies of philosophy during this period laid the foundations for his conception of freedom and the inherent individual rights.

From 1948 to 1955 he worked as an expert for the UN in New York. While there, he was in close contact with modernist literary circles and was particularly influenced by the works of T. S. Eliot and Ezra Pound, and especially by the activities associated with the American magazine *Poetry* (1912–).

In 1955 he returned to Lebanon, much affected by issues connected with modernism and eager to rid Arabic literature of constraints preventing it from reflecting its own time. Desiring to herald a second Arab poetic renaissance, in 1957 al-Khāl gathered a number of poets, critics, and translators to found *Shiʿr*, which turned out to be the most professional avant-garde Arabic journal dedicated to poetry, as a forum for both emerging and established Arab poets (including Adūnīs) and a laboratory that made modernist thought accessible to Arab readers through translations of contemporary foreign poetry. Furthermore, the journal acted as an observatory that aimed to reassess the Arab cultural heritage from the inside in order to link the Arab cultural future to its pre-modern interactions with other cultures. Using *Shiʿr*, al-Khāl sought to support new literary trends by providing a publication outlet for experimentation (including such genres as free verse and prose poetry, especially the works of Unsī l-Ḥājj, 1937–2014). His goal was to free Arabic literature from adherence to its traditional principles and conventional genres, to detach Arabic poetry from outdated prosody, and to bring poetic diction closer to spoken language in lexicon, structure, and tone.

Although al-Khāl authored novels, plays, poems, and essays—alongside producing translations of the Bible and significant foreign works—he is remembered above all as the leader of the modernist *Shiʿr* movement that was to become a central cultural institution in the literary life of Beirut in the 1960s. Al-Khāl gathered a supportive network around *Shiʿr* formed of five prestigious cultural organisations: the newspaper *al-Nahār*, the literary club Khamīs Majallat *Shiʿr* (Thursday's *Shiʿr*), the publishing house Dār Majallat *Shiʿr* (established in 1958), the magazine *Adab* ("Literature") launched in 1962 in order to extend the spirit of *Shiʿr* to other fields, and *Gallery One*, founded in 1963 to bring the ideas of the *Shiʿr* movement to the fine arts.

From his earliest publications to his death, al-Khāl considered the cause of freedom to be a prerequisite to self-fulfilment and thus to the establishment of a modern society.

Bibliography

Works by Yūsuf al-Khāl
al-Aʿmāl al-shiʿriyya al-kāmila 1938–1968, Beirut 1973; *Dafātir al-ayyām. Afkār ʿalā waraq*, London 1987; *al-Ḥadātha fī l-shiʿr*, Beirut 1978; *Qaṣāʾid fī l-arbaʿīn*, Beirut 1960; *Rasāʾil ilā Dūn Kīshūt*, Beirut 1979; *al-Wilāda al-thāniya*, Beirut 1987; *Yawmiyyāt kalb*, Beirut 1987.

Translated poems
Mounah A. Khouri and Hamid Algar (trans.), *An anthology of modern Arabic poetry* (Berkeley 1974), 53–7; Issa J. Boullata (trans.), *Modern Arab poets* (Washington DC 1976), 41–8; Salma Khadra Jayyusi (ed.), *Modern Arabic poetry. An anthology* (New York 1987), 295–300; Abdullah al-Udhari (trans.), *Modern poetry of the Arab world* (London 1986), 51–8.

Studies
Jacques Amateis, *Yūsuf al-Khāl wa-majallatuhū Shiʿr*, Beirut 2004; Dounia Badini, *La revue Shiʿr/Poésie et la modernité poétique arabe, Beyrouth (1957–1970)*, Paris 2009; Dounia Badini, La vie littéraire autour de la revue *Shiʿr* (1957–1970), *MEL* 13 (2010), 69–89; S. K. Jayyusi, *Trends and movements in modern Arabic poetry*, 2 vols., Leiden 1977.

Dounia Badini

Kharāj in South Asia

Kharāj was vital to the relationship between the Muslim state and its subjects, the status of territories ruled over by the state, and the social and economic history of **South Asia**, during and after Muslim rule.

During Muslim rule, *kharāj* referred to a tax charged on agricultural commodities. Unlike the land tax that was later imposed by the British, it was paid not in cash but in kind, in agricultural goods. The classical Arabic term *kharāj* was used in the Indian subcontinent alongside other local and regional terms such as the Arabic terms *ḥāṣil* or *maḥṣūl* (referring to the amount collected), the Indian word *bhāolī*, and the Persian *ghalla bakhshī* (referring to crop sharing). Like in the formative period of Islamic law in Arabia, both terms of *kharāj* and *jizya* (poll tax) have been used interchangeably in South Asia for centuries. In contrast to *jizya*, the legitimacy of *kharāj* was not hotly contested, as peasants were accustomed to paying part of their produce to rulers and/or dominant regional sovereigns in exchange for protection and as a sign of their submission.

The history of the practice of *kharāj* may be divided into three main phases. While historians disagree on the modalities of assessment and collection of *kharāj*, they all trace it back to Sulṭān ʿAlāʾ al-Dīn Muḥammad Khaljī (r. 695–715/1296–1316), who is considered the first Muslim ruler to have enforced the payment of *kharāj* in South Asia. The second phase begins with the Mughal emperor Akbar (r. 963–1014/1556–1605), who transformed *kharāj* substantially, as part of broader reforms in the agrarian system. According to Akbar's close counsellor and historiographer Abū l-Faḍl ʿAllāmī (d. 1011/1602), efforts were undertaken to standardise the modalities of *kharāj* and to standardise measurement across the Mughal Empire. Akbar's financial and agrarian politics and their long-term impact have been a controversial subject in South Asian scholarship. The third phase of *kharāj* dates to the twelfth/eighteenth century, when its regional character became more evident, due, in part, to the weakening and disintegration of the

Mughal Empire. The increasing wealth of regional rulers, *zamīndārs* (wealthy land owners), and the collectors, as well as the uncertainty of *kharāj* payment modalities contributed in many cases to the destabilisation of central power. The contribution of *kharāj* to the decline of the Mughal empire is, nevertheless, still a subject of energetic debate.

Legal and historical sources from the Delhi sultanate onward such as the *Fiqh-i Fīrūzshāhī* (The jurisprudence of Fīrūz Shāh (r. 752–790/1351–1388)) speak of two forms of *kharāj* that were practised in South Asia: *kharāj-i waẓīfa* consisted of a fixed annual tax, and *muqāsama*, more common in South Asia, was proportional to agricultural output. It is thought that it was not to exceed half of the total output, even if overall production was low. This regulation could be modified, depending on the quality of land, weather conditions, the power balance of tax collectors and the central power. The payment of these taxes was also depending on the status of the land owners, whether they were *dhimmīs* (protected non-Muslims), *kitābīs* (people of the Book), or similar to *kitābīs*.

Indo-Muslim legal literature from the sultanate period onwards depicts the ruler as the ultimate sovereign over territories and sees the payment of *kharāj*, which was sometimes used interchangeably with the term *jizya*, as the exclusive duty of the landowners. The *ʿulamāʾ* (religious scholars) defended this tradition against increasing state efforts to appropriate territories. Official documents from the period offer further insight into the heated political debate and power struggles surrounding the issue of land and *kharāj*. The famous compendium *al-Fatāwā al-ʿĀlamgīriyya*—a compilation of the authoritative doctrines of the Ḥanafī school of law commissioned by the Mughal emperor Awrangzīb Alamgīr (r. 1068–1118/1658–1707) and carried out by a team of religious scholars led by Shaykh Niẓām Burhānpūrī (d. 1092/1680)—recommends that deserted territories should be kept under the supervision of the state and their yield given back to their owners if and when they return. The *Fatāwā* prescribes that the state should, in the event of natural catastrophe, either decrease the amount of *kharāj* or waive peasants' tax duties altogether.

The debate on *kharāj* in South Asia is similar to that on taxes in other regions in the Islamic world in the same period. For instance, the position of legal scholars regarding the treatment of the land and tax and their call for an equal and equitable treatment of the landowners regardless of their religion and political affiliation are similar to debates on land tax in cases such as those in Egypt under the Ottoman rule, as described by legal scholars such as the Egyptian Ibn Nujaym al-Miṣrī (d. 943/1536).

Bibliography

Sources

Abū l-Faḍl ʿAllāmī, *Āʾīn-i Akbarī*, ed. Henry Blochman, 3 vols., Calcutta 1876, Calcutta 1927–49² (vol. 1 trans. Henry Blochman and rev. Douglas C. Phillot, vols. 2–3 trans. Henry S. Jarrett, rev. Jadunath Sarkar), repr. New Delhi 1977–8; Ziyāʾ al-Dīn Baranī, *Tārīkh-i Fīrūz Shāhī*, ed. Sayyid Ahmad Khan, *The Táríkh-i Feroz-sháhí*, Calcutta 1862, trans. I. A. Zilli, Delhi 2015; Shaykh Niẓām Burhānpūrī (supervising compiler), *al-Fatāwā al-Hindiyya al-ʿĀlamgīriyya*, vol. 2, Beirut 1999.

Studies

Muzaffar Alam and Sanjay Subrahmanyam, L'état moghol et sa fiscalité. XVIᵉ–XVIIIᵉ siècles, *Annales. Histoire, Sciences Sociales* 49/1 (1994), 189–217; Blain Auer, Regulating diversity within the empire: the legal concept of zimmi and the collection of jizya under the sultans of Delhi (1200–1400), in Thomas Ertl and Gijs Kruijtzer (eds.), *Law addressing diversity: pre-modern Europe and India in comparison (13th–18th centuries)* (Oldenbourg 2017), 31–55; N.B.E. Baillie, Of the kharáj or Muhammadan land tax. Its application to British India, and effect on the tenure of land, *JRAS* 7/1 (1875), 172–89; Thomas Ertl and Gjis Kruijtzer (eds.), *Law addressing diversity. Premodern Europe and India in comparison (13th–18th c.)*, Berlin 2017; Irfan Habib, *The agrarian system of Mughal India*, New Delhi 1999; Muzaffar Alam, Eastern India in the early eighteenth century "crisis." Some evidence from Bihar, *Indian Economic and Social History Review* 28/1 (1991), 43–71; Baber Johansen, *The Islamic law on land tax and rent. The peasants' loss of property rights as interpreted in the Hanafite literature of the Mamluk and Ottoman period*, London 1988; Mouez Khalfaoui, *L'Islam indien, pluralité ou pluralisme. Le cas d'al-Fatāwa al-Hindiyya*, Frankfurt am Main 2008; William H. Moreland, *Agrarian system of Moslem India. A historical essay with appendices*, Cambridge 1929; Tapan Raychaudhuri and Irfan Habib (ed.), *The Cambridge economic history of India*, vol. 1, c.1200–c.1750, Cambridge 1982.

Mouez Khalfaoui

Khāzindār

The term ***khāzindār*** (also spelt *khizandār* or *khaznadār*), a compound word of the Arabic *khizāna* (treasury) and Persian *dār* (keeper), denoted a military office of the Mamlūk sultanate of Egypt and Syria (648–923/1250–1517). Military men who served in this capacity for the sultan, *amīr*s, or other notables held the office. Ibn Taghrībirdī (d. 874/1470) lists it amongst the offices introduced by Sulṭān Baybars I (r. 658–76/1260–77), although the name of the office appears occasionally also in Ayyūbid sources.

The sultan in Egypt had several *khāzindār*s, who were supervised by the *khāzindār al-kabīr* (grand *khāzindār*), followed by the *khāzindār al-thānī* (second *khāzindār*), the *khāzindār al-thālith* (third *khāzindār*), and so on, in a hierarchical structure. Before the third reign of Sulṭān al-Nāṣir Muḥammad b. Qalāwūn (709–41/1310–41), the office of the *khāzindār al-kabīr* was usually filled by an *amīr al-ṭablkhāna* (*amīr* of the drums or *amīr* of forty), which was the second rank. According to Ibn Nāẓir al-Jaysh (d. 786/1384), the office was sometimes filled instead by an *amīr ʿashara* (*amīr* of ten), which was the third rank. Al-Nāṣir then upgraded the office to make it one of the twelve military offices held by *amīr*s of one hundred (*amīr miʾa*, or commanders of one thousand, *muqaddam alf*), which was the first rank. This upgrade might have been related to the sultan's establishment of the *dīwān al-khāṣṣ* (bureau of the privy funds), given that Ibn Khaldūn (d. 808/1406) and al-Qalqashandī (d. 821/1418) noted the cooperation of the *khāzindār al-kabīr* and the *nāẓir al-khāṣṣ* (civilian chief of the *dīwān*) in the management of the sultan's treasuries of money, fabrics, and so on. After al-Nāṣir's death in 741/1341, however, the office was again held by an *amīr al-ṭablkhāna*.

Under the Circassian Mamlūks (r. 784–923/1382–1517), powerful eunuch *khāzindār*s, such as Zayn al-Dīn Marjān al-Hindī (d. 833/1430) under Sulṭān al-Muʾayyad Shaykh (r. 815–24/1412–21) and Jawhar al-Qunuqbāʾī (d. 844/1440–1) under Sulṭān al-Ashraf Barsbāy (r. 825–41/1422–38), appeared on the political stage. The rise of eunuch *khāzindār*s was probably related to the growth of the sultan's sources of income independent of the government's financial bureaus. These eunuchs concurrently held the offices of *zimām* (chief eunuch) and *khāzindār al-kabīr* and became influential in the Mamlūk government. However, the original military post of *khāzindār al-kabīr* continued to exist and was sometimes referred to as *amīr khāzindār*. Two people were thus simultaneously assigned to each office.

The chancery manuals by al-Saḥmāwī (d. 868/1464) and Ibn Kannān (d. 1153/1740), which contain information on ninth/fifteenth-century Mamlūk administration, state that the office of *khāzindār* comprised three roles: 1) the *khāzindār al-ṣinf* or *khāzindār al-kabīr* was responsible for the sultan's treasury of cloth; 2) the *khāzindār al-ʿayn* was responsible for the sultan's money and jewels, settling his accounts, and purchasing items for him, in cooperation with the civilian *nāẓir al-khizāna* (controller of the treasury); and 3) the *khāzindār al-kīs* was responsible for the fund designated to distribute alms to the poor during the sultan's processions. A eunuch usually held the office of *khāzindār al-ʿayn*, because the sultan's money and jewels were held in the harem; that eunuch therefore also held the office of the *khāzindār al-ṣinf*.

Four eunuch *khāzindārs* were appointed by the viceroy in Damascus; the foremost held the rank of *amīr al-ṭablkhāna*. These eunuchs were responsible for the sultan's robes of honour held in the citadel of Damascus.

There were occasionally offices with titles similar to *khāzindār* in other dynasties, such as *khazīnedār* in Ottoman Egypt and *khazānadār* and *khazīnadār* in India under the Delhi Sultanates.

Bibliography

Sources

al-Asadī, *al-Taysīr wa-l-iʿtibār wa-l-taḥrīr wa-l-ikhtibār fī-mā yajib min ḥusn al-tadbīr wa-l-taṣarruf wa-l-ikhtiyār*, ed. ʿAbd al-Qādir Aḥmad Ṭulaymāt (Cairo 1968), 70; Ibn Kannān, *Ḥadāʾiq al-yāsmīn fī dhikr qawānīn al-khulafāʾ wa-l-salāṭīn*, ed. ʿAbbās Ṣabbāgh (Beirut 1991), 125–6; Ibn Khaldūn, *The Muqaddimah. An introduction to history*, trans. Franz Rosenthal (Princeton 1958, 1967²), 2:25; Ibn Nāẓir al-Jaysh, *Kitāb tathqīf al-taʿrīf bi-l-muṣṭalaḥāt al-sharīf*, ed. Rudolf Veselý (Cairo 1987), 190; Ibn Taghrībirdī, *al-Nujūm al-ẓāhira fī mulūk Miṣr wa-l-Qāhira*, ed. Fahīm Muḥammad Shaltūt et al. (Cairo 1963–72), 7:182–6; Khalīl b. Shāhīn al-Ẓāhirī, *Kitāb zubdat kashf al-mamālik*, ed. Paul Ravaisse (Paris 1894, repr. Cairo 1988), 114; al-Qalqashandī, *Ṣubḥ al-aʿshā fī ṣināʿat al-inshāʾ* (Cairo 1913–22, repr. 1985), 3:481; 4:20, 21, 186, 191; 5:92, 457, 462–3; al-Saḥmāwī, *al-Thaghr al-bāsim fī ṣināʿat al-kātib wa-l-kātim*, ed. Ashraf Muḥammad Anas (Cairo 2009), 1:396; Tāj al-Dīn ʿAbd al-Wahhāb b. ʿAlī al-Subkī, *Muʿīd al-niʿam wa-mubīd al-niqam*, ed. Muḥammad ʿAlī al-Najjār et al. (Cairo 1948, 1996³), 26.

Studies

David Ayalon, Studies on the structure of the Mamluk army, pt. 3, *BSOAS* 16 (1954), 57–90, here 62; R. Stephen Humphreys, *From Saladin to the Mongols. The Ayyubids of Damascus, 1193–1260* (Albany 1977), 290, 461; Daisuke Igarashi, The evolution of the sultanic fisc and *al-Dhakhīrah* during the Circassian Mamluk period, *MSR* 14 (2010), 85–108, here 94–5; Daisuke Igarashi, *Land tenure, fiscal policy, and imperial power in medieval Syro-Egypt* (Chicago 2015), 127–9; Donald P. Little, Khaznadār, Khāzindār, *EI2*; William Popper, *Egypt and Syria under the Circassian sultans, 1382–1468 A.D. Systematic notes to Ibn Taghrî Birdî's chronicles of Egypt* (Berkeley 1955), 1:92–3, 106; Ishtiaq Husain Qureshi, *The administration of the sultanate of Delhi* (Lahore 1942), 63, 196; Stanford J. Shaw, *The financial and administrative organization and development of Ottoman Egypt, 1517–1798* (Princeton 1962), 195, 290, 349.

Daisuke Igarashi

Kirmānī, Awḥād al-Dīn

Awḥād al-Dīn Kirmānī (d. 635/1238) was one of the most controversial Persian

Ṣūfīs of the sixth/twelfth and seventh/thirteenth centuries. The controversy centred on the practice of *samāʿ* and his penchant for gazing at beautiful young boys *(shāhid bāzī)*, which, sympathisers argue, was a way of meditating upon the divine. The uproar surrounding Kirmānī is all the more surprising as he was appointed by the ʿAbbāsid caliph al-Mustanṣir (r. 623–40/1226–42) as *shaykh al-shuyūkh* (*shaykh* of *shaykhs*), which gave him precedence amongst Baghdad's Ṣūfīs). This appointment allowed him to oversee the Marzubāniyya complex, which was one of the most prestigious *khānaqāh*s (Ṣūfī convents) in Baghdad; it had previously been overseen by the major Persian-born religious scholar, Ṣūfī theorist, and preacher Abū Ḥafṣ ʿUmar Suhrawardī (d. 631/1234), who spent much of his life in that city. Kirmānī served as *shaykh al-shuyūkh* for the four years preceding his death.

Little is known about Kirmānī's youth, although there are several anecdotes in the hagiography that describes his virtues (Anon.) and was probably composed soon after his death. According to this hagiography, he was born in Kirmān, son of the local ruler, Sulṭān Ṭurānshāh, who was deposed by the Ghuzz (Oghuz) tribesmen (c. 584/1188). Later authors, such as Ibn ʿArabī (d. 638/1240), the celebrated Ṣūfī of Andalusian origin, do not mention Kirmānī's royal background (Abū Maḥbūb, Tarjuma, 42). The hagiography describes how Kirmānī was accepted as a disciple by Shaykh Rukn al-Dīn Sūjāsī (d. c. 1014/1605), who taught him the Ṣūfī path, and describes Kirmānī's many travels and meetings with leading Ṣūfīs and political and military leaders, culminating in his close association with the caliphate in Baghdad. This work is evidence of the increasing confidence of Ṣūfīs at this time, benefitting, as they did, from the patronage of local military rulers. The hagiography even describes Ibn al-Jawzī (d. 596/1200), the great Ḥanbālī religious scholar from Baghdad, as a follower of Rukn al-Dīn Sūjāsī, in spite of the fact that Ibn al-Jawzī was a staunch advocate of a sober form of Islam and had criticised the Ṣūfī practice of *samāʿ* and gazing at young boys (Ibn al-Jawzī, 380–96).

The hagiography does not shy from addressing controversial issues, such as Kirmānī's witnessing the divine through the physical form of beautiful boys, contrary to Junayd's prescription to take care to observe *samāʿ* at the proper time, in the proper place, and, most importantly, with the proper people (Avery, 59) (Junayd, d. 298/910, Persian-born, was a central figure amongst the mystics of Baghdad). Clearly, beautiful young boys were not Ṣūfīs, which explains, in part, the criticisms levelled against Kirmānī by the likes of Jalāl al-Dīn Rūmī (d. 671/1273), the major Persian mystical poet, and ʿAlāʾ al-Dawla Simnānī (d. 736/1336), the Persian mystic and author. These criticisms were written long after Kirmānī's death, and there may well have been other issues behind the criticisms, such as the struggle amongst the nascent Ṣūfī orders for hegemony in Anatolia and Iran. Likewise, the criticisms by the wandering dervish and alter ego of Rūmī, Shams al-Dīn Tabrīzī (d. 645/1247) of Kirmānī, may have centred on the competition to inherit the spiritual legacy of their master, Rukn al-Dīn Sūjāsī (Ridgeon, Controversy, 17–29).

The Kirmānī controversy seems strange, not only because of his elevation to a senior spiritual rank in Baghdad but also because of Kirmānī's association with

Ibn ʿArabī, who is known for his esoteric understanding of Islam and his scrupulous adherence to the externals of *sharīʿa*. So intimate was the relationship that Ibn ʿArabī asked Kirmānī to care for his son-in-law, Ṣadr al-Dīn Qūnāwī (d. 674/1274), who is known to have expressed great fondness for Kirmānī (Chittick). Despite this connection between the two leading advocates of the doctrine that came to be known as *waḥdat al-wujūd* (unity of existence), there is no evidence of any elaborate or detailed exposition of that doctrine in Kirmānī's works. He left no prose composition, although a large collection of Persian quatrains on typical Ṣūfī themes has been attributed to him (Kirmānī, *Dīwān*).

Kirmānī died in Baghdad, and it is unknown whether a tomb was built over his grave, which might have provided the foundation for a following of Ṣūfīs who propagated his form of ecstatic Ṣūfism. He had one son, who seems to have spent his time in northeastern Iran, which might have contributed to the lack of interest in the development of a "Kirmāniyya" Ṣūfī order around his grave. It is probable, too, that the competition from deceased saints in Baghdad—such as ʿAbd al-Qādir al-Jīlānī, d. 561/1166, the Ḥanbalī jurist Ṣūfī and preacher who became the eponymous ancestor the Qādiriyya, and the aforementioned al-Suhrawardī—who probably had already-established pilgrimages, would have prevented the success of a new order. The lack of a Kirmāniyya order may also be attributable to Kirmānī's refusal to issue *ijāza*s (licences to teach) to his disciples, perhaps indicating his own preference for an individual to succeed him as *shaykh*, thereby facilitating the emergence of an order (Ridgeon, *Awḥad al-Dīn Kirmānī*, 116).

Perhaps because of the contributions to the Kirmānī controversy by influential literary Ṣūfīs, Kirmānī continued to be associated with the ecstatic *samāʿ* to the extent that Jāmī (d. 898/1492), the Persian mystical poet and hagiographer from Herat, wrote that, when Kirmānī became excited during the *samāʿ*, he would rip open the shirts of his partners and dance breast to breast with them (Jāmī, 588). Such comments may have led to Kirmānī being associated with other Ṣūfīs, such as Fakhr al-Dīn ʿIrāqī (d. 687/1289), who were attracted to the divine manifested in the male form.

Bibliography

Sources

Anon., *Manāqib-i Awḥād al-Dīn Ḥāmid b. Abī l-Fakhr-i Kirmānī*, ed. Badīʿ al-Zamān Furūzānfar, Tehran 1347sh/1969; Awḥad al-Dīn Kirmānī, *Dīvān-i rubaʿiyāt-i Awḥad al-Dīn Kirmānī*, ed. Aḥmad Abū Maḥbūb, Tehran 1366sh/1987–8; Ibn al-Fuwāṭī (attrib.), *al-Ḥawādith al-jāmiʿa wa-l-tajārib al-nāfiʿa fī l-miʾa al-sābiʿa*, ed. Mahdī al-Najm, Beirut 2003; Ibn al-Jawzī, *Talbīs Iblīs*, trans. as *The Devil's deceptions*, Birmingham 2014; Jāmī, *Nafaḥāt al-uns*, ed. Maḥmūd ʿĀbidī, Tehran 1370sh/1990–1.

Studies

Kenneth S. Avery, *A psychology of early Sufi samāʿ. Lstening and altered states*, London 2004; William Chittick, The last will and testament of Ibn ʿArabī's foremost disciple and some notes on its author, *Sophia Perennis* 4/1 (1978), 43–58; Aḥmad Abū Maḥbūb, Tarjuma-yi aḥvāl, in Aḥmad Abū Maḥbūb (ed.), *Dīvān-i rubāʿyāt-i Awḥad al-Dīn Kirmānī* (Tehran 1366sh/1987–8); Lloyd Ridgeon, The controversy of Shaykh Awḥad al-Dīn Kirmānī and handsome, moon-faced youths. A case study of *shāhid-bāzī* in medieval Sufism, *Journal of Sufi Studies* 1 (2012), 3–30; Lloyd Ridgeon, *Awḥad al-Dīn Kirmānī and the controversy of the Sufi gaze*, London 2018.

Lloyd Ridgeon

Kunta-Ḥājjī

Kunta-Ḥājjī al-Iliskhānī (Kishiev) (c. 1800–67) was a Chechen Ṣūfī master, the eponymous founder of the Kunta-Ḥājjī branch of the Qādiriyya brotherhood active in Chechnya, Ingushetia, and Daghestan; this branch is well-known for its *dhikr* dance practice (the Qādiriyya is a widespread Ṣūfī order of which ʿAbd al-Qādir Jīlānī, d. 561/1166, a Ḥanbalī scholar active in Baghdad, became, after his death, the namesake and patron; *dhikr*, lit., remembrance, is the central Ṣūfī devotional exercise, in which participants recite a name or series of names of God, or a litany; it may be performed alone or communally and may involve chanting, movements, and music).

1. Life

Kunta-Ḥājjī left no comprehensive Ṣūfī work: what we know about him comes from the writings of his disciples, from Daghestani sources (including those written by his opponents), from imperial Russian reports, and from legends disseminated by his followers. This has led to controversies and speculation about his life, teaching, and political position.

Kunta-Ḥājjī was probably born in about 1800 in the Chechen settlement of Isti-Su (Melcha-Khi) but moved with his father, Kishi, and his mother, Khedi, to Iliskhan-Yurt, also in Chechnya (Akaev, *Sheikh Kunta-khadzhi*, 97–9). Other traditions locate his birth in the village of Inkho, in Daghestan's Gumbet mountain region (Meskhidze, Kunta-khadzhzhi, 227). While there is a widespread assumption amongst his followers that Kunta remained illiterate *(ummī)*, Daghestani manuscript collections contain Arabic letters writen by him, so he probably had some formal education. His father took him on the *ḥajj* (Akaev, *Sheikh Kunta-khadzhi*, 30–3).

Kunta is mentioned as a disciple of Tashaw Ḥājjī al-Indīrī (d. 1845) (al-Bammadī, 2), a Naqshbandiyya Khālidiyya *shaykh* and *jihād* leader in Chechnya and the Kumyk lands of northern Daghestan who insisted on his autonomy from Imām Shāmil (Shamwīl, r. 1834–59) and from Shāmil's major Khālidiyya *shaykh*, Jamāl al-Dīn al-Ghāzīghumūqī (d. 1866) (Kemper, *Herrschaft*, 255–60, 295–300) (the Naqshbandiyya, whose eponymous founder, Bahāʾ al-Dīn Naqshband, died in Bukhārā in 791/1389, is now widespread; its orthodox Khālidī branch was founded by the Kurdish *shaykh* Khālid Naqshbandī, d. 1827, himself trained in India in the Mujaddidī current initiated by Shaykh Aḥmad Sirhindī, d. 1034/1624, posthumously known as the *mujaddid* (renovator) of Islam in the second millenium; from Iraq the Khālidiyya spread rapidly in the Ottoman provinces, the Caucasus, the Volga basin, and Central Asia, as well as to Southeast Asia from Mecca). Tashaw might have given Kunta a Qādiriyya initiation, with or without the specific *dhikr* dance practice. Another master whom Kunta revered is a certain Ghāzī-Ḥājjī from the North Caucasus (Kunta-Ḥājjī, *Tarjamat maqālāt*, 26–32).

2. Practice

Kunta practised a loud remembrance of God *(dhikr jahr)*, in a form that developed into ecstatic group dances in circles *(raqṣ* and *dawrān)*, accompanied by a tambourine or other musical instruments (cf. Ippolitov). Kunta's Ṣūfī movement challenged the Naqshbandiyya Khālidiyya, which was dominant at that time in Daghestan and parts of Chechnya and insisted on the legitimacy only of the silent *dhikr khafī* that has become strongly associated with Shāmil's *jihād* (cf. Zelkina, *In quest*; Kemper, North Caucasian Khālidiyya). Kunta is said to have rejected *jihād* and to have opposed violence in general (Albogachieva, 16); popular literature praises him as "a Chechen Mahatma Gandhi," but it is difficult to find textual evidence for a pronounced pacifist character of Kunta-Ḥājjī's teaching, beyond an insistence on mutual support and solidarity amongst Muslims. The miracles reported from Kunta are based mostly on claims of clairvoyance and the ability to be present at two places simultaneously, including Mecca.

In the late 1850s Kunta and some of his *murīds* (disciples) were reportedly summoned to Shāmil's headquarter in Vedeno (Chechnya), where the *imām* and his Daghestani *shaykhs* and scholars examined Kunta's teaching and observed his *dhikr* ritual. Some sources claim Shāmil found nothing reprehensible or even joined Kunta's *dhikr* circle. Daghestani sources, however, insist that Shāmil condemned Kunta's teaching and forced the latter to undertake his second pilgrimage to Mecca.

3. Historical context

Kunta's success is usually explained as resulting from the circumstance that, by the time of his return (in 1861?), the Chechens were exhausted by the long *jihād* against Russia and therefore ready to embrace Kunta's position of non-resistance as well as his Ṣūfī practice. In the early 1860s, Kunta established a network of deputies (*wakīls*) in Chechnya and Ingushetia, and representatives of today's Ingush *wird* (sub-branch) insist it was Kunta who introduced the Ingush to Islam (Mal'sagov, 16–7). Naqshbandī opponents concede that he had disciples also in the Avar and Andi regions of Daghestan (al-Bāginī, *Ṭabaqāt*, 416ff). Whether Kunta had political ambitions is difficult to ascertain. The Russian authorities grew concerned about his increasing influence, and, in January 1864, Kunta, his brother and some of his *murīds* were imprisoned and exiled to Russia's north.

4. Writings of his disciples

Kunta claimed to maintain regular communication with the Prophet and to receive divine inspiration *(ilhām)*, especially in dreams. To his *murīds* he recommended the purification of the heart. His disciple ʿAbd al-Salām al-Chachānī (d. after 1871) (Tutgireev), from Alkhan-Yurt (near Grozny), accompanied Kunta into exile and produced two works that report his master's sayings in direct speech, translated from Chechen-Ingush into Arabic; these compilations circulated in manuscript form. One of these, untitled, provides Kunta's responses to reproaches from unnamed *ʿulamāʾ*; here Kunta defends his *dhikr* practice and the participation of women in it (cf. Shikhaliev, 73–4). The other text, titled *Ajwiba* ("Responses"), presents Kunta's views on fourteen issues, such as divine love, *dhikr*, shaykhdom, the virtues of the Prophet, and prayers for the deceased (al-Chachānī, *Ajwibat*). This text reflects Kunta's suffering in exile; Kunta describes Russian rule over Muslims as a *fitna* (affliction, in this context) and excused Muslims who could not follow the ritual properly while imprisoned or in exile. Al-Chachānī's two texts were later compiled into one book and published in Syria (al-Chachānī, *Kitāb jawāb*). More widespread in the Caucasus is *Maqālāt* ("Sayings"), another compilation of Kunta's sayings collected by one of his *murīds*, mostly on Ṣūfī ethics and the *shaykh's* intercession for his disciples. This Arabic book was first published in Daghestan in 1910, accompanied by a Kumyk translation (Kunta-Ḥājjī); later translations were made into Chechen, Ingush, and Avar (Shikhaliev, 72–3). Some manuscripts contain Chechen-language hymns (*naẓm*s) devoted to Kunta, obviously for performance in Ṣūfī rituals.

Reportedly, some three thousand of his *murīd*s, armed with nothing but daggers, protested in 1864 against Kunta's exile at a Russian fort; the Tsarist troops killed 164 of them, including women. Kunta died in Ustiuzhno (in the Novgorod area) in 1867, but his followers claim to this day that he has not died; there are legendary accounts of people who met him in the 1970s (Akaev, Sheikh Kunta, 98).

5. Disintegration and later development of the movement

After Kunta's death, his movement disintegrated into several *wird*s known under the names of his disciples of the first and second generations. Next to the Kunta-Ḥājjī *wird* proper, of local importance in Chechnya are the Bammat-Girei, ʿAlī-Mitaev, and Chim-Mirza branches, and a few others. The major Ingush *wird* is the Baṭṭāl-Ḥājjīs (Meskhidze, Shaykh Batal). Often headed by hereditary leaders, these Ṣūfī groups differ in their male headdress and the musical instruments they use; some groups allow women to participate in their circular dances. These *wird*s survived Soviet repression in the 1930s and the violent deportation in 1944 of the entire Chechen and Ingush nations to Kazakhstan and elsewhere in Central Asia; one *wird*, the Vis-Ḥājjīs, came into being amongst Chechen exiles in Kazakhstan and entered Chechnya only when the deportees had returned to the North Caucasus, in the second half of the 1950s (Ermekbaev, 220ff.). Some historians describe Kunta's teaching in general as "Chechen Islam" and as closely connected to the clan *(teip)* structure of Chechen and Ingush society; some argue that he was a supporter of local customary law *(ʿādāt)* and therefore opposed Shāmil's *jihād* movement and the enforcement of *sharīʿa*. In the Arabic texts that report his sayings, Kunta shows respect for the *madhāhib* (Ar. plur. of *madhhab*, school of legal thought) but presents Ṣūfism as standing above them. One Arabic letter (Makhachkala, Inst. Ist. Arkh. Ethn. RAN (Institute of History, Archaeology, and Ethnography, Russian Academy of Sciences) *fond* (collection) 16, *opis'* (inventory) 3, MS 1024) reveals his claim to authority in regulating legal disputes and his familiarity with Islamic legal terminology.

Groups of the Kunta cluster played a role in the early phase of the Chechen separatist war against Russia in 1994–6, where the Kunta *dhikr* dance was used as a symbol of national unity. By the mid-1990s, however, Chechen separatism became increasingly connected to Salafist anti-Ṣūfī ideas. After Russia's reintegration of Chechnya through a military operation beginning in the fall of 1999, the Kremlin appointed former separatist *muftī* Aḥmad Kadyrov (d. 2004) as head of the republic; in that capacity, Kadyrov promoted the heritage of Kunta-Ḥājjī as "national Islam" and had many tombs of Kunta-Ḥājjī's relatives and disciples renovated; the major *ziyāra* (regional "pilgrimage" to the tomb of a holy person) site is the shrine of Kunta's mother, Khedi (Vachagaev, *Sheikhi*). Today, diasporic Chechen and Ingush Ṣūfīs also carry on with *dhikr* ceremonies in cities such as Moscow and St Petersburg (Oparin).

Bibliography

V. Kh. Akaev, Sheĭkh Kunta-Khadzhi Kishiev v dukhovnoĭ kul'ture chechentsev. Sut' ucheniia i ego sovremennoe znachenie, *Islam v Sovremennom Mire/Islam in the Modern World* 12/1 (2016), 95–108; V. Kh. Akaev, *Sheĭkh Kunta-Khadzhi. Zhizn' i uchenie*, Grozny 1994; M. Albogachieva, "I am entrusted with only prayer beads by Allāh, and I will take neither a dagger nor rifle in my hands" (Kunta- Ḥājjī Kishiev, his preaching and followers), *Manuscripta Orientalia* 17/2 (2011), 13–20; Shuʿayb b. Idrīs al-Bākinī, *Ṭabaqāt al-khʷājagān al-naqshbandiyya wa-sādāt al-mashāʾikh al-khālidiyya al-maḥmūdiyya*, ed. ʿAbd al-Jalīl al-ʿAṭāʾ, Damascus 1419/1999; Shihāb al-Dīn al-Bammadī al-Dāghistānī, *Furāt Dāghistān fī aynaʿ bustān*, Petrovsk 1909; ʿAbd al-Salām al-Chachānī, *Ajwibat al-ustādh al-mufīd li-masāʾil al-murīd al-mustafīd*, Makhachkala, Dzhamal Malamagomedov Manuscript Library; ʿAbd al-Salām al-Chachānī, *Kitāb jawāb al-sāʾilīn wa-tarjamat al-murīdīn*, ed. Muḥammad b. al-Ḥājj Aḥmad al-Ghumūkhī, Shām al-Sharīf/al-Qunayṭara, Syria 1330/1911–2; Zh. A. Ermekbaev, *Chechentsy i Ingushi v Kazakhstane. Istoriia i sud'by*, Almaty 2009; A. P. Ippolitov, Uchenie "zikr" i ego posledovateli v Chechne i Argunskom okruge, in V. Kh. Kokoshvili (ed.), *Sbornik Svedenii o Kavkazskikh gortsakh* (Tiflis 1869), 2:1–17; Michael Kemper, *Herrschaft, Recht und Islam in Daghestan. Von den Khanaten und Gemeindebünden zum ǧihād-Staat*, Wiesbaden 2005; Michael Kemper, The North Caucasian Khālidiyya and "Muridism." Historiographical problems, *Journal of the History of Sufism* 5 (2006), 111–26; Kunta Ḥājjī, *Tarjama maqālāt al-shaykh al-fāḍil wa-l-ustādh al-kāmil al-Ḥājj Kunta al-Michighīshī al-Iliskhānī* (Arabic text with Kumyk trans. by Shikhammat Qadi Baibulatov), Temir Khan Shura, Dagestan 1910; Magomed S. Mal'sagov, Drevo zhizni, in *200 let sviatomu ustazu Kishi-khadzhi (1800–2000)* (Nal'chik', Kabardino-Balkar Republic 2001), 5–53; Dzhul'etta Meskhidze, Kunta-khadzhzhi, Kishi (rubezh XVIII–XIX vv.–1867), in St. M. Prozorov (ed.), *Islam na territorii byvsheĭ rossiĭskoi imperii. Entsiklopedicheskiĭ slovar'* (Moscow 2006), 1:227–8; Dzhul'etta Meskhidze, Shaykh Batal Hajji from Surkhokhi. Towards the history of Islam in Ingushetia, *Central Asian Survey* 25/1–2 (2006), 179–91; Dmitriy A. Oparin, Migration and contemporary Muslim space in Moscow. Contextualizing North Caucasian loud dhikr and the religious practices of Central Asian folk mullas, *Contemporary Islam* 11 (2017), 61–80; Shamil Sh. Shikhaliev, Kratkiĭ obzor arabograficheskikh sochineniĭ Kunta-khadzhi Kishieva, in M. S. Albogachieva (ed.), *Islam v Rossii i za ee predelami. Istoriia, obshchestvo, kul'tura. Sbornik materialov mezhregional'noĭ konferentsii, posviashchennoĭ 100-letiiu so dnia konchiny vydaiushchegosia religioznogo deiatelia sheĭkh Batal-khadzhi Belkharoeva* (St Petersburg 2011), 71–5; Mairbek Vachagaev, *Sheikhi i ziiaraty Chechni*, Moscow 2009; Anna Zelkina, *In quest for God and freedom. The Sufi response to the Russian advance in the North Caucasus*, London 2000; Anna Zelkina, Some aspects of the teaching of Kunta Hâjjî on the basis of the manuscript by ʿAbd al-Salâm written in 1862 AD, *Journal of the History of Sufism* 1–2 (2000), 483–507.

Michael Kemper
Shamil Shikhaliev

L

Lexicography, Urdu

Urdu lexicography, encompassing multiple genres in verse and prose that provide explanations of words and phrases, is similar to most other major New Indo-Aryan languages in the late arrival—in this case, dating the to the mid-nineteenth century—of the comprehensive monolingual dictionary. Derived primarily from the speech forms prevalent in the Delhi region of northern India, Urdu is identical in grammar to Modern Standard Hindi and is differentiated primarily by its use of the Perso-Arabic script and a greater prevalence of lexis derived from Persian, and (through Persian) Arabic. It is for this reason that lexicography became an important venue for debates about official status and patronage, both within the colonial state and in post-independence India and Pakistan.

1. Early history

Indic vocabulary frequently appears in the entries of the many Persian *farhang*s and *lughat-nāma*s (Persianate genres that approximate the modern alphabetical dictionary) prepared in the Indian subcontinent (Baevskii, 79–116). The earliest texts, however, may belong to the *niṣāb* genre of children's vocabularies in verse. The *Qaṣīda dar lughat-i Hindī* ("An ode on Hindi terms"), a brief medical vocabulary in forty-four verses that share an end rhyme, was prepared by Yūsuf b. Muḥammad Yūsuf Khurāsānī (fl. early tenth/sixteenth century). Known by the pen name Yūsufī, he was a poet and physician associated with the courts of the Mughal emperors Bābur (r. 932–7/1526–30) and Humāyūn (r. 937–46/1531–40 and 962–3/1555–6). In its opening verse, the author promises in Persian to provide "the names of all things in Hindi and benefit from each remedy's special name." The so-called *Khāliq bārī* (named for two of the *asmā' llāhi al-ḥusnā*, or divine epithets, both meaning "Creator"), appearing in most manuscripts with more then two hundred rhyming distichs in varying metres, is commonly attributed to Amīr Khusraw of Delhi (d. 725/1325) and is a vocabulary of synonyms drawn from Arabic, Persian, and what the text calls Hindavī or Prākrit. Some scholars, most notably Shirānī, have argued against this attribution, but later research suggests that a core set of verses must have originated before the eleventh/seventeenth century (Āh, 81; Ḥusayn, 363; Nārang, 129–31). Numerous similar works appeared beginning in the late tenth/mid-sixteenth century, with English increasingly replacing Persian as the language glossed by Urdu by the early twentieth century (Hakala, On equal terms, 223–7; Majeed).

By the late eleventh/seventeenth century, Europeans began turning their attention to the northern Indian speech forms that would later come to be subsumed under the modern names Hindustani, Hindi, and Urdu (Bhatia and Machida; Hakala, Authorial problem, 481–4). Similar works by Indian authors appeared at this time, describing and defining these speech forms through Persian (see, e.g., Keshavmurthy on the *Tuḥfat al-Hind*, "Gift from India," of 1085/1674–5). The *Gharāʾib al-lughāt* ("Wonders of words") by ʿAbd al-Vāsiʿ Hānsvī (fl. late eleventh/seventeenth century), considered by many to be the first major lexicographical work on Urdu, described terms prevalent in the Haryana hinterlands, some eighty miles north and west of Delhi. Setting the pattern for subsequent debates about linguistic authority, the great Persian philologist Sirāj al-Dīn ʿAlī Khān-i Ārzū (d. 1169/1756), in his *Nawādir al-alfāẓ* ("Rarities of terms," 1743), dismissed ʿAbdul Vāsiʿ's terms as "not of the knowing ones of the imperial camp and of the language of Akbarābād (Agra) and Shāhjahānābād, (but instead merely) the language of the native land of the author of the treatise" (Ārzū/Hānsvī, 248–9; Dudney).

2. Collaboration between South Asians and Europeans

Collaborations, often unacknowledged, between European and South Asian lexicographers were common during the colonial period. John Gilchrist (d. 1841) compiled much of his *A dictionary, English and Hindoostanee* in Faizabad while on leave from his post as assistant surgeon in the East India Company's Bengal Army. Complaining in the introduction about the lack of available materials on which to base his own work, he claimed "to extract *viva voce*, every known word in their voluminous tongue" by asking his Indian interlocutors to furnish him with "every signification they could possibly attach to such sounds or words as *a*, *ab*, *abab*, *ababa*, *abach*, *abad*, *abada*, *abaf*, &c." (Gilchrist, viii). Just a few pages later, however, he acknowledges that he had drawn the terms in his dictionary from Samuel Johnson's 1755 *A dictionary of the English language:* "from Johnson every word was explained in succession, to a number of learned Hindoostanees, who furnished the synonymous vocables in their own speech" (Gilchrist, xiv). Gilchrist was appointed in 1800 the first professor of Hindustani at the College at Fort William, a school in Calcutta that trained young East India Company officials for service in India during the first four decades of the nineteenth century. Gilchrist and his colleagues oversaw the production of Devanāgarī- and Arabic-script editions of literary and pedagogical materials, including several dictionaries.

Another early example is the wholesale incorporation of the *Shams al-bayān fī muṣṭalaḥāt al-Hindūstān* ("The sun of speech, on the idioms of Hindustan," 1792) by Mirzā Jān Ṭapish (d. 1816) into Joseph Taylor and William Hunter's *A dictionary, Hindoostanee and English* (1808), enabled perhaps by the Delhi poet-scholar's long incarceration in a Calcutta jail for having allegedly helped Shams al-Dawla (d. 1831, son of the Nawāb of Bengal Mubārak al-Dawla, r. 1770–93) and Nawāb Wazīr ʿAlī

(r. 1797–8) of Awadh to conspire against the British (Joseph Taylor, d. 1811, then a captain in the Bengal Artillery, later gained the rank of major in the East India Company; William Hunter, d. 1812, was an official and minister in India, then secretary to the Asiatic Society in Calcutta, Bengal, who made one of the first translations of the Bible into Hindi).

The efforts of S. W. Fallon (retired in 1875 from a post as inspector of schools, Education Department of Bengal, d. 1880) to expand Urdu lexicography to include folksongs, proverbs, and other artefacts of the spoken language complemented those of his contemporary, John T. Platts (d. 1904), whose own monumental dictionary was based on a copious survey of printed texts including newspapers; Platts held various posts in India, including that of officiating inspector of schools, northern circle, Central Provinces, before being elected teacher of Persian language at Oxford University in 1880. Neither work has been entirely supplanted by subsequent scholarship.

Two former assistants to Fallon, Sayyid Aḥmad Dihlavī (d. 1918) and Chirañjī Lāl (d. 1898), both from Delhi, helped advance monolingual Urdu lexicography. Several comprehensive dictionaries by single authors followed, including the massive *Nūr al-lughāt* ("Light of words," 1922–31) by Nūr al-Ḥasan and *Jāmiʿ al-lughāt* ("Totality of words," 1935) by ʿAbd al-Majīd (Ḥasan; Majīd; Bailey).

3. After independence

India's National Council for the Promotion of Urdu Language, Pakistan's Muqtadira-yi Qawmī Zabān (National Language Authority), and various regional institutions have sponsored dictionary projects since independence. These organisations have continued in the tradition of earlier voluntary associations such as the Vernacular Translation Society, which, beginning at Delhi College in the early 1840s, commissioned Urdu translations of English textbooks in medicine, law, science, economics, and history (Minault). Pakistan's *Qaumi* (national) *English-Urdu dictionary* (1992), although edited by the esteemed Urdu scholar Jamīl Jālibī under the imprimatur of the National Language Authority, was criticised for drawing on an American work, *Webster's encyclopedic dictionary of the English language*, rather than a British model (Hameed). For Jalibi, though, English "has now become common throughout the world mostly through the intervention of American power and influence" (Jālibī, v). The great twentieth-century scholar of and advocate for Urdu, ʿAbd al-Ḥaq (d. 1961), began compiling the *Lughat-i kabīr-i urdū* ("Great dictionary of Urdu"). Following his death, the project, a monolingual historical dictionary of the Urdu language modelled on the Oxford English Dictionary, was published between 1973 and 2010 in twenty-two volumes. In June 2017, a full century after it was first conceived, an online version of ʿAbd al-Ḥaq's dictionary, known now by the title *Urdū lughāt. Tārīkhī uṣūl par* ("Urdu dictionary: on historical principles"), was inaugurated by the government of Pakistan.

Bibliography

Sources

Sirāj al-Dīn ʿAlī Khān Ārzū, *Nawādir al-alfāẓ*, and ʿAbd al-Wāsiʿ Hānsvī, *Gharāʾib al-lughāt*, ed. Sayyid ʿAbdallāh, Karachi 1951; Sayyid Aḥmad Dihlavī, *Farhang-i āṣafiyya. ʿArabī, Fārsī, Turkī, Hindī, Sanskrat, awr Angrezī lughāt makhlūṭ bih Urdū*, 4 vols., New Delhi 1974; S. W. Fallon, *A new Hindustani-English dictionary, with illustrations from Hindustani literature and folk-lore*, Banaras 1879; John Borthwick

Gilchrist, *A dictionary, English and Hindoostanee, in which the words are marked with their distinguishing initials; as Hinduwee, Arabic, and Persian. Whence the Hindoostanee, or what is vulgarly, but improperly called the Moor language, is evidently formed*, 2 vols., Calcutta 1787–90; Nūr al-Ḥasan, *Nūr al-lughāt*, 4 vols., Karachi 1959²; Jamīl Jālibī, *Qawmī Angrezī Urdū lughat = Qaumi English-Urdu dictionary*, Islamabad 1992; Ahmeduddin Khan, *The east and west khaliq baree*, Moradabad 1906; Munshī Chiranjī Lāl, *Makhzan al-muḥāvarāt*, Delhi 1898²; *Lughat-i kabīr-i Urdū*, ed. ʿAbd al-Ḥaq, Karachi 1973; ʿAbd al-Majīd, *Jāmiʿ al-lughāt*, Lahore 1933; John Thompson Platts, *A dictionary of Urdū, classical Hindī, and English*, 2 vols., London 1884; Mirzā Jān Ṭapish Dihlavī, *Shams al-bayān fī muṣṭalaḥāt al-Hindūstān*, ed. ʿĀbid Raẓā Bīdār, Patna 1979²; Joseph Taylor, *A dictionary, Hindoostanee and English*, rev. William Hunter, 2 vols., Calcutta 1808; *Urdū lughat. Tārīkhī uṣūl par*, ed. Abū l-Layth Ṣiddīqī and Nasīm Amrohvī, 22 vols., Karachi 1977–2010; *Urdū lughat. Tārīkhī uṣūl par*, Government of Pakistan 2017 (www.udb.gov.pk/).

STUDIES

Ṣafdar Āh, *Amīr Khusraw bahaythiyat-i Hindī shāʿir. Naẓariyya-yi Maḥmūd Shīrānī ke tanqādā muṭālaʿa ke sāth*, Bombay 1966; Solomon I. Baevskii, *Early Persian lexicography. Farhangs of the eleventh to the fifteenth centuries*, trans. N. Killian, ed. John R. Perry, Honolulu 2007; T. Grahame Bailey, Review of *Jamiʿ ul-lugāt*. A new Urdu dictionary by ʿAbdul Majīd, *BSOAS* 9 (1938), 440–1; Tej K. Bhatia and Kazuhiko Machida, *The oldest grammar of Hindustānī*, 3 vols., Tokyo 2008; Arthur Dudney, The wonders of words, or the role of Khān-i Ārzū's *Navādir al-alfāẓ* in the development of Urdu, in Satyanarayana Hegde (ed.), *An informal festschrift in honor of the manifold lifetime achievements of Shamsur Rahman Faruqi*, http://www.columbia.akadns.net/itc/mealac/pritchett/00urduhindilinks/srffest/txt_dudney_khaniarzu.pdf; Walter N. Hakala, The authorial problem in the *Khāliq bārī* of "Khusrau," *Indian Economic and Social History Review* 51/4 (2014), 481–96; Walter N. Hakala, On equal terms. The equivocal origins of an early Mughal Indo-Persian vocabulary, *JRAS* 25/2 (2015), 209–27; Walter N. Hakala, *Negotiating languages. Urdu, Hindi, and the definition of modern South Asia*, New York 2016; Masʿūd Hāshmī, *Urdū lughat navīsī kā pas manẓar*, Delhi 1997; Masʿūd Hāshmī, *Urdū lughat navīsī kā tanqīdī jāʾiza*, New Delhi 1992; Prashant Keshavmurthy, Mīrzā Ḫān ibn Faḫr al-Dīn, in Fabrizio Speziale and Carl W. Ernst (eds.), *Tuḥfat al-Hind, Perso-Indica. An analytical survey of Persian works on Indian learned traditions* (2013) (http://perso-indica.net/work.faces?idsec=15&idw=84); *Lughat navīsī ke masāʾil*, ed. Gopī Chand Nārang, New Delhi 1985; Javed Majeed, Modernity's script and a Tom Thumb performance. English linguistic modernity and Persian/Urdu lexicography in nineteenth-century India, in Michael S. Dodson and Brian A. Hatcher (eds.), *Trans-colonial modernities in South Asia* (Milton Park, Abingdon UK 2012), 95–115; Gail Minault, Delhi College and Urdu, *Annual of Urdu Studies* 14 (1999), 119–34; Ḥusayn Mumtāz, *Amīr Khusraw Dihlavī. Ḥayāt awr shāʿirī* (Karachi 1975), 325–58; Najīb Athrat Nadvī, Tabṣire. Urdū ke lughāt, in *Urdū lughat. Risāla-yi Hindustānī Ilahābād (1931–1947) se intikhāb* (Patna 1993), 25–35; Gopī Chand Nārang, *Amīr Khusraw kā Hindavī kalām. Maʿ nuskhahā-yi Barlin, dhakhīra-yi Ishpringar*, Chicago and Delhi 1987; Jābir ʿAlī Sayyid and Wārith Sarhindī, *Kutub-i lughat kā taḥqīqī va lisānī jāʾiza*, Islamabad 1984; Abū Salmān Shāhjahānpūrī, *Kitābiyāt-i lughāt-i Urdū*, Islamabad 1986; Ḥāfiẓ Maḥmūd Shīrānī (ed.), Dībācha-yi duvvum, in *Ḥifẓ al-lisān. Maʿrūf ba-nām-i Khāliq bārī* (Delhi 1944), 52–66; *Urdū lughat. Yādgārī maḍāmīn*, ed. Abū l-Ḥasanāt, Karachi 2010.

WALTER N. HAKALA

Lucknow until 1856

Lucknow (Lakhnaw, now Lakhnau), located on the banks of the river Gomtī, came to epitomise all that was magnificent, refined, and cosmopolitan in the regional courts of eighteenth and nineteenth-century North India under the nawabs (an honorific title for semi-autonomous Muslim rulers of princely states) of Awadh (Oudh; r. 1722–1856).

Lucknow is said to be "the ancient Lakshmanavati, founded by Lakṣmaṇa, the brother of Rāmacandra of Ayodhya." Recalling this mythical past is the Lakṣmaṇa Ṫīlā, "the high ground situated within the defenses of the dismantled Macchi Bhawan fort" of the city (Führer, 265).

1. Emerging regional centre (eighth/fourteenth to early tenth/sixteenth centuries)

The earliest mention of Lucknow comes from the famous Moroccan traveller and writer Ibn Baṭṭūṭa (d. 770 or 779/1368 or 1377), who arrived during the reign of the Delhi sultan Muḥammad b. Tughluq (r. 725–52/1325–51). His account reflects the emergence of Lucknow around the middle of the eighth/fourteenth century as a regional centre, managing the agricultural surplus from the surrounding area. Lucknow is mentioned by Ibn Baṭṭūṭa as amongst the territories under the control of governor ʿAyn al-Mulk (Ibn Baṭṭūṭa, 105). When and how it attained this position is not known, as Lucknow is not mentioned in sources from before the sultanate period.

Lucknow must have gained further prominence due to the rise of the Sharqī dynasty in the late eighth/fourteenth century and the creation of the independent Sharqī sultanate of Jawnpur (796–888/1394–1483), as it was near the capital city Jawnpur and was well connected with several urban centres of the region, such as Dalmaw, Etawah, Sandila, Kannawj, and Bahraych (Habib and Nizami, 623, 683, 712, 714).

In the ninth/fifteenth century, when Sulṭān Bahlūl Lodī (r. 855–94/1451–89) divided his territories amongst princes and senior nobles in accordance with Afghan tribal tradition, Lucknow, along with Kalpi, was given to prince Āʿẓam Humāyūn (d. 926/1520). The revenue potential of the city is apparent from the list of revenue circles (administrative divisions called *sarkārs*), based on the records of Bahlūl's successor Sikandar Shāh (r. 894–923/1489–1517), reproduced by Mughal emperor Bābur (r. 932–36/1526–30) in his memoirs (Bābur, 521).

Lucknow is mentioned increasingly in the sources for the period of struggle for establishment and consolidation of Mughal authority under Bābur and Humāyūn (r. 937–47/1531–40 and 962–3/1555–6). A passage in the *Bābur-nāma* (Bābur's memoirs) suggests that there was a fort in Lucknow, which was used as a retreat and for reorganising offensives by the Afghans against the forces of Bābur (Bābur, 99, 594, 600, 681). The emperor personally visited Lucknow while in pursuit of Afghan leaders (Bābur, 601). Humāyūn had apparently come to Lucknow while struggling for supremacy over his brothers.

After his success against the Mughals, Sulṭān Shīr Shāh Sūrī (r. 947–52/1540–5) set out to organise his empire. He established mints, including one in Lucknow (Wright, 101, entry 713), where copper coins began to be issued. The role of Lucknow at that time was not confined to the management of agricultural surplus but seems to have extended to non-agricultural products, and the city emerged as a centre for mobilising resources from manufacturing and trade.

2. Administrative and commercial centre (late tenth/sixteenth to eleventh/seventeenth centuries)

The administrative role of Lucknow was expanded when the Mughal emperor Akbar (r. 963–1014/1556–1605) reorganised imperial territories during the last quarter of the tenth/sixteenth century. Its status was raised to that of a *sarkār* headquarters in the *ṣūba* (province) of Awadh (a *sarkār*, or district, was a fiscal and administrative division comprising several *parganas*, or cantons, that emerged under the Lodīs). Abū l-Faḍl Allāmī (d. 1011/1602), a close adviser, confidant, and historiographer of Akbar, remarks that it is "a large city on the bank of the Gumti, delightful in its surroundings" (Abū l-Faḍl, *Āʾīn-i Akbarī*, 2:184). Lucknow is also listed by Abū l-Faḍl amongst those twenty-eight towns where copper coins were struck during Akbar's reign (Abū l-Faḍl, *Āʾīn-i Akbarī*, 1:133).

Beginning in the middle of the eleventh/seventeenth century, European traders regularly sent their representatives to Lucknow to arrange for the purchase of calicoes produced in the nearby areas of Daryabad and Khayrabad (Foster, 5:146; Mundy, 2:141, 156). English factors were also very interested in mercoole, a coarse cloth used as a wrapper for quilts (Foster, 8:299). Calicoes and mercoole were bought at Lucknow and carried to Agra for sale.

During the late eleventh/seventeenth and early twelfth/eighteenth centuries, the Mughal Empire faced several crises: the Maratha (Marāṯ'hā) and Jat (Jāt') insurgencies, the growing ambition amongst the regional and quasi-regional magnates, the invigoration of *zamīndārs* (landholders and local potentates) and holders of *madad-i maʿāsh* (living-support grant), and the aspirations of *jāgīrdārs* (revenue assignees) for permanent holdings and a secure base in their respective regions. Such local land-owning groups strove to increase their share of regional resources. These developments were seen as opportunities for *ṣūbadārs* (provincial governors) to take full advantage of the decline of imperial authority at the local level (Alam, 11, 12, 16, 118, 243). Saʿādat Khān Burhān al-Mulk (d. 1151/1739), who was appointed *ṣūbadār* of Awadh in 1134/1722 by Mughal emperor Muḥammad Shāh (r. 1131–61/1719–48), assumed an independent stance in his *ṣūba*. He also extended his domain by suppressing the local chiefs, on all sides, beyond the limits of the Mughal *ṣūba* (Srivastav, 90). Under his successors, Abū l-Manṣūr Khān Ṣafdar Jang (r. 1152–67/1739–54) and Shujāʿ al-Dawla (r. 1167–89/1754–75), better known as Nawwāb Wazīr, Awadh passed from the status of a Mughal province into a de facto independent state.

When Saʿādat Khān Burhān al-Mulk took charge of the *ṣūba*, the city of Lucknow was under the control of the *shaykh-zādas* (lit., descendants of the *shaykhs*, referring to Indian Muslims), a preeminent and influential indigenous land-owning class in Awadh. They were part of the Mughal administration in the region, and some of them held important positions, but they always defied the authority of the new *ṣūbadār* (Alam, 7, 23, 225). Saʿādat Khān, who was fully aware of their strength and resources, decided to suppress them immediately. He crossed the Ganges in the rainy season and marched to Kakori, where he shrewdly entered into an alliance with the *shaykhs* of the town, who familiarised him with the strengths and weaknesses of Lucknow. He resumed his march and silently entered the city at night, forced the *shaykh-zādas* to submit, and captured their stronghold, Machchhī Bhawan (palace of the fish).

3. Lucknow as capital of Awadh

The creation of a court and capital in Lucknow dates to the reign of Nawwāb Āṣaf al-Dawla (r. 1189–1212/1775–97).

His shifting of the capital from Fayzabad to Lucknow defied all the apprehensions of those contemporaries who doubted the wisdom of his choice of Lucknow as the capital. For instance, Mīrzā Abū Ṭālib (d. 1806), the author of *Tafzīḥ al-ghāfilīn* ("Disgrace of the heedless"), considered the shift of capital a "manifest mistake," as the climate of Fayzabad was "better than that of Lucknow" and because the "ground at Lucknow was uneven and its bazaars and streets were narrow and confined." He further comments, "Had he (Āṣaf al-Dawla) first of all selected a level site for his residence, a city worthy of name would have been raised for less expense than was incurred in the building of Lucknow" (Hoey, 8). Nevertheless, the new capital emerged as the most fabulous court city in the Subcontinent, surpassing the Mughal capital in its wealth and the resilience of its artistic products. Lucknow supported a vital intellectual and cultural life and developed its own style in many spheres of culture, endowing them with its distinctive stamp and sophistication *(nafāsat)*, making it the cultural centre of North India (Trivedi, *Making*, 11–40).

The culture of Lucknow was distinguished from those of other cities of North India by the fact that, from its earliest times as the capital of the nawabs of Awadh, it was exposed to European culture and became a favourite destination for British and other Westerners.

4. The city as a centre of art and culture

Under the encouragement of the rulers of Awadh, Lucknow became famous for its diverse achievements. Intense economic activity attracted all types of professional groups to the city, such as skilled weavers, shawl makers, damasceners, and silver workers, and it attained a prominent position amongst the urban centres of North India. Its growth as a centre of luxury products and trade and as a cultural node occurred in an amazingly short time. It had become a large city by the close of the twelfth/eighteenth century, and, as late as 1870, it was the largest city in India, after the three presidency towns of Calcutta, Madras, and Bombay (Benett, 2:358). In 1856 its population was estimated at one million (Sleeman, 137), and it was said to have comprised eight hundred *muḥalla*s (quarters) and eighty-three *ganj*s (market centres) (Judicial Commissioner to Chief Commissioner, Oudh). In fact, no other Indian city had the appeal and enjoyed the cultural efflorescence that Lucknow did during the late eighteenth and early nineteenth centuries.

In the course of a century, Lucknow was adorned with scores of palatial monuments, country houses, majestic gateways, *imāmbārā*s (Shīʿī prayer spaces), mosques, tombs, and *karbalā*'s (quadrangular structures where *taʿziya*s, or miniature replicas of the tomb of Imām Ḥusayn, grandson of the Prophet, are buried during the Shīʿī commemorations, in the month of Muḥarram, of Ḥusayn's defeat and murder at Karbalāʾ by Umayyad forces in 60/680). Saʿādat ʿAlī Khān gave the Awadh capital a distinctly Western look, especially in the southern part of the city (Heber, 1:386).

The rulers of Awadh, especially Nawwāb Shujāʿ al-Dawla and Saʿādat ʿAlī Khān (r. 1798–1814), followed a cautious policy against the commercial penetration of the British East India Company. By imposing high tariffs, Saʿādat ʿAlī Khān restricted the company's trade and took steps to safeguard the interests of the local mercantile community and professionals (Hoey, 1:xvii). This move facilitated the growth of crafts in the city, which emerged as a renowned centre of industrial arts (Birdwood, 150). The historian Lāljī praises the arts and crafts of the city. He remarks in 1851, "Lucknow, since the reign of Nawwāb Āṣaf al-Dawla, has become the greatest rendezvous for expert craftsmen and excellent artists. Even today the accomplished artists of various trades and professions abound here, whose matchless skill [enables] them to create wonders of arts unattainable in any other place" (Lāljī, fol. 110b). Lucknow luxury products (e.g., metalware, glassware, jewellery, ornate weaponry, textiles) were in great demand throughout the Subcontinent.

Some artistic developments in Lucknow owe their origin to the prevalence of Shīʿism (Hassan Ali, 1:31; Najma al-Ghanī Khān, 3:1).The crafting of *taʿziya*s had flourished since the days of Nawwāb Āṣaf al-Dawla; they were manufactured of expensive materials such as silver, ivory, ebony, sandalwood, cedar, and glass (Najm al-Ghanī Khān, 3:31). Most of these arts declined considerably after the annexation of the kingdom to the East India Company's territory in 1856, but some are still practised, such as gold and silver embroidery and cotton thread embroidery *(chikankārī)* (Trivedi, *Making*, 226–85).

Lucknow also earned distinction as a centre of Shīʿism in North India. A crystallisation, expansion, and Indianisation of the Shīʿī religious ceremonies took place in Lucknow. *Mujtahid*s (scholars qualified to interpret legal issues not explicitly addressed in the Qurʾān) assumed religious power. *ʿAzādārī* (observance of mourning rituals connected with Muḥarram) was popularised and performed with fervour and on a grand scale. The period of mourning was extended from ten to forty days, up to the twentieth day of Ṣafar, the second month of the Islamic calendar (Aḥmad, 13). *Imāmbārā*s became the focus of these mourning rituals, which were conducted throughout the region (Trivedi, Invoking, 127–46; Trivedi, Genre, 194–221).

Lucknow emerged as a Shīʿī pilgrimage centre in India during the nineteenth century because of the growing emphasis by the nawabs on erecting shrines in the fashion of the shrine cities in Iraq and Iran. The Shāh Najaf Ashraf *imāmbārā*, a creation of King Ghāzī al-Dīn Ḥaydar (r. 1814–27), marked the beginning of the erection of monumental replicas of these religious structures in Lucknow. The demand for Iranian architects to reproduce these replicas increased enormously.

Lucknow emerged as the most famous centre of Islamic learning in late-twelfth/eighteenth-century India, a reputation that is still enjoyed. The *dars-i niẓāmī* curriculum and teaching methods were developed and propagated by Mullā Niẓām al-Dīn (d. 1161/1748), an outstanding scholar of the Farangī Maḥall family, which was the focus of scholastic activity in the city (Robinson, 22, 23). This curriculum emphasised the study of *maʿqūlāt* (the rational sciences) and made compulsory the study of Arabic, Persian, grammar, mediaeval mathematics, philosophy, jurisprudence, theology, exegesis, and tradition. The popularity of the *dars-i niẓāmī* curriculum was so great that Lucknow's Ṭīlā mosque could, during the twelfth/eighteenth century, accommodate seven hundred students who aspired to posts in government or education (Robinson,

22, 23). In the late eighteenth and early nineteenth centuries Lucknow became the major centre of Shīʿī scholastic theology.

Lucknow was known for its literary culture. While Persian maintained its dominance for scholarly and other compositions in prose, Urdu gained ground as the main vehicle of literary expression. The literary culture of Lucknow thrived on the institutions of *mushāʿira* (poetic assemblies) and *majlis* (the Shīʿī mourning assembly of Muḥarram). In the *mushāʿira*s, held throughout the year, literary prowess was tested (Muḥsin ʿAlī, 8). *Majālis* (Ar. plur. of *majlis*) were much like *mushāʿira*s, as venues where poetical talents were judged. Here the form of the *marthiyya*, mournful poetry that narrates the martyrdom of Imām Ḥusayn and his kinsmen in Karbalāʾ, was standardised. The installation of the printing press in Lucknow in 1819 during the reign of King Ghāzī al-Dīn Ḥaydar also encouraged literary activities.

Under the patronage of the rulers of Awadh, who observed Shīʿī rituals, the *marthiyya* rose to new heights. As an audience-oriented literary tradition, it changed in accordance with the social environment and patronage patterns and amalgamated, in the process, many traits of oral-epic rendition, indigenous myth, music, and dramatic performance. Many leading poets of Lucknow, including Hindus, adopted the *marthiyya* as the sole medium of poetry. *Mathnawī* (narrative poems in rhymed couplets), *rekhtī* (verse in the spoken dialect of women), *hajw* (poetic satire), *hazal* (humorous verse), and *wāsukht* (impassioned and vigourous verse) were other popular poetic genres. Urdu prose in Lucknow developed on the lines of Persian *qiṣṣa*s (stories) and adhered to an ornate prose style emphasising Persian diction. Important progress was made in Urdu journalism with the short-lived Lucknow weekly *Ṭilism* ("Talisman"), published in 1856–7.

Lucknow became a noted centre of classical Indian music and dance under the nawabs. There was a significant rise in the status of the courtesan, known by the generic term *ṭawāʾif*, trained to entertain. Under the patronage of the nawabs, *kat̲h̲ak* (a dance form performed by the Kat̲h̲ak community of musicians and dancers) developed as a *darbārī nr̥tya* (courtly dance). King Wājid ʿAlī Shāh (r. 1847–56), a skilled musician and dancer, choreographed numerous dances into a type of female group dancing called *rahas*. He also established a *parī-khāna* (fairy house) for the training by eminent *ustād*s (masters) of young courtesans in various forms of song and dance (Wājid ʿAlī Shāh, 71). *T̲h̲umrī* (a folk musical genre) and *ghazal* (lyrical poem rhyming AA, BA, CA...) came increasingly into vogue due to their use in *kat̲h̲ak*. The *khayāl* (a musical genre of the Delhi region) became popular, especially amongst dancing women. *Marthiyya-khᵛānī* (the tuneful recitation of *marthiyya*) was also recognised as a musical genre. The urban theatre of North India was born in Lucknow towards the middle of the nineteenth century. The *Indra sabhā* ("Assembly of the god Indra"), written by Āghā Ḥasan Amānat (d. 1858) and first staged in 1853, was the first Urdu play produced with an intimate mixture of Indian and Persian conventions, and it paved the way for Urdu drama.

Lucknow lost much of its glamour after the annexation of the kindgom of Awadh in 1856 and the turmoil of 1857, but its artistic legacy and cultural traditions survived.

Bibliography

Sources

Abū l-Faḍl ʿAllāmī, *Āʾīn-i Akbarī*, ed. Henry Blochman, 2 vols., Calcutta 1872–7, trans. Henry Blochmann (vol. 1) and Henry S. Jarrett (vols. 2–3), *The Ain i Akbari*, Calcutta 1873–94, ed. Douglas C. Phillott (vol. 1) and Jadunath Sarkar (vols. 2–3), 1927–49[2], repr. New Delhi 1977–8; Abū l-Faḍl ʿAllāmī, *Akbar-nāma*, ed. ʿAbd al-Raḥīm, 3 vols. in 2, Calcutta 1873–87, trans. Henry Beveridge, 3 vols., Calcutta 1897–1921, repr. New Delhi 1979; Mir Hassan Ali, *Observations on the Mussalmans of India, description of their manners, customs, habits and religious opinions made during a twelve years residence in their immediate society*, vol. 1, London 1832; Bābur, *Bābur-nāma*, trans. Annette Susannah Beveridge, 2 vols., London 1922, repr. New Delhi 1970; W. C. Benett, *Gazetteer of the province of Oudh*, 3 vols., Lucknow 1877–8; William Foster (ed.), *The English factories in India*, vol. 5 (1634–36), vol. 7 (1642–45), vol. 8 (1646–50), Oxford 1906–27; Sayyid Kamāl al-Dīn Ḥaydar, *Tārīkh-i mamlūkāt-i Awadh*, Allahabad, State Archives, MS Pers.; Reginald Heber, *Narrative of a journey through the Upper Provinces of India from Calcutta to Bombay, 1824–25*, vol. 1, Philadelphia 1829; Ibn Baṭṭūṭa, *Riḥla*, trans. Mahdi Husain, *The Reḥla of Ibn Baṭṭūṭa (India, Maldive Islands and Ceylon)*, Baroda 1953, repr. 1976; Lāljī, *Mirʾāt al-awḍāʿ*, Aligarh, Maulana Azad Library, Pers. MS (1851); Muḥammad Najm al-Ghanī Khān, *Tārīkh-i Avadh*, vol. 3, Lucknow 1919 (Urdu); Mirzā Abū Ṭālib Khān, *Tafḍīḥ al-ghāfilīn* (a work written in 1796–7 during a stay in Calcutta), trans. William Hoey, *History of Āsafʾud Daulah Nawab Wazir of Oudh*, Allahabad 1885, repr. Lucknow 1971; Mīr Muḥsin ʿAlī ("Muḥsin"), *Sarāpā-yi sukhan*, Lucknow n.d.; Peter Mundy, *The travels of Peter Mundy in Europe and Asia*, 1608–1667, vol. 2, ed. Richard C. Temple, London 1914; Rābiṭ ʿAbd al-Aḥad, *Vaqāʾiʿ-i dilpadhīr*, trans. Muḥammad Taqī Aḥmad, *Tarikh Badshah Begam. A Persian manuscript on the history of Oudh*, Allahabad 1938, repr. Delhi 1977; Edward C. Sachau (ed.), *Alberuni's India. An account of the religion, philosophy, literature, chronology, astronomy, customs, laws and astrology of India, about A.D. 1030*, vol. 1, London 1910, repr. Delhi 1989; WājidʿAlī Shāh, *Parī-khāna*, trans. from Urdu to Persian by TaḥsīnʿAlī Khān Sarvānī, Karachi 1958; William Henry Sleeman, *A journey through the kingdom of Oude in 1849–1850*, 2 vols., London 1858.

Reports

Judicial Commissioner to Chief Commissioner, *Proceedings of the chief commissioner's office in the judicial department*, Lucknow, Secretariat Record Office, MSS 2–11, 24 June 1856; Oudh, Secretariat Record Office, MS 173, 13 June 1856.

Studies

Muzaffar Alam, *The crisis of empire in Mughal North India. Awadh and the Punjab, 1707–1748*, Oxford 1986; George C. M. Birdwood, *The industrial arts of India*, London 1880; A. P. Charles, *Monograph on gold and silver ware produced in the United Provinces*, Allahabad 1905; Ananda K. Coomaraswamy, *The arts and crafts of India and Ceylon*, New York 1964; Cuthbert Collin Davies, *Warren Hastings and Oudh*, Oxford 1939; Alois Anton Führer, *The monumental antiquities and inscriptions. In the North-Western Provinces and Oudh*, Allahabad 1891, repr. Delhi 1969; Charles William Gwynne, *Monograph on the manufacture of wire and tinsel in the United Provinces*, Allahabad 1910; Mohammad Habib and Khaliq Ahmad Nizami (eds.), *A comprehensive history of India*, vol. 5, *The Delhi sultanate* (A.D. 1206–1526), New Delhi 1970, repr. 1982; William Hoey, *A monograph on trade and manufactures in northern India*, Lucknow 1880; Iqtidar Alam Khan, *The political biography of a Mughal noble. Munʿim Khan Khan-i Khanan, 1497–1575*, New Delhi 1973; Francis Robinson, *The ʿulama of Farangi Mahall and Islamic culture in South Asia*, London and New Delhi 2001; Ashirbadi Lal Srivastav, *The first two nawabs of Awadh*, Agra 1954; Madhu Trivedi, Invoking sorrow. *Marsiya* in North India, in Satish Saberwal and Supriya Verma (eds.), *Tradition in motion. Religion and society in history* (Oxford and Delhi 2005), 127–46; Madhu Trivedi, A genre of composite creativity. Marsiya and its performance in Awadh, in Mushirul Hasan and Asim Roy (eds.), *Living together separately. Cultural India in history and politics* (Oxford and New Delhi 2005), 194–221; Madhu Trivedi, *The making of the Awadh culture*, Delhi 2010, repr. 2013; Nelson Wright, *Catalogue of the coins in the Indian Museum, Calcutta*, vol. 2, Oxford 1907.

Madhu Trivedi

M

Maghribī, Aḥmad Khattū

Aḥmad Khattū Maghribī (b. Delhi, 737/1336; d. Sarkhej, 10 Shawwal 849/9 January 1446), popularly known as Ganjbakhsh (bestower of treasures), was a Ṣūfī (spritual preceptor) of the Maghribī *silsila* (spiritual order) who came to be recognised as the spiritual protector of the regional sultanate of Gujarat (r. 810–980/1407–1573). The Maghribī *silsila*, founded by Shaykh Abū Madyan Shuʿayb (d. c 594/1198) in North Africa, had a minor presence in the Indian subcontinent. Ahmad Khattū is arguably the best known Ṣūfī from the Maghribī tradition in the region. Most of our information about his life and teachings comes from two texts, *Tuḥfat al-majālis* ("The gift of assemblies") and *Mirqāt al-wūṣūl ilā Llāh wa-l-Rasūl* ("The ladder to union with God and his Messenger"), written by his close disciples Maḥmūd Irajī and Muḥammad Qāsim, respectively, about the middle of the ninth/fifteenth century. Conceived as Aḥmad Khattū's *malfūẓāt* (recordings of his public assemblies), the two texts vary considerably in their narrative structure and form. Aḥmad Khattū himself wrote little: he is believed to have composed a *risāla* (treatise) on Maghribī Ṣūfīs and to have written some Persian poetry, examples of which can be found in his disciples' texts.

Aḥmad Khattū's disciples report that he was born into a noble family in Delhi but was separated from his family in a dust storm. He eventually settled with Bābā Isḥāq, a Ṣūfī of the Maghribī order, in the village of Khattū, near Nagaur in northwestern Rajasthan. Bābā Isḥāq adopted the young Aḥmad, facilitated his education in Delhi, and initiated him into the spiritual path of the Maghribī *silsila.* After the death of his spiritual mentor in 766/1374–5, Aḥmad Khattū is believed to have left Khattū and travelled widely in the central Islamic lands on pilgrimage. Maḥmūd Irajī and Muḥammad Qāsim also give extensive accounts of the Ṣūfī's travels in Samarqand, where he accompanied the Mongol ruler Amīr Tīmūr (r. 771–807/1370–1405) following the latter's attack on Delhi in 800/1398. In this account, Aḥmad Khattū, initially taken prisoner by Tīmūr, was credited with interceding on behalf of Delhi residents and saving them from Tīmūr's wrath.

Aḥmad Khattū probably migrated to Gujarat early in the ninth/fifteenth century, around the time Ẓafar Khān, the representative of the Delhi sultan and future sultan of Gujarat (r. 810–3/1407–11) was consolidating his own political authority in the region. The *Tuḥfat* and the *Mirqāt* emphasise that it was upon Ẓafar Khān's request that the Ṣūfī decided to settle in Gujarat. Aḥmad Khattū established his residence in Sarkhej, about six miles southwest of the future capital Aḥmadābād, built by Sulṭān Aḥmad Shāh (r. 813–46/1411–42) in 813/1411 with the advice and blessings of the Ṣūfī. In the following decades, the prestige of Aḥmad Khattū grew along with the prosperity of the Gujarat sultanate. Upon Aḥmad's death, Sulṭān Muḥammad Shāh II (r. 846–55/1442–51) commissioned the building of a mausoleum in Sarkhej, which was completed by his successor, Sulṭān Quṭb al-Dīn Aḥmad II (r. 855–63/1451–58). The Ṣūfī's tomb was expanded considerably over subsequent decades by Sulṭān Maḥmūd Begṛā (r. 863–917/1458–1511), who added to the Sarkhej complex several palatial structures including pavilions, quarters for royal men and women, and royal funerary structures. His son Sulṭān Muẓaffar Shāh II (r. 917–932/1511–26) and his son's wife Rānī Rāj Bāi (d. 999/1590?) were buried alongside Sulṭān Maḥmūd Begṛā, in the tomb complex. The combination of textual and architectural commemoration of Aḥmad Khattū in the second half of the ninth/fifteenth century was critical in solidifying in later texts and popular memory the Ṣūfī's position as one of the prominent *awliyā'* (friends [of God]) of Gujarat.

Bibliography

Mumtaz Currim, Ahmadabad. *Dargahs* of Shaykh Ahmad Khattu and Hazrat Shah Alam, in Mumtaz Currim and George Michell (eds.), *Dargahs. Abodes of the saints* (Mumbai 2004), 80–93 (esp. 80–8); ʿAbd al-Ḥaqq Muḥaddith Dihlavī, *Akhbār al-akhyār fī asrār al-abrār*, ed. ʿAlīm Ashraf Khān (Tehran 1383sh/2004–5), 314–21, trans. into Urdu by Mawlānā Muḥammad Fāḍil, *Akhbār al-akhyār* (Delhi 1994), 339–49; Maḥmūd b. Saʿīd Īrajī, *Tuḥfat al-majālis*, Ahmedabad, Gujarat, Pir Mohammed Shah Library and Research Institute, MS 1231, trans. into Urdu by Mawlānā Sayyid Abū Ẓafar Nadwī, *Tuḥfat al-majālis*, Ahmedabad 2005[3]; Aḥmad Khattū, *Risāla-yi Aḥmadiyya fī manaqib al-mashāʾikh al-maghribiyya*, Sarkhej, Gujarat, Shaykh Ahmad Khattu Roza Library, MS 733 (modern copy from the original MS prepared by Ahmed Eusufji Patel, n.d.); Sikandar b. Muḥammad Manjhū, *Mirʾāt-i Sikandarī*, ed. S. C. Misra and M. L. Rahman (Baroda 1961), 34, 56–8; Khaliq Ahmad Nizami, Shaykh Ahmad Maghribi as a great historical personality of medieval Gujarat, in *Medieval India. A miscellany* (London 1975), 3:234–59; Khaliq Ahmad Nizami, Aḥmad Khattū, *EIr* (updated version is available at www.iranicaonline.org/articles/ahmad-khattu-also-known-as-ahmad-magrebi-famous-medieval-gujarati-saint-whose-name-is-associated-with-the-foundation); Muḥammad Qāsim, *Mirqāt al-wuṣūl ilā Llāh wa-l-Rasūl*, ed. Nisar Ahmad Ansari, New Delhi 2004, trans. into Urdu by Mawlānā Sayyid Abū Ẓafar Nadwī, *Sīrat-i Aḥmadiyya*, Gandhinagar n.d.

Jyoti Gulati Balachandran

Maḥmūdābād family

The **Maḥmūdābād family** was a leading landed family of North India that was prominent in public life under the Mughals, the *nawwāb*s (an honorific title for semi-autonomous Muslim rulers of princely states) of Awadh, and the British. These Ṣiddīqī *shaykh*s trace their descent from the first caliph, Abū Bakr al-Ṣiddīq (d. 13/634), through Naṣrallāh, a *qāḍī* of Baghdad, who is said to have come in the seventh/thirteenth century to India, where his descendants were *qāḍī*s of Delhi. In the eighth/fourteenth century, Qāḍī Naṣrallāh's great-grandson, Qāḍī

Nuṣratallāh, acquired land in Awadh, and, under the Mughals, his descendants Nawwāb Dawūd Khān, Nawwāb Maḥmūd Khān, and Bāyazīd Khān rose high in the imperial service. Nawwāb Maḥmūd Khān founded, in the Sitapur district of Awadh, in the time of the Mughal emperor Akbar, the town of Maḥmūdābād, which gave its name to the junior branch of the family, which has been dominant over the past 150 years and whose palace lies on its outskirts.

1. Nawwāb ʿAlī Khān

In recent times, the family's fortunes were established by Nawwāb ʿAlī Khān (d. 1858) a Shīʿī poet, scholar, and able estate manager. Between 1838 and 1858 he took advantage of the disturbed conditions of Awadh to add to the few lands he inherited, using all means at his disposal, until he possessed what Sleeman described as a "magnificent estate" (Reeves, *Sleeman*, 269–73). Although he played a prominent part in the Mutiny against the British of 1857–8, the Maḥmūdābād estate that was his great achievement did pass in large part to his son, Amīr Ḥasan Khān (d. 1903). The British policy of clemency and their aim of creating an Indian aristocracy in Awadh thus enabled the family to consolidate the gains made under the Awadh regime and to emerge in the late nineteenth century as one of the largest Muslim landlords in India.

2. Rājā Amīr Ḥasan Khān

The wealth of the Maḥmūdābād estate allowed the descendants of Nawwāb ʿAlī Khān to play a leading role in Indian and Muslim affairs under the British. Rājā Amīr Ḥasan Khān's activities were those of a cultivated landed gentleman. He followed literary pursuits, in particular writing elegies on the Shīʿī Imām al-Ḥusayn (d. 61/680), and was a great public benefactor in Awadh, supporting schools and a public library. In 1871 he became vice-president and, from 1881 to 1892, president of the British Indian Association, the organisation of the Awadh *taʿalluqdār*s (landlords in Awadh who, after the Mutiny, were granted permanent property rights in their estates). He also served on the viceroy's council and prominently opposed the Indian National Congress.

3. Muḥammad ʿAlī Muḥammad Khān

The raja's son, Muḥammad ʿAlī Muḥammad Khān (d. 1931), played a more varied and even more distinguished role in public life. He maintained the traditions established by his father and gave generously to educational projects such as Lucknow University and Lucknow Medical College and founded the Lucknow Madrasat al-Wāʿiẓīn. He not only gave generously to the Muhammadan Anglo-Oriental College at Aligarh but was also active in the movement to raise funds to transform the College into Aligarh Muslim University, of which he was the first vice-chancellor, from 1920 to 1928. He was president of the British Indian Association (1917–21, 1930–1), and served on the United Provinces Legislative Council (1904–9) and the governor-general's Council (1907–20). From 1920–5 he was the first home minister in the United Provinces government and consequently had the embarrassing task of imprisoning many personal friends, who were supporters of the Indian National Congress and the Khilāfat Movement. In 1925 he was given the title of Maharaja.

More important were Muḥammad ʿAlī's activities as a leading Muslim politician and patron of other politicians. He became involved in the politics of protest for the first time in 1909, demanding joint electorates in the negotiations leading to the Morley-Minto Council reforms (Indian Councils Act 1909), when the majority of North Indian Muslims were asking for separate ones. From 1909 to 1917 he was closely associated with the radical wing of Muslim politics. He took the part of the radicals in the Muslim university movement; he protested vigorously to government over the Kanpur mosque incident of 1913, when prolonged firing on a Muslim mob protesting against the demolition of part of the mosque in order to widen a road prompted the first signs of widespread serious criticism of British rule amongst North Indian Muslims; and he helped negotiate the pact between the All-India Muslim League and the Indian National Congress at Lucknow in 1916, by which time his political stance had so annoyed the government that it threatened to confiscate his estates. From 1915 to 1919 he was president of the All-India Muslim League and presided over its sessions in 1917, 1918, and 1928. Throughout much of his life he helped to support, financially and in other ways, young men who were entering politics, such as the lawyer Sayyid Wazīr Ḥasan (d. 1947), secretary of the All-India Muslim League in 1912–9; Rājā Ghulām Ḥusayn (d. 1917), editor of *New Era*, a newspaper modelled after Muḥammad ʿAlī's (d. 1931) *Comrade*, which aimed to help the "Young Party" take control of the Muslim League; Chawdharī Khāliq al-Zamān (d. 1973), whom he made, for a time, his education secretary; and the leading pan-Islamist politicians Muḥammad and Shawkat ʿAlī (d. 1938). His political support was not, however, restricted to Muslim League politicians; he was also a nationalist and counted amongst his friends leading members of Congress, such as Motilal (d. 1931) and Jawaharlal Nehru (d. 1964). In the last years of his life he strove, against Muslim opposition, to get his community behind the Nehru Report of 1928, Congress's response to the communal problem, which supported the creation of Muslim provinces but rejected separate representation for Muslims. Finally, he threw his weight behind the Muslim Nationalist Party, founded in 1929. He died in May 1931.

4. Rājā Muḥammad Amīr Aḥmad Khān

The maharaja was succeeded by his eldest son, Rājā Muḥammad Amīr Aḥmad Khān (d. 1973), who, although he began in politics as an Indian nationalist, soon became absorbed in Muslim separatism. In 1936, as a young man, he was drawn into the All-India Muslim League by Jinnah (Muḥammad ʿAlī Jinnāḥ, d. 1948), a close family friend for more than two decades and a trustee of the Maḥmūdābād estate. From 1937 to 1947 he played a leading role in the League as treasurer, chairman of the working committee, and major benefactor. In particular, he served as the link between the League and Muslim youth; he was president of the All-India Muslim Students Federation and devoted himself especially to organising the student forces that played a considerable role in the League's campaign for support. Amīr Aḥmad Khān did not, however, follow the League policy in all respects. A deeply religious man, in the 1940s he became involved in the Islāmī Jamāʿat, a short-lived organisation which advocated, against the view of Jinnah, that Pakistan should become an Islamic state.

After the partition of India, Amīr Aḥmad Khān lived for a time in Iraq and Pakistan. In 1957 he became a Pakistani citizen but played little part in the country's politics; he rejected President Ayyūb Khān's (r. 1958–69) demand that he refound the Muslim League on the grounds that Pakistan needed a party "with socialist aims wedded to Islamic justice" (daily *Dawn*, 15 October 1973). From 1968 until his death in 1973 he was the director of the Islamic Cultural Centre in London, where his principal achievements were completing the London Mosque, establishing an Islamic Science Foundation, and helping to launch plans for the World of Islam Exhibition of 1976.

5. Rājā Muḥammad Amīr Muḥammad Khān (Sulaymān)

Amīr Aḥmad Khān was succeeded by his son Rājā Muḥammad Amīr Muḥammad Khān (known as Sulaymān). Born in 1942, the latter was educated at La Martinière College (Lucknow) and Aldenham and Pembroke Colleges (Cambridge). On returning to India, he spent two sessions as a member of the Uttar Pradesh Legislative Assembly, but much of his life has been dominated by the struggle to achieve the return of the family estate, which had been taken over by the government of India in the Indo-Pakistan war of 1965 and declared enemy property in 1968. Despite decisions in the raja's favour in the Bombay High Court of 1987 and in the Indian Supreme Court of 2005, the greater part of the estate has not been returned.

6. The family and Twelver Shīʿism

The Maḥmūdābād family have not just been major players in provincial and national affairs in India, they have also been notable supporters of Twelver Shīʿism. This is manifested in the great Muḥarram ceremonies they have held at the family palace at Maḥmūdābād and in the town of Maḥmūdābād, as well as in the five religious trusts they have created to support them. It has been apparent especially in their support for the Madrasat al-Wāʿiẓīn, a seminary founded in 1919 that has sent missionaries throughout India, as well as Burma (Myanmar), West Africa, and the Middle East.

Bibliography

Brief family histories

Shaykh ʿAlī Ḥasan, *Taʾrīkh-i Maḥmūdābād*, MS, Mahmudabad, Muqeem Manzil, n.d.; Nurul Hasan Siddiqui, *Landlords of Agra and Avadh*, Lucknow 1950; H. R. Nevill, *Sitapur. A gazetteer, being volume XL of the gazetteers of Agra and Oudh*, Allahabad 1907.

Studies

Choudhry Khaliquzzaman, *Pathway to Pakistan*, Lahore 1961; Choudhry Khaliquzzaman, The raja of Mahmudabad. Some memories, in Cyril Henry Phillips and Mary Doreen Wainwright (eds.), *The partition of India. Policies and perspectives, 1935–47*, London 1970 (information on the political careers of Muḥammad ʿAlī Muḥammad and Amīr Aḥmad Khān); Muhammad Amir Ahmad Khan, Local nodes of a transitional network, in Justin Jones and Ali Usman Qasmi (eds.), *The Shīʿa in modern South Asia. Religion, history and politics*, New Delhi 2015, studies the workings and impact of the Madrasat al-Wāʿiẓīn; Muhammad Amir Ahmad Khan, *The making of North Indian Muslim identity. Poetry, politics and religion, 1850–1950*, Ph.D. diss., Cambridge University 2014 (a study of the poetry of Amīr Aḥmad Khān, amongst other things); Thomas R. Metcalf, *Land, landlords and the British Raj in India in the nineteenth century*, Berkeley 1979; Peter D. Reeves, *Landlords and governments in Uttar Pradesh. A study of their relations until zamindari abolition*, Delhi 1991; Peter D. Reeves (ed.), *Sleeman in Oudh*, Cambridge 1971, examines the family as *taʿalluqdārs*; Francis Robinson, *Jamal Mian. The life of Maulana Jamaluddin Abdul Wahab of Farangi Mahall, 1919–2012*, Karachi 2017 (Amīr Aḥmad Khān through the eyes of a lifelong personal and political friend); Francis Robinson, *Separatism among Indian Muslims. The politics of the United Provinces' Muslims 1860–1923*, Cambridge 1974.

Francis Robinson

Majdhūb, Muḥammad

Muḥammad b. Qamar al-Dīn Aḥmad **Majdhūb** (b. 1210/1795–6, d. 1247/1831) was the founder the Majdhūbiyya Ṣūfī order in Sudan, centred in the city of Sawākin, on the Red Sea coast.

Muḥammad Majdhūb was born into the Majādhīb, a prominent holy family of traders of the Jaʿaliyyūn tribal confederacy of the central Nile valley. He was sometimes known as al-Majdhūb al-Ṣaghīr (the younger), in contrast to his great-grandfather of the same name, Muḥammad b. ʿAlī (fl. c.1102/1690–1). It was the latter's son Ḥamad (d. 1190/1776–7) who first adopted the Shādhiliyya Ṣūfī order that his descendants followed. The Majādhīb became politically dominant in the region of al-Dāmar when the Sinnār sultanate declined, in the early thirteenth/late eighteenth century, but Majdhūb's branch of the family appears to have focused on trade and piety.

Born in the town of al-Matamma, Majdhūb moved between there and al-Dāmar in his youth, studying and teaching. In 1820, he met the founder of the Khatmiyya *ṭarīqa*, Muḥammad ʿUthmān al-Mīrghanī (d. 1852), and joined him on the *ḥajj* to Mecca. There, however, he broke with al-Mīrghanī, while developing a close relationship with al-Mīrghanī's teacher Aḥmad b. Idrīs (d. 1837). Majdhūb settled in Medina and remained there for about seven years.

The nature of Majdhūb's relation to Ibn Idrīs is disputed. In his letters, he accepted Ibn Idrīs as his *shaykh* but seems not to have adopted the *ṭarīqa* (Ṣūfī way or method) from him. Ibn Idrīs apparently considered Majdhūb an intellectual "brother." The later Idrīsīs insist that Majdhūb was a follower of Ibn Idrīs, while the Majādhīb deny this. The Ṣūfī *ṭarīqa*s of Ibn Idrīs and his students and that of Majdhūb, all Shādhilīs, are probably closely related but not directly linked. Majdhūb does not appear, in his writings, to have placed particular emphasis on the concept of the *ṭarīqa Muḥammadiyya* (the way of meeting with and following the Prophet) that was so important to the students of Ibn Idrīs.

In 1828, Majdhūb left Medina and returned to Sudan, settling in the port town of Sawākin. Although he had, despite his young age, acquired followers in Medina, it was in Sawākin that he established his reputation, marrying into local families and building a mosque that became the centre of his teaching. He attracted an increasing number of students from local families and from Beja tribes of the surrounding regions. The brotherhood, which he considered the Shādhiliyya but came to be known as the Majdhūbiyya after him, thus became primarily a local order in the Sawākin region.

Majdhūb left Sawākin after only two years there and returned in 1831 to his family home in al-Dāmar. That town had been evacuated after a conflict with the new Turko-Egyptian rulers of Sudan, but the ban had been lifted, and the family was allowed to return some years earlier. We do not know whether Majdhūb intended to settle permanently in al-Dāmar, because, only two months later, in 1831, he died, at the age of only about thirty-six. He left behind a considerable body of literature, much of it didactic or devotional.

BIBLIOGRAPHY

Albrecht Hofheinz, Encounters with a saint. Al-Majdhub, al-Mirghani and Ibn Idris as seen through the eyes of Ibrāhīm al-Rashīd, *Sudanic Africa* 1 (1990), 19–59; Albrecht Hofheinz, *Internalising Islam. Shaykh Muḥammad Majdhūb, scriptural Islam, and local context in the early nineteenth-century Sudan*, Ph.D. diss., University of Bergen 1996; Albrecht Hofheinz, Transcending the *madhhab*—in practice. The case of the Sudanese shaykh Muḥammad Majdhūb (1795/6–1831), *ILS* 10 (2003), 229–48; Albrecht Hofheinz, The writings of the Majādhīb, in R. Sean O'Fahey (ed.), *Arabic literature of Africa. 1. The writings of eastern Sudanic Africa to c. 1900* (Leiden 1994), 243–76; Ali Salih Karrar, *The Sufi brotherhoods in the Sudan*, London 1992; Awad al-Karsany and Abdallahi Osman, *Al Majdhubiyya and al Mikashfiyya. Two Sufi tariqas in the Sudan*, ed. M. W. Daly, Khartoum 1985; Mark Sedgwick, *Saints and sons. The making and remaking of the Rashīdi Aḥmadi Sufi order, 1799–2000*, Leiden 2005; Einar Thomassen and Bernd Radtke (eds.), *The letters of Aḥmad ibn Idrīs*, London 1993.

KNUT S. VIKØR

Mande (Mandingo)

Mande (Mandingo) is the name of a West African language and of its native speakers who, as a widely dispersed trading diaspora, were responsible for diffusing Islam throughout much of the western Sudan. Their homeland lay in the mediaeval empire of Mali, which, at its apogee in the eighth/fourteenth and ninth/fifteenth centuries, controlled the trans-Saharan trade in gold. Its kings converted to Islam, and the greatest of them, Mansā Mūsā I (r. 712–37/1312–37), made the *ḥajj*, stopping in Cairo in 724/1324. From Mali, Mande traders, known as Wangara, set out for other territories in search of gold and other commodities for exchange. The conversion of Yaji Dan Tsamiya (750–87/1349–85), ruler of the Kano kingdom, one of the principal Hausa city states and an important centre of trade in its own right, is attributed to the Wangara in the Kano Chronicle (Palmer, 58–98). Although the elites of the empire were Muslim—the ruling aristocracy, the traders, and clerical lineages—it is unlikely that the mass of the peasantry ever converted to Islam. With the decline of the empire, the rulers and warriors of successor states in the Mande heartland ceased to profess Islam, although there remained a significant minority of Muslim traders and clerics.

During its heyday, the expansion of Mali led to a movement of Mande traders and clerics westwards into the Senegambian region, a trend that continued after the empire's decline. Although the chronology is uncertain, the prominent cleric al-Ḥājj Salīm Suware (fl. seventh/thirteenth or ninth/fifteenth century) left the town of Diakha in the Masina region to found the town of Diakhaba on the Bafing River. Although he left no extant writings, his teachings had a fundamental influence throughout the Mande diaspora, characterised by what scholars have called the "Suwarian tradition" of Islamic learning. The tradition involved the separation of clerical activities from warfare and politics and advocated a peaceful co-existence between Muslims and non-Muslim rulers, an arrangement particularly apt in states and chiefdoms in which Muslims were a minority. The Akan goldfields to the south also attracted Mande trading and clerical elites. These communities, known as Jula

(Juula, Dyula) also followed the Suwarian tradition of Islamic learning. From the seventh/thirteenth to the thirteenth/nineteenth century these trading and clerical diasporas contributed to the expansion of Islam throughout West Africa, particularly in the savanna, although Islam remained a minority religion in most places, even amongst Mande speakers.

Paradoxically, the widespread Islamisation of the Mande was an unintended consequence of colonial rule, especially by the French (from the 1880s to 1960). The development of a plantation economy accompanied by the rapid proliferation of new urban centres in the forest zone of Côte d'Ivoire stimulated a steady flow of migrants from the northern savanna region. These migrants were integrated into an urban Jula culture marked simultaneously by Islam and the Mande language. Conversion to Islam was an essential step for integrating into these communities, and the new converts then spread the religion back into the hinterland, especially in French Sudan (now Mali). This association between Islam and the Mande language has not only been perpetuated but also radically transformed throughout the past millennium.

Bibliography

Robert Launay, *Beyond the stream. Islam and society in a West African town*, Berkeley 1992; Nehemia Levtzion, *Ancient Ghana and Mali*, London 1973; H.R. Palmer, The Kano chronicle, *Journal of the Royal Anthropological Institute of Great Britain and Ireland* 38 (1908), 58–98; Brian James Peterson, *Islamization from below. The making of Muslim communities in rural French Sudan, 1880–1960*, New Haven 2011; Lamin Sanneh, *The Jakhanke. The history of an Islamic clerical people of the Senegambia*, London 1979; Ivor Wilks, The Juula and the expansion of Islam into the forest, in Nehemiah Levtzion and Randall L. Pouwels (eds.), *The history of Islam in Africa* (Athens OH, Oxford, and Claremont, South Africa 2000), 93–115; Ivor Wilks, The transmission of Islamic learning in the Western Sudan, in Jack Goody (ed.), *Literacy in traditional societies* (Cambridge 1968), 161–97.

Robert Launay

Maryam al-Adhraʿiyya

Maryam bt. Aḥmad b. Muḥammad b. Ibrāhīm b. Ibrāhīm b. Dāwūd b. Ḥāzim al-Adhraʿī al-Miṣrī al-Ḥanafī, known as al-Shaykha **Maryam al-Adhraʿiyya** (b. c.719/1319, d. 805/1402–3), was a reliable authority for various *ḥadīth* compilations from diverse genres.

The details of Maryam's life are based on Ibn Ḥajar's *Muʿjam al-Shaykha Maryam*, which is available at Dār al-Kutub al-Miṣriyya, in Cairo (*ḥadīth* no. 1421). Maryam was born in Cairo to a family descended from the Adhri(u)ʿāt (present-day Dirʿā), a village in Syria. No biographical dictionary mentions a husband, so it is possible that she never married. Ibn Ḥajar gives her the *kunya* Umm ʿĪsā.

Maryam's father took her to assemblies of *ḥadīth* scholars, although we do not know her age when she first attended. In the *Muʿjam*, however, there is a reference to two teachers who died in 722/1322, when Maryam was three (Ibn Ḥajar, 41a, 63a). Al-Fāsī mentions that Maryam heard al-Wānī (d. 727/1326), when she was five (al-Fāsī, 1:64), indicating that her career as a traditionalist (*muḥadditha)* began early.

Five of Maryam's teachers are named in the biographical sources; all had died by the time she was sixteen. She was the last to transmit from most of these scholars (Ibn Ḥajar, *Inbāʾ*, 2:254). Both Abū l-ʿAlāʾ al-Faraḍī (d. 700/1300) and Maryam heard *ḥadīth*s from al-Dabbūsī (d. 729/1328). There is a span of a century between the deaths of al-Faraḍī and

Maryam, producing an example of what is known in *ḥadīth* literature as *al-sābiq* and *al-lāḥiq* (early and late [students of transmitters]) (al-Maqrīzī, 470). Al-Fāsī asserts that Maryam was, in this respect, a unique example amongst Egyptian teachers (al-Fāsī, 1:65).

Maryam began her education—especially by attending the hearing sessions of scholars—at an early age. She mentions in the *Muʿjam* that she heard a certain *ḥadīth* from her teacher Abū l-Nūn al-Dabbūsī (d. 729/1328) in the year 726/1325, when she was seven (Ibn Ḥajar, 3a).

This phenomenon of transmission authority passing from the very old to the very young has been observed in other cases as well during the Mamlūk period (Sayeed, 88). Twenty-eight of the 319 teachers (almost 9%) mentioned in *Muʿjam al-Shaykha Maryam* are female. The dates of death of four of them are unknown, but the confirmed death dates for the other women indicate that Maryam's contact with them must have occurred when she was young.

Comparison with male biographies in the *Muʿjam* shows that the criteria used to justify the inclusion of these female teachers were the same as those used for the male teachers. Female teachers included in the *Muʿjam* are described as being from families known for a tradition of learning and producing religious knowledge. Maryam heard *ḥadīths* from teachers who were also skilled in medicine (Ibn Ḥajar, 57a, 64a).

From the *Muʿjam* we learn that Maryam travelled to Damascus before 736/1335 to take *ḥadīth* from ʿAbd al-ʿAzīz b. ʿAbd al-Laṭīf al-Ḥarrānī (d. 763/1362) (Ibn Ḥajar, 44a) and perhaps other scholars (the *Muʿjam* treats many teachers who either lived or died in Damascus).

Maryam received *ḥadīth* also from five members of the al-Sunhājī family: Muʾnisa bt. ʿAlī (d. 732/1332) (Ibn Ḥajar, 74a), her son ʿAbdallāh b. ʿAlī b. ʿUmar al-Ṣunhājī (d. 724/1324) (Ibn Ḥajar, 38a), ʿĀʾisha bt. ʿAlī b. ʿUmar al-Ṣunhājī (d. 739/1338) (Ibn Ḥajar, 53b), Khadīja bt. ʿAlī b. ʿUmar al-Ṣunhājī (d. 734/1334) (Ibn Ḥajar, 29b), and Hājar bt. ʿAlī b. ʿUmar al-Ṣunhājī (d. 777/1375) (Ibn Ḥajar, 74b).

Although Maryam probably convened assemblies for many students, she appears in the biographies of only twenty-three, three of them female. Twenty of these students are taken and gathered from al-Sakhāwī's *al-Ḍawʾ*.

Maryam's teaching career indicates that, in the years between childhood and advanced age, she must have continued her search for knowledge by studying the works for which she was awarded *ijāza*s (official permission) to transmit to her students, without undertaking any teaching activities; that is, she did not teach during the period of her sexual maturity.

The various accounts tell us that Maryam conducted her activities in a variety of settings with both men and women. After being authorised by her teachers to transmit the knowledge she acquired from them, she went on to teach both men and women. She was thus empowered by certain conditions under which there was no gender barrier to acquiring religious knowledge and instructing others.

Amongst the works that Maryam transmitted are major *ḥadīth* collections, including the *Ṣaḥīḥ* of Muslim (d. 261/875), which she heard from her teacher al-Wādī Āshī (d. 749/1348). She also heard from her teacher al-Wānī his *Mashyakha* (for a list of other works she heard from her teachers, see Ibn Ḥajar, *Majmaʿ*, 2:560–70). The subjects covered by these compilations emphasise that her reputation was based on the transmission of a range of works in diverse areas of Islamic knowledge. She transmitted personal collections of *ḥadīth*, *musnad*s (*ḥadīth* collections arranged by *isnād*), *al-Amālī* ("The dictations"), *al-Arbaʿūn* ("The Forty [Traditions]"), *al-Fawāʾid* ("Collection of wise sayings"), *al-Muwāfaqāt* ("The reconciliations"), and *Sudāsiyyāt* (*ḥadīth* collections that have six narrators between the Prophet and compiler of the collection), as well as works on ascetic piety, such as the *Makārim al-akhlāq* ("The best manners") by al-Ṭabarānī (d. 360/971). Maryam also transmitted *mashyakha*s (collections of biographies of the teachers of a certain scholar), including that of her teacher al-Wānī.

The *Muʿjam* has no list of the books and *ḥadīth* collections that Maryam transmitted (for this list, see Ibn Ḥajar, *al-Majmaʿ*, 2559–71; Ibn ʿAzzūz, 400–4). It is clear from this list that Maryam's most notable lectures addressed Muslim's collections of *ḥadīth*. She was, however, famous also for other collections, foremost amongst them *al-Ḥadīth al-musalsal bi-l-awwaliyya* ("The *ḥadīth* that is arranged by the order in which the students hears it from his teacher"). Ibn Ḥajar, amongst others, is noted for having heard her recite *al-Awwaliyya*.

Maryam died in 805/1402, at the age of eighty-four. Ibn Ḥajar praises her as a pious and chaste woman who had a great love of knowledge (Ibn Ḥajar, *Inbāʾ*, 2:254–5).

Bibliography

Sources

Ibn Fahd al-Makkī, *Laḥẓ al-alḥāẓ bi-dhayl ṭabaqāt al-ḥuffāẓ*, ed. Zakariyyāʾ ʿUmayrāt (Beirut 1998), 1:142; al-Fāsī, *Dhayl al-taqyīd fī ruwāt al-sunan wa-l-masānīd*, ed. Kamāl Yūsuf al-Ḥūt (Beirut 1990), 1:64; Ibn Ḥajar al-ʿAsqalānī, *Dhayl al-durar al-kāmina*, ed. ʿAdnān Darwīsh (Cairo 1992), 138; Ibn Ḥajar al-ʿAsqalānī, *Inbāʾ al-ghumr bi-abnāʾ al-ʿumr*, ed. Ḥasan Ḥabashī (Cairo 1969, repr. 1998), 2:245–6; Ibn Ḥajar al-ʿAsqalānī, *al-Majmaʿ al-muʾassis lil-muʿjam al-mufahras*, ed. Yūsuf al-Marʿashlī (Beirut 1992), 2:559–571 (no. 270); Ibn Ḥajar al-ʿAsqalānī, *Muʿjam al-Shaykha Maryam*, Cairo, Dār al-Kutub al-Miṣriyya, MS 1421; Ibn al-ʿImād, *Shadharāt al-dhahab*, eds. ʿAbd al-Qādir al-Arnāʾūṭ and Maḥmūd al-Arnāʾūṭ (Beirut 1982), 7:54; ʿUmar Riḍā Kaḥḥāla, *Aʿlām al-nisāʾ fī ʿālamay al-gharb wa-l-Islām* (Beirut 1959), 5:37; al-Maqrīzī, *Durar al-ʿuqūd al-farīda fī tarājim al-aʿyān al-mufīda*, ed. Maḥmūd al-Jalīlī (Beirut 2002), 3:469–70; al-Sakhāwī, *al-Ḍawʾ al-lāmiʿ li-ahl al-qarn al-tāsiʿ* (Beirut n.d.), 12:124 (no. 757); al-Ziriklī, *al-Aʿlām* (Beirut 2002), 7:210.

Studies

Muḥammad Ibn ʿAzzūz, *Juhūd al-marʾa al-Dimashqiyya fī riwāyat al-ḥadīth*, Damascus 2004; Mohsen Abdelaty Haredy Khalifa, *Female transmission of ḥadīth in the Mamluk period. An annotated edition and study of Ibn Ḥajar's Muʿjam ash-Shaykhah Maryam*, Ph.D. diss., Leiden University 2014; Asma Sayeed, Women in *ḥadīth* transmission. Two case studies from Mamluk Damascus, *SI* 95 (2002), 71–94.

Mohsen Haredy

Mīr Jaʿfar

Mīr Jaʿfar ʿAlī Khān (also Mīr Muḥammad Jaʿfar Khān, b. 1102/1691?, d. 1178/1765) was nawab—Pers. *nawwāb*, Bengali *nabāb*, from Ar. *nuwwāb*, pl. of *nāʾib*, lit., deputy, a Mughal title for provincial governors and quasi-autonomous rulers in India—of Bengal between 1170/1757 and 1174/1760–1 and from 1176/1763 until his death. His gubernatorial career marked the effective transition, often dubbed a "revolution" by contemporaries, from late Mughal to English East

India Company rule in eastern India. He is remembered more widely for his role in the battle of Plassey (Palashi, 1170/1757), the event traditionally viewed as inaugurating British expansion in the Subcontinent.

Mīr Jaʿfar's origins are obscure. The son of one Sayyid Aḥmad Najafī (date of death unknown), he migrated from Ottoman Iraq to Mughal Bengal as a mercenary sometime during the *ṣūbadārī* (governorship) of Nawwāb Shujāʿ al-Dīn Muḥammad Khān (r. 1139–52/1727–39). As a commander in the nawab's army, from 1174/1734 he led several punitive expeditions against European merchants, Maratha (Marāṯʹhā) raiders, and insubordinate officials. Awarded high military rank by Nawwāb ʿAlīvardī Khān (r. 1153–69/1740–56), other important postings followed: *fawjdārī* (district command) in two garrisons, *nāʾib-niẓāmat* (deputyship) in Orissa, and *mīr bakhshī*, the highest military-administrative office. He was to lose all his positions, although he would later regain some of them. Occasional tensions aside, his loyalty to ʿAlīvardī's regime was strong and was strengthened further by marriage ties. At the death of ʿAlīvardī and the accession of his grandson Sirāj al-Dawla (r. 1169–70/1756–7), Mīr Jaʿfar vowed, hand on Qurʾān, to continue faithful service.

The oath proved false. He turned "one untrue to the salt" *(namak-ḥarāmī)*—that is, a traitor—a volte-face on Sirāj al-Dawla's regime that arose from a twofold circumstance. Relations disintegrated between an assertive new nawab and his grandees at the provincial capital, Murshidabad. Meanwhile, downriver on the Hooghly River, a distributary of the Ganges, the growing arrogance of British traders in Calcutta demanded an aggressive response. Yet Sirāj al-Dawla's assault on the Company's Fort William only exacerbated matters. The British regrouped, finding chance relief in a military build-up in India meant initially for global war against the French. A Murshidabad clique led by Mīr Jaʿfar and an emboldened Company under Colonel Robert Clive (d. 1188/1774) then agreed to depose the nawab together and bring "revolution" to Bengal. On 5 Shawwāl 1170/23 June 1757, Sirāj al-Dawla's army met Clive's forces in the village of Palashi. The prearranged "conspiracy" ensured British victory, as the nawab's most powerful general refused to fight. Treated with reverence in British imperial historiography, the battle in fact amounted to a half-day scuffle, thanks to Mīr Jaʿfar.

Succeeding Sirāj al-Dawla as nawab, Mīr Jaʿfar styled himself Shujāʿ al-Mulk Ḥusām al-Dawla Mīr Jaʿfar ʿAlī Khān Bahādur Mahābat-Jang, the last title an appropriation of ʿAlīvardī's honorific, meaning "terror of war." He plainly desired a new regime akin to the old. Simultaneously, though, he and his son oversaw a purge of his former master's clan. Delivering vast fortunes and privileges to Company officials, Mīr Jaʿfar nevertheless struggled to meet their demands. With further British takeover of revenue sources, his *ṣūbadārī* fell into desperate arrears. Once his patron, Clive, left India, the Company engineered a "second" revolution (1174/1760). On accusations of misrule, some accurate, others not, he was forced to abdicate in favour of his son-in-law. Three years later, the British unseated him, too. In the lead-up to another victorious battle against *nawwābī* and allied Mughal forces at Buxar (Bakshar, 1178/1764), the Company made Mīr Jaʿfar nawab once more. Within months the Company became Mughal *dīwān* (fiscal administrator) of Bengal. Mīr Jaʿfar's descendants continued to occupy the *nawwābī masnad* (seat) but were kept firmly at British beck and call.

Mīr Jaʿfar is the quisling par excellence of South Asian history and memory. His name remains a familiar slur, synonymous with "betrayer." This resulted partly from late colonial nationalist narratives. "Becoming nabab means no more concern for money!" bellows Mirjjāphar in *Sirājaddaulā* (1905), Girishchandra Ghosh's Bengali play dramatising the birth of British rule. Witness to the age of "revolution" *(inqilāb)*, the historian Ghulām Ḥusayn Ṭabāṭabāʾī (d. 1212/1797–8) had little praise for Mīr Jaʿfar's character or his rule. He portrayed a nawab increasingly indifferent to "worldly affairs" and given to pleasures—intoxicants while at court and ox flesh while on tour.

Bibliography

Sources

John Caillaud, *A narrative of what happened in Bengal, in the year MDCCLX, wherein is contained, an account of the revolution which took place at that time*, London 1764; *Calendar of Persian correspondence, being letters, referring mainly to affairs in Bengal, which passed between some of the Company's servants and Indian rulers and notables*, 11 vols., Calcutta 1911–69; *Fort William–India House correspondence, and other contemporary papers relating thereto*, 21 vols., Delhi 1949–85; *Girishchandrēr Sirājaddawlā*, ed. B͟habānigopāl Sānyāl, Calcutta 1975; Samuel Charles Hill (ed.), *Bengal in 1756–1757. A selection of public and private papers dealing with the affairs of the British in Bengal during the reign of Siraj-uddaula*, 3 vols., London 1905, repr. 1968; John Zephaniah Holwell, *An address to the proprietors of East India Stock, setting forth the unavoidable necessity and real motives for the revolution in Bengal, in 1760*, London 1764; *ʿIbrat-i arbāb-i baṣar*, London, British Library, MS Or. 2040; India Office Records, London, British Library; Karam ʿAlī, *Tārīkh-i Bangāl va Bihār Sada-yi Hīzhdahum. Muzaffar-nāma (Bihar and Bengal in the 18th century. A critical edition and translation of Muzaffarnama. A contemporary history)*, ed. and trans. Shayesta Khan, Patna and New Delhi 1992; Orme Manuscripts, London, British Library; Persian correspondence, New Delhi, National Archives of India; Robert Clive Papers, Aberystwyth, National Library of Wales; Salīmallāh, *Tārīkh-i Bangāla*, ed. S. M. Imām al-Dīn, Dacca 1979; Luke Scrafton, *Observations on Mr. Vansittart's narrative*, London 1766; Luke Scrafton, *Reflections on the government of Indostan. With a short sketch of the history of Bengal, from the years 1739 to 1756, and an account of the English affairs to 1758*, Edinburgh 1761 and London 1763; Ghulām Ḥusayn Khān Ṭabāṭabāʾī, *Siyar al-mutakhkhirīn. Dar bayān-i tārīkh-i mamlakat-i Hind az ibtidāʾ-yi sana 1118 hijrī tā 1194 hijrī*, ed. ʿAbd al-Majīd, 2 vols., Calcutta 1833; Ghulām Ḥusayn Salīm, *Riyāḍ al-ṣalāṭīn. Tārīkh-i Bangāla*, ed. ʿAbd al-Ḥaq ʿĀbid, Calcutta 1890; Henry Vansittart, *A narrative of the transactions in Bengal from the year 1760, to the year 1764*, 3 vols., London 1766; William Watts, *Memoirs of the revolution in Bengal, anno. dom. 1757, by which Meer Jaffeir was raised to the government of that province, together with those of Bahar and Orixa*, London 1760; Yusūf ʿAlī Khān, *Tārīkh-i Bangāla-yi Mahābat-Jangī*, ed. ʿAbd al-Subḥān, Calcutta 1969.

Studies

Partha Chatterjee, *The black hole of empire. History of a global practice of power*, Princeton 2012; Nandalal Chatterji, *Mir Qasim. Nawab of Bengal, 1760–1763*, Allahabad 1935; Sushīl Chawdhurī, *Nabābi āmalē Murshidābād*, Calcutta 2004; Kalikinkar Datta, *Alivardi and his times*, Calcutta 1939, 1963²; Abdul Majed Khan, *The transition in Bengal, 1756–1775. A study of Seiyid Muhammad Reza Khan*, Cambridge 1969; Purna Ch. Majumdar (comp.), *The Musnud of Murshidabad (1704–1904), being a synopsis of the history of Murshidabad for the last two centuries, to which are appended notes of places and objects of interest*, Umraoganj 1905; Peter James Marshall, *Bengal. The British bridgehead, eastern India, 1740–1828*, Cambridge 1987; Subhas Chandra Mukhopadhyay, *The career of Rajah Durlabhram Mahindra (Rai-Durlabh), diwan of Bengal, 1710–1770*, Varanasi 1974; Nikhilnāth Rāy, *Aitihāsik chitra. Murshidābād-kāhinī*, Calcutta 1978; Atul Chandra Roy, *The career of Mir Jafar Khan (1757–65 A.D.*,

Calcutta 1953; Robert Travers, *Ideology and empire in eighteenth-century India. The British in Bengal*, Cambridge 2007.

Rishad Choudhury

Mughulṭāy b. Qilīj

ʿAlāʾ al-Dīn Abū ʿAbdallāh **Mughulṭāy b. Qilīj** b. ʿAbdallāh al-Bakjarī al-Ḥikrī al-Ḥanafī (b. 689–762/1290–1361) was a historian and an expert in *ḥadīth* and genealogy (Ibn Ḥajar, 4:352; Ibn Taghrībirdī, 9:762). Of Turkish origin, he was born in Egypt and lived in Cairo (al-Suyūṭī, 133) and belonged to the Arabised class of *awlād al-nās* (lit., sons of the people), the descendants of the Mamlūk elite. Amongst his teachers were ʿAlī b. ʿUmar al-Wānī (d. 735/1334–5), Yūsuf b. ʿUmar al-Khatanī (d. 731/1331), and Yūnis al-Dabābīsī (d. 729/1329). He also frequently visited the chief judge Jalāl al-Dīn al-Qazwīnī (d. 739/1338), who interceded in 734/1334 with the sultan al-Nāṣir Muḥammad b. Qalāwūn (third reign, 709–41/1310–41) to obtain him a professorship of *ḥadīth* in the al-Ẓāhiriyya *madrasa*. Despite the opposition he encountered in this appointment from local scholars who attacked him over his competence on *ḥadīth*, he kept his position (al-Ṣafadī, *Aʿyan*, 3:276). He also taught at the citadel mosque, the Ṣarghatmishiyya *madrasa*, and the al-Ṣāliḥiyya mosque in Cairo. The sources say that many people attended his classes but that local religious scholars attacked him for his teaching and writings, although we do not know exactly why (Ibn Ḥajar, 4:352).

His only nonreligious literary work, *al-Wāḍiḥ al-mubīn fī dhikr man ustushhida min al-muḥibbīn* ("The accurate and clear in speaking of the lovers who became martyrs," Beirut 1997), made him the victim of a scandal and earned him a prison sentence. *Al-Wāḍiḥ al-mubīn* comprises alphabetically arranged stories about those who died of pure passionate love (*ʿishq*) and thus became martyrs, in accord with the apocryphal saying of the Prophet, "He who loves passionately, remains chaste, and dies for this love dies as a martyr" (Mughulṭāy, *al-Wāḍiḥ al-mubīn*, 17) A long introduction precedes these *akhbār* (stories) and discusses the reliability of this saying (Giffen, 34). According to al-Suyūṭī, the attacks on Mughulṭāy began in 745/1344–5, when the scholar Khalīl b. Kaykaldī al-ʿAlāʾī (d. 760 or 761/1359 or 1360) took a stand against him because of a passage in this work in which he was accused of slandering ʿĀʾisha, the favourite wife of the Prophet, for mentioning the possibility that she committed adultery (Mughulṭāy, *al-Wāḍiḥ al-mubīn*, 28; Manjarrez Walker and Sells, 55–7) because he included in his works poems that offended public morality. Mughulṭāy refused to plead guilty, and the matter was brought before the Ḥanbalī judge al-Muwaffaq (d. 800/1398), who arrested him. His book was removed from the market and burned publicly, but the *amīr* al-Jankalī b. al-Bābā (d. 746/1345) later had him released from prison (Ibn Ḥajar, 4:352).

Several of his books reflect his knowledge of religious sciences and philology. His books apparently numbered more than one hundred, only a few of which have survived. Almost all his biographers cite his *Sunan Ibn Māja* ("The *sunna* of Ibn Māja," Riyadh 1999); a commentary on the *Ṣaḥīḥ* of al-Bukhārī (d. 256/870), *al-Talwīḥ fī sharḥ al-Jāmiʿ al-ṣaḥīḥ* (London, British Library, MS Or. 14160, vols. 2–6); and *al-Zahr al-bāsim fī l-sīra al-nabawiyya* ("The smiling flowers on the Prophet's life," Leiden University Library, MS Or. 370), a biography of the Prophet written as a commentary upon and criticism of al-Suhaylī's (d. 581/1185) *al-Rawḍ al-unuf* ("The meadow of new herbage," Hamdan). He also wrote *al-Ishāra ilā sīrat al-Muṣṭafā wa-taʾrīkh man baʿdahu min al-khulafāʾ* ("The guide to the life of the Prophet and the history of the caliphs who came after him," Cairo 1908, Damascus and Beirut 1996) and *al-Durr al-manẓūm min kalām al-Muṣṭafā l-maʿṣūm* ("The strung pearls from the words of the sinless Chosen One," n.p. 1994) (Ibn Ḥajar, 7:353; al-Shawqānī, *al-Badr al-ṭāliʿ*, 2:312; al-Suyūṭī, 139; Ibn Taghrībirdī, 11:9; al-Ziriklī, 7:275). According to Ibn Ḥajar (4:353), he had a good knowledge of genealogy but only an average understanding of the other sciences related to *ḥadīth*.

BIBLIOGRAPHY

WORKS WHOSE DETAILS ARE NOT CITED IN THE ARTICLE

WORKS BY MUGHULṬĀY

Mughulṭāy, *Ikmāl Tahdhīb al-kamāl fī asmāʾ al-rijāl*, 12 vols., Cairo 2001; Mughulṭāy, *al-Ināba ilā maʿrifat al-mukhtalif fīhim min al-ṣaḥāba*, 2 vols., Riyadh 2000; Mughulṭāy, *al-Talwīḥ fī sharḥ al-Jāmiʿ al-ṣaḥīḥ*, London, British Library, MS Or. 14160, vols. 2–6; Mughulṭāy, *al-Wāḍiḥ al-mubīn fī dhikr man ustushhida min al-muḥibbīn*, ed. Otto Spies, *al-Mughulṭāʾī's Specialwerk über Martyrer der Liebe*, Stuttgart 1936 (edition of the first part of the book).

SOURCES

Ibn Ḥajar al-ʿAsqalānī, *al-Durar al-kāmina fī aʿyān al-miʾa al-thāmina*, 6 vols., Hyderabad 1350/1930; Ibn Quṭlūbughā, *Tāj al-tarājim fī ṭabaqāt al-Ḥanafiyya* (Baghdad 1962), 77; Ibn Taghrībirdī, *al-Nujūm al-zāhira fī mulūk Miṣr wa-l-Qāhira*, 16 vols., Cairo n.d.; al-Ṣafadī, *Aʿyān al-ʿaṣr wa-aʿwān al-naṣr*, 3 vols., Frankfurt 1990; al-Ṣafadī, *al-Wāfī bi-l-wafayāt*, 24 vols. (Beirut 1971), 23:61; al-Shawqānī,

al-Badr al-ṭāliʿ, 2 vols., Cairo 1348/1929; al-Suyūṭī, *Dhayl Ṭabaqāt al-ḥuffāẓ lil-Dhahabī*, Jerusalem and Damascus, 1333–4/1915.

STUDIES

Monica Balda-Tillier, The forbidden passion. Mughultay's book on the martyrdom of love and its censorship, *Al-Qanṭara* 37 (2014), 187–212; Lois Anita Giffen, *Theory of profane love among the Arabs. The development of the genre* (New York 1971), 33–4; Abdelhamid Saleh Hamdan, Mughulṭāy, *EI2*; Gurdofarid Miskinzoda, *On the margins of Sīra. Mughultāʾī (689–762/1290–1361) and his place in the development of sīra literature*, Ph.D diss., University of London, School of Oriental and African Studies 2007, 54–62; Ashley Manjarrez Walker and Michael A. Sells, The wiles of women and performative intertextuality. ʿAʾisha, the *hadith* of the slander, and the *sura* of Yusuf, *JAL* 30 (1999), 55–77; Khayr al-Dīn al-Ziriklī, *al-Aʿlām*, Beirut 1997; *GAL*, 2:66, *GALS*, 2:47–8.

MONICA BALDA-TILLIER

Muḥammad Bakhsh

Muḥammad Bakhsh (1830–1907), popularly known as Miyāṇ Muḥammad, was a Panjābī Ṣūfī poet from Mīrpūr (in Azad Kashmir). He is celebrated particularly for his long narrative poem *Sayf al-Mulūk*, completed in 1863.

1. EARLY LIFE

He was born into a Qādirī Ṣūfī lineage based at Khaṙī, near Mīrpūr (McLoughlin and Khan), then under the rule of the Hindu princely state of Jammu and Kashmir. The patron saint of Khaṙī was Muḥammad Pīrā Shāh Ghāzī Qalandar (d. 1162/1749), known as Damṙiyāṇ vālā Sarkār (lord of the copper coins), who was a follower of the influential Qādirī lineage founded by Sayyid Muḥammad Muqīm (d. 1055/1645) from Ḥujra Muqīm Shāh, in Okāṙā district. Miyāṇ Muḥammad compiled a continuation in Persian prose of the *Tadhkira-yi Muqīmī* ("Memoir of Muqīm") covering the Qādirī-Qalandarī saints of Kharī and related local lineages. This was translated into Urdu by his disciple Malik Muḥammad as *Būstān-i qalandarī* ("The orchard of the Qalandars"). After the early death of Miyāṇ Muḥammad's father in 1847, he was succeeded as head of the Kharī lineage by his eldest son, Bahāwal Bakhsh, until his death in 1881, when the responsibility for running the shrine was, in turn, reluctantly assumed by Miyāṇ Muḥammad himself.

2. The *Sayf al-Mulūk*

Miyāṇ Muḥammad enjoys an unrivalled reputation in his home region of Azad Kashmir and the adjacent areas of the Poṯ'hohār plateau in northwestern Panjāb, where his great Panjābī poem *Sayf al-mulūk*, comprising 9249 pairs of rhyming *davayye* verses, locally enjoys the unchallenged status of a national epic. It is an extended reworking of the long Persian story of *Sayf al-Mulūk va Badīʿ al-Jamāl*, which is included in the *Thousand and one nights* and exists in numerous other versions in several South Asian languages (Shackle, Story). The poem's many local references and the characteristic colouring of its standard Panjābī by the incorporation of many distinctive local words have caused it to be considered as much a truly local creation as is the *Hīr* (completed 1180/1766) of Vārith Shāh in the central and eastern districts of the Panjāb. Like the latter work, it is associated with a popular melody *(lay)* to which its verses are regularly recited.

The poem is laid out lavishly on a grand scale. The narrative proper is preceded by a long authorial introduction, in which, after the usual preliminaries, the poet describes the written sources he has used, then explains his conception of true poetry (Syed, Author), and expands on his vision of the story of Sayf al-Mulūk as a Ṣūfī allegory for the spiritual quest in the face of all the obstacles that must be tackled bravely by the true spiritual hero of lofty intent *(mard-i himmat)*.

While the broad outline of the story itself is carefully preserved, the narrative is greatly expanded by numerous asides explaining the spiritual significance of the action and the psychological states experienced by the hero in his various experiences. Characteristic of Miyāṇ Muḥammad's style is the incorporation of many sententious reflections brought to life by vivid poetic imagery, for example, *Qadar p͟hulāṇ dā bulbul jāṇe, ṣāf damāghā vālī / Qadar p͟hulāṇ dā giraj kīh jāṇe, murde k͟hāvaṅ vālī* ("The value of flowers is known to the nightingale whose mind is clear. How can their worth be known to the vulture, who is intent on eating dead flesh?"). Such frequently quoted sententious verses are important to the poem's reputation as a work of spiritual guidance.

At the end of the long narrative proper, Miyāṇ Muḥammad adds an exceptionally long conclusion, which includes a famous list (verses 9016–89) of the main figures of earlier Panjābī literary history, apparently inspired by the similar list appended to the *Aḥsan al-qaṣiṣ* ("The best of stories") by the earlier local poet Aḥmad Yār (d. 1845).

3. Other poetry

A prolific writer of many other Panjābī poems, Miyāṇ Muḥammad took full advantage of the publishing industry newly established in Lahore to disseminate his work. As a young man, he composed a series of shorter Panjābī poems on various topics, regularly acknowledging the inspiring encouragement of his elder brother and providing updated lists of his earlier titles, including *Qiṣṣa Sohṅī Māhīṇvāl* (1857), narrating the famous local romance of Sohṅī and Mahīṇvāl; *Tuḥfa-yi mīrāṇ* ("Homage to the lord," 1857–8), an account of the miracles performed by Shaykh ʿAbd al-Qādir Jīlānī (d. 561/1166), a Ḥanbalī scholar active in Baghdad who became revered, after his death in that city, as the wonder-working patron saint of the Qādirī order; *Qiṣṣa Shaykh Ṣunʿān* (1857–8), a remarkable adaptation of the well known story from ʿAṭṭār's (d. 618/1221) Persian *Manṭiq al-ṭayr* ("The conference of the birds"), giving a prominent role to Shaykh ʿAbd al-Qādir (Shackle, Representations); *Mathnavī nayrang-i ʿishq* (1858–9), a Panjābī reworking of the Persian *mathnavī* by Ghanīmat Kunjāhī (Shackle, Persian poetry; Singh); *Qiṣṣa Shāh Manṣūr* (c. 1858–9), an account of the miraculous career of the great Baghdadi Ṣūfī saint of Persian origin Manṣūr al-Ḥallāj (d. 309/922); *Qiṣṣa Shīrīn Farhād ba-rivāyat-i ṣaḥīḥ* (1860), a correction of an erroneous version of the story of Shīrīn and Farhād, as found in a Panjābī poem, with reference to the Persian original written by Niẓāmī (d. 605/1209). A *Gulzār-i faqr* ("Garden of spiritual poverty") is regularly mentioned after *Qiṣṣa Shīrīn Farhād* in the lists included by the author in his other Panjābī poems, but it is now apparently lost.

Following the completion in 1863 of his masterpiece *Safar al-ʿishq yaʿnī Qiṣṣa Sayf al-Mulūk* ("The journey of love, or, The story of Sayf al-Mulūk"), Miyāṇ Muḥammad's remaining long poems appeared at longer intervals. His next composition was *Tuḥfa-yi Rasūliyya* ("Homage to the Apostle") (1864–5), an account of the miracles attributed to the Prophet; *Qiṣṣa Sakhī Khavāṣ Khān* (1865–6), based on the local legend of Khavāṣ Khān of Rohtās, an Afghan soldier who sacrificed his life for love; *Qiṣṣa Mirzā Ṣāḥibāṇ* (1871–2), a fine poem distinguished by the copious use of an ornamented style, which provides an extended treatment of the classic romance of Mirzā and Sāhibāṇ but which, in spite of the efforts evidently lavished upon it, has never been very popular. After becoming head of the lineage upon the death of his elder brother, Miyāṇ Muḥammad was unable to write as much as he had previously: *Hidāyat al-muslimīn* ("Guidance for Muslims," 1877) is a spirited verse polemic that advances numerous textual sanctions for the cult of devotion to the tombs of Ṣūfī saints, arguing forcefully against the claims of the Wahhābī reformists that this practice was essentially un-Islamic; his last substantial poem was *Chiṯ'ṯhī Hīr Rānjhā* ("Letters of Hīr and Rānjẖā," 1897), a lyrical development of the famous story of Hīr and Rānjẖā in the form of letters by the leading characters.

4. Assessment

Miyāṇ Muḥammad was an exceptionally fluent versifier. Several anecdotes record his talent for extempore composition of occasional poems addressed in Panjābī to numerous respondents (collected in Parvīz). In addition to the more substantial poems listed above, he wrote numerous shorter works. These poems, mostly undated, include a *Bārāṇ māh* ("The twelve months"), in the traditional genre arranged by the calendar, *Sīḥarfī Sassī Punnūṇ*, and several other acrostic poems in the *sīḥarfī* form (genre in which the first word of each of the thirty stanzas is headed by a letter of the Arabic alphabet), five of which are collected as his *Panj ganj* ("Five treasures").

In the broader historical context of the classic Muslim poetry of the Panjāb, Miyāṇ Muḥammad may be seen as one of the last pre-modern masters whose comprehensive oeuvre sums up all pre-existing tradition. In this respect, he may be compared to Khᵛāja Ghulām Farīd of Bahāwalpūr (d. 1901), who achieved a comparable summation in his lyrics in Siraiki, the language of Bahāwalpūr and southwestern Panjāb, as another saint-poet living in a princely state at some remove from the modernising atmosphere of British India.

Although there was no direct link between them, the influence of Miyāṇ Muḥammad's literary example may be seen in the prolific output of another narrative poet from the area, Dā'im Iqbāl of Gujrat (d. 1984), who wrote several long romances with a profoundly Ṣūfī colouring, of which the best is probably his extended treatment of the story of Sohṇī and Mahīṇvāl titled *Bayt al-māl. Qiṣṣa Sohṇī Mahīṇvāl*, completed in 1934.

Miyāṇ Muḥammad never married and died without issue. His memory was, however, preserved in the writings of his closest disciple Malik Muḥammad, a contractor from Jhelum who spent much time with him and who, in addition to his Urdu translation of the *Tadhkira-yi Muqīmī*, produced a noteworthy edition of the *Sayf al-mulūk* accompanied by an authoritative biographical sketch in Urdu that is regularly reprinted with more recent editions of the poem.

Bibliography

Editions of Sayf al-Mulūk

Sayf al-Mulūk maʿ-i savāniḥ-ʿumrī, ed. Malik Muḥammad, Jhelum 1914; *Safar al-ʿishq, yaʿnī Qiṣṣa Sayf al-Mulūk, maʿ-i savāniḥ-ʿumrī-yi ḥaḍrat muṣannif*, ed. Maḥbūb ʿAlī, Muzaffarabad 1994; *Sayf al-Mulūk*, ed. and trans. into Urdu by Miyāṇ Ẓafar Maqbūl, Lahore 2000; *Sayf al-Mulūk (Safar al-ʿishq)*, ed. Muḥammad Sharīf Ṣābir, Lahore 2002.

Other works by Muḥammad Bakhsh

Chiṯ'ṯ'hiyāṇ, ed. Afḍal Parvīz, Islamabad 1985; *Hidāyat al-muslimīn*, ed. Maḥbūb ʿAlī, Muzaffarabad 1980; *Mathnavī Nayrang-i ʿishq panjābī*, ed. Maḥbūb ʿAlī, Jhelum 1964; *Mirzā Ṣāḥibāṇ*, Lahore 1874; *Panj ganj maʿ-i Sīḥarfī Sassī Punnūṇ va Bārāṇ māh*, ed. Maḥbūb ʿAlī, Jhelum c. 1960; *Qiṣṣa Sakhī Khavāṣ Khān*, ed. Muḥammad Faḍl Ilāhī Ḥaydarī, Jhelum 1964; *Qiṣṣa Shāh Manṣūr*, ed. Akhtar Jaʿfarī, Lahore 1988; *Qiṣṣa Shīrīn Farhād ba-rivāyat-i ṣaḥīḥ*, Lahore 1879; *Qiṣṣa Sohṇī Mahīṇvāl*, ed. Muḥammad Faḍl Ilāhī Ḥaydarī, Jhelum 1964; *Shaykh Ṣunʿān maʿ-i Chiṯ'ṯ'hī Hīr Rāṇjhā*, ed. Maḥbūb ʿAlī, Muzaffarabad ca. 1975; *Tadhkira-yi Muqīmī*, trans. into Urdu by Malik Muḥammad, *Būstān-i qalandarī*, Jhelum 1930; *Tuḥfa-yi Mīrāṇ*, ed. Miyāṇ Muḥammad Sikandar, Khaṛī Sharīf, circa 1990; *Tuḥfa-yi Rasūliyya*, ed. Maḥbūb ʿAlī, Muzaffarabad 1978.

Studies

Ghulām Ḥusayn Aẓhar, *Miyāṇ Muḥammad*, Lahore 1980; ʿAzīz Aḥmad Chawdharī, *Miyāṇ Muḥammad Bakhsh*, Khariyan 1986; Seán McLoughlin and Muzamil Khan, Ambiguous traditions and modern transformations of Islam. The waxing and waning of an "intoxicated" Sufi cult in Mirpur, *Contemporary South Asia* 15/3 (2006), 289–307; Miyāṇ Sikandar Muḥammad, *ʿĀrif-i Khaṛī*, Dina, circa 1990; Christopher Shackle, Persian poetry and Qādirī Sufism in late Mughal India. Ghanīmat Kunjāhī and his *mathnawī Nayrang-i ʿishq*, in Leonard Lewisohn and David Morgan (eds.), *The heritage of Ṣūfism*, vol. 3, *Late classical Persianate Ṣūfism (1501–1750)* (Oxford 1999), 435–63; Christopher Shackle, Representations of ʿAttar in the West and in the East. Translations of the *Manṭiq al-ṭayr* and the tale of Shaykh Sanʿan, in Leonard Lewisohn and Christopher Shackle (eds.), *ʿAttar and the Persian Sufi tradition* (London 2006), 165–93; Christopher Shackle, The story of Sayf al-Mulūk in South Asia, *JRAS* 17/2 (2007), 1–15; Arun Singh, *Black light. Islamic philosophical themes from the Nayrang-e ʿishq*, London 2013; Najm Hosain Syed, The author of *Saiful Maluk* and his concepts of criticism, in Najm Hosain Syed, *Recurrent patterns in Punjabi poetry* (Lahore 1968), 47–62.

Christopher Shackle

Muḥammad Shāh Qājār

Muḥammad Shāh Qājār, titled Ghazī (warrior), was the third Qājār shah of Iran (r. 1250–64/1834–48). His short reign resembles an interregnum between those of his grandfather Fatḥ ʿAlī Shāh (r. 1212–50/1797–1834) and his son Nāṣir al-Dīn Shāh (r. 1264–1313/1848–96). He was the eldest son of ʿAbbās Mīrzā (Prince ʿAbbās), Nāʾib al-Salṭana (d. 1249/1833), Fatḥʿalī's crown prince and governor general of Azerbaijan, who led the Iranian forces in the Russian-Persian wars that resulted in the defeat of the Iranian armies and the signing of the Gulistān (1228/1813) and Turkmenchay (1243/1828) treaties. In these treaties, imperial Russia had guaranteed the succession of ʿAbbās Mīrzā to the Qājār throne; because ʿAbbās Mīrzā died before his father, Fatḥ ʿAlī named his son Muḥammad Mīrzā as his own successor under pressure from Russia and Britain, both having found Iranian stability advantageous to their expansionist policies in the region.

Iranian successions were often contested by two or more claimants. Before Muḥammad Mīrzā could remove from Tabriz, his seat in Azerbaijan, his uncle ʿAlī Shāh Ẓill al-Sulṭān declared himself shah in Tehran and held out for three months, until he relented and was forgiven by his nephew. There were other rebellions, too, the most important of which arose from the claim to the throne made by his uncle Ḥusayn ʿAlī Mīrzā Farmānfarmā (d. 1251/1835) backed by another uncle, Ḥasan ʿAlī Mīrzā Shujāʿ al-Salṭana, which was resolved by the sword.

In securing the throne for Muḥammad Mīrzā, his able secretary Mīrzā Abū l-Qāsim Qāʾim Maqām Farāhānī (d. 1251/1835) played a pivotal role, for which the shah made him chancellor of the realm. He did not, however, last long in this post; in the long Iranian tradition of the assassination of strong viziers, the chancellor was put to death by suffocation in 1251/1835 on the shah's orders. The shah replaced Qāʾim Maqām with his childhood tutor and mentor Mullā ʿAbbās Īrvānī (d. c.1264/1848), known as Ḥājjī Mīrzā Āqāsī, a man with Ṣūfī tendencies who persuaded the shah to support Ṣūfī orders and individuals. He was a simple man with little ability to rule, who managed the economy and the army badly.

Muḥammad's reign was marked by turmoil and the rebellion of princes and notables and even some *ʿulamāʾ*. The most notorious of the latter was the virtual assumption of autonomy in Isfahan by its leading *mujtahid* Sayyid Muḥammad Baqir Shaftī, with the support of local *lūṭī*s (ruffians), whose extirpation took time and much effort. The shah's foreign policy favoured Russia, which was the primary reason for his failure to capture Herat between 1253/1837 and 1255/1839. He would probably have succeeded, had it not been for pressure applied by Britain, which landed troops on Kharg Island, in the Persian Gulf. Herat was the gateway to India, and Britain feared that its fall into Persian hands would facilitate Russia's access to the Subcontinent.

An historic event under Muḥammad Shāh was the rise in 1260/1844 of Sayyid ʿAlī Muḥammad Shīrāzī (d. 1266/1850), known as Bāb (lit., gate) on account of his claim that he was the intermediary between the Hidden Imām and the Shīʿī community; he later declared himself the Imām. His message attracted many converts, first in Fars province and then elsewhere, and caused the state and the *ʿulamāʾ* serious concern. He was eventually arrested in 1262/1846 on Āqāsī's orders, to be taken from Shiraz to Tehran, but the governor of Isfahan, Manūchihr Khān Gurjī (d. 1263/1847), although not a Bābī himself, blocked the road and held Bāb in Isfahan, under his own protection. After the death of the governor, however, Bāb was taken to Tehran and thence to Tabriz where he was interrogated by three *ʿulamāʾ*, flogged on the orders of the young Nāṣir al-Dīn Mīrzā, the heir apparent, and imprisoned in Chahrīq castle, in far northwestern Iran. The Bābī movement persisted after Muḥammad Shāh's death and was violently suppressed by his successor Naṣīr al-Dīn Shāh's strong and capable chancellor and army chief Mīrzā Taqī Khān Amīr Kabīr (d. 1268/1852). Nevertheless, the movement survived, later dividing into two sects, the successful one founding the Bahāʾī faith as a religion in its own right.

The final unrest under Muḥammad Shāh was the revolt in 1262/1846 of Ḥasan Khān Sālār, the trustee of Imām Riḍā's shrine in Khurāsān, and his brother Muḥammad Khān, the acting governor of that province. These were sons of the formidable Divilū Qājār nobleman Allāhyār Khān Āṣif al-Dawla, ʿAbbās Mīrzā's brother-in-law and Muḥammad Shāh's maternal uncle, who aspired to the chancellorship and was an enemy of Āqāsī (the Divilū were the non-reigning branch of the Qājārs). The conflict between Āṣif al-Dawla and the shah was eventually resolved by his respectful exile to the ʿAtabāt (the Shīʿī holy cities in Iraq), from where he is believed to have encouraged his two sons to rebel against the state. This *fitna* (strife) too was suppressed by Amīr Kabīr, who had Ḥasan Khān Sālār and his brother killed, despite his promise that their lives would be spared if they surrendered.

Muḥammad Shāh died in 1264/1848 of chronic gout. His reign was ridden with instability, turmoil, and chaos and led to economic and military decline. His Ṣūfī tendencies did not, however, stop him from being the first Persian shah to wear European-style clothes. He was less harsh and less enamored of women than his grandfather and his son.

Bibliography

Hamid Algar, *Religion and state in Iran, 1785–1906. The role of the ulama in the Qajar period*, Berkeley 1969; Abbas Amanat, *Pivot of the universe. Nasir al-Din Shah Qajar and the Iranian monarchy 1831–1896*, Berkeley 1997; Mahdī Bāmdād, *Sharh-i hāl-i rijāl-i Īrān*, vol. 3, Tehran 1992; Maud Diver, *The hero of Herat*, London 1913; Peter Hopkirk, *The great game*, London 1990; Mansūra Ittādiyya, *Infiṣāl-i Harāt. Gūshihāʾi az ravābiṭ-i khārijī-yi Īrān* (1200–1280 H.Q.), ed. Muṣṭafā Zamānī Nīya, Tehran 2002; Homa Katouzian, *The Persians. Ancient, mediaeval and modern Iran*, New Haven 2010; Ann K. S. Lambton, *Qajar Persia*, London 1987; Denis MacEoin, *The messiah of Shiraz. Studies in early and middle Babism*, Leiden 2009; Alī Asghar Shamīm, *Īrān dar durih-yi Qājār*, Tehran 1963; Muḥammad Taqī Sipihr (Lisān al-Mulk), *Nāsikh al-tavārīkh*, ed. Jahangīr Qāʾam Maqāmī, Tehran 1337sh/1958.

Homa Katouzian

CUMULATIVE LIST OF ENTRIES 2020-1

Dehhani 2016-3 : 66
Delhi, architecture 2014-3 : 93
Deli Birader, Gazali 2014-2 : 89
Deli Orman 2014-4 : 72
Demak 2011-2 : 136
Demir Baba Tekke 2015-1 : 96
Democritus 2015-2 : 79
Demokrat Parti 2016-2 : 67
Denmark, Muslims in 2014-2 : 91
Deobandīs in Africa 2015-4 : 104
Deposit 2013-4 : 103
Dermagandhul, Serat 2013-1 : 94
Dervish 2011-4 : 129
Devil (Satan) 2018-5 : 19
Dewan Dakwah Islamiyah Indonesia 2017-2 : 48
al-Dhahabī 2016-1 : 73
Dhahabiyya 2012-2 : 118
Dhawq 2015-1 : 97
Dhawq, Ibrāhīm 2011-3 : 145
Dhimma 2012-3 : 87
Dhow 2016-5 : 50
Dhū l-Faqār 2012-4 : 77
Dhū l-Kifl 2012-2 : 121
Dhū l-Nūn al-Miṣrī 2012-4 : 79
Dhū l-Rumma 2011-3 : 147
Didactic poetry, Arabic 2011-4 : 135
Dietary law 2012-1 : 121
Dihkhudā, ʿAlī-Akbar 2018-6 : 38
al-Dihlawī, Shāh Walī Allāh 2015-4 : 106
Dihqān 2015-1 : 104
Dīk al-Jinn 2011-4 : 137
Dilāʾ 2019-4 : 46
Dilmaçoğulları beyliği 2014-3 : 101
al-Dimyāṭī, Nūr al-Dīn 2015-2 : 80
Dīn-i ilāhī 2015-2 : 81
al-Dīnawarī, Abū Saʿd 2016-2 : 68
Diogenes 2012-2 : 123
Dioscorides 2014-4 : 73
Dipanagara 2012-2 : 126
Dire Dawa 2014-1 : 94
Ḍirghām b. ʿĀmir 2014-4 : 75
Disciple in Ṣūfism 2018-2 : 24
Dīwān Group 2012-4 : 81
Ḍiyāʾ al-Dīn al-Makkī 2016-2 : 69
Diyāb, Maḥmūd 2012-1 : 126
al-Diyārbakrī, al-Ḥusayn 2015-3 : 75
Diyarbekri, Abdussamed 2013-2 : 93
Djambek, Djamil 2014-3 : 102
Djenné 2015-3 : 78
Djibouti 2017-1 : 54
Djula 2016-2 : 70
Dobhāshī 2014-4 : 77
Döger (Ghuzz) 2018-1 : 33
Dogon 2018-4 : 13
Dome 2017-5 : 74
Dome of the Rock 2014-4 : 78
Dongola 2015-3 : 80
Donkey (eschatological aspects) 2013-3 : 82
Dönme 2012-3 : 92
Doughty, Charles Montagu 2018-1 : 34
Doxography 2015-2 : 83
Drama, Urdu 2014-1 : 95
Drawing 2019-5 : 14
Dreams 2012-3 : 96
Druzes 2013-4 : 104
al-Duʿājī, ʿAlī 2012-1 : 126
Dualism 2012-1 : 127
Dūbayt in Arabic 2014-1 : 96
al-Dukālī,ʿAbd al-Wāḥid 2018-5 : 27
Dukayn al-Rājiz 2011-4 : 138
Dulkadir 2017-2 : 49
Dunqul, Amal 2012-2 : 129
al-Duwayhī, Ibrāhīm al-Rashīd 2011-4 : 139
Düzme Mustafa 2019-6 : 29
East Africa 2016-2 : 74
Əbdürrəhim bəy Haqverdiyev 2015-1 : 109
Ebubekir Kani 2020-1 : 28
Ebubekir Ratib Efendi 2016-4 : 50
Ebüziyya Mehmed Tevfik 2015-3 : 83
Ecevit, Bülent 2019-5 : 27
Edebiyat-ı Cedide 2017-5 : 82
Edhem Paşa 2016-3 : 70
Edirne 2018-3 : 28
Edirne, Treaty of 2016-2 : 79
Education, general (up to 1500) 2017-4 : 29
Education, early Ottoman 2016-2 : 80
Education, later Ottoman 2018-3 : 35
Education in the Indian subcontinent 2017-4 : 48
Education in Muslim Southeast Asia 2017-1 : 58
Education in West Africa 2020-1 : 30
Efendi 2017-5 : 84
Eger 2016-4 : 52
Egypt until 1517 2016-3 : 72
Egypt, art and architecture 2018-1 : 36
Əhməd Cavad Axundzadə 2015-2 : 88
Elements 2014-2 : 93
Əli bəy Hüseynzadə 2015-2 : 89
Elias of Nisibis 2014-4 : 85
Elijah 2012-2 : 131
Elisha 2012-4 : 84
Elixir 2013-4 : 109
Elvān Çelebi 2019-4 : 48
Emanation 2016-1 : 81
Emin Nihad 2017-1 : 62
Empedocles 2011-4 : 142
Emrullah Efendi 2018-1 : 41
Encümen-i şuara 2017-1 : 63
Encyclopaedias, Arabic 2015-2 : 90

Maghribī, Aḥmad Khattū 2020-1 : 132
Maḥbūb b. al-Raḥīl, Abū Sufyān 2019-1 : 145
Maḥfūẓ, Najīb 2008-2 : 164
Maḥmūd, ʿAbd al-Ḥalīm 2014-4 : 148
Maḥmūd Gāvān 2015-3 : 142
Maḥmūdābād family 2020-1 : 133
al-Majdhūb, ʿAbd al-Raḥmān 2014-2 : 146
Majdhūb, Muḥammad 2020-1 : 137
Majelis Permusyawaratan Ulama 2019-5 : 140
al-Mājishūn 2009-2 : 151
Makal, Mahmut 2019-6 : 121
Makhdūm-i Aʿẓam, Aḥmad 2012-1 : 150
Makhlūf, Muḥammad Ḥasanayn 2013-3 : 130
Malay and other languages of insular Southeast Asia 2019-1 : 147
al-Malībārī, Zayn al-Dīn 2019-3 : 146
al-Mālikī, Abū Bakr 2017-5 : 152
Maʿmar b. Rāshid 2019-6 : 122
Mamlūks, Ottoman period 2019-6 : 124
Manastırlı İsmail Hakkı 2019-6 : 129
Mande (Mandingo) 2020-1 : 138
Mangkunagara I 2019-4 : 145
al-Mannūbiyya, ʿĀʾisha 2013-4 : 153
Mardāvīj b. Ziyār 2018-6 : 152
Maryam al-Adhraʿiyya 2020-1 : 139
Maşizade Fikri Çelebi 2014-3 : 151
Masʿūd-i Saʿd-i Salmān 2011-2 : 152
Mataram 2019-4 : 146
Medina since 1918 2019-6 : 130
Megiser, Hieronymus 2017-2 : 151
Mehdizadə (Abbas Səhhət) 2015-2 : 152
Mehmed Esad, Sahaflar Şeyhizade 2016-2 : 153
Mehmed Halife 2019-5 : 141
Mehmed Zaim 2019-5 : 142
Mezzomorto Hüseyin Paşa 2017-1 : 136
Minaret 2019-6 : 132
Mīr Jaʿfar 2020-1 : 141
Mīrak al-Bukhārī 2018-2 : 153
Mughulṭāy b. Qilīj 2020-1 : 144
Muhājirūn 2019-6 : 142
Muḥammad Bakhsh 2020-1 : 145
Muḥammad Shāh Qājār 2020-1 : 149
Muḥammad al-Walī 2019-4 : 147
Muhammadiyah 2019-6 : 145
al-Munajjim, Banū 2019-3 : 148
al-Murādī, Muḥammad Khalīl 2015-3 : 147
Mushfiq-i Kāẓimī, Murtaḍā 2019-2 : 141
Muways b. ʿImrān 2016-1 : 152
Muzakkar, Abdul Kahar 2018-2 : 154
al-Naḥḥās, Abū Jaʿfar 2019-4 : 149
Nāʾīn 2019-5 : 144
Naon, Avram 2013-4 : 155
Nigm, Aḥmad Fuʾād 2019-5 : 146
Niẓām Shāhīs 2017-3 : 146
Novel, Arabic 2014-1 : 152
Oromo 2014-2 : 148
Osman Hamdi 2019-6 : 149
Paşa 2014-2 : 151
Persian grammar 2018-3 : 148
Pir Sultan Abdal 2013-2 : 135
Reşid Rahmeti Arat 2016-3 : 146
Ṣabrī, Ismāʿīl 2019-4 : 151
al-Ṣaffār al-Bukhārī 2012-2 : 144
al-Samarqandī, Abū Ṭāhir 2013-2 : 137
Sarāy Malik Khānum 2013-2 : 139
Sayyid Baraka 2017-1 : 138
Sayyid Sulṭān 2014-3 : 153
Shaqīq al-Balkhī 2016-2 : 155
Shawqī, Aḥmad 2015-3 : 150
al-Shaykh Imām 2019-5 : 149
Sri Lanka 2015-1 : 148
Sub-Saharan African literature, ʿAjamī 2012-2 : 145
Suhrāb 2019-1 : 152
Sulṭān Ḥusayn Bāyqarā 2017-1 : 143
Sylhet Nagari 2015-1 : 152
Ṭalḥa b. ʿUbaydallāh 2014-4 : 150
Tamīm b. al-Muʿizz 2012-4 : 116
Tayyarzade Ata Bey 2015-4 : 151
al-Thamīnī, ʿAbd al-ʿAzīz 2010-1 : 194
Tokgöz, Aḥmed İḥsān 2013-1 : 144
Tūrsūn-zāda, Mīrzā 2018-6 : 155
Uluboy, Abdülbaki Fevzi 2016-3 : 149
ʿUmar b. Hubayra 2019-5 : 151
United Kingdom, Muslims in the 2017-1 : 146
Vasi Alisi 2016-3 : 151
Wahab Chasbullah 2017-5 : 155
Yazīd b. ʿUmar b. Hubayra 2019-5 : 153
Yusuf Amiri 2016-4 : 144
Zarrūq, Aḥmad 2013-3 : 132
Zuhr, Banū 2019-2 : 145

Printed in the United States
By Bookmasters